NEW ENGLAND AND THE MARITIME PROVINCES

New England and the Maritime Provinces

Connections and Comparisons

Edited by
STEPHEN J. HORNSBY
JOHN G. REID

McGill-Queen's University Press
Montreal & Kingston • London • Ithaca

ISBN 0-7735-2865-2 (cloth)
ISBN 0-7735-3040-1 (paper)

Legal deposit second quarter 2005
Bibliothèque nationale du Québec

Printed in Canada on acid-free paper that is 100% ancient forest free (100% post-consumer recycled), processed chlorine free.

This book has been published with the help of a grant from the Canadian-American Center of the University of Maine.

McGill-Queen's University Press acknowledges the support of the Canada Council for the Arts for our publishing program. We also acknowledge the financial support of the Government of Canada through the Book Publishing Industry Development Program (BPIDP) for our publishing activities.

Library and Archives Canada Cataloguing in Publication

New England and the Maritime provinces : connections and comparisons / edited by Stephen J. Hornsby, John G. Reid.

Includes bibliographical references and index.
ISBN 0-7735-2865-2 (hbk)
ISBN 0-7735-3040-1 (pbk)

1. Maritime Provinces – History. 2. New England – History. 3. Maritime Provinces – Relations – New England. 4. New England – Relations – Maritime Provinces. I. Hornsby, Stephen J. (Stephen John), 1956– II. Reid, John G. (John Graham), 1948–.

FC2028.N48 2004 971.5 C2005-900281-6

Typeset in 10/12 Baskerville by True to Type

Contents

Contributors

ROBERT H. BABCOCK is professor emeritus in the Department of History at the University of Maine. The author of *Gompers in Canada: A Study in American Continentalism Before the First World War* (1974), he is currently general editor of the *Canadian-American Public Policy* series of occasional papers.

BETSY BEATTIE is Canadian Studies librarian at the Fogler Library of the University of Maine. Her most recent major publication is *Obligation and Opportunity: Single Maritime Women in Boston, 1870–1930* (2000).

BÉATRICE CRAIG is a member of the Department of History at the University of Ottawa. Her research focuses on rural history and women's history, and her publications include the prize-winning "Salaires, niveaux de vie et travail féminin dans l'arrondissement de Lille au XIXe siècle" (1998).

JACQUES FERLAND is a member of the Department of History of the University of Maine. His publications in the history of labour and capitalism include "Les Chevaliers de Saint-Crépin du Québec: Une Étude en Trois Tableaux" (1991) and "Rural and Urban Processes: A Comparative Analysis of Australian and Canadian Development" (with Christopher Wright, 1996).

JULIAN GWYN has recently retired from the Department of History at the University of Ottawa. His major publications include *Excessive*

Expectations: Maritime Commerce and the Economic Development of Nova Scotia, 1740–1870 (1998) and *Ashore and Afloat: The British Navy and the Halifax Naval Yard Before 1820* (2004).

STEPHEN J. HORNSBY is director of the Canadian-American Center at the University of Maine. A geographer with research interests on both sides of the Canada-United States border, his most recent publication is *British Atlantic, American Frontier: Spaces of Power in Early Modern British America* (2005).

COLIN D. HOWELL is a member of the Department of History at Saint Mary's University and executive director of the Gorsebrook Research Institute. A former editor of *Canadian Historical Review,* he is the author of *Northern Sandlots: A Social History of Maritime Baseball* (1995).

EDWARD D. (SANDY) IVES is professor emeritus in the Department of Anthropology at the University of Maine. Among the latest of his many publications in the folklore of Maine and the Maritimes is *Drive Dull Care Away: Folksongs from Prince Edward Island* (1999).

RICHARD W. JUDD is a member of the Department of History at the University of Maine. Currently the co-editor of *Maine History,* he is also the author of *Common Lands, Common People: The Origins of Conservation in Northern New England* (1997).

ELIZABETH MANCKE is a member of the Department of History at the University of Akron. Her publications on early modern imperialism and on northeastern North American colonial history include "Another British America: A Canadian Model for the Early Modern British Empire" (1997) and *The Fault Lines of Empire: Political Differentiation in Massachusetts and Nova Scotia, c. 1760–1830* (2004).

BILL PARENTEAU is a member of the Department of History at the University of New Brunswick and the editor of *Acadiensis.* Among his publications is the prize-winning "'Care, Control and Supervision': Native People in the Canadian Atlantic Salmon Fishery, 1867–1900" (1998).

GEOFFREY PLANK is a member of the Department of History at the University of Cincinnati. He is the author of *An Unsettled Conquest: The British Campaign Against the Peoples of Acadia* (2000).

JOHN G. REID is a member of the Department of History at Saint Mary's University. He is the co-editor (with Phillip A. Buckner) of *The Atlantic Region to Confederation: A History* (1994) and coordinating author of *The "Conquest" of Acadia, 1710: Imperial, Colonial, and Aboriginal Constructions* (2004).

DAVID SANGER is a member of the Department of Anthropology at the University of Maine. His numerous archeological studies include "Testing the Models: Hunter-Gatherer Use of Space in the Gulf of Maine" (1996).

SCOTT SEE is a member of the Department of History at the University of Maine. His major publications include *Riots in New Brunswick: Orange Nativism and Social Violence in the 1840s* (1993).

JOSHUA SMITH is assistant professor of Humanities, United States Merchant Marine Academy, Kings Point, New York. His doctoral dissertation at the University of Maine was entitled "The Rogues of 'Quoddy: Smuggling in the Maine–New Brunswick Borderlands, 1783–1820."

REGINALD C. STUART is a member of the Department of History at Mount Saint Vincent University. A longstanding researcher in cross-border topics, his major publications include the prize-winning *United States Expansionism and British North America, 1775–1871* (1988).

D.A. SUTHERLAND is a member of the Department of History at Dalhousie University. He has written extensively on nineteenth-century Nova Scotia, and has co-authored (with Judith Fingard and Janet Guildford) *Halifax: The First 250 Years* (1999).

M. BROOK TAYLOR is a member of the Department of History at Mount Saint Vincent University, and has recently held the Visiting Professorship in Canadian Studies at the University of Tsukuba in Japan. Among his major publications is *Promoters, Patriots, and Partisans: Historiography in Nineteenth-Century English Canada* (1989).

DEBORAH C. TREFTS has continued investigating and writing about watershed degradation and declining marine species in the Canadian-American Greater Gulf of Maine Region. She also teaches professionals, students, and others the art and science of deciphering the public policy process.

WILLIAM WICKEN is a member of the Department of History at York University. He has appeared as an expert witness in key eastern Canadian legal cases involving native entitlements, and his publications include *Mi'kmaq Treaties on Trial: History, Land, and Donald Marshall Junior* (2002).

GRAEME WYNN is a member of the Department of Geography at the University of British Columbia. Among the most recent of his many publications in Canadian and Atlantic Canadian historical geography is *Remaking the Land that God Gave to Cain: A Brief Environmental History of Canada* (1998).

Acknowledgments

This book is based on presentations made at a conference held at the University of Maine in April 2000. However, its origins go back to 1996, when then-President Fred Hutchinson of the University of Maine visited Saint Mary's University and met with faculty members interested in cross-border studies. Out of that meeting came the idea for a jointly sponsored conference. A preliminary one-day symposium was held at Saint Mary's in October 1997, and preparations then followed for the full-scale conference in Orono.

As well as thanking Dr Hutchinson for his initial interest, we are grateful to all those involved in the early stages of the project, including Thérèse Arseneau, Stephen Davis, Colin Howell, Jackie Logan, and Madine VanderPlaat. We also thank those who were instrumental in making the April 2000 conference the success it was. As well as the participants, we thank in particular Raymond Pelletier, Elizabeth Arntzen, Amy Morin, and Nancy Strayer at the Canadian-American Center, University of Maine. The conference was supported in part by grants from the U.S. Department of Education and the Canadian Embassy, Washington, DC.

During the process of revising the essays for publication, we were assisted by the reviews offered by three press readers. We are very grateful as well to our editors at McGill-Queen's University Press, including John Zucchi, Joanne Pisano, and copy editor Jane McWhinney. At the University of Maine, we are grateful to Pamela Dean for indexing the volume, and to Michael Hermann for preparing the maps.

For financial support that made publication possible, we thank the Canadian-American Center of the University of Maine.

NEW ENGLAND AND THE MARITIME PROVINCES

1

Introduction

STEPHEN J. HORNSBY AND JOHN G. REID

The impulse for this collection, *New England and the Maritime Provinces: Connections and Comparisons*, arose from a conference held at the University of Maine in April 2000, co-sponsored by the Canadian-American Center of that university and by the Atlantic Canada Studies Program and Gorsebrook Research Centre of Saint Mary's University. In its less immediate origins, however, the book recognizes two deeper currents of thought and change. First, it is the product of a longstanding academic interest in Canadian-American interconnections, in the comparative study of societies on either side of the famously undefended border (which, as C.P. Stacey reminded us many years ago, was more myth than reality at least until 1871 and by some definitions until 1940),[1] and in the particular circumstances of the Maritime–New England area. Second, the collection responds to contemporary changes relating to globalization and its effects, whether welcome or contested, on international relationships and differentiations.

For a conference on these themes, the University of Maine was a natural choice. The historiography of Canadian-American relations had been profoundly influenced during the 1930s and 1940s by the active interest of two major philanthropic foundations, the Carnegie Endowment for International Peace and the Rockefeller Foundation – with Maine venues important to both. The University of Maine itself was the location of a Carnegie-sponsored conference in July 1938 on *Educational Problems in Canadian-American Relations.*[2] In addition to papers on education, it included a reflection by Harold Adams Innis, "Economic Trends in Canadian-American Relations," noteworthy for its forecast: "Canada will become increasingly dependent on the United States and ... the problem will become, more, rather than less acute." The great political economist also chose that occasion to demonstrate his detailed knowledge of A.A. Milne's *Winnie the Pooh* by concluding his paper with a lengthy quotation dealing with the trials and tribulations of Eeyore and illustrating Canadian sensibilities by citing the long-suffering donkey's plea that "A little Consideration, a little Thought for Others, makes all the difference."[3]

Arresting as Innis's implied comparison of Canadian-American relations with events in the Hundred Acre Wood must have been, no similar theme seems to have emerged from the Rockefeller-sponsored conference held at the Samoset hotel in Rockland, Maine, four years later. Devoted to an examination of the "Eastern Maritime Region," the conference explored cultural characteristics shared by the Maritimes and New England, notably northeastern New England. The general concept of a continentalist cross-border regionalism, which animated the series of conferences of which this was one, found few endorsements in Canada. Nevertheless, the discussions at Rockland had a significant influence in stimulating Rockefeller support for historical research at the University of New Brunswick, focusing on the cultural approach of a leading participant in the conference (and a former student of Innis's), Alfred Goldsworthy Bailey.[4]

Sustained in part by the personal interest of the long-serving president Arthur A. Hauck (1934–58), activity in the Canadian-American field continued steadily at the University of Maine, led increasingly by two faculty members, Edgar B. McKay and Alice R. Stewart. Both McKay and Stewart, whose contributions were expressly called to mind at the opening of the April 2000 conference, were prime movers in the establishment during the 1960s of the New England-Atlantic Provinces (later New England-Atlantic Provinces-Quebec) Program, the forerunner of today's Canadian-American Center.[5] Alice Stewart's scholarly interests bore directly on the Maritime provinces, and in 1971 she joined A.G. Bailey and others on the Advisory Board of the University of New Brunswick's new journal, *Acadiensis.* The journal's editor, P.A. Buckner, made it clear that it would "include within its geographic scope not only the Maritime Provinces and Newfoundland but also ... Maine."[6] Stewart, in turn, reinforced the point by contributing to the first issue a review essay on cross-border historical studies.[7]

All of these developments had both institutional and intellectual results in the 1970s and 1980s. The work of the scholars of the founding generation of *Acadiensis* was specifically scrutinized – and celebrated – at the biennial Atlantic Canada Studies Conference in Halifax in May 2000.[8] One of the resulting innovations had been the founding of the interdisciplinary Atlantic Canada Studies Program at Saint Mary's University in 1975, with its MA program and Gorsebrook Research Institute added in 1983. Also by that time, the Canadian-American Center at the University of Maine had taken on its present form. Among the products of its focus on teaching and research on Canadian-American topics was the international conference, *The Northeastern Borderlands: Four Centuries of Interaction*, held in 1987, and the publication of the proceedings two years later.[9] The borderlands concept had been developed many years before by Herbert E. Bolton as a tool for the study of interactions between the United States and Mexico during the Spanish colonial period. Bolton had further developed his transnational approach in his presidential address to the American Historical Association, in which he called explicitly for a comparative approach to the analysis of European colonial experiences in the Americas.[10] At the 1987 conference, the borderlands concept was used to analyse the interactions that had taken place in northeastern North America from native-European contacts to later cross-border movements and connections, with results that also included historiographical discussion and critical appraisal of the borderlands notion itself. Further borderlands studies at the University of Maine yielded a series of monographs in the ensuing years.[11]

During the 1990s interest in borderlands analysis continued to increase. In 1999 a forum essay by Jeremy Adelman and Stephen Aron in *American Historical Review* traced the origins of Bolton's borderlands notion and its relationship to the frontier theory of Bolton's mentor, Frederick Jackson Turner. Distinguishing conceptually between frontiers (as areas where borders were undefined and where relationships between peoples were characterized by intercultural accommodations) and borderlands (as areas contested by rival imperialisms), Adelman and Aron maintained that "conflicts over borderlands shaped the peculiar and contingent character of frontier relations." They argued too that North America experienced a dynamic transition process by which borders eventually became defined and borderlands became "bordered lands," in which old informal accommodations were restricted by the formalities of nation states.[12] The essay by Adelman and Aron sparked a lively debate, in which the issues ranged from the relationship of borderlands with Richard White's earlier formulation of "the middle ground"[13] to the admitted deficiencies of the Adelman-Aron approach in its treatment of the autonomous actions of aboriginal populations. Although, on the whole, Adelman and Aron were praised for introducing a new intellectual rigour through their distinctions between constructs, the exchange made it clear that the borderlands concept was not a dogma but an interpretive model capable of generating productive debate.[14]

If the essays in this book can be seen as responses to these long-standing currents of scholarly thinking, the collection as a whole can also be fairly characterized as the product of an era in which transnational interaction has become a central issue in the broader public arena. While transnational initiatives in themselves have a long pedigree reaching back at least to the Bretton Woods Conference of 1944, the pace of commentary and debate has quickened greatly in recent years. In a climate where catchwords are all too often valued above the austerities of analysis, there can be no more ubiquitous a word at the turn of the twenty-first century than "globalization." It is a process, we are told, marked by the decline of the nation state and the rise of transnational economic blocs such as the European Union and the North America that is emerging from the North American Free Trade Agreement. It embraces the enormous power wielded by multinational corporations in the global economy, the communications and technological revolutions, the impact of third-world immigration to Western countries, the spread of a generic popular culture around the globe, and the ill-defined but formidable influence of bodies such as the World Trade Organization (WTO). And, as the WTO found out in Seattle in December 1999, all of it is intensely controversial. Subsequent debates and demonstrations, along with the manifold repercussions of the attacks on New York's World Trade Center and the Pentagon in September 2001, have introduced new and ongoing complications.

While academic contributions to debates on globalization issues have yet – with the arguable exception of some economic analyses – to provoke street-level confrontations, historians have given increasing attention in recent years to transnational approaches that seek to shift the focus away from a traditional and simplistic concentration on the nation state as a unit of study. Comparative history, of course, has a long pedigree. Almost three-quarters of a century have passed since Marc Bloch published his classic statement on comparative methodology, followed in the North American context some five years later by Bolton's "The Epic of Greater America."[15] Recent discussions, however, have focused increasingly on the limitations of a comparative methodology in the absence of a sophisticated basis for comparison. While this is a point with which neither Bloch nor Bolton would have disagreed, it was expounded with particular force in 1991 when the historian Ian Tyrrell challenged Americanists to abandon American exceptionalism by throwing off the notion of the United States as a frame of analysis for either unitary or comparative studies, and instead to embrace a more thematic version of transnational history. This approach would be especially useful, Tyrrell argued, in at least three contexts: the use of a regional approach to examine questions that transcend national boundaries; the study through environmental history of issues that pay no regard to borders; and the study of organizations, movements, and ideologies that encompass many nations.[16] Eight years later, Tyrrell was one of fifteen scholars who collaborated in the writing of a special issue of the *Journal of American History* devoted to transnational perspectives on United States history. While the range of issues considered was wide, the project's editor, David Thelen, defined the overall goals concisely: "We wanted to explore how people and ideas and institutions and cultures moved above, below, through, and around, as well as within, the nation-state, to investigate how well national borders contained or explained how people experienced history. We wanted to observe how people, moving through time and space according to rhythms and relationships of their own, drew from, ignored, constructed, transformed, and defied claims of the nation-state."[17] Thelen went on to link these issues explicitly with public debates over globalization and to identify collaborative scholarship as an important key to the crossing of the threshold away from the constraints of purely national history.[18]

Our hopes for the April 2000 Orono conference and for this book have much in common with those articulated by Thelen, and with those of practitioners of other broadly based approaches. Historical geographers, for example, have long operated independently of the national paradigm and in turn, through such works as Donald Meinig's monumental *The Shaping of America*, have crucially influenced the recent efforts of historians to set North American developments in the context of a North Atlantic world.[19] This, however, being a volume devoted specifically to issues affecting the Maritime–New England geographical area, a significant historiographical caveat is in order. While transnational approaches are typically seen in the context of United States historiography as mounting a challenge to a tradition in which centripetal forces operating in the late nineteenth and early twentieth centuries had tended, as Tyrrell remarked, to merge "imperial, regional, and local experience into a national stream of history,"[20] the same approaches take a rather separate trajectory in the context of Canadian historical traditions. Canadian historiography has had its own centripetal forces, notably including the ascendancy of the "Laurentian thesis" in Anglo-Canadian historiography from the late 1940s to the early 1960s.[21] Yet in many important respects Canadian historiography has developed in generically different configurations from those of its counterpart in the United States, and has had longstanding centrifugal tendencies.

Canadian historiography, for example, has reflected – and continues to reflect – the coexistence of different nationalisms within the borders of Canada. English-language historical writing has traditionally followed quite separate imperatives from those animating either Quebec or Acadian historians (which two French-language historiographical traditions have not always co-existed easily either). Although important convergences have taken place in the past generation or so, particularly with the growth of social history and of pluralist approaches to national identity and experience, differences remain.[22] Thus, debates in Canada over the relationship of social and national history – even though the existence of such debates is far from peculiar to Canadian historiography – have had a distinctively multi-layered character.[23] And, whereas in the United States transnational approaches may be seen as a conscious counterweight to the national focus, Canadian historians are in the different position of being longstanding participants in a historiography that is (or at least ought to be) transnational not by adoption but by definition. Such considerations have direct relevance to the present volume insofar as the issues have involved regional distinctiveness. Ramsay Cook in 1967 deplored the sterility of then-contemporary debates over the Canadian national identity in making the celebrated (and cerebrated) observation that "perhaps, instead of constantly deploring our lack of identity, we should attempt to understand and explain the regional, ethnic, and class identities that we do have. It might just be that it is in these limited identities that 'Canadianism' is found."[24]

The concept of "limited identities" was quickly embraced by regional historians, including those of the Maritime provinces, but the thrust of the resulting scholarship – particularly as it related to the post-Confederation era – was not to abandon Canadian history in exchange for a separate regional history, but rather to insist that Canadian history could not be fully understood until its regional dimensions were properly explored.[25] Hence the reservations expressed by Phillip Buckner in two critiques of the borderlands approach, at least insofar as it might be used to advance a continentalist agenda by implying that national boundaries and identities were either meaningless or undesirable.[26] Hence too the reality that, from a Maritime perspective, the border experience can more readily be seen from at least the early nineteenth century onward as a contributing element to a "limited identity" within British North America and Canada, than as a source of intrinsic alienation. Or, to put it another way by adopting the terminology of Adelman and Aron, the

1.1 Contemporary location map of New England and the Maritime Provinces.

Maritime–New England area after the era of the American Revolution can properly be viewed as increasingly a bordered land rather than a borderland. For all that, of course, the study of cross-border connections and comparisons does not have to be an instrument for conflating separate societal phenomena, any more than a continental frame of reference must be a stalking horse for a continentalist agenda. If either of these principles held true, there would be no justification for a book such as this one. What this collection seeks to do, rather, is to take a critical and analytical approach to both connection and comparison.

The present book makes no claim to be comprehensive in its treatment of Maritime–New England topics. Significant lacunae inevitably exist. However, it does offer a series of studies that collectively convey a strong indication of the range and diversity of the connections and comparisons that can and should be drawn, from the earliest human societies to the twenty-first century. The essays reflect the collection's overall focus on the complementary themes of connection and comparison, and in some of them both of these threads can be traced. The principal themes, in many cases intertwined, are cultural, social, economic, and environmental. The collection is organized chronologically, at least to the extent allowed by contributions that consider overlapping periods.

Although the Maritimes and New England consistently represent the principal focus of the collection, the authors in some instances reach outside this geographical area for comparative purposes. Scott W. See's treatment of the Gavazzi riots in Lower Canada is an example. Also, no obligation was placed on the authors to embrace all of the Maritimes and New England in their analyses; most focus on particular areas or entities on either side of the border. They establish themes that illustrate the fluidity in time and space that is unavoidable in any effort to come to terms with a bordered land that has had many more complexities than just a border. At the same time, as Graeme Wynn observes, "complex pieces are invariably part of larger wholes," and in this sense the collection seeks also to contribute to the overall historiographies of the Maritimes and New England as well as to the historiography of the connections and comparisons that link the two.[27]

The essay by David Sanger launches the collection by reviewing successive millennia during which cultural and environmental changes interacted throughout the territory later known as the Maritimes and New England. While it hardly needs saying that the line separating Canada from the United States had not yet been imagined during the long period of exclusively aboriginal occupation, Sanger draws attention to the deeper currents of cultural evolution that justify treating the Maritime Peninsula as a discrete region. Elizabeth Mancke extends the point into the early phase of non-aboriginal intrusion. Taking issue with the conventional use of a colonial model to explain more complex and cross-cultural phenomena associated with European expansion, Mancke proposes instead an approach based on "spaces of power." Early modern empires in northeastern North America, she argues, had more to do with multiple and contested usages of space and resources than with colonial settlement as such; European and aboriginal spaces of power could frequently coexist, depending on the environmental demands of each. William Wicken's essay provides an example of the potential durability of aboriginal spaces of power. Wicken takes eighteenth-century treaty negotiations as the backdrop for an analysis of the significance of an important 1999 decision of the Supreme Court of Canada – in the case of Donald Marshall Junior – for the Passamaquoddy of northeastern Maine, who referenced a 1760 treaty with the British crown as the basis for claiming the right to a commercial fishery in Canadian waters under the Marshall ruling. Finally in this opening series of essays that combine cultural and environmental approaches, Geoffrey Plank investigates the culturally generated stresses associated with the posting of New Englanders to garrison duty in the St. John Valley in the late 1750s. Alternating between extremes of violence and boredom, these militia soldiers found the landscape alien and disconcerting, although this did not prevent later groups of New Englanders from responding more positively to it as settlers. Thus, from the earliest human societies to the mid-eighteenth century, and in the absence of any well-defined border, cultural, and spatial considerations offer the key to determining the existence of a recognizable region.

Béatrice Craig's essay continues the focus on the St John Valley, but it introduces an entirely different set of social, economic, and cultural interactions that characterized the late eighteenth century and the first half of the nineteenth. It was clear by now that a border existed, even though not until the Webster-Ashburton Treaty of 1842 could Great Britain and the United States agree on its location.[28] Cross-border spaces of influence and interaction also existed, however, and there was room for doubt whether this was what later historians – again we borrow from Adelman and Aron – would see as a borderland or a bordered land. Craig's analysis of perceptions regarding francophone communities on the upper St John underlines one difference that was conditioned by the existence of an international border: the distinction between British observers, whose more detached views of the St John Valley French were influenced by the multi-ethnic character of the empire, and those from the United States who were troubled by deviations from the ideals of republicanism and progress. This era also saw the elaboration of cross-border economic relationships. Julian Gwyn's analysis of Nova Scotia–New England trade from the 1720s to the 1860s identifies New England as an important and productive trading partner for Nova Scotia, rather than holding its northern neighbour in an imperialist embrace. As Joshua M. Smith shows, however, the border was also a porous enough creation for illegal trade to flourish. Smuggling, Smith contends, might indicate the existence of cultural affinities across the border but more importantly represented a business activity that flowed through channels created by resource configurations existing independently of the international divide. There were affinities, too, as Scott W. See demonstrates, among the ethno-religious conflicts that arose in Canada East, Nova Scotia, and Maine. While nativist-inspired riots always had distinct local variations, See identifies more general patterns of social class tension and Catholic-Protestant hostility, as well as detecting information networks by which one such event could influence another regardless of the jurisdiction in which either may have taken place. By the mid-nineteenth century, therefore, the Maritime colonies were clearly divided from New England, but connections and affinities could persist.

As the collection moves into the middle decades of the nineteenth century, and toward the twentieth, three essays explore further economic dimensions of the Maritime–New England relationship, again through both connections and comparisons. While none seeks to offer a definitive answer to the question of comparative rates and qualities of economic development on either side of the border, which awaits the detailed attention of an economic historian, each of the essays bears on the economic significance – real and perceived – of the international divide.[29] D.A. Sutherland combines cultural with economic history in exploring Nova Scotia's preoccupation with the politics of economic development during the years between the establishment of responsible government and the Treaty of Reciprocity. An envious popular perception of the economic and cultural vibrancy of New England coexisted in Nova Scotia with a profound mistrust of any move toward the relinquishment of British North America's political distinctness from its more populous neighbour. Yet, as Jacques Ferland's essay demonstrates, the cross-border economic relationship must also be examined for the complexities of its more localized characteristics. The leather-manufacturing business of the Shaw brothers, for instance, was based in eastern Maine, but from the 1850s to the 1880s it relied on natural resources extracted from western New Brunswick. Economic dependency and environmental depredation resulted. Finally, Robert H. Babcock takes an approach that relies on comparison rather than connection in studying the economic history of the cities of Portland and Saint John between 1880 and 1920. Portland's growth was more the rapid and complex of the two. Accounting for the difference, Babcock is sceptical of traditional interpretations that have attributed Saint John's slower growth to public policy restraints originating in Ottawa. Rather, he argues, different port-hinterland relationships and the fortuitous synchronization of Portland's development with larger phases of industrialization have greater explanatory power. Taken together, the four contributions portray a border across which the flow of trade was continuous, but which also embodied a separation characterized by competition for economic development and for control of natural resource commodities.

The late nineteenth and early twentieth centuries saw the emergence of further resource-related historical developments that had cultural and environmental consequences spanning the border. Edward D. Ives offers a summary of a scholarly lifetime of cross-border folklore analysis and fieldwork in drawing out the influence of Maritime balladeers in the lumbercamps of Maine. The cross-border commonality of ballads and balladeers reflected the migration of men who worked in the woods, from New Brunswick to Maine and from Maine to the midwest. If timber was one major resource commodity common to the Maritimes and New England, fish was another. Deborah C. Trefts, conscious of the significance of fisheries crises in the late twentieth and early twenty-first centuries, demonstrates that public policy makers in both Canada and the United States were forced to confront serious fisheries decline in the Gulf of Maine as early as in the 1860s and 1870s. In this case, the international divide was sharply evident in the contrast between the respective responses. A centralized regulatory regime emerged in Canada, while laissez-faire accompanied by a faith in the ability of science and technology to solve the problem characterized the response of the United States. Yet, in the area of sport fisheries and hunting, as Bill Parenteau and Richard W. Judd show, regulation was the preferred policy option on both sides of the border, though at the cost of class-related tensions and disruption of longstanding patterns of resource exploitation by both native and non-native rural dwellers. Travel writers portrayed Maine and the Maritimes as an undifferentiated paradise for sportsmen, and the states and provinces responded to the influx of wealthy tourists in the late nineteenth and early twentieth centuries by aggressively restricting the hunting and fishing activities of existing populations. By intertwining cultural, social, and environmental history, the essays focusing on this period show the commonalities that stemmed from comparable resource usages on either side of the border, even though the consequences – in terms of comparability of cultural patterns or state responses – varied from sector to sector.

With the essay by Betsy Beattie, the collection moves further into the twentieth century. Beattie's essay starts with the Maritime notion of "the Boston States" as a target for out-migration, and shows that differing definitions of this term can be explained by the different prevailing destinations of male and female migrants. While young male migrants frequently travelled long distances to settle in far-flung areas of the United States, young women typically migrated to the Boston area. Colin D. Howell's essay is also concerned with movement across the border, but its focus is on a shared sporting culture that developed between the Maritimes and New England during the interwar years. This culture declined only during the 1950s and 1960s, when Canada-wide promotion of the spectator sports identified by the federal state as inherently Canadian resulted in a radical imaginative relocation of the Maritimes in a Canadian rather than a cross-border sporting universe. Contrasting historical imaginings are also central to the essay by Reginald C. Stuart and M. Brook Taylor, which examines wider intellectual contexts within which Maritime–New England connections and comparisons must be examined and at the same time moves the volume toward its conclusion. Stuart and Taylor reflect on the intellectual and educational problems created by the contrast between the thoroughgoing separation of Canadian and United States historiographies, and the more global tendency to perceive the two countries as being more closely interrelated than any others in the world. The essay demonstrates that a continental frame of reference – as opposed to a continentalist agenda – can encourage a nuanced analysis and provide a counterweight to the assumptions of those who might see North American history as that of the United States writ large.

The collection concludes with a synthesis by Graeme Wynn. While identifying common themes among the essays, and setting them in the context of earlier cross-border analyses, Wynn also reviews current theoretical debates and the future research trends they may open up. Borders, for Wynn, do matter. Yet their significance must be measured in subtle and sophisticated ways that take account of complexity in space and variation through time. The contributions to this volume show that a politically bordered land can still be a social, cultural, and environmental borderland at some times and places, but also that political bordering can ... must – even should? – have profound social, cultural, and environmental consequences. Wynn places the present collection as a staging-point in ongoing research: "I would urge more careful and explicit comparative work, as well as inquiry in wider, innovative, and more speculative veins to encourage a rethinking of both the region and the linkages between the different parts."[30] If this book contributes to making that wish come true, we shall be well satisfied with its success.

2

Pre-European Dawnland: Archaeology of the Maritime Peninsula

DAVID SANGER

When investigating contacts and comparisons across what is a recently established border between Canada and the United States, it is important to recognize that people inhabited the Maritime Peninsula for at least 11,000 years before Europeans set foot on the land. The region constitutes a natural cultural area in which similarities can be traced for thousands of years. In modern terminology, it includes eastern Quebec, the Maritime provinces of New Brunswick, Nova Scotia and Prince Edward Island, and Maine east of the Kennebec River (see map, p. 9). The cultural affinities and communication networks that characterized this area for many millennia provide a forceful indication of the validity of cross-border regional study. The earliest evidence of human occupation in the Maritime Peninsula dates to the Paleoindian period (11,000 to 9,500 BP).[1]

From the anthropological perspective, people entered the Americas from eastern Asia earlier than 12,000 years ago.[2] Ice sheets associated with the last major glacial period, the Wisconsinian, covered the Maritime Peninsula, effectively limiting the first appearance of humans to the post-glacial period. Stone artifacts of the culture of this Early Paleoindian period are remarkably homogeneous throughout the Maritime Peninsula. Archaeologists traditionally assign a time range of between 11,000 and 10,000 years ago for this period, based on dates from relatively few sites, of which the Debert site, near Truro, Nova Scotia, is the best known.[3] However, except for some scattered finds, Debert remains unique in the Maritimes; many more sites of this period are known in Maine, all west of the Penobscot River

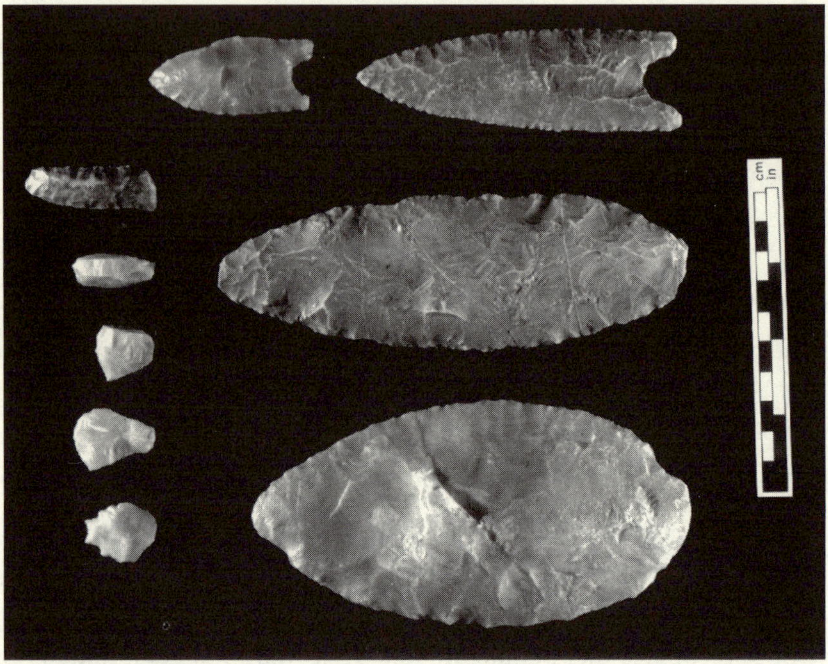

2.1 Chipped stone artifacts from the Paleoindian period site at Debert, Nova Scotia.

drainage.[4] People of the early Paleoindian period preferred silica-rich rocks, such as chert or chalcedony, for their artifacts (Figure 2.1). Of these, the fluted points, sometimes called "Clovis," attract inordinate attention. Maritime Peninsula Paleoindians participated in a technological pattern recognized in much of North America south of the glacial ice.[5]

Very little is known of Early Paleoindian subsistence patterns in the Maritime Peninsula region due to a scarcity of food remains preserved in the acidic soils of the region. Just a handful of definite caribou, some caribou or deer, and beaver bones have been identified.[6] Reconstructions of vegetation during this millennium indicate that tundra and perhaps open-spruce parklands were evolving into more closed forests.[7] The tundra or spruce parkland model has fostered a caribou-focused hunting culture analogue similar to that of the historic Algonquian hunters – formerly known as "Naskapi" but now as "Innu" – of Labrador and Quebec, or the Inuit.[8] Some scholars have challenged the appropriateness of this model.[9] Despite occasional finds of mammoth or mastodon bones, there is no evidence that Paleoindians of the

Maritime Peninsula hunted them as their counterparts did elsewhere in North America. With basically the same tool kit, Early Paleoindian people adapted to a wide variety of North American environments, ranging from ice-margins in the north to closed deciduous forests in the Southeast, to the Plains grasslands, and the dry Southwest.

Known Early Paleoindian sites in the Maritime Peninsula are located on well-drained, sandy soils, often elevated, as opposed to modern river floodplains.[10] This preference for location has led to confusion over the age of sites because the sandy sediments are prone to natural and cultural disturbances that may result in spurious associations between charcoal, used for dating, and artifacts.[11]

The limited availability of the preferred cherts and other fine-grained rocks used to manufacture chipped stone tools may have played an important role in Early Paleoindian behaviour. Silicates (known locally as "agates") from the Minas Basin area of Nova Scotia were used extensively by the inhabitants of the Debert site,[12] while chert from the Munsungun Lake quarries of northern Maine occurred in sites along the Androscoggin River in Maine, and south to Portland.[13] Archaeologists have speculated about the mechanisms that resulted in this wide distribution.[14] It is most likely that bands roamed widely as part of their normal seasonal round and made regular visits to the quarries to replenish their rock supplies. The latter hypothesis fits the proposed caribou-dominated lifestyle. No direct evidence exists for the spiritual aspect of Early Paleoindian culture in the Maritime Peninsula, although elsewhere in North America caches of tools with red ochre occur.[15]

Archaeologists of the Maritime Peninsula recognize the presence of another lithic tradition, the Late Paleoindian. Known primarily through their lithic technology, the Late Paleoindian people did not manufacture fluted points or some of the other characteristic tools of the earlier period. The origins of their long, slender spear points, or bifaces, can be traced west up the St Lawrence Valley to the Great Lakes, where they have been dated to between 10,000 BP and 9,500 BP, and from there to the Plains.[16] In Quebec, radiocarbon dates of roughly 8,100 years ago have been reported for the Rimouski site.[17] Scattered finds occur in New Brunswick and Nova Scotia.[18] The Varney Farm site in western Maine has produced ambiguous radiocarbon ages ranging from approximately 8,400 to 9,400 years ago.[19] At the Blackman Stream site on the Penobscot River, near Orono, a Late Paleoindian biface occurred a metre below an ancient soil horizon radiocarbon-dated to between 7,400 and 8,400 years ago.[20]

Currently, the Blackman Stream situation constitutes the best stratigraphic record because of its burial deep in alluvial sediments.

Artifacts at the other sites are so close to the surface that disturbances of one kind or another have created ambiguous contexts similar to those that plague investigation of Early Paleoindian sites in the region.

In Maine a very different culture, the Early Archaic, had developed by around 9,500 BP. Unless we are willing to accept the notion of two very different cultures occupying essentially the same space, a terminal date of around 9,500 BP for Late Paleoindian would best accommodate the Maine data. Elsewhere in the Maritime Peninsula the culture type may have persisted longer. However, for the region as a whole, 9,500 BP may be taken as the Early and Middle Archaic periods lasting until 6,000 BP and the onset of the Late Archaic period.

By regional convention, the Archaic Period represents the disappearance of the distinctive Paleoindian technology, the introduction of ground stone tools, and the absence of agriculture and pottery.[21] For convenience, archaeologists divide the Archaic into three subperiods. In contrast with the broadly similar technological pattern of the Paleoindians, regional differences became paramount in the Archaic. Although a number of models have been proposed to explain the shift, most follow a basic premise, expressed broadly as a "settling in" of populations, a factor of adaptation to local landscapes. The use of immediately available lithics appeared as part of the overall process. In the Southeast, some evidence supports an *in situ* evolution from the Paleoindian Period.[22] Environments were changing rapidly; forests and game animal distributions began to assume a more modern character. For eastern seaboard regions south of the Maritime Peninsula, the presence of Southeastern styles of bifaces has suggested a spread of ideas from south to north.[23]

Two concepts compete as integrative devices for Early and Middle Archaic sites in the Maritime Peninsula. The Atlantic provinces region has been subsumed under the Maritime Archaic tradition concept.[24] For Maine, and adjacent New Hampshire, an alternative term has been proposed – the Gulf of Maine Archaic tradition.[25] It is critical to note that these two taxa are not equivalent: the Maritime Archaic tradition applies to the entire culture, whereas the Gulf of Maine concept refers only to the lithic technology involved. Archaeologists have rejected the Maritime Archaic formulation for Maine while acknowledging that significant similarities exist.[26]

To date, neither tradition has been clearly identified in the Maritime provinces. When intact Early and Middle Archaic sites are found in the Maritimes, they may look more like Maine sites than their Maritime Archaic tradition counterparts from the north side of the Gulf of St Lawrence and the Labrador coast.[27] Intuitively, the southern view makes more sense because of the contiguous land mass and environ-

2.2 Chipped and ground stone artifacts representing the Archaic period. The speciments are from various sites in Maine.

mental similarities. Finally, explanation for recent finds at Cap-de-Bon-Désir, near Tadoussac on the upper north shore of the St Lawrence River, has favoured the Gulf of Maine tradition rather than the Maritime Archaic, despite the presence of seal bones in the deposits.[28]

In central Maine, the earliest Archaic sites date from 9,000 years and earlier.[29] The stone tool industry features the use of local lithics, such as vein quartz and a variety of metamorphic rocks. Most surprising, perhaps, is the scarcity of chipped stone bifaces or spear points, especially analogues of those occurring in southern New England and in western Maine along the Androscoggin River.[30] The latter area lies outside the Maritime Peninsula as defined in this chapter. It may be that bone and antler served for piercing weapons instead of chipped stone spear points. Celts and gouges, usually considered woodworking implements, occur together with a variety of chopping and cutting artifacts, more functional than elegant. Over time other metamorphic stone artifact forms, such as slate points, ulus, and plummets entered the record (Figure 2.2). Overall, the artifact inventory is much broader than that associated with the Paleoindian Period. The fact that no close technological similarity exists, given the obviously different mode of adaptation, offers no support for a hypothesis of population continuity.[31]

A number of Early and Middle Archaic sites have yielded food remains in the form of highly shattered and heavily burned (calcined) bones. The minute size of most bone fragments has frustrated detailed dietary reconstruction; however, diligent analysis has demonstrated the aquatic nature of the remains, especially the presence of muskrat, beaver, fish, and turtle.[32] Unlike Paleoindian sites, these Archaic stations occur in modern drainage valleys, nearly always at the bottom of a sequence of alluvial silty sand deposits that set off various occupations, one from the other. In central Maine, particularly in the Penobscot River Valley and its tributaries, sites occur in close proximity to wetlands. The high biological carrying capacity of these wetlands, especially cattail (*Typha*) marshes,[33] combined with riverine resources, permitted a settlement pattern of the localized variety suggested by the "settling in" process of Archaic hunters and gatherers throughout eastern North America. Although it is highly unlikely that these populations were fully sedentary, their annual round was much more restricted than that hypothesized for the Paleoindians. The switch to local metamorphic rocks appears to be a logical consequence of the focus on wetlands as opposed to upland hunting of wandering caribou herds.[34] In an attempt to document the evolution of wetlands near archaeological sites, University of Maine researchers have studied central Maine wetlands and developed a detailed history that progresses from open water (lakes), to cattail marshes and fens, to *Sphagnum* moss peat bogs.[35] Important new research demonstrates that during the Early and Middle Archaic periods water levels in Maine lakes and rivers were substantially lower than they were when Europeans arrived. [36] This must have had profound impacts on the abilities of Native peoples to canoe the waterways and on the various animal and plant species living in aquatic environments.

Although we know relatively little about the spiritual life of Early and Middle Archaic people, the red ochre burial pattern that becomes so prominent in the Late Archaic period has its roots in the Early and Middle Archaic period; it has been dated in southern New England to 8,500 years ago.[37]

With the advent of the Late Archaic period (approximately 6,000 BP) the pre-European record in much of the Northeast becomes more complete. Indeed, for large areas such as much of New York State and the Maritime provinces, this period represents the first positive evidence for any human occupation since the Paleoindian Period.[38] The recognition of many more sites, and therefore an assumed population increase, has prompted scholars to invoke an environmental explanation for the scarcity or even absence of Early and Middle Archaic–aged sites.[39] Once Maine archaeologists discovered deeply buried sites in riverbank settings, the gap in the record vanished. That Maine would be unique in this respect seems unlikely.

In a number of central Maine sites, starting no earlier than 6,000 BP, large, side-notched projectile points (likely spear points) appeared (Plate 2). Named "Otter Creek" points after sites in Vermont,[40] these distinctive forms occur throughout eastern Maine and western New Brunswick, and into Nova Scotia.[41] To date, only Maine sites have radiocarbon estimates that range from about 5,800 BP to 4,500 BP. Archaeologists suggest that Otter Creek points were added to existing Middle Archaic tool kits.[42] The new cultural combination becomes the Laurentian tradition, a term first employed by William A. Ritchie.[43] Laurentian tradition–related sites of the Maritime Peninsula occur above head of tide, while the distinctive Otter Creek points are reported mostly east of the Kennebec River.[44] Two finds, so far unique, are noteworthy.

In central Maine, at Sebasticook Lake, amateur archaeologists found the remains of hundreds of wooden stakes sticking up from the mud after lake levels had been artificially lowered. Investigations demonstrated that some of the stakes dated to 5,000 years ago.[45] This chance find suggests that similar stationary fish trap structures occurred throughout the Maritime Peninsula wherever suitable conditions existed.[46] A second unique find involves the discovery of a tiny piece of 6,000-year-old gourd, thought to represent a domesticated variety, from a site on the upper Piscataquis River.[47] Its origin remains mysterious, as the region is well outside the expected climate-growth zone for this species. Trade is the most likely explanation.

The Laurentian tradition distribution supports the hypothesis of a "two population" model for Maine.[48] Artifact differences between contemporaneous sites in the interior and the coast, which cannot be explained on strictly environmental or task-specific grounds, suggest two alternative modes of adaptation. One lifestyle, the Laurentian tradition, represents an adaptation to the interior and its wetlands; the other, the Small-stemmed Point tradition, reflects a focus on the coastal zone and marine resources.[49] The concept of two basic adaptations makes moot much of the previous controversy that failed to distinguish between interior and coastal populations, and assumed that one culture type covered both.[50] The distinction between coastal and interior has only recently been emphasized, although its genesis dates to over two decades ago.[51] Finally, Laurentian tradition sites, as recognized by Otter Creek points, disappear from the Maine record about 4,500 BP. This disappearance creates a hiatus in the record of about half a millennium before people of the Susquehanna tradition populated the interior sometime after 3,800 BP. Perhaps more apparent than real, this gap nevertheless constitutes yet another challenge to archaeologists.

Intact coastal sites occur only with the Late Archaic period because of the rise in sea-level. From a high-water point toward the end of the Pleistocene epoch, when marine waters covered much of the coastal plain, a regression resulted in a sea level 60 metres below current sea level at about 10,500 BP, or synchronous with Paleoindian times.[52] Sea levels then rose abruptly before slowing, such that by the mid-Holocene epoch (approximately 5,000 BP–4,500 BP) we begin to recognize intact coastal sites in Penobscot Bay; an example is the Turner Farm site.[53] Although fishermen have dredged up potentially earlier artifacts from around the Maritime Peninsula, archaeologists can only discern actual intact sites from the period after sea levels stabilized somewhat later than 5,000 BP.[54]

The excavator of the Turner Farm site, the pre-eminent Maritime Peninsula coastal site of the Late Archaic period, argued that the earliest occupations represented a longstanding regional adaptation to the resources of the Gulf of Maine.[55] Part of that adaptation included the consumption of shellfish, whose calcareous remains neutralized the normally acidic soils and effected excellent preservation of food bones, including those of marine species such as swordfish, seal, and cod. Terrestrial mammals, especially deer, were also taken. Sites of a similar culture, termed the Moorehead phase, occurred in other mid-Maine coastal areas from Monhegan Island on the west, to Frenchman Bay in Down East Maine.[56] Small-stemmed points occur in collections as far east as Washington County, Maine.[57] On the basis of these point styles, the Bain site near Yarmouth, Nova Scotia could have been related.[58] Sea-level rise in the remainder of the Maritime Peninsula might have eroded similar sites, but this hypothesis should not be assumed, as the Maine coastal sites could have represented the northern extent of a longstanding east coast maritime adaptation.[59] Once again, however, the scarcity of intact sites in the Maritime provinces frustrates our efforts. Two distinct origins for the maritime adaptation have been suggested: one north of the Gulf of St Lawrence – the Maritime Archaic tradition – and one to the south, the Small-stemmed Point tradition and its associated Moorehead phase.[60]

The well-known red ochre cemeteries of the Maritime Peninsula have captured the imagination of the public and profession alike for over a century. Popularly known as the culture of the "Red paint people," this mysterious culture typifies regional archaeology for many. Although archaeologists once considered the red ochre burials to be Late Archaic in age, we now realize that they are at least 8,500 years old in the coastal far Northeast[61] and up the St Lawrence Valley to the Ottawa River.[62] As such, the burials co-occur with a number of different culture types, environmental zones, and adaptations. Unfortunately, few of these cemeteries have been excavated professionally using modern techniques; Port au Choix (Newfoundland) and Cow Point (New Brunswick) represent the only examples.[63] Human remains were preserved at Port au Choix, permitting detailed examination of the population.[64] Throughout most of the red-ochre cemetery range, however, since skeletons did not survive the acid soils, biological comparisons of populations have been impossible.

The mortuary pattern involved copious amounts of red ochre, or crushed hematite. Other traits include interment (both primary and secondary) in discrete, formal, cemeteries (usually not in contemporary habitations), and the inclusion of specific suites of artifacts, some of which are highly diagnostic. The majority of artifacts are of metamorphic rocks, many of which are unused, manufactured specifically for the grave. A remarkable series of long, delicate, beautifully symmetrical slate bayonets at Cow Point have embellishments on one side; significantly, that side faced upward in the grave. These artifacts and their careful placement indicate that the deceased remained spiritually linked with those who conducted mortuary ceremonies. While we may not be capable of understanding the symbolism involved, we can appreciate both the quality of workmanship and the rare glimpse into a symbolic system in operation millennia ago. These burial practices, known as the Moorehead burial tradition, integrated the Archaic Period throughout the Maritime Peninsula.[65] Their ubiquity reminds archaeologists that although tool types may change, and people's adaptive patterns reflect local environments, a cosmological and spiritual centrality united the region.

In much of the Maritime Peninsula, the Late Archaic period ends with the appearance of the Susquehanna tradition around 3,800 BP.[66] This tradition, which evolved from earlier Archaic culture types in the mid-Atlantic area, swept into southern New England and Maine, overrunning the coastal Moorehead phase and a currently untitled culture type (if indeed any) that existed in the interior. Sites from the Susquehanna tradition occur above earlier occupations and extend well inland.[67] For a period of a few centuries, the dichotomy between coast and interior vanishes. Susquehanna artifacts reached the Maritimes, but not with the intensity seen in Maine.[68] Susquehanna tradition sites date between about 3,800 and 3,400 BP. Almost overnight, in radiocarbon terms, several classes of tools, technology, settlement patterns and burial customs were completely replaced, as cremation of bodies and associated artifacts became the general rule. Most archaeologists favour a population replacement, a migration, as an explanation for this phenomenon.[69]

But how and why might this change have taken place? Although migrations still occur in the modern world, they are notoriously difficult to demonstrate in the pre-literate archaeological domain. Realizing that population movements were being over-used as the explanation for all culture change, archaeologists have become reluctant to invoke them. However, in this instance, the alternatives, independent (or *in situ*) evolution and diffusion of ideas, are equally difficult to demonstrate.

For Maine, the entire replacement of so many artifacts, the new settlement pattern and burial customs, and new, high precision radiocarbon dates that demonstrate a chronological gap between Susquehanna and Moorehead burial tradition sites[70] all suggest the presence of a new population bearing a different culture. Unfortunately, the scarcity of skeletal remains renders DNA analysis inoperable. Given traditional assumptions about pacifistic hunter-gatherer behaviour, the thesis of a territorial conquest at the expense of a resident population requires a level of documentation currently unavailable. It may be that colonists bearing the Susquehanna tradition expanded into an area essentially devoid of humans.

The "why" portion of the inquiry depends on whether one accepts the population replacement hypothesis. Although changes in environment and subsistence patterns have been suggested in the past,[71] these are currently not very compelling explanations. Perhaps unknown events in the mid-Atlantic Coastal region, homeland of the Susquehanna tradition, hold some answers. For the Maritimes, a migration is less likely; the traits appear somewhat attenuated when compared with Maine, the similarities being more in morphology and less in technology, and the typical Susquehanna burials of Maine and southern New England not yet described in the Maritimes. In this instance some diffusion of ideas may constitute a better explanation. If so, the implication would be that for much of the Maritimes a population replacement did not occur at this time.

As this review indicates, most of our knowledge of the Archaic period in the Maritime Peninsula derives from Maine sites. While sites such as Cow Point (New Brunswick) contribute useful data to the overall picture, for much of the Maritimes we have at present to rely either on Maine or Newfoundland-Labrador finds to provide the framework. This picture changes dramatically with the final pre-European period in the Maritime Peninsula, the Ceramic or Maritime Woodland period, which began about 3,000 BP and continued up to the arrival of Europeans.

With the onset of this period, the amount of available information increases quite substantially. Ironically, this comparative wealth of material is not reflected in the published literature, which has tended to focus on the earlier periods. For the first time, we have a considerable amount of data from the Maritime provinces to compare and contrast with a similarly enhanced database for Maine. Interpretation of the finds emphasizes the growing distinctiveness of the region from the Iroquoian speakers to the west and the agricultural coastal Algonquians of southern New England.

Fired earthenware vessels, or ceramics, made an appearance in the Maritime Peninsula around 3,000 BP.[72] Because pottery appeared almost simultaneously across the Northeast it probably represented a rapid diffusion from one or more dispersal centres in the west or the south. Disposal of the dead in an eye-catching manner has a long archaeological history in eastern North America. Sometime after 3,000 BP, Native populations south of the Great Lakes began to bury their dead in earthen mounds, accompanied by a distinctive suite of artifacts that archaeologists recognize as being either of the Adena or the Hopewell burial traditions.[73] Artifacts reminiscent of the Adena tradition appeared along the St Lawrence Valley and into the Maritime Peninsula; a low mound (about one metre high) was erected over burials at the Augustine site, Red Bank, on the banks of the Miramichi River.[74] A somewhat similar site, although not nearly as intact by the time archaeologists visited the area, was found near Halifax.[75] Other burial sites in the Maritimes lack mounds.

To some archaeologists, the Ceramic or Woodland Period burials represent two different culture types, Meadowood and Middlesex, the latter associated with the distinctive Adena-like artifacts and mound building.[76] One recent review of eastern Canadian culture history has combined both into a single Adena burial pattern, in which participation by local populations was overseen by a "priesthood or priest-shaman class."[77] According to this model, the Meadowood culture, defined in New York and the St Lawrence Valley, did not exist in the Maritimes. However, some recent finds on the Jemseg River, a tributary of the St John, indicate close artifact connections with Meadowood sites in the St Lawrence Valley.[78]

Such differences of opinion and uncertainty occur commonly when the data are ambiguous, reliable radiocarbon dates few, and detailed published accounts scarce. A further problem arises when archaeologists import terminology from one area (e.g., New York State) into another (e.g., Maritime Peninsula) and then expect precise analogues.

To date, negative evidence suggests that Maine did not participate in the Adena (Middlesex) burial pattern. After so many Late Archaic cemeteries of the Moorehead or Susquehanna types, the burial record is nearly silent. However, it would take only one spectacular find of a burial mound from the early Ceramic period in Maine to catapult this area into a consideration of the cultural dynamics found in New Brunswick and Nova Scotia. The current evidence suggests that, while Maine and the Maritimes participated in the same general eastward spread of artifact styles, the details and the mechanisms may have differed. An evaluation of the linguistic evidence provides a clue.

Through detailed comparisons of closely related languages of the Algonquian family, a case can be made for a proto-Algonquian linguistic homeland in the Great Lakes area.[79] The distribution of Eastern Algonquian languages (Mi'kmaq, Maliseet-Passamaquoddy, Eastern Abanaki, and possibly Etchemin) in the Maritime Peninsula supports the hypothesis of an eastern movement of people down the St Lawrence Valley sometime between 3,000 and 2,000 BP.[80] With the notable exception of the Susquehanna tradition discussed earlier, Northeastern archaeologists have hesitated to accept migration as an explanation for culture change and have favoured *in situ* evolution. This hesitation may be changing, as attested by recent debate over the possibility of late pre-European migration of Iroquoian speakers into upstate New York.[81]

The evidence from the Maritimes can be interpreted to support population movements along the St Lawrence Valley and into northern New Brunswick. The migrants brought with them ideas of burial and worldview that differed from local traditions. In Maine, people adopted some of the artifacts (such as the pottery, copper beads, and projectile point forms) but apparently never participated in the Adena-like (or Middlesex) mound-building complex and distinctive suite of artifacts, perhaps because there was no influx of people to carry the required structured symbolism. Finding Adena-like mounds throughout Maine would make it necessary to rethink this hypothesis. Finally, a review of the early Ceramic period in New Brunswick has noted a difference in the archaeological record between northeast and the southwest portions of the province, a division speculated to reflect the ethnic division between the Mi'kmaq and the Maliseet ethnic groups of the Contact Period.[82]

In Maine a number of sites have substantial quantities of the earliest ceramic forms known in the Northeast, a distinctive conical form built of superposed clay coils consolidated and thinned by twisted cord wrapped around a paddle. This technique imparts a highly distinctive surface texture to the exterior and interior of the vessel, while the relatively coarse, sandy-gravel temper is also diagnostic. Throughout much of the Northeast it is called "Vinette I," the earliest of a long series of named pottery types that become increasingly restricted to

2.3 Artifacts in stone, bone, tooth, and pottery from the Ceramic period. The specimens are from various sites in coastal Maine.

regions. For the Maritime Peninsula a different scheme has been suggested, one that recognizes a series of changes in form and surface treatment (or decoration), and then uses these attribute constellations to characterize seven periods, Ceramic Periods (CP) 1–7; the latter represents Aboriginal pottery being produced in parts of the Maritime Peninsula during the Contact period.[83] Vinette I pottery equates with CP1.

Maine sites with CP1 pottery also contain small chipped projectile points and a particular form of biface scraper that bears resemblance to contemporary artifacts from elsewhere in the Northeast.[84] In addition, occasional copper beads made of rolled native copper occur. No convincing argument has been made that the bearers of this culture descended from the previous Susquehanna tradition. Despite the accelerated pace of research in Maine in recent years, very little is known of events between the earliest appearance of CP1 pottery and the end of the Susquehanna tradition as manifested in the Maritime Peninsula. It is almost as if the area suffered a dramatic drop in population for a couple of centuries, although not all archaeologists agree.[85] (Figure 2.3)

Starting around 2,000 BP, the evidence supports the development of a local way of life on the Maritime Peninsula that is relatively unaffected by events to the south and west. The great majority of all known sites in the area date from this period to the coming of Europeans. For the first time, the numbers of preserved sites permit archaeologists to make statistically significant observations when describing settlement patterns. For example, a decade of site survey and test excavation in the Boothbay Harbor area of the central Maine coast revealed over 200 sites, which have formed the basis of a detailed analysis of preferred settlement areas, season of occupation, and subsistence. The results could be compared with other coastal settings in Maine and western New Brunswick to help distinguish local from regional cultural patterning.[86]

Coastal shell middens, because they are composed of thousands of mollusk shells (mostly soft-shell clam and mussel), retain a great deal of site structure normally lost in interior sites because of acidic soils and natural disturbances. Archaeologists have been able to detect functionally specific areas of sites, such as dwellings, manufacturing areas, and places for the dumping of debris. The amount of information generated greatly exceeds anything possible from preceding times.

Positive evidence for dwellings appears for the first time in the form of small (about three by four metres), oval, semi-subterranean houses probably covered by a conical pole and bark tent similar to the well-known wigwams depicted in early Contact Period illustrations.[87] Their small size suggests nuclear or extended family occupation. To date, the clearest evidence derives from excavations in coastal shell middens. The excellent preservation of organic remains in coastal middens permits archaeologists to construct detailed accounts of diets based on preserved bones of prey species. These "ecofacts" form the basis for hypotheses related to strategies for exploitation of the varied environments in the Maritime Peninsula.[88]

As the pre-European era comes to an end, archaeologists feel more comfortable with consulting early texts for accounts of aboriginal people and their activities. Textual analysis is, of course, a methodology with some pitfalls because of the magnitude of the changes that occurred in native life, and the tendency to homogenize behaviour on the basis of scattered observations from various sources. For example, a well-known letter written by Jesuit Pierre Biard details a seasonal round for Mi'kmaq in the eastern Bay of Fundy early in the seventeenth century.[89] Although the Biard account fits well with one model of pre-European Nova Scotia settlement pattern,[90] it has been applied uncritically to the Maliseet of the St John River[91] and the Penobscot people of Maine.[92]

When tested against archaeological data from the Maine coast, the Biard model fails. Based on multiple seasonal indicators, especially the time of year that clams and other animals were taken, the evidence strongly points to a year-round occupation on the coast of Maine. People moved within a circumscribed area to take advantage of seasonally abundant prey and to obtain shelter for the winter.[93] Reconstructions of settlement patterns elsewhere in the Maritime Peninsula have emphasized the high degree of variability that paralleled the environmental differences present in the Maritimes.[94]

During the discussion of the Archaic period, as already noted, two alternative adaptations, one coastal and one interior, best explained the evidence for Maine. A similar paradigm can be applied with even more confidence to the Ceramic period because we now have so many more data points on which to build. It is important to note that the identification of two modes of adaptation, coastal and interior, does not necessarily imply two ethnic groups. In addition to the evidence derived from seasonality of the Maine coast, there are a number of material culture differences, including the basic way in which vegetable fibre was twisted to produce cordage.[95] Unfortunately, interior sites do not feature the excellent faunal preservation seen in the coastal shell middens. Available remains are consistent with summer occupation in the interior, at a time when a simplistic extension of the Biard account for Nova Scotia would have people on the coast.[96]

Another approach to the "two population" concept is to consider the possibility of differences in the non-material culture domain. Frederik Barth has pointed out the difficulty in separating ethnicity from an ecological adaptation, a difficulty that would especially hold true when the defining traits involve subsistence and other aspects heavily influenced by local environments.[97] Archaeological glimpses into cosmology and ideology are rare in the Maritime Peninsula and depend highly on idiosyncratic interpretations of mortuary behaviours. However, another avenue of investigation, discard of animal bones, may offer independent evidence for differing cosmologies.

Ethnohistorical accounts from the interior of Quebec and the Maritime Peninsula confirm that crucial spiritual relationships exist between people and prey animals. The spirits of animals that allow themselves to be taken by people must be supplicated, ritually recognized, and shown great respect, even after consumption of their flesh. As described for the Mistassini Cree by Adrian Tanner,[98] this is a three-step process: location of the game, perhaps using divination; the encounter and kill; and respectful behaviour in the camp and during consumption, which involves ritual during the meal and in the "clean-up" phase. Great care is taken not to let the dogs eat bones of the animal, as that act would upset the "Spirit Masters," or leaders. Failure in obligations to the animal spirits courts disaster; the "Spirit Masters" will not tolerate the animals to be captured.

Accounts, many recorded in the Jesuit Relations, detail how important it was in the early European period not to let dogs have bones of captured animals, and thus offend the Spirits. Ritual disposal of bones ranged according to the animal involved and local custom. A common way of making sure the camp dogs did not violate the spirits was to incinerate the bones.[99] In the nineteenth century, there is an account of Mi'kmaq hunters in Nova Scotia burning all bones of "Deer" so as not to offend and incur the wrath of the "guardian Genius" of each species.[100] In Maine, Frank Speck has elicited comparable ideology regarding appropriate care with prey bones from early twentieth-century Penobscot hunters.[101] The express prohibition against careless disposal of certain animal bones occurs also among northeastern hunter-gatherers from Quebec to the Maritime Peninsula.

Interior Maine archaeological sites rarely have bone preserved unless it was chemically altered through burning. Of more than 12,000 bone fragments from the Hirundo site, for example, nearly all (91%) were calcined after being incorporated into fire hearths.[102] Observation of this pattern can be reproduced at site after site in interior Maine. Coastal sites, by contrast, rarely display any burned bone.[103] Typically, bones occur in an unburned state, simply tossed out onto the midden along with shells, broken implements, and general camp debris. Signs of carnivore chewing, probably by dogs, are not uncommon. Among coastal people of Maine and adjacent New Brunswick, concern for insulting the "Spirit Masters" at this, the final or disposal stage, appeared not to involve deliberate burning or general restriction of dog access. With the caveat that historical observations must be treated cautiously when applied to the archaeological record, the widespread and pervasive notion of honouring the spirits of animals by systematically burning food bones may constitute another way to distinguish between inhabitants of the coast and those of the interior.

The absence of Aboriginal agriculture in the Maritime Peninsula distinguishes the region from neighbouring areas, the Iroquoian-speaking farmers to the west, and Algonquian agriculturalists in southern New England. When Samuel de Champlain sailed south and west from the Bay of Fundy along the Gulf of Maine, he recorded agriculture for the first time at the Saco River, well south of the Kennebec River mouth.[104] Maize agriculture, which probably only reached New England some time after 1,000 BP, had profound effects on the nature of at least some Native societies. Greater population densities, increased sedentism, and more social complexity resulted.[105] Traditional explanations for the northern limits of native agriculture are based on 100–120 frost-free-day isobars. However, according to modern climate records, much of coastal, and some interior regions of the Maritime Peninsula could have supported agriculture. Frost-free days may be only part of the environmental constraint. Along the coast of Maine where there are sufficient frost-free days, long periods of foggy weather in the summer screen needed sunshine from the ripening corn. The final centuries of the pre-European period witnessed a deterioration in the climate, the Little Ice Age, which might have further inhibited the spread of agriculture.[106]

Small groups of people organized into bands with fluid membership may be quite independent in daily activities. But when it comes to sustaining social groupings, bands need to establish social networks. Ethnographic evidence from northeastern North America points to the importance of kin-based networks that linked people biologically, socially, and politically over substantial areas.[107] These networks also functioned to exchange information within the area, so that, while localized adaptations occurred in response to ambient environments, a high level of cultural commonality distinguishes the Maritime Peninsula from surrounding areas. The development and continued presence of the famous Wabanaki Confederacy undoubtedly owes its existence to the longstanding social alliances forged in the pre-European era.[108] It constitutes a clear reminder that the insertion of an agreed-upon international border in the nineteenth century simply made social relations a little more bureaucratic, but hardly less effective. Native people continue to maintain cross-border social relationships and a highly developed sense of homeland, something patently obvious in the archaeological record.

Despite a full century of archaeological research in the Maritime Peninsula, there is still much to learn. Nevertheless, through the efforts of many scholars a considerable amount of data already exists. It reveals the complexities that should be expected from eleven millennia of history. At the same time, it demonstrates that a regional approach, recognizing the cultural and environmental affinities spanning the current Canada–United States border, is essential to any scholarly understanding of the initial 90 percent of human history in the Maritime Peninsula.[109]

3

Spaces of Power in the Early Modern Northeast

ELIZABETH MANCKE

For scholars of the early modern Americas, the turn toward imperial history provides conceptual possibilities for reassembling the transoceanic and multinational connections that, although widely prevalent, were too cross-grained for more strictly colonial history. This interpretive shift is especially promising for studies of northeastern North America (from the Kennebec River in present-day Maine to Newfoundland and Labrador), areas where Europeans did not always establish "colonial" settlements; if they did, the settlements were precarious and often failed. Europeans have had a longer presence in the northeast than almost anywhere else in North America. However, an analytic framework for integrating this presence within a larger understanding of the early modern Atlantic world has proved elusive, largely because it fits so awkwardly within interpretive frameworks biased in favour of colonial development.[1]

This essay addresses that problem by conceptualizing the early modern northeast in terms of intersecting and competing "spaces of power," both territorial and marine. By "spaces of power" I mean systems of social power, whether economic, political, cultural, or military, that we can describe functionally and spatially.[2] Social power has multiple forms that frequently operate at variance with one another. Our sense that they should be integrated is a product of the emergence of the modern state, which occurred simultaneously with early modern expansion. Transoceanic expansion derived part of its energy and tension from the parsing of and competition among different forms of social power. Would merchants or court officials determine overseas agendas? Whose interests were to be championed in conflicts between merchants and colonists? How might the plunderings of pirates be turned to diplomatic advantage? Would missionaries make good agents of a crown vis-à-vis native peoples?

The conceptualization of the early modern Americas in terms of spaces of power differs from existing models of European expansion in two significant ways. First, the concept of spaces of power does not presuppose colonies. Scholars have accepted, almost as a given, that colonies – settlements with local governments that become the bases of new societies – were the normative European spaces in the Americas.[3] This colonial perspective has blinkered scholarship on the northeast. Some scholars have analysed why the northeast was not normative, that is, why colonies failed.[4] Others have attempted to show that settlements in places such as Newfoundland were more like colonies than we realize and thus can be analysed using models drawn from colonial studies.[5] Studies that have not framed their arguments around colonial development, despite research of high integrity, run the risk of being viewed as so particularistic, if not anomalous, that they are difficult to integrate into larger conceptual frameworks.[6]

This habit of explaining European expansion in the Americas in terms of colonies also has contributed to the wide acceptance of the idea that a Greater New England stretched from Long Island to Labrador.[7] That idea offers a convenient colonial tent under which messy particulars can be housed. Colonial New England, however, did not exert the ideological, economic, political, or military dominance that the notion of a Greater New England suggests, nor was it, or more particularly Boston, the first or only centre of power with an interest in the northeast. Rather, there were multiple claimants, including natives, to different spaces and activities in the region for which the New England paradigm cannot suitably account.

The second way that the idea of spaces of power modifies existing interpretive frameworks is that it can accommodate systems without easily identifiable centres, in particular native systems of power that exerted great control and influence in the northeast. Unlike a centre and peripheries model, a spaces of power analysis does not presuppose relatively integrated spheres of interest with a centre that can be identified spatially or functionally.[8] In a centre and peripheries model, one system's frontiers abut on another system's, and on these frontiers, of which colonies were one type, were marchlands of contested control. The early modern northeast (and the Atlantic world, more generally) had multiple and overlapping forces of influence and control, and some without frontiers between them, frequently because they were functionally rather than spatially differentiated. In early eighteenth-century Nova Scotia, for example, French-speaking Catholic priests operated in a space of religious and cultural power that was quite distinct from the space of political power defined by the British colonial government located in Annapolis Royal. Centres did exist, but, as this example suggests, political, economic, cultural, and military spaces of power did not necessarily share a single centre.

An analysis of the early modern northeast in terms of spaces of power forces us to rethink our understanding of how overseas expansion reshaped the geographies of the extra-European world and affected the meanings invested in those various geographies.[9] Such an approach also has methodological significance. By reconstructing manifestations of power in functional and spatial terms, we can identify the shifting balance between different forms of power – for example, economic and political power – or European and native power, that is not always possible to identify from fragmentary manuscript records alone. The concept of spaces of power can also widen our perspectives on the early modern northeast and on European expansion more generally.

THE SIXTEENTH-CENTURY FISHERY

One of the signal characteristics of the early modern northeast is the great diversity of peoples – natives or Europeans, fishers, merchants, explorers, missionaries, settlers, sailors, or soldiers – who had interests in the region. The nature of that diversity was heightened by the fact that Europeans who frequented the area were often disaggregated, and their shared European subjecthood did not necessarily give them shared overseas interests, as the tangled history of Acadia or the intra-English conflicts over Newfoundland testify.[10] Scholars have used evidence of that disunity and intranational competition in part to explain why colonies failed. But many, if not most, of the Portuguese, Spanish, French, and English who frequented the northeast had no intention of being colonists – much less failed ones – but rather were migratory and sojourning members of their home societies. They oriented themselves to North American spaces in relation to the needs of their home societies, rather than as spaces for new societies.[11] Thus the appearance of disunity and competition is partially a consequence of the kinds of social power that Europeans projected into the northeast.

No aspect of the Americas was more clearly an extension of Europe than the early fisheries, which were organizationally highly fragmented, spatially scattered, and based not in North America but in Europe. In the sixteenth century, Portuguese, Basque, Breton, Norman, and West Country fishermen had intersecting zones of utilization, suggesting their own lack of engagement with the international competition of overseas expansion. The fishery was the one area of the Americas for which the Spanish and Portuguese did not observe a strict division of the extra-European world based on papal bulls and the 1494 Treaty of Tordesillas. Although Spain reputedly conceded the fishery to be Portuguese, the latter tended to fish along the eastern shore of Newfoundland and the Spanish Basque in the Gulf of St Lawrence and along the Strait of Belle Isle. This apparent east-west division, however, reflects economic more than political spheres of influence. Basque whaling enterprises were located along the Gulf and Strait shores, thus explaining a concentration of the Spanish west of the Portuguese – a coincidental, more than intentional, conformity to the Iberian division of the extra-European world.[12]

Despite nearly a century of Iberian involvement in the fishery, the Spanish and Portuguese governments had little presence in the northeast, even when united under one crown from 1580 to 1640. Since the monarch of neither country commissioned surveys of the region, cartographers relied on fishermen's charts and oral reports for descriptions of the coastline. From the early sixteenth century, cartographers had produced maps with quite accurately detailed sections of coastline, but the problem lay in accurately connecting all the pieces. Until the 1540s cartographers had drawn Newfoundland as part of the mainland and then as an archipelago until 1592, when the first map showed it as a single island. This cartographic confusion over an area frequented by thousands of men per year for nearly a century reflects both the marginal place of the fishery in the international politics of overseas expansion and the perception of the fishery as a maritime space that was not subject to the same cartographic assertions of dominion as were other parts of the Americas, Africa, and Asia.[13]

When war with England and France broke out in the 1580s, Newfoundland and Labrador were exposed and expendable flanks, sacrificial spaces of the far-flung Iberian empires. Philip II requisitioned fishing vessels and their men for military needs, and ships that did reach the fishing grounds were vulnerable to plundering by English and French privateers. By the time Spain signed the Treaty of Vervins with France in 1598 and the Treaty of London with England in 1604, the Iberians had relinquished their dominance in the fishery to the French and the English.[14]

Given the maritime orientation of the northeastern spaces that Europeans occupied in the sixteenth century, thinking about them as maritime spaces on the northwestern side of the Atlantic Ocean is more analytically useful than thinking of them as terrestrial spaces on the northeastern edge of North America. The ties that linked the fishery to Europe were decentred and significantly depoliticized, they ran from dozens of fishing ports along the coasts of Portugal, Spain, France, and England to hundreds of harbours, coves, bights, and tickles in Newfoundland, Labrador, the Gulf of St Lawrence, and, by the end of the century, southward along the Atlantic coast. European territorial penetration was extremely limited, and officials in Madrid, Lisbon, Paris, and London were slow to capture the political implications of the fishery.[15]

Not until the Treaty of Whitehall in 1686 did Newfoundland figure in a major European treaty, despite the centuries of multinational contact in the fishery. Then, during the negotiations for the 1713 Treaty of Utrecht, the Newfoundland fishery emerged as a highly prized resource, with access sought by France and Spain, despite Britain's territorial claim to the island. The legacy of these maritime and economic spaces of power, defined in the sixteenth century and sustained and embellished in the seventeenth, would assume international prominence in the eighteenth, nineteenth, and twentieth centuries. The international politicization of the fishery, however, was not made spatially coterminous with the spaces claimed and utilized by native peoples, by the Europeans who came as fur traders, or the hardy few who slowly fashioned persisting settlements.[16]

NATIVE SPACES OF POWER, C.1550–1700

The sixteenth-century fishery had its most immediate and profound political impact among native peoples in the northeast as the fur trade developed out of the fishery. Along the Gulf shore and Strait of Belle Isle, Inuit, Innu (Montagnais-Naskapi), St Lawrence Iroquoians, and Wabanakis traded with whalers and fishers. They traded furs for European wares, primarily metal goods common in the fishery: knives, axes, hatchets, kettles, hooks, and nails. The Souriquois, ancestors of the Mi'kmaq, acquired Basque-made shallops, enhanced their watercraft skills by learning to sail, and traded southward along the coast of what became New England. Late sixteenth-century explorers reported a trade jargon of Basque and native words which suggests the economic and cultural importance that trade had assumed.[17]

The fur trade reinforced old and created new Native alliance systems that stretched deep into the continent. On the north side of the St Lawrence watershed, Algonquin and Innu traders moved European goods as far inland as Huron settlements on Georgian Bay. South of the gulf and river of St Lawrence were at least two trading systems: Wabanaki traders ranged from Cape Breton to the Gaspé and south to about Cape Cod; farther west and reaching into the continent was the

Iroquois confederacy, rival to the Huron-Algonquin-Innu network. Native competition to control the fur trade appears to have made the St Lawrence River Valley a political boundary and transportation corridor as well as a precarious zone of habitation. Some time in the second half of the sixteenth century it was depopulated, probably by a combination of native warfare and European diseases.[18]

European traders attempted to attach themselves onto these vast native spaces of political, economic, cultural, and military power by building trading posts at critical junctures on the native transportation systems. At the mouth of the Saguenay River, a major outlet into the Gulf of St Lawrence for the Algonquins and Innu, French merchants constructed a fort in 1600. In Acadia, French merchants established trading posts at Port Royal, at the mouth of the St John River, and on Penobscot Bay. Samuel de Champlain strategically chose Quebec as a site that would give access to the Huron trading system and allow the French to control European travel on the St Lawrence. Dutch settlements along the Hudson River were sited for trade with the Iroquois.[19]

The primary control of terrestrial space, including the riverine transportation networks, remained native. While Europeans participated in indigenous power struggles, most notably Champlain's alliance with the Algonquins and Innu against the Iroquois, they had insufficient power – whether military, political, economic, or cultural – to supplant native control. Fur trading forts were small spaces of European presence, outposts of transatlantic merchant networks that depended on native goodwill and sufferance for their survival.[20] Monarchs, ministers, and diplomats in Europe nevertheless attempted through charters to convert these commercial enclaves into colonial spaces of power with vast territorial pretensions that generally ignored native claims.

The boundaries of European claims in the northeast underwent a transition over the seventeenth century. The colonial charters first granted by the French and English monarchs defined grants by lines of latitude, whether for Acadia (40–46° north latitude), Virginia (34–45° north latitude), or Newfoundland (46–52° north latitude), geographic overlays that had no relevance to the geopolitical divisions of native peoples.[21] Those abstract, mathematically defined boundaries running on lines of latitude can still be seen in many east-west boundaries from New Hampshire to Florida, testimony to the construction of European landscapes that ignored native landscapes. North of New Hampshire, however, those initial charter boundaries soon gave way to boundaries defined almost entirely by the physical landscape: rivers, watersheds, heights of land, islands, and peninsulas. These physical features found expression in the political divisions that emerged among European contenders, many of whom redefined their claims relative to their associations with native spaces of power and commercial networks, which, in turn, depended on water transportation, defined by rivers, watersheds, heights of land, islands, and peninsulas. Thus imperial spaces of power negotiated among ministers and diplomats in Europe were influenced by the ways Europeans in the northeast had adapted themselves to native spaces of power.

Newfoundland seems to be the one exception to this dialectical relationship between native spaces of economic and political power and European claims. The difference, however, may be more illusory than real when positioned within the larger context of the northeast. The Beothuks, the island's native people, never undertook regular trade with Europeans, nor were they objects of sustained Christian missionization, as were other natives throughout the northeast. During the summer months, when fishermen frequented the island, the Beothuks seemingly retreated into the interior, returning to the shore in the fall to scavenge for metal goods at vacated fishing sites. As permanent European residency increased, Beothuk seasonal access to the shore decreased and the marine component of their diet declined. A growing dependence on a limited number of terrestrial mammals probably caused long-term nutritional immiseration, increasing the Beothuks' vulnerability to the growing impact of the European presence, particularly through exposure to new diseases. As well, the reorientation of native economic and political networks in the sixteenth century probably attenuated earlier patterns of native contact across the Strait of Belle Isle and further exacerbated the degree of Beothuk isolation.[22]

The lack of Beothuk involvement in the fur trade meant that European fur merchants never established posts on the island, and thus the commercial interplay between the fishery and the fur trade, characteristic of places such as Acadia/Nova Scotia or Canada, did not develop in Newfoundland. The island became symbolic of the entire banks fishery, even though other places facilitated access to the fishery, as the building of Louisbourg by the French on Cape Breton demonstrated. But Cape Breton's networks of power included the fur trade with the Mi'kmaq, and therefore that island's space was defined as being more diverse than Newfoundland's.

Political boundaries in the northeast, Newfoundland's included, became defined by the functional specificity of commercial and cultural relations between Europeans and natives rather than being taken from the abstract and mathematically defined boundaries articulated in royal charters. Those political boundaries, in turn, encompassed strikingly different configurations of power from those of colonies whose boundaries more closely conformed to the spaces of power defined in charter grants.

CHARTERS AND SPACES OF POWER

For scholars of the early modern Americas, charters seem to capture the moment of origin for a new colonial society. A characteristic of charters that makes them very satisfying as documents of origin is that they often defined political, economic, military, and cultural spaces as coterminous, and concentrated power over all of them in the grantees. When colonies developed from chartered ventures, as in Virginia or Massachusetts, those spaces of political, economic, military, and cultural power were coterminous, even after the revocation of the charters and the royal appointment of governors. If a colony was divided, as was Carolina into northern and southern parts, the spaces of power remained coterminous, though divided. The government of South Carolina, for example, did not control cultivation of tobacco in North Carolina, the colony's dominant staple crop. In turn, North Carolina did not control the provision of clergy for South Carolina. Rather North Carolina regulated its own economy, and South Carolina provided for its own clergy.

The point that spaces of power in colonies were coterminous may seem so obvious as not to bear mention; that they might be otherwise may seem absurdly counterfactual. In the northeast, however, economic, political, cultural, and military spaces of power were not coterminous, and European states negotiated their functional division. After the British conquest of Acadia in 1710 and its cession in 1713, for example, spaces of power were parsed among the British, French, Mi'kmaq, and Acadians. The British ostensibly had sovereign control over Nova Scotia, although they were challenged militarily by the Mi'kmaq and the French. Power over the religious or cultural space, however, resided in non-British hands. The British had agreed that the Acadians could remain Catholic, and the bishop in Quebec appointed priests with approval (often nominal) from Nova Scotia's governor.[23] The Treaty of Utrecht (1713) acknowledged British sovereignty over Newfoundland, but France's guaranteed seasonal shore rights from Port Riche to Cape Bonavista gave the French a large economic space that discouraged British economic use, seriously limited Britain's political control, and culturally defined that area of Newfoundland as French.[24]

The question arises as to why Europeans more successfully defined spaces of political, cultural, economic, and military power in some parts of North America as relatively coterminous, as was the case in the colonies from New Hampshire to Georgia, while in other areas, such as the northeast, Rupert's Land, Louisiana, or even New Mexico, functionally different spaces of power were not coterminous. Part of the answer can be found by correlating the timing of charters to other

European uses of North American space.[25] In other words, we need to ask whether charters initiated European interest in a part of the Americas or whether they were later developments. When we frame the question this way, a significant geographic pattern emerges. Along the Atlantic seaboard from New Hampshire to the Carolinas, charters generally represent the first sustained European interest in an area. The English had attempted a colony at Roanoke in the 1580s, for instance, but no claimants from that venture or any other European venture existed to provide a substantive challenge to the primacy of the Virginia Company's settlement at Jamestown in 1607. In these parts of North America, charters did represent a moment of European origin, and such charters defined European spaces of political, economic, cultural, and military power as coterminous.

The charters for Acadia (1603) and the Newfoundland Company (1610), coming shortly before and after the Virginia Company charter (1606) respectively, did not, on the other hand, represent the initiation of European interests in the northeast. Rather, they represented attempts to redefine and reconfigure the spaces of power that the English and French had already created in the sixteenth century. In the case of Acadia, Henri IV granted the charter in his attempt to consolidate France's tenuous claims to "New France." In the 1580s, a growing number of French merchants had become involved in the fur trade, and Henri IV resolved to harness his colonial interests to their mercantile aspirations. In exchange for establishing settlements and recruiting and transporting colonists, he granted a small group of merchants exclusive French trading rights to a section of North America stretching from 40–46° north latitude. The monarch quickly learned, however, that these monopoly privileges threatened the commercial interests of other French merchants, who protested the 1603 charter; he revoked it in 1607.[26]

The charter for the Newfoundland Company proved similarly contentious among the English. In the petition for incorporation, the grantees, predominantly merchants from London and Bristol, had stressed the importance of establishing English settlements on Newfoundland to pre-empt "anie forraine Prince or State." Before James I issued the charter, the Privy Council consulted Trinity House, an organization that represented many independent fishermen and merchants. In its tepid endorsement, it stressed the importance of keeping the fishery open. West Country fishing interests soon perceived both the charter and attempted settlements as direct threats to their "ancient rights" in the migratory fishery. Settlements with an island-based government, they contended, might have controlled their land distribution and local courts and conceivably have implemented policies harmful to the migratory fishery. Colonial space based on charters, therefore, could have dramatically reconfigured the access to and utility of commercial maritime space.[27]

In the cases of both Acadia and Newfoundland, numerous French and English merchants had vested interests in North American trade which predated the issuing of charters for colonization. Those merchants and associated firms had sufficient political leverage in France and England to demand that their economic spaces of power take precedence over charters for colonies. In the colony of Canada, by way of contrast, the French more successfully integrated political, economic, cultural, and military power, in part because Samuel de Champlain sited Quebec, the first settlement, beyond the parts of North America where European merchants were already active.[28]

Most merchants had little interest in making North American spaces of economic power coterminous with political, cultural, or military power except insofar as such integration of power supported their commercial interests. At various times in the first half of the seventeenth century, for example, the French government unsuccessfully tried to oblige merchants to recruit and transport colonists to North America in exchange for trading privileges.[29] When merchants did build permanent establishments, they sited them not so as to optimize long-term colonial development but so as to intersect with native trading systems or exploit the fishery. Europeans living in those commercially oriented settlements were often sojourning employees of a merchant firm and hence not colonists planning to remain in North America.

What emerged in the northeast in the first half of the seventeenth century were fragmented and conflicting claims that were legally and constitutionally ambiguous. Some were based on longstanding commercial practices. Claims based on charters did not completely disappear, but tended to be used for diplomatic, legal, and contractual defences and were juxtaposed to commercial claims based on usage. Conquest quickly developed as a third basis for European claims, as armed expeditions attacked vulnerable outposts. The fragmented and functionally-specific quality of these claims kept them contested. Did conquest have more validity than longstanding commerce? Did commercial interests always trump royal charters? What claims from charters could be asserted in the face of commercial challenges? How might charters be used in international negotiations? The ambiguity of these conflicting assertions of rights and claims in North America forced their adjudication into the highest echelons of European governments, especially those of France and England, and often into diplomatic negotiation. As a consequence, the affairs of Europeans in the northeast quickly came under various forms of ministerial oversight, both internal and external, and more so than in colonies further south.[30]

In the European calculus of overseas expansion, these small, struggling – at times conflict-ridden – outposts legitimated grandiose territorial claims, and European governments did not hesitate to assert that they represented sovereign spaces of power. The weakness of tertiary developments in these functionally specific spaces of power, whether a trading post, a fishing outport, a military garrison, or the odd attempt at a colony, led metropolitan governments to undertake programs to stabilize them. The French began much earlier than the English, in part because the crown and ministry in France controlled greater financial resources than did their counterparts in England and could more readily invest in overseas projects. Louis XIV royalized the administration of Canada in 1663, that of Acadia in 1670. In 1662 France built an administrative centre for the fishery at Plaisance (Placentia), Newfoundland, on the west side of the Avalon peninsula. While Plaisance soon had the largest resident population of any French fishing settlement (of which there were few), it functioned not so much as a colony – the nucleus of a new society – but as a way for the French government to assert administrative control, if not sovereignty, over the highly decentralized and dispersed commercial spaces of the fishery. This objective would find even more elaborate expression in the building of Louisbourg in the early eighteenth century.[31]

The growing involvement of the French and English governments in the northeast, whether to adjudicate conflicts among subjects, to negotiate international agreements, or to build administrative centres, contributed to the development of colonies in ways that commercial activity or the granting of charters had not done. Metropolitan participation generally involved attempts to integrate divergent spaces of power, though at the international level coordination and accommodation, rather than integration, was often the outcome, particularly in the fishery. Consequently, colonies in the northeast, both in their emergence and their long-term development, were directly shaped by the agendas of metropolitan governments rather than primarily by the interests of private promoters or settlers themselves. For the French, royal and ministerial involvement overseas was widespread after 1663 and included French interests throughout the Americas. For the British, however, direct government involvement in the internal development of colonies was incremental and did not involve a serious commitment of monies until Parliament funded the building of Halifax in 1748.[32]

PERSISTING SETTLEMENTS AND THE COLONIAL TRANSITION

In the northeast, pockets of permanent European residents emerged in four ways: 1) a few European settlements persisted from seventeenth-century colonial ventures; 2) unsponsored settlements developed in conjunction with economic ventures, particularly in the fishery; 3) the French and British governments increasingly invested in administrative infrastructure (both civilian and military) to manage their national interests in the northeast and to legitimate territorial claims (these permanent establishments, such as Plaisance and Louisbourg, encouraged the settlement of permanent residents even if the administrative personnel was only temporary); 4) the French and British governments sponsored settlements, with varying degrees of success, in attempts to create viable colonies.

What is striking about these persisting European settlements is how functionally specific most were, primarily providing places of residence. They often lacked the most basic provisions of civil government, such as the deeding of property, the formal adjudication of disputes, and the recording of vital statistics. The relationship of these persisting European residential spaces – a kind of demographic space of power – to economic, political, cultural, and military spaces of power varied enormously, although it is fair to say that most settlements either were weakly integrated with other spaces of power or were kept subordinated to them. The weakness or absence of linkages between residential spaces and political power, or their subordination to economic power, gave these communities few resources to negotiate their own interests. Persisting settlements were consequently not so much the loci of new societies – the case with British settlements further south or with French settlements in Canada – as another functionally specific kind of space, the interests of which were often compromised by competing economic, political, military, and cultural systems. If we analyse the control of space that these permanent settlements had, their marginality and inadequacy as seedbeds of colonialism come into sharper focus.

The French farming settlements established along the Bay of Fundy, the communities from which Acadian culture emerged, were marginal in multiple ways. The eighteenth-century Acadians were descended largely from French settlers brought to Acadia in the 1630s and 1640s, after the English returned the area to the French in the Treaty of Saint-Germain-en-Lay (1632). France's ministry under Cardinal Richelieu wanted to solidify French claims in North America by establishing agricultural communities, but the political reality was that the

French interests that dominated Acadia were invested in the fur trade or the fishery and not in farming. The land the Acadians farmed was also marginal; they had reclaimed most of it from the sea by dyking the marshes. These bayside farms did not legitimate more grandiose territorial ambitions on the part of the settlers.[33] As a practical matter, territorial control remained Mi'kmaq, notwithstanding European claims. Indeed, neither fur traders, fishermen, nor farmers threatened the practical reality of the pre-eminence of native territorial control in Acadia. The land the French occupied either complemented native use, as in the case of fur traders, or operated on lands that were marginal to native concerns, as in the case of the Acadian farmers.[34]

As the development of Acadia/Nova Scotia shows, the Acadian farming communities had the least capacity of any group to influence the area's geopolitical definition. During the seventeenth century, commercial interests, whether French merchants and traders or New England traders and fishermen, asserted greater influence over the geopolitical future of Acadia than did Acadian farmers. Their lands were recorded as seigneurial grants, a form of landholding that gave the occupiers little say over the long-term distribution or use of the land beyond their farms. Militarily, the Mi'kmaq and their native allies could keep Acadian settlements geographically constrained, while military forces from New England and Britain or Louisbourg and France could influence whether claims of sovereignty would be French or British. In short, the agricultural settlers in Acadia had far less jurisdictional authority than did their farming counterparts in other parts of European America.[35]

When the British formally took over Acadia in 1713, this configuration of people and space remained largely intact, much to the frustration of the British officials sent to govern Nova Scotia, who found themselves confronted with the largely untenable task of reconfiguring the spaces of power – native and European – that had developed over the sixteenth and seventeenth centuries. They complained that their control scarcely extended beyond the walls of the garrison at Annapolis Royal, and recognized that the Mi'kmaq, Catholic priests, and French officials in Louisbourg or Quebec often had more power than they did. To give teeth to British sovereignty and to transform Nova Scotia into a viable colony, British officials had to make the agents of different spaces of power acknowledge British suzerainty, if not sovereignty. In the 1710s and 1720s they negotiated with the Mi'kmaq, Wulstukwiuk, and Abenaki, although significantly, they had to coordinate the negotiations with officials in New England because native spaces of power did not conform to European-determined jurisdictions. Between 1727 and 1730, Nova Scotia's colonial officials finally coaxed the Acadians into swearing an oath of allegiance, which was critical to deeding the land they occupied. The prolonged discussions that finally resulted in this oath-taking, albeit with contested qualifications, often turned on the question of the vulnerable position of the Acadians in relation to native, French, and British spaces of power.[36]

Meanwhile, within the British world, the functional uses of Nova Scotia's space were being redefined. New England merchants traded with impunity in the province, despite occasional prohibitions against trading with the Acadians. Parliamentary legislation had given the Royal Navy pre-eminent claims to the woods from New Jersey through to Nova Scotia. Until Nova Scotian officials completed surveys of naval stores, for which they had no funds, they could not grant land to new Protestant settlers.[37] The lack of funding for surveys of the woods points to the need to think about fiscal matters spatially. British colonies were to be self-financing, but because that was not feasible in a territory such as Nova Scotia, which was only nominally a colony, financial resources were needed from the centre. Parliament's 1748 decision to fund the building of Halifax and subsidize the immigration and settlement of foreign protestants was critical in redefining both Nova Scotia and the empire.[38] Under the British constitution, this reconfiguration of fiscal spaces of power fundamentally confirmed that Nova Scotia's constitutional relationship to the metropolitan government was as part of an imperial state under Crown-in-Parliament rather than as an autonomous dependency of the crown.[39] The older British colonies, in contrast, could imagine themselves as states, in part because of the coterminous nature of spaces of power within them, including fiscal discretion. Nova Scotia's spaces of power had never been so unified or clearly defined.

Persisting settlements in Newfoundland were also marginal in relation to other spaces of power. Despite the failure of early seventeenth-century chartered settlements, some "colonists" remained and an increasing number of fishers began overwintering to protect access to harbours and to extend the season. These permanent residential spaces, however, did not have the formal government of colonial spaces. The metropolitan government adamantly refused to provide more than seasonal governance and ignored the property claims of permanent residents until the 1699 *Newfoundland Act.* West Country merchants supported residential spaces, which provided permanent facilities to protect their commercial interests and created a captive labour market, but did not support island-based government, which could erode mercantile power and buttress residential rights.[40]

While residential spaces in both Newfoundland and Acadia/Nova

Scotia were inadequate for generating colonial development, the relationship of permanent settlements to other spaces of power was quite different in the two places. Metropolitan officials, first French and then British, believed that the greatest economic resources of Acadia/Nova Scotia were land-based and that its economic future lay in farms and a forest industry, complemented by some fishing. Thus they felt it necessary to encourage the occupation and private ownership of land by Europeans. In Acadia/Nova Scotia a colonial society became a metropolitan goal that was pursued unsuccessfully for most of a century, first by the French and then by the British. Only in the mid-eighteenth century, when Britain finally committed considerable fiscal and human resources, did the colonial transition in Nova Scotia take place.

In the case of Newfoundland, however, it was acknowledged that the valuable resource was maritime and hence could not be alienated into private hands as land could be. The vast expanse of the fishing grounds, their international exploitation, and the Europe-based investment in the fishing industry positioned Newfoundland within economic, political, and military spaces that were transatlantic in their breadth. International competition required interstate negotiations. Merchants involved in the fishery pressed their concerns at the highest levels of government in England, France, and Spain. Scores of communities along the west coast of Europe depended on the income generated by the thousands of young men who crossed the Atlantic every year to work in the Newfoundland fishery.[41] As navies became more militarily important to national defences in the seventeenth century, metropolitan officials came to believe that the fishery served as an indispensable nursery for sailors. In this transatlantic configuration of power, international disputes over claims to Newfoundland were intrinsically linked with maritime access to the fishery.

In negotiations leading to the Treaty of Utrecht (1713), access to the fishery became a major point of contention. Both France and Spain claimed property rights in the fishery on the basis of the "ancient" participation of their subjects in the migratory fishery. France conceded Britain's sovereign claim to the entire island and agreed to vacate Placentia in exchange for guaranteed seasonal shore rights from Point Riche to Cape Bonavista. This treaty clause forced an international acknowledgment of the commercial spaces of power that French fishers had occupied for much of two centuries, while at the same time qualifying Britain's claim to sovereignty over Newfoundland. Spain, in turn, negotiated for and received British acknowledgment of its subjects' rights to fish in Newfoundland waters. Both of these concessions angered members of the British Parliament, and long remained red-flag issues whenever the parliamentary Opposition wanted to illustrate the Ministry's reputed penchant for sacrificing the overseas interests of the nation.[42]

The fragmenting of terrestrial and maritime space in Newfoundland among various contenders, the vesting of specific usufruct rights to people in Europe, and the separation of the utilization of space and sovereignty over it had the long-term consequence of rooting political and economic power over the island in Europe rather than in North America, a reality that still has resonance in contemporary Newfoundland politics. While France agreed to give up shore rights in 1904, it has claims to territorial waters based on its 1763 retention of St Pierre and Miquelon. Spain has retained fishing rights in Newfoundland waters, and fishing rights for the United States figured repeatedly in Anglo-American treaties after 1783.

In an international climate that guaranteed access to the Newfoundland fishery for some European powers, the interests and claims of permanent residents on the island were comparatively insignificant. Population growth, war, and the virtual collapse of the British migratory fishery in the early nineteenth century finally forced the colonial transition. During the American Revolution (1775–1783) and the French Revolutionary and Napoleonic Wars (1793–1815), privateering threatened the economic viability of fishing fleets, and many people chose to settle in Newfoundland rather than risk the seasonal transatlantic voyages. Privateering also disrupted the provisioning trade from New England, the Mid-Atlantic states, and Ireland and caused famine-level food shortages. Finally, in the early 1820s the British government recognized the pressing need for a colonial government on Newfoundland and in 1824 the first year-round governor arrived. In 1832, two centuries after the first English subjects began settlements on the island the calling of an assembly completed the colonial transition.

As this analysis of the colonial transition in Nova Scotia and Newfoundland shows, colonies needed more than settlers of European extraction for them to exist. On the eve of the American Revolution, Newfoundland had 12,000 permanent residents but it was not made a colony with an island-based government by the British, despite its sizable population. In contrast, the Island of Saint John (later renamed Prince Edward Island) became a colony in 1768, despite its meagre population of 197.[43] The British government could more easily create it as a colony than it could Newfoundland, because the former was small and lacked other acknowledged claimants. Acadia/Nova Scotia had technically been a colony with a year-round government since the seventeenth century, but the linkages between the resident colonists and the colonial officials, most on secondment from the metropole, had been so fragile and limited that what existed was not an integrated colonial society but a series of discrete, but overlapping, spaces of power, the most powerful of which, on a day-to-day basis, were native, not European.

The colonial transition in Newfoundland and Acadia/Nova Scotia contrasts sharply with the origins of colonies from New Hampshire to the Carolinas, with Canada, and with island colonies such as Bermuda, Barbados, or the Leeward Islands. As noted earlier, many of those colonies had coterminous spaces of economic, political, military, and cultural power, and residential spaces were integral rather than marginal to them. In these cases, the establishment of colonies as the initiation of a European presence in the Americas expressed a particular configuration of the extension of European power overseas and was quite specific to place and time. The increasing need of European metropolitan governments to negotiate among peoples with competing interests in the Americas made the kind of colonies established in the seventeenth century quite irrelevant by mid-eighteenth century.

CONCLUSION

If our standard for conceptualizing and assessing the early modern Americas is colonial settlement, then the northeast looks quite anomalous. Yet, if we take a broader perspective, both spatially and chronologically, the overlap of and competition among functionally specific and nationally diverse spaces of power was widespread. Indeed, viewed globally, European colonial spaces, especially in Africa and Asia, were exceptional forms of contact. Instead, the emergence of colonies tended to be intermediate stages in European expansion and imperialism.

From a northeastern perspective, the metropolitan negotiation of space and power in the Americas was longstanding, dating back to the early seventeenth century, when Henri IV revoked the charter to Acadia to placate French merchants, and continuing through British attempts to stabilize Nova Scotia after 1713. Looking beyond the northeast, then, the actions of the British government in issuing the Proclamation of 1763 or passing the *Quebec Act* (1774) were familiar strategies, expressions of the practice of accommodating various claimants to different spaces of power rather than being wholly new developments.

As is well known, this metropolitan practice of accommodating multiple claimants came into conflict with attitudes and practices that had emerged in the British colonies along the eastern seaboard, where metropolitan adjudication of conflicting claims to spaces of power had not been common. Colonists perceived metropolitan adjudication of space in the trans-Appalachian West as an unwarranted exercise of central power and an infringement of the right of colonists to have largely unitary control over the spaces in which they lived. Futher-more, they expected to be able to create similar spaces as they expanded westward. After the American Revolution, the retention of extensive local control of space and the replication of that practice as Americans expanded westward contrasted sharply with the practice in "white settler colonies" of British North America, and indeed in the British Empire more generally. In nineteenth-century British colonies, the local rights of colonists were limited, and to the extent that they did exist they were subordinated to the metropolitan government's prerogative to adjudicate among multiple claimants.

As this essay shows, that constitutional practice of the nineteenth-century empire was not just a reaction to the American Revolution, but was one that had long predated the crisis between the metropole and the thirteen colonies. If we view early modern expansion through the conceptual lens of "spaces of power," and see colonies as just one kind of space that Europeans created overseas, then the northeast ceases to be anomalous and indeed can offer lessons about the development of Canadian society, about the textured nature of European imperialism, and, ironically, about the distinctive place in the history of expansion of the thirteen colonies that rebelled and became the United States.

4

Passamaquoddy Identity and the Marshall Decision

WILLIAM WICKEN

On 17 September 1999 the Supreme Court of Canada issued its decision in *R. vs. Donald Marshall Junior.* This decision was based on the court's interpretation of a treaty signed between the British Crown and three aboriginal communities, the Mi'kmaq, the Maliseet, and the Passamaquoddy. Today, the Mi'kmaq and the Maliseet live within Canada's borders: the Mi'kmaq in eastern New Brunswick, the Gaspé region of Quebec, Prince Edward Island, Nova Scotia, and southern Newfoundland; the Maliseet along the St John River in New Brunswick. The Passamaquoddy, however, live in Maine. An important question raised by the Court's decision was whether the Passamaquoddy could benefit from the decision, since at the time the treaty was signed they were living within what is now the province of New Brunswick.

The court's decision has had important consequences for both the Mi'kmaq and the Maliseet. The decision recognized that the Mi'kmaq and Maliseet had a constitutional treaty right to engage in the commercial fishery, a right the federal government of Canada had previously sought to deny. The decision also prompted the federal government to initiate negotiations with each aboriginal community in the hope of resolving outstanding economic and political disagreements. One of the federal aims in these discussions is to extinguish any existing aboriginal title in Atlantic Canada.

Although the Marshall decision was clearly directed toward Atlantic Canada's aboriginal communities, it unavoidably poses the question as to whether the Passamaquoddy – as an aboriginal community which up until the early 1800s lived on both sides of the susequently-determined border between New Brunswick and Maine – is a beneficiary of the 1760 treaty that was crucial to the Supreme Court's ruling regarding the commercial fishery. Moreover, since the intent of the present federal discussions is to resolve outstanding aboriginal title claims, some consideration will be needed regarding the Passamaquoddy and their claims to southwestern New Brunswick. Ultimately, these questions reveal the paradoxical position that the Passamaquoddy occupy: an aboriginal community with a transnational identity.

The question before the Supreme Court in *R. vs. Marshall* was whether Donald Marshall's treaty right to fish and to sell fish had been accommodated by federal fisheries legislation. In a 5–2 majority decision written by Justice Ian Binnie, the Court determined that Mr Marshall's treaty rights had not been accommodated, since the Fisheries minister exercised an absolute and unilateral right to impose the conditions under which Mr Marshall could fish and sell fish.

In finding that Mr Marshall had such a right, Justice Binnie – on behalf of the majority – focussed upon the minutes of a Nova Scotia Council meeting that had framed the Mi'kmaq communities' understanding of the treaty. During meetings held on 11 February 1760, the Governor of Nova Scotia, Charles Lawrence, had asked the delegates if they had anything to propose, "to which they replied that their Tribes had not directed them to propose anything further than there might be a Truckhouse established for the furnishing them with necessaries in Exchange for their Peltry, and that it might, at present, be at Fort Frederick." For Justice Binnie, this exchange showed that the intent of both sides in negotiating the 1760 treaty was that trade would result in providing the Mi'kmaq with "necessaries." Since this portion of the treaty formed a central aspect of the parties' common intent, the Court believed that any subsequent arbitrary changes would be inconsistent with the spirit of the treaty. For this reason, the Court found that the unilateral imposition of Canadian fisheries legislation violated the intent of the British-Mi'kmaq 1760 treaty and therefore was unconstitutional, since this treaty was protected by Canada's 1982 Constitution.[1]

Curiously, the 11 February 1760 meeting that had formed a critical part of the Court's judgment did not directly involve the Mi'kmaq, although other documents showed that the same terms negotiated at that meeting would later be incorporated into treaties signed with twelve separate Mi'kmaq communities. Rather, the 11 February 1760 meeting had included delegates from the Maliseet and from the Passamaquoddy – a community now located on the United States side of the U.S.–Canada border.

The Marshall ruling touched off a controversy in Atlantic Canada and across Canada. Non-aboriginal fishermen, media pundits, and politicians expressed cóncern regarding the Supreme Court's decision to entrench a treaty right to fish and to sell fish into a constitutional right. Into this fray stepped the Point Pleasant Passamaquoddy community of eastern Maine, whose leaders argued that the Supreme Court ruling also provided their community a right to engage in the commercial fishery within Canadian waters.[2]

The Passamaquoddy community's statement suggested differing interpretations as to how borders should be applied to aboriginal communities who have historical ties on both sides of the U.S.–Canada divide. David Bevan, director-general of Resource Management for Canada's Fisheries Department responded that since there was no legally recognized Passamaquoddy band in Canada, the Point Pleasant people were not covered by the Marshall ruling. "Legal analysis," he commented, "indicated to us quite clearly that the right would not apply to American citizens." This view was contested by Ernie Altvater, chief of the Point Pleasant band, who was quoted as saying that the Passamaquoddy are not American citizens: "We've been fishing and hunting on both sides of the imaginary line for a long time and will continue to do so."[3] For Altvater, the border separating Maine and New Brunswick has no legal bearing. The Passamaquoddy, like other aboriginal communities whose territory straddles the Canada–U.S. border, believe that their people are neither "Canadian" nor "American," and are therefore not subjects or citizens of any such nation.[4]

My purpose in this essay is to evaluate the historical basis of Altvater's statement, which suggests that the Passamaquoddy form an identity independent of Canadian and American concepts of political citizenship. I propose to do so in two ways: by examining the nature of Passamaquoddy settlement patterns between the signing of the 1760 treaty and the creation of the United States in the 1780s; and through reference to the 1760 treaty itself. This was the last treaty the Passamaquoddy concluded with Great Britain prior to the creation of the United States. The argument can be stated quite simply: until the formation of the United States, the Passamaquoddy inhabited the area later known as southern New Brunswick, were independent of British political authority, and ranged across the area that would eventually separate the United States and Canada. In this sense, there is some historical basis to Altvater's statement that the border has little meaning for the Passamaquoddy. However, there remain a number of questions regarding how the Passamaquoddy conceptualized their community identity after 1783, which need to be resolved before determining the applicability of the Marshall ruling to the Passamaquoddy community.

In 1760 the Passamaquoddy lived adjacent to the St Croix River and Passamaquoddy Bay in what is now southwestern New Brunswick and eastern Maine. The precise location of their community, however, is difficult to determine, as is its size.

One reason for the shortage of information is that the region surrounding Passamaquoddy Bay was not well known to Europeans; few visited the region, and fewer still lived there. As a result, there are few extant records for reconstructing Passamaquoddy history. There were very few censuses made of the Passamaquoddy. The most extensive and accurate counts were made of the Mi'kmaq inhabiting mainland Nova Scotia, and of the Penobscot and Norridgwock who lived to the west of the Passamaquoddy within the present-day state of Maine. The fact that the Passamaquoddy lived in areas unsettled by New England or Acadian farmers rendered them a relatively unknown community to non-natives. For this reason, there are no extensive records to analyse their demographic history in the same way that can be done for neighbouring peoples.[5]

Two documentary records, however, allow some suggestions to be made regarding the location and population size of the Passamaquoddy from 1763 to 1780. The first account is contained in an anonymous report written by a French missionary in 1763, stating that there were two separate places inhabited by the Passamaquoddy: Peskadamkkante and Meges [Machias]. In total, these two areas had a population of twenty-four or twenty-five men capable of bearing arms.[6] The second account dates from 28 July 1780 and was compiled by Frederick Delesdernier, identified as a lieutenant in the Indian Department of the United Colonies. He also lists the Passamaquoddy as living in two locations, one community at Passamaquoddy and the other at Scoodick, "on the lakes." This last account provides a nominal listing of the heads of families for each household as well as the number of women and children. In total, Delesdernier lists 152 people living in coastal and inland regions adjacent to Passamaquoddy Bay and the St Croix River.[7]

Locating the two Passamaquoddy villages is difficult. James Wherry contends that there were at least four or five principal encampments during the 1700s. He suggests that, sometime after 1704, Passamaquoddy lived for extended periods near Salmon Falls on the St Croix River, the present-day site of the power station in Milltown [St Stephen], New Brunswick. By the mid-1700s, this site had been abandoned in favour of St Andrews. However, increasing British settlement forced the community to relocate, and eventually led to the establishment of more permanent settlements on the United States side of the border.[8]

What is clear is that the Passamaquoddy lived on both sides of the U.S.–Canada border. Moreover, there was a constant movement back and forth by individual families, as well as a tendency to live together as one large community for extended periods. As the 1763 anonymous account suggests, the villages of Machias and Passamaquoddy often merged together to form one village.[9]

That the Passamaquoddy formed a separate and distinct aboriginal community is shown in British and French documentation. For instance, during the summer of 1720, the governor of Nova Scotia, Richard Philipps, sent individual letters to both the Passamaquoddy and to the St John River Indians (Maliseet). Significantly, each community replied separately. The Passamaquoddy response was signed by three men, one of whom was identified as the "Chief of the Passamaquoddy."[10] Similarly, after a draft of the 1760 treaty had been signed in Halifax in late February,[11] a later ratification was attended by a Passamaquoddy delegation at Fort Frederick at the mouth of the St John River. This information is contained in the diary of a New England soldier, John Burrell, who was stationed at the fort. On 2 June 1760, Burrell wrote that "a Grate number of Indians came in from Passamaquoddy," and on 28 June that "ye Grate King of ye Indians Came into ye Garrison to make a Grate peace with ye English." Though it is unclear whether this "grate King" represented the Passamaquoddy or the Maliseet, nonetheless Burrell's diary shows that the treaty ratification was attended by delegates who were clearly identified as Passamaquoddy and were considered to be a community distinct from the Maliseet. [12]

While the Passamaquoddy presence along what would later be the U.S.–Canada border is clear, the community's political relationship with the British is less apparent. Central to an understanding of this relationship are the 1760 treaty and the minutes of the conference that preceded its signing on 23 February. Not all aspects of this treaty are relevant here, but the historical context of its negotiation can give us some insight into Altvater's assertion regarding the Passamaquoddy community's present-day political status.

The 1760 treaty was signed long before the nineteenth-century industrialization of the American and Canadian economies. Industrialization precipitated a new dynamic in relations with aboriginal people, as governments attempted to restrict the political and economic independence of aboriginal communities. Their unrestricted access to common lands conflicted with capitalist notions of private property and nationhood. To take just one example, during the 1820s and 1830s the state of Georgia attempted to impose its political control over Cherokee lands. In a series of seminal hearings before the

Supreme Court of the United States, the Cherokee argued that they were a political entity separate from the United States. This status, they argued, had been recognized in a series of treaties signed by their ancestors with the British and American governments. The Cherokee's proclaimed independence from American law, however, was contested by both state and federal authorities. This conflict intensified as the American population increased, as new technologies were developed, as relations of production were reorganized, and as the United States came to represent something more than just a collection of individual states. In sum, by the early 1830s the United States government was no longer willing to tolerate competing conceptions of nationhood, which would implicitly undermine private economic interests.[13]

These policies, however, only emerged in the early 1800s and did not underlie British treaty making with the Passamaquoddy in 1760. On the one hand, the British colonial state lacked the military might to enforce an agreement restricting Passamaquoddy land use. And on the other hand, the British were quite content for the Passamaquoddy to continue to live by hunting and fishing. Why so? Because the British imperial economy in 1760 was premised on different assumptions from those that would later prevail. The British expected that Passamaquoddy families would trap fur-bearing animals and that the furs would be exported to Great Britain or its colonies. Indeed, this exchange was symptomatic of the way in which goods were produced and sold within the British imperial economy. British officials therefore negotiated terms with the Passamquoddy that would make such exchanges feasible. For this and other reasons, the 1760 treaty did not result in the surrender of Passamaquoddy lands or the creation of reserves, two important measures that would be included in treaties signed much later with other aboriginal communities in western Canada and in the United States.

That the British chose not to negotiate the surrender of Passamaquoddy lands in 1760 shows that they expected that the Passamaquoddy would live mainly by fishing and hunting. This was explicitly written into the treaty by what has been called the Truckhouse clause.[14] This clause formalized a commercial relationship between the British and Passamaquoddy. In exchange for Passamaquoddy neutrality in the ongoing war between Great Britain and France – which had begun in the mid-1750s and would not formally end until 1763 – the British agreed to maintain a truckhouse at Fort Frederick. There, a government-appointed agent would sell goods to the Passamaquoddy in exchange for the furs, skins, and feathers produced by them. In other words, colonial officials expected that the Passamaquoddy would continue to live in areas they had occupied before

1760, and would also hunt there to produce items to exchange for a selected number of European-produced commodities. Indeed, though later treaties were signed with twelve different Mi'kmaq communities with the same commercial clause as contained in the Passamaquoddy treaty, the majority of the furs traded to the British after 1760 would come from Passamaquoddy and Maliseet territories.[15]

At the same time, the 1760 treaty contained clauses suggesting that the British intended to settle farming and fishing families in areas adjacent to the Passamaquoddy and thereby place some restriction on where and how the Passamaquoddy would live. This intention is contained in the renewal of earlier treaties made in 1726 and 1749.[16] The relevant clause states that the Passamaquoddy would not "molest any of His majesty's Subjects or their Dependants in their Settlements already made or Lawfully to be made." Since no British settlements were located in southwest New Brunswick – with the exception of Fort Frederick – any new settlements could only be accomplished through "lawful" means. However, the treaty does not define, nor do the conference summaries suggest, how the delegates would have understood the term "lawful."

These two clauses therefore would seem to be contradictory. The treaty implicitly accepted that Passamaquoddy families would produce furs for the mercantilist economy but also suggested a process by which settlement of the region would proceed.

British officials would have eventually been forced to deal with the contradiction implicit in the treaty's wording. However, the political and economic turmoil stemming from the creation of the United States undermined the development of a coordinated British policy in the region. Instead, the interplay between a fast-growing settler population in New Brunswick and the efforts of the British to strengthen the loyalty of their remaining North American colonies in the wake of American independence undermined the Passamaquoddy's political status in the region. This political change was soon accompanied by alterations in the state's regulation of natural resources, ushering in an economic and political regime that stressed the sanctity of private property and the state's regulation of common resources for the "common good."

For the most part, governments in Canada and the United States identified the "common good" with private capitalist interests and with the non-aboriginal communities that those interests supported. As a result, the national state legislated measures that would lead to aboriginal peoples' disenfranchisement and, it was hoped, to their adoption of capitalist norms of behaviour. The effect of that legislation implicitly created differences between aboriginal communities living on the American side of the border and those living on the Canadian side, regardless of the particular ways in which these communities may have modified or resisted these legislative measures. For the Passamaquoddy, the creation of a border between Great Britain and the United States in 1783 therefore had momentous consequences, since their cultural identity, political status, and community structure have been profoundly affected by American society.

The historical problem, however, lies in determining the Passamaquoddy's treaty right to the regions of southwestern New Brunswick that they inhabited in 1783. Did they surrender their right to those lands once they migrated across the border and established permanent settlements on the American side? Did the British have the right to occupy Passamaquoddy lands once they had vacated them and had made the conscious decision to settle in the United States? Indeed, one can argue that the Passamaquoddy decided to side with the United States in their dispute with Great Britain and so became "American," thereby also implicitly surrendering any rights they had gained from signing the 1760 treaty.

But even if this were not true, have not the Passamaquoddy themselves become American, if only because their community has been profoundly changed by its interaction with American state and national authorities, and with American culture? Or have the Passamaquoddy retained a political and cultural identity that supersedes their status as American "citizens"? Do they have more in common with Maliseet and Mi'kmaq residents of "Canada" than they do with their neighbouring American citizens? In other words, do aboriginal people whose communities have historically straddled the U.S.–Canada border maintain a political and cultural identity that supersedes identities created by the formation of the United States and Canada? Altvater seems to believe so, or at least that is what he can be taken to imply when he says that the Passamaquoddy have moved back and forth across the "imaginary line" for the past 230 years.

But in making such an argument, the Passamaquoddy have still to demonstrate that their present claim is not simply political opportunism but is an outgrowth of a pattern of behaviour that continued after 1783. To establish that the border held little meaning for them, the Passamaquoddy community would need to document movement back and forth between Maine and New Brunswick after 1783. Such border crossings may not always have been easy or even possible to make, as both Canadian and American border-guards may have made them difficult. Nonetheless, the Passamaquoddy need to document their case rather than just stating it.

Perhaps, however, the question that needs to be addressed is not that one, but rather how industrialization affected Passamaquoddy identity. After all, one reason why the Passamaquoddy moved back and forth across the St Croix River before 1783 was to fish, to hunt, and otherwise to provide for themselves. Once industrialization occurred, and new fishing and hunting regulations were legislated, did the Passamaquoddy come to identify more with Americans and less with other aboriginal people?

Research on these issues would assist in resolving the Passamaquoddy's present claim. Certainly, the evidence shows that at least up until 1783 the Passamaquoddy lived on both sides of what would become the New Brunswick–Maine border. This movement was implicitly encouraged by British policy makers in both London and Nova Scotia who wanted Passamaquoddy furs. Moreover, British policy makers did not seek to regulate the movement of the Passamaquoddy, either by defining where individual families might hunt or by creating reserve lands. If any regulatory capacity existed that would have limited the community's movement, it was defined by their aboriginal neighbours. These would have included the Maliseet who lived along the St John River and the Penobscot who inhabited areas adjacent to the Penobscot River. In this sense, therefore, up until the creation of the United States in 1783, the Passamaquoddy formed a political identity independent of British authority.

Passamaquoddy identity did change after 1783 and in ways that expanded their relationship with Americans and minimized their relationship with aboriginal people. However, as Eric Hobsbawm reminds us, there is a big difference between living in a nation and feeling a part of it. "Nationalism," after all, is a nineteenth-century phenomenon and not an eighteenth-century one.[17] This is what makes the Passamaquoddy situation so intriguing, since they came to live within the United States at the very time when it was becoming a nation and some among them – though certainly not all – came to see themselves as American. But whether, how, or when the Passamaquoddy came to think of themselves collectively in this way are still, I believe, unanswered questions.

What does all this mean for the Passamaquoddys' claim that they should benefit from the Supreme Court's decision in *Marshall*? They may have a case. But to get there, they need to demonstrate that the border has not substantively altered their people's cultural and social relationship in the lands they call "home."

5

New England Soldiers in the St John River Valley, 1758–1760

GEOFFREY PLANK

Events in the St John River Valley between 1758 and 1760 played a pivotal role in the history of the Maritime region and New England. The valley was contested territory in the late 1750s, claimed by the Wulstukwiuk and other nations of the Wabanaki Confederacy, by the French Empire, and by the British.[1] In 1758 a contingent of English-speaking soldiers, including a large number of New Englanders, came to the river to secure it unambiguously to the British crown. In military terms their expedition succeeded, and in broad geopolitical terms it laid the foundation for the eventual establishment of anglophone New Brunswick.

Our purpose here is to reconstruct and interpret the mental maps of a few individuals who went to the St John region in the 1750s, in an effort to determine the nature of their thinking about the landscape. The ideas of the New Englanders and where they placed the St John Valley in the geography of the expanding British Empire is of particular interest. To what extent did they consider the valley part of a greater New England? Can their participation in this expedition be attributed to provincial or regional expansionism, or did the New Englanders think of the valley as foreign territory, in a way that prefigured the international border that would eventually divide New Brunswick from Maine?[2] In addressing this question it will be helpful to focus on the New Englanders' understanding of the regional landscape, the connections they observed (or failed to observe) between the valley, peninsular Nova Scotia, and their homes to the west. Their interactions with the peoples of the region, and particularly with the

Acadians, are also significant, in part because their way of dealing with the local peoples reveals much about their perspective on the region's geography, and in part because the St John Valley in the late 1750s was a scene of extraordinary violence. The soldiers' campaign against the Acadians in the area demands historical attention, not only because it tells us much about the plans and apprehensions of the British and the New Englanders, but also because the events of the late 1750s became a turning-point in Acadian history, the moment when the centre of francophone culture in the Maritime region shifted decisively away from the places inhabited by the Acadians in the seventeenth century.[3]

In the middle years of the eighteenth century there was no multicultural or international consensus on the position of the Maritime region within the wider geography, history, or politics of North America; any reconstruction of the ideas of the time will always be peculiar to specific individuals and groups. A wealth of historical detail has come down to us in the diaries of two Massachusetts soldiers sent to the St John region in 1759 and 1760: an ordinary soldier named Enoch Poor, whose journal can be found in the collections of the Huntington Library, and Sergeant John Burrell, whose diary was published early in the twentieth century by the New England Historical and Genealogical Society. Much supplementary evidence is available in the official correspondence of officers stationed on the St John, at Annapolis Royal, and elsewhere, including the writings of Colonel Robert Monckton, Captain John Knox of Annapolis Royal, General Jeffery Amherst, and others.

In July 1755, within one month of the British seizure of the French fort of Beauséjour on the isthmus of Chignecto, an expeditionary force under the leadership of Captain John Rous sailed to the St John River in an effort to oust the French military from its fort on the site of present-day Saint John, New Brunswick. When the French received news that the British were coming, they burned their fortifications and moved upstream before Rous and his ships arrived.[4] Over the next three years the French maintained a military presence on the river, and Acadian refugees, escaping the reach of the British authorities who sought to remove them from the Maritime region, came in large groups. Acadian families arrived by canoe, by sailing vessel, and on foot. Some used the river valley as a highway, and, often with the assistance of Mi'kmaq or Wulstukwiuk guides, proceeded to Quebec. Others built new homes on the riverbanks, and the St John Valley became one of the most important centres of refuge for Acadians who escaped deportation.[5]

According to William Martin, a British soldier with first-hand knowledge of the St John River in 1758, approximately one hundred Acadian families lived on its banks, with the largest concentration in a village called Ste Anne, at the site of modern-day Fredericton. According to Martin, Ste Anne was "a straggling but beautiful village," with houses lining each bank of the river for two miles. There was a prominent chapel and a parish house, and although there were no fortifications, a French military officer commanded a small fighting force at Ste Anne.[6] A few miles upstream was a missionary outpost and a Wulstukwiuk village as large or larger than the Acadian settlement. Together, Martin reckoned, they constituted a significant challenge to British authority.

As Martin's report and others from the late 1750s make clear, the British were well aware of the Acadian and French presence on the St John River.[7] The British claimed the river as their own and planned to remove the Acadians who lived there just as they had deported most of those who lived on the peninsula of Nova Scotia. But for more than three years, from the summer of 1755 until the fall of 1758, Britain's military commanders had priorities elsewhere, and no sufficient force was available to send to the St John. A naval expedition launched in June 1758 was emblematic of British frustration in this period. Captain Bond of the HMS *Hind* was ordered "to look into the St. John's, fire several guns there, and afterwards repair to the fleet at Louisbourg."[8]

It was not until after the British evicted the French from Louisbourg in 1758 that the imperial authorities could concentrate enough attention and resources on the St John River to launch a concerted campaign to secure it. In September 1758, shortly after the seizure of Louisbourg, Colonel Robert Monckton brought a flotilla of ships and at least 1,200 men to the river.[9] In October he oversaw the construction of a new fort where the old French one had been, which he called Fort Frederick. He also sent an expeditionary party north in search of Ste Anne.[10] His vessels drew too much water to go so far upstream, but their mere presence drove several families of Acadian refugees north of the British advance. Along the way the soldiers discovered abandoned farmsteads, and they burned what they found.[11] Several parties went upriver in October and November 1758, and finally, in February 1759, a body of British soldiers reached Ste Anne.[12] Most of the inhabitants had already fled. The attackers killed six villagers, took six more hostage, and destroyed the settlement as thoroughly as they could.[13] According to Brigadier-General Moses Hazen, the New Englander in command of the expedition, the men burned "one hundred forty-seven dwelling-houses, two Mass-houses, besides all their barns, stables, granaries, &c."[14] Nonetheless, the commanders at Fort Frederick were not convinced that the village had been totally destroyed; at least three more expeditions were sent upstream from Fort Frederick in July and September 1759. One party in July came close to Ste Anne – perhaps within 9 miles – but returned without seeing the settlement. The soldiers captured some Acadians they encountered on the way, however, burned their houses, destroyed their crops and slaughtered their cattle.[15] The September expedition met fierce resistance from the local "French," and resulted in the death of at least seven attacking soldiers.[16]

Then, on 18 October 1759, three French-speaking delegates, two from Quebec and one from Ste Anne, arrived at Fort Frederick flying a flag of truce with the news that Quebec had fallen. They announced that they were (as John Burrell expressed it) "ready to resine themselves to ye English Nasion."[17] Enoch Poor recorded in his journal that they wanted to know whether the soldiers "would let them come in as prisoners or whether they should stay and live upon their land." The three delegates told the commanders at Fort Frederick that approximately 150 men, women, and children were ready to accept British directions, because "they had nothing to eat."[18] Three weeks later an Acadian family entered the fort,[19] and two days after that, several more came under British military escort.[20] Colonel Monckton issued a vague promise of sanctuary to the Acadians who arrived at his post, but, as Amherst later explained it, the "pass" Monckton issued "was by no means meant, or understood to give the French any right to those lands."[21] On 27 January 1760 most of the Acadian men who had come to Fort Frederick were boarded onto ships.[22] The next day, the women and children were put on board,[23] and the ship sailed for Halifax. Within weeks of their arrival in the provincial capital the captured Acadians were bound for France.[24]

A note of warning before looking at the soldiers' journals in detail. Military service, in and of itself, was an extraordinary event in the life of a typical New England man. Many of the men who kept journals as soldiers never recorded daily events at any other time in their lives;[25] they kept diaries during their periods of service because they expected their military experience to be extraordinary. It is hardly surprising, therefore, that they described the landscapes around them as strange. Providentialism, the belief that unexplainable occurrences contain signs of God's intentions, also informed many of their wartime observations. This disposition led them to focus on wondrous events. Burrell, for instance, recounted the descent of a "comet" in the woods to the northwest of Fort Frederick on 22 January 1760. He wrote that it lit up the sky before it exploded with "a noyes [that] was heard Like to

3 cannon."[26] Poor described a similar event in the sky to the southeast of the fort one month later. He wrote that his "comet" was "as big as a washtub."[27] Perhaps it was mere coincidence that Burrell and Poor were on the St John River to witness the arrival of two large meteors, one striking the earth. It could have happened anywhere. But one can still conclude from the soldiers' descriptions of these celestial events that they believed they had entered an alien, almost magically charged land. Given their predisposition and circumstances, analyzing the journals and the fact that the soldiers were on the lookout for unusual things, it is no surprise that they described the St John region as an unfamiliar place. But beyond their sense of the strangeness of the scene and their eagerness to return home, they did describe specific features of the landscape that made the St John River Valley seem different from New England.

One fundamental set of circumstances affected the perceptions and experiences of almost all the soldiers posted in this region during this period: they came to the St John River by way of the Bay of Fundy, their supplies came to them from across the water, their political and military power was based on naval forces, and almost all their communication with the outside world came from across the local seas.

It would be difficult to imagine a set of circumstances in which a body of New England soldiers in the late 1750s might have arrived at the river on foot from the west, after a long and perilous trudge through the woods. It is easier to picture a scenario in which the men came in coastal vessels, skirting eastward from the rivers of what is now central Maine. Had they arrived by land, the New Englanders' perceptions of the St John region might have been different. Their mental maps would have emphasized the contiguity of the landmass linking the St John region to Maine, an area where New Englanders had been expanding their settlements intermittently for generations. They might have considered their arrival on the St John as a leap forward, continuing and accelerating a long process of eastward expansion. But these soldiers had arrived by way of the open water, some of them had come from Louisbourg, where they had participated in a successful siege earlier in the year, and others had been detached from garrison-duty in peninsular Nova Scotia. They had seen Louisbourg, Halifax, Annapolis Royal, or Fort Cumberland more recently than they had seen New England. And all of them would maintain closer contact with those forts than they would with the eastern outposts of Maine; eighteen months passed after the construction of Fort Frederick before any large party left the garrison with the intention of going to Maine.[28] By contrast, ships shuttled between the fort and Annapolis Royal at least monthly, if not more frequently.

The soldiers' journals confirm Captain John Knox's statement that vessels were "continually running" between Knox's base at Annapolis Royal, Boston, Halifax, and the new British fort on the St John.[29] All of those ports were within a few days' sail of Fort Frederick, but one striking feature of the soldiers' journals is that they recorded much more communication with sites in Nova Scotia than with sites in New England, as demonstrated by the following records:

ENOCH POOR'S RECORD OF SHIP TRAFFIC AT FORT FREDERICK, 20 MAY 1759–1 JANUARY 1760

Vessels arriving from:		*Vessels departing for:*	
Annapolis Royal	4	Annapolis Royal	4
Halifax	2	Halifax	2
Boston	2	Fort Cumberland	3
		Boston	1

JOHN BURRELL'S RECORD OF SHIP TRAFFIC AT FORT FREDERICK, 3 AUGUST 1759–1 JANUARY 1760

Vessels arriving from:		*Vessels departing for:*	
Annapolis Royal	4	Annapolis Royal	2
Halifax	1	Halifax	2
Boston	1 (3 ships in a convoy)		

This pattern changed in 1760, when the New England soldiers' terms of enlistment were nearing conclusion and the men began to concentrate on returning home. It is also important to note that many of the ships coming to and from Annapolis Royal or Fort Cumberland were travelling in a circuit that began and ended in Boston.[30] Nonetheless, it is significant that the soldiers did not identify those vessels as coming from or travelling to New England. The immediate origin or destination of the ships in the Bay of Fundy region was what registered in their minds. Similarly, regardless of the ultimate source of procurement, the soldiers recorded in their diaries that their arms and ammunition came from Annapolis Royal.[31] So, according to their journals, did their food and other supplies.[32] Officials high in the military command, like John Knox, understood the place of the Bay of Fundy in a larger trade network that incorporated Boston. But ordinary soldiers were less likely to think that way, in part because it was more difficult for them to arrange for the trans-shipment of goods or letters.

On 16 January 1760 Burrell received a letter from his wife in Massachusetts. It had come by an indirect route, and was six months in transit.[33]

Water defined the landscape for the New England soldiers. Their ships and their shore-hugging fort were their main sources of sustenance and security. In the winter and early spring when ice blocked the harbour at the mouth of the St John, men crowded at the top of the ramparts and stared out toward the sea, anxiously hoping that the ice would break and that they would regain their connection with the outside world.[34] The men stayed by the water even though doing so carried inherent dangers. It took several weeks for the ship captains serving the garrison at Fort Frederick to acquire the skills and local knowledge necessary to negotiate the falls and narrows below the fort.[35] They relied on Acadian pilots to teach them how to navigate the river mouth, but even after they had learned to avoid wrecking their ships, they were no match for the local Algonkian and Acadian travellers, who navigated the rapids in small sailing vessels and canoes, and could slip past the water's obstacles much more easily than the British or the New Englanders could.[36]

Water presented other hazards as well. On 17 September 1759, according to Burrell, a "grate raine" so "washed ye part of ye Fort that it fell down a grate part of the same." The next day, Burrell wrote, "ye Fort keeping still falling down."[37] On the 4th of November he recorded that "ye wind Blue & a hYg Tide that washed ye stores or Blue it to Peases that some of ye Provisions fell out into the Tide."[38] But water could also bring unexpected delights. On 16 August a naval patrol came to Fort Frederick with two captured French ships. Poor recorded that the proceeds came to "two thousand pounds old tenor."[39] The men celebrated because they expected a share. In Burrell's words, they "had a frollek."[40]

In contrast to the water, the woods seemed more mysterious and uninviting, and at times literally impenetrable. On the day he first landed on the banks of the St John, Monckton recorded in his diary that there was "not the Least sign of any Road, or Path – The Woods very thick & bad marching." Over the next few days he sent several parties of soldiers out to search for trails, but he concluded "that it was not practicable for us to Proceed by Land" and so he decided to build his fort at the site of the abandoned French fortification, close to the mouth of the river, above the falls.[41]

As Poor described the local forest, it was capable of absorbing people and making them disappear. According to his journal, on 14 May 1759 a body of sixty soldiers struck out into the woods and spied a group of "Indians" in the distance. The captain "told them to halt."

The soldiers stopped marching, apparently expecting either an armed engagement or the start of negotiations. But the "Indians" simply ran away. The soldiers gave chase for "some miles but could not find them."[42] Four days later another group of soldiers left the confines of the fort to go fishing on the river. They were attacked by a group of Algonkian warriors and fled to the protection of the fortress walls. Poor wrote of the incident, "The Indians shot upon them but they got all into the fort but one which the Indians carted off."[43] The story emphasized the importance of the fortress walls. Those who reached the fortifications were safe, while the one man left outside was lost. That evening at twilight a company of thirty provincials and regulars entered the woods looking for the warriors and the captured man. They heard a shout, but they could not locate the Algonkians or the missing soldier.[44] On 15 June 1759 another party of soldiers out fishing on the river was ambushed by a group Poor identified as "the French and the Indians." One of the soldiers was killed and scalped, and another badly wounded. During the engagement many of the men of the garrison fought from the confines of a sloop in the waters of the river. Others tried to fight from the fort, firing cannons from the battlements. Poor writes that the attackers simply fled downstream, "and after they had got to the bay, the enemy fired their guns for joy."[45] A company of men, this time fifty in number, left the fort in search of the attackers. Poor reported again that "they could not find them."[46]

The soldiers' costliest adventure into the forested interior came in September, 1759 when over ninety men went upstream in the hope of looting the Acadians. The men returned after six days with "but a little Plunder." The expedition had cost the lives of five men and resulted in the wounding of seven others. At least three of the wounded men suffered in the fort for days or weeks before dying. Burrell writes on 5 October: "Leannard Commens died with ye wound ye enemy gave him ye 8 of September, he lived four weeks after his body was shott thrue with a ball." According to Burrell, "the soldiers were beat by ye enemy fireing upon ye party as they were in a small creek."[47] Not every expedition into the woods ended in ambush, but when the soldiers ventured out, even to gather firewood, cut hay, or carry water to their ships, they travelled in large groups and some of them shouldered arms.[48]

When they entered the woods the men were encroaching on alien territory, and the animals as well as the people seemed strange. Like celestial events, the arrival of wild creatures drew the attention of the diarists. Their descriptions of the men's reactions underscore how unfamiliar they were with the animals of the northern woods. Perhaps it is not surprising that they fired their muskets at a bear that emerged from the trees across the river and started swimming toward the fort.[49] But the soldiers' response to a moose that walked out of the woods reveals more about their relationship to the landscape. Both soldiers recorded what happened after the animal appeared. An officer left the fort with seven or eight men and boarded a small watercraft. They paddled up to the moose and opened fire with five or six guns, "but they did not kill him."[50] Whether the soldiers were frightened by the creature, hungry for its meat or interested in its antlers, their actions were hardly those of accomplished frontiersmen.

These soldiers were not, for the most part, the ancestors of the present-day anglophone residents of New Brunswick.[51] Nonetheless, in their response to the region one can see hints of differences in outlook that would eventually differentiate the peoples of the Maritime provinces from the New Englanders. It was significant for the future of the region that the English-speaking soldiers who came in the late 1750s did not want to settle there. They and their commanders valued the St John River primarily as a waterway. It was water-travel that made the river important strategically, and water-travel only that made it (to the extent that it ever was) familiar, safe, or useful for these New Englanders.[52] Furthermore, the local pattern of communication and trade, at least as it was perceived by the occupying soldiers, linked the St John River more closely to peninsular Nova Scotia than to Boston. This trade route – running from the peninsula to the St John, and in peacetime continuing upstream and overland to the St Lawrence River – had been travelled for more than a century, at least since the first permanent French colonization in the area. The route would continue to play an important role in tying together the loyal British-ruled colonies during and after the American Revolution. The St John River's most important geographical connections ran north-south, not east-west, and its dominant trade route linked it to an evolving economic and political region separate from the New England colonies.

What do these sources tell us about the Acadians? Before addressing that question, a few disclaimers are in order. First, as every historian of the Maritime region knows, there were no Acadian diary-keepers in the period of the Acadian removal, and very few letter-writers – none, as far as I am aware, in the St John region. Therefore, the inner lives of Acadian individuals – their private thoughts and emotions, and their understanding of the values inherent in community life – can only be deduced from an analysis of their spoken words and their behaviour. Second, it is clear from several episodes in this story that the Acadians in the region were divided among themselves over the extent to which they would oppose or work with the English-speakers. Nine Acadians, for example, guided Monckton up the river in 1758.

They were former prisoners from Fort Cumberland, and they had obtained release from custody in exchange for their services. They may have been acting under severe coercive pressure, but there is every indication that they gave Monckton reliable intelligence and advice.[53] Other Acadians would refuse to cooperate under any circumstances.

Did the Acadians think of the St John River as a new home or as a temporary refuge? Did they think of it as part of the old colony of Acadia? The evidence is mixed. First, it is important to notice how much investment went into construction at Ste Anne. A complete, elaborate community was built there along the river, and it serves as strong evidence that the Acadians believed they had come to stay. But most of the villagers who lived in Ste Anne in the 1750s were newcomers, and a large portion of them (exact numbers are unrecoverable) came from the Bay of Fundy region where their lives had been very different. The old methods of agriculture that had dominated their lives along the Bay of Fundy could not be quickly or easily transferred to the river banks, and especially after Monckton and his forces blocked access to the mouth of the St John, Acadians living along the river were cut off from old patterns of communication and trade.

Nonetheless, the St John continued to be important to the Acadians who lived there, as a mode of travel within and between their villages, and as a corridor of communication with the French settlements on the St Lawrence, upstream. The Acadian villages in the St John Valley were long and narrow, with houses strung closely along the riverbank. The settlement pattern suggests that the villagers, like the New Englanders, were more comfortable by the water than deeper in the woods. The danger inherent in entering an unfamiliar wooded landscape may have influenced the decision of some Acadians to quit the region altogether when Monckton and his forces challenged them on the banks of the river. A significant portion of the refugees uprooted from the river valley fled not into the surrounding countryside, but straight upriver and on to Quebec. Others, of course, stood and fought, or at least defiantly ignored the orders of the British imperial authorities.

Though a few Acadians cooperated with the British, the correspondence and journals of the commanders and soldiers make it clear that the Acadians were targets of the expeditions of the late 1750s, whether or not they overtly opposed the soldiers.[54] The journals blandly describe attacks on Acadian herdsmen and farmers, showing no apparent regard for whether the individuals targeted were engaged in or supporting military activity. For example on 6 November 1758, Monckton wrote: "Danks & Brewer whom I had order'd ... to March down the Neck, & kill all the Cattle they met with – Return'd late this Evening – And reported that they came across 3 or 4 french men, that were driving off about 40 Head of Cattle – that the Men made their Escape – But that they kill'd most of the Cattle – And had burnt the Houses."[55] Enoch Poor recorded a similar incident the following year:

The 12th of July our scout came in about 10 o'clock in the day. On the 10th day as they lay ashore the sun was about half an hour's height and at 6 they sent a scout out and they saw fine horses, fine oxen and a man belling about and they saw a canoe coming with 2 men in her and a sail up and they came along by the main body and Captain Churches hailed them and told them surrender and they should have good quarters, but they tried to get off. Then our men fired 20 or 30 guns and shot them very bad. Then they would not come to. Then our men shot upon them and they cried quarters and then our men went out in a bateau and brought them ashore.[56]

The prisoners were brought to Fort Frederick, and Poor wrote nothing more about them. What is striking, though, is the innocuousness of their activity, even as Poor described it. As on the peninsula of Nova Scotia, in the St John Valley, Acadians were subject to arrest regardless of their activity. Even when they were leading oxen at dawn, or sailing a canoe on calm water, their presence in the landscape violated the intentions of the British authorities. The British sought to remove the Acadians from everywhere in the region, but they were particularly concerned to destroy the Acadian villages on the banks of this strategically important river.[57]

General Hazen, the New Englander who commanded the expedition that razed Ste Anne in February 1759, reported after the operation that his men had scalped the six Acadian settlers whom they had killed.[58] The statement is striking, because scalping had long held a peculiar symbolic importance in the Maritime region, and because this incident, if it occurred, is unique. New Englanders had been scalping native peoples in the area for generations, but unlike the French on Ile Royale, they had refrained from authorizing the taking of scalps from persons identified as being of European descent. In 1749, when Edward Cornwallis arrived from Britain to serve as governor of Nova Scotia, he adopted the local practice of paying bounties for the scalps of the Mi'kmaq, but retained the prohibition against scalping whites. Self-consciously abiding by the long-standing "custom," Cornwallis exempted the French missionary Jean-Louis Le Loutre from his scalp-bounty policy, even though he had accused Le Loutre of leading Mi'kmaq warriors in unprovoked attacks.[59] The French and the Acadians had been traditionally exempt from scalping. The events of 1759 therefore demand particular attention.

During the Seven Years' War the practice of taking "French" scalps began outside of the Maritime region, in all likelihood in the Appalachian Mountains and the Ohio Valley, where the British colonists had less experience facing the French in battle. In the summer of 1755 the governor of Virginia ordered a unit of rangers to "kill all the Fr., Ind's, &c. they met with."[60] Within certain circles, the tactic received widespread support. In the spring of 1756, shortly after he was appointed commander-in-chief of the British forces in North America, the Earl of Loudon received advice from a former colonist residing in London that he should pay Iroquois warriors for the scalps of the French.[61] Scalps were cut from the heads of French soldiers and at least one noncombatant in the vicinity of Lake Champlain in the autumn of 1756.[62] In 1757 the governor of South Carolina offered native warriors a prize for the scalp of "any French man or French Indian" they killed.[63] During his expedition to Québec in 1759 James Wolfe felt compelled to prohibit the scalping of French settlers and soldiers, but despite his orders, in one episode alone approximately twenty French settlers were killed and scalped.[64]

While old strictures against scalping French colonists collapsed in the context of the war, Britain's official policy toward the Acadians changed in ways that exposed them to new forms of violence. The Acadians taken from peninsular Nova Scotia in the early years of the conflict had been relocated in the thirteen colonies in the hope that they would be absorbed into English-speaking communities and become "profitable and, it is possible in time, faithful subjects."[65] That effort, however, proved traumatic for almost everyone concerned. After carrying the Acadians south, shipmasters reported that they could not imagine a service "more disagreeable or desperate."[66] At least one captain lost control of his vessel when the Acadians he was carrying seized the ship, ran it aground at the mouth of the St John River, and burned it.[67] Other masters managed to deliver their passengers, but in the process they only transferred their difficulties to the colonists and colonial authorities on land. Most of the Acadian exiles were assigned to rural communities in Massachusetts, Connecticut, New York, Pennsylvania, Maryland, and South Carolina. In general, they refused to stay where they were put. A large number migrated to the colonial port cities, where they established impoverished French-speaking Catholic neighbourhoods, exactly the sort of communities Britain's colonial officials had hoped to discourage. More worrisome still, a number of Acadians threatened to make their way north, to French-controlled regions including the St John Valley, Ile Royale, the coasts of the Gulf of St Lawrence, and Canada.[68] British military commanders worried that any young Acadian men who made it north would zealously fight for the French.[69] By 1758 the British had given up placing Acadians among English-speakers. The experiment was widely considered a failure.

After the surrender of Louisbourg in 1758, the French negotiators agreed to the evacuation of Ile Royale and Ile St Jean. In accordance with the agreement, in a relatively orderly fashion, most of the French civilians on those islands were sent to France. The adjacent mainland, however, remained contested ground between the British and the French Empires, and the capitulation agreement signed at Louisbourg did nothing to clarify its status. The absence of agreement on the location of the imperial border made the British military commanders eager to empty those territories of French-speaking settlers. They hoped to discourage Britain's negotiators in Europe from returning any territory to France at the conclusion of the war. Furthermore, by destroying the settlements as a pre-emptive measure, they hoped to make it difficult for the French to re-establish their colonies if the diplomats officially granted them back any land.[70]

The Acadians in the St John Valley were thus symbolically, and in practical terms, central to the contested issue of sovereignty. The idea of making them British had been effectively abandoned, and as long as they were present in the valley, the region seemed potentially French. These circumstances made the Acadians politically significant, but did not give them power. For a short period they may have been at a disadvantage even in comparison to the local native peoples, because (as far as the British were concerned) the Acadians had no political standing and no way to enter into formal negotiations with the British military command. Unlike the Algonkian peoples who were by the late 1750s and early 1760s making peace with the British, they had no recognized leaders to negotiate for them, and in any event, as long as they remained in the region the British were unwilling to cede them ground.

The Acadians' position would begin to improve after the fall of Quebec, when the need arose among the British to develop a policy for the colonists residing there. Though some imperialistic enthusiasts hoped to deport all the French settlers in Canada, for a variety of practical reasons political deliberations took a different turn.[71] As a result, a new set of discussions began on the place of French-speaking Catholics within the British imperial realm.[72] Unfortunately, when the six men at Ste Anne were scalped those debates lay in the future, and the Acadians remained at their most marginalized position.

There is no way of determining the extent to which such high political considerations affected the thoughts of sergeants and private men. Nonetheless, even considering the soldiers' perspective, the geographical context of the scalping incident was significant. As French-speaking Catholics, the Acadians would have seemed alien to the soldiers no matter where they encountered them, but they appeared even more so in seeming to reside comfortably in a valley that the New Englanders considered dangerous and strange. The burden of the soldiers' journals suggests that the violence they inflicted on the Acadians reflected their sense of vulnerability in a landscape that was foreign to them, and very far from home.

In late March 1760, the New Englanders in the garrison of Fort Frederick sent an ultimatum to their commanding officer informing him in very specific terms that they would abandon their posts when their terms expired on May 1, regardless of whether they received official permission to do so.[73] Six weeks later a large number of the men made good on the threat. In the first week of May a fishing vessel set anchor in the harbour at the mouth of the St John River. Recognizing the arrival of the ship as an opportunity, the men packed their bags and marched out of the fort, ostentatiously ignoring their commanding officers, who watched as the soldiers walked away. More than seventy soldiers, many of them armed, commandeered the ship and sailed to Boston.[74] Most of those left behind at Fort Frederick were ready to follow the deserters. According to their commander "not one soldier in this garrison will stay on any account whatsoever, but will force any vessel that may arrive here to carry them off."[75] Eventually he convinced approximately fifty men to stay, if only temporarily. John Burrell was among the cooperative ones.[76]

As these events were unfolding, the commander of the garrison wrote to the governor of Massachusetts complaining that "home sickness" had afflicted all his New England men.[77] Six weeks later Amherst echoed the complaint. Neither speeches nor financial inducements could convince the New Englanders to remain on the St John, because, he wrote, they would never be "cured of their home sickness."[78] These officers' references to "home sickness" stand among the earliest uses of the phrase on the North American continent. The words had appeared together in print in English for the first time only in 1756, in a translation from the German where they appeared in quotation marks as a newly coined translation of a German-language term.[79] By using the phrase, the officers were self-consciously displaying their sophistication. Nevertheless it is appropriate that their comments, perhaps the earliest diagnosis of "home sickness" in North America, referred to New England soldiers. Almost everywhere they were deployed in the colonial period, New Englanders eventually became restless, and anxious to return to the familiar landscape of their provincial towns.[80]

When assessing the views of the soldiers, it is critical to place their response to the region within the context of their short military careers. In contrast to many regular British soldiers, the New Englanders enlisted for only limited periods, and they regarded their months in the army as an extraordinary time of their lives. Most of those posted in the St John region had already completed a significant part of their term of service, in Nova Scotia or Ile Royale. Though their maps might have told them otherwise, it is likely that many of them believed that redeployment in the St John Valley had taken them farther from their homes. This illusion was reinforced by patterns of transport and communication. Ships from Nova Scotia routinely sailed directly to Boston, but to get to Massachusetts from the St John River usually required stopping off first at Fort Cumberland, Annapolis Royal, or Halifax. This made the river seem more distant from New England, while the density of the surrounding woods and fear of attack caused the soldiers to view the valley as dangerous and strange. Their commanders believed it was their mission to transform the region and make it less alien, primarily by removing the Acadians and the French. In the long run, the officers assumed, new settlers would come, and indeed, in the more peaceful decade after 1760, other English-speaking newcomers, including many New Englanders, arrived with a happier disposition and responded to the local landscape in more optimistic ways. By that time, however, the New Englanders who had participated in the expeditions of 1758 and 1759 had defiantly and angrily returned to their native land.

6

Before Borderlands: Yankees, British, and the St John Valley French

BÉATRICE CRAIG

Borderlands studies are growing in popularity, and the upper St John Valley, in northern Maine and north west New Brunswick, seems an ideal laboratory to examine cross-border activities and transnational populations, as well as economic, political, and cultural interactions.[1] The river is the border between the United States and Canada; the valley, however, had been settled for over fifty years when the boundary was drawn in 1842 and cut this farming and lumbering settlement known as the Madawaska Territory in two – a division local people and lumbering interests ignored as long as they could. Lower Canadians migrated to the valley; valley people migrated to New England; local residents moved back and forth across the river, were born here, raised there, married back where they had grown up, and had children born on both sides of the river. The river, until the railway finally reached the valley in the late 1870s, was the only convenient means of communication within the settlement and between the settlement and the outside world. People did their business wherever it suited them, and the lumber interests particularly ignored the boundary. American lumber interests owned timber land in Canada, and provincials logged in the United States. Both relied on crews drawn from Maine, New Brunswick, or Quebec and fed with bread, fish, pork, and beans imported from Quebec, while their horses filled their bellies with locally raised fodder. And everybody got paid after the timber was sold in Saint John, whence it was exported to the United States or Britain. Local people even voted where they resided with scant attention to citizenship, a practice that caused a scandal in Maine in the late 1870s.[2]

Even nowadays, the population of the upper St John Valley is distinct from the surrounding ones. Made up of French-speaking Catholics, it differs from the Yankees, Scots-Irish, Green Irish, and Scandinavians to the south; a mix of Acadians and French Canadians, it is distinct from both Quebeckers and New Brunswick Acadians.

"Borderlands," "cross-border activities," and "transnationality" are, however, contemporary concepts – and using them indiscriminately could result in reading one's preoccupations back into a past that did not necessarily share them. There is no evidence that in the nineteenth century the permanent residents of the St John Valley thought of themselves as "transnational"or of their region as a "borderland." They were not the result of the interactions of people on the borders of two national entities, but rather the result of a political vacuum. They had been there first.

"Borderlands" and the like are also concepts imposed from the outside by scholars and, in their wake, by politicians and journalists. The nineteenth century, however, does not seem to have developed this concept, if the comments from the surprisingly numerous people who travelled through the St John Valley are any indication. If there were lessons to be learned from the patterns of interaction between the Madawaskayans and their neighbours, or from the operations of transnational businesses, they were lost on the visitors. Instead, visitors integrated their observations into pre-existing intellectual or ideological frameworks, which had no use for borderlands. This makes their published comments better windows into the mindset of the era than sources about the region. The British, in their European or North American varieties, tended to view the St John Valley French as one of the motley groups in the British Empire; the Americans viewed them either as a political trump card, as museum pieces, or as a subversive popish-colonialist fifth column. Descriptions of the St John Valley also reflected shifts in opinion over time. Later authors were more likely to be conscious of the linguistic, religious, and cultural differences between them and the people they described. Although British and American accounts both evolved toward greater ethnic consciousness, if one can use a very twentieth-century term, they nonetheless differed in their vision of the French. American travellers and commentators seemed much more influenced by what they had read beforehand about the people they were encountering. They were much more inclined than the British to stereotype, to moralize, and to deplore the fact that the St John Valley residents were not clones of themselves. And unfortunately the Americans did not always take their cues from authors who viewed the French favourably, such as Bancroft and Longfellow, but as often took them from other authors who disdained them. Each side, however, shared a common vision: the Madawaska settlers were not some unique blend, but belonged to their people, and in the case of the Americans, this might mean they had to be remade in the American image.

The upper St John Valley seems to have been well frequented from the late eighteenth century onward. Until the building of railways in the later part of the nineteenth century, the valley was the only winter route between Halifax and Quebec City, and one of the few summer ones. Consequently, it was frequently used by British people,[3] who could be government officials, couriers, or private individuals travelling for business or pleasure. The latter were usually attracted by the Grand Falls, which had quickly become a well-known public attraction. Even official travellers would sometimes make a point of stopping along their way to view them. Many of those British travellers indulged in a pastime common among the respectable classes of the time – the writing of travelogues – and left accounts of their trip through the upper reaches of the St John Valley. As for more official travellers, they often visited the region specifically to collect information for reports they were expected to produce.

British travellers went through the upper St John Valley even before it was settled. American travellers did not appear until much later, with the exception of the surveyor of the Bingham purchase, who made his way to the region in 1790. No other Americans seem to have reached the upper St John until the late 1810s, and those were timber cruisers and lumberers. Some of those men settled permanently in the area; none bothered to pen his impressions for posterity, though. Then, in 1820 Maine became a state, took a hardline position in the northeastern boundary dispute, and tried to assert sovereignty over these very remote and not very accessible northern reaches. The state sent agents to the disputed territory to investigate "trespasses" and "aggressions" by the British, to inquire into the inhabitants' land claims, and, after the settling of the boundary dispute, to report upon the progress of education in the settlement. Official reports were picked up by journalists, who drew their own portraits of the Madawaska French for the entertainment of their readers; private visitors followed in the footsteps of the government agents and published their impressions.

The earlier travellers through the St John Valley were not unduly concerned with the inhabitants' Frenchness – if they noticed it at all. Patrick Campbell, John Mann, and Lieutenant Coke, three tourists who travelled through the St John Valley between 1791 and 1832, occasionally referred to the fact their guide, boatman, or landlord was a Frenchman, but nothing in their narrative allows the reader to conclude they had visited a French settlement.[4] Some visitors not only did not "see" the French, but "saw " the local Irishmen instead, and could mislead their readers into thinking the upper St John Valley was the site of a hardscrabble Hibernian pioneer community of poor families eking out a living among stumps.[5]

Travellers who did notice that the St John Valley inhabitants were French did not necessarily make much fuss over the issue. Park Holland, the Bingham purchase surveyor, described the terrain, the weather, the housing, and the crops very matter-of-factly, drew the portrait of an old French hunter married to an Amerindian women, commented favourably on the politeness of the inhabitants, gave a thumbnail sketch of the settlement history, and continued his journey after two paragraphs![6] He could have been describing any other Maine pioneer settlement.

Travellers, although indifferent to the ethnicity of the inhabitants, were acute observers in other respects. They gave precise descriptions of the landscape and the fauna, and, in the case of the pleasure travellers, of their own adventures and the problems they encountered on a still fairly difficult and rugged route. One might conclude that they did not dwell on the issue because they did not think it was important. They took for granted that the world was made of all types and accepted the fact with equanimity.

Two early observers stand out from this group. *They* noticed. One thought the French were excitingly exotic; the other was slightly ill at ease and, one may surmise, vaguely concerned. The first gentleman was an 18–year-old lieutenant in the 104th foot regiment of New Brunswick. A native of Jersey, he had arrived in British North America shortly after the outbreak of the war of 1812; his regiment was sent to the Canadas the following winter. Lieutenant John LeCouteur kept a diary and sketched the scenery on his way.[7] He stayed less than two days in the upper St John Valley, but kept his eyes open and chatted with the priest. His description is the first of a trend which gathered subsequent strength: the equation of the St John Valley "Acadian" settlement with the Arcadia of antiquity.[8] LeCouteur describes the French inhabitants as settled in "peaceful retirement," their habits and manners as "simple and kind." The settlers grew enough in summer, he wrote, to be able to spend the winter in "mirth and friendly intercourse." LeCouteur explicitly made the parallel with the ancient world, asserting, "This is the only Arcadia now existing in the world."[9]

LeCouteur was a rather sentimental young man, prone to idealizing all he met (especially the young ladies). The realization that the St John Valley settlers were different did not inevitably lead to such effusive and drippy statements, however. Peter Fisher, the first historian of the province of New Brunswick, was obviously unsettled by what he found, and yet he had little negative to report. His 1825 *History of New Brunswick*[10] describes a flourishing settlement growing significant surplus and trading it in Fredericton. So does his 1838 *Notitia.*[11] The *Notitia,* published at the peak of the boundary dispute, asserts that the settlers were "warmly attached" to the British government. Like LeCouteur, Fisher found the Madawaska French peaceful and contented, leading an orderly life. Crime was unknown among them and they had had no need for magistrates until traders and other strangers settled among them. So far, Fisher was describing the Madawaska French in practically the same terms as LeCouteur, without the teenaged sentimentality. All this praise made the conclusions of both his descriptions surprising. His account in the *History of New Brunswick* ends by stating: "The men are about the middle size, generally spare built and active; the women, on the contrary are very stout and short. They are very lively and hospitable, but very slovenly in their house and cookery. In short, they appear a different race from the English. A stranger going above the falls finds himself suddenly among a new race of people, different in their language, religion, habitations and manners."[12] By 1837 Fisher still found the French a breed apart, albeit one whose intercourse with the English was improving. "Within a few years," he commented, "some of them have begun to imitate the English in constructing frame houses, which is making a great improvement on the face of the country".[13]

LeCouteur and Fisher heralded two trends that came to characterize American descriptions of the Madawaska French in the later part of the century. One of those trends was strengthened by an opportunistic reading of St John Valley history during the boundary dispute, and by the publication of Longfellow's *Evangeline.* The other was reinforced by the practical problems of integrating the St John Valley into the Maine body politic.

The first Americans to reach the upper St John Valley after Park Holland and leave accounts of their journeys were officials sent by the state of Maine in the 1820s and 1830s. They took note of the inhabitants' Frenchness, but probably would not have wasted much ink over it had they not been able to use it to bolster Maine's claim to the territory. They presented the Madawaska French as Acadians who had been evicted from their settlements on the lower St John when the Loyalists had arrived, and who had deliberately resettled above Grand Falls because they knew the region was not under British jurisdiction. Accordingly, they asserted, the British claim to the disputed territory was a sham: the upper St John Valley and the entire disputed territory was, and had always been, American. It was no "borderland," but a *bona fide* part of the United States, inhabited by people who had knowingly and deliberately escaped British oppression.

The first of those state officials were the party of George W. Coffin, who had been sent to the disputed territory in 1825 to investigate the activities of the "Provincials."[14] They were allowed to grant *bona fide* settlers up to 100 acres. Their local guide and informant was John Baker, an American lumberer and miller originally from southern Maine. Baker told the visitors the French inhabitants were very desirous to become part of the United States, and the two officials reported that the French settlers themselves had expressed such a desire. They also discovered they had neither the time nor the authority to issue grants to the Madawaska settlers, who were too numerous and in any case usually occupied more than 100 acres. The rest of their description of the French is mostly quite matter-of-fact: the families were large; the inhabitants were "very industrious, civil and hospitable people, and well deserving of the fostering care of government"; their agriculture was flourishing, and they grew the best potatoes the officials had ever seen, despite the fact they were not, according to Coffin, "what we should call good husbandmen." Coffin was also at a loss to find a frame of reference within which to understand the community he was visiting. For lack of anything better, he equated the French with a tribe of white Indians: when his party met Simonet Hébert, a prominent local citizen, he referred to him as the "grand Sachem of this French settlement." Like Fisher, he may have thought the French were a "race apart."

Coffin was followed in 1828 by Charles S. Davies, who was appointed by the state to investigate British "aggressions."[15] Davies seems to have been the first to articulate the theory that the St John Valley French were refugees from the British colonies. Davies described them as "French Neutrals" (the term that the American colonies had used to refer to the Acadian deportees in 1755): "[They] had been expelled from their farms and improvements on the establishment of the province of New Brunswick; and ... have been joined from time to time by their countrymen from Canada, who have not chosen to continue under the government established on its conquest."[16]

Davies's account flies in the face of existing evidence. It ignores the fact that a considerable number of Fredericton Acadians had received grants on the lower St John from the New Brunswick government, that the rights of all occupants – including Acadian occupants – to sell their improvement to whoever took over their land for whatever reason had been reasserted by the governor in council, and that many of the Madawaska settlers had sold a grant or some improvements before – or even after – taking land at Madawaska.[17] Owing to the size of the population that had to be granted land, the process was not very smooth. Some Acadians complained of injustice, but so did some of the Planters and the Loyalists. The lower St John Acadians may have been particularly dissatisfied with the massive arrival of the Loyalists in the area, but the evidence shows on balance that, as a group, they were not at that time treated worse than their Planter and Loyalist neighbours.

In 1831 the Maine government sent another two agents, John G. Deane and Edward Kavanagh, to the St John Valley to ascertain the claims of the settlers to the land they occupied. The governor was very careful in the choice of his envoys. Edward Kavanagh was a Catholic; he had attended school in Quebec, and could speak French fluently. Perhaps for this reason, there is no suggestion in the writings of the two men that the Madawaska French belonged to a different branch of humanity altogether. Kavanagh kept a journal of the expedition. Later, Deane and Kavanagh presented the governor with a formal report of their findings.

Kavanagh's journal[18] is packed with detailed information about the layout of the land, the soil, the climate, the state of the roads, the means of conveyance, accommodation en route, forms of landownership, crops and other economic activities, and religion. He found the land fertile, the people industrious and peaceful, and the housing primitive (too many log houses, not enough American frame houses). He and Deane were almost always well received, although the settlers were worried the Americans might evict them if the boundary dispute was settled in their favour.

The information contained in the report to the governor is more detailed.[19] It first briefly describes each holding (name of occupant, length of occupation, extent of improvements etc.), and notes that most of the settlers were from French Canada. These details were followed by a lengthy description of the area, its geography, soil, climate, hydrography and fauna, and of its people and their activities. Three pages denounce British trespasses. Like Kavanagh's journal, the report is very matter-of-fact, and conveys a positive image of the inhabitants as "inoffensive and obliging people who live in peace with each other."[20] The settlement is also described as economically prosperous. The report ends with a recommendation concerning the best way to introduce American laws and usage in the settlement.

The historical narrative contained in the report toes the party line as earlier defined by Charles Davies. The inhabitants are described as follows:

> descendants of the ancient Acadians, who were driven from their farms by the introduction of the Refugees and the Laws of the province. They abandoned their farms to the British and sought a refuge in a place [where] they believed the British had no right to exercise jurisdiction. They understood where the

lines of the province were, and the old inhabitants described the lines correctly according to the treaty of 1783. They remained sometimes undisturbed, but were finally induced to take deeds of their land, but no other acts of jurisdiction seemed to have been exercised over them for many years, and very few acts before the administration of Governor Douglas, who was very active in extending the British usurpation.[21]

This account was inaccurate. The French had petitioned the New Brunswick government for grants; they had voted at elections; they had received the provincial bounty on bread grain grown on new land. And the province had appointed some of them to the positions of Parish officers, Justice of the Peace, and Militia officials.[22] But this narrative strengthened the American claim to the disputed territory and was promptly adopted by Mainers, if one is to believe some newspapers of the time. In December of 1831, for instance, the *Republican Journal* (Belfast, Maine, and Democrat despite its name) described the results of the Loyalist migration: "The poor Arcadians [*sic*], driven, once more from their homes and reduced to beggary, plunged again into the wilderness, an hundred and seventy miles from Fredericton, and occupied their present position, which they, knowing the terms of our treaty with Great Britain and being familiar with the geography of the country, considered as without the bounds of English jurisdiction."[23]

Dean and Kavanagh's text also completely obliterated the French Canadian ancestry of the Madawaska settlers. They were now all Acadians. And "Acadians" and "Arcadians" were synonymous, as in LeCouteur's narrative. Being rather practical men, Deane and Kavanagh had not imagined an "Arcadia" on the banks of the St John River! But the *Belfast Republican* journalist, who very likely had never set foot in the disputed territory, had no difficulty romanticizing the settlement he had heard about. On the one hand the Madawaska settlers were described in pre-lapsarian terms; they were the "natural men" of eighteenth-century philosophers, guided by the innate goodness of human hearts and uncorrupted by the deleterious influence of civilization. On the other hand, they were doomed: sooner or later, they would move from the Golden Age to the modern one. Not only was their present existence romanticized; so was their history. The Madawaska Acadians were described as a people reduced to a wretched state and hounded around the wilderness by the cruel British. And the narrative was replete with heart-tugging images and expressions.

As long as this version of Madawaska history was the dominant one, the Americans were more likely to treat the French with sympathy. Acadian history neatly paralleled the basic plot line of the melodramas so popular at the time, which opposed an arch-villain totally devoid of redeeming qualities and a pure, innocent, and helpless heroine who passively suffered at his hands. They could also stage a pure and fearless hero who rescued the damsel in the last page. The British were the villain, the Acadians the virginal heroine, and the Americans the hero into whose arms they had run for protection!

In addition, educated New Englanders knew about the "real" Acadians. Volume 4 of George Bancroft's *History of the United States*, published in 1852, contained an account of the *Grand Dérangement* very favourable to the Acadians.[24] Bancroft drew what he saw as obvious parallels between the fate of the Acadians and that of the American colonists: both had been victims of British oppression. Now their descendants were seemingly seeking to join the republic to the south. How could the Americans turn their backs on this small people? Ideological consistency required that they be adopted into the family.

The problem, though, was that the fair damsel could never be as fair in real life as in her rescuers' imagination. Bancroft's Acadians were brave and gallant and admirable ... and gone forever. One could not confront his heroic description with reality. The St John Valley Acadians were very real – and had become citizens of Maine. By 1843 the *Republican Journal*, which had so far been rather positive, if rather maudlin, found the Madawaska French backward in many respects:

> The people live chiefly by agriculture ... Their husbandry is rude; their implements poor; and their breeds of cattle, sheep and hogs of the worst description. Their chief crops are wheat, barley, oats, potatoes and grass ... Their houses are most frequently built of hewn timber: sometimes of logs, and sometimes they are shingled or clapboarded. They are warm and comfortable. There are a few grist mills, of an inferior description. They buy and sell but little, producing nearly everything they consume, and hardly anything more.[25] Their trade, such as it is is with Fredericton and Quebec, principally with the latter place.[26]

The journalist may have thought he was being sympathetic and understanding; after all he had referred his readers to Bancroft and pleaded for the welcoming of the Madawaska people into the Maine family. Nonetheless, his text reveals a great deal of ambivalence: the French were allegedly not good farmers, and were satisfied with a subsistence agriculture – which in a country so relentlessly devoted to "progress" was a damning statement, not a compliment. The author also imagined a self-contained community with minimal business contacts with the outside world. The rest of the article described the French as people who enjoyed life, instead of working hard to improve their lot. And, worse, they were engaging in pastimes that Puritans had always considered sinful, like dancing and gambling on horses. They were improvident and "careless of the future," and furthermore those traits were genetic ("characteristic of the nation from which they sprung").

Mainers were beginning to understand that to decide out of Romantic enthusiasm, Republican generosity, or anti-British resentment, that the French deserved the protection and sympathy of the American Republic was easy enough. Dealing with the practical problem of integrating this group into the existing society was a much more difficult proposition. What would be the place of these newcomers in American society? What kind of citizens were they going to be? Until the Webster-Ashburton treaty was signed, Mainers seemed to have taken for granted that the French would integrate into American society without major difficulties. Nonetheless, they assumed that the French suffered from obvious handicaps, as they had until then been living in ignorance of what they perceived as the proper rules of a free and democratically ordered society. Land agents were worried by the French's lack of experience with the American system of government and legal system. Deane and Kavanagh were amazed when they discovered that landed property was respected despite the absence of deeds, and sold or transferred by verbal contracts with a minimum of apparent problems.[27] In their eyes, a society resting upon the force of the spoken word rather than on the authority of the written one was in some way deficient and vulnerable.

The commissioners appointed to issue grants of land under the terms of the 1842 treaty were frustrated by the inability of the French to speak English, by their ignorance of American laws, and by their "irregular" way of acquiring and conveying land.[28] Each land agent mentioned the lack of formal government agencies among them as a problem. Deane and Kavanagh specifically listed the need for roads, courts, and a registry of deeds, as well as for Justices of the Peace and schools. They also recommended that the area be organized as a county in the near future. In their eyes, these were the most pressing concerns. Later officials were also concerned about the lack of roads, magistrates, municipal charters, and schools, especially schools where the English language would be taught.[29]

Mainers believed that for the French to be integrated into the American citizenry, they would have to change their habits and adopt the numerous agencies of government viewed in the United States as a bulwark of freedom against despotism. Initially, many officials believed English-speaking schools would easily take care of any problem that might arise.[30] Others, such as the *Republican Journal*, feared that integrating and assimilating the French would be an arduous task.[31]

Mainers believed that the French would not be fit for self-government unless they were properly schooled and trained. By emphasizing the formal and legalistic aspects of democracy, however, they overlooked the fact the French did have some experience with self-government and were already running their own affairs. But owing to the distance between the settlement and the county seat (more than 150 miles until 1833), the French had taken the habit of settling as many of their problems on their own as possible, calling in the arm of the English law only as a last resort. Observers, whether from Maine or from New Brunswick, stated that the French solved their grievances through arbitration: a panel of two or three people, including the priest, heard the contestants and made a decision that usually gained compliance.[32] It is doubtful, then, whether the French – accustomed to running their own affairs informally, verbally, and in French according to local standards of justice and equity – saw as progress the notion of conducting their legal business formally and in English, abiding by externally generated laws and customs.

Contrary to expectations, the French then proved unwilling to die out or assimilate. They were selective in their adoption of the American system: they conducted town meetings in French, squatted on empty land, and were very lukewarm in their support of public schools. They saw little point in book learning, and when they sent their children to school, it was to learn to read and write French, not English.[33]

The refusal of the St John Valley French to cooperate in their own cultural assimilation led the Americans to seriously doubt their intellectual abilities and potential for "progress." Once the Webster-Ashburton treaty was signed, the political need to equate the Madawaska settlers with the Acadians vanished. The settlers were more and more identified, not with the Acadians, but with the French Canadians, and French Canadians ranked much lower in nineteenth-century American public opinion than the idealized pre-deportation Acadians they had never met. Popular American authors writing about Canada normally described its French-speaking inhabitants as cheerful, congenial, and hospitable – but also ignorant, superstitious, unenterprising, and indolent.[34]

The timing of the identification of the Madawaska inhabitants with the French Canadians rather than with the Acadians further added to their disfavour. Before 1830 Americans had usually perceived members of other cultural groups as innocent children who needed to grow up, like any children, and become responsible albeit worldly-wise adults. French Canadians were not really responsible for their backwardness; they were subjected to the double tyranny of the British crown and the Popish Church, which imprisoned them in Old World customs. Free institutions would make them free men, as they would make free men of members of any cultural group.[35] This latter notion had fallen into disfavour by the 1840s, and preconceived notions about the characteristics of the French "race" appeared.[36] The French Canadians emerged as a "fun-loving people" favouring merriment over hard work, and lacking Puritan commitment to acquisitiveness. Many American descriptions of the Madawaska French began to follow this model.

By the late 1850s the Madawaska French, like their Canadian counterparts, were beginning to be accused of undesirable characteristics. Childlike carefreeness was no longer to be smiled at, but censured. The French aversion to English-speaking schools rendered them suspect in the eyes of their Anglo-Saxon neighbours, many of whom saw Madawaskans as unfit citizens weakening the political fabric of society.[37] Throughout the state and the Union, a significant number of citizens were beginning to view foreigners as Trojan horses sent to their shores by the absolutist powers of Europe to undermine the cause of freedom. Know-Nothingism appeared in Maine in the early 1850s. Although the party never nominated its own candidates for state elections, it was a political force to be reckoned with. Officials could no longer benignly neglect the northern French and their assumed ignorance of the democratic process.

By and large, though, the most damaging blow to the French image came from the press. In the fall of 1858 editors from the major papers in the state travelled to the northern part of Maine. This was a junket to promote the area and encourage immigration. Their comments about the French, however, were anything but sympathetic. The Madawaska settlers were accused, among other things, of selling their votes to the highest bidders, of lacking pioneer spirit because they did not clear the forest, of preferring to divide their holdings among their children, and of being poor farmers.[38] The first accusation cannot be proved or disproved, but naturalized citizens were frequently stereotyped by native-born as sellers of votes. The forest the French supposedly should have been clearing was on land unfit for cultivation. The Madawaska French seldom divided their holdings, unless they were much larger than average.[39] The editors had been fooled by the typical French Canadian farm lay out, in long, narrow strips, fronting the river. As for the French being poor farmers, the agricultural censuses tell a very different story: in 1860 Madawaska farms were more productive than many New England ones.[40]

Rather than being an accurate description of reality, the editors' portrait of the French was the anti-portrait of the individual who adhered to the Protestant work ethic. Liberal-capitalist ideology wanted men to be free of the shackles of traditions and superstitions;

the French were described as sharing the habits of the peasantry of France, "retained almost intact since the days of Louis XIV." The Protestant work ethic emphasized industriousness and acquisitiveness; the French were "light hearted, improvident, unenterprising people, content to remain stationary while all around is progressing." The new ideal called for a repression of instinct. The French were "more fond of the fiddle than the hoe." They were also too prolific, almost always described as having too many children.[41] This evocation of a people exerted a strange fascination on the Americans, coupled with explicit or implicit disapproval. Properly civilized people were not supposed to make children for the fun of it; this was a sign of lack of self-restraint. The French reproduced as uncontrollably as animals, and had not yet learned how to control their instincts and delay gratification. Improvidence and high fecundity were therefore two aspects of the same problem, and were used to explain the alleged poverty of the French.

Mainers writing for their countrymen denounced the French menace at length. Madawaska people were indeed a "border" people, but one contaminating the American Experiment with undesirable traits common in Old World and Colonial societies. When they wrote for an outside readership, Americans did not need to be so alarmist, and the Madawaska French became mostly objects of ridicule. Charles Lanman, a sportsman and author of several books on the less-settled parts of North America, took a trip from New York to Boston through Quebec, Labrador, and Maine in the late 1840s, travelling through the Temiscouata and Saint John Valleys.[42] He described the French Canadians as a miserable and barbaric bunch. As for the St John Valley Acadians, they had "degenerated into a more ignorant and miserable people"[43] than the French Canadians, whom they closely resembled in appearance and customs. Lanman described the two groups in the same terms: their main business was popery, drinking, cheating their neighbours, barely making a living from tilling the soil, and "fleecing the strangers to perfection." He went to mass at St Basile and found the congregation "composed entirely of Acadians decked in the most ridiculous gew-gawish dresses imaginable."[44] After the service, the men spent the rest of the day racing horses of which the swiftest belonged to the priest. Lanman did not comment on this activity, but neither Englishmen nor New Englanders would have found it an appropriate way to spend the Sabbath.

This outright negative attitude was one side of the coin. The romantic qualities of the Acadian past continued to attract attention, and were widely publicized after the publication of H.W. Longfellow's *Evangeline* in 1847. Maine people quickly realized that some of the

"Evangeline people" were living in their backyard. Some hardy travellers even went north to visit those picturesque characters, and *Harper's Monthly Magazine* published an account of such a journey.[45] The author, Charles Hallock, referred to Madawaska as the "land of romance," and praised the civility, simplicity, and virtue of the inhabitants. His account explicitly refers to the poem. Stepping inside one of the houses, a member of the author's party "contemplated the huge Canadian stove, six feet high, that stood in the partition wall, so as to warm both rooms ... then he looked at the loom and the spinning wheel, and thought of Longfellow's *Evangeline*; at the antique chairs and the bedsteads set into the walls like berths."[46] What made him think of *Evangeline* was an activity that New England women had by then abandoned and was therefore a throwback to the past: the manufacture of homespun.

Hallock's text is an odd mixture of detailed and direct observations of material culture and habits that ring true. He describes, for instance, houses with front porches where "the family sit at evening and receive the calls of their neighbors who come in boats,"[47] and his comments passing as observations about the mores and values of the people were visibly shaped by his reading of the poem. Hallock and his friends attended a local wedding and the ensuing dance, and reported that the event exuded a child-like innocence, as uncontaminated by outside influence as Gabriel and Evangeline's wedding might have been, had it taken place. The bride is a "rosy-cheeked maiden" wearing "kirtle and petticoat, guiltless of hoops."

Evangeline's success even influenced some government officials. The land agent who investigated the claims of the settlers on proprietors' land in 1874 described the customs and high standard of morality of the French in words plagiarizing the poem. He also dwelt at length on the quaintness of the French, describing their houses, for instance, in condescending terms: "They have queer looking cottages with windows that open and shut like doors, their roofs and piazzas being broken, projected, picturesque, and often ornamented with trellis, cornice and fanciful adornements, so that their solid homeliness is often fringed with elegance."[48]

When visitors equated the Madawaska French with Acadians, they depicted them not as a hindrance to the progress of civilization, but as a counterfoil to the modern world. Our 1874 land agents concluded: "We would say for the people of Madawaska that, with their primitive style of living, they enjoy the priceless blessings of health, which more than compensate for the absence of modern luxuries, and are doubtless much happier than millions who live in rich mansions and roll in luxury."[49]

The St John Valley Acadians, like Bancroft's and Longfellow's pre-deportation fabrications, provided the Americans, caught in the compulsory march towards progress, with a psychological refuge. Somewhere, in remote and isolated valleys sheltered by forest primeval, survived some remnants of a past steeped in rustic and tranquil felicity, frozen in time and untouched by the world around them, guiltless not only of hoops in their skirts, but of any trace of modernity.

This "frozen in time" theme was common to descriptions of the Madawaska French both as Acadians and as French Canadians, as it was to most post-1840 American writings about Acadians and French Canadians. Acadia was Arcadia, or the garden of Eden; French Canada was stuck in a retrograde feudalism and in popery. Neither belonged to the modern world, which swirled around them and passed them by. The Acadians were too good to live in it, while the French Canadians not good enough.

What about the British? They were not attempting to build the "Perfectly Free" society in North America, and the cultural, linguistic, and religious distinctiveness of the French should not therefore have threatened them unduly. And indeed, from the 1840s onward British visitors to the St John Valley noticed that the inhabitants were different from themselves, but they neither denounced the situation as dangerous nor idealized the Acadians as the lost tribe of Arcadia. This did not mean that the British thought of the Madawaska French as their equals. They often suggested that the French were not as "advanced" as could be desired and occasionally hinted that the example of the British would be profitable for them.

Three British men left particularly detailed accounts of the Madawaska territory in the 1840s and 1850s, and another did so in the 1870s. Edmund Ward, born in Nova Scotia at the end of the eighteenth century of Loyalist parents, was a printer, journalist, and deputy agent for immigration in New Brunswick in 1840. His book on the St John River was intended to attract settlers.[50] Abraham Gesner, another Nova Scotia–born son of Loyalists and a contemporary of Ward, studied medicine, surgery, and geology in London, and became known as the inventor of kerosene. He left another detailed account of New Brunswick for the benefit of immigrants.[51] Finally, James Finlay Weir Johnston, a Scottish agricultural chemist and mineralogist, was invited by the New York State agricultural society to come and visit their part of the United States in the late 1840s, and to report on its capacities to support agriculture. Some New Brunswick promoters, hearing of his journey, convinced the lieutenant-governor also to finance a similar visit there.[52]

Edmund Ward depicted the French as "composed chiefly of Acadian French" and as a "harmless and inoffensive people, who pay implicit obedience to their clergymen."[53] They had been joined, he said, by impoverished French Canadians who had since achieved a fair measure of success, and by a few Scots and Irish. Several of the French settlers were substantial farmers, who supplied the nearby lumber-camps with oats and hay.[54] Gesner's Madawaska settlers were similarly a mix of French Canadians and Acadians, sprinkled with a few Provincials and Americans.[55] Some of their ancestors had been Indians, which explained their distinctive physique – they were dark-haired and dark-skinned. Their everyday style of dress was distinctive too, and Gesner believed it to derive from the old French peasantry.[56] The men were still wearing their hair in queues, an eighteenth-century fashion. They were "remarkably moral, orderly and frugal" and "passionately fond of music and dancing." After Mass, the remainder of the day was spent racing horses or canoes, dancing and card playing.[57] Agriculture was very productive, and the crops beautiful,[58] despite an imperfect system of tillage and a "lack of agricultural enterprise seldom seen among English settlers."[59]

However, Gesner's French were also unambitious, unenterprising, unacquisitive, and pleasure-loving. Gesner was not sure how to explain the Madawaska settlers' behaviour. On the one hand, he attributed it to their cultural heritage, and to some innate conservatism only slowly eroded by the example of the English. "It is scarcely possible," he added, "to wean them from the customs of their forefathers, and improvements in the system of agriculture are very slow introduced among them."[60] Whatever he encountered that was unfamiliar, like the outdoor clay oven and the well-pole, he identified as not only typically French, but as inherited, unchanged, from the seventeenth century! But in other parts of his book, he described the rest of New Brunswick settlers in terms that were not significantly different. New Brunswickers, whether French or British, were unpolished, but hospitable and fond of a good story or a good tune, and not commercially minded.[61]

Ward and Gesner then described the St John Valley in very similar terms. So did J.F.W. Johnston, who published two books as a result of his North American peregrinations. In his *Notes on North America*, the Madawaska French appear as a mixed and divided community. The old Acadian French were "fine, industrious men." The Lower Canadians were represented by the English settlers as a "miserable" set.[62] Johnston believed this prejudiced view stemmed from the poverty of the recent French Canadian immigrants. The St John Valley soil was of excellent quality, and the crops beautiful, although some of the French Canadian settlers "appeared to be both needy and indifferent cultivators." The stock left a lot to be desired on the other hand.[63]

Although Johnston's description conveys an overall impression of prosperity, he was not entirely satisfied. Upper and middle St John Valley settlers all the way down to Woodstock, whatever their ethnic origin, had abandoned the cultivation of wheat and replaced it with buckwheat. This would not do, because buckwheat grew too easily and with too little effort, and thus promoted indolence.[64] Paradoxically, Johnston denounced buckwheat as requiring too much from the farmer's wife. Wheat could be turned into bread that kept for several weeks. Buckwheat had to be prepared for every meal. Johnston believed a farmer's wife had better things to do with her time than cook! And constant cooking disturbed the orderliness of the kitchen.[65]

Johnston described in detail the activities of only two farmers. One was a M. Cyr, who owned 350 acres, twice the local average.[66] The other, Capt. L. Coomb, possessed 1,025 acres.[67] Johnston obviously believed that anything short of an English estate-type agriculture was primitive and unworthy of notice. This type of agriculture was rather uncommon in North America, where farms were operated solely with a family labour force. European travellers tended to disdain those small family farms and the extensive form of agriculture they practised.[68] Western Europeans practised a labour-intensive, high-yielding agriculture on small acreage. North American farmers, who had access to much more land but were chronically understaffed, relied on extensive cultivation instead, and their yields were, literally, medieval. European observers did not look beyond land productivity and did not notice that labour outputs in the American northeast were similar to those in Britain. Johnston was no different.[69] His attitude was that New Brunswickers did not know how to farm. Their land was "generally ill-treated – the take-all-and-give-nothing system being pursued, partly from ignorance and partly from idleness."[70]

The last scientific depiction of the Madawaska settlement in the period under study here was penned by Charles Lugrin, the secretary of the Agricultural Board of New Brunswick and author of several promotional volumes on New Brunswick. In 1872 he presented the provincial Legislature with a report on Victoria County, which included the New Brunswick Madawaska as well as several civil parishes below the Grand Falls.[71] Lugrin gave the legislators a detailed description of the crops, soils, and farming techniques prevailing in the area, identifying what was specific to each group: the Irish produced excellent potatoes; the French grew large amount of peas, some flax, and "were expert in weaving good, strong, and durable linen."[72] Victoria County agriculture was not as good as Lugrin wished it was. He partly blamed the deleterious influence of the lumber trade, not the inhabitants' ethnicity. The lumber trade and shingle making provided farmers with opportunities of making "easy" money and lured them away from their fields, which were consequently neglected. The second cause behind the underperformance of Victoria County agriculture was also independent of ethnicity: the lack of cheap communication with existing markets. Lugrin recommended a railway connection to solve this problem.[73] Lugrin's position was thus very similar to that of the Americans in the 1830s and early 1840s.

Lugrin also described the ethnic makeup of the county. The four western civil parishes were inhabited by a mix of French-Canadians and Acadians. As a group they stuck "tenaciously to their old manners and customs." They had no obvious character flaws, and "though not very enterprising, [were] tolerably industrious and economical."[74] Lugrin noted that they were beginning to feel what he believed was the favourable influence of the English, with whom they were in daily contact. Public, non-confessional schools would complete their transformation.

As for private British travellers, they remained blissfully unconcerned by Frenchness in the St John Valley. They were usually aware of it, but cultural differences, rather than being a problem in their eyes, were yet another tourist attraction. And none made reference to *Evangeline.* Either the poem was not read in the British Empire and even in New Brunswick – or the British did not equate contemporary Acadians with fictitious ones.[75]

What do all these accounts tell us? If we strip them of their moralizing slants and opportunistic constructions of history, they convey very similar information about the Madawaska settlers. The upper St John Valley was a prosperous settlement, blessed with a flourishing agriculture, engaging in some lumbering and shingle making on the side, but a bit old-fashioned, especially when it came to clothing and housing styles. Serious crime was unknown among them, and they kept a nice balance between work and leisure, profit making and social activities. They were polite, hospitable, and gregarious. The women were very busy with large families and textile production, among other duties, and had little time for "homemaking." Madawaska houses probably looked more like workshops than Victorian parlours. However, what is lacking is any reference to the transnational nature of this community, and more particularly, of its economic activities.

Early visitors seem to have been able to see what was in front of them. Their accounts of the Madawaska settlement were normally descriptive and abstained from moralizing. Initially, the Americans were neutral as well, even if they manipulated the Madawaska history for their own ends. Until about 1815, Americans took for granted that their society was the best in the world because their institutions were superior to all others. Any people, no matter how endemic their barbary, could progress to the standard of the Americans if they enjoyed similar free institutions. Humankind was one unique race, improvable and inevitably destined to progress. By 1850 this vision had been replaced in the minds of most by Anglo-Saxon racialism. Humankind was made of different races, some inherently superior to others. The outward signs of supremacy included their British- or American-style political institutions, and their individualism and acquisitiveness. A people that displayed different institutions or a lack of entrepreneurial spirit was not only inferior, but likely to be incorrigible. Between 1815 and 1850 the two ideologies coexisted, one gradually replacing the other, although without completely eliminating it.[76]

The American perception of the French fitted into this framework. People who were different were, almost by definition, inferior. Inferior people burdened the Americans in their march to progress, and the people of the St John Valley were different. It was true that the more nostalgic or romantic Americans were willing to tolerate small pockets of difference in remote areas. An Acadian reservation in Northern Maine might thus be acceptable. Yet, no matter how sympathetic Longfellow may have been toward the Acadians, he did no favour to their descendants; they could find acceptance only if they lived up to the expectations the poem raised, one of which was to be living fossils. The St John Valley French could either remain trapped in the past and be admired by some, or step into the present and be vilified.

Anglo-Saxon racialism prevailed in Britain as well.[77] It seems to have had limited impact on the travellers' views of the Madawaska French, however. British visitors who travelled through the valley believed the French were socially and technically very conservative, but had no doubt that healthy evolution would take place as the French mingled with English-speaking people. The British writers' sense of superiority also had other sources than ethnic consciousness alone. Their lumping the Madawaska French in the same bag as the rest of the rather backward and not very hard-working New Brunswickers suggests that class as much as ethnicity could explain their attitude.

At one level, then, British and American views were very different. The Americans were conducting a grand experiment in North America: they were building the prototype of the democratic Society. For the experiment to succeed, all had to share the same values and the same ideology. Cultural and linguistic differences – and Catholicism – had to be neutralized or quarantined. The British, on the other hand, were not conducting any experiment. Their society was ethnically very diverse. English, Welsh, and Anglo-Norman, Cornish and Manx, Scot and Irish, despite having very little in common either in culture or religion, shared the British Isles. The only thing Britain asked all her constituent peoples, the glue that kept everything together, was allegiance to the Crown. By the late seventeenth century, attempts at imposing religious conformity had been abandoned. Subsequently, ideological or cultural conformity was neither required nor sought. And being French and Catholic in an Empire that soon included India, much of Africa, and part of the Arab world was not being very exotic. At another level, however, the British and the Americans shared the same inability or unwillingness to recognize the existence of "people in between." Each half of the St John Valley was expected to conform to the expectations of a larger political body: an ideologically and cultural homogeneous republic, or an Empire composed of a hierarchy of distinct groups. In the eyes of all the visitors to the area before the coming of the railway, there were no such entities as borderlands.

7

Comparative Economic Advantage: Nova Scotia and New England, 1720s–1860s

JULIAN GWYN

Nova Scotia–New England commerce underwent dramatic shifts between the 1720s and the 1860s.[1] Although hindered at times by warfare, trading relations between the two regions survived and at times flourished. Historians' attempts to define and account for this enduring relationship have been only partially successful despite an abundance of manuscript sources.[2] The interest of economists in international trade history, meanwhile, has declined as the contention that exports form the driving force of economic growth has been eclipsed by theories that prefer to define what sustains economic growth rather than what causes it. Nevertheless, the notion that comparative economic advantage – the theory that each country can derive maximum economic benefit from concentrating on the goods and services it produces and supplies most efficiently – is one approach to trade history that retains currency among economists. At the same time this approach offers considerable explanatory power for economic historians. An investigation of Nova Scotia–New England commercial ties in this context provides a useful basis on which to assess the reasons for the continuing importance of New England to Nova Scotia.

As early as the 1720s comparative economic advantage already played a large part in linking Cape Breton/Ile Royale and Acadia/Nova Scotia with New England. Although the historical geographer Andrew Hill Clark[3] held New England responsible for having retarded French development of Louisbourg's agricultural and forest hinterland by supplying the fortress with provisions and building materials readily available in Cape Breton had the French taken proper note of the island's potential, subsequent scholars have taken a different view. With this in mind, in the 1960s I investigated the impact of Louisbourg's development on the New England economy, an exploration later elaborated by Donald Chard.[4] Cape Breton needed certain products that could be produced elsewhere and shipped more cheaply; Louisbourg imported goods from the Antilles françaises and France more cheaply than they could be purchased in New England. New Englanders depended on fish purchases at Louisbourg to complete the supply of their West Indies market. Consequently, between 1730 and 1744 one vessel in five which entered the port of Louisbourg came from New England, and one in two in the interwar years 1750–54.[5] In return, before 1744 almost half the 181 fishing boats and trading vessels purchased in Louisbourg were sold by New Englanders, who also shipped provisions there.[6] In this trade Massachusetts led. However frequent such inter-empire trade, the practice contradicted the then dominant geopolitics. Until the idea of economic imperialism took root with the nineteenth-century concept of tariff-free trade, economic domination was thought best advanced by wars of territorial expansion. Thus, on the Massachusetts–Nova Scotia frontier and elsewhere, economic advantage was largely determined by the clash of arms.

The supply of the French at Louisbourg was but one aspect of the interest Nova Scotia afforded Americans. The fisheries of Nova Scotia were paramount. Before a British government became centred in Halifax in 1749, the main fishing station was at Canso in Chedabucto Bay.[7] Guarded by a small British military detachment and visited occasionally by a British naval frigate,[8] the fishery was not conducted by those inhabiting peninsular Nova Scotia. Of the 819 fishing boats noted in six seasons there between 1721 and 1730 (the first years for which there is statistical evidence) some 89 percent were New England–owned. Another 2 percent came from Nova Scotia, Newfoundland, Pennsylvania, and New York.[9] The rest were from ports in the British Isles.

New Englanders were initially the great economic beneficiaries of the renewal of the Anglo-French power struggle over Nova Scotia in 1744. French regional decline was achieved primarily through British military and naval power, although New England privateers swept French fishing vessels off the coast and in 1745, aided by a British naval squadron, laid successful siege to Louisbourg. British taxpayers secured New England's frontiers, and compensated New Englanders when they raised forces for their own defence.[10] New Englanders were doubly rewarded by being granted all the contracts in 1746 to rebuild the fortifications and town that they had severely damaged in 1745.[11]

Table 1 Halifax Port Entrances and Clearances, 1770–71

	Entrances (Annual Average)				*Clearances (Annual Average)*			
	n	%	*tonnage*	%	*n*	%	*tonnage*	%
New England	92	63.9	3,518	46.0	120	68.6	4,551	54.3
Other U.S.	23	16.0	1,028	13.4	24	13.7	1,058	12.6
Total	144	100.0	7,645	100.0	175	100.0	8,388	100.0

Source: NA, CUST16/1.

Subsequently, with a large share in provisioning the Louisbourg garrison, 11 percent of ships clearing Boston sailed for Louisbourg until 1749.[12] When Louisbourg was evacuated and the garrison redeployed at Halifax, Nova Scotia's economic ties with New England were further strengthened. After 1749, about 60 percent of all merchant vessels that anchored in Halifax harbour in most years had sailed from a New England port. Until 1775 Nova Scotia thus remained dependent on New England's supply.[13] No other North American colony was more important to Boston than Nova Scotia.[14] No region was more important to the port of Halifax than New England, as Table 1 shows.

Without competition from a Nova Scotia merchant fleet, American-owned vessels, led by New Englanders, also earned the freight. As Nova Scotia's exports were minuscule, her merchants needed heavy British government spending within the colony to enable them to afford the New England imports.[15]

Nova Scotia's economic tether to New England was strengthened by the land grab engineered when the deportation of the Acadian population began in 1755. The economic loss of this successful agricultural population and the disappearance of the Louisbourg market in 1760 both seriously dislocated Nova Scotia's economy and prolonged the dependence of Halifax on external supplies.[16] The labour shortage caused by the Acadian deportation was filled largely by New Englanders. Though a battalion of Acadian labourers worked in Halifax until 1762,[17] none was employed in the building of the naval yard begun in 1758, or in the repair of British warships there. Rather, New England artificers were recruited by Benjamin Hallowell, the Boston shipbuilder, some of whom stayed in Halifax beyond war's end in 1763.[18] The arrival in the 1760s of some 8,000 New England Planters, the bulk of whom settled around the Bay of Fundy, deepened Nova Scotia links to New England. What limited agricultural surpluses were produced by these new settlers were absorbed in the Halifax market, or, because of easier access, were exported (as earlier by the Acadians) to New England.[19]

The war with rebel America between 1775 and 1783 did not quite sever Nova Scotia's economic ties with New England. An exchange of sorts occurred, most of it involuntary. Vessels making for or departing Nova Scotia were seized by New England privateers. In response, the British navy seized American vessels, many of which, with their cargoes, were owned by New Englanders. The coasts of both New England and Nova Scotia were subject to raids, and even occupation, with the consequent loss of property by destruction or from the booty of war.[20] There is scattered evidence of clandestine commerce between the enemies across the Gulf of Maine, largely confined to the early years of hostilities. This war increased shipping costs and raised prices throughout Nova Scotia, which wages failed to match.[21]

With the Loyalist refugee exodus to Nova Scotia – few came from New England after 1776 – new short-term opportunities arose for New Englanders. The rapid construction of a town of almost 10,000 people at Shelburne depended in part on the supply of American building materials, from prefabricated house frames to bricks and window panes.[22] This was a repetition in 1783–84 of what New England had contributed to the building of the town of Halifax in 1749–50, but on a much grander scale.[23] The failure of Shelburne to become a centre for the West Indies trade profited Halifax only marginally. Its further deficiency as a fishing port contributed to New England's continued postwar domination of Nova Scotia's coastal fisheries.[24]

One curious post-1783 development was the temporary migration of a significant part of the Nantucket-based whale industry to Dartmouth, Nova Scotia.[25] Before the British government forced the whalers' emigration to Wales in 1792, Timothy Folger and Samuel Starbuck with the Boston Loyalist refugee Benjamin Mulberry Holmes, from 1786 combined their capital and inaugurated a flourishing Nova Scotia–based whaling operation. Extant shipping records show that annually between 1789 and 1791, seventeen ships with crews of 215 men and boys returned to Dartmouth each year, while twenty whaling ships carrying crews of 226 departed for the south Atlantic.[26] None departed in 1793 and only one in 1794, when the last whaling expedition for many years was mounted from Halifax harbour.

Historical geographer Graeme Wynn is the one other scholar who has manifested more than a passing interest in Nova Scotia's economic ties to New England. Wynn followed Clark in part in a series of articles emphasizing New England's role in Nova Scotia's economic underdevelopment.[27] I interpret the evidence differently. However well New England did out of the exchange, the ready presence of the New England market was a greater potential boon to Nova Scotia's economy than Nova Scotia ever proved for New England. Nova Scotia's advantage was in the rapid growth of New England's population and the enormous expansion of its economy, which was potentially so important to Nova Scotia. In 1770 when New England held an estimated population of 581,000 souls, Nova Scotia had perhaps 12,000. After a century of growth, Nova Scotia's 388,000 was dwarfed by New England's 3,487,000.[28] New England in 1774, according to one estimate, may have been the poorest region of what became the United States, but it was far better off than Nova Scotia, which was a very poor market. A century later that gap had certainly widened.

However welcome this small market was to New England, it was never New England's alone to exploit. Its principal European competitors were English suppliers, based principally in London and Liverpool. Even in post-1783 North America, New England interests, based largely in Boston, had to face the widening role of New York and Philadelphia combined, in providing a market for Nova Scotia's trade goods and in offering shipping services. Pre-1776 New England dominance was not sustained.

For Nova Scotia, trade with the British West Indies after 1783 depended on the import of certain American commodities being free of duty if carried by British subjects and in British-registered vessels. With the rise of Nova Scotia's direct trade with the Caribbean, the prewar role of New England diminished. The colony now supplied itself with raw sugar, rum, and coffee, although small quantities of molasses continued to be imported from New England in most years.[29] Only in 1789 was the first tariff on American imports into Nova Scotia legislated. It established a 10 percent *ad valorem* duty on all goods except, in the words of the Act, "scantling, planks, staves, heaving boards, shingles, hoops, square timber, wheat, rice, rye, Indian corn, barley, wheat and rye flour, neat cattle and sheep alive."[30]

Let the year 1790 serve as a surrogate for postwar Nova Scotia–Cape Breton's trade with the United States. Imports from the States amounted to $253,700, composed of a few principal items. These were bread, flour, and cornmeal worth $187,400 (73.8%), grain $34,500 (13.6%), wood products $16,000 (6.3%), and livestock $14,000 (5.5%). Although tobacco was imported regularly, none was imported that year.[31] Total exports that year amounted only to $29,300, of which 94.8 percent was accounted for by cod and rum.

Low-value gypsum, shipped from Fundy ports, may have been an important export item, but exports of only twenty tons valued at $250 were recorded in 1790. In most years before 1807, up to 100,000 tons were rumoured to have been exported, employing as many as 500 small vessels.[32] Between 1832 and 1853 an average export of about 40,000 tons was recorded, before the American Civil War killed the trade. Shipped as far afield as Philadelphia and as near as Eastport, Maine, and entered duty-free, these exports allowed for an illegal trade of perhaps $20,000 to $80,000 annually back into the Fundy ports, mainly in the form of flour and specie. As the worthies of Hants County, led by Mr Justice Wilkinson, noted in an 1843 petition to the imperial Board of Customs, "the great disadvantage arising from this trade was that it placed the carrier completely in the power and at the control of the American trader, who would seldom pay more than 6s. [$1.20] or 8s. [$1.60] per ton, a sum ruinous to the proprietor and discouraging to those immediately concerned in the shipment and freight."[33] Low in price – from the 1840s to the 1860s between $0.58 and $0.66 a ton – but large in bulk, it was suitable only for small coastal craft.

The extent to which vessels registered in New England participated in this post-1783 Nova Scotia trade is unclear. If we use the extant shipping records for Halifax for 1790 as an example, then no American-owned ships entered or cleared the port that year.[34] The entire Cape Breton and Halifax trade was conducted by vessels of the British empire, with vessels owned in Halifax leading. That year, as Table 2 shows, tonnage entries into Halifax from New England had declined markedly from their pre-1776 levels. Now in 1790 far fewer than one ship in ten entering Halifax came from a New England port. Moreover, fewer goods were being imported from Boston than from Philadelphia and New York combined. Whereas before the American War of Independence almost two-thirds of shipping was to and from American ports to the south of Nova Scotia, by 1790 such traffic with American ports had fallen to less than 30 percent of all ship movements.[35] The Nova Scotia merchant fleet, then composed mainly of small vessels averaging about fifty measured tons, was suited to this coastal and West Indies trade.[36] By 1790 numbering 433 ships and measuring 22,129 tons, the fleet was steadily augmented first by building and then, from 1793 onwards, by prizes seized in war.[37]

The outbreak of the French war in 1793 again influenced Nova Scotia–Cape Breton trade with New England. Prize goods entered the export trade from Halifax, adding to the overall value of exports, which by 1794–95 had risen to more than $184,000 from $29,000 four years earlier. That year, exports of prize coffee and prize sugar were worth $33,800 (18.4%). Exports from Nova Scotia were then dominated by fish valued at $126,800 (69%).[38] The rise in fish exports doubtless stemmed from the destruction of the French fishery upon

Table 2 Halifax Inward Shipping, 1790

	n	%	*tonnage*	%
New England	16	8.9	1,178	7.8
Other U.S.	18	10.1	239	8.3
Deep seas	90	50.3	10,948	72.9
Coasting	55	30.7	1,650	11.0
Total	179	100.0	15,015	100.0

Note: Tonnage for only 20% of coasting vessels is available, with an average of 30 tons each.
Source: NSARM, RG31–105/1 (13).

the outbreak of war and the loss of its base on St Pierre and Miquelon. The French were replaced partly by New Englanders and partly by Nova Scotia fishermen, who for the first time secured a significant niche in the offshore fishery.

The war with France disrupted trade as Britain's North American squadron based at Halifax seized American vessels thought to be carrying contraband goods. Between 1793 and the outbreak of war between the United Kingdom and the United States in May 1812, some 226 American vessels were seized and processed by the Halifax vice-admiralty court. Of these, about half were owned and half were built in New England. Some two-thirds of the tonnage (or about 18,776 tons) had been built either in Massachusetts, Connecticut, or Maine.[39] Though some of these ships were restored to their American owners, even when their cargoes were condemned New England losses amounted to an estimated $2.8 millions. The chief beneficiaries were the British naval captors, though the buyers both of vessels and cargoes initially were almost always Nova Scotians. Some of these were resold in New England. Once again inflation, due to the dislocation of war, had an impact on Nova Scotia; and its effects became acute during the thirty-two months' war with the United States in 1812–15.

The so-called War of 1812 saw another 766 ships condemned by the Halifax vice-admiralty court, the preponderance of these being American.[40] Of these about half were either built or owned in New England. The extent to which Nova Scotian shipowners suffered losses at the hands of New England privateers has yet to be studied in the manner undertaken by John Faibisy for the War of Independence. Some of the captured ships and cargoes were resold to New England buyers, while the 1814 British capture of Eastern Maine allowed Halifax merchants to re-export British manufactures to the larger New England markets.[41]

Table 3 Shipping Entering Port of Halifax, 1825 & 1834 Compared

	1825				*1834*			
	n	%	*tonnage*	%	*n*	%	*tonnage*	%
New England	33	8.0	3,965	10.0	57	8.6	5,206	7.4
Other U.S.	40	9.7	4,492	11.3	67	10.2	8,283	11.7
Deep seas	227	55.3	25,573	67.1	372	56.5	48,343	68.4
Coasting	111	27.0	5,550	14.1	163	24.7	8,802	12.5
Total	411	100.0	39,580	100.0	659	100.0	70,634	100.0

Note: As tonnage was recorded for about one-quarter of coasting vessels, we estimate the average vessel tonnage at 50 and 54 tons in 1825 and 1834 respectively.
Source: NSARM, RG31–105/2 (8, 17).

Table 4 Nova Scotia Shipping to and from U.S.A., 1835–65

	Inwards				*Outwards*			
	n	%	*tons*	%	*n*	%	*tons*	%
1835	833	37.1	161,051	46.7	876	25.4	80,417	29.4
1845	1,845	43.4	155,949	41.7	1,920	44.1	168,562	43.6
1855	2,993	51.3	322,948	55.2	2,807	50.4	297,862	52.1
1865	3,334	48.8	463,115	49.8	3,161	50.1	501,183	53.0

Sources: NA, CO221/48, CO221/59; House of Assembly Journals and Proceedings (HAJP) for 1855 (Halifax, 1856), Appendix 86, 381, 387; HAJP for 1865 (Halifax, 1866), Appendix 2, 245, 256.

Colonial shipping data for trade between Nova Scotia and individual American ports after 1815 are rare. The only useful guide is provided by the shipping listed as paying fees for the upkeep of the Sambro lighthouse off Halifax harbour.[42] This evidence, when compared with 1790, demonstrates the revival of postwar trade with New England. As the overseas commerce of Nova Scotia diversified and the economy matured, New England's pre-1776 domination of Nova Scotia's trade was never regained. As an example, in 1818–19 some 215 vessels exported sugar from Halifax; only one-third of that number shipped to New England ports.[43] Data in Table 3 illustrate a relative decline at the port of Halifax of imports from New England ports. This is significant, as Halifax remained the chief port in the colony for the import of American commodities. Moreover, this freight was carried not by American vessels, but by British-registered vessels, either from British North America or from Bermuda. In 1834, of the fifty-seven vessels freighting goods to Halifax from New England, only fourteen were American-owned, while almost all the others were owned in Nova Scotia, especially in Halifax.

When we consider American trade with Halifax and all the outports, the picture, as Table 4 shows, is rather different. The trend saw the relative strengthening of trading ties with the United States from the 1830s through the 1860s, as the absolute volume of commodity trade expanded. The shift was from 30 percent of all vessel movements and 49.3 percent of tonnage in 1835, to 39 percent of all vessel movements and 51.4 percent of tonnage in 1865. What is unknown is the changing New England proportion of this expanding trade. What is certain is that the bulk of the trade was shipped by British-registered vessels, and not in foreign bottoms. In 1835, 35 percent of ships involved were American or other foreign carriers, and by 1865 only 15 percent.[44]

Part of the explanation for this phenomenon is found in the policies of successive American administrations, which excluded British colonial vessels from access to American coastal trade, while failing to protect the American deep-sea merchant fleet. This exclusion directed Nova Scotia shipowners as well as those from other British North American colonies into American foreign trades. Between the 1840s and the 1860s the proportion of American imports carried in American-registered vessels fell from 70 percent to less than 30 percent.[45] As the overall size of this trade grew rapidly in these decades, the market was supplied by foreign shipping, in which Nova Scotia's shipowners were well placed to profit. The Reciprocity Treaty and the American Civil War merely amplified these opportunities. Trade until after 1830 was modest. Between 1830 and the onset of the Reciprocity Treaty in 1854, the commerce of Nova Scotia with the United States, as measured in per capita terms, increased by almost 30 percent in value. Under reciprocity the proportion rose more steeply.[46] Between 1844–54 and 1855–66 the per capita value of Nova Scotia's imports from the United State rose by 74 percent, while its exports to the United States rose by 85 percent. Comparable estimates for the colony's recorded worldwide trade are about 39 percent each for imports and exports.

To bread, flour, cornmeal, and tobacco, which still dominated American exports to Nova Scotia, were added imports of barrelled beef and pork, drugs and dyestuffs, hardware, leather, cordage and canvas, woodenware, and cabinetware. In 1846 the head of the imperial customs service in Halifax, T.N. Jeffrey, noted: "At the present day a traveller from the United States in visiting the small towns or settlements or those of more consideration could almost fancy himself in the United States by finding himself surrounded with every article of

Table 5 Nova Scotia Trade with USA. Annual Average ($)

	Imports (A)	*Exports (B)*	*Total Trade (A + B)*	*% change*
1834–6	544,300	447,200	991,500	
1844–6	611,700	1,136,300	1,748,000	76.3
1854–6	2,023,100	3,320,600	5,343,700	205.7
1864–6	3,098,400	4,223,600	7,322,000	37.0

Source: NA, CUST6/3–5, 13–15, CUST12/3–5, 13–15; 1854–6: HAJP for 1855, Appendix 86, 360–4; HAJP for 1856, Appendix 86, 368–8, 372–3; HAJP for 1857, Appendix 60, 332–3, 336–7; HAJP for 1864, Appendix 2, 87–8, 190–1; HAJP for 1865, Appendix 2, 95–6, 206–7; HAJP for 1866, Appendix 2, 106–7, 180–1, 316–17, 422–3.

domestic goods from that country."[47] Tobacco imports, for instance, rose from 346,000 lb annually in 1832–34 to 849,000 lb in 1870–71, although some of these were re-exported to other British North American colonies and the West Indies.

That Nova Scotia continued to import processed food from the United States after 1815 should not be a surprise. The economics of comparative advantage dictated this sensible practice. By the 1830s Nova Scotia was self-sufficient in beef and pork, and had a small trade in the export of livestock to Newfoundland and the Caribbean. Part of the export trade to the West Indies was in provisions, although the bulk was made up of dry fish and wood products. Nova Scotia produced enough grain by the 1830s to become self-sufficient in bread and biscuit manufacture, but continued to import annually very large quantities of flour and cornmeal. Indeed, by the early 1870s it was less self-sufficient in these commodities than it had been earlier, despite absolute increases in grain production. American flour thus remained important both for domestic consumption in Nova Scotia as well as to supply its export market in the West Indies. As little of this flour seems to have originated in New England, New Englanders were unlikely to have become involved in its shipment to Halifax from ports like New York and Philadelphia.

Although Nova Scotia continued to import barrelled beef and pork as well as biscuit and bread from the United States, by 1870 the province had become a net exporter of these commodities.[48] Dependent on imports of fresh vegetables and apples before 1795, Nova Scotia became a net exporter of both after 1815. Fruit and vegetables represented fully 7 percent of her 1832–66 exports to the United States. From being a net importer of American wood products, Nova Scotia became a net exporter after 1815. Among fish products, cod declined in relative importance as mackerel assumed the dominant share of exports to the

States. New exports to the American markets after 1815 also included coal, raw sugar, and firewood. Coal production rose steadily from 33,100 gross tons annually in 1830–31 to 582,300 tons in 1870–71. Whereas in the 1830s some 75 percent of production was exported to Boston and New York, despite a $1.68 tariff per ton, this proportion fell to less than 28.6 percent by 1870–71.[49] Between 1832 and 1866, coal represented one-quarter of the value of Nova Scotia's exports to the United States. Boston shippers shared this freight with Nova Scotian and Cape Breton shipowners. In Cape Breton those of Arichat predominated, while in peninsular Nova Scotia owners in Halifax were prominent. Low-value firewood became an additional export for the smaller outports in the late 1840s, despite a 30 percent American tariff.[50]

American shipowners during the eleven years of reciprocity between 1854 and 1866 made no headway as carriers in the Nova Scotian trade with the United States. That trade was carried on principally by Halifax, Yarmouth, and Pictou, which together accounted for 69 percent of the value of the trade, and each of these three ports was largely serviced by Nova Scotian vessels. Pictou alone, owing to its coal export trade, attracted a significant number of American-owned vessels, which arrived there in ballast. In the three dozen other Nova Scotia ports that traded directly with American ports, shipping was also dominated by Nova Scotian shipowners.[51]

Where New England continued to play a vital role in the Nova Scotian economy was in the fisheries. However well Nova Scotia managed to supply its export markets in fish, its fishermen never caught enough cod to supply fish merchants. Between 1801 and 1820, 35 percent (570,000 quintals) of Nova Scotia's cod exports were purchased elsewhere in British North America.[52] In the mid-1860s fish merchants spent up to $550,000 annually for such purchases especially from Newfoundland, to supply Nova Scotia's cod markets.[53] Year after year right into the 1870s, the same under-harvesting characterized Nova Scotia's cod fishery, even as the annual catch increased and more men were drawn into the fishery.

If Nova Scotia's cod exports went principally to the West Indies, a new American market developed from the late-1830s for mackerel, herring, and salmon. From 9.3 percent of the average value of Nova Scotia's exports to the United States in 1834–36, fish and fish products reached 50.6 percent in 1854–56 before declining to 41.2 percent in 1864–66. In value this was a thirty-fold increase in thirty years, and marked a major shift in Nova Scotia–U.S. trade. Details are found in Table 6. Even at these elevated levels, however, Nova Scotia never supplied more than a small fraction of the U.S. market, most of which New England fishermen were largely able to furnish.

Table 6 Nova Scotia's Annual Fish Exports to the United States ($)

	1834–36	*1844–46*	*1854–56*	*1864–65*
cod	30,200	3,000	95,300	143,100
mackerel	700	139,000	707,300	877,700
herring/alewives	500	1,800	131,700	186,500
salmon	9,500	41,600	71,600	45,100
misc.	500	1,800	17,400	24,100
total	41,400	187,200	1,023,300	1,276,500
% of U.S. exports	9.3	30.6	50.6	41.2

Sources: See Table 3.

Table 7 United States Tariffs on Nova Scotia Sea Products, 1834–1864

	1834	*1842*	*1846*	*1857*	*1864*
	$	*$*	*%*	*%*	*$*
herring (bbl)	1.00	1.50	20	15	$1.00
mackerel (bbl)	1.50	1.50	20	15	2.00
salmon (bbl)	2.00	2.00	20	15	3.00
cod (cwt)	1.00	1.00	20	15	0.50
misc (bbl)	1.00	1.00	20	15	1.50
fish oil (gal)	0.15	0.15	20	15	20%
fish products	12.5%	12.5%	20	15	20%

Source: Gwyn, *Excessive Expectations*, 180, Table 7.1 extracts.

Nova Scotia's fishermen were easily outclassed by the New Englanders, who were farther removed from the grounds. Complaints about the Americans were frequent. "How long, O Jonathan! wilt thou abuse our patience?" a newspaper typically wailed when reporting a fleet of 115 American vessels fishing in 1838 between Cape George and Cape Hood.[54]

The cause of this disappointing record for Nova Scotia is found partly in American protective tariffs. Herring faced a $1.00 per barrel tariff in 1834, which rose to $1.50 in 1842. A new tariff rate was introduced next in 1846 when it was set at 20 percent and lowered to 15 percent during much of the eleven-year Reciprocity Treaty regime. In 1864 the tariff was set at $1.00 per barrel. Mackerel suffered a $1.50 per barrel tariff in the twenty years before reciprocity began, and a $2.00 tariff in 1864. Similarly high tariffs were experienced for all fish, as Table 7 illustrates.

The essential problem was more deeply embedded. Contemporary observers were amazed at the repeated failure of Nova Scotians to reap the abundant harvest of the seas about the colony's coasts. Even Nova

Scotia's officials contrasted New England enterprise in the fishery and Nova Scotia's lethargy. "American fishermen," James Daly, the Canso area fishery inspector, wrote in 1852, "deserve a great deal of praise. Their vessels are of the very best description, beautifully rigged and sail remarkably fast; well found in every particular, and carry large crews, a great many of whom are from the provinces." By contrast Nova Scotian boats were "of the worst models, badly masted, poorly rigged, wretchedly found in sails and rigging and about half manned."[55]

Undercapitalization was endemic; Nova Scotians with capital avoided direct ownership of fishing vessels, and the fishery in Nova Scotia was largely left to poor men. Many fishermen hired on American boats and later became American citizens, a process which then opened the way for other family members and former companions to follow.[56] Paul Crowell estimated in 1852 that one-quarter of the then 15–16,000 American fishermen were from Nova Scotia, while a recent study found that only 8 percent in 1860 and 10 percent in 1870 of crews on Maine fishing vessels were born in Atlantic Canada.[57] Contemporaries were acutely aware of the exodus from Nova Scotia, perhaps beginning with the return of failed Loyalist refugees in the 1780s mainly to the "Boston" states. No mention is found of New Englanders who emigrated to nineteenth-century Nova Scotia, a subject still left unstudied.

In conclusion, in the 120 years after the founding of Halifax in 1749, the economic ties between Nova Scotia and New England were second in importance only to the colony's economic links to the British Isles. This view contrasts with that of Michael Francklin, Nova Scotia's lieutenant governor in the 1760s and echoed in our day by historians Graeme Wynn and George Rawlyk, that the colony was "too much dependant on New England."[58] Rather, Nova Scotia's ability to trade with such large and growing markets was a distinct advantage. If the colony's economy grew more slowly than that of New England, the cause was not an externally imposed underdevelopment.[59] Much more complicated issues were involved, as I have tried to explain in my general study of Nova Scotia's economy between 1740 and 1870.[60]

At no time did New England hold Nova Scotia in an "economic hammerlock,"[61] to use Rawlyk's phrase. Rather, before the 1775–83 war as afterwards, New England remained an important trading partner. There were four principal reasons for this. First, because of the importance of the fisheries off Nova Scotia's extensive coasts, Nova Scotia's fishermen were subject to unrelieved competition first from Massachusetts and later from Maine. The failure of Nova Scotia's capitalists, except for the Robin Company in Arichat from the 1760s and John Zwicker in Lunenburg from the 1850s, to undertake long-term direct investment in the fisheries meant that the colony's fisheries were conducted by poor men. This fact and the failure to defend the coastal fisheries from New England interlopers, prevented the colony from achieving a level of export earnings that otherwise would have been possible. This failure also gave rise to the seasonal migration of Nova Scotians into the much more effectively capitalized fisheries of Massachusetts and Maine. Only on the two occasions when a concerted effort was made to police Nova Scotia's coastal fisheries (during the war years 1812–15 and the decade and a half before the onset of reciprocity in 1854) did Nova Scotia's fishermen secure an adequate share of the fishery and hence a market in the United States. A second reason for the colony's continuing strength in trade was that as its direct trade with the Caribbean expanded, especially after 1783, it remained dependent on some American provisions, especially flour, and as this commodity reached Nova Scotia mainly from Philadelphia and New York, New England's relative role as a shipper declined. Third, although the revolutionary war disrupted natural trading routes between Nova Scotia and New England and established a political frontier, there were still sound economic motives for active cross-border trade and investment. The enduring duty-free gypsum trade from the Fundy ports was a case in point. When coal became an export commodity after 1815, Boston became a major market. When the coal monopoly ended in 1858, New England capital was enticed into expanding Nova Scotia coalfields. When gold was discovered in Nova Scotia in the 1860s, New Englanders likewise became involved.

A fourth reason was only partly economic. Family ties derived especially from the 1760s Planter settlement ensured that the economic relationship would not languish, despite the tariff walls that soon separated the British colony from the American Republic. Subsequent cycles of prosperity and depression gave rise to unplanned migrations across the very porous borders. As New England's economy industrialized and as Boston's international trade expanded, emigrants both from the British Isles and from the lower provinces of British North America helped to fill the labour market. Many came from Nova Scotia, some with useful skills, though few with much capital. The magnitude of their annual remittances back to Nova Scotia is unrecorded, nor have we any clear idea of the scope and direction of Nova Scotian capital invested in New England after 1815.

Although this subject is important to the pre-Confederation economic development of Nova Scotia, it is perhaps marginal to that of New England. As it was dealt with only tangentially in my *Excessive*

Expectations: Maritime Commerce and the Economic Development of Nova Scotia 1740–1870, knowledge of its history, especially after 1783, remains slight.[62] Now that the study of international trade and history is out of fashion, the subject may never find its historian. Yet, to understand Nova Scotia's economic ties to New England is to deepen our understanding of regional distribution in the Northeast, a subject still a matter of speculation, even as wars and tariff barriers attempted to direct trade elsewhere. Much more than has been suggested here can be teased from the surviving evidence. Invisible trade, especially in the form of cross-border investments, is likewise shrouded in obscurity.[63] The subject should not be allowed to continue withering on the vine. The topic is too important to the region, and the sources, whatever their limitations, too attractive to remain unexplored. Above all, such research can be powerfully elucidated by applying the concept of comparative advantage.

8

Humbert's Paradox: The Global Context of Smuggling in the Bay of Fundy

JOSHUA M. SMITH

Eighteenth- and nineteenth-century accounts of smuggling often give conflicting views on the subject. Dr Johnson's definition of a smuggler as a "wretch who, in defiance of the laws, imports and exports goods without payment of the customs" is very typical of contemporary feelings toward those engaged in smuggling, at least among those who allied themselves with the rising authority of the nation-state.[1] Others disagreed, arguing that it was the laws that forbade smuggling that were in the wrong. Smuggling thus represented the struggle between those who favoured a free-trade system relatively unencumbered by regulation and those who clung to an ideal of trading privileges generally labelled as mercantilism. Certainly smuggling threatened the standing order and undermined deference to political and social leaders. A telling example of how smuggling eroded deference is recounted in the journal of Methodist missionary Joshua Marsden, who stumbled across some smugglers one night in Digby, Nova Scotia, and recorded the following:

> Digby is given up to smuggling, and at night, when the smugglers came on board, to carry their contraband goods ashore, we were greatly disturbed with their profane and worldly conversation; they continued to grow worse, and at last we reproved them, but this brought upon us a flood of reproach and invective: one of them, to show his importance, quoted a scrap of latin, but upon my calmly telling him we did not deal in scraps, his fury became ungovernable; and I believe, had it not been for fear of the consequence, they would have murdered us both.[2]

This account is representative of how those in power reacted to smuggling. Marsden, a Methodist missionary and an outsider, probably did not understand initially that these men working on the Sabbath were smugglers. The smugglers themselves remained anonymous, but at least one had some education and, while violence was not their first choice, they were clearly prepared to harm Marsden. This chance encounter between missionary and smuggler is also a small illustration of the struggle between those in authority and the proletariat, a struggle that was unfolding in the Atlantic world throughout the eighteenth and well into the nineteenth century.[3]

Marsden defies the assumption, however, that he was a priggish upholder of the status quo. He was actually from modest origins and had sailed before the mast as a common sailor. Nor was he ashamed of his common roots; he wrote about them quite freely in his published autobiography.[4] Marsden was rather more circumspect in his handling of the deacon who worked under him in the Saint John, New Brunswick, Methodist church, a pious Loyalist named Stephen Humbert. In his autobiography Marsden made no mention of the deacon, whom he snubbed on the grounds that he engaged in the smuggling trade, thereby creating no small amount of tension within the Saint John Methodist community between the missionary and the deacon.[5] Thus on both sides of the Bay of Fundy Marsden ran into problems with smugglers, a uniquely interesting phenomenon, given the fact that Methodists were a Christian sect with specific injunctions against smuggling. Methodism's founder, John Wesley, himself deemed smuggling as bad as highway robbery, and discouraged his congregations in Cornwall and Devon from engaging in the practice.[6]

Methodists are an interesting group because their values were particularly well adapted to the social transformations that were then creating a new liberal order in Western society. Methodist emphasis on self-discipline and sobriety fit well into the rise of an industrial society. British Methodist missionaries in the West Indies played an important role in the abolition of slavery, one of the great early liberal achievements that demonstrated the viability of social progress.[7] As principles of free trade came to increasingly dominate the British commercial consciousness, smuggling, one of the great scourges of mercantilist commercial policy and frowned upon by Methodists, rapidly died away. Methodists thus were at the heart of the great controversies and events of the early nineteenth century, not only in Canada, the United States, and Britain, but throughout the Atlantic world. Their role has not been easy to track; apparently Methodists neither supported nor undermined the status quo, and even the notable Marxist historian E.P. Thompson has accused them of robbing the proletariat of their anger against those who would be their masters.[8] Methodists in British North America possessed the same set of internal contradictions as Methodists elsewhere. A pious Methodist like Stephen Humbert engaged in the forbidden but common practice of smuggling, yet at the same time was a fierce defender of the status quo, of which he could claim membership as a long-time elected representative in the colonial assembly. Humbert's sins and crimes intertwined inextricably with his achievements and merits. A Loyalist refugee from New Jersey, he had proven his loyalty to the British crown during the American War of Independence, yet he traded both licitly and illicitly with the old American foe. How are we to understand the seeming contradictions between his professed devotion to Methodism and the British monarchy and his sinful and illegal activities as a smuggler?

Humbert's paradoxical behaviour bears examination, for his attitude to smuggling touches on some of the great themes in the early nineteenth century, especially free trade and its relationship to morality and criminality. The region surrounding the Bay of Fundy was one of the great smuggling centres of the Atlantic world in the first decades of the nineteenth century, ranking with regions like St Mary's on the Georgia–Spanish Florida border, and Heligoland in the Baltic.[9] An understanding of smuggling in eighteenth- and nineteenth-century North America will help us better understand Humbert's actions, and may shed some light on the commercial connections that linked Canada's Maritime provinces to New England despite the political boundary that technically separated the two regions into separate political and economic spheres.

SMUGGLING AS A SOCIAL STATEMENT

While lexicographer Samuel Johnson and other members of the British privileged classes denounced smuggling, other contemporary accounts leaned in the opposite direction. In addressing the new United States Congress in 1789 on the problem of smuggling, Congressman Fisher Ames stated: "The habit of smuggling pervades our country. We were taught it when it was considered rather as meritorious than criminal."[10] Ames referred back to the time before the American Revolution, when British imperial attempts to curb smuggling had helped to spark the spirit of revolt. Ames addressed the fact that the Revolution was partly initiated by angry crowds engaged in direct protest against anti-smuggling policies. These actions resulted in the burning of the revenue cutter *Gaspee* and other demonstrations of popular will.[11] But smuggling was far more than an ideological statement or a struggle between the haves and the have-nots. It was an activity participated in eagerly by all levels of society. Future British prime minister Robert Walpole himself used an admiralty barge to smuggle wine up the Thames, thereby avoiding heavy duties.[12] The political elite of both Nova Scotia and New Brunswick engaged in smuggling; accusations of smuggling resulted in a duel in Halifax in 1819 between the son of the provincial attorney general and a local merchant.[13] Similarly, Maine's political and economic leaders actively participated in smuggling.[14] Smuggling in North America was in fact "*big* business," as Francis Jennings has pointed out.[15] Those charged with enforcing anti-smuggling laws found it a daunting task not only because of violent proletarian resistance but also because of apathy or resistance from above.[16]

Sympathy for smugglers surfaces in surprising places. Adam Smith, a famed political economist and a customs officer himself, wrote extensively about smugglers in *The Wealth of Nations*, the book that forms the basis of Western liberal economic thought. He insisted that smugglers were essentially honest citizens but that unjust laws "made that a crime which nature never intended to be so."[17] Smith's answer – free trade – was the force that ended smuggling as a significant social and economic phenomenon. Free trade involved removing as many trade restrictions as possible, including the taxes and trading restrictions that smugglers found so onerous. It should therefore be little surprise to learn that smugglers in both Britain and Passamaquoddy referred to themselves as "free traders," putting into practice the very concepts that Smith advocated, even if they were illegal.

INTERNATIONAL EXAMPLES OF SMUGGLING

An examination of illicit trade on a wider scale places smuggling in the Bay of Fundy well within the normal commercial impulse of the Atlantic world. Members of virtually all societies were engaged in evading commercial regulations, including groups as diverse as First Nations women carrying furs from New France into New York,[18] Acadians trading furs with Massachusetts Bay,[19] colonial Philadelphians smuggling French molasses,[20] British merchants introducing textiles illicitly into New Granada,[21] Yankee smugglers trading with South America,[22] American merchants landing tobacco at night on the Irish coast,[23] Loyalists from New Brunswick and Nova Scotia bringing gypsum to eastern Maine,[24] and even the slave runners bringing slaves into the United States via Florida.[25] The scale was immense. While economic historians John McCusker and Russell Menard have attempted to downplay smuggling as "a tiny fraction of all goods handled," other historians have vehemently asserted that smuggling was not only an enormous part of colonial trade, but was also intrinsic and necessary for colonial economies.[26]

Smuggling existed throughout the Atlantic basin at many levels and in different societies. For the struggling poor the problem was to wrest a living, while for political leaders the problem was how to better control national wealth to strengthen the state. At first glance, then, one might place smuggling within the tradition of proletarian struggle against the standing order as outlined by neo-Marxists such as Thompson, and more recently Peter Linebaugh and Marcus Rediker.[27] But while smugglers engaged in all the tumults, riots, and traditional forms of community protest that excite neo-Marxist scholars, these "fair traders" also seem to have collaborated with the rising middle class and actively – even enthusiastically – engaged in the new market economy. Out of this confusion one may surmise that smuggling was a part of a discourse about the transition to a capitalist market economy.

Britain, the foremost commercial nation of the eighteenth- and early nineteenth centuries, and the first to enter the industrial revolution, underwent an astonishing degree of smuggling, which threatened both the government's revenues and its authority. British smugglers frequently operated in large well-armed gangs that openly defied customs officers and even military units. Smugglers broke into customhouses, murdered informants, intimidated the legal system, bribed officials, and even rescued compatriots from London's Newgate prison. This struggle between smugglers and the government occurred not only in isolated coves and creeks in Cornwall and Sussex, but even in the docks of London, where a small army of bureaucrats and enforcement officers attempted to regulate and tax goods imported from Britain's growing empire. The scale of smuggling-related violence has prompted writers to consider it in terms of a war between government and so-called "free traders."[28]

Illicit trade and smuggling-inspired violence required that the Crown mount a sustained and expensive effort to suppress it, often just when the government was fighting wars overseas that demanded the very revenue that smuggling denied it. In 1767 the British Crown employed 2,687 men to stop smuggling; in 1783 it employed 4,235, and boats in proportion; yet Parliament reckoned that smugglers introduced twenty million pounds of tea and thirteen million gallons of brandy into Britain between 1780 and 1783.[29] Parliament reported that smuggling gangs of up to seven hundred roamed the English countryside.[30] By 1784 there were nine cavalry regiments and fifty-six revenue cutters in England and Scotland dedicated to suppressing smuggling, at a cost of well over a quarter million pounds.[31] They failed. Parliament responded with several investigations headed by

Lord Sheffield and ever harsher laws. By 1819 the cost of the preventive service amounted to £546,402. The cost in lives escalated as well; throughout the 1820s gun battles erupted on England's southern coast. Smugglers and prevention officers both died; the authorities hanged several prominent smugglers and transported hundreds more to distant colonies.[32]

Smuggling was not successfully curbed in England until the 1840s, when an enormous army of coast guards, in combination with lower tariffs, made smuggling difficult and unprofitable. The defeat of the smuggling trade was in some ways a triumph for those espousing Adam Smith's liberal economics: by lowering tariffs and throwing British ports open to the world's shipping, new policies eliminated many of the financial incentives to smuggle goods. Yet at the same time the state had to create a massive enforcement machinery to ensure that trade was carried out legally, so that it could be taxed and regulated. Illicit trade became increasingly furtive, involving concealment and bribery in the ports rather than large gangs on the beaches.[33] In addition, the type of smuggled commodities changed: smuggling increasingly became a matter of moving small, high-priced items rather than shiploads of bulky wool or barrels of claret. By 1857 British smuggling was a mere shadow of what it had been, thanks to increased state control and the effects of free trade.[34]

What forces drove British smuggling? British neo-Marxists such as Cal Winslow perceive smuggling in the same light as poaching and wrecking, a "right" common people possessed according to custom and tradition.[35] Ending smuggling therefore required a change in societal views as well, and the industrial revolution, as Eric Hobsbawm observed, was "not merely an acceleration of economic growth, but an acceleration of growth because of, and through, economic and social transformation."[36] The industrial revolution heralded a new age that demanded rationalization, professionalization, and respect for the law. It should be no surprise, then, that Methodists, a sect particularly attuned to this new age with its emphasis on improvement, self-control, sobriety, and abolition of slavery, were early opponents of smuggling as well.[37]

The industrial revolution thus played an important part in ending the social economy of smuggling. The smuggler did not fit well into the scheme of modern commerce, which tended to confine international trade to fewer ports with larger and more modern facilities. But these causes were probably secondary to the rise of free trade; Britain entered into a period of unfettered trade that made most smuggling unnecessary.[38] The transition from mercantilism to economic liberalism put many smugglers out of work and made them conform to new economic realities. Those who remained in the trade practised it through bribery, subtlety, and concealment of cargoes within vessels. These new methods, true to the age, were dubbed "scientific smuggling."[39]

SMUGGLING IN THE BAY OF FUNDY

The Bay of Fundy, as a part of the greater Atlantic economy, conformed to certain economic patterns, and smuggling was no exception. Throughout the seventeenth century trade existed between the various groups surrounding the Bay of Fundy, including First Nations.[40] While governments may have considered much of this trade smuggling, that term seems much too specific for a region so hotly contested, with many overlapping claims of sovereignty. Nor were commercial regulations well developed; trade restrictions, such as limiting the range of trade goods that Indians received for furs, especially rum, seem to have been honoured more in the breech than in the practice.[41] Furthermore, there were no real customs agents in the area; seizure of contraband was a military function, and probably never went to a civilian court. Archaeologists studying the remains of seventeenth-century trading posts concluded that commerce with one's potential or actual enemies was "a way of life on a frontier where opportunity took precedence over political allegiance."[42] "Pragmatic" seems an apt term to describe the activities of the region's inhabitants, who suffered a high degree of turmoil and uncertainty in their lives.[43]

During the eighteenth century, as the British exerted control over the area, smuggling developed as a means of ameliorating the harsh circumstances of life on a frontier. The Acadians, technically under British control after the Treaty of Utrecht in 1713, traded with whom they pleased.[44] French influence in the Bay of Fundy endured until British forces captured Fort Beauséjour in 1755, and New England merchants continued to trade with their French colonial neighbours despite the law. Some of their smuggling vessels were heavily armed. The Boston smuggling sloop *Nancy and Sally* carried five swivel guns and a variety of muskets and musketoons on board.[45] When a British naval vessel attempted to board the *Nancy and Sally*, the smugglers resisted with force and killed two Royal Navy sailors. A court convicted three of the smugglers of manslaughter, branded them on their left hands with the letter "M," and imprisoned them for three months. Upon their release, the Royal Navy promptly impressed them.[46]

The New England settlers who came to the region in the mid-eighteenth century, known in Nova Scotia as Planters, also smuggled in much the same way that their Massachusetts Bay relatives did. But the scale was unremarkable, involving basic trade goods such as rum, wool cards, or a few gallons of molasses. The economies of the lands surrounding the Bay of Fundy were too small to support a significant trade, licit or otherwise.[47] Furthermore, between 1713 and 1775 the region was unified under British rule. British regional domination meant that the two local colonial entities, Massachusetts Bay and Nova Scotia, operated under similar regulations and markets. Nonetheless, British warships such as HMS *Jamaica* occasionally patrolled the Bay of Fundy in the 1760s to suppress smuggling.[48]

The American Revolution changed this situation. When the United States broke with Britain, new smuggling opportunities arose for those willing to risk crossing the border, as governments attempted to regulate and tax trade. American timber merchants were especially eager to sell masts to the Royal Navy in Halifax, and gladly received contraband British goods that fetched high prices in Boston.[49] The Loyalists at the British post at Penobscot actively participated in this contraband trade, as did various people at Passamaquoddy. The local American commander described Passamaquoddy as a hotbed of smuggling, and frequently reported his frustration at not being able to stop illicit trade.[50] Soon after the end of the war in 1783, Britain created the new colony of New Brunswick on the northern shore of the Bay of Fundy. One of the first problems New Brunswick administrators faced was controlling smuggling, especially at Passamaquoddy, which was divided at the Treaty of Paris in 1783 by the newly created border between the United States and the remaining British North American colonies. The problem was exacerbated by the Loyalists from Penobscot, who at the end of the war removed to St Andrews on the northeastern shore of Passamaquoddy Bay. Merchants from St Andrews quietly continued their illegal trade with American merchants after the war.[51] Other regions in the Maritimes suffered from an influx of contraband American goods as well, to the point where one Nova Scotia merchant complained in 1787: "You can scarce enter a House, but you see an American package."[52]

Smuggling only became of real importance in the region with the approach of the War of 1812, when both the scope and the scale became truly remarkable. Smugglers illicitly brought thousands of cattle to Nova Scotia, funnelled millions of barrels of flour through the Maritimes, and secreted thousands of tons of gypsum across the border from New Brunswick into Maine. From 1806 to 1820 a roaring smuggling trade developed, largely as a result of a struggle between American demands for free trade and British mercantilist policies that were slowly eroding in the early nineteenth century. This constantly fluctuating commercial war had consequences for the entire Atlantic community, from the Caribbean sugar colonies to the Newfoundland fishing industry. On an official level, this struggle evolved through a series of trade negotiations and treaties between Britain and the United States.[53] But at the local level it often created greater incentives to smuggle because protective tariffs created greater incentives to engage in illicit cross-border trade. During this time smuggling in the Bay of Fundy closely followed the English model of escalating violence and resistance, first on the American side through the War of 1812, and then in the Maritimes after the war.

Smuggling clearly represented a struggle over trade regulations, but what can it tell us about attitudes toward national boundaries? The immediate answer is that the borders imposed by the Treaty of Paris in 1783 were contested by the people who lived on either side of them. Benedict Anderson's contention that nations were an "imagined community" seems particularly apt here, because there were limits to what that imagination could will into being.[54] The residents of Passamaquoddy refused to believe that their neighbours across the borders were somehow different than themselves. The American citizens of Passamaquoddy must have had great difficulty in imagining that the plantation owners of the South were somehow closer to themselves than the fishermen of Campobello or Grand Manan on the British North American side of the border. The first component of understanding borderlands thinking refers not to a place, or a process, but to an attitude that rejected the arbitrary authority of the state. The most obvious manifestation of this disregard for governmental interference in the economy was smuggling. The more government forces attempted to halt unregulated trade the more apparent it became to locals that the state was an unwelcome and alien force.

The importance that government attached to the smuggling trade was measured by the scale of the effort to halt it. The level of enforcement in the region, especially at Eastport, Maine, increased dramatically on the American side of the border. In 1807 the federal presence in Eastport consisted of an unarmed customs collector and perhaps half a dozen part-time assistants. By 1812 the federal government had bolstered that presence with a new and more effective collector, a permanent U.S. deputy marshal, a small fortification garrisoned by a half company of artillerists, and a revenue cutter. During the war additional troops, up to five hundred, patrolled the area to suppress smuggling. In fact the only shots fired in anger by the cannon of Fort Sullivan at Eastport were fired at smugglers.[55] However, the American forces at Passamaquoddy completely failed, in no small part because the local judicial system often favoured the smugglers, as did minor customs officials and militia.[56]

On the New Brunswick side of Passamaquoddy, too, officialdom mustered its strength to combat smuggling. The region's Superintendent of Trade and Fisheries operated a cutter that occasionally captured smugglers.[57] But the customs officers in both New Brunswick and Nova Scotia were pitifully weak – and often corrupt.[58] The Royal Navy sometimes interfered with smuggling, but the best tool it had to stop smuggling, impressment, was no longer in use after 1815. Nor was the authority of the Royal Navy necessarily respected; smugglers on more than one occasion rescued vessels seized by naval units.[59] The British imperial government as a whole did not seem to be interested in promoting colonial commerce over that of the United States, and the colonial governments were not capable of halting illegal commerce even when they acted in concert.

An example of this ineffectiveness is the attempt of Nova Scotia and New Brunswick officials to control the carrying trade in gypsum after the War of 1812. Gypsum, mined at the head of the Bay of Fundy, was highly desired by American farmers as a fertilizer in the Mid-Atlantic and Upper South regions.[60] Until the 1820s Nova Scotia was the foremost producer of gypsum in North America. Producers generally shipped it to Passamaquoddy, where American merchants bought it in lots of twenty to sixty tons. The two provinces failed in part because of American diplomatic pressure, but also because smugglers at Passamaquoddy persisted in selling gypsum to the Americans.[61] Despite the intentions of the provincial governments, the small farmers and coastal mariners who carried gypsum to the American lines clung to their illicit trade and rejected the centralization of commercial authority.[62] The gypsum smugglers' method for rejecting government regulations was not subtle: it involved kidnapping government officers, shooting at customs officials, and arming vessels with cannon and muskets. In 1820 a "plaster war" broke out between New Brunswick officials and plaster smugglers. At its height, plaster smugglers lashed together rafts of up to ten schooners and brigs for self-defence and sailed down Passamaquoddy Bay in open defiance of the provincial official appointed to regulate the plaster trade. That official was Stephen Humbert, the Methodist deacon, himself a sometime smuggler. He proved powerless to resist such determined opposition and could only watch as the plaster vessels made their escape.[63]

As in Britain, smuggling in the Bay of Fundy eventually lessened through a combination of state intervention and economic liberalization. Illicit trade at Passamaquoddy diminished because it became less profitable and more risky, but it is less clear that a social transformation occurred in either northern New England or the Maritimes that made smuggling unacceptable. Small-scale smuggling persisted, but the new economic liberalism with its emphasis on free trade meant that the days of large-scale illicit trade ended in this region by the middle of the nineteenth century. Reciprocity, a trade policy whereby British colonies in North America could trade with the United States on virtually the same footing as American shippers, proved especially effective in removing the incentives to smuggle. The continued development of the American customs system and its counterparts in New Brunswick and Nova Scotia further discouraged contraband trade at Passamaquoddy.

Despite regulations, ideology, and a variety of other forces, much of the populace at Passamaquoddy refused to accept the idea that the border created in 1783 meant that people on the other side of it were "foreigners." The state created mechanisms that attempted to separate American citizens from British subjects but, despite the law, Maritimers and New Englanders mixed and seemed to feel it was their right to trade, especially at Passamaquoddy. Because the state imposed the border in the very area where governmental authority was weakest, locals could and often did choose to ignore that border.[64] Because border populations could ignore the authority of distant governments with some impunity, they could also offer criminals safe haven. Passamaquoddy's isolation, low population density, cross-border marriages and connections fostered by locals, and common frontier experiences resulted in a common rejection of commercial regulations as bothersome and unnecessary restrictions: smuggling was thus tolerated, and even approved of in border communities. Border residents even extended this acceptance of illicit trade to "adventurers," smugglers from as far afield as New York City, Liverpool, England, or even Sweden and the Caribbean, who in turn reinforced resistance to governmental control.

PASSAMAQUODDY SMUGGLERS

Passamaquoddy's reputation as a smugglers' haven drew merchants such as John Clap of New York to the region. He attempted to smuggle a cargo of provisions across the border from Maine into New Brunswick "in eight different boats, vessels, & rafts," but American officials seized his goods and successfully prosecuted him.[65] Another example is Nathan Appleton, who during the War of 1812 smuggled British manufactured goods into the United States via St Andrews, New Brunswick. He in turn channelled his profits into a manufacturing venture sponsored by Francis Cabot Lowell of the famous "Boston Associates," who constructed the first large textile mills in the United States.[66] The lure of profit drew adventurers to Passamaquoddy.

It is less easy to divine the reasons why common fishers, farmers, and timbermen smuggled. Many undoubtedly engaged in it for profit like the adventurers; others to support their families, or because they were trapped in unusual circumstances. Fishers regularly engaged in smuggling on a small scale, trading American provisions and products like shoes to their Maritime counterparts in return for fish. This saved the American fishers a great deal of labour, provided New Brunswick and Nova Scotia families with food and other goods at reduced prices, and had the added bonus that the practice was virtually impossible to detect.[67] American farmers frequently drove their cattle to the border to sell in British North America, even when their own government forbade it. American farmers regarded this practice as their right, even during time of war with Britain, when their cattle provided provisions for the British military. When government officials attempted to interfere, farmers fought back.[68] American timbermen, too, engaged in smuggling when their New Brunswick employers chose to pay them in goods rather than in specie. When they attempted to recross the border into the United States, American customs authorities sometimes seized their hard-earned British goods as contraband.[69]

In New Brunswick and Nova Scotia smugglers also came from all walks of life; poor mariners and wealthy merchants alike engaged in illegal commerce. Moreover, there were British adventurers from afar who came to the region to smuggle. John Young, a Scottish merchant who ventured to Castine to partake of the profitable trade with the enemy under the aegis of British troops during the town's occupation in 1814 and 1815, was not a man for half measures. Not only did he buy smuggled goods from willing Americans, but he in turn avoided the 5 percent duty imposed by British customs officials there. Young packed contraband tobacco, soap, candles, and other American goods in barrels of codfish. His justification was of ancient vintage: "We are you know creatures of imitative habits & as all around me are smuggling I am beginning to smuggle too."[70] Like their American counterparts, some Maritimes smugglers used their ill-gotten gains to fund more noble ventures. Christopher Scott, founder of the Bank of New Brunswick, made his fortune as a smuggler "on the lines."[71] Samuel Cunard, as a young captain of his father's coasting schooner, engaged in the Passamaquoddy smuggling trade, thereby launching the career of the man who founded the most famous shipping line in history.[72]

Ordinary Maritimers smuggled, too. Like their American counterparts, they participated in a pre-commercial economy that emphasized community bonds. They sought to wrest a living by farming, timbering, or fishing, and feared taxes that had to be paid in cash.[73] Seeking out lower prices, high-quality goods, and easy profits at the expense of the government was a rational survival strategy that often gained the acceptance – or at least the acquiescence – of entire communities. Smuggling quickly became something of a local tradition at Passamaquoddy: one New Brunswick local who lived close to the border recalled smuggling as one of the region's most important trades, "which some are in the habit of styling Contraband – but which we call *free trade.* Our geographical position exposes us to great temptations in this respect."[74]

With the exception of John Wesley and the Methodists, it is difficult to find a group who found smuggling immoral. Common people traded illegally to survive, and local traditions often condoned the practice; English parsons were notorious for abetting smuggling, and English churches sometimes sheltered contraband goods.[75] Capitalists smuggled for profit, but even smuggling adventurers often had a very strong strain of Christian morality; the most religious merchants were often the most successful businessmen.[76]

THE "QUODDY PLASTER WAR" OF 1820

This struggle against commercial regulation broke into what amounted to a revolt in New Brunswick in the summer of 1820, when the province attempted to impose shipping restrictions on the export of plaster of paris (gypsum) to the United States. Traditionally the plaster was brought in small boats from the head of the Bay of Fundy to Passamaquoddy, where it was either lightered into American vessels or unloaded onto a handy beach for trans-shipment. Both processes encouraged the introduction of American contraband into New Brunswick. After the War of 1812 both New Brunswick and Nova Scotia attempted to control the trade, imposing laws that made it illegal to land exported plaster east of Portland, Maine. These laws proved unenforceable, not least of all because there was no means to prevent plaster-bearing vessels from continuing their traditional trade at Passamaquoddy.[77] Finally, in 1820 New Brunswick appointed a preventative officer to halt the illicit plaster trade: Stephen Humbert.

Stephen Humbert was involved in at least two smuggling incidents himself. By his own admission, he was caught introducing American goods into Saint John, New Brunswick sometime before 1805.[78] American court records also indicate that Humbert was caught attempting to smuggle American flour out of the United States in 1808, during Jefferson's embargo.[79] Yet Humbert was hardly a desperado. Humbert was a Loyalist, longtime member of the provincial assembly, respected merchant, militia officer, composer of church music, and Methodist.[80]

Why he chose to become the preventative officer in charge of stopping illicit trade in gypsum remains a mystery; perhaps it was an instance of using a thief to catch a thief. Whatever the reason, Humbert would have reason to regret the decision before his tenure in office was through.

New Brunswick and Nova Scotian plaster traders fiercely resisted the plaster laws during what became dubbed the "plaster war."[81] Within days of Humbert's commencing his duties, plaster smugglers kidnapped Humbert's deputy and son when he attempted to seize a Nova Scotia plaster vessel at the mouth of Saint John Harbour. Humbert's son was released on the shore of Nova Scotia unhurt, but well out of his jurisdiction, penniless, and with no means of getting home.[82] Humbert himself fared little better. In the course of the summer of 1820, he was shot at, threatened repeatedly with death, attacked by mobs, and ignored by his superiors. Crown customs officials at Passamaquoddy colluded with smugglers to embarrass Humbert, and Royal Navy officers provided support so tepid that it was clear their sympathies lay with the plaster traders rather than the provincial preventive officer. As Humbert pursued a plaster vessel, an angry mob in Lubec, Maine, threw rocks at his boat, giving one of his men a dangerous head wound. Other crowds sought to break out prisoners, and prisoners resisted recapture with violence. Humbert reported several attempts to assassinate him, and stated that the region was in actual rebellion against the provincial government. Finally smugglers hit upon the perfect solution for rendering Humbert harmless: when departing Passamaquoddy Bay, as we have described, they lashed up to ten schooners or brigs together and sailed out the bay.[83]

Humbert's predicament is interesting not because it was unusual, but because it places the illicit plaster trade well within the Atlantic tradition of resistance to trade regulation. The scale of the violence at Passamaquoddy was even comparable to that in Britain. The apathy, indifference, and outright hostility to his problems on the part of fellow officials and military and naval officers was also a typical experience of those who tried to break up smuggling throughout the Atlantic world, whether it be in England, Antigua, New Brunswick, or even the United States. The lot of the conscientious customs officer was often an unhappy one; by the early autumn of 1820, Humbert had tendered his resignation. His embarrassment did not end there, however. His actions as preventative officer were hugely unpopular, and he lost his seat in the legislative assembly that year. This was one contest the smugglers won: the assembly repealed the unpopular plaster law, and the trade resumed.[84]

Humbert's experience was somewhat unusual in that he faced not only the hostility of fellow countrymen but that of Americans as well. American citizens seemed eager to punish the New Brunswick official who interfered with the profitable plaster trade. Humbert reported several times the presence of Americans among the crowds who resisted him, including those who patrolled the waters of Passamaquoddy in small boats hoping to intercept the preventive officer. The people of Lubec, Maine, seemed especially eager to tangle with Humbert. After the rock-throwing incident, the people of Lubec mounted a cannon near the shore in case Humbert should return. American officials also swore a warrant for Humbert's arrest, should he be found in American territory.[85] Even if it was based on economic self-interest, American participation in the "Plaster War" indicates that popular feeling against commercial restrictions transcended whatever hold the international border had on local sentiments. Republican Mainers gladly joined Loyalist New Brunswickers and Planter Nova Scotians in resisting the plaster laws.

CONCLUSION

Smuggling in the Bay of Fundy was a complex phenomenon. It insinuated itself into many aspects of the region's history. But did smuggling bind the region together, creating a "special relationship" between New England and the Maritimes? While there is ample evidence that there were cultural sympathies between New England and the Maritimes, it is also apparent that smuggling was business, conducted in line with Adam Smith's dictum that a merchant "is not necessarily the citizen of any particular country."[86]

More compelling is the idea that smuggling was a regional and traditional response to the centralization of commercial wealth and power.[87] Certainly there is an element of that in the case of Passamaquoddy. But the presence of so many adventurers from distant ports indicates that smuggling was not purely a regional response, but part of a larger process that encompassed the entire Atlantic basin: the transition to a market economy. Some of the great smuggling merchants invested their profits in the new commercial economy then developing. It is quite clear, however, that smuggling represented a challenge to government on both sides of the border. It led to disorder, loss of revenue, and higher taxes. Smugglers and government were locked in combat, and sometimes the smugglers won, as in the case of the Plaster War. Nor was this struggle confined to the Bay of Fundy: smuggling was part of a worldwide struggle that struck at state authority and whose defeat required massive law enforcement efforts and social transformation. In the Bay of Fundy, where jurisdictions were unclear or underdeveloped and governmental authority weak near the international border, smuggling thrived well into the nineteenth century.

Smuggling thrived at Passamaquoddy and other smuggling havens in part because it was more convenient to conduct illicit trade there than to obey the burdensome commercial laws imposed by the state. Another reason smuggling thrived at Passamaquoddy was that the border between two great commercial powers ran through it. Smuggling was closely related to the border, an invisible line between the United States and British North America that profoundly impacted the daily lives of Passamaquoddy residents.

9

Variations on a Borderlands Theme: Nativism and Collective Violence in Northeastern North America in the Mid-Nineteenth Century

SCOTT W. SEE

With the advent of the Irish famine migration to North America in 1847, anti-Catholicism coursed through established channels. As Irish Catholics poured into the continent, nativism crystallized, giving Protestants and native-born a sense of urgency that had been absent before mid-century. The prolific Nova Scotia writer Thomas Chandler Haliburton, for example, targeted the Irish Catholics in a classic nativist statement: "[Romanism] thought that if it could break down the civil power, reduce all ranks to a common level, and gradually weaken any constitutional connection between the several governments and Protestantism, it would recruit its forces from the population of its adversaries, overthrow them in succession, or perhaps overwhelm them all together."[1]

Countless editors, politicians, and Protestants echoed Haliburton's thoughts on Romanism and its purported assault on democracy.[2] Apocalyptic rhetoric soared. Another author succinctly captured the drama of the moment: "It is high time, my fellow Protestants, for us to assume in our own defence, and in behalf of our Catholic fellow subjects, a position of firm and fearless antagonism to the encroachments of the Papacy."[3] The call to arms repeatedly led to collective conflict in North America, just as Lyman Beecher's fiery anti-Catholic sermons had helped to kindle the destruction of the Ursuline Convent in Charlestown, Massachusetts in 1834. The links between emerging nativism, Irish migration patterns, and a global contest between Roman Catholicism and Protestantism were firmly forged in mid-nineteenth-century North America.[4]

The relationship between these themes will be better understood by considering them in a borderlands context. As the preface to one collaborative work suggests: "Thanks to the long history of borderland interaction and the close economic relationship and social connections between Quebec, the Maritimes, and New England, the Northeast is an appropriate region in which to study the complex relationship between Canada and the United States, and furthermore, to refine the borderlands concept."[5] Borderlands studies assess regional interrelationships in order to gauge international behaviour, as well as to compare economic, social, cultural, and even political themes. Indeed, the emergence of borderlands projects in the past two decades suggests that a lively interdisciplinary discussion is well underway; it should enrich our understanding of North American history by allowing us to step outside the disciplinary confines described by the boundaries of modern nation-states.[6]

Although the nature of human interaction in transborder regions provides a compelling focus, another possibility for using the borderlands concept is to study historical dynamics that have less to do with cross-border activities and more to do with common historical themes. Exploring the transatlantic migration of peoples, such as the Irish, and assessing the reception of those peoples in North America by using a borderlands canvas, opens up some intriguing avenues for comparison. The answers to historical questions can be approached on a broader basis if they reach across boundaries. Thus borderlands are useful for studying themes that transcend a region itself and hint at overarching patterns of activity and behaviour. And although the thrust of this collection of essays is to explore themes in the Maritimes and New England, a borderlands approach that addresses religious and ethnic dynamics argues strongly in favour of including Quebec.[7] Although Quebec undeniably sits outside of the focal mainstream for the overwhelming number of essays in this collection, its Protestant–Irish Catholic tensions speak directly to the core issues addressed in this chapter.

This study explores nativism and collective violence in the mid-nineteenth century by looking at three violent episodes in the Northeastern borderlands: the Gavazzi riots in Quebec City and Montreal in 1853; the Portland, Maine, "Rum Riot" of 1855; and Nova Scotia's Gourlay Shanty clash in 1856. Although the borderlands region is replete with examples of nativism and collective conflict, a focus on the mid-1850s presents an opportunity to determine whether collective violence involving Irish Catholics and Protestants was shaped more by local exigencies or by larger North Atlantic patterns.[8] Differences between these clashes were manifold, suggesting that local factors clearly defined nativism and conflict. Yet, by looking at the episodes' strikingly similar characteristics, we can observe themes that transcend boundaries. Hence the borderlands idea is useful not just for studying regional interrelationships, but also for creating an intellectual arena for coming to grips with important, sweeping themes.

The selected incidents can best be understood in the framework of nativism, religious tensions, and ethnic identification. These three factors, so thoroughly interwoven in the skein of self-identification for nineteenth-century peoples, comprise the most potent catalyst for collective conflict in the period under discussion. Nativism, defined by the American historian John Higham as the "intense opposition to an internal minority on the ground of its foreign ... connections," or a "defensive type of nationalism," has been a recurrent social and political force in the last two centuries of North American history.[9] It has been variously applied to American history, but with particular rigour to political parties such as the Know-Nothings, and to emerging definitions of nationalism.[10] Canadian historians, in the words of one scholar, have also found nativism a "useful tool" for understanding the social responses to immigrant ethnic minorities.[11] The arrival of the famine Irish triggered dramatic instances of nativism in both the United States and pre-Confederation Canada, fuelled by a mixture of Protestant anxiety over the global spread of Roman Catholicism and a racially based antipathy to Celtic peoples.

In an overarching sense, religious fervour characterized the entire nineteenth century in North America and Europe. Religion often proved a more compelling determinant of an individual's social, economic, and political status than did secular considerations. In both the United States and Canada religion cannot be understated as an important backdrop for the Victorian era.[12] This theme was manifest in a centuries-old struggle between Protestants and Catholics; religious conflict infused North Atlantic history.[13] Ethnicity was typically intertwined with religion, as in the case of the Irish Catholics. Although members of this group were in North America before the late 1840s, the dramatic famine immigration brought hundreds of thousands of Irish Catholics, mostly destitute, to the United States and British North America. In 1847 alone, the two absorbed approximately 214,000 arrivals, of whom roughly 90 percent were Roman Catholic. By 1855, after the famine had abated and Irish Catholic immigration dropped precipitously, thousands of newcomers had landed, ensconced themselves in urban enclaves, and moved into hinterland communities in search of farmland and work.[14]

The combination of religion and ethnicity spawned one of the most powerful incentives for a nativist response in North America.

Although anti-Catholicism drew sustenance from European doctrines and an international literature, it also found nourishment in local issues. News of raging Papal controversies crossed the Atlantic. Protestants especially feared the Pope's purported authority in dictating temporal matters such as politics; many perceived that Catholic adherents were credulous servants who mindlessly performed the bidding of religious leaders.[15] Alarmed Protestants thought of Irish Catholics as a fifth column of zealous warriors bent on destroying individual freedoms and governing institutions.[16] One newspaper noted: "Perhaps a final conflict is at hand between Protestant truth and Popery leagued with Infidelity."[17] According to nativists, Catholics lied, cheated, and even murdered without remorse, secure in the knowledge that they would receive temporal forgiveness from corrupt priests. Fear of "the very worst kind of [Popery], *Irish* Popery," underpinned the nativist response to the famine immigrants.[18] Irish Catholics, variously characterized as the "ignorant masses," "untameable barbarians," and "lower orders," were suspect because they appeared "unrestrained by any code of morals."[19] Newspapers consistently portrayed Irish Catholics as easily duped and enamoured with intoxicating beverages.[20] At a fundamental level, the admixture of nativism, religious fervour, ethnicity, and the famine migration created a foundation for the three conflicts that broke out in the mid-1850s in the Northeastern borderlands.

The Gavazzi riots in Quebec City and Montreal in 1853 occurred in the context described above. Of the roughly 80,000 migrants who arrived in 1847 in Canada East (present-day Quebec), virtually all were channelled through the two cities.[21] The quarantine station of Grosse Ile, thirty miles downstream from Quebec City, was a scene of almost unsurpassed misery as the famine tide crested.[22] Although many of the immigrants pushed inland to Canada West (present-day Ontario) or south to the United States, thousands located in the province. The Irish accounted for almost 44,000 of Canada East's population in 1844; by 1851–52 their numbers had grown to 51,499. By 1871 fully one half of the province's English speakers claimed Irish descent. Moreover, Montreal and Quebec City had the highest proportion of Irish-born in any of British North America's cities.[23]

Perhaps most important, the Irish settled in great numbers in port communities where their predecessors had established a modest presence before the famine. The bulk of Irish-Catholic males gravitated to unskilled positions in the work force; for example, they comprised a key labour component in the construction of canals from the late 1820s through the 1840s.[24] Quebec City experienced an 800 percent growth of Irish between 1821 and 1851, but Montreal probably felt the famine migration's legacy most acutely. Irish Catholics represented over 20 percent of its total population by the early 1860s, and, much to the alarm of many contemporaries, they outnumbered the Protestant Irish, Scots, and English combined.[25] The Irish eked out an existence in squalid areas that became identified with their cultural and religious traditions, such as Griffintown in the city's southwestern section along the banks of the St Lawrence River.[26]

The centrepiece of the rioting in Quebec City and Montreal in 1853 was Alessandro Gavazzi, an apostate Italian priest, who travelled throughout Europe and North America delivering searing lectures on the evils of Roman Catholicism. His message was clearly proclaimed in a banner phrase that accompanied his published lectures in 1853: "Popery is still what it always was, a detestable system of cruelty, impiety and imposture, fabricated by the father of lies."[27] On 4 June of that year, Gavazzi addressed the Methodist Wesleyan Church in Quebec City on the subject: "The Popish System of Blindness." Two days later a second lecture, entitled "The Inquisition," was given at Chalmers' Church, also known as the Free Church, after the Wesleyan Church refused to sponsor another lecture for fear that violence might ensue. The event touched off a riot between the audience of about 1,000 who attended the lecture and the crowd of 600, mostly Irish Catholics who gathered to protest. After Gavazzi made a comment linking priests to Ribbonmen, a violent agrarian group with roots in Northern Ireland, shouts of "It's a lie!" and "Turn him out!" came from crowd members outside the church. Someone whistled – probably a pre-arranged signal – and rocks hurled by the crowd smashed the church windows.[28]

The roughly forty policemen on the scene did nothing to prevent the conflict, nor did they enter the church immediately after the riot started. As one witness observed: "The row was a purely religious row, and nothing else could have been expected from Policemen [who are] intimately connected with the Rioters, by religious feelings and by sundry local associations."[29] Chief Constable Russell supposedly said to the rioters, "Now boys, do not disgrace yourselves," which led one witness to conclude that he knew the rioters and was sympathetic to their grievances. Gavazzi was driven from the pulpit by men wielding sticks; he was forced into a small basement room with another foreigner, who received a severe beating. The arrival of British troops defused the riot. No one was arrested, and Gavazzi left for Montreal on 8 June on a steamboat. Troops stationed in the city, in anticipation of another riot, positioned men near the wharf, but fortunately, Gavazzi departed without another confrontation.[30]

The Chalmers' Church riot was but a precursor to a more explosive event upriver in Montreal. Greeting Gavazzi when he stepped off the steamer on 9 June with several armed friends were Presbyterian and

Methodist ministers and the city's police superintendent, Lt.-Col. William Ermatinger. Nervous citizens anticipated violence. News immediately circulated that Gavazzi would lecture at the Zion Congregational Church near the Hay Market. Mayor Charles Wilson, a Catholic of Scots and French Canadian descent, asked for supplemental law enforcement. Eighty police were called into service, including special constables and the highly trained and mostly Protestant Water Police. About one hundred troops from the recently arrived 26th Regiment were stationed in a fire engine house about a quarter of a mile from the church.[31] Both sides were clearly prepared to engage in battle. One Protestant grimly observed: "We will be prepared in the church to meet force with force."[32] Weapons, including guns, pistols, and a shotgun, were stored in the Zion Church's basement.

Outside the church a crowd of approximately 300 gathered and began to chant, "Let us have at Gavazzi."[33] The almost inevitable riot was touched off when a man left the lecture early and was fired upon by someone in the crowd.[34] The lecture attendees immediately poured out of the church and discharged their weapons into the crowd of Irish Catholics, killing two and wounding others. The nearby troops soon arrived and split into two divisions – back to back – on the street in front of the church. In the confusion of the riot, several soldiers heard the command to fire. Volleys rang out from both detachments, a total of thirteen were killed and dozens wounded. The dead included Irish Catholics James Macrae and Thomas O'Neil, and on the opposing side, Daniel McGrath, the son of the former chief of police, and Charles Adams, the son of a city councillor. The youngest casualty was thirteen; the oldest was in his late thirties. Reinforcements protected the church, and the crowds dissipated after the troops fired.[35]

The city essentially fell under martial law the following day. About 400 Montrealers formed the Committee of Vigilance and demanded an inquiry and punishment of the rioters, but apparently they received no formal response. They also wanted protection for Gavazzi so that he could lecture again. Instead, the ex-priest departed for the United States on 11 June. An inquest, which included the testimony of over a hundred witnesses from all the involved parties, explored the causes of the riot and the military's use of force. Questions focused primarily on the command to fire, which witnesses variously claimed came from an "Irish villain" in the crowd or from Mayor Wilson. One sardonically noted: "It was the Virgin Mary who gave the commands to fire."[36] Following a coroner's jury, which concluded that the mayor was at fault for ordering the troops to fire, the military held a court of inquiry. When the Supreme Court threw these cases out in the fall session, the military went ahead with a general court-martial to vindicate military discipline. Meanwhile, the trials of rioters proceeded, and by autumn all the indicted Protestant and Catholic rioters had been acquitted.

The riot triggered several extensive reports, two of which were penned by Protestants.[37] One found that Mayor Wilson was not responsible for the deaths, and noted that "religious differences are the cause of a large portion of the evils of life," and that "beneath the mere surface of society in every country, lie the smouldering embers of religious and political hate."[38] Although some Montrealers sought a restoration of harmony in the troubled environment of religious and ethnic conflict, others wanted to stir the pot of discord. Citizens needed better protection, many argued, and thinly veiled threats poured forth that Protestants would take more aggressive action if the government failed to act.[39] Not surprisingly, the affrays in Quebec City and Montreal were followed by other religious and ethnic violent episodes in the colony, such as the dramatic murder of a Protestant convert named Robert Corrigan in the Beauce region two years later. After that episode, the Orange Order established a lodge in the area, "with the object of self protection."[40] The Corrigan murder and the growth of the Orange order illustrated the intertwined class, religious, ethnic, and political factors that shaped the conflicts of the 1850s.[41]

Portland's "Rum Riot" of 1855 shared many of these themes. Although Irish Catholics had been in Maine from the colonial period, the state's geographical position on the North Atlantic seaboard made it a conducive destination for thousands of impoverished Irish immigrants from the 1830s to the 1850s. The greatest concentration of Irish in the state were found in urban areas such as Portland, especially in the neighbourhoods of Munjoy Hill and Gorham's Corner, and in Ellsworth and Bangor. Significantly, these locations experienced the greatest frequency of conflict in the 1850s.[42] While the anti-Catholic lectures of Gavazzi provided the spark for conflict in neighbouring Canada East, the temperance issue emerged as the centrepiece of the Portland riot.

Nativism buttressed the temperance movement in Maine and other states because its tenets called for a direct social control of immigrant groups by the native-born population. Although the first state temperance union was formed in 1832, the famous Maine Law of 1851 codified temperance and became a national model for prohibition forces.[43] Neal Dow, a former mayor of Portland, championed the law; indeed, his name became virtually synonymous with plans to legislate temperance. Dow also rapidly became identified with Maine's nativist activities. After the Maine Law came into force, the links between temperance reformers and the nativist movement solidified.

Native-born resistance to immigrants in Maine found expression in the growth of the Know-Nothing party during the 1850s, an organization that included zealous Protestants, temperance advocates, and abolitionists.[44] The party's platform called for the repeal of naturalization laws, the exclusion of immigrants from holding elected office, the protection of Protestant interests, and the opposition to Catholic militia companies. Thus the Know-Nothing agenda included both anti-immigrant and anti-Catholic components.[45] As the Know-Nothings became a viable political force, the cultural gap between recent Irish Catholic and French Canadian immigrants and native-born Protestants widened. Itinerant Protestant street-preachers, who travelled throughout the borderlands region, contributed substantially to religious and ethnic tensions in mid-century. In 1854 Portland's Father John O'Donnell sought police protection after being attacked, while Father John Bapst of Ellsworth was tarred and feathered in one of the era's most shocking examples of nativism.[46] Other clashes involving Irish Catholics and nativists broke out that same year in Bangor and Bath, as well as in Manchester, New Hampshire, and in Dorchester and Lawrence, Massachusetts.[47]

Dow and other temperance reformers unofficially allied themselves with the Know-Nothing cause, especially in their attempts to control the drinking habits of the "lower orders of Irishmen." In Portland's municipal elections of 1852, Dow alleged that opposing Democrats had imported great numbers of Irish railroad labourers to create a majority.[48] Nativist sentiments in state elections reached a zenith in 1855. Hoping to regain the mayor's seat in Portland, Dow secured the Republican nomination early in the spring. His confidence was boosted by the recent passage of a law requiring that foreign-born voters register their naturalization papers with municipal authorities three months prior to an election.[49] Because the law was instituted on 17 March, and Portland's election was scheduled for April, recent Irish immigrants would be excluded from voting. On election day masses of Democratic "foreigners" were turned away from the polls – the opposition called them "Irish cattle" and proponents of the "rot gut" party – and Dow secured a victory by a thin majority.[50] The link between prohibition, abolition, and revivalist religions was important, for it created a substantial voting bloc of citizens. Dow's election set the stage for the "Rum Riot."

In office Dow promised to suppress the illegal trade and consumption of alcohol. Yet remarkably, he quickly flirted with trouble when he ordered a shipment of alcohol for Portland's legal agency under his own name, an action that technically ran afoul of the terms of his own law. Word of the shipment, which Dow had stored in City Hall, leaked out. On 2 June a crowd of several hundred Irish Catholics, clearly relishing Dow's embarrassing predicament, gathered outside the building and vociferously insisted that the stocks should share the fate of other illegal shipments and be destroyed. The assembled group, ranging in age from small boys to older men, eventually numbered between one and two thousand, many no doubt drawn to the unfolding events out of curiosity. Liquor circulated freely, and observers claimed that some of the protestors brandished pistols.[51]

After a period of milling around the streets near City Hall – a classic precursor to riots – an offshoot of the crowd tried to break into the basement of the building with pieces of timber that they used as a battering ram. The beleaguered police force that protected the City Hall made a number of arrests. Encouraged by several leaders, the swelling crowd surged forward in an attempt to free their captured compatriots. As one defender noted: "A phalanx would instantly be formed around, and a rescue effected, by a skilled manoeuvre in separating the persons, or some act of more or less determined violence."[52] Approximately twenty Rifle Guards, mustered and marched to the scene by the mayor and two aldermen, arrived and armed themselves with supplies from the armoury.[53]

The riot reached a crescendo after the sheriff and mayor read the *Riot Act.* Following a barrage of stones, which knocked down several of their numbers, the guardsmen fired warning shots. Testimony later revealed that many in the crowd believed that the troops were using blanks.[54] Undeterred, the rioters continued their attempts to break into the agency room. As the intensity reached a feverish pitch, the guardsmen and police fired a volley into the swarming crowd.[55] The initial broadside killed a sailor named John Robbins; apparently his last words were, "I will either go through or go to hell." One observer later testified that Robbins had "rendered himself prominent by his violence of language and conduct."[56] After firing several more volleys – some of which were aimed into the air – the police and militia cleared the area with fixed bayonets. At least six Irish Catholic labourers received wounds in the altercation, but the crowd's rapid withdrawal with the injured led to speculation that other deaths had probably resulted from the riot.[57] As one testimonial indicated: "Several bodies were borne away, apparently lifeless; two of they supposed to be dead."[58] Overall, the riot lasted several hours before the final charge that resulted in Robbins's death. As further indication of the riot's intensity, workers later collected two bushels of stones and brickbats near the agency room that had been the focus of the attack.

The riot traumatized the community, and, like the Gavazzi clashes, it spawned a flurry of meetings, investigations, and reports. A gathering of citizens, hastily assembled in the aftermath, deeply criticized

Dow's behaviour both before and during the riot, and called for his resignation.[59] Dow published a spirited defence of his actions and applauded the troops for their restraint.[60] The coroner's report on the body of John Robbins, which concentrated heavily on the question of whether a policeman or militiaman had been responsible for his death, inconclusively noted that he had died of a gunshot wound caused by a musket, pistol, or revolver ball.[61]

In addition, and as a reflection of the riot's severity, the Board of Aldermen charged an eighteen-member committee to investigate the disturbance. The committee, which took pains to note that it was not a judicial tribunal, met on 9 June and received testimony from over sixty witnesses, including John A. Poor of the *State of Maine* and other "gentlemen of standing, respectability and character."[62] The committee determined that the mob was close to achieving its objective to destroy the alcohol stores, and that the police used their firearms responsibly. As the members rationalized, "the death of one man, and he a leader in the riotous assault, no doubt saved the lives of many innocent."[63] As to the question of the expediency of having the Rifle Guards employed to aid the police, the committee applauded the tactic and pointed out that in the terms of a written agreement produced before the conflict, the militia would be considered "*armed police*" in such events.[64] Thus the committee deemed the police and guardsmen "guiltless and justified in law" if they killed or wounded rioters.[65] The committee also called the popular rumour that the riot was carried out by boys "preposterous."[66] In investigating the riot's background, they traced it to the law for the suppression of drinking houses and tippling shops that had been put into operation in early May. Although they investigated Dow's ordering of liquor stocks, the committee members concluded that the mayor had acted within his legal rights.[67] In sum, the committee's carefully couched arguments and conclusions essentially exonerated the police, militia, and mayor.

The various defenses of local authorities prompted one fervent critic of the temperance movement, Joseph Ware, to publish an entirely different assessment of the riot and its aftermath later that year. Disputing the claim that Robbins was the ringleader of the riot, Ware charged the official inquiry with bias in exonerating Dow, whose obvious hypocrisy with the temperance movement had been exposed by his involvement in ordering the alcohol shipment.[68] Ware attributed the fracas, which he dubbed the "Maine Law Riot," to the law itself and to temperance fanatics: "Considered in the light of a mere tumult, the affair was insignificant; but considered in the relation it sustains, in the popular and moral history of our State, it is the most important event that ever happened within its borders."[69] Under the Maine law, Ware contended, "public money was paid out to spies and informers, [and] the city was overrun with pimps and self-constituted police."[70] Moreover, the Maine Law supporters had succeeded in "engrafting the principles of the Know Nothings on their original creed."[71] As a critic of the temperance impulse, Ware claimed that Dow had fallen into a snare of his own making because of his duplicitous behaviour.[72]

Ware's pamphlet disputed virtually every point made by the committee of the Board of Aldermen. Curious onlookers comprised most of the crowd, the author contended, and Dow made a premeditated decision to fire upon them without a warning. The deceased – John Robbins of Deer Isle – was second mate on the barque *Louisa Eaton.* In town to visit his fiancée, he happened upon the riot when he passed by City Hall. Thus he was not a ringleader or criminal, as Dow and others had claimed.[73] Ware maintained that the aldermen had charged the committee with an agenda to exonerate Dow; to support this assertion he pointed out that the members did not take information under oath. Moreover, he argued that the crowd's use of pistols remained unproven.[74] In defence of this position, Ware noted that not one of the police or militiamen was wounded by gunfire, but rather by stones and brickbats. If nothing else, Ware's elaborate counterpoint to the official story of the use of civilian and militia forces to quell the "Rum Riot" indicated deep divisions in the community over political and ethnic issues.

Significantly, the riot also galvanized supporters of professionalized police forces, especially in Portland. Maine police in mid-century consisted of politically appointed marshals and deputies, and sometimes voluntary citizen reserves. In Portland, a restive locale noted for its crowd activity, a nascent city police emerged from a traditional night watch format in 1849.[75] Significantly, the ordinance to establish Portland's police force explicitly noted that one of its functions was, if "called upon by the Mayor or City Marshal, to assist in quelling any riot, or disturbance."[76] In the wake of the June riot, a published law report recommended a strengthening of the fledgling police force. "Against unforeseen emergencies, such as tumults and riots," it asserted, "an extraordinary police becomes necessary."[77] The report also elaborated on the definition of a potentially hostile collective as a "dozen or more persons, armed with clubs or any other dangerous weapons, or to the amount of thirty, whether armed or not."[78] The duties of the mayor, aldermen, selectmen, constables, sheriff, and deputies in confronting potential disturbances included circulating among the crowd, as long as they felt safe to do so, in order to temper the situation. The decision to call out military forces to confront civilian crowds in urban settings, a delicate and problematic issue that had plagued authorities for decades, should be the sole responsibility of the governor.[79] Thus, as the law report demonstrates, the "Rum Riot" provided an impetus to buttress professional police forces and their official duties in Maine.

The tensions between Irish Catholics and nativists subsided somewhat in the aftermath of the "Rum Riot," yet they did not disappear. The Irish continued to be the focus of vitriolic attacks, such as one newspaper's observation that "the ignorance and excitable character of many of them render them easy dupes of the more designing, and ready to be pushed forward into any scene of violence in opposition to law and order."[80] Conversely, others portrayed the civilian and military forces as agents that enthusiastically repressed popular protests. One account, for example, claimed that the mayor "took a sledge hammer to kill a fly" in the 1855 confrontation.[81] Although the summer brought more clashes between Irish crowds and the police, no more deaths resulted. Dow did not run for re-election, and the Democrats subsequently made state-wide political gains. As part of a national impulse, many Maine Know-Nothings joined the embryonic Republican Party. The temperance issue remained alive, although the Democrats repealed the law in 1856. Portland's conflict was but one of a series of dramatic clashes in the borderlands area that were shaped by ethnic, religious, and cultural values in the 1850s.

Nova Scotia's experience with famine immigrants differed in significant ways from that of its neighbours. A province born of North American skirmishes that were defined by larger French and British imperial conflicts, Nova Scotia by the nineteenth century had a population that included prominent clusters of Roman Catholics. This was especially the case in Halifax, the colony's major port, which since the late eighteenth century had been home to a substantial number of Irish Catholics. In 1837 fully 35 percent of its population was Catholic; by 1851 the figure had grown to over 42 percent. Halifax County mirrored that growth. About 12,200 famine immigrants, a modest number by North American standards, arrived in 1847. Thus by mid-century Halifax claimed about 90 percent of Nova Scotia's Irish Catholic population.[82] For much of the 1850s the recent infusion of famine Irish galvanized an anti-Catholic response, and Halifax County, with its commanding Irish Catholic presence, became the focal point for nativism in the colony.

Nova Scotia's identity was intricately bound up in British agendas and outlooks throughout this era. The Crimean War (1854–56) and the Sepoy Mutiny in India (1857) were of particular concern in the

Empire, and many Protestants considered the Irish Catholics a disloyal group.[83] Harsh critics dubbed Nova Scotia's Catholics the "Irish Sepoys." The Irish, one newspaper inveighed, seemed "ready for every scheme of riot and disorder."[84] Another bluntly proclaimed: "This is a Protestant country ... if [Catholics] prefer to admire the infallibility of the Church ... they ought to betake themselves to more congenial localities."[85]

Nova Scotia's developing political system found partial definition in Protestant-Catholic divisions. A tenuous coalition during the 1830s between Protestant Reformers and Catholics had all but disintegrated two decades later. The Catholic political base varied according to the settlement patterns of Acadians, Irish, and Scots. Protestants, who clearly held majority status, often suppressed their denominational quarrels in order to concentrate their energies on what many perceived to be the more crucial Irish Catholic peril.[86] Conservative elements, in order to undermine the alliance between Reformers and Catholics, promulgated the notion that Irish famine immigrants would have deleterious social and economic impacts on Halifax in particular and on the province in general.[87]

Simmering tensions, partially defined by these issues, led to the Gourlay Shanty riot in 1856. Seemingly at the centre of the swirling events was the estimable Joseph Howe, Liberal politician and popular editor of the *Novascotian.* Although he had actively sought the readership and political support of Catholics in the years before mid-century, his editorials during the 1850s took on decidedly nativist overtones. In 1854, acting in the capacity of Chairman of the Railway Commission on the Executive Council, Howe went to Boston and New York to recruit young men to work on a railway line under construction between Halifax and Truro, with a branch line to Windsor and the Annapolis Valley. Howe's political enemies claimed that he was illegally recruiting Irish Catholics – about 120 actually arrived in Nova Scotia – to serve in the Crimean War. William Condon, a politician and president of the Charitable Irish Society, on 7 April 1855 telegraphed his concerns to an Irish newspaper in New York and exposed Howe's activities. An embarrassed Howe beat a hasty retreat to Nova Scotia; when he arrived home he was furious with Condon and the Catholics.

Further religious and ethnic tensions festered when a series of dramatic clashes on the railway line broke out in 1856. On a religious holiday – Corpus Christi Day – Protestant railway workers mocked Catholic beliefs in a testy confrontation. Immediately afterward, on 26 May, about a hundred Irish Catholics attacked a shanty belonging to the Protestant Gourlay family, which was located north of Enfield on the county border between Halifax and Hants. From ten to fifteen

Scots Presbyterians sustained injuries in the clash; some had been beaten with pick handles. Women and children in the building first hid and then fled. Testimony later revealed that the attackers let them go so that they could concentrate on fighting with the men.[88]

Shockwaves from the conflict, which occurred in a relatively isolated location along the railway, were immediate and profound. Intermingling with an unrelated event in Halifax, they precipitated a virulent nativist reaction in the colony. Two magistrates dispatched approximately a hundred militiamen to the scene. Howe also left for the Enfield area to lead an investigation. He returned to Halifax on 5 June, just in time for an address by the former British ambassador to the United States. Sir John Crampton had been recently dismissed because of his alleged involvement in the illegal scheme to recruit volunteers to fight in the Crimean War. Condon also attended the meeting, which infuriated Howe. Fresh from his investigation of the Gourlay Shanty attacks, Howe launched a tirade against the Irish Catholics for being disloyal. Significantly, he linked the loyalty issue to the riots. Condon denounced Howe and his associates for proposing Protestant societies similar to the American Know-Nothings.[89] The cases against the eight arrested attackers, heard in December 1856, yielded acquittals and hung juries. Protestants and Catholics constituted the juries, and with one exception the former voted for convictions and the latter for acquittals.[90]

The Gourlay Shanty affair had two interrelated legacies. In the political sphere, Conservatives delighted in driving a wedge between the Liberal Howe and his former Catholic allies. The eight Catholics in the House of Assembly and two Protestants from Antigonish and Digby – counties with prominent Catholic constituencies – crossed the aisle to join the Conservatives. In 1857 the Liberal government fell and the Conservatives formed the government. Religious tensions permeated the debates in the Assembly for the next several years. In one telling moment, Howe drew comparisons between the Irish and French by referring to one of his colleagues as a "representative of the gentle manners, dignified demeanor, and cultivated mind, of the French Catholics."[91] In 1859 the Catholic-supported Conservatives lost a bitter campaign fought largely on the "Catholic Ascendancy" issue.[92] Liberal William Young returned as premier in 1860, soon to be replaced by Howe. One newspaper triumphantly announced: "Nova Scotia is herself again. Her big heart once more beats healthily. She has thrown off the yoke of tyranny ... Nova Scotia, Protestant Nova Scotia, is free."[93] The Gourlay Shanty riot helped to reshuffle the colony's political deck, and the Grits would depend on the Protestant vote for at least another quarter century.[94]

Intensified nativism, analogous to unfolding events in Maine and Canada East, was another direct result of the Gourlay Shanty clashes. One newspaper pronounced: "We are glad for the sake of our province that the assailants were all *foreigners* and the offscourings of the earth." If they continue along this course, another speculated, "the country must be cleared of them at all hazard."[95] In a remarkable comparison to tragic events in the United States that would soon lead to a civil conflict, a circular proclaimed that the riot "[had] not been surpassed ... by any crime committed in Kansas."[96] Yet another editor coupled the various dynamics at work: "It is not a question between the Liberals and Tories ... It is a question between Novascotians and foreigners, between men of peace and assassins, between Protestants and Romanists, between men who love and honour Queen Victoria and men who are abject slaves of the Pope of Rome."[97] Moreover, Howe's emphatic and articulate response to the riot led directly to the formation of the Protestant Alliance, an organization with a mandate to "counteract the machinations and operations of Popery" and "alien power" by employing "tracts, lectures, sermons, and periodicals."[98] "This diabolical outrage ... was a Catholic foray in the heart of a Protestant country," Howe stated in one editorial.[99] In another letter he concluded: "It is clear ... that so long as Protestant Nova Scotians are divided, the Catholics must rule the country."[100] Howe's most truculent nativist response, *To the People of Nova Scotia*, appeared in 1857; it is significant that in his call for Protestant unity he maintained that Scots and French Catholics were not a party to recent "treasonable" activities.[101] In a striking transborder reference, the *Casket* – a Scots Catholic newspaper – dubbed Howe's appeal "The Know Nothing Manifesto."[102]

Other clashes followed the Gourlay Shanty riot. A smaller confrontation in early June 1856 involved Irish labourers who used weapons and threats to ensure that only their compatriots would be employed along the railroad line.[103] Brawls erupted between Scots and Irish navvies in early January 1857 near St. Croix on the railway's Windsor branch.[104] Another disturbance, involving Orangemen and Catholics, occurred at Halifax County's Grand Lake in November of that year.[105] Clearly the tensions among the railroad construction crews, defined by competition, religion, and ethnicity, continued to fester in the late 1850s.

These three clashes in the borderlands region of Quebec, Maine, and Nova Scotia suggest strong themes for contrast and comparison. While local determinants profoundly molded them, broader patterns of collective conflict and nativism in the mid-nineteenth-century world played equally important roles. An attempt to understand these events through the exclusive study of *either* local *or* regional dynamics, in other words, would lead to an incomplete picture.

The distinct qualities of these conflicts are undeniably striking. The Gavazzi riots in both Quebec City and Montreal were prompted by scheduled lectures by an apostate priest who deliberately offended Roman Catholics; Portland's "Rum Riot" broke out in the context of divisive temperance legislation that had thoroughly infused local politics; and the Gourlay Shanty confrontation illustrated ethnic and religious tensions that were defined by an intensely competitive marketplace for underpaid railway workers. Unique local or regional political tensions defined these clashes, especially in Maine and Nova Scotia, and the use of police, militia, or professional troops varied dramatically. In Quebec City the police were sympathetic to the Irish Catholic crowd, for example, whereas in the other cases government forces acted primarily in the interests of Protestants and nativists. Finally, the Irish Catholics in Canada East were co-religionists of the numerically superior French Canadian population, whereas in Maine and Nova Scotia, Protestants held a comfortable majority.

The distinctive elements of these three clashes are significant, yet the factors that suggest regional patterns are equally compelling. In the broadest sense, all occurred in the wake of substantial Irish Catholic famine immigration. With the extraordinary infusion of Catholics into societies dominated by Protestants, as in the cases of Portland and Halifax, came a sense of alarm that reinforced nativism. Even in Canada East, with an overwhelmingly Catholic population, the Irish were considered more contentious and problematic than French Canadians who, despite the recent history of the rebellions and other riots, were typically characterized as passive and law-abiding. Nativist elements in all three examples helped to create a setting for collective violence. In Quebec City and Montreal, anti-Catholic dogma led to riots. In Portland, the Know-Nothing Party represented a political and social articulation of institutional nativism, and in Halifax County a pervasive anti–Irish Catholic press and political culture defined – at least in part – the Gourlay Shanty clashes.

It is of note that all three disturbances began with predominantly Irish Catholic crowds either threatening violence or attacking their Protestant and nativist enemies. Belligerent crowds at both the Gavazzi lectures started riots, angry Irish Catholics smashed their way into City Hall in Portland to begin the "Rum Riot," and Irish Catholic navvies attacked Protestant co-workers on the Nova Scotia railroad line in the Gourlay Shanty episode. Although Protestants and nativists were clearly eager to do battle in all three instances, especially in the Gavazzi affrays, the fact that Irish Catholics essentially struck the first blow served to reinforce stereotypes that they were part of a headstrong and uncivilized group.[106]

Events in the immediate wake of all three conflicts also followed parallel tracks. Although Irish Catholic and Protestant rioters, public officials, and troops were tried or subjected to hearings in each circumstance except the Gavazzi riot in Quebec City, no convictions resulted. Various factors explain the lack of formal or legal retribution, including the difficulty in identifying guilty parties, the challenge of securing convictions with wildly contradictory eyewitness accounts, the reluctance of community officials to exacerbate tensions by extensive reprisals directed at only one group, and the natural tendency in all three locations to exonerate public officials and armed forces that were charged with maintaining public order. Nonetheless, all of the clashes under review garnered extensive official and public attention. Trials, coroner's inquests, political debates, special commissions, published reports, and opinion pieces captivated Quebecers, Mainers, and Nova Scotians during the 1850s.

Collectively, the intense political and popular discussion led to a compelling notion that the forces of social control needed to be strengthened. Tensions continued to flare up and riots occasionally broke out in the aftermath of each event, thus giving contemporaries the sense that collective conflict based on religious and ethnic themes was endemic. Although people considered the use of professional troops or militia problematic because it threatened an expansion of civilian-military confrontation, a clear sentiment to reinforce the constabulary and strengthen professional police forces emerged in all locations. These examples thus fit squarely in a North Atlantic theme of the rise of professional police forces in the nineteenth century, spawned in part to control large-scale public demonstrations.[107]

Finally, nativist or vigilante groups were given a boost as a result of these confrontations. Building on a prevailing concept that Irish Catholics represented a mortal attack on Protestantism, democratic institutions, or connections to the British Empire, as in the cases of Canada East and Nova Scotia, various nativist groups channelled public concerns and offered a vigorous counteroffensive. The Orange Order, with an established record of opposition to Irish Catholics, enjoyed membership surges in Quebec City, Montreal, and Halifax following the clashes. Protestant Montrealers formed a Committee of Vigilance after the Gavazzi Riots, while concerned Nova Scotians, especially Haligonians, joined the newly formed Protestant Alliance on the heels of the Gourlay Shanty episode. Similarly, Mainers flocked to the Know-Nothing party in 1855 after the "Rum Riot" and other disturbances involving Irish Catholics. With the exception of the Orange

Order, with its deeper fraternal roots and international connections, all the other nativist organizations were defunct within a few years. Nativist elements in the Know-Nothing movement were largely drawn to the emerging Republican Party, whereas in Canada the Committee of Vigilance and the Protestant Alliance were transient organizations that collapsed under the weight of official disapprobation and a more pacific social climate in the 1860s.

These clashes in the borderlands region of Canada East, Maine, and Nova Scotia suggest powerful comparative themes. International migration patterns are the most obvious. In overdrawn and stereotypical fashion, Protestants thought that Irish cultural baggage meant that violence would follow the population group wherever it went. Perhaps most important, contemporaries saw their world as circumscribed by religious and ethnic forces. Even if individuals deplored those distinctions, they were part of the inescapable fabric of nineteenth-century life. Religion and ethnicity infused politics and social events, and profoundly determined the work environment of the period. Thus both played a defining role in class distinctions. Although all of the conflicts under scrutiny generated a profusion of local reports, trial transcripts, and personal accounts, they took place in a larger context.

Individuals struggled to understand conflict and nativism in a broader perspective. Journalists, authors, politicians, and religious leaders repeatedly referred to events that took place outside their immediate world. Information made its way throughout the region and from abroad, albeit with a lag in time. News items and editorial pieces from various sources were frequently reprinted verbatim in newspapers. Moreover, lecturers such as Gavazzi deliberately used an international arena to promulgate their ideas. Whether native-born Protestant or immigrant Irish Catholic, people looked outside their local communities and beyond their experiences to make sense of their present and provide guidelines for the future.

Historians frequently use modern boundaries to restrict and define their studies, and there are many persuasive reasons to do so. In the circumstance of numerous clashes between Protestants and Irish Catholics in the Western world of the nineteenth century, however, it makes little sense to restrict historical studies to hidebound national constructs. Moreover, there are compelling reasons for including a case study from a province outside the basic parameters – New England and the Atlantic region – of this collection of essays. These tumultuous issues were guided by an intricate combination of factors: local and foreign, immediate and distant. Our understanding of nativism and collective conflict in the nineteenth-century Atlantic world is enriched when a comparative framework is employed. Canada East's

Gavazzi clashes, Maine's "Rum Riot," and Nova Scotia's Gourlay Shanty disturbance illustrate the advantages of employing a borderlands historical assessment.

An itinerant anti-Catholic lecturer, nicknamed "Angel Gabriel," visited several New England states and British North American provinces in the 1850s. The ribbons on his hat captured the essence of the borderlands theme that this paper has addressed: "Rule Britannia," "Hail Columbia," and "To Hell with the Pope."[108]

10

Nova Scotia and the American Presence: Seeking Connections Without Conquest, 1848–1854

D.A. SUTHERLAND

In 1849 Abraham Gesner, part-time geologist and full-time promoter of regional resources, proclaimed to his fellow Nova Scotians that, while they currently lived amid numbing poverty, development policies were available which, if implemented, would produce wondrous results.

> Her [Nova Scotia's] now unproductive and vacant wilderness lands would pour down to the sea-board immense supplies of grain, and other agricultural produce, our small towns would rise into places of note, with whole streets of shops, and our rivers would be the seats of manufactures; our bays and harbours would swarm with ships, transporting our coal and other minerals abroad. Upon our own soil iron could be smelted and manufactured for home consumption and exportation. The fisheries would be rendered profitable, and the whole country assume the cheering aspect of prosperity ... We would cease to hear of the rivalry of our neighbours, and the reproaches that are now cast upon the country for its lack of enterprize.[1]

Such rhetoric, with its predictions of a future which, 150 years later, still remains unrealized, suggests that Nova Scotians, as Julian Gwyn has argued, were prone to engage in "excessive expectations."[2] Perhaps so, but how did these "excessive expectations" arise, how persuasive were they to contemporaries, and what legacy did they leave, in terms of defining Nova Scotia's identity? An exploration of the years 1848 to 1854, with special emphasis on Nova Scotia's changing relationship with the United States as revealed in political interaction and public discourse, will be instructive in addressing these questions.

As of February 1848, when the imperial government in London yielded to parliamentary and colonial demands for "responsible government," Nova Scotian public affairs entered a new era. Victorious in the general election of 1847, local reformers voted "no confidence" in the existing administration and shortly thereafter, on instructions from the Colonial Office, were invited to form a cabinet which enjoyed virtually unfettered control over the internal affairs of Nova Scotia.[3] With power came enormous challenges, above all that of engineering economic development. Much of Nova Scotia remained mired in frontier backwardness, while more mature sections of the colony were caught in the throes of an acute cyclical slump in business. In addition, blight had for several years wiped out local potato crops, producing, in some areas, outright famine. Hard times in the form of hunger, bankruptcy, unemployment, and emigration to the more prosperous United States dominated the Nova Scotia scene in the late 1840s. Distress was made all the more acute by fears that Britain's ongoing abandonment of mercantilism in favour of free trade would permanently cripple colonial economic prospects. The new government in Halifax, being dependent on public opinion for re-election to office, felt compelled, especially when pushed by boosters such as Abraham Gesner, to give high priority to the quest for measures that might stimulate economic recovery and self-confidence among Nova Scotians.[4]

For six years, from 1848 to 1854, debate raged over which policies were most appropriate for Nova Scotia as it wrestled with the colony's economic adversity. Given the long-term erosion of economic links with Britain and its years of increasing trade with New England, it was predictable that much of what was said focused on relations with the United States. As well, Nova Scotian reformers had a tradition of looking, on occasion, to American models for economic and social innovation.[5] Finally, old conflicts, such as the Revolution and the War of 1812, had faded from the colonial mind such that anti-Americanism had largely ceased to be a significant factor in Nova Scotia politics.[6] In these circumstances many colonial leaders were prepared to seek closer connections to the United States, not as a prelude to annexation but rather as a device to make viable the fledgling regime of responsible government. The process of reaching out to the United States involved the two primary themes of railroads and reciprocity.

Nova Scotia's love affair with railroads had begun in the mid 1840s, inspired by a frenzy of construction activity in both Britain and the United States. Railroad enthusiasts insisted that the application of steam power to land transportation would usher in near universal prosperity, pointing to the rise of London and New York as proof of what rail lines

10.1 *Map of Roads, Railroads and Minerals*, by Alexander Munro, [1855]. From Alexander Monro, *New Brunswick, With a Brief Outline of Nova Scotia and Prince Edward Island* (Halifax: Richard Nugent, 1855; Reprinted Belleville, Ontario: Mika Studio, 1972), facing p. 1.

could do to generate wealth and power. Although simplistic and deceptive, such logic had a powerful appeal, especially to British Americans hungry for devices to jump-start their struggling economies.[7] In Nova Scotia railroad advocates initially promoted the idea of a line from Halifax to the St Lawrence, to provide an all-weather connection between the Maritimes and the Canadas. As originally conceived, railroad construction seemed to orient Nova Scotia away from the United States, but railroad strategy would soon be recast such that it became part of the pursuit for improved connections with the republic.

Shortly after assuming office in 1848, Nova Scotia's Liberal government committed itself to the achievement of economic rejuvenation through massive expenditures on public works. Earlier, that might have meant canal construction but railroads had now become the project of choice. Provincial Secretary Joseph Howe, perhaps the most dynamic member of the new administration, insisted that Nova Scotia embark immediately on the building of two rail lines, one providing local service between Halifax and Windsor, on the Bay of Fundy and the other, a trunk line running from Halifax to Quebec City. Echoing Abraham Gesner's boast about how railroads constituted "the mainsprings of civilization," Howe claimed that the construction and operation of these two lines would usher in the material and moral achievements predicted in Gesner's 1849 pamphlet. Those who doubted the possibility of such extravagant successes were dismissed as mere "croakers" bereft of vision, and told to look to New England, where railroads, it was said, had "worked wonderful results, causing the wilderness to blossom as the Rose and the heart of man to rejoice therein."[8] Shrewdly reading the public mood, Howe's political opponents endorsed the concept of a railroad-oriented development strategy, insisting only that the construction and operation of any new transportation system be left to the realm of private enterprise.[9]

Unfortunately, poetic images proved easier to muster than the capital required to launch rail construction in Nova Scotia. Difficult terrain and the relative lack of population density deterred private sector investment, while public sector finance got snarled in disputes, notably the city of Saint John's insistence that it must be on the main line of any Halifax to Quebec railroad. By the summer of 1850 no rail construction had been accomplished, a failure which threatened to become a major embarrassment for the Nova Scotia government, especially since hard times continued to plague the colony and were providing a powerful "push" behind the growing exodus of locals to the new goldfields of California and, a little later, Australia.[10]

Then came news of an international convention to be held in Maine to discuss yet another rail project, this one featuring a link through Portland west to Boston, north to Montreal and east to Saint John and Halifax. Dubbed the "European and North American" (ENA) railroad, this enterprise seemed to offer a solution to the deadlock that had developed over rail construction in Nova Scotia. Responding with alacrity, a delegation of provincial notables, headed by Premier J.B. Uniacke, attended the Portland convention to pledge their support to the ENA. On their return to Halifax, Uniacke and his colleagues told an enthusiastic and bipartisan mass rally that Yankee ingenuity now promised to give Nova Scotia what it so desperately needed, namely trunk-line rail connection with the rest of North America.[11] For most colonials it seemed to matter little that this link would proceed by way of the United States. Now, with an alternative before them, locals were prepared to admit that the intercolonial had always been a long shot whose chief allure had been the hope that an "all-British" line might, on strategic grounds, receive from the government in London the money needed to bring it into being.[12]

The rush by Nova Scotians, especially those resident in Halifax, to embrace the ENA was entirely consistent with trends in colonial-American relations which had been operating for several years. In the period 1830–1850, for example, the American share of overall Nova Scotian commerce had risen from about 12 percent to *circa* 30 percent. A port like Halifax still continued to import more from Britain than the United States but the latter had emerged by mid-century as Nova Scotia's leading export market. [13]A large fleet of mainly Nova Scotian–owned vessels ran between local and American ports, bringing in items such as flour, tobacco, and manufactures, in exchange for fish, potatoes, wood, and coal. Ever since 1840 Samuel Cunard's transatlantic steamers had provided biweekly service between Halifax and Boston, and by mid-century travellers could also shuttle between those two ports in a pair of sail-powered packets.

Closer trade and improved transportation facilities led to a host of other connections that stand out even from a cursory survey of colonial sources.[14] For example, in 1850, while Halifax newspapers devoted most of their coverage of out-of-province to events in Britain, readers received both detail and comment on such American developments as the death of President Zachary Taylor, the celebrated murder trial and execution involving Professor J.W. Webster of Harvard University, and controversy over resistance to the new Fugitive Slave Law enacted in an effort to conciliate growing sectional tension in the republic. As of November 1849 a telegraph link between Halifax and the United States accelerated the flow of information coming north. Meanwhile, Nova Scotians were deluged with American newspaper advertisements, mainly for patent medicines but also seeking clients for life and fire insurance policies, Boston and New York hotels, commercial brokers, and even educational institutions. Books and periodicals from the United States were vigorously promoted, mainly by E.G. Fuller, the colourful proprietor of Halifax's American Book Store, who every Fourth of July flew the Stars and Stripes outside his shop. Travelling minstrel shows added to the American presence in Halifax; their entertainment, although offending the fastidious, generated passionate delight among the ordinary folk who flocked to hear and see lively tunes, blackface comedy, and the latest in dance steps. Somewhat more earnest were the multitudes who rallied to the Sons of Temperance movement. Late in the 1840s, it had spilled into Nova Scotia from Maine, quickly to become a mass movement demanding total suppression of the liquor trade that had long been a feature of the colonial identity. In parallel spheres, Nova Scotian advocates of health and educational reform used American precedents to buttress their case for such institutions as an insane asylum and a training school for public school teachers.[15]

The growing enthusiasm for things American in mid-nineteenth-century Nova Scotia was demonstrated with particular flair by the comments of two colonials who visited the United States and wrote up their experiences in the Halifax press. Richard Nugent, editor-proprietor of the Halifax *Sun*, who went on a tour of Portland, Boston, and New York City in the spring of 1850, spoke enthusiastically in his letters back home about American technology, business hustle, and capacity to have a good time. Summing up his impressions, Nugent said Americans were very much a "go ahead people" whom Nova Scotians must learn to emulate when it came to joining the march of progress.[16] Similarly, John Sprott, a Presbyterian cleric from the Musquodoboit valley just outside Halifax, said the New Englanders and New Yorkers he encountered in 1850 struck him as being a people "in motion and [whose] keen sharp look would pierce the shell of a tortoise." Opportunities abounded, far more-so than in Nova Scotia, Sprott claimed, such that Boston held some 4,000 Bluenosers who had gone south to better themselves. Summing up what the republic had to offer, he observed. "If a man does not make money in America, the fault must be his own."[17] Reiterating this theme in 1854, the Halifax *Morning Journal* declared that local people must overcome their "childish obtuseness and timidity," a personality flaw that the editor blamed on a chronic colonial preference for an "aristocracy of rank" over an "aristocracy of commerce." In order to make responsible government truly effective, it was suggested, this time by Richard Nugent, Nova Scotians had an obligation to practise self-reliance, a quality that in turn demanded "that spirit of enterprize, which forms a feature so distinctive in the American character."[18]

Idealized projections of what America was all about came readily to Nova Scotians, since much of what they experienced at home seemed relatively dowdy and inert. Certainly that was the opinion of outsiders who visited Halifax and vicinity in the early to mid-1850s. A reporter from the Boston *Atlas*, who came to the colony during the summer of 1850, commented, for example, that Nova Scotia's capital had a "mean appearance," with "old and dingy" buildings that seemingly never received a coat of paint. The people he found to be even worse.

Summing up their personality, he wrote: "There is a sad want of that freshness, liveliness and cheerfulness which marks a New England town."[19] Significantly, Halifax editors tended to agree with their abrasive American colleague, complaining about prevalent dirt and disorder and going beyond that to suggest that too long a dependence on the imperial military garrison might have eroded the work ethic among local citizens.[20]

These comments, which embodied a volatile blend of ambition, envy, and frustration, could not be ignored by those in power. They already faced a powerful Conservative presence in the legislature fighting a determined rearguard resistance against the new democracy as embodied by responsible government. While Halifax merchants had not followed their Montreal counterparts into a campaign for economic and political integration with the United States, they were hungry for reassurance that Nova Scotia's vital interests would not be sacrificed to change. And now expressions of dissatisfaction from erstwhile Liberal stalwarts like Nugent, who spoke for Halifax's large and restless Irish Roman Catholic community, gave a powerful incentive for a vigorous assertion of leadership by Provincial Secretary Howe and his cabinet colleagues.[21]

Howe, while ever mindful of his Loyalist roots and prone to romantic assertions of the importance of Nova Scotia's connections with the British empire, was also fiercely devoted to boosting the prospects of his native province. Thus, in the summer of 1850 he attempted to combine his diverse enthusiasms by journeying to London to lobby for British capital and loan guarantees to ensure the construction of Nova Scotia's section of what would be an essentially American-dominated trunk line railroad. Howe insisted that his initiative was in no way subversive. Far from being a prelude to annexation, construction of the ENA railroad would, he argued, bolster Nova Scotia's allegiance to the empire by ushering in economic prosperity and thereby curbing the grumbling and self-pity that seemed to affect so many of his compatriots. With a railroad in being that linked Nova Scotia not only to the United States but also to Canada, British America would prosper and thereby achieve the strength needed to resist the republican "manifest destiny." Moreover, Howe calculated that by successfully delivering the megaproject which had become identified in the popular mind as the prime route to progress, the new regime of responsible government might find the means to triumph over enmity and disillusionment.[22]

Unfortunately, Howe's vision collapsed in the worst possible way. At first, his private lobbying and public speeches in England produced, in the winter of 1851, an apparent agreement whereby the British government would provide the loan guarantees needed to launch construction of rail lines to link Halifax with both Quebec and Portland. Then in December of that year the Colonial Office issued a clarification: funding would be provided only for an all-British line, which moreover would have to hug New Brunswick's gulf coast and thus not pass through Saint John.[23] The news proved devastating for Nova Scotia boosters such as Howe. Suddenly their dream of a rail link to the United States had been snatched away to protect the integrity of an intercolonial project seemingly doomed to failure because of its bypassing of Saint John, the largest and most dynamic city in the Maritime region. Infuriated by what he saw as British obtuseness, Howe reluctantly shifted from trunk-line projects to short-line initiatives designed to link the city of Halifax with the outport communities of Windsor, Truro, and Pictou. The next four years would be dominated by a desperate, highly partisan – and ultimately futile – effort to entice outside, private-sector investment into the precarious field of Nova Scotia railroading.[24]

The failure in the early 1850s to proceed with either an intercolonial line or one passing through neighbouring New England unquestionably added to the existing current of resentment felt by Nova Scotians toward the London government. The Crown remained a revered symbol and things British, from literature to technology, remained highly popular, but trust in imperial policy makers was becoming eroded. Much more was involved here than traditionalist resentment over London's abandonment of oligarchy and retreat from protectionist trade regulations. Reformers like Howe had envisioned a new order built around a transatlantic partnership that would serve the vital interests of both Britain and British North America. But when called upon to be supportive, London has retreated into what, from a colonial perspective, seemed to be stinginess and paranoia. Nova Scotian frustration prompted by the collapse of trunk-line railway initiatives became all the greater when combined with the province's second great aspiration involving the United States, the regulation of trade.

Britain's unilateral decision, taken late in the 1840s, to implement a policy of free trade with the world had provoked consternation and occasional violent protest throughout British North America. Although unable to shape British commercial policy, the colonies received through responsible government the power to set their own tariff schedules. In Nova Scotia that led to a protracted debate over the relative merits of free and regulated trade. Free trade proponents came to prevail as early as 1847, essentially because protectionists were divided in their goals, while Halifax's powerful merchant lobby, allied with the colony's fishermen, insisted that low duties, especially on the massive quantities of foodstuffs imported from the United States, were vital for Nova Scotia's economic survival. That arrangement remained far from perfect for locals, however, mainly because, while American goods paid minimal rates on entering Nova Scotia, colonial goods faced a tariff of 20 percent at the United States border. This tariff wall, especially in the case of fish, was regarded as a major impediment to Nova Scotia's economic growth. Thus the new government formed in 1848 was anxious for negotiations that would ease access to the American market for Nova Scotian producers.[25]

Other British American colonies, especially Canada, in which Britain's abandonment of mercantilism threatened dire economic dislocation, also desired a trade deal with the United States. That mutual interest led to an intercolonial conference at Halifax in September 1849 where delegates made a reciprocal agreement to minimize import duties on non-manufactured goods and endorsed in principle the idea of extending that arrangement to the United States. Unanimity broke down, however, when discussion turned to the concessions that might have to be offered to persuade Congress that reciprocity served American interests.[26] Of all the things Congress was likely to request, none ranked higher than access to colonial inshore fisheries. Throughout the 1840s, New England fishermen had become ever more aggressive within the three-mile limit, entering both to fish and to trade with outport residents. That encroachment, especially when it compromised local control over the lucrative mackerel fishery, provoked outrage among Nova Scotian merchants. Their demands for protection against American competition led to demands on the part of Nova Scotia's delegates to the intercolonial trade talks of 1849 that, while reciprocity with the United States was desirable, the deal must not include giving Yankees access to the coastal waters of the Maritimes.[27]

Such intransigence soon proved to be untenable. In the summer of 1850, responding to rumours that a one-on-one reciprocal trade deal might emerge between Canada and the United States, William Young, speaker of the Nova Scotia House of Assembly travelled to Washington in search of a compromise.[28] Besides forging contact with Washington insiders, especially Israel D. Andrews, who was destined to play a key role in bringing reciprocity into being, Young laid out the conditions that likely would be required to convince Nova Scotians to open their fisheries to American enterprise. The counter-concessions sought by Young featured inclusion of coal on the list of goods exempt from duties, elimination of all bounties paid out to American fishermen by their own governments, colonial access to the internal coasting trades of the United States, and finally, the right to have colonially built vessels placed on the American shipping registry.[29] More than anything else, this audacious list of demands demonstrated the widespread belief among Nova Scotians that their escape from hard times would require a sweeping integration into the American economy. This goal, involving both railroads and reciprocity, had come to dominate the strategic thinking of Nova Scotian leaders as they struggled to cope with the demands imposed on them by responsible government.

Would Britain support Nova Scotians in seeking implementation of the strategic vision articulated in 1850 by William Young and his colleagues? London may have had little enthusiasm for costly and commercially dubious colonial railroad ventures, but on reciprocity its outlook was more positive. A United States trade deal with British America promised to ease dangerous political unrest in Canada and might also act as a prelude to lowered duties on British goods entering the American market. Thus, as early as 1849 high level contacts were initiated to ascertain Washington's willingness to come to terms on reciprocity. From the beginning, London officials realized that nothing could be accomplished unless the Americans were offered access to the Maritime inshore fisheries.[30] But did the imperial government agree with Nova Scotian leaders that any such concession must be offset by American accommodation of such colonial demands as access to the coastal trades and shipping registry of the republic? That question produced answers which, throughout the early 1850s, revealed more ambiguity than certainty.

A vivid example of the mixed signals coming from London was provided by the decision, taken in the summer of 1852, to despatch a squadron of royal naval vessels to patrol Maritime coastal waters and enforce the terms of the 1818 convention, which minimized the operations of American fishermen within the three-mile limit. Halifax's business elite rejoiced in what they initially interpreted as unqualified British support for their protracted campaign to drive New England fishermen from local waters.[31] The government in Washington read the situation in a similar manner and responded by despatching American gunboats to Nova Scotia, a gesture that led to some delicate moments in Halifax harbour as the two navies came into contact with one another. But no collision occurred, basically because London had ordered its forces to proceed cautiously, issuing warnings rather than seizing the property of American interlopers.[32] Moreover, information gleaned from royal navy officers operating along the Nova Scotian coast undermined the claims of self-appointed Nova Scotian patriots. Outside Halifax, Yankee fishermen were welcomed by coastal residents, who saw these foreigners as an important source of cheap supplies and cash sales for surplus fish. In addition, many locals went to sea on American fishing craft, lured by higher wages and more efficient fishing gear.[33] In the end, British intervention proved to have been nothing more than a gambit designed to bring the United States to the bargaining table. Once that had been accomplished, negotiations were all too likely to proceed along lines reflecting British, American, and Canadian, rather than Nova Scotian, priorities.[34]

Indecisive debate finally gave way to tangible action in 1854 with respect to Nova Scotia's protracted pursuit of railroads and reciprocity, although in neither case did the colony fully achieve its goals. First to break was the deadlock over rail construction. Frustrated by their inability to entice foreign contractors into the colony and chagrined by successful launches of rail projects in both Canada and New Brunswick, a core of Nova Scotian politicians rallied behind Joseph Howe's long-held conviction that the local government should itself undertake to build railways. In April 1854, after intense argument and a realignment of forces within the Assembly, legislation was passed authorizing the creation of a Railroad Commission, headed by Howe, which would build, at public expense, rail lines from Halifax to the Fundy outports of Windsor and Truro. Trunk-line connection with the continental interior was so expensive as to be beyond Nova Scotia's grasp, but such was Howe's optimism that he boasted these initial few miles of track would so stimulate economic growth that before long local folks would be boarding trains for destinations in both Canada and the United States.[35]

The political shakeup associated with the beginning of rail construction brought William Young into the cabinet as premier of Nova Scotia. Almost immediately, he had to deal with a sudden reactivation of negotiations on reciprocity. In May 1854 the British government despatched Canada's Governor General, Lord Elgin, to Washington with instructions to press vigorously for a North American trade deal.[36] The timing of this initiative was ominous for Nova Scotia. War loomed between Britain and Russia, and it would be ever so tempting for London to make concessions on reciprocity that might translate into American good-will during a European military crisis. This at least was how the situation was read in Halifax, to the extent that Young hesitated when invited to join the colonial delegation named to accompany Elgin on his mission to Washington. Although personally persuaded that reciprocity on almost any terms would be advantageous to Nova Scotia, Young feared becoming personally identified with a settlement that some Nova Scotians might see as a betrayal of their vital interests. Thus he dithered, and in the end no Nova Scotian delegates went to Washington, on the feeble excuse that a letter formally asking for their presence had never been received.[37]

Perhaps relieved that potentially awkward characters had removed themselves from the proceedings, Elgin shrewdly played upon sectional tensions within Congress to sell reciprocity as a measure beneficial to the well-being of all interested parties. British America would get duty-free access to the American market for all its "natural products," including coal; the United States would receive, among other concessions, access to the Maritime inshore fisheries; and Britain might expect Washington to remain benignly neutral as Britain and France launched their invasion of Russia's Crimean peninsula. The only parties to feel aggrieved were the Nova Scotians who, on learning of what had been agreed to, promptly complained that inclusion of coal on the duty-free list was insufficient compensation for loss of exclusive control over their increasingly valuable inshore fisheries.[38]

Rather than immediately creating a forum for the venting of patriotic spleen, Premier Young delayed calling the Nova Scotia legislature into session to debate the merits of the reciprocity treaty. Ultimately he procrastinated until December 1854, by which time two developments had taken place that made it virtually impossible for the legislature to do anything other than ratify the deal negotiated in Washington. First of all, in mid-summer, as a gesture of good faith toward American interests, London announced that New England fishers could immediately begin operating in Maritime inshore waters. Later that autumn, in expectation of the treaty going into effect, Washington began issuing rebates of duties for natural products imported from those North American colonies which had formally endorsed the treaty.[39] Under these circumstances, for Nova Scotia to become a lone hold-out would have been quixotic in the extreme. When the legislature finally met, opposition leader J.W. Johnston denounced the train of events, while Joseph Howe said the treaty amounted to "one of the greatest insults ... ever known to have been perpetrated on a colony."[40] Significantly, however, complaints were directed more at Britain than the United States. Thus in its protest, the upper house of the colonial legislature focused on what it saw as London's "invasion of the Constitutional Rights of Nova Scotia and ... violation of the Pledges of the Parent Country," over surrender of the fisheries.[41]

Speaking for the majority of legislators, Premier Young insisted that while the terms of the reciprocity deal might be imperfect, the treaty would in his opinion operate as "a most invaluable and prolific boon," above all because it moved Nova Scotia toward integration with the American economy. The past few years of relative isolation, bereft of imperial protection and squeezed by foreign competition, had been a period of acute distress. But now, with a treaty that promised, on a long-term basis, special status with the flourishing economy of the neighbouring republic, Nova Scotia had a real opportunity to achieve progress. Young further predicted that over time protectionist sentiments within the United States Congress would subside, such that colonial access to the American carrying trade and vessel registry would come to be seen as innovations beneficial to both American and Nova Scotian interests.[42]

Young's optimism was supported by the fact that in 1854 stagnation had finally given way to bustle throughout the Nova Scotian economy. Spillover from economic growth in the United States and Europe, combined with surging demand for goods and labour triggered by the Crimean War, had spawned a pattern of increased trade, rising prices, and full employment. In and around Halifax the start of railroad construction provided a further stimulus for overcoming hard times. Under such conditions boosterism, which earlier had a resemblance to whistling in the wind, suddenly seemed confirmed by actual circumstances. The dream of having Nova Scotia catch up with the rest of North America, articulated by Abraham Gesner back in the dire days of 1849, now appeared attainable. In the opinion of contemporaries, the turn-around and the prospects for enduring achievement derived primarily from the accomplishment of strengthened connections with the United States, connections which had begun to compensate for the loss of protection and assistance once provided by links to the British Empire. It was as if a new era had dawned for Nova Scotia, one that promised to make responsible government more than a poverty-trap.[43]

Did these developments mean that these mid-century colonials wanted to merge into the United States? For some, most notably individuals like Abraham Gesner who migrated to the United States in search of enhanced opportunity, the answer was yes. But those who persisted in Nova Scotia adopted a more complex posture, seeking economic and cultural Americanization while retaining a separate political identity. That was the orientation of most speeches delivered by Nova Scotian leaders during a debate held in the winter of 1854 on the future prospects of British North America. Joseph Howe, complaining bitterly that "a Colonist is nothing," spoke wistfully about Nova Scotia maturing to play a partnership role in a revitalized British empire. His peers preferred the vision of an amalgamated British North America. Such a union, observed opposition leader Johnston, would give the northern colonists the "national character" to cope with external challenges, above all the challenge of dealing with the United States. What was needed, said an anonymous letter writer inspired by the political rhetoric of the day, was "the power and will to settle our own business with neighbour Jonathan in our own way, totally independent of John Bull's intervention."[44] Here Nova Scotians were summing up Nova Scotia's experience over the years between 1848 and 1854. British America's ongoing struggle to escape economic adversity had persuaded most colonials that success in everything from railroads to reciprocity required a closer association with the United States. But reliance on Britain to negotiate the terms of that association was fraught with risks, most obviously the danger that imperial rather than colonial priorities would dominate proceedings. Corrective action, Johnston and others thought, required what eventually would be known as Confederation.

In retrospect we can see that Nova Scotian public affairs during the years 1848 to 1854 were dominated by what might be called the politics of development. The advent of democracy in the form of responsible government forced local leaders as never before to address issues of popular concern. No problem more preoccupied Nova Scotians than their "have-not" economic status, in comparison to neighbouring parts of North America. Local patriots such as Gesner insisted that hard times could be overcome through bold initiatives orchestrated by those in power. Inspired by signs of success in the neighbouring republic, colonial boosters called for implementation of a strategy designed to integrate British America economically with the United States through both railroads and reciprocity. Nova Scotian leaders, confounded by internal disagreements and confronted by the formidable obstacle of British and American self-interest, struggled through six years of protracted negotiation until, in 1854, they emerged with controversial but seemingly tangible accomplishments in the areas of both railroads and trade.

Both the strengths and the weaknesses of responsible government were demonstrated during this short period. Public opinion, infused with a hunger for development and largely convinced it could be obtained by opening the American border, forced action upon provincial leaders. But the short-line railroads of the 1850s did not reach beyond the region, and reciprocity remained a partial and precarious accomplishment. By the mid-1860s dissatisfaction, fed in large measure by rising economic expectations and political anxieties related to the American Civil War, had convinced many Nova Scotians of the need to exchange local autonomy for membership in a federal union of British North America.

Confederation ultimately came to prevail, and yet its limited success in bringing the kind of progress dreamed of by men like Gesner led to an ongoing local debate over whether Nova Scotia would be better served by integration with America rather than with Canada. For complex reasons, including the invention of the Loyalist myth as a reinforcement for faltering Canadian nationalism, secession never became more than a fringe element in provincial politics. Nevertheless, as long as the American border remained open, thousands of Bluenosers headed south to become "whitewashed Yankees," their mass behaviour illustrating a deeply seated ambiguity in the Nova Scotian consciousness over how best to forge a working relationship with the United States.[45]

11

The Command of Money in Shaw's Borderlands, 1859–1887

JACQUES FERLAND

In social history, the power of place over people's lives is considered less a given than a reality that varies over time. To grasp the historical significance of a geographical concept such as the "borderlands" between Canada and the United States, then, becomes a matter of conducting numerous research projects whose aggregate findings should ultimately yield a solid foundation for historical interpretation. Using what David Harvey calls the "command of money" gives us a useful conceptual tool[1] to explore one such "borderland" area between the state of Maine and the province of New Brunswick during the post–Civil War period. This case study focuses on how the business strategies of a dominant family enterprise, the Shaw brothers from Massachusetts, proved conducive to the exercise of such command of money as to entitle them to determine if, where, and when the border ought to be perceived as a pertinent reality.[2]

When capital is acquired or controlled mainly by a handful of industrialists, as is frequently the case in sparsely settled resource-extracting areas of the Northeast, money itself confers considerable agency to this class of entrepreneurs. For example, it serves to populate and depopulate a borderland area by providing leverage to redirect migratory patterns for thousands of people. It enables employers to redefine the ethnic and social makeup of residential and occupational populations by empowering their managers to reconfigure human activities over hundreds of miles on both sides of the border. Among local residents, command over money can also serve to recast the modalities according to which people expect to produce, to consume, and to associate. In the wake of business decisions, it can further shorten the life span of a rural industrial nucleus, and, by extension, undermine the social and economic vitality of a given borderland area. Beyond these objective considerations lies the more subjective issue of whether command of money can also serve to shape contemporary perceptions of borderlands according to what is most convenient to influential industrialists. This latter, more subjective, dimension of the historical meaning of a "borderland" area is of particular interest when focusing on the rise and decline of the Shaw brothers' sole leather tanning activities in eastern Maine and western New Brunswick during the second half of the nineteenth century.

As long as their cross-border leather manufacturing system remained profitable, as it did between 1859 and 1883, the Shaw brothers constantly blurred national distinctions both in their business practices and in their financial statements. But when they proved incapable of avoiding financial collapse, in July 1883, their holdings were rapidly divided into two separate ventures: a "Canadian" and an "American." While F. Shaw & Brothers were being closely monitored in the United States, their Montreal books proved inaccessible to frustrated creditors. Suddenly, access to what they had portrayed as a mere branch of the parent company was denied. Revealingly, though, the Shaws never considered New Brunswick as part of this Canadian branch. Rather they tied their New Brunswick holdings to a borderland office in Vanceboro', Maine. Arguing that this borderland property significantly added to the liabilities of their U.S. parent company, the Shaws maintained that all their resource-extracting facilities in New Brunswick, along with those put to similar use in Maine, had been a failed experiment and should be deemed "valueless." Creditors in the Maritime provinces were thus placed in a position of greater subordination than most of their counterparts in the United States. Along with their spokesman, E.L. Wetmore, Maritime creditors stand out in contemporary records as the embodiment of New Brunswick subservience to the Shaws' command of money.

NATURE'S CHEMISTRY: HEMLOCK SOLE LEATHER TANNING IN THE NORTHEAST

With the coming of age of the North American industrial heartland during the second half of the nineteenth century, urban-industrial centres increasingly conducted the terminal stages of commodity production. Yet these urban industries did not always "produce" consumer goods; more accurately, their role frequently consisted in assembling, amalgamating, and finalizing what had been initiated months before in more modest hinterland settings.[3] In the manufacture of leather products, boot and shoe manufacturing constituted the cumulative outcome of six to twelve months of human labour, of which only a few weeks, perhaps days, were performed within urban factories. By contrast, the production of heavy leather in the hinterland, mostly destined to be cut into soles, required months of productive activities before hides could be turned into leather.[4]

Research has shown that leather tanning remained "tradition-bound" throughout much of the nineteenth century. The old craft's industrial development is generally regarded as a long evolution, rippled with an infinity of local variations but without any salient feature in the annals of the "Industrial Revolution."[5] Typically, scholars preoccupied with "stages" of industrial development have often assumed that the wood-framed implements, vats and buildings, water power, and organic processes of heavy leather making belong to the "eotechnic" era. This is the age of wood, wind, and water when businessmen "relied upon the hard work of men and beasts and upon the motive power of running water" to capitalize on an "essentially static technological complex."[6] Such an urban-centred representation of the industrial era fails, however, to capture a more essential feature of rural industrialization in the hinterland. While urban dwellers observed industrial progress as a rapid march toward the mechanization of production, rural settlers and backwoodsmen experienced industrialization in the realm of human consumption, even creative destruction, of the natural world.

In many ways, the manufacture of heavy leather shared with lumbering and agriculture a common exploitation of nature's wealth and a dependence on nature's clock. Rural tanneries were not simply factory buildings where people, tools, and machinery were combined to achieve a more efficient division of labour; the physical layout of leaches, sweat vaults, vats, and lofts, as well as the man-made hydrographic network of dams and canals, may be advantageously regarded as an extractive industrial plant in whose specialized construction work lay a conscious effort to harness nature's chemistry on a grand scale. (Table 1)[7] Relying primarily on the natural tanning properties of hemlock bark, tannery hands had good reasons to perceive the essence of the work they did as a slow "feeding" process.[8] Rather than "making" leather, much of their work consisted in assisting in the lengthy process of combining both animal and vegetable constituents into a marketable compound of gelatine and tannin known as "leather." It is largely because of this "feeding" process and the resulting weight differential between the hide and the leather – the very source of profits in this branch of the trade – that numerous sole leather tanneries were

Table 1 Maine's Leading Heavy Leather Tanners (1860)

Name	*Place*	*Bark (cords)*	*Leather (tons)*	*Value ($)*	*Gross Income ($)*	*Monthly Wages ($)*
Shaw family:	Detroit	~3,000	~250	120,000	44,600	450
	Plymouth	2,000	200	80,000	28,490	255
	Burnham	3,000	250	110,000	37,550	400
	Dexter	2,500	240	95,000	25,304	408
	Alton	2,500	~200	81,000	23,700	330
		13,000	1,140	486,000	159,653	1,943
Maine Competitors:						
William Plaisted	Stetson	3,000	~250	100,000	33,200	400
A. Webb & Co.	Lowell	2,000	~200	100,000	25,530	360
H. & H.R. Hunt & Co.	Liberty	2,000	~200	76,000	4,631	312
A.H. Buzzell	Amherst	2,000	163	65,100	7,168	286
C.P. Church	Bradford	1,800	125	40,000	4,950	250
Chancy Case	Mariaville	1,200	90	40,000	5,273	176
S. Lothrop	St. Albans	1,000	75	30,000	4,436	147
		14,000	1,103	451,100	84,888	1,931
Grand Totals:		27,000	2,243	937,000	244,541	3,874

Source: U.S. Census, Products of Industry, Maine, 1860.
Gross income is calculated by subtracting wages from the value added.

erected far in the wilderness where they could most profitably consume from four to twelve times in bark weight what they produced in leather tonnage.[9]

Paradoxically, from an urban-centred perspective, it is in this slowest and least mechanically promising branch of the leather trades that one can often find the earliest manifestations of "big business" and mass production. Tannery buildings were evolving from a barn-type wooden structure into three- to five-hundred-foot-long extractive and processing mills where profit margins became a function of how much hemlock tan bark one consumed and how much hide stock could be kept in these "liquor" vats. Because the turnover from hides to leather remained very slow, literally submerging capital for several months, mass production was achieved not so much through increased productivity but by expanding both extractive activities and processing facilities in an environment combining a highly functional transportation system for hides and leather with cheap labour and an extensive and heavily wooded acreage of hemlock stands.

The first prominent sole-leather manufacturers known for their command of money in this trade capitalized on cheap tanbark by erecting unusually large tanneries in the Berkshires of Massachusetts and the Catskills of New York, where they also imported hides from South America. This import strategy furthered their command of money by achieving complete autonomy from the old merchant class and a domestic supply of hides that reflected the meat industry.[10] The phenomenal growth of its extractive operations, which itself stemmed from the concentration of capital, entailed a very critical implication for the future of this rural industry. Capitalists, whose primary business strategy of expansion consisted in multiplying the number of rural tanneries in operation, could drastically shorten the life span of these mass-extracting establishments simply by locating them too close to one another. Technology offered a solution to the ensuing depletion of hemlock trees in the vicinity by developing hemlock "extract mills" that industrialists could locate farther afield. The sole purpose of the mills was to condense tannin distilled from hemlock bark into a thick compound that could be more easily and cheaply transported by rail.[11] Yet this technique proved wasteful and, as it often grew into an independent business, it had the unfortunate effect for leather manufacturers of opening to continental and international trade what had largely remained until then a captive local market in hemlock tanbark.

Following an early period of typically optimistic industrial promotion, the environmental impact of sole-leather tanning left in its wake not a few critical observations such as this one from Maine state officials late in the nineteenth century: "It is a transient business, for, unlike spruce, when once cut over, hemlock does not readily reproduce itself, and when the bark supply is exhausted, unless it can be brought from a distance by rail at a reasonable price, the site is abandoned and the buildings left to decay."[12] What these officials failed to mention was that many of these "buildings left to decay" originally belonged to a group of siblings whose command of money was such, during the 1870s and early 1880s, as to both reconfigure a borderland area and to curtail its life span as a hemlock-extracting and leather-producing rural economy.

THE SHAW FAMILY AND ITS CROSS-BORDER BUSINESS EXPANSION

The family of Brackley Shaw, Sr had been engaged in the leather tanning business since the second decade of the nineteenth century.[13] At first sight, there is not much to distinguish this Cummington family from countless other Massachusetts family enterprises that conducted tanning on a moderate scale. But their initial location, family networking, and cross-border mobility would all contribute to the making of an unprecedented borderland business empire in the leather trades. Brackley Shaw, Sr and his brothers Charles and Spencer learned their trade in the same county where William Edwards, reputedly a "pioneer" in the mass-production of sole leather, conducted his path-breaking experimentation.[14] In fact, Charles Shaw briefly acquired a tannery in 1846 that Edwards had built for William Hubbard of Cummington. But soon thereafter Brackley Shaw, Sr lost "nearly all he ha[d] to fire," and died of "fever" at the head of a large family of nine children in 1848.[15] From this point, the Shaw family composition and kinship networking contributed both to the recovery and business expansion of the firm. Five of Brackley's nine children were males, between the ages of seventeen and twenty-five, who immediately undertook to rebuild the family business. They formed various co-partnerships during the 1850s with the intention of opening branch plants headed by family members and other relatives. This strategy and its corresponding scattered manufacturing system would remain the family's chief asset during the next thirty years.

Sixteen years after their father's death, the Shaw brothers had formed four distinct family enterprises in which Fayette, William, and Brackley, Jr were key members. Kinship ties beyond these three male siblings also helped them exert a greater command of money, particularly in the Sebasticook Valley of Maine, where they pooled resources with their uncle, Charles Shaw, and his sons.[16] By placing various relatives at the head of local tanneries in contiguous rural settings, the Shaw brothers achieved significant economies of scale. In less than a decade, on the eve of the Civil War, the firms of F. Shaw and Brothers, Charles and Brackley Shaw and Company, and Shaw Brothers and Company rapidly outdistanced all of their Maine competitors by processing half of the state's sole leather output and generating two-thirds of the industry's gross income in Maine.[17] (Table 2)

Shortly before the Civil War, in 1859, the Shaw brothers transplanted their kin-oriented, scattered manufacturing system into Canada East (Quebec).[18] This decision was no doubt partly motivated by the existence of two railroads – the St Lawrence and Atlantic, which extended from Montreal to Portland, Maine, and a shorter line recently completed between Waterloo, in Shefford County, and the Richelieu River valley.[19] Centring their operations in Shefford County – in the northern foothills of Appalachia – they rapidly transformed this borderland area into the leading hemlock bark-producing territory in the newly emerging Dominion of Canada. From Roxton Falls – the site of their largest Canadian tannery and the primary residential location of William Shaw – the Shaw brothers gradually added to their Canadian industrial property other tanning facilities in Waterloo,

Warden, Adamsville, Mawcook, Fulford, Farnham, Drummondville, and St Leonard d'Aston (Table 2) This Canadian branch also had its own "store" in Montreal from where Brackley Shaw, Jr not only marketed sole leather but also supplied South American hides to the family tanneries as well as some of their Canadian competitors. Hence, by 1880, five other Quebec tanneries had become "accountable to the firm," thus giving the Shaws ownership of, or control over, fourteen tanneries in Canada. It was said to be "doing the largest business of any leather manufactory" in the country.[20]

The Shaws' borderland manufacturing system achieved its greatest cross-border synergy shortly after the Civil War when, anticipating the completion of a railroad line from Bangor, Maine, to Saint John, New Brunswick, William Shaw and his brother-in-law, Romanzo Kingman, hired building crews to erect "very large" tanneries in the backwoods of eastern Maine. Growing out of the "wilderness" (or more accurately upon the ancient Wabanaki lands of the Mattawamkeag River valley and of the head waters of the St Croix River), five new tanneries were almost simultaneously erected in Kingman, Jackson Brook, Forest City, Vanceboro', and Grand Lake Stream village, Maine, between 1869 and 1872. (Table 2) With a combined extractive capacity of over 50,000 cords of hemlock bark per year, these establishments were bound to alter rural life in this borderland area. As the local population was sparse, even non-existent in places such as Grand Lake Stream, the Shaws had to orchestrate virtually everything necessary to conduct business in such remote areas. In addition to erecting the colossal tannery buildings and infrastructures, their crews further built at least 178 tenement houses, along with "hotels," school houses, store houses, and camps, thus shaping the emergent villages and hamlets into company towns. Indeed, the new tanneries were located in a borderland area where agro-forestry had previously achieved such a tenuous hold on the environment that the most basic services were lacking. As late as 1883, the Shaws' industrial holdings included 111 horses sheltered in company barns in addition to countless wagons, sleighs and sleds, pungs and carts, harness and robes. The Shaws' industrial property further encompassed wharves, landings, steamboats, boats, bark scows, and flat cars; blacksmith, carpenter, and cooper shops; saw mills, "poor farms," and company stores. Finally, a considerable acreage of forest land along or nearby the Canada-U.S. border was acquired to ensure a cheap supply of hemlock bark, along with additional real estate and bark leases in eastern Maine and western New Brunswick.[21]

Clearly, the Shaws' command of money had contributed decisively to making this borderland of capital flow and technological diffusion

Table 2 Financial and Spatial Progress of F. Shaw and Brothers

Date	Estimated Worth	Location: Canada	Location: United States
7/10/1854	$4,000		Cummington, Mass. (a) Dexter, Me. (b)
7/11/1860	$6,000		Cummington, Mass. (c) Dexter, Me. (b) Detroit, Me. (a) Plymouth, Me. (a) Burnham, Me. (b)
3/14/1866	$350,000	Montréal, Qué. (a) Roxton Falls, Qué. (a) Waterloo, Qué. (a) W. Farnham, Qué. (a)	Detroit, Me. (a) Plymouth, Me. (a) Cummington, Mass. (c) Dexter, Me. (b) Burnham, Me. (b) Winn, Me. (d)
11/1/1870	+$500,000	Montréal, Qué. (a) Roxton Falls, Qué. (a) Waterloo, Qué. (a) *Drummondville, Qué. (a) *St. Ephrem, Qué. (e) *Durham, Qué. (e)	Boston, Mass. (a) Forest City, Me. (f) Vanceboro, Me. (f) Jackson Brook, Me. (g) Hinckley Tp, Me. (a) Kingman, Me. (h)
11/5/1883	$6,199,256	Montréal, Qué. (i) Roxton Falls, Qué. (i) Waterloo, Qué. (j) Drummondville, Qué. (i) Warden, Qué. (i) Mawcook, Qué. (i) Adamsville, Qué. (i) Fulford, Qué. (i) *Pokiok, N.B. (a) *Millville, N.B. (a) *Woodstock, N.B. (a)	Boston, Mass. (a) Kingman, Me. (a) Hinckley Tp, Me. (a) Jackson Brook, Me. (a) Forest City, Me. (f) Vanceboro, Me. (f) Colton, NY (a) Wells, NY (a) St. Regis F. NY (a) Arietta, NY (a) *Piseco, NY (a) *Houlton, Me. (a) *Tp. 39, Hancock, Me. (a) *Sherman Mills, Me. (a)

(a) F. Shaw and Brothers (3 brothers: Fayette, William, and Brackley Shaw (b) Charles and Brackley Shaw (uncle/nephew) (c) L. Shaw and Brothers (4 brothers, Lorenzo, Fayette, William, and Brackley) (d) In partnership with H. Poor and Son and brother-in-law, L. Kingman (e) In partnership with J.J. Millar (f) F. Shaw and Brothers (4 brothers: Fayette, William, Brackley, and Thaxter) (g) In partnership with James Ayers (h) Shaw, Kingman & Co. (in partnership with brother-in-law, L. Kingman (i) Shaw Bros. and Cassils (in partnership with son-in-law, J. Cassils) (j) E. and S. Shaw & Co. (in partnership with uncle, Spencer Shaw, and brother, Eldridge Shaw)

Sources: (Baker Library) *Early handwritten Credit Ledgers of the Mercantile Agency*, volumes on Canada East, Massachusetts, Maine, and New York

a human experience as well. Although rural tanneries seldom required more than a hundred hands per establishment, their full-time adult male workforce drew hundreds of families to mushrooming company towns. Moreover, in exploiting autonomous ecological processes so far in the wilderness, they were hiring bark "peelers" and other seasonal woodworkers during a good portion of the agricultural season.[22] In this new seasonal ritual – the most labour-intensive activity in sole leather tanning operations – the Shaw family exerted its greatest demographic and migratory impact. News of spring and summer work in the Maine and New Brunswick forests drew countless woodsmen from Quebec and the Maritimes, thus establishing the Northeast sole leather tanning district as a new specialized regional labour market, which largely coincided with the Shaws' operations. The borderlands formed an area known for its considerable influx of migrant workers during the warmer months when the seasonal workforce might have equalled, even exceeded, the local, residential population.

But this specialized regional labour market and its corresponding company towns always depended closely upon a plentiful and cheap supply of hemlock bark. Unfortunately for the local inhabitants, the Shaws had not envisaged the possibility that by locating five of the largest sole leather tanneries on this continent within a short distance of each other they would rapidly strain local resources and run out of tan bark. Carpenters had just finished building company tenements in Grand Lake Stream village when William Shaw gave the first hint that depletion of hemlock trees was well underway. He called upon Quebec construction crews to build a chain of "extract mills" in the late 1870s and early 1880s. Located in Houlton, Sherman, and "Texas or Tp. 39," in Maine, and in Woodstock, Poquiock, and Millville, New Brunswick, these mills essentially acted as satellites of Maine's five giant tanneries, whose sole purpose was to extract tannin from neighbouring counties on both sides of the border to maintain the large tanneries in full operation.[23]

At the time of William Shaw's death, in August 1882, the Shaw family thus stood at the head of an impressive, but highly volatile, borderland manufacturing system on both sides of the Appalachian Mountains. Shortly before their business collapse, the Shaws were still extending their command of money in new directions, such as the Adirondacks and southwestern Ontario.[24] By then, South American hides were funnelled from their hide houses in Montreal and Boston to no less than eighteen and as many as twenty-four tanneries, which, along with seven extract works, could consume 150,000 cords of hemlock bark per year – over half a million trees according to an earlier estimate[25] – for a total output of thirteen thousand tons of leather.[26]

The Shaws' capital, which they calculated at seven million dollars in January 1883, included one and a half million dollars' worth of hemlock bark lands, nearly one and a half million dollars in buildings, and over three million dollars in "quick" assets.[27]

THE "FAILURE" OF THE SHAWS' MAINE–NEW BRUNSWICK BORDERLAND

The "Canadian" and the "American" branches of the Shaw family enterprise were styled differently only in 1874, when their Montreal-registered firm was dissolved in order to integrate Brackley Shaw's son-in-law, John Archibald Cassils.[28] The Scottish-born Canadian was said to be a man of modest means who reportedly joined the firm primarily for his managerial skills. Beyond the fact that the Canadian venture was now styled Shaw Brothers and Cassils, however, this legal distinction did not signal any dissolution of partnership or entail any loss of assets for the U.S. company. According to the terms of this new partnership, the "stock, assets, and effects then held by said F. Shaw and Brothers, in the city of Montreal" now constituted their capital in the new firm, leaving F. Shaw and Brothers with a three-fourth share of the profits made by Shaw Brothers and Cassils. In fact, the U.S. parent virtually owned all of its "Canadian" tanneries, leasing them to Shaw Brothers and Cassils at the nominal price of one-quarter cent per pound of leather.[29] Even though the Canadian and American branches were geared to each country's domestic markets, they were still headed by a single family enterprise, whose members had elected permanent residence on both sides of the border.

Moreover, the Shaw family continued to blur national distinctions in the late 1870s and early 1880s, when the "American" associates acquired forest lands and built extract works in New Brunswick and the "Canadian" partners claimed title to some of the tanneries in the Adirondacks.[30] Such a business strategy suggested that the nucleus of the borderlands enterprise was the three original founders rather than any specific centre or political region. This view was given its clearest expression in the Shaws' reports to the Dun credit agency. Between 1877 and 1883, the senior partners produced several sworn statements to the financial community of greater New England to the effect that F. Shaw and Brothers held over one million dollars in Canadian assets.[31] And by their renewed articles of co-partnership, on 2 January 1882, Fayette Shaw, Brackley Shaw, and William Shaw officially represented F. Shaw and Brothers as a company doing business as "Tanners and Leather Merchants in Massachusetts, Maine, New York, and the Dominion of Canada."[32]

The Shaws' sphere of capital accumulation only became more firmly delineated along geopolitical lines when the "American" firm suspended its operations due to "involuntary insolvency" on 28 July 1883, sending shockwaves through financial circles in New York, New England, and the Maritimes.[33] The creditors' astonishment turned into anger when newspapers reported that Fayette Shaw had withdrawn $55,000 twenty-four hours before the assignment and fled to Canada, from where he had not yet returned. And when the Montreal office refused to open its books to the creditors' investigating committee, the Shaws' cross-border strategy of salvation was condemned in the bitterest terms. According to a local report printed in St Stephen: "The feeling of the meeting [in Boston] was pretty well expressed by a creditor from Pawtucket, who said that, as businessmen, the creditors could not afford to compromise with the commercial rascality here disclosed; that, as a dangerous precedent in business, this offer [of $0.33 cents in the dollar] should be rejected. When the head of the firm returned from his Canadian asylum and disclosed his hidden assets, it would be time to treat with them."[34]

The meeting adjourned with a resolution to take any measures, civil or criminal, to compel Fayette Shaw to disclose his interest in the Montreal-based company of Shaw Brothers and Cassils. But the "Canadian" legal fiction successfully withstood all the acrimony and protest. All "information in regard to the interest of F. Shaw & Bros [was] persistently withheld from" the creditors' committee, who were unable to make "any estimate of its value." Even in their account books in the United States, the senior partners had systematically avoided any monetary reference to their interests in Shaw Brothers and Cassils. The door to the Quebec side of the Shaws' borderlands, including two New York tanneries claimed by the Montreal firm, had been slammed shut, barred, and bolted.[35]

No such difficulty awaited the investigation of the Shaws' interest in New Brunswick. Observing that the books of their business dealings in that province had been kept by Thaxter Shaw, in Vanceboro', Maine, and that the three senior partners had been engaged in a rather vague but still separate partnership with their young brother, accountants simply distinguished this entity from the Boston-based firm by creating a separate "class of indebtedness" for the border tanneries at Vanceboro' and Forest City and their corresponding "extract works," bark lands, and quick assets in Poquiock and in Millville, New Brunswick, all of which was styled "F. Shaw and Brothers of Vanceboro'."[36] This distinction was clearly in the interest of Maritimes creditors because the "Vanceboro'" branch was found to be solvent, meaning that its assets ($692,408.56) were deemed to be sufficiently in excess of its liabilities

($135,313.52) to place its owners in the position of paying their creditors the full amount of their claims. The bulk of these assets consisted of "land account," "tannery property," and "bark," of which significant proportions were found in New Brunswick. For example, to the Vanceboro' tannery were attributed bark stumpage rights extending to well over 50,000 acres of forest land in York County, and the Poquiock extract works similarly entailed assets in land and in stumpage rights over an area totalling some 15,000 acres.[37]

The Shaws' response to this rather positive "valuation" of the branch managed by Thaxter Shaw may seem puzzling at first sight. Contending that the creditors' committee of accountants did not really understand the tanning business, they argued that all their New Brunswick holdings were nearly worthless; that "extract-works" in New Brunswick and in Maine should be understood as liabilities rather than as assets; and that the property and contracts associated with these facilities – such as forest lands and bark leases – could no longer achieve the value ascribed by the evaluators because of the poor state of their tanning operations in Maine. As of the fall of 1883, the mills in Woodstock, Poquiock, and Millville, New Brunswick, and those in Sherman, Houlton, and "Texas," Maine were absolutely valueless: "If we resume business, we shall abandon them as extract-works. One or two of them are of some value to be converted into tanneries. The remainder are valueless except for old iron and junk; and consequently the bark at these works is without value, both in the woods and on the spot, the same being too remote for profitable use at the tanneries; and the bark-leases connected therewith are a liability, and the lands connected are generally of little value."[38]

While the Shaws were obviously endeavouring to devalue their inflated assets so as to pay their creditors only a small fraction of their claims while maintaining secrecy as to their "Canadian" resources, they articulated the following interpretation of the root cause of their financial predicament in the Maine-New Brunswick borderlands: "We have made large reductions in the estimated value of [Maine] tanneries; and besides the reasons therefor, which are apparent to every man in the trade, we have to say that the tanneries are very large ones, and the bark resources are insufficient to run them to their full capacity; hence they are no more valuable than much smaller tanneries would be in the same locality. It was to supply this lack, and atone for the large size of the tanneries, that we established these extract-works, which have proved so disastrous a failure."[39]

Months before this "failure," a number of New Brunswick commentators had voiced two major objections to the Shaws' expansion in the province. At the time when extract works were being erected in Woodstock and Poquiock, Saint John newspaper editors expressed views, both environmental and political, which hardly amounted to local industrial promotion. From an environmental point of view, they urged local farmers, who would engage in bark-peeling work, to "look well to their forests of lumber." With spruce and pine nearly all gone, hemlock trees were now increasingly valued as building material. "It is thought by many that the forests should not be cleared of the hemlock, as it not only deprives the future generation of lumber for building purposes, but it causes those destructive fires to rage so furiously destroying the hard wood as well as the soft wood."[40] Here, the editor of the *Daily Telegraph* was further alluding to the popular belief, no doubt partly borne out in fact, that, once the bark was peeled, the tree itself was left "on the ground to decay and add fuel to some future fire." Because hemlock tanbark and hemlock lumber were intended for two different markets, their supply and demand did not always ensure that they could be exploited in tandem, and bark peeling was thus known as a "destructive agent" that left much waste in its wake.

But it was in the realm of political economy that the strongest opposition was voiced to the Shaws' command of money. Hopes of witnessing the erection of industrial tanneries in Woodstock and elsewhere were soon dashed by the realization that the American capitalists intended only to extract tannin, not to process hides, in the western portion of the province. "The extract is sent out of the country to be used for tanning purposes abroad, leaving very little behind but the means of destruction ... In this way much of the raw material is destroyed and what is left made to build up the manufactories of another country." This destructive side of extracting tanbark became especially objectionable in the province because: "Our own tanneries require our first consideration, and it is unjust to them to allow this extract manufacture in the Province."[41] However, not every Maritimes spokesmen agreed with the Saint John editors. Reflecting the more immediate needs of woodworkers and the interest of landowners in the borderland area, the Carleton *Sentinel* adopted what sounds like a very familiar refrain in today's pulp and paper mill towns: whether they were Canadian or American business men, the Shaws had "put in circulation a large amount of money," first by building and fitting up their extract mills, then by paying considerable sums to the revenue in import duties, also through the employment of a good deal of labour and, finally, by materially assisting trade for the greater benefit of "our farmers and all other classes."[42] Such subservience to the Shaws' command of money also transpires in a testimony by E.L. Wetmore of the Fredericton law firm of Wetmore and Winslow, who was "sharply critical" of the "treatment of New Brunswick creditors of F. Shaw & Bros" by the United States creditors.

In response to the Shaws' contention that the creditors' experts had greatly overestimated their assets because they did not understand the tanning business, numerous institutions and individuals, including officials from 145 U.S. banks, merely pointed to the Shaws' own financial reports and sworn statements shortly before their "failure," wherein they had raised capital by representing their assets at between five and seven million dollars. That these industrialists were now formally reporting their total assets as amounting to only two million dollars was nothing short of fraudulent representation. Not a few among them would have agreed with a Boston editor who speculated that the "failure was a masterly scheme for the safe reduction of a business grown too large for its managers."[43] In the midst of this mounting suspicion, Wetmore sided with the Shaws by asserting that these threatening New England and New York creditors had not been properly informed by their own experts:

> It is notorious that the Messrs Shaw raised the price of bark lands in New Brunswick, that they were continually and openly seeking to purchase in all directions, and that in consequence properties that had been lying in the market for years without a purchaser being found for them, were sold to the Messrs Shaw at such prices as their owners had never before thought of ... If a sale were effected under ordinary circumstances, on the most favorable terms to the buyer as to time, price, etc., the estate would come very successfully out of it if it realized *one-half* the price paid for it by the Messrs Shaw, and I sincerely believe that if sold at a forced sale it could not realize *one-quarter* of the price said.[44]

But when he attempted to voice this opinion in Boston, Wetmore was "choked off," "compelled to take his seat," and never received a "fair hearing." Upon his return to New Brunswick, he not only echoed the Shaws' rationale but voiced a damning condemnation of his American counterparts for the "outrage" and the "deliberate insult" thus committed "to myself and to the New Brunswick creditors, whom I represented."[45]

In sharp contrast to the Saint John editors, then, Wetmore was not at all concerned by the environmental impact of the Shaws' operations or any question of political economy; his was essentially a cultural criticism of the American propensity to take over everything, everywhere, including his freedom of speech. Trapped in a borderlands relationship of subordination, Maritime creditors and their spokesman thus emerged on the side of the Shaws in their struggle against angry creditors, their law suits, and attachments. The perspective of the Maritime creditors was that of people not living in an economy where property value increased over time, but in one of perennial boom and bust cycles. From such a perspective, the Shaws' estimates of their assets before July 1883 would not have been fraudulent; more likely, they reflected the overly optimistic and speculative tendencies of a boom cycle. But now that the speculative bubble had burst, it was time to face reality and to recover what surely amounted to the value of their "real" assets, even if part of these assets were said to comprise "old iron and junk" and forest land of "little value." The depressed state of the lumber trade itself undoubtedly served to reinforce such an attitude. Between 1883 and 1884, lumbering operations in New Brunswick experienced a "falling off" of over 47 percent, from 386 million to 203 million superficial feet.[46] Maritimes creditors were still hoping for some sort of recovery three years later, when Duncan MacIntyre, from Montreal, purchased the entire Shaw estate in the province of New Brunswick, inclusive of the unused bark, which had been just lying in the woods and near the mills. But when it became obvious that the Maine tanneries would no longer operate with the assistance of New Brunswick mills, MacIntyre simply offered the property "for sale again by him in toto or in parcels."[47] Here was another instance of a single, virtually self-contained, boom and bust cycle. In the end, as these New Brunswick mills turned into decaying buildings, both the Saint John editors and Maritimes creditors had been accurate: New Brunswick land value had been inflated as a result of the Shaws' command of money, and hemlock forests had been recklessly depleted to sustain a "foreign" industry.

CONCLUSION

As satellites of F. Shaw and Brothers' operations, the New Brunswick mills and their surrounding hemlock reserves could not assume a separate existence from Maine's "very large" tanneries, either by legal fiction or by national distinction, because they were "valueless" without their parent company. Being used exclusively for extractive purposes, New Brunswick mills and bark lands simply could not be portrayed as a "Canadian" component of the Shaw family's aggregate cross-border business. Even within the hinterland area of the Northeast, their command of money had thus exerted such a differential impact on rural industry as to make one side of this Maine–New Brunswick borderland completely dependent on the other. And the environmental effect of this dependency obviously extended to New Brunswick leather manufacturers and future generations of builders as well, by greatly depleting the province's western hemlock reserves. In the Shaws' industrial borderlands and throughout the Northeast hinterland, New Brunswick had thus served, once more, as a "staples colony."

When the gap between extractive and processing operations grew wider in the Maine–New Brunswick borderland, tanneries, mills, and bark lands all lost considerable value. Labour went unpaid, tannery hands moved on to other sources of employment, seasonal wage-earners chose different destinations or subsistence strategies. In fact, community development proved so tenuous in Grand Lake Stream village and Forest City, Maine, that the former never could organize into a township and the latter, ultimately, reverted back to "unorganized" status. The corresponding situation in western New Brunswick proved even more transitory. Extract mills erected in the late 1870s and early 1880s had outlived their useful existence only three or four years later. Along with the premature depreciation of equipment and buildings, the closing of these extract works resulted in the waste of thousands of cords of bark and the precipitous decline in the value of wood lots and forest lands, not to mention its contribution to a dramatic "falling off" in the province's lumber operations. Given these circumstances, one might easily assume that discontent and protest would have been most widespread among Maritimes creditors and advocates of "home industry." In reality, the province's economic vulnerability as a "staples colony" and its people's subordination to the command of money exerted by the Shaws and other similarly influential industrialists translated into an attitude of subservience, which contrasted sharply with the barrage of protest and of indignation voiced by New England and New York creditors. For, as political economist Mel Watkins once wrote, the "staple trap" is not restricted to a question of economic "linkages," or lack thereof, but pertains also to the attitudes and peculiar mentality bred in the staples-producing hinterland economies of Canada.[48]

12

Re-examining the Economic Underdevelopment of the Maritime Provinces: A Case Study of Portland, Maine, and Saint John, New Brunswick

ROBERT H. BABCOCK

Ever since Stanley Saunders was first called upon more than sixty years ago by the Rowell-Sirois Commission to explain the economic decline of the Maritime provinces, a good many scholars have continued to wrestle with this question.[1] Why, they ask, has the easternmost region of Canada experienced less development than the remainder of the nation? Given the many interactive variables of broad scope and magnitude to sort out, the number of historical periods to examine, and the different theoretical models to draw upon, it is not surprising that the search for solutions to this difficult question has become a veritable academic growth industry.*

From the outset the vast majority of scholars have approached it by comparing mostly non-contiguous portions of selected Canadian cities or regions. Such analyses have been based upon explicit or implicit contrasts between the Maritimes and other parts of Canada rather than comparing any two elements, whether cities or regions, located on different sides of the international boundary dividing the Northeastern Borderlands into New England and Atlantic Canada. It is true that one scholar elected to compare the economies of the Maritimes and nearby Newfoundland,[2] and another contrasted the historical development of the textile industry in the Maritimes and North Carolina.[3] But the others almost invariably have relied upon implicit comparisons between the Maritimes and the central Canadian core provinces of Ontario and Quebec, including the latter's two large metropolitan areas, Toronto and Montreal. Some of these interpreters, mainly economists and geographers, point to distinct spatial factors to account for the pattern of economic disparities.[4] Most pay homage to Harold Innis's staples theory of development, including Saunders himself, who attributed the Maritimes' decline immediately following Confederation to the demise of its wood, wind, and sail-based economy.[5] In a similar vein, B.J. Kierstead cited the "inevitable" growth of large Central Canadian firms whose powerful tentacles wrested control over eastern Canada's smaller, weaker fringe markets and financial institutions.[6] To explain Canada's regional variations Larry McCann constructed a complex spatial process involving the interplay between "heartlands"; that is, metropolitan centres that exert varying degrees of economic, social, and political dominance over more rural, largely resource-producing hinterlands. "The attributes of cities – size, function, and regional settlement patterns," McCann says, "tell us a great deal about the geographic character of heartland and hinterland regions." As for eastern Canada, he concludes: "The power of central Canadian cities also brought about, in part, the demise of a short-lived industrial revolution in the Maritimes."[7] It is not made clear just how much "in part" actually entails.

Rather than relying upon geographically based "forces," other scholars have touted the role of various political and economic contingencies in affecting the economic history of the Maritime Provinces. Thirty years ago Bill Acheson traced the differential impact of Ottawa's National Policy upon the economies of central and eastern Canada, wondering along the way if the absence of a strong "Boston-like" regional metropolis within the Maritimes might have put the region's economic growth into the hands of Montreal and Toronto businessmen intent upon pursuing their own interests.[8] Then Ernie Forbes argued that the loss of the Maritime provinces' political control over Intercolonial Railway (ICR) rate structures to Central Canadian interests was a key variable that precipitated the region's sharp economic decline after World War I.[9] Although Roy George, an economist, had blamed the same phenomena upon the entrepreneurial weaknesses in the Maritimes' business class,[10] that was not so, David Frank retorted, detailing how a coterie of inept businessmen from outside the Maritimes had been responsible for the demise of the Cape Breton coal industry.[11]

As a method of doing comparative history, broad comparisons between the Maritimes and central Canada run the risk of becoming trapped in an "apples-oranges" dichotomy. That is, given the many disparities embedded from the start in those two complex regions, it is often difficult if not impossible for the analyst to separate causes from consequences. Did the removal of artificially low ICR freight rates, for instance, provoke the Maritimes' underdevelopment, or did their presence prevent the region's entrepreneurs from fostering any "real" comparative economic advantages over central Canada? Did the National Policy exert a brief "hot-house" stimulus upon the industrialization of the Maritimes until competitive, continental, market-driven forces reversed its distorting impact? As Marc Bloch, the father of comparative history, observed long ago, the comparative method offers the most persuasive hypotheses when the items being juxtaposed share many features in common. Only then will "the experimental condition of 'all other factors being equal' ... be more nearly achieved."[12]

From this perspective, then, comparing two units from within the Northeastern Borderlands may offer an attractive alternative to the Central Canada/Maritimes contrast. Many of the heartlands and hinterlands within the Borderlands region share substantial geographical and historical similarities, thereby improving the changes of isolating those crucial variables, whether driven by geography or policy, that exerted the most significant impacts upon one side or the other of the international boundary. Moreover, the fact that New England contained Boston, the dominant regional metropolis within the Northeastern Borderlands, while the Maritimes never possessed an urban heartland of comparable magnitude within its boundaries, offers researchers using the cross-border paradigm a unique opportunity to assess this variable as well.

By comparing the economy and demography of Portland, Maine, with those of Saint John, New Brunswick, during the four critical decades from 1880 to 1920, this essay brings the conundrum of Maritime underdevelopment into a closer focus. For instance, a large number of the shared factors rooted in the Portland–Saint John comparison – their similar spatial locations, hinterland resources, spectrum of economic activities, and decades-long port rivalries – are absent from the Maritimes–central Canada comparisons. In addition, a wide variety of data drawn from U.S. and Canadian censuses as well as from many other sources strongly suggests that the 1880–1920 era was a major turning point, in starkly different directions, for each of these two small urban heartlands, as a result of factors previously unmentioned or underplayed by students of Maritimes underdevelopment. A third advantage to such a focus is that fluctuations in both cities in the activity of the metals industry offer insights into key variables affecting their changing economic destinies. Next, the supportive role played by Boston's entrepreneurs during this period of Portland's growth contrasts with the competitive posture of Montreal merchants toward the Saint John business community. Last and most significantly, our comparison reveals that both the relatively greater size and the better timing of American capital invested in Portland's hinterland between the 1890s and 1920s played a significant role in propelling the Maine city's economic and demographic growth trajectories well beyond those of Saint John.

To lay the foundation for these hypotheses we begin by comparing the evolution of heartland-hinterland dynamics in the two North Atlantic ports and tracing the overall pattern of demographic changes that took place between 1880 and the early 1920s. This exercise stems from Jane Jacobs's premise that urban centres grow successfully when local industries start exporting products and, at the same time, become markets for home-produced goods that replace their imports. The richer the emerging web of economic activity, the more resilient, adaptive, and expansive the urban economy.[13] During this period we shall see that the Maine city and its hinterland both surpassed the Fundy port. Hence, if we can understand why the Portland economy grew more rapidly between 1880 and 1920, we should be able to offer convincing reasons why its sister city, Saint John, significantly lagged.

Narrowing our focus onto a vital sector of the urban economy, we compare the metalworking industries in Portland and Saint John, portions of which experienced widespread rationalization and consolidation at the turn of the century. Beginning in roughly the 1890s and extending until well after World War I, huge aggregations of capital rapidly established control over many sectors of the North American economy, particularly, but by no means exclusively, in steel, railroads, chemicals, electrical goods, and pulp and paper, creating huge national and international markets for products formerly produced in much smaller workplaces for distribution to regional North American markets. Decade-long comparisons of metalworking employment and related business activity reveal the second Industrial Revolution (often labelled "monopoly capital") at work in the evolving economies of both Portland and Saint John. Its differing impacts upon New England and Atlantic Canada, and particularly the sources and timing of its influence, profoundly affected both the size and rates of growth and change in metalworking, thereby accounting for a significant divergence in the two cities' destinies.

The concluding section compares the strategic responses of each city's elites to the changing economic contexts within which they worked. At a critical moment after external monopoly capitalists had begun undermining Portland's locomotive and railway rolling-stock production, the rapid expansion of the American pulp and paper industry, coupled with growing demands within the burgeoning American market for other resources from Portland's hinterland, offered many new opportunities that were eagerly embraced by entrepreneurs in the Maine city's metalworking sector. By contrast, Atlantic Canada's pulp and paper industry did not "take off" until the 1920s and 1930s for reasons that will be presented.

Lacking the investment capital to develop new products in their own region until the 1920s and 1930s, Saint John entrepreneurs turned elsewhere. They single-mindedly set about working to restore the city's traditional nineteenth-century mercantile trading functions by enlarging its winter port facility to rival Portland's. In the absence of new regional markets and facing strong competitive pressures from central Canadian and American manufacturers, their choice is understandable, and there is evidence in this essay to suggest that it proved to be moderately beneficial to Saint John's metalworking shops. Nevertheless, the aggregate economic and demographic census data for the two cities during this period show conclusively that Portland had surpassed Saint John as a result of its accelerating, more balanced economic development. For Portland, the rapid takeoff of the pulp and paper industry in its northern New England hinterland, more than any other single factor, offers the best explanation for the different urban grown patterns observed in these two cities at the turn of the century.

COMPARING METROPOLITAN-HINTERLAND DYNAMICS

Throughout most of the nineteenth century, both Portland and Saint John had been small lumber ports with comparable hinterlands. Square timber and deals from the territory drained by the St John River passed through Saint John sawmills to burgeoning markets abroad, transforming the city into one of the major imperial timber exporters on the North Atlantic. At the same time much of Portland's lumber, barrels, shooks, and staves produced from timber harvested in northern New England wound up in the West Indies sugar industry. Saint John merchants established hegemony over the terms of trade throughout the St John River valley and around adjacent Fundy shores of New Brunswick and Nova Scotia, while their counterparts in Portland controlled most economic activity in northern New Hampshire and Vermont as well as in Maine and along the "Downeast" shore. Both cities shared other factors in common: for instance, neither enjoyed any special status or economic stimulus – unlike Boston or Halifax – as a political, cultural, or military centre. In both, a wholesale trading and manufacturing complex based on lumber and shipbuilding formed the core, encompassing many stores, factories, warehouses, and workshops, as well as sizeable retail sectors marketing household goods and foodstuffs. Photographs reveal that late nineteenth-century Portland and Saint John even looked much alike.[14]

During the heyday of wooden sailing ships, iron foundries forged woodworking tools and marine hardware vital to both cities' shipbuilders and lumbermen in the hinterlands. In Saint John, James Harris and Thomas Allan set up the first foundry in Saint John in 1831 to produce nails, ships' knees, and mill goods. They sold the nail business to another entrepreneur who moved it to the outskirts of Saint John and hired Seth R. Foster, a skilled metalworker from Massachusetts, to run the shop.[15] George Fleming arrived from Scotland in the early 1830s and joined Harris & Allan's machine shop. Later he organized a partnership and operated casting, molding, machine shops, and a blacksmith's forge where skilled craftsmen built the first steam engine in the province.[16] Thomas McAvity, another Scots emigrant, founded a hardware store on Prince William Street in 1835 and settled down with his bride to beget six sons and five daughters in the intervals between peddling brass goods. His two eldest sons eventually persuaded their father to begin the manufacture of the hardware as well, and in 1864 T. McAvity & Sons bought a foundry to produce ship's bells and brass fittings for Fundy area shipyards.[17] These firms reveal the close connection between that era's railways, shipbuilding, and metalworking.

The impact of nineteenth-century railways and shipping on Portland's metalworking industry can be illustrated most clearly by the history of the Portland Company. Originating in the vision and enterprise of John A. Poor, a Maine lawyer, as a part of his ultimately successful scheme to locate Canada's winter port in Maine, the firm was chartered in 1846 with $150,000 in capital raised by public subscription. A foundry emerged on six acres at the eastern end of Portland harbour. Capable of casting up to 20 tons of iron, the firm opened in October 1847 with seventy men engaged in building locomotives and a wide variety of freight cars for the railway already under construction between Portland and Montreal. In 1848 twenty-four oxen ceremoniously hauled the first completed engine, a wood-burner, through Portland streets lined by an enthusiastic crowd. During the interim, before track-laying had been completed, the company employed over a hundred machinists, blacksmiths, foundry men, boiler makers, pattern makers, and labourers to build locomotives and rolling stock for a railway in Panama under feverish construction at the peak of the California gold rush.[18]

After the last spike had been driven into Portland's rail link to Montreal in 1853, the company prospered by selling engines and rolling stock to the line's lessee, the Grand Trunk Railway (GTR). Since its engines were less expensive than English models, the GTR bought 135 of the first 325 locomotives manufactured by the Portland firm. Additional orders came from as far away as Chicago and Galveston, but about 40 percent of the total business was provided by Canadian lines, including the Intercolonial, Canadian Pacific Railway (CPR), New Brunswick & Canada, and the Ontario, Simcoe & Lake Huron railways.

During the economic downturn at the end of the 1850s, orders fell precipitously. Still, the company remained solvent thanks to the repair business and to a new activity – building and repairing engines of steamships engaged in the Canadian winter port trade. A measure of prosperity returned during the American Civil War when the company filled government orders for cannon, machinery, and engines for gunboats. At this time the firm began making both high and low pressure boilers and "castings of all kinds," and was reported to be "getting out of debt."[19] Although it had to cut salaries in order to meet expenses during the depression-ridden 1870s, this cloud had lifted by 1880 and the factory was said to be "full of work."[20]

For both nineteenth-century ports, the advent of railways at mid-century offered risks and opportunities. On the one hand, the new steam-powered transportation technology enabled larger metropolitan centres, whether Boston or Montreal, to extend their tentacles into northern New England or Atlantic Canada and threaten the smaller towns' economic and demographic expansion. On the other, in an age when bulk transport was significantly cheaper by water than by land, Portland and Saint John merchants fully expected to convert their closer proximity to northern European ports into a permanent trade advantage over larger cities to the south and west. Hence both groups believed that a rail link to Montreal would tap the Canadian hinterland to their own advantage. As we have just seen, Portland initially won this competition.[21]

Later, witnessing a decline in their port's timber trade which left a portion of its economy in the doldrums, Saint John merchants searched for an economic alternative. Aided by the federal government in Ottawa, they persuaded the newly completed Canadian Pacific Railway to help construct a major port terminal in their city rivalling the Grand Trunk Railway's facility in Portland. From the 1890s into the 1920s, the Maine and New Brunswick ports – along with Halifax – competed for Canada's winter port trade. Aided by Ottawa, the two Atlantic Canadian cities eventually won the lion's share of this business. But by then the Maine city's growth curve had surpassed Saint John's for reasons which this paper strives to explain.

The population of the two cities and their hinterlands can reveal, as Jacobs says, the general dynamics of their overall economies during the period from 1880–81 to 1920/21. Initially, Saint John was 18 percent larger than Portland, its metropolitan functions greatly enhanced

Table 1
A Comparison of the Populations of Portland and Saint John and their Hinterlands

	1880/81	*1890/91*	*1900/01*	*1910/11*	*1920/21*
Portland	33,810	36,425	50,145	58,571	69,272
Saint John	41,353	39,179	40,711	42,511	47,166
Cumberland Cty	75,723	90,949	100,689	112,014	124,376
Saint John Cty	52,966	49,574	51,759	53,572	60,486
Maine	648,936	661,086	694,466	742,371	768,014
New Brunswick	321,233	321,263	331,120	351,889	387,876
Proportion of City Population to the County (%)					
Portland	44.6	40.0	49.8	52.3	55.7
Saint John	78.1	79.0	78.7	79.4	78.0
Proportion of City Population to State/Province (%)					
Portland	5.2	5.5	7.2	7.9	9.0
Saint John	12.9	12.9	12.3	12.1	12.2

Source: U.S. and Canadian census data

Table 2 A Comparison of Foundries and Machine Shops in 1880–81

	Portland	*Saint John*
businesses	8	5
employment	415	66
prod. value	$600,400	$146,800
value-added	$85,412	$19,100

Source: U.S., Canadian census data

by its commanding role in the nineteenth-century Imperial timber trade. Demographically, however, its immediate and extended hinterlands (Saint John County and the province of New Brunswick) remained smaller than Portland's, and it would appear to have achieved its maximum state of metropolitan dominance over that territory by 1891. Saint John's proportion of New Brunswick's population actually declined slightly thereafter. In sharp contrast, Portland's share of Maine's population nearly doubled between 1880 and 1920. By the turn of the century the Maine city's population was almost 25 percent greater than Saint John's, and the gap widened over the ensuing two decades.

As we have noted, metalworking had sprung from the same roots in the early nineteenth-century experience of these two cities, but the industry had grown at different rates. Although Saint John was the more populous town in 1880/81, it had fewer foundries and machine shops, and they employed just 17 percent of the number of workers in Portland foundries (Table 2). Why? Certainly the Great Fire of 1877 in Saint John had reinforced the effects of the worldwide depression of the 1870s, diverting scarce local capital into the reconstruction of Saint John's infrastructure rather than underwriting new metalworking ventures. Despite this handicap, the sons of Vulcan in the Fundy port managed to produce 24 percent of Portland's product value and 22 percent of its value added. Although foundries and machine shops developed from different baselines after 1880/81, metalworking in both towns experienced significant growth. At the same time both ultimately suffered a reduction in their capacity to fabricate railway-related goods for national and international markets, and each sought new markets to replace them.

METALWORKING SECTORS DURING THE 1880S AND 1890S

During this period of heightened competition, markets fluctuated sharply, and businesses with better access to capital and technology were able to consolidate their activities, gain ground over smaller firms, and successfully compete in emerging national and regional markets. Both cities were affected by changes wrought by monopoly capital, as the experience of eleven specific foundries and machine shops illustrates.

Selected Portland Foundries and Machine Shops

During the remaining two decades of the nineteenth century, when steam power was rapidly supplanting water wheels throughout northern New England, Portland foundries and machine shops produced hundreds of custom-made boilers and steam engines. At the same time an expanding consumer market (see population data, Table 1) required large quantities of stoves, tools, horseshoes, copper and tin goods, iron ware, and steam heating apparatuses. As more and more ocean-going steamships displaced sailing vessels calling at nineteenth-century Canada's winter port, Portland's larger foundries refitted to build and repair marine engines.

Sharply changing business cycles, a narrowing of product lines, and the gradual constriction of external markets during the 1880s are revealed in the fortunes of the Portland Stove Foundry. Founded in 1877, only six years later the firm was importing pig iron from

Scotland to make stoves for the New England market and rice kettles for sale in Africa. In 1885 fifty men worked in a factory considered "one of the most flourishing" in Portland. But a year later the workforce was cut 20 percent and the economic uncertainties provoked those who remained to organize a mutual benefit society. By the end of the 1880s, however, business had picked up again and the foundry began to specialize in two ways – by promoting a brand-name furnace, and by accepting nickel-plating contracts from several Maine firms. On the eve of the 1893 depression, the workforce had grown to about eighty men who manufactured furnaces and stoves for sale throughout New England. Although the firm survived the depression, most of its trade afterward was confined to Maine.[22]

Because northern New England remained an important lumber-producing region during the 1880s, Portland machine shops turned out shingle machines, planers, and circular saws for scores of lumber mills located between Berlin Falls, New Hampshire, and Fort Kent, Maine. A commercial traveller, Jefferson Chase, arrived in Portland in 1881 to open a shop with his son to manufacture mill supplies. Chase & Son specialized in rotary sawmills, endless-chair haul-in rigs, sawing machines, and steam engines to run this equipment. By the mid-1880s they were selling mill machinery to firms in dozens of Maine and New Hampshire towns. Three years later they had six millwrights building lumber mills and putting in machinery at several additional Maine and New Hampshire locations. Yet they failed to escape the uncertainties of the era of competitive capital, and in 1892 the firm's assets were sold to meet its debts.[23]

Chase & Son's difficulties are mirrored in the census data (Table 3). During the 1880s the number of foundries and machine shops in Portland rose from eight to twelve, but more important, capital inputs doubled to over $1 million, while labour inputs remained constant at slightly over 400 souls. At the same time the value of goods produced had actually decreased from $600,000 to $513,000 by 1890, probably reflecting both intensified competition and currency deflation. Some metalworking businesses survived by blending their manufacturing specialties with dealerships for larger, out-of-state machinery firms, while others simply merged with stronger competitors or went out of business.

The history of the Portland Rolling Mills reveals both the competitive pressures felt by the city's metalworking firms during the late nineteenth century and a timely infusion from the metropolitan Boston region. The firm had been launched by local businessmen after the Civil War. Its one hundred employees produced fish plates, railway iron and spikes, shafting, blacksmiths' tools, and ship supplies for local and regional markets. By 1870 it was paying 20 percent dividends to its stockholders, but the worldwide depression later that decade forced the original owners out of business.[24] When demand returned in the 1880s, the new owners, having acquired "a valuable plant [for] a mere song," geared up to manufacture horseshoes and other goods. In 1884–85 the 150 employees were said to be turning out more work than at any previous time (save one month) since the firm had been founded. Its mill produced up to 12,000 tons of bar iron and railway supplies for car works in Laconia, New Hampshire, and Springfield, Massachusetts, nut and bolt iron for a firm in Lowell, Massachusetts, and angle plates for the Boston & Lowell, Boston & Maine, Providence & Worcester, and Old Colony (Virginia) railways.

Nevertheless, by the end of the 1880s all of the New England foundries faced growing competition from mills outside this region with better access to cheaper fuel, and Portland Rolling Mill's workforce dropped to thirty-five men.[25] The Boston & Maine, for instance, reduced its rail requisitions from 300 tons to 40 tons a month, and in the midst of the depression of the 1890s the firm was forced to shut down until "new orders come in, which may be three or four weeks hence." Then in 1899 a disastrous fire completely destroyed the mill. Fortunately for the Maine city, Boston capitalists rebuilt it later that year and also equipped it to roll steel.[26]

Initially the Portland Company profited during the 1880s from James J. Hill's construction of the Great Northern (GN) transcontinental railway, building 103 huge, eight-wheel, 36–ton locomotives for the GN. (Some of these monsters were sent by rail to New York City and then shipped in sailing vessels around Cape Horn to the Pacific Coast.) The Portland Company's profits soared and employment reached an all-time high of 525 men. Other railways, including the CPR, Maine Central, Portland & Ogdensburg, Eastern, Quebec Central, and Windsor & Annapolis, bought Portland-made rolling stock. According to the R.G. Dun credit agency in New York City, the company was "in a very prosperous condition, out of debt, doing all they can manage and making money." [27]

Census data in Table 3 reveal the broad outlines of these trends. Intense competition enabled the larger, more capital-intensive, technologically advanced firms like the Portland Company to gain market advantages over smaller firms. While total capitalization of Portland metalworking establishments more than doubled, employment remained steady rather than increasing. Both the value of goods produced, and – more significantly – profits as reflected in the value-added figures, had certainly dipped during this decade.

Table 3 Portland's Foundries and Machine Shops, 1880–1890

	1880	*1890*
businesses	8	12
capital invested	$527,000	$1,302,949
employees	421	404
value products	$600,400	$513,168
value-added	$85,412	$54,179

Source: U.S. Census, 1880, 1890

Selected Saint John Foundries and Machine Shops

During the mid-nineteenth century, demands stemming from the burgeoning North American railway industry spurred Saint John's foundries and machine shops as it had Portland's. James Fleming's Phoenix Works turned out the first monster locomotives in Canada, weighing up to 40 tons apiece, for John A. Poor's other scheme, the European & North American Railway (ENA). By the 1880s the firm's eighty men ran bar and sheet iron through lathes, drills, planers and shaping machines to fashion locomotives, boilers, ship tanks, and marine and stationary steam engines. The foundry also manufactured metal gates for the Saint John waterworks and coal mining machinery for the Joggins, Nova Scotia, shafts owned by Saint John merchants.[28]

In the 1860s another Saint John entrepreneur, James Harris, bought out the heirs of his partner (Harris & Allan) and was reported to be "doing a large business" in the manufacture of railway rolling stock for the ENA's Western Extension to Saint John. Upon the completion of the government-financed Intercolonial Railway from Montreal to Saint John and Halifax during the depression-ridden 1870s, Harris received a large order from Ottawa to build 586 trucks and 200 coal cars for the Intercolonial Railway (ICR). "This contract has greatly increased the value of his property," the local R.G. Dun informant reported, "and will greatly benefit him this winter." At that time Harris owned a foundry, car shop, blacksmith shop, and rolling mills that had cost him $115,000 and for which he still owed "a great deal." Five years later Harris was believed to have earned $50,000 clear on the ICR contract, and his credit rating soared.[29]

Riding the crest of the railway boom, James Harris plowed his profits back into the firm and, like Portland Company officials, sometimes appeared short of working capital. In 1883 he built 550 railway freight cars, six passenger cars, and 4,500 car wheels, mostly for the ICR, and hundreds of tons of bar iron. A year later the ICR ordered 300 coal hoppers. By the mid-1880s the firm manufactured every item required for railway rolling stock except for the springs. The bulk of its orders came from regional railways, but Harris also received a request from the CPR to build sleeping cars for its construction crews. Orders poured in at such a rate throughout the decade that Harris was forced to build a new rolling mill just to maintain an adequate supply of bar and plate iron. By 1888 he employed 350 men, somewhat fewer than the Portland Company, and the *Montreal Herald* considered the Harris firm to be "probably the most extensive car works in Canada."[30]

As in Portland, so in Saint John: steam power's coming of age transformed many Saint John foundries during the 1880s and early 1890s by creating a demand for a wide variety of metal goods. The Saint John Iron Works, a small firm founded during the age of sail, manufactured engines, boilers, tanks, brass castings, and all kinds of mill and marine supplies. Employing just twelve hands in 1878, the Abrams & Kerr foundry needed fifty men by 1882 to turn out steam engines, rotary mills, mill machinery, shafting, planers, and molders for customers throughout the Maritimes. In 1882 William Hazelhurst built a second foundry at Coldbrook to manufacture railway car wheels and axles. Three years later Vincent White, a lumberman and wholesale flour dealer, bankrolled a young nephew with an MIT engineering degree into setting up a foundry. White insisted that his kin take on a partner with practical experience, and George Waring, the proprietor of a small machine shop in Indiantown, joined the firm. The two erected a plant in Saint John to manufacture boilers, saws, edgers, and planers for area sawmills. They also engaged in steamship work.[31] Waring credited the National Policy tariffs with enabling him to compete against American producers.[32] After Thomas McAvity died in 1887, his six sons took command of the business and soon employed 130 hands in their foundry, machine and molding shops, and finishing and shipping rooms, filling orders for central Canadian markets. Saint John's nail, nut, and bolt business soared during the 1880s.

As Table 4 reveals, during the 1880s both the number of foundries and machine shops and the workforce had doubled in Saint John. Unlike the situation in Portland, the value of goods produced and profit margins had also increased during this period, perhaps inflated by the National Policy, yet the total dollar value of metalworking business still lagged behind Portland's (see Table 3). While both the Saint John and Portland metalworking businesses, stimulated by the growth of steam-powered machinery, had flourished during the 1880s, our case histories suggest that growing competition from both within and without the New England–Atlantic Canada borderlands region had

Table 4 Saint John's Foundries and Machine Shops, 1881–1891

	1881	*1891*
businesses	5	10
capital invested	n/a	$153,600
employees	71	151
value products	$146,800	$173,600
value-added	$19,100	$27,830

Source: Census of Canada, 1881, 1891

begun to favour the larger, more highly capitalized and technologically advanced firms.

THE IMPACT OF THE SECOND INDUSTRIAL REVOLUTION

By the 1890s larger firms, particularly in the locomotive industry, were competing across continental markets and had begun to challenge a sizable portion of the Portland and Saint John metalworking sector. When the rate of railway expansion began to slow at this time, firms like the Portland Company in Maine and the Harris Works (and their successors in Atlantic Canada) faced stiffer competition from these bigger, more modern firms located outside the northeastern borderlands region and closer to the larger urban transportation centres that could compete on a continental scale. Philadelphia's huge Baldwin Works, for instance, was turning out 557 locomotives for both domestic and export markets as early as 1883. By the turn of the century, the North American locomotive industry had been consolidated into two giants, Baldwin in Philadelphia and the American Locomotive Company (ALCO) with plants in both Schenectady and Montreal.[33] After 1900 the Grand Trunk turned to ALCO rather than to the Portland Company for its engines, and the Maine Central began to order a dozen engines at a time from ALCO's Schenectady works. Only scattered requisitions continued to be placed with the Portland Company by smaller railways in the northeastern borderlands such as the Windsor & Annapolis, the Quebec Central, and the Bangor & Piscataquis lines. Complicating matters for regional foundries, the price of railway rolling stock also declined substantially.[34]

The rationalization and concentration of locomotive and rolling stock manufacture under the aegis of monopoly capital exerted a similar impact on Saint John's metalworking sector. In 1888, for instance, James C. Harris, the New Brunswick molder who had created one of the largest foundries in Canada, died, leaving his firm rudderless at a critical moment. Subsequently the Harris foundry, machine shops, and car works were sold, dismantled, and transferred bodily to a firm in Amherst, Nova Scotia, and then later to Montreal.[35] Only the rolling mill remained in Saint John, and five years later a Boston syndicate attempted to take it over. When that failed, the mill merged with Foster's Nail Works.[36] Local merchants stepped in to bail out Waring & White's iron foundry during the 1890s. McAvity's brass works continued to prosper, but James Fleming abandoned the locomotive business rather than risk ruinous competition from the new giants. A few smaller firms either went out of business or left the Fundy port.[37]

At roughly the same time that the locomotive and railway rolling stock business had declined in both cities, the stories of metalworking in Portland and Saint John began to diverge. Even before 1880 some of Portland's metal shops had begun to benefit enormously from the exploitation of northern New England's staples by American monopoly capitalists, giving Portland a head start over Saint John (see Table 2). Without doubt the New England region's pulp and paper industry transcended all the others in capital invested, value of products, and number of workers employed. In the United States, paper consumption rose rapidly during the mid-nineteenth century. The popularity of paper shirt collars, for instance, stimulated the growth of pulp production. During the 1880s the sulfite chemical process had been perfected and soon dominated the industry.[38] By late 1894 there were thirty-one pulp mills and nineteen paper mills in Maine turning out over a thousand tons each day.[39] The Pine Tree State soon ranked second in total U.S. production, and by the turn of the century the large, highly capitalized American pulp and paper companies had invested about $12 million in capital and employed about 5,000 hands. With the formation of the giant International Paper Company in 1898, the pulp and paper industry reached a new level of concentration in a giant single firm that accounted for about 70 percent of all American newsprint production.[40]

For one key foundry, the Portland Company, already under enormous competitive pressure by the 1880s (as we have noted) from the new American locomotive giants, the rise of the pulp and paper industry was a godsend. During that decade it began to fill some special orders from mills using the new sulfite process. The paper industry required huge tanks called digesters that held the liquors that reduced trees to pulp. In 1885 the Portland Company built its first large digester for the nearby S.D. Warren paper company, and by the next winter it was building "lots of tanks," a rotary furnace, and boxcars for the same firm.[41] The burgeoning pulp and paper industry also ordered iron smokestacks, stand pipes, flume work, and penstocks from Portland's oldest foundry. Although the company sold some pulp digesters and paper mill goods to New York, Quebec, New Brunswick, and even California and Japanese firms, the bulk of its orders came from Maine and New Hampshire mills. Of twenty-one regional pulp and paper companies using the Portland Company's specially built equipment during this period, fifteen were located in Maine, five in New Hampshire, and one in Vermont.[42] "Manufacturing pulp-mill machinery," the editor of the *Industrial Journal* noted in 1888, "is getting to be a considerable part of the company's work."[43]

While the paper industry was the largest of the firm's new clients, the region's canneries, cotton and woollen mills, and ice companies all demanded more and more boilers. A flyer from the Portland Company during this era listed twenty-six cotton and woollen mills using its boilers: nineteen were in Maine, two each in New Hampshire, Massachusetts, and Rhode Island, and one in South Carolina.[44] During the summer of 1887 the firm complained of being "driven" by orders for steam retorts from corn-packing companies "all over" Maine. At the same time it continued installing and repairing marine boilers for ocean-going steamers and fishing boats.[45]

Declining orders for railway rolling stock coupled with growing orders from expanding hinterland resource-based industries, gave Portland Company management no choice but to respond to changing industrial conditions. The firm was reorganized under the direction of the experienced manager of the Portland Rolling Mills. Charles Milliken discharged the superintendent of locomotive construction, a 25–year veteran, along with several foremen. He enlarged and re-equipped the firm's railway shops to turn out more items serving the resource hinterland of northern New England.[46] While the Portland Company continued to produce the occasional locomotive until 1906 and specialized railway rolling stock until 1911, a mix of boilers, snowploughs, marine engines, pulp and paper digesters, stand pipes, and all kinds of repair work made up the bulk of the business from the 1890s until well into the twentieth century. "An impression prevails quite generally that we manufacture nothing but Locomotives," a Company advertisement of that era noted. "We wish to correct this by saying, we are well equipped for all kinds of Pulp and Paper Mill (heavy) Machinery and for Castings, Boilers, Digesters, etc. For Pulp Work. Our newly equipped Boiler Shop is able to handle all kinds of boiler and tank work economically." The company could produce "anything made of iron or steel that goes to equip a railroad, pulp or paper mill, lumber mill or factory."[47] Some if its specialty items even found markets outside New England: for instance, six boilers for the city of Chicago, rotary steam snow shovels for Paterson, New Jersey, tanks to pulp mills in New York State, and passenger elevators for New York City buildings.[48]

The company's new strategy, relying heavily upon the needs of the region's surging, resource-based economy, pushed up employment from 270 in 1892 to 350 hands by the summer of 1893. By then it was building the largest digesters in the world, measuring 47 feet high and 14 feet in diameter. Company crews erected penstocks at the new Rumford Falls sulfite mills and installed the first of nineteen boilers at a large new pulp mill in Berlin, New Hampshire.[49]

During the depression of the 1890s employment at the Portland Company fell to 250. Although the firm still repaired locomotives and steamers engaged in the winter port trade, "the plant ... kept pace with the rapid growth of the pulp and paper industry of the state and [could] manufacture anything required in a pulp mill at short notice." As a result, employment was back up to 300 by late 1899 and the company boasted of becoming the region's largest manufacturer of pulp digesters.[50] By June of 1901 the payroll had reached 400, largely on the basis of its work for the pulp and paper industry.[51] Two years later it was reported that the previous year had been "very prosperous" with the "largest business in their history." Its boiler shop was fabricating penstocks, erecting stand pipes, and building boilers, digesters, feeders, draught tubes, and wheel cases. Another department installed passenger and freight elevators in a variety of Maine and some Massachusetts buildings. The car shop built log bunks and flat cars for use in the woods, and stone cars for Maine's granite industry. The foundry made castings for the engines of the U.S. battleship *Georgia* under construction at the nearby Bath Iron Works. The firm's new electrical department installed lights on the steamer *Catherine*, wired a government dredge, and sold voltage regulators throughout North America.[52] This new pattern of business continued throughout the first two decades of the twentieth century and confirmed the ability of Portland's venerable metalworking concern to sail through the rough seas blown up by the second Industrial Revolution.

Although eighteen foundries and machine shops still operated in Portland by 1900, most of them remained quite small firms employing ten or fewer men.[53] Since an increasing number of Maine firms had begun to place their orders for boilers and steam engines with Boston foundries, the smaller Portland metalworking shops survived largely by specializing in products demanded by the city's hinterland market, such as canning machinery, canners' dies and solder, metal seals for bottled goods, yacht engines, brass goods, and repair work. After 1900 some machinery firms like Dunton-Chenery Company no longer

Table 5 Portland's Foundries and Machine Shops, 1900–1920

	1900	*1909*	*1920*
businesses	18	21	18
capital	$1,179,487	$1,615,000	$3,006,169
employed	528	483	710
goods produced	$683,528	$1,200,000	$4,195,381
value-added	$130,027	$587,000	$2,354,246

Source: U.S. Census, 1900, 1910, 1920

Table 6 Employment in Portland Metals and Machinery Sector, 1920

branch	*males*		*females*		
auto bodies	5		1		
boilers	6				
iron, steel bar	320		4		
cans	300		100		
capping irons	5				
machinery	608		29		
tinware	4				
marine hardware	322		19		
metal work	3				
metal jar covers	37		44		
sheet metal work	49		4		
steel beams	60				
stoves	87		3		
Totals	1,806	+	204	=	2,010

Source: Maine Bureau of Industrial and Labor Statistics, Report for 1919–20, 32–40

made their own products but instead began to market steam, gasoline, kerosene, and hot air engines, electric motors, and sawmill machinery manufactured elsewhere.[54]

The trend toward specialization persisted after 1900. Some of the larger Portland metalworking firms producing consumer goods flourished, while others without a secure market or sufficient capital struggled. Portland Stove Foundry pushed its Atlantic Wood Furnace for households in northern New England and branched out into larger furnaces for schools and churches.[55] Megquier & Jones sold metal building materials and machinery to the region's pulp and paper mills. F.E. Hitchings began repairing the boilers of Stanley steamer autos. Southworth Brothers was established after the turn of the century to manufacture printing and bookbinding machinery for the New England region as well as for foreign markets. National Metal Seal

Company's canning jar tops were popular throughout the United States.[56]

Recall that (South) Portland's rolling mill had been bailed out at the turn of the century by Boston capitalists, who had rebuilt it after a fire in 1899. By 1910 this firm had a 25-ton open hearth furnace under construction that was designed to produced 100 tons of bar iron daily by a workforce of 225 men. A year later the firm closed briefly for lack of business, but wartime demand for munitions gave the enterprise a new lease on life, and by 1919–20 it had become one of the largest employers in the Portland area with 320 males and 4 females. It is likely that a portion of the company's product was sold to Boston firms.[57]

At the conclusion of World War I the number of foundries and machine shops in Portland had declined by three to eighteen. On the other hand, capitalization had nearly doubled from $1.6 million in 1909 to slightly more than $3 million a decade later. The number of wage earners in the city's chief metalworking industry had risen to 710, the value of products had increased over six times, and value-added had risen eighteen times. By 1920 most of the machinery in these plants was powered by electricity rather than by steam, a change reflected in the appearance of a new firm – Maine Electric – among the manufacturers of machinery in the Forest City. Four metals shops now employed more than 100 hands; most of those remaining were tiny by comparison.[58]

Thanks for the most part to the increasingly diversified resource economy of northern New England, to expanding urban and rural consumer markets in Portland's hinterland, and to the boiler and ship repairing work stemming from the city's winter port trade with Canada, Portland's metals industry continued to expand substantially after 1900. As Table 6 shows, by 1920 over 2,000 men and women found jobs in the city's metals sector. Portland's (and South Portland's) machinery and marine hardware firms alone accounted for nearly half the jobs in this sector. While fruit and vegetable canning had tapered off in the Maine city, this regional industry was still responsible for the employment of nearly 500 Portlanders who turned out cans, capping irons, and metal jar covers for hinterland "corn shops." Portland Stove Foundry's ninety employees continued to manufacture a variety of stoves and furnaces to ward off the effects of New England winters, while another two firms employed nearly 400 hands to roll and assemble structural steel. With the exception of two of the largest firms (American Can Company with 400 employees and Bancroft & Martin Rolling Mill's 324 men and women), most of the city's metal shops still remained under the ownership and direction of local rather than outside capital.

It is worth noting in passing at least one of the "spread effects" beyond the metalworking sector generated in Portland by Maine's burgeoning paper industry. At the turn of the century the Portland Stone Ware Company began to manufacture brick linings for the Portland Company's pulp digesters. Soon the plant was "taxed to its utmost capacity to produce these linings in sufficient quantities to supply the demand."[59] It also made special tile – each brick contained 600 holes – through which pulp chemicals could drain. Its clay linings found their way into locomotive and stationary boilers and smelting furnaces. By 1904 the firm employed 300 hands, demonstrating another beneficial facet of the northern New England's pulp and paper industry for Portland's economy.[60]

As we have already seen, the nineteenth century rationalization and concentration of North American metalworking in the locomotive sector exerted a comparable impact on Saint John. But without its hinterland under active development by outside (largely, "monopoly") capital like Portland's, the Fundy port's urban economy and population growth continued to lag behind that of the Maine city. Most notably, a vigorous pulp and paper industry never really got off the ground in the late nineteenth and early twentieth century New Brunswick. At first, the future had looked promising, and pulp mills using the mechanical grinding process had emerged in Saint John and Sussex during the 1860s, followed by more modern sulphite mills in Saint John and Chatham near the turn of the century. In 1894 an American-owned firm – Stetson, Cutler – began producing small quantities of pulp at Mispec near Saint John before closing doors in 1903 for reasons unknown.[61] In 1898, while Stetson, Cutler was still in operation, the city's merchants sent the mayor overseas to persuade a Manchester capitalist to put up £65,000 for a city pulp mill. However, this facility, completed in 1900 and located at Union Point in Saint John (the site of the Irving Company's present-day mill), soon experienced serious financial problems, and by 1914 it was turning out only 60 tons of wood pulp a day. Two years later it was sold to consortium consisting of the American-owned International Paper and a Michigan firm.

As Bill Parenteau has pointed out, these early pulp-only mills remained marginal operations for a number of reasons, including the fact that New Brunswick lacked sufficient hydroelectric power. Furthermore, Crown timber leases remained under the control of the province's powerful sawn lumber interests rather than falling into the hands of pulp and paper entrepreneurs. In addition, the giant American market for newsprint remained off limits to Canadian mills until a U.S. tariff reduction in 1913 lowered trade barriers for this commodity. But instead of erecting new pulp and paper mills in New Brunswick during this period, large foreign capital-intensive firms like International Paper Company bought up lumber companies on the Miramichi River in order to harvest and then ship huge quantities of provincial pulpwood (in the order of 500,000 cords/year) to its new pulp and paper mill in Rumford, Maine.[62] For all these reasons, then, Saint John's metalworking industries received no significant business from the provinces's minuscule pulp and paper sector. One pulp company, organized during the 1880s to build a mill at Chatham, New Brunswick, is known to have purchased its engines, boilers, and machinery directly from England, Scotland, and Germany rather than from provincial metalworking shops.[63] Clearly, from the perspective of Saint John's turn-of-the-century elites, the city's economic destiny required a new strategy.

A NEW WINTER PORT

By the 1880s the centre of Portland's economy had begun to shift from waterfront-related commerce to the fabrication and retailing of goods for the northern New England region. Conversely, Saint John elites, lacking capital to pursue comparable opportunities in their own regional hinterland, kept their gaze fixed on the city's waterfront and set out to transform it into the Atlantic terminus of Canada's new transcontinental Canadian Pacific Railway. The arrival in 1889 of the first CPR trains in Saint John completed the initial stage of the Fundy city's campaign to displace Portland as Canada's primary winter port. The second stage began almost immediately when officials drew upon substantial public funds to modernize the city's port facilities. By 1904 the city of Saint John alone had spent approximately $900,000 in dredging, wharves, warehouses, and related facilities, supplemented by funds from Ottawa and the CPR. At a time when English-speaking imperialists were anticipating the economic and strategic integration of the British Empire, two of the board of trade's officers successfully promoted a subsidized "Fast Atlantic" steamship route between England and the port of Saint John. Ottawa agreed, and regular trips between Saint John and Liverpool began during the winter of 1895–96. In subsequent years, port-related business stimulated a flow of capital into Saint John's construction, metals, and provisioning industries. It also spawned new enterprise such as shipbuilding and repairing.[64] In short, the New Brunswick port used its harbour to reach beyond a relatively more barren hinterland than Portland's in terms of economic activity in order to stimulate its local metropolitan functions.

How successful was this strategy? Tables containing data on the number of foundries and machine shops (Table 7), or metals and

Table 7 Foundries and Machine Shops in Saint John, 1891–1911

	1891	*1901*	*1911*
businesses	10	11	8
employees	151	126	470
capital	$153,600	$129,306	$591,500
goods produced	$173,600	$189,745	$512,324
value-added	$27,830	$86,147	$145,911

Source: Census of Canada, 1891, 1901, 1911 (Note: data from 1921 not yet available)

machinery sector (Table 8), the amount of capital invested, the number employed, the value of goods produced, and value-added for the years 1891, 1901, 1911 and/or 1914 reveal that Saint John, while still lagging behind its sister city in Maine, had accomplished some important gains, especially in numbers employed by foundries and machine shops.

Comparing Tables 7 and 8, we can see that the Fundy port's metalworking industries reaped an even greater advantage from its new winter port. (Note, however, that an indeterminate number of firms listed in Table 8, while engaged in metalworking, are not "foundries and machine shops.") On the eve of World War I, the city virtually matched its Maine rival in the number of firms doing metalworking business, although the sector's employment level in 1914 was just two-thirds that of Portland's in 1920. (Comparable census data from Saint John for the postwar census [1921] are currently unavailable to researchers.)

As we have seen, the rationalization and concentration of North American metalworking exerted a similar impact on both these metropolises in the northeastern borderlands region. For reasons already discussed, no pulp and paper industry or an equivalent economic stimulus appeared on the scene during the first two decades of the twentieth century to alter Saint John's laggard status. Without its hinterland under active development by outside capital, the Fundy port's urban economy and population growth lagged behind the Maine city's expansion despite a notable stimulus from the new winter port activity.

Still, Table 7 reveals that some Saint John metalworking firms, like their counterparts in Portland, had successfully weathered the passage through the second Industrial Revolution. Eight foundries and machine shops persisted to 1911, most of them turning out specialty work for the new winter port–related activities. Like Portland's, Saint John's were much more highly capitalized firms that employed a workforce three and one-half times larger than at the turn of the century.

Table 8 Employment in Saint John Metals and Machinery Sector, 1914

Firm and specialties	*No. employed*
axes, edge tools, springs:	
Campbell Bros.	25
Josiah Fowler Co.	50
machinery and gas engines:	
Phoenix Foundry (James Fleming)	150
Union Foundry & Machine Wks	100
J. Fred Williamson	20
copper and brass goods:	
G. Hevenor Ltd.	12
safe mfgr and locksmith:	
H.T. Iddiols	5
elevators, bolts, rivets:	
Wm. Lewis & Sons	20
E.S. Stephenson Co.	10
wire nails:	
Maritime Nail Co.	140
James Pender Co.	80
Cda Nail/Wire	50
brass, iron foundries:	
T. McAvity & Sons	400
stoves, ranges	
McLean, Holt & Co.	75
iron products:	
Portland Rolling Mills	110
Saint John Iron Works	100
J.E. Wilson Ltd	30

total no. metalworking firms, 1914: 17;
total no. employees in metalworking firms, 1914: 1,377

Source: Saint John NB Canada, *Canada's Winter Shipping Port* (Saint John: Issued under the Direction of the Common Council, 1914), 97–8.

Both the value of goods produced and profits earned appear to have climbed sharply. Although it is impossible to know for certain, these notable gains, accelerating over the next three years (see Table 8), were probably derived from winter port–related business.

Yet by comparison to the growth of Portland's foundries and machine shops during the early twentieth century, Saint John metalworking enterprise still lagged. By 1909 there were twenty-one such establishments in Portland employing 579 workers and only eight in Saint John giving jobs to 470 men (see Tables 5, 7). The Maine city's firms commanded 37% more capital, produced 43% more goods in dollar value, and yielded approximately 25% more profit than the

Saint John foundries. By 1920 they required 2,246 horsepower to operate their plants, of which all but 100 hp was provided by electricity. The absence of cheap electrical power in the Saint John region undoubtedly retarded growth of comparable secondary manufacturing.[65]

CONCLUSION

This explicit comparison of the evolution of the two fundamentally similar urban economies has revealed much about the patterns of economic growth and change in Portland and Saint John between 1880 and 1920. During that period, Portland's population and economy grew much more rapidly than that of Saint John; a direct comparison helps to explain why one gained an advantage over the other. It is appropriate to compare these two northern borderland cities during this period because they shared several fundamentals in common: their forest-dominated hinterland resources were remarkably similar, and both had served to different degrees for varying periods from the 1850s into the 1920s as winter ports of Canada. While a detailed comparison of all the business sectors in these cities over four decades remains beyond the scope of this paper, one key sector – metalworking – has served as a reasonably accurate indicator of the relative stages of the two urban economic growth cycles during the major transformation wrought by the second Industrial Revolution.

In 1880 Saint John contained 18 percent more people than Portland, yet the Maine port's metalworking sector (Table 2) was significantly larger in all four categories, probably because of its two strategic advantages: a somewhat more populous and developed hinterland region than Saint John that was dependent upon Portland's services; and the Maine city's effective control over the lion's share of Canada's seasonal winter port business at that time. Then two major factors intervened. At first, the second Industrial Revolution exerted a deleterious impact upon the two cities' foundries and machine shops, reshaping both urban economies by consolidating the manufacture of railway locomotives and rolling stock into a smaller number of highly capitalized, technologically efficient plants located in central Canada and the United States. But then, large amounts of new U.S. "monopoly capital" poured into the Maine city's timber-rich hinterland – mostly from the pulp and paper industry but also from lumber, granite, ice, slate, and vegetable harvesters and processors – thereby creating new opportunities in Portland's metalworking shops to manufacture machinery and tools. At the same time the expanding New England resource towns enlarged Portland's regional market for consumer goods. Third, fuelled by the wheat boom and massive immigration to the Canadian prairies, Portland's winter port activities at the turn of the century also stimulated new foundry, machine shop, and marine hardware enterprise. Consequently, readier access to American capital, entrepreneurship, and markets generated a more balanced, self-sustaining economic and demographic growth cycle in Portland than in Saint John during this period. Meanwhile, as Larry McCann points out, the more fragile urban expansion of the Maritimes "reflected the growth of tariff-sheltered industry and focussed on the region's two major ports (with Halifax exceeding Saint John in its rate of growth) and along the line of the Intercolonial Railway."[66]

As Portland's industries capitalized on the fortuitous emergence of a pulp and paper industry (and, to a lesser extent, upon its other hinterland resources) in northern New England, the forest-rich hinterland of Saint John in New Brunswick and along the Fundy shore remained less exploited until after World War I. As a result of the lack of demand generated by a comparable "growth engine," Saint John's consumer market remained less than half the size of Portland's, grew more slowly, and after World War I frequently succumbed to the control of central Canadian manufacturers who were able to offer their goods and services from warehouses and branch plants erected in the Maritimes.[67] By the time the New Brunswick pulp and paper industry finally got off the ground during the 1920s and 1930s, it tended to rely upon standardized machinery manufactured in Europe and the United States rather than tailor-made equipment produced by Saint John's foundries and machine shops. Portland's fortuitous ability to prosper from the exploitation of northern New England's resources had served to insulate it from the longer-run consequences of the consolidating effects of monopoly capital on the railway locomotive and rolling-stock industry.

Lacking other remedies, Saint John elites returned to a mercantile strategy to invigorate their urban economy and thereby stem the outward flow of their city's residents. A tradition shaped by the Fundy port's historic transoceanic links to Europe, reinforced by a strong local cultural identity derived from the Loyalist City's historic Imperial connection, helped bolster these efforts. Census data suggest that the growth of a winter port facility in Saint John harbour during the first two decades of the twentieth century had exerted a beneficial impact upon the city's metalworking industry. Nevertheless, Saint John's overall population growth continued to lag behind Portland's.

Certainly the timing of the arrival of three key agents of change central to the fate of both cities – the railway, the winter port, and the pulp and paper industry – had also been an important factor. For the Maine city the successive arrival of each during the 1840s, 1850s, and 1880s proved beneficial. For the Fundy port each of these exogenous factors was experienced several decades later (1870s, 1890s, 1920s) during a less favourable climate for the generation of balanced economic growth. Seen from this comparative, cross-national perspective, then, it may perhaps not have been spatial factors, railway freight rates, or tariff policies so much as the different timing and impact of forces generated by the second Industrial Revolution that best explain the remarkably different patterns of economic development these two borderlands cities experienced between 1880 and 1920.

13

Maine-Maritimes Folklore: The Lumberwoods Connection

EDWARD D. IVES

This brief chapter distills four decades of work on the folklore of the lumber camps in Maine and the Maritimes, drawing in particular on my *Joe Scott: The Woodsman-Songmaker.*[1] Since the song repertoire under discussion will be unfamiliar to most people, my analysis will necessarily be cast in very general terms. Most typical of these songs are the English-language story-songs, ballads if you will, and a special set of them officially known as British broadsides but more colloquially called "come-all-ye's," from their habit of opening with a stanza like:

> Come all of you brave shantyboys wherever you may be
> Come sit upon the deacon seat and listen unto me
> I'll sing the Jam on Gerry's Rock, a story you should know
> 'Bout the bravest of all shantyboys, our foreman young Munroe.

They tend to be long and sad, telling of some bold adventure or love affair, and they are apt to be moralistic in the "take warning by my fate" mode. The entire genre arose in eighteenth- and nineteenth-century Britain, where printers hired hacks to produce them for sale on slips, or broadsides (hence their name), but hundreds of them were also turned out in the New World.[2] Ballads of this type are found all over North America, but there are regional patterns, one of which is highlighted here.

Call it the northern tradition. It extends from Newfoundland through Prince Edward Island, Nova Scotia (including Cape Breton),

New Brunswick, Maine, Ontario, the northern areas of New Hampshire, Vermont, New York, and Pennsylvania to Michigan, Wisconsin, and Minnesota (notice, by the way, that Ohio, Indiana, and Illinois are *not* included).[3] This tradition has an identifiable singing style, and its repertoire is distinctive enough that most exceptions turn out not to be exceptions at all but are rather easily explained.

The common denominator to all these regions was the nineteenth-century lumbercamp. Without being too fussy about competing claims along the line, we can say that the North American lumber industry had its first great development in Maine and New Brunswick in the early nineteenth century; then, as the century moved on, while the industry continued unabated in the east, it extended westward, reaching the vast pineries of Michigan, Wisconsin, and Minnesota in the 1860s.[4] Thousands of Maine men followed that expansion, and thousands of men from the Maritimes came to Maine to fill the gap they left. Some stayed, while others returned home each spring. Thus, during the second half of the nineteenth century, there was a steady traffic of labouring men coming and going between Maine and the Maritimes and Maine and the upper Midwest. And with these men went their intellectual and aesthetic baggage.

Lumbering was hard physical six-days-a-week daylight-to-dark work for these men. Almost all of their non-working time was spent in the bunkroom, a none-too-large, pole-floored, rough-hewn room dimly lit by kerosene lanterns, probably overheated by a big ram-down woodstove and filled with anywhere from a dozen to seventy-five or eighty men who had put in a hard day's work and had little opportunity to wash. This was the woodsman's home for several cold and dreary months, often without a break right through from October through March. No official provision was made for recreation. Men could gab, read (if they could find a book or newspaper), and play cards and the like of that, but if there was going to be any more elaborate entertainment, they would have to provide it for themselves. And provide it they often did.

Their weekday evenings would generally be work-oriented, looking, that is, toward the next day's work. Sharpening an ax, mending a torn sweater, teamsters looking to their horses, or repairing harness would allow for nothing much in the line of organized entertainment. On Saturday night, though, with no work day ahead, there was apt to be singing, step-dancing, storytelling, recitations, sometimes (according to the late Angus Enman of Spring Hill, Prince Edward Island) in quite an organized and insistent format: "Saturday night, you see, when you'd come into the camp after supper you had to tell a story or sing a song or dance. If you didn't, they'd ding you; they'd put the dried codfish to you ... They had these old dried codfish, and if you wouldn't sing or dance or do something ... they'd take the dried codfish and throw you down and whale you with it!"[5]

That wasn't how it was in every camp, and of course there was the occasional camp where there was no singing at all, but the preponderance of the evidence is that the old come-all-ye's – sung in the traditional solo, hard-voiced, unaccompanied way – were a standard feature of lumbercamp entertainment all through the region under discussion. It would be impossible for me to say how often elderly woodsmen have told me they learned this-or-that song in such-and-such a camp, and men who were known in their home communities as singers would be asked on arriving back from the woods if they'd learned any new songs that year. Without question it was the lumbercamp that acted as the beating heart of northern song tradition, and it was the men moving from camp to camp and camp to home who carried songs back and forth from one end of the region to the other.

Given such an established tradition, it should not be surprising to find that within it there was a creative tradition in which new songs growing out of the lumberman's life itself were constantly being created. Several of them became very well known and versions of them have been collected from the Maritimes to Minnesota. Just one example is "The Banks of the Little Eau Pleine." Set in central Wisconsin, it was composed by a timber cruiser named W.N. "Billy" Allen some time in the 1870s.[6] In 1958 I collected a splendid version of it from Charlie Gorman at his home in Lot Seven, Prince Edward Island. Charlie, in turn, had learned the song in a lumbercamp near Sherman Mills, Maine, around 1900. Just to make the whole back-and-forth pattern even more neat, Billy Allen himself was born in St Stephen, New Brunswick, in 1843.

My own special scholarly interest was in people like Billy Allen – woodsmen who made up songs. Who were they? What inspired them, and – most relevant here – how widely were their songs known? Larry Gorman and Lawrence Doyle (both from Prince Edward Island) were satirists who blistered or poked fun at people they worked with and lived among; their songs were well known locally, but, being thoroughly topical, never entered any wider tradition. Joe Scott, on the other hand, took the long come-all-ye's for his model, writing about death on the job, murder, unhappy love, and other thoroughly universal and broadside-ballad themes, and I have collected well over two hundred versions of his songs. The lumbercamp tradition spread them all the way from Berlin, New Hampshire, to Tignish, Prince Edward Island.

Yet it proved impossible to discover even one version of these songs farther west. It was a simple matter of demographics. Lured by better wages, Maine woodsmen began moving west after the Civil War. The Panic of 1873 intensified this exodus, extending it into the 'eighties, after which it slowed down significantly. We can see this slowdown reflected nicely in the song tradition. Earlier songs like "The Jam on Gerry's Rock," "The Little Brown Bulls," and "Canaday-I-O" are about equally well known in the Midwest and the Northeast, but "The Banks of the Little Eau Pleine," composed in the 'seventies in Wisconsin, is far better known in the Midwest. "James Whalen," a river-drive song about an accident on the Mississippi in 1878, and "Harry Bale," about an 1879 sawmill accident in Lapeer, Michigan, have been well collected in the Midwest but are found in only one or two versions in the east. Conversely, "Peter Emberly," composed near Boiestown, New Brunswick, in 1881, is one of the best-known woods ballads in the Northeast, but it has rarely been found in the Midwest.

It is too bad that we do not have datable songs from the later 'eighties to make this almost-too-neat case still neater, but the point is made that as the movement of northeastern woodsmen back and forth to the Midwest slowed down, so did the exchange of songs, until by the late 'nineties both had almost ceased entirely. It was in the late 'nineties and early 1900s that Joe Scott's ballads were created and went into circulation. Thus, while they were in plenty of time to move freely in the Northeast, they were at least twenty years too late to be carried to the Midwest camps – restricted by economics and demography.

Some questions, however, remain to be answered conclusively. There has been much discussion over the past decade or so about "the two Maines." While there have been various attempts at drawing the line between the two, the general concept has been northern-southern. A little more adventurously, I have often said that – if we don't expect too much of it – a line from Mount Washington to Calais rather neatly separates Maine's two cultural watersheds: to the south New England, to the north the Maritime Provinces. In general that line has held up rather well, and never better than in accounting for distributional exceptions – especially northern songs found south of my line. For instance, I was puzzled when a man from Sanford, Maine – deep in the New England area – sang three of Joe Scott's ballads for me. As it turned out, he had grown up in the north and learned them while working in the woods and on the drives along the Mattawamkeag River. Then there was a man from Wells – also well south of my hypothetical line – who knew many songs that matched very nicely with standard woods repertoire. Sure enough, it turned out he was originally from central New Brunswick, and he learned his songs in the lumberwoods there. Beyond this one rather narrow field of ballad repertoire, I have not submitted my concept to anything even remotely resembling rigorous statistical examination, but an idea that has worked well for one aspect of culture will often be applicable to others. I submit it as a challenge for consideration.

A final element must be factored in to this matter of repertoire and distribution. In my fieldwork over the past forty years, I have found ten good singers from the Maritimes to every one from Maine, and even those who *were* from Maine were often second-generation Maritimers or had other strong Maritime connections. Taking that one step further, most of those thousands of province men who came to work in the Maine woods had two things in common: they were from poor rural areas and they were heavily of Irish or sometimes Scottish ancestry. How often retired woodsmen have replied, when asked about singing in the camps, with something like "Yeah, those old PIs, they were the ones!"[7] The comments of Emile Leavitt of Old Town, Maine, are to the point here: "There was an awful lot of people from the Province of New Brunswick and Nova Scotia. You know, English-speaking people, Scotch, Irish. They worked in the Maine woods then, and they had a lot of these songs, you know, ballads. Saturday nights they'd sing all night almost, 'til twelve o'clock. It was always ballads about somebody's girl or something – about the girl they left behind, you know."[8] The old song tradition still flourished for them *at home*, and the lumbercamps simply offered an arena for its extension.

So much for the lumberwoods. Here is a second and final challenge. If lumbering formed a strong Maine-Maritimes musical bridge, how about fishing? Certainly there was contact. Maine vessels were in and out of ports like Halifax and St. John's, not to mention dozens of smaller ones, and it was not unusual for province men to sign on Maine vessels. Without question there were occasions – both afloat and ashore – analogous to Saturday nights in the lumbercamp bunkhouse, occasions where singing would have been an accepted and expected form of recreation and expression. But I have never seen any evidence that fishing created a cultural continuity like that created by the lumbercamps. Let some younger scholar – wearing my blessing on his or her head – show that I am wrong.

14

Canadian and American Policy Making in Response to the First Multi-species Fisheries Crisis in the Greater Gulf of Maine Region

DEBORAH C. TREFTS

As Maritimes and New England fisheries depletion reached crisis proportions in the nineteenth century new policies were necessitated.[1] Each nation reacted, in different ways, to the diminution or disappearance of multiple species of food-fish that, prior to the nineteenth century, had sustained coastal and river communities in the Greater Gulf of Maine Region (GGOMR, see map).[2] At a time when fishery science, marine biology, and environmental history were in their infancy, governments and fishers confronted the following conundrum: Could the same number of people, in the same time, on the same fishing ground, with the same gear, catch the same number of fish as they could formerly?[3]

In much of New England the answer to this question was "no" for anadromous salmon, river herrings, and shad throughout much of the nineteenth century; for inshore and nearshore[4] halibut, cod, haddock, hake, and mackerel by mid-century; and for coastal scup, tautog, and sea bass by the eve of the Civil War. In much of the Maritime provinces the answer was "no" for salmon, shad, and river herrings by mid-century; and for inshore and nearshore cod, haddock, and mackerel by the mid-1860s.[5] These concurrent and sequential fishery declines contradict two current assumptions. The first is that prior to the twentieth century, if not World War II, sea fisheries were regarded as inexhaustible; their natural supply was sufficient to meet demand.[6] The second is that the collapse of multiple Canadian and American fisheries in the GGOMR in the early 1990s was unprecedented. Evidence of declining and depleted fisheries in Canada, the United States, England, France, Germany, Italy, and Russia during the 1800s belies such sweeping generalizations.[7]

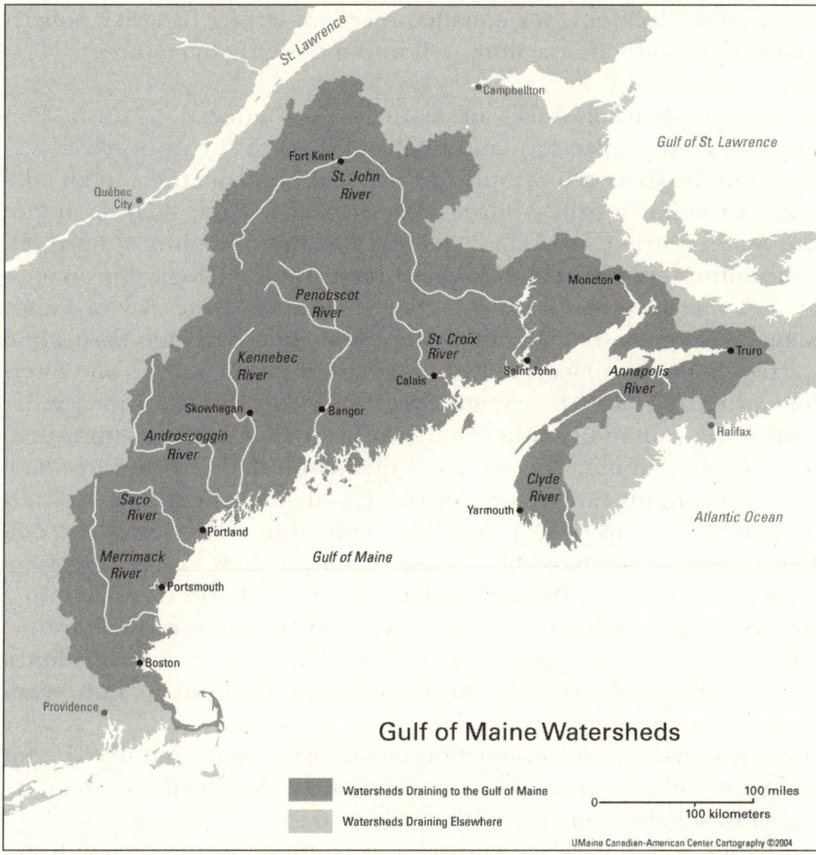

14.1 Watershed of the Gulf of Maine and major river basins. After Richard D. Kelly, Jr, *Gulf of Maine Watershed* (Augusta, Maine: Maine State Planning Office, 1991).

Accurate hindsight enhances contemporary insight, foresight, and problem solving. Awareness of the historical decline of river, coastal, and ocean species in the GGOMR, and of Canadian and American policy making in response to it, puts the region's present-day fisheries crisis in clearer perspective. It seems useful, therefore, to consider the long-term diminution of fish stocks beginning with the seventeenth- and eighteenth-century antecedents of the nineteenth-century crisis. The ensuing policy-making process can then be summarized – from problem recognition and assessment to policy promotion and selection – for both Canada and the United States, first at the state/provincial level prior to the late 1860s, and later by the federal level after Confederation and the Civil War. Canada took less than a year (1867–1868) and the United States nearly two years (1871 and 1872) to establish different, yet equally precedent-setting fisheries policies that would guide their actions well into the twentieth century.

Stories of plentiful stocks of marine fishes enticed Spanish, Portuguese, French (Breton), and English fishers to the GGOMR's coastal waters in the sixteenth century.[8] In the Gulf of Maine the annual infusion of roughly a trillion litres of freshwater run-off, tidal mixing of deepwater nutrients and coastal waters, and intermingling of northern and southern marine fishes fostered remarkable biological productivity and species diversity. In the central Gulf of Maine–Bay of Fundy watershed, more than sixty rivers formed nine drainage basins and thirteen estuaries that served as nurseries for juvenile fishes and filters for waste.[9] Accounts by voyagers and colonial officials of the earlier years of the non-indigenous fisheries provide useful information about the location, abundance, size, and quality of marine fishes to which later populations can be roughly compared. The GGOMR was typically described in terms of its profitable commodities. What was scarce in Europe was a merchantable "resource" in the New World. Fish were regarded as free goods until they were captured and extracted on a species-by-species basis; thereafter, each fish represented a distinct commodity with a specific value.[10] As Massachusetts Bay colonist William Wood observed in 1634, no country known to Europeans yielded "more variety of fish, winter and summer ... not only for the present spending and sustenation of the plantations, but likewise for trade into other countries."[11] Gulf of Maine fisheries, therefore, were the most sought after in the Western world.

Atlantic cod, one of many species of bottom-dwelling "groundfish," was the most highly prized of the GGOMR's extensive array of fishes, and the first natural resource encountered by European explorers that was valuable enough to recoup the trans-Atlantic shipping costs. It immediately secured a foothold in the North Atlantic commercial economy, enabling New England colonists to purchase scarce European goods.[12] Cod formed the basis for North America's lucrative trade with Roman Catholics in southwestern Europe, whom the Pope admonished to eat fish, and with plantation owners in the tropical West Indies and American South, who supplied their slaves with inexpensive fish protein that kept well. Before refrigeration and the development of markets for fresh fish during the late nineteenth century, groundfish that were less readily preserved – notably haddock, hake, and pollock ("scale fish") – trailed behind cod, but were still important.

Voyagers' reports of particularly large and high quality codfish taken in shallow waters convinced fishers from England's southwest coast (West Country) that the stocks in New England's inshore and nearshore waters surpassed those off Newfoundland.[13] Plying the waters off New England for cod made sense for other reasons as well. Although Newfoundland's larger cod grounds were closer to England and Europe than were New England's, its fishery was more costly and perilous. Cod fishing off Newfoundland entailed waiting until late spring (mid-May) for the season to start, fishing from ships in dangerous offshore waters, enduring fog and stormy weather all season long, curing cod onshore at the mercy of the elements, and ending the season when ice conditions became too treacherous.[14] Although less extreme than off Newfoundland, conditions in the Maritime provinces, primarily the domain of the French, were considerably more difficult than in southern New England. The cod season started in early spring – sooner than in Newfoundland but later than in Massachusetts and New Hampshire. Arriving soon after the Pilgrims, Acadian settlers employed small boats in inshore waters for a subsistence, rather than a commercial fishery.

Off Massachusetts, early cod fishers used small boats in inshore waters and vessels in nearshore waters. Because weather and sea conditions were milder, the cod season began in mid-winter (February) and continued virtually year-round. West Countrymen, subsistence fishers from Virginia seeking protein for the starving colonists at Jamestown, and settlers in the Plymouth and Massachusetts Bay colonies thus concentrated their efforts off Massachusetts, New Hampshire, and Maine.[15] New England's premier fishing areas during this period were cod spawning and feeding grounds in nearshore, coastal, and estuarine waters where biological productivity was particularly high and many species of finfish and shellfish spent all or part of their life cycle. Cod abounded in the waters off the central coast of present-day Maine; fishing stations were established on Matinicus, Monhegan, and Damariscove islands, the Isles of Shoals, and on the coast at Pemaquid. Off New Hampshire, cod were prodigious near the Isles of Shoals.[16] The best cod fishing grounds on the Massachusetts coast were in Ipswich, Massachusetts, and Plymouth bays, and off Martha's Vineyard.[17] In the vicinity of these and other cod grounds, voyagers and settlers often noticed large populations of other groundfish species (especially haddock), flounders (notably halibut and plaice), mackerel, and herrings and river fishes.[18]

To attract their prey, early cod fishers used baited handlines. Herring – the *Clupeidae* family of pelagic, surface-schooling fishes – was one of the chief baits used, thus the exploitation of cod and herring progressed simultaneously. Many early accounts did not distinguish between Atlantic (sea) herring and river herring (also called "alewives" and *gaspereaux*), let alone between the two species of river herring common to the region, alewives and blueback herring, making population comparisons particularly difficult. Nevertheless, the abundance of herring in Passamaquoddy Bay, at the mouth of the St Croix River basin, impressed French explorers Pierre Dugua, Samuel de Champlain, and Sieur de Poutrincourt in the early 1600s. On the cod grounds off Matinicus Island, opposite Penobscot bay and river, Champlain found many sea herring. At night European ships harvesting cod on the banks commonly set gill nets for sea herring. John Josselyn surmised in 1670 that there were "infinite numbers" of river herrings along the Maine coast. When the region's settlers established a fishery for salt cod that was substantial enough for them to enter the export trade, the use of herring – both sea and river – as bait increased.[19]

Next to cod, the GGOMR's earliest settlers were most amazed by the abundance of anadromous species – marine fishes that spawn in freshwater.[20] The first governor of Acadia – the colony surrounding the *baie françoise* (present-day Bay of Fundy) – described the sea as "paved" with salmon and other fishes. More than 80 percent of the rivers of the present-day Maritime provinces were naturally accessible to large runs of Atlantic salmon, the most highly prized anadromous fish. Each spring and summer great quantities of river herrings, American shad (another member of the herring family), sturgeons, and striped bass also populated the naturally passable rivers, streams, and brooks from southwestern Nova Scotia to the Bay of Fundy to Passamaquoddy Bay and the St Croix River.[21]

The vast numbers of these species that frequented nearly all of the rivers and streams from the St Croix to the Housatonic in spring and summer were even more awe-inspiring. In New England, the rivers most renowned for their productivity were the Piscataqua and the Merrimack. The Piscataqua River–Great Bay Estuary system opposite the Isles of Shoals sustained one of the Atlantic's most diverse ecosystems and one of the continent's greatest salmon runs. Salmon, shad, river herrings, sturgeons, and striped bass skirted Plum Island, at the northern end of Ipswich Bay, and ran up the Merrimack and its tributaries through Massachusetts and New Hampshire until the White Mountains blocked their upstream passage. Shad, river herrings, and sturgeons migrated through Massachusetts and Boston bays into several estuaries and rivers. Wood claimed in 1634 that the shad in one such river, the Saugus, were "bigger than the English shad, and fatter."[22] Along with cod, William Bradford and Edward Winslow found shad in Plymouth Bay in the 1620s "in great abundance and take[n] with great ease at our doors," and Isaac de Passieres (~1628) saw "so many [river herrings] that it is quite amazing."[23] The Connecticut River, one of the best salmon rivers in the United States, hosted even greater numbers of shad, as well as large runs of striped bass and sturgeons. Because of its abundant resources, indigenous peoples called this river "the smile of God."[24]

As William Cronon has revealed, however, the economy that equated natural resources with production and money, treating "members of an ecosystem as isolated and extractable units," used these assets in an environmentally self-destructive manner that seemed careless and wasteful to European visitors.[25] New England's settlers were usually, though not always, more aggressive in their exploitation of natural resources than were Maritime settlers. Among other reasons, they immigrated in much larger numbers, they lived in a milder climate, and had better access to new lands and waterways when critical resources were exhausted, and they industrialized much sooner. Environmental historians have documented the profligate behaviour that precipitated three unanticipated, interrelated terrestrial ecological crises during the colonial period – deforestation,[26] topsoil depletion,[27] and beaver extirpation.[28]

These crises contributed to a postcolonial ecological crisis – watershed transformation. In clearing wooded and vegetated stream banks; routinely discarding sawdust and refuse in streams;[29] installing impassable dams, locks, and canals; controlling water-flow; degrading, flooding, and reclaiming wetlands;[30] and polluting waterways with industrial-strength contaminants,[31] New Englanders manipulated entire river systems. One largely unintended consequence was the widespread degradation and destruction of essential fish habitat. Combined, habitat loss and extensive overfishing resulted in two postcolonial marine ecological crises – the extirpation of anadromous fish stocks and the subsequent extirpation of inshore and nearshore coastal-ocean stocks. Together the two produced a socioecological crisis affecting not only multiple fish species but also riparian and coastal communities throughout the GGOMR. Although the historical antecedents of the region's first multi-species fisheries crisis were numerous, its most immediate human-induced cause was wasteful and excessive fishing, the focus here.

The problem of diminishing anadromous river species – initially river herrings, shad, and salmon, and later striped bass, sturgeons, and rainbow smelt[32] – developed over centuries in Maritime Canada and long preceded other fishery problems. Their decline corresponded with the growth of the region's population during and after the American Revolution (1775–1783) and with increased encroachment by American fishers following the depletion of New England's rivers. During the Revolutionary War the bank fisheries were shut down; salmon and river herrings were taken in such large numbers that localized declines occurred; and Nova Scotia became an independent base of fishing operations with Halifax at its centre, free from control by New England fishing interests. After the war most coastal towns had neither the capital for engaging in distant trade and using larger vessels nor the experience; thus the inshore mackerel, herring, sea bass, clam, and lobster fisheries expanded.[33]

Thousands of displaced Loyalists, many of whose possessions, property, and fortunes had been confiscated, emigrated *en masse* across the Gulf of Maine. The British government shipped essential foods, but it could not meet the demand, even after returning the poorest and sickest immigrants to America. It gradually discontinued its food bounty around 1785.[34] The anadromous fisheries then became the focus of increasingly intense fishing effort.[35] Along New Brunswick's river systems, grants of land ranging from 200 to 1000 acres apiece were given to the new colonists, partly because the enormous fish runs fostered prosperity. Salmon were the most highly sought, but shad and river herrings were also quite important. Fishing effort further intensified after the War of 1812 when the populations of New Brunswick and Nova Scotia swelled with mass immigration, mainly from Scotland and Ireland.[36]

The salmon fishery of the St Croix River watershed was the first in the province to experience a significant decline, but fisheries in other rivers were not far behind. The growth of the immense New Brunswick logging industry led to the construction of mill dams. After impassable dams were extended across the entire width of the river, the numbers of salmon began to diminish because they could no longer ascend the St Croix to their upstream spawning grounds. Already by 1815 it was evident throughout much of New Brunswick that the boom in the province's timber industry was occurring at the expense of its most important anadromous fisheries, and that efforts to catch salmon had greatly increased. Unrestricted overfishing, facilitated by insurmountable dams, was largely to blame.[37]

For similar reasons, a decade later Nova Scotia's abundant salmon, shad, and river herring fisheries also diminished markedly. Salmon returned annually to the rivers in sufficient numbers to meet local needs, but the province could no longer sustain a local export trade. In search of commercial quantities, some fishers sailed to the Gulf of St Lawrence, Newfoundland, and Labrador. The great majority in the Scotia-Fundy region, however, changed prey. Their substitution after the mid-1800s of alternative anadromous and inshore species – mainly adult sea herring, lobsters, striped bass, sturgeons, and sardines for depleted salmon, shad, and river herrings – triggered a second series of declines. Thereafter, many inshore fishers gradually extended their seaward range to within about ten nautical miles of shore.[38]

In both Nova Scotia and New Brunswick, provincial laws were enacted to stem the decline of commercially important fisheries, but they were rarely applied. Because the royal charter that had incorporated Parrtown (Saint John) stipulated that the harbour fishery between the high and low water marks on the eastern side of the St John River was to be regulated and managed by the City's Common Council, it was afforded special rights. The Council chose not to extend most of the fisheries laws pertaining to southern New Brunswick to this fishery.[39] In July 1850 New Brunswick's lieutenant governor directed Moses Henry Perley, the emigration officer at Saint John, to inspect the fisheries of the Bay of Fundy. Perley had grown up fishing, hunting, and trading with the Indians, and had previously investigated the fisheries of the Gulf of St Lawrence. Assisted by his son, he visited all of the rivers flowing into the Bay (including those in Nova Scotia) and met with many fishers and mill owners. His remarkable report graphically depicted the destruction of anadromous fishes and sea herring on their spawning grounds. Perley found that salmon had continued to decline in most rivers, and that shad and river herrings were scarce in many.[40] He believed that the care and preservation of the latter fishery were particularly important because cod appeared at the river mouths they frequented.[41]

Perley actively promoted, and helped draft, legislation that codified his recommendations. The New Brunswick Legislature's fisheries committee studied his report, endorsed his advice, and revised its sea and river fisheries laws in the *Fisheries Act of 1851*. Additional laws and regulations were periodically promulgated, the most extensive of which was the 1863 *Act Relating to the Coast and River Fisheries.* The harbour fisheries of Saint John were exempted. Salmon were the chief focus; no other anadromous species were specifically mentioned.[42] Despite the appointment of fishery wardens, these laws were no more effectively implemented and enforced than were those enacted prior to Perley's investigation.[43] In Nova Scotia two periods of active lawmaking by the Legislature to protect anadromous fisheries, particularly salmon (1851–1856 and 1864–1866) were negated by indifferent magistrates and by repeals.[44]

In New England, meanwhile, the decline of anadromous species had been evident long before the American Revolution. During New England's first 250 years, its anadromous and inshore fisheries were freely and intensively exploited. Harkening back to royal grants, residents throughout the region claimed the freedom to fish. The levelling of forests, plowing of fields, and monoculture of corn depleted topsoil within five to six years, yet colonial fields were not left to lie fallow. Unused corn stalks and other vegetation were fed to cattle and horses rather than being plowed back into the soil. Because livestock grazed on these fields day and night, livestock manure could not be gathered from paddocks and barns for use as fertilizer. Along the coast, colonial farmers used Atlantic menhaden and kelp as fertilizers. Farmers living along estuaries and stream banks adopted the foul-smelling practice of applying tens of thousands of river herrings, shad, and salmon to their fields to increase their productivity. Although these fishes did extend the productive life of the cornfields, wild animals dug them out of the soil, the fields continued to reek, and fish oil eventually spoiled the fields.[45] Farmers also used river herrings as feed for their livestock. Moreover, river fishes were a staple for hired hands, poor families, prisoners, and indigenous peoples.

Demand for salmon began in the 1630s when Bostonians developed a taste for it and wagonloads were transported from the Merrimack River, but until about 1745 many colonists considered shad unfashionable. As each species became more widely accepted, domestic and international markets quickly developed. Salmon production expanded with New England's rapidly growing population. Towns and small villages soon dotted the Merrimack and Connecticut river systems. Streams were blocked with dams to provide water for settlers, sawmills, gristmills, agricultural irrigation, and canals. Many dams prevented the passage of anadromous fishes, greatly reducing their ability to reach their upstream spawning grounds.[46] Weirs, spears, and dipnets were used to catch the fish that aggregated in the waters below mill dams and canal locks, searching for a way past them. Nets and seines proved so efficient that they gradually became the preferred fishing gear. By the early eighteenth century, when shad was still unpopular, nets were being crafted specifically to target salmon.[47]

Colonial records show that during the late seventeenth century anadromous fishes diminished rapidly in certain rivers. After the turn of the eighteenth century salmon failed periodically in the Merrimack; by 1720 such failures were customary. For decades the problem of declining fish populations was most evident in central New England's smaller streams. In the Boston market, the availability of salmon taken in rivers from Maine to Acadia masked its great diminution in the Merrimack, which was hastened by a ninety-yard-long net at Amesbury and an impassable dam at Concord. A pickled salmon trade developed between Maine, New York, and the mid-Atlantic region, putting further pressure on this resource. By 1750 Piscataqua salmon had declined alarmingly; sawmills, sawdust, and weirs were blamed. According to salmon historian R.W. Dunfield, "New Englanders were constructing more dams, clearing more land, polluting more water and netting more salmon than all of the other colonies combined, and the results were showing: in the rivers south of the Penobscot in Maine, salmon were disappearing."[48] Salmon downeast of the Penobscot were next in jeopardy.

The American Revolution exacerbated the decline of anadromous fish stocks. New Englanders had developed commercial fisheries for several species – most importantly cod, scale fish, sea herring, and mackerel. Until the presence of the British navy curtailed nearly all but the river and inland fisheries,[49] they had worked in inshore, nearshore, and offshore waters from the Mid-Atlantic to Davis Strait, including the GGOMR. During the war, boat fishers still supplied many coastal villages with a variety of fresh fish, but more remote communities relied almost entirely on river fish and shellfish.[50] In explaining the subsequent extirpation of many river herring stocks, Lorenzo Sabine focused on the myth of inexhaustibility. "On some of the rivers, where the fishery is now nearly extinct, the supply at the revolutionary era was considered inexhaustible ... farmers and fishermen were in the constant habit of filling wagons and boats at pleasure with scoop-nets and other simple implements."[51] Impassable dams, whether operational or abandoned but not removed, still facilitated overfishing of all of the river fishes. Because the American army needed protein, however, the colonists who contracted with the Continental Congress to supply fish were exempted from local restrictions on fishing gear and on fishing below dams.[52]

America's victory freed New England's merchants from the constraints of England's mercantilist policy, which had limited them to providing raw materials to British manufacturers. Existing enterprises and markets were revived and broadened. As the region's prostrate marine fishing industry slowly recovered and expanded, immense quantities of salmon, shad, and river herrings were captured for bait for the cod fishery, and for pickling and trading to the West Indies.[53] Moreover, value-added commodities were increasingly manufactured locally. Textile milling had begun in Massachusetts as early as the 1650s but had expanded lethargically until the end of the war. After 1790, when Rhode Island merchant Moses Brown replicated the water-powered cotton spinning machine and small-scale factory system first developed in England, rivers were dammed throughout New England to supply power to hundreds of cotton and weaving factories and to factories producing firearms, furniture, clocks, machine tools, shoes, and paper.[54] As Samuel Eliot Morison noted: "Every country town with a good-sized brook or river set up a textile or paper mill or iron foundry ... The center of interest in Massachusetts shifts from wharf to waterfall; by 1840 she had become predominantly a manufacturing state."[55] The effects of this shift on the fisheries soon became exacerbated.

Small-scale textile factories paved the way for large-scale industrialization in just three decades (1790~1820). The Waltham-Lowell factory system – featuring large-scale planned industrial communities at

Lowell (1822) and Lawrence (1847) – transformed the Charles and the Merrimack River basins. Most notably, channelization projects, canals, insurmountable dams, and enormous reservoirs harnessed, slowed, redirected, and irreversibly altered the Merrimack's rapidly flowing waters in southern New Hampshire and northeastern Massachusetts. In sucking the kinetic energy out of its powerful current and flooding its extensive riparian marshes,[56] they reduced its speed and its capacity for diluting pollutants before they reached the coastal waters above Ipswich Bay. Yet routine dumping of refuse, untreated waste, animal carcasses, dyes, chemicals, and many other industrial byproducts turned the Merrimack and many of its tributaries into virtual sewers. The Boston entrepreneurs and engineers who financed and controlled the Waltham-Lowell system successfully opposed actions to restore water quality and depleted fish stocks.[57]

New England's transformation from an agricultural to an industrial society exacerbated the problems caused by land-based environmental degradation, traditional mill dams, and overfishing. Northeastern anadromous stocks dwindled. Entire rivers – including the Piscataqua, Merrimack, and Connecticut – were depopulated. By 1850 the Penobscot was the only Maine river that could support a commercial salmon fishery. Just as British North American salmon had sustained many a Loyalist after the Revolution, it had now become New England's chief source of salmon.[58]

Anadromous species were not the only marine fishes disappearing; the more intensively exploited "deep-sea" species diminished as well. Halibut and cod declined markedly in the western Gulf of Maine during the early nineteenth century and sea herring began appearing more erratically.[59] Halibut, a massive flounder generally regarded as a trash fish before 1821 due to its unwieldy size and weight, became a prized food-fish by 1825. Fishers from Gloucester, Massachusetts, first targeted the large Massachusetts Bay stock, but within just a few years so few remained that the fishery was abandoned. By the late 1820s, Gloucestermen had also decimated the nearby Middle (Stellwagen) Bank stock. Despite the treacherous currents and fast-brewing storms for which Georges Bank was infamous, the Gloucester fleet then concentrated on the vast numbers of high quality halibut frequenting Georges. After twenty years of intensive fishing this fishery also collapsed. Thereafter, Gloucestermen sailed in search of halibut to the inner Atlantic banks, followed by the Grand Banks, and finally to the waters off western Greenland, Davis Strait, and Iceland.[60]

The inshore and nearshore "summer" cod fishery, which had commenced each spring and continued through much of the fall, declined rapidly during the early 1830s. Gloucester's Proctor brothers (1882) noted the peak of the Cape Ann fishery in 1832 and its subsequent decline: "[It] reached its maximum in 1832, when it employed a tonnage of 6463 tons, furnishing employment to 799 men, and resulting in a catch of 63,112 qtls. fish, of a value of $157,780, receiving also a bounty of $25,172 from the government. From this time, the business, except as a winter industry, began to decline, giving place to the mackerel fishery and other modern branches of the industry."[61] Joseph Smith's account (1887) of the collapse of Cape Ann's cod fishery is nearly identical to that of the Proctor brothers.[62] The American Fish Bureau's 1887 report indicates that the affected waters extended well beyond those off Cape Ann, that other (unidentified) species had declined as well, and that because of the loss of the summer shore fishery, New Englanders were compelled to sail further offshore to more distant fishing grounds.[63] Cod were still numerous off Maine and scale fish were plentiful in the Gulf of Maine. Both were abundant off British North America in the waters that early Massachusetts settlers had avoided. From the 1830s until the Civil War, Maine led New England's deep-sea fishing industry. Off Massachusetts, the spring haddock and fall pollock fisheries expanded in lieu of the summer cod fishery.[64]

The Proctor, Smith, and American Fish Bureau accounts, and the timing of the ascendancy of Maine's fleet, add credence to the assertion by Canadian fisheries expert Joseph Gough that "the growing scarcity of stocks" led to the offshore movement of the Massachusetts fleet.[65] Although Samuel Eliot Morison noted the decline of the codfishing fleets of Merrimack (Newburyport), Boston Bay, and South Shore (including Plymouth) after the mid-1830s and the growth of the Cape Ann and Cape Cod fleets, his explanation that "concentration was the tendency of the age" warrants further consideration.[66] The diminution of the summer shore fishery in the western Gulf of Maine may well have precipitated the fishing industry's regional readjustment, including the growth of Plymouth's mackerel fleet.[67] It may also have sped up Gloucester's transition from cod hand-lining to cod trawl-lining, a more competitive but also far more dangerous fishing method. The development of faster and larger vessels, enabling the speedier transport of fishers to and from the deep-sea fishing grounds and onboard storage of large quantities of fish, may also have been hastened.

In all six New England states and in the Maritime provinces, government officials recognized the problem of diminishing river and coastal fisheries. Typically they enacted – but failed to adequately enforce – well-intentioned laws to protect anadromous species. Although protection of groundfish was uncommon, the Massachusetts Bay Colony prohibited the use of cod and bass as fertilizers for farm crops in 1639, and in 1652 it established times during the cod, haddock, hake, and pollock spawning seasons when these species could not be taken (close-times).[68]

In New Hampshire and Massachusetts the primary objective of early river fishery laws was to preserve the supply of fish. Fishways were to be built in or around dams, and other obstructions removed or made less harmful through restrictions on the time, method, and/or extent of fishing. The second and third legislative objectives were to harmonize conflicting interests, usually by authorizing citizen-run town fisheries, and to prevent fraud by establishing a system for inspecting dried and pickled fish.[69] Legislation did not effectively counter the overuse and abuse of New England's river fishes. As they grew scarcer, more laws were proposed. Massachusetts passed at least one new river-fishery law or one amendment to an existing law per year from 1786 through 1872, except in 1828.[70] By the end of the Civil War, Massachusetts and Maine had enacted hundreds of laws.[71] During the first forty years of Maine's statehood, its legislature passed more than a hundred acts pertaining to river fishes. Roughly fifty of the river fishery laws enacted by the Massachusetts Legislature before Maine became independent also applied to Maine's rivers.[72] Throughout New England, wasteful fishing practices were the norm, however. Local and state conservation laws were routinely ignored.

In 1856 Massachusetts appointed three commissioners to investigate and report on artificial propagation of fish as a potential remedy to the problem of declining river fishes.[73] They determined that the formerly abundant Connecticut River salmon had disappeared many years earlier, and predicted that shad would soon "leave the river entirely" because their ascent had been obstructed during the preceding three years by a dam at Holyoke, and by locks and canals at Enfield.[74] Seven years later, the legislatures of New England's upstream states, New Hampshire and Vermont, passed resolutions calling upon Massachusetts, Connecticut, and Maine to recognize the urgent problem caused by dams in the Connecticut, Merrimack, Saco, and other rivers.[75] New Hampshire and Vermont formed fish commissions the following year. Massachusetts also created a fish commission in 1865; it was followed by Connecticut in 1866, Maine in 1867, and Rhode Island in 1869.[76]

Because the main impediments to the ascent of the Connecticut and Merrimack rivers were dams located in Massachusetts, its commissioners were primarily responsible for investigating the interstate problem.[77] Each of the other five fish commissions focused on the extent and causes of the decline of anadromous fisheries in its own state and published the results in either annual or biannual reports. In late February 1867, the five commissions then in existence met in

Boston and created an informal association – the New England Commissioners of River Fisheries – to establish a common policy for the restoration of indigenous fishes and the introduction of new species.[78] New Hampshire and Massachusetts agreed that decisions about Merrimack River fisheries would be made jointly, and New Hampshire and Maine agreed on joint decision-making for the Salmon Falls, Saco, and Androscoggin rivers. The four states sharing the Connecticut River also decided to cooperate on fisheries-related matters,[79] and their commissioners promised to fulfill the following obligations: "It shall be the duty of *New Hampshire* to procure impregnated ova of shad and salmon and place them in the head waters of the [Connecticut] river; of *Vermont* and *Massachusetts*, to build suitable and sufficient fish-ways for the free passage of the fish; of *Connecticut*, to prohibit the use of gill nets and stake nets or pounds in the Connecticut river, and upon the sound near its mouth. It is understood that the duty to be performed by each State is conditioned upon the cooperation of the other States."[80] According to this arrangement, if one state reneged on its promise all could. Each of the commissions set about implementing, at a minimum, its agreed-upon task. Despite significant delays and difficulties, especially with respect to the Connecticut River, fishways were installed in many dams, and shad and salmon eggs were hatched and planted. Efforts to curb excessive and inappropriate fishing, however, were nearly as ineffective then as they had been formerly.

Federal involvement was contemporaneous in Canada and the United States as the federal governments of both countries realized after Confederation and the Civil War, respectively, that the state of their marine fisheries had worsened. Prime Minister John A. Macdonald and President Ulysses S. Grant each designated officials for fisheries issues. Macdonald's appointee immediately delegated the task of conducting a reconnaissance in Nova Scotia and New Brunswick while he remained in Ottawa to organize a federal fisheries bureaucracy. Grant's appointee personally undertook and directed scientific field inquiries in Massachusetts, followed by Maine and the Maritimes, during two successive summers, and spent the interim period in Washington, DC.

In Canada, under the *British North America Act* of 1867, jurisdiction over coastal fisheries was given to the Dominion government. The first Minister of Marine and Fisheries, Senator Peter Mitchell – a father of Confederation from New Brunswick who was familiar with the fishing industry – simultaneously confronted the tasks of creating his own federal ministry and determining the extent of Canada's domestic and regional fisheries problems. He modelled the organic act for his new Department of Marine and Fisheries after the Province of Canada's well-respected Fisheries Branch, and appointed its head, William F.

Whitcher, as the department's Commissioner of Fisheries. The provincial Fisheries Branch had been established in 1857, a decade before Confederation, to regulate the visibly diminishing supply of salmon in Quebec and Ontario. No similar institution existed in either New Brunswick or Nova Scotia.[81]

Preoccupied with these matters and with his senatorial obligations, Mitchell promptly assigned three men knowledgable about fisheries issues to the task of personally inspecting and reporting on the fisheries of Nova Scotia and New Brunswick. In 1867–1868, Thomas Knight and H. W. Johnston surveyed Nova Scotia, and William Venning covered New Brunswick. Knight concluded that Nova Scotia's river fisheries were in a state of "crisis," principally because of the use of fixed nets and weirs, that the sea herring fishery was declining, and that the practice of throwing offal into the waters near river mouths was "pernicious." He recommended that the Dominion enact fisheries legislation similar to that of the province of Canada.[82]

Johnston's report to Mitchell confirmed both Knight's and Perley's observations about the state of Nova Scotia's river fisheries. He concurred: "The failure of the coast fisheries [especially cod, haddock, mackerel, and sea herring], and the consequent destitution of all engaged in them may be attributable in great measure to the deplorable state of [the] nurseries which produce the food of our salt-water fishes, and attract them to our shores." Johnston urged the enactment and stringent enforcement of legislation requiring fishways in all dams impeding the passage of migratory fishes and authorizing the appointment of fishery wardens with the power of summary action. He further recommended that the wardens report to an inspector, who could also act as a magistrate.[83]

According to Venning, all kinds of fisheries had been neglected in New Brunswick. He asserted that the fishes in the Bay of Fundy consumed juvenile herring, and that they therefore depended upon the protection of the sea herring spawning ground at the Southern Head of Grand Manan Island. Tightly constructed weirs wasted vast numbers of small herring that were useful only for producing oil. If, instead, these juvenile fish were allowed to mature, their value would be greatly enhanced. Convinced that the illegal deposit of gurry (fish offal) on the shore drove off the herring, he recommended a law requiring fishers to have all gurry composted onshore or used in the production of guano.[84]

Venning thought that all but one of New Brunswick's rivers – the Mispeck – were so unproductive that they could not "afford the supply of milt and spawn necessary for restoring" the supply of anadromous fishes, particularly salmon, to another river via artificial propagation. As Perley had observed seventeen years earlier, residents along the Kennebecasis, Hammond, and Petitcodiac rivers were still animated by an "insane desire" to destroy every salmon, only now there were fewer to catch. In the Canadian-American St Croix River, only a "remnant" of fish were left, and such "enormous quantities" of mill rubbish and sawdust were being deposited that for some distance below St Stephen the accumulated debris could obstruct navigation. Only one dam in the province had a working fishway. Like Perley, Venning was concerned that the shad in the St Croix were being captured full of spawn. If this continued unchecked, the fisheries at the upper part of the Bay of Fundy – where he assumed the shad migrated to feed after they had spawned – would eventually be destroyed.[85]

Drift nets took so many salmon, shad, and river herrings in the Harbour of Saint John that Venning was surprised that a single fish made it past this "labyrinth of nets" to the river. Yet the harbour catch was relatively small because of the prodigious yield being taken by myriad large nets drifting for long distances down the outer bay. He urged that drift nets be prohibited in the bay within two miles of the coast. For the harbour fishery, however, he recommended only a weekly close time from sundown on Saturday through sunrise on Monday because more stringent regulations would disadvantage impoverished fishers. Moreover, Venning favoured adapting the pre-1867 provincial *Fishery Act of Canada* to New Brunswick and improving the existing fishery warden system, despite the radical changes in longstanding practices and customs that would ensue.[86]

Similar debates were underway in the United States. The issue that brought the federal government squarely into the fishery affairs of the New England states was not the depletion of salmon, shad, and river herrings. It was the prolonged disappearance – for more than a decade – of southern New England's most important summer fishes. During and after the American Civil War, fishers from Connecticut to Maine complained to their state legislators and to members of Congress about a marked decline in the abundance of New England's coastal and ocean food-fishes. In southern New England scup, tautog, and sea bass were the species of greatest concern during this period, while in eastern New England the supply of groundfish, mackerel, and sea herring worried the inshore fishers.

In the late 1860s in southern Massachusetts and in Rhode Island, fishers who used traditional handlines for capturing a variety of fin-fish demanded that their state legislators protect the coastal fisheries. They accused a smaller group of fishers, who during the preceding fifteen to twenty years had upgraded their gear to more efficient and costly nets and weirs, of excessive and inappropriate fishing. Arguing that the diminution of inshore fishes had occurred simultaneously with the introduction of this new technology, the handliners blamed these "trappers" for the disappearance of the scup, tautog, and sea bass. The trappers successfully challenged the efforts of the dory fishers to convince state and federal authorities to prohibit the use of their gear.

The majority of inshore fishers, including poorly paid labourers who needed inexpensive sources of protein to sustain their families and the more well-to-do who fished for recreation, used single lines let from small boats or from the shore. Many handliners had been displaced by the sharp postwar slump in the American merchant marine and by the decline of the whaling industry; others had retired from the rigours of fishing on the offshore fishing banks. Most of these fishers vehemently disapproved of those who had been investing in fixed nets. Pounds, traps, fykes, and weirs[87] were the chief nets employed.[88] Typically they were grouped together in sheltered bays and inlets, and across the mouths of estuaries and rivers. The most important of the pound-net fisheries were found in Massachusetts along the north and south shores of Cape Cod, in Buzzards Bay, on the north shore of Martha's Vineyard, and around Nantucket Island. South of the Cape they were used in Rhode Island in Narragansett Bay, in Connecticut along the eastern half of the coast, and in New York at the eastern end of Long Island.[89]

While nets were more costly than lines, they captured far more fish. Handliners claimed that unfairly large numbers were being taken, and that anadromous species in particular were being prevented from reproducing because fish were being caught that had not yet spawned.[90] Trap owners and dealers responded in part that this claim could not be proven.[91] Taken together, disappearing inshore fisheries, evolving fishing methods, and conflicting socioeconomic values formed the genesis of another interstate fisheries problem. Although the Rhode Island Legislature leaned toward regulating traps, the Massachusetts Legislature did not, so neither state restricted their use. Interstate competition prevailed over cooperation, and paved the way for federal intervention.

The assistant secretary of the independent Smithsonian Institution, Spencer Fullerton Baird, became aware of New England's fisheries controversy while collecting marine specimens during summers spent in Woods Hole, Massachusetts in 1863 and 1870, and in Eastport, Maine, in 1869.[92] Baird was the politically savvy and well-connected curator of the Smithsonian's National Museum, a renowned ornithologist, and an amateur marine biologist. He viewed the controversy in southern New England as a problem of two states being unable to compromise on a common fishery policy.[93] From his perspective as a self-trained naturalist and avid specimen collector, the scientific aspects of the fisheries decline were intriguing. Resolution of this problem offered superb opportunities for research in the nascent field of marine biology and the promise of scientific discovery.

Keen on exhibiting marine fauna in the Smithsonian's National Museum, establishing a marine laboratory, and initiating a broad fisheries research program, Baird realized that this interstate fishery problem was the opportunity for which he had been waiting. He pursued his vision of a solution strategically, and with energy and tenacity. By acting quickly and decisively to resolve the problem of the disappearance of key New England food-fishes, he believed he could also demonstrate the utility of scientific discovery and enlightenment to ordinary citizens.[94] To the Smithsonian curator, however, practical science and popular enlightenment were largely synonymous with specimen collection and exhibition. It is for good reason that he was later described as having had an "insatiable passion for the slaughter, stuffing, and storing of specimens."[95]

In January and early February 1871 – with the invaluable support of his closest Washington friend, the esteemed and politically powerful Senator George Edmunds of Vermont – Baird tirelessly lobbied Congress. His aim was to convince the House and Senate to pass a joint resolution authorizing the president to appoint an unsalaried, independent Commissioner of Fish and Fisheries to conduct a scientific study of New England's multi-species fisheries problem.[96] The resolution was carefully worded so that only he would be qualified for the position. Baird succeeded, but not before he had agreed to expand the geographic scope of the investigation to include any other declining fisheries in the United States, including those of the Great Lakes.[97] Appointed by President Grant, Baird pursued his inquiries in New England with dispatch.

Baird's plan of action was not as straightforward as was Mitchell's in Canada. He focused on New England's problem fisheries in phases, rather than all at once, as had Knight, Johnston, and Venning. During his first summer as U.S. Fish Commissioner (1871) he investigated southern New England's scup, tautog, and sea bass problem. Baird's plan for studying these coastal fisheries was based on his "natural method" of fishery-related inquiry. Before relocating from Washington, DC, to Woods Hole, Massachusetts – his summer field station – he amassed a wealth of statements and reports about New England's fisheries and those of European nations. Moreover, he developed an ambitious scientific plan consisting of a set of eighty-eight questions relevant to the natural history of individual species. This had not been done before. The commissioner realized that to complete these histories "thorough knowledge" was needed about the "associates" – both animal and vegetable – of the food-fishes, and about the chemical and physical characteristics of the water.[98]

At Woods Hole, Baird investigated the coastal waters from Cape Cod to Narragansett Bay in order to determine whether the locally important summer scup, tautog, and sea bass fisheries were diminishing. A cadre of academic scientists joined him, although many conducted their own basic marine research projects. Accompanied by an experienced photographer who took over two hundred photographs at successive intervals during the summer, he inspected some thirty coastal pounds, traps, and weirs in operation. Baird examined the contents of the stomachs of the fish found in them, dredged Buzzards Bay, and did what he loved best – discovering, collecting, and disseminating numerous marine specimens. In addition, he travelled to ten different locations between Hyannis, Massachusetts, and Newport, Rhode Island, to interview local fishers both individually and in groups.[99]

Baird also grew concerned for New England's anadromous fishes. He soon became aware that New England's salmon, shad, and river herrings had seriously diminished and that the state fish commissions were attempting to implement various remedies, including the artificial propagation and planting of salmon and shad ("fish culture"). In December 1871 Senator Edmunds forwarded letters from fish-culture advocates in Vermont and Connecticut proposing the establishment of two federal fish hatcheries from which impregnated spawn would be transferred to the states. This time the federal fish commissioner did not initiate an on-site investigation to scientifically study the matter. Already convinced that artificial propagation was superior to natural reproduction, he agreed to help the states lobby Congress for funding.[100]

Baird turned his attention to the Gulf of Maine in 1872. Setting up a temporary field station in Eastport, Maine – the centre of the country's sea herring fisheries – he focused more on the region's sea herring and groundfish than on its anadromous river fishes because the decline of New England's cod fisheries had most affected the fishing communities north of Cape Cod. Some of the same scientists continued the research they had begun, and dozens more joined them, including academics, collectors, state fish commissioners, state inspectors, and college students. The U.S. Coast Survey loaned him a steamer for surveying Georges Bank because it was one of the best fishing grounds, and the Treasury Department loaned the *Mosswood*, a revenue cutter.[101]

Baird was particularly interested in the sea herring entering the Bay of Fundy. Surmising that ocean temperatures would be of considerable importance in solving the problem of declining fisheries and the mystery of why Bay of Fundy herring frequented certain parts of the coast but ignored others, he outfitted the *Mosswood* with a deep-sea thermometer and began recording water temperatures. Baird predicted that announcements of impending weather changes and of the occurrence and movements of herring, mackerel, cod, and other deep-sea fishes would better prepare fishers and fish markets. He convinced the Army to build a telegraphic station in Eastport to assist with this research.[102] The commissioner spent part of the summer of 1872 in southern and eastern New Brunswick (including Grand Manan Island), northeastern Nova Scotia, and Prince Edward Island. He learned about the current state of the fisheries of Maritime Canada, the types of regulations affecting them, and methods of implementing these regulations – and he added numerous salmon specimens to his collection.[103]

Based on the investigations on both sides of the Canada–U.S. border, there was no doubt that important fisheries were declining. Venning, Johnston, and Knight found that the anadromous river fisheries of New Brunswick and Nova Scotia were in a state of crisis. Nova Scotia's sea herring fishery was "on the whole going backwards,"[104] and vast numbers of juvenile sea herring were being wasted in New Brunswick. Moreover, Nova Scotia's coastal fisheries had failed. The province's most commercially important species – cod, haddock, and mackerel – had not appeared inshore. In their small, open boats, fishers dared not venture too far offshore in search of them.[105] Most lacked access to vessels that could transport them to more productive fishing grounds, as did many of their counterparts in New England.

Baird's subsequent investigation in southern New England found that there had been an "enormous diminution" in the number of shore fishes during the preceding fifteen to twenty years. Upon returning from Eastport he informed Congress that New England's anadromous fishes were nearly extinct, and that within the previous thirty to forty years, cod, haddock, and hake had become "practically a failure." He claimed that it was well known that they had diminished measurably along the coast and in some locations had "ceased entirely."[106]

Investigators in both countries also quickly determined the reasons for the multi-species decline. They were convinced that the decline of the sea herring and anadromous fishes, especially river herrings, had caused the disappearance of the GGOMR's most important "deep-sea" (coastal-ocean) species: the cod, haddock, mackerel, and hake that formerly had ventured inshore. They attributed this change largely to the deplorable state of the spawning grounds that produced the juvenile prey that attracted groundfish and mackerel to the coast. Tightly constructed weirs continued to waste vast numbers of them.

In Nova Scotia and New Brunswick, the decline of river fishes was blamed on several factors. In addition to weirs, fixed nets, and extensive drifts, nets were being used to capture river fishes, particularly juvenile and spawning fish. Dams impeded the ascent of anadromous fishes to their upstream spawning grounds. Enormous quantities of sawdust and mill rubbish were continually being dumped into the rivers, and fishers routinely tossed fish gurry into the waters near river mouths. Finally, provincial fisheries laws were widely disregarded.

In the United States, Baird gathered information relevant to seven possible causes of the decline of southern New England's scup, tautog, and sea bass. These were: change in the abundance of the food of fish, change in the location of the fish themselves, diseases, atmospheric conditions (periods of particularly hot or cold weather and volcanic eruptions), predators, pollution, and "human agency." The first four he quickly dismissed.[107] Baird concluded that together, the ravages of the bluefish and excessive fishing of parent-fish (stock-fish) were to blame.[108] "The object of those engaged in the fisheries has been to obtain the largest supply in the shortest possible time, and this has involved more or less of waste, and in some cases, reckless destruction of the fish."[109] Fishers were scrambling to catch large quantities for three reasons. First, fish had been "managed" as though there were no possibility of future exhaustion. Second, the nation had been growing very rapidly. Recent improvements in transportation and preservation meant that fish could now be packed in ice and sent in good condition all over the country via the new railroads; thus demand had increased proportionately. Third, boiling and pressing fish produced not only valuable oil but also a residue that worked well as a fertilizer.[110] While formerly the supply of fish had "greatly exceeded the demand," it had failed "to a certain extent at least and in certain localities."[111]

Baird attributed the decline of anadromous species to "exhaustive fishing," impassable dams, and lumbering and manufacturing interests that opposed restorative measures, especially the construction of fishways.[112] After his summer in eastern Maine and the Maritime provinces, he thought it "perfectly safe to assume" that the cause of the disappearance of cod, haddock, and hake was tied to the decline of anadromous species – principally river herrings.[113] In a letter to one of Maine's fish commissioners in mid-November Baird wrote: "With the decrease of these fish there has been a corresponding diminution in the numbers of the cod and other deep-sea species near our coasts; but it was not until quite recently that the relationships between the two series of phenomena were appreciated as those of cause and effect."[114] Thus in both Canada and the United States the leading fisheries authorities attributed the disappearance of the region's staple inshore fishes to the diminution of herring species.

What now remained to be determined were the policy implications of these findings. Initially, both Mitchell and Baird promoted a similar solution – uniform government regulation. Only the former succeeded. Mitchell took a precautionary, regulatory approach to fisheries management. At his urging, Parliament enacted *The Fisheries Act of 1868*, which gave his new Department of Marine and Fisheries broad powers over the Dominion's coastal and river fisheries, including shellfish.[115] Provincial laws were either repealed or continued.[116] The Act regulated the taking of immature fish, salmon, cod, seals, and whales. It authorized a system of fishing licenses and leases, forbade acts that injured fishing grounds and polluted rivers (including throwing fish gurry overboard), and required the installation of working fishways. Further, it provided for the appointment of sworn Fishery Officers who exercised magisterial powers as *ex officio* Justices of the Peace, and thus had the power to arrest poachers.

The "young of any of the fish named" in the Act were not to be fished for, killed, purchased, sold, or possessed. The use of mackerel, herring, and caplin seines for taking codfish was prohibited (the meshes were too small), and minimum mesh sizes were established for codfish seines and salmon nets. Minimum distances were imposed between individual nets and between nets and the mouth of any waterway in which salmon spawned, salmon fishing was prohibited at artificial passes and salmon leaps, taking salmon near or on their spawning beds was made illegal, and a salmon close season was prescribed. Drifting for salmon was prohibited, as was their capture with "bag-nets and trap-nets and fish-pounds." Spears, grapnel hooks, negog, and nishagans were not to be employed by non-Indians to kill several species of fish, including salmon, herring, and shad. A thirty-six-hour Sunday close time was also authorized for all seines, nets, and other fishing gear. Fines and penalties collected were to be used for the Dominion's new coastal and offshore federal Fisheries Protection Service. The Minister of Marine and Fisheries was further authorized to set aside and lease waters for the natural or artificial propagation of fish.

The *Fisheries Act* provided a wide variety of regulatory tools designed to protect particular species and all immature fishes. It specified norms, contingencies, and sanctions, but not long-range goals. At its core, however, the Act was designed to further Canada's long-term common interest in restoring and sensibly managing its most lucrative fisheries. Among the anadromous river fishes, it focused mainly on the protection of salmon – from overfishing and from the loss and degradation of spawning habitat. Other than protecting juvenile fishes of all kinds, and prohibiting non-Indians from taking shad with four gear types commonly used by Indians, it did little to conserve shad during its spawning season. Despite their acclaimed role in drawing cod, haddock, mackerel, and other ocean species inshore, river herrings were even less well protected than shad.

In the United States, Baird – who believed that nothing could be done about the voracious bluefish – promoted a seasonal weekend close time for southern New England's pounds, traps, and weirs. He recommended that during the six weeks when the coastal fishes spawned each spring, traps and pounds should be prohibited between 6:00 p.m. Friday and 6:00 a.m. Monday. The commissioner thought that this temporary closure would enable a percentage of fish to lay their eggs and pass through their spawning area.[117] To his great disappointment, during the winter of 1871–1872 he failed to garner sufficient support within the Massachusetts and Rhode Island legislatures for the bill that he had drafted, negotiated with the state fish commissions, and promoted. Although he had threatened to write a more restrictive federal bill if the states did not enact his weekly close time proposal, there is no evidence that he took any steps to carry out his threat.[118]

Baird supported intra- and interstate efforts to regulate the anadromous river fisheries and to require the installation of fish passageways in dams, but both came under state jurisdiction and control. Rather than pursuing options designed to help the state fish commissions achieve either or both objectives, he spent two months during the spring of 1872 lobbying Congress for funding for a federal fish culture program. Fortunately for Baird and his colleagues, one-term congressman Robert Roosevelt of Manhattan (Theodore's uncle), who was also one of New York state's Fish Commissioners, was an ardent fish culture advocate.[119] The coalition was successful, and Baird was put in charge of the new program, for which the appropriation of $15,000 was three times as much as Congress had allotted a year and a half earlier for his national food-fish inquiry.[120]

En route to Eastport in June, the Fish Commissioner hastily convened a meeting in Boston to decide how to spend this appropriation. The Fish-Culturists Association and New England fish commissions agreed that shad would be transplanted into the Mississippi River and its tributaries. The shad hatcheries in Connecticut and New York were placed at Baird's disposal. Expansion of the interstate salmon hatchery that had been established in Bucksport, Maine, a year earlier was approved.[121] Over the summer Baird spent several days at his Eastport field station with Charles Atkins, superintendent of the Bucksport hatchery, and with commissioners Stilwell and Stanley of Maine. They guaranteed that they would hatch and distribute all of the salmon eggs that the federal government provided them. Baird indicated that he intended to cover the costs of procuring eggs and distributing them to the states that agreed to assume the responsibility for restocking their rivers. Stilwell and Stanley "understood the policy of the government to be to place in [their] hands every year, a number of salmon eggs, equal to the annual product of each river in salmon, when the rivers [were] in full stock." They anticipated restocking all of Maine's original salmon-producing rivers.[122]

The association and state commissioners met again in New York in

October. Hopeful about the future of shad propagation, Baird focused the meeting on the "next most important fish" to be cultured – the salmon – and thus on the hatchery operations in Maine.[123] Atkins had purchased nearly 700 salmon from weir fishers on the Penobscot River, many of which had survived. Most of their eggs were distributed to the states on a *pro rata* basis for less than $5.00 per thousand – and in the years to come less than $3.00 (far less than the cost of obtaining eggs from Ontario). Vermont and New Hampshire – which, to the embarrassment of their commissioners, had not appropriated monies for fish culture – were allotted a much smaller number of eggs than were the states that had contributed to the hatchery prior to the approval of federal funding. From the share belonging to the federal government, eggs were sent to states outside New England. Just as Venning had found with respect to the rivers in New Brunswick (other than the Mispeck), fish were so scarce in all of Maine's salmon rivers except the Penobscot that the Bucksport hatchery could not be replicated. For the first time, however, New England's fish commissioners had enough eggs to re-establish broods of salmon in their exhausted rivers.[124]

Baird's objectives for his federal fish culture program were twofold: the replenishment of depleted grounds with indigenous species and the formation of new fisheries in grounds that had never been "sufficiently productive." Essential to both were the application of science and careful observance of natural laws.[125] The successful propagation and transplantation of food-fish on a vast scale, therefore, were challenges to which he was by nature well suited, given his deep personal interest in practical science that benefited the general public. When the U.S. Commissioner of Fish and Fisheries submitted his second report to Congress four months after his October meeting, all but fifteen of its 102 pages, and most of the supplementary papers accompanying it, focused on the history, theory, and practice of fish culture in North America and Europe.[126] Two weeks later, Congress approved $17,500 for fish culture for the fiscal year ending June 30, 1874, compared with just $5,000 for Baird's national food-fish inquiry.[127] During the remainder of the nineteenth century Congress continued to direct the lion's share of its fisheries-related appropriations to fish culture.

CONCLUSION

The respective responses of Canada and the United States to their similar and contemporaneous fisheries crises provide a unique opportunity for comparing the policy directives of the two neighbours. Although the investigations conducted in each country were quite different, the conclusions they reached about the existence and causes of the concurrent and sequential fishery declines were not. They started from the same finding: the same number of people, in the same time, on the same fishing ground, with the same gear, could *not* catch the same number of fish then as they could formerly. The region's most important anadromous, bait, and "summer" groundfish fisheries had been declining for quite some time, especially in New England. Deprived from spring through fall of sufficient quantities of their accustomed inshore prey, cod and scale fish had all but disappeared from coastal waters, leaving many small boat fishers destitute. Yet the federal policies selected by each country in response to the ecological and socioeconomic dislocation caused by each crisis contrasted sharply.

Canada chose a precautionary, regulatory approach focused on minimizing excessive fishing of particular declining species, limiting the capture of juvenile and spawning fishes, securing the unimpeded ascent of all anadromous fishes upstream, and curbing the pollution of rivers, coastal waters, and spawning grounds. The distinguishing characteristic of Canada's fisheries policy was its reliance on bureaucratic solutions to fisheries problems. An outside service of local river and coastal wardens reported and answered to district overseers having magisterial powers, who reported/answered to provincial fishery inspectors. These inspectors reported/answered to an inside service in Ottawa directed by a Commissioner of Fisheries, who was in turn responsible to both the Deputy Minister of Marine and Fisheries and the Minister of Marine and Fisheries.[128]

The United States adopted a non-regulatory, research and development-oriented approach. Due to jurisdictional and scientific uncertainties, management of New England's marine fisheries was left to the states, despite their poor track records in implementing their respective policies and interstate agreements. The federal government focused on advancing scientific knowledge about the marine environment and the causes of fishery declines, helping fishers track the movements of bait fish and groundfish, and assisting the states in artificially rebuilding depleted shad and salmon stocks and transplanting these species nationwide. The distinguishing characteristic of the United States' fisheries policy was its reliance on scientific and technological solutions to fishery problems.

Although each country handled its own crisis separately, Canadian and American fishery authorities were cognizant of each other's investigations and perspectives. After his summer field trip to the Maritime Provinces in 1872, for instance, the U.S. Commissioner of Fish and Fisheries concluded that the dearth of herrings and anadromous fishes had caused the groundfish decline. By then, most of New England's "summer" cod and anadromous stocks had been gone for decades, thus their predator-prey relationship had not been apparent.

The GGOMR's multi-species fisheries crisis also involved Canadian and American connections that were far more consequential than extending professional courtesies and sharing information. New England fishers were partly responsible for the decline of some Maritime stocks. Since the early colonial period vessels from New England had fished for anadromous species, sea herring, and cod in the coastal and nearshore waters of the Maritime provinces. After the Revolutionary War, Loyalists populated New Brunswick, established commercial fisheries in the Bay of Fundy, installed impassable mill dams on streams, began turning forested watersheds into timber production centers, and decimated essential fish habitat. In response to the depopulation of their rivers and the disappearance of their summer cod fishery during the nineteenth century, New England fishers ventured to British North American waters in greater numbers. They subsequently switched from traditional fishing methods to new technologies that significantly increased catch sizes, and they introduced these innovative methods into Canadian waters.

If current assumptions about the natural supply and stability of fisheries past were correct, however, it should not have mattered that New Englanders encroached on Canadian fishing grounds and fished more aggressively than their counterparts in the Maritimes. Canada and the United States should not have confronted the concurrent and sequential decline of river, coastal, and ocean fish stocks in the GGOMR during the nineteenth century. Instead, GGOMR sea fishes should have been abundant enough to be considered virtually inexhaustible, as in colonial times when explorers and early settlers commonly encountered vast numbers of high-quality river fishes and herrings intermingling in inshore waters with groundfish and mackerel.

The colonial perception that the Greater Gulf of Maine Region's supplies of marine fishes and other valuable commodities were virtually inexhaustible precipitated centuries of excessive waste. Degradation and manipulation of forested watersheds destroyed natural habitat essential for the reproduction of adult anadromous fishes and the survival of their young. Remarkably effective fishing methods enabled fishers to aggressively target their prey species by species and stock by stock. During the nineteenth century, salmon, shad, and river herring stocks crashed in one river after another. Sea herring, long used as bait in the all-important cod fishery, also declined. Cod stocks that seasonally had been attracted inshore to feed on herrings and juvenile fishes disappeared. Substitute fisheries – for the same species elsewhere and for different species nearby – were developed and heavily exploited. Declines in New England typically preceded and exacerbated those in the Maritime Provinces. By the mid-1860s, Canada and the United States each faced vexing multi-species fisheries crises that preceded their present-day crises by more than 130 years.

15

More Buck for the Bang: Sporting and the Ideology of Fish and Game Management in Northern New England and the Maritime Provinces, 1870–1900

BILL PARENTEAU AND RICHARD W. JUDD

Fish and game administrators and members of sporting clubs from the northeastern United States and eastern Canada assembled in Montreal for the first annual meeting of the North American Fish and Game Protective Association on 2 February 1900. From the published proceedings it is evident that a great deal of planning went into ensuring that this would be a successful beginning. The implications of the meeting were profound throughout northeastern North America, and nowhere more so than in the cross-border region encompassing northern New England and Canada's Maritime provinces. The meeting began with a twenty-two-item agenda covering a wide range of issues related to the enactment and enforcement of fish and game laws. Having achieved a measure of success in individual jurisdictions, it was now time, conservationists agreed, to consider resource management issues in a broader perspective: to standardize fish and game regulations throughout the northeast according to the scientific principles of conservation.[1]

This historic Montreal meeting offers a starting point for examining fish and game management in the Maritimes and the northern New England states of Maine, New Hampshire, and Vermont, as state administrators and sportsmen concerned with fish and game stocks in this borderlands region comprised the largest group of participants. The proceedings offer a summary report on three decades of efforts to restructure resource use through state regulation, and they give a clear indication of the extent to which elite sporting interests had gained control over fish and game resources in the region by the end of the nineteenth century. Although the proceedings overflow with platitudes about a new beginning, the Montreal meeting in reality signified the culmination of a process underway for more than a quarter century. Inspired by the aristocratic notions of hunting and angling espoused by powerful sporting interests, all of the jurisdictions represented at the Montreal meeting had, by 1900, implemented the essential elements of modern fish and game administration.

The first annual meeting of the association can also be seen as an attempt to legislate into reality a mythical region promoted in the tourist literature of the late nineteenth century. Travel writers treated northen New England and the Maritime provinces as a continuous region abounding with fish and game and populated by friendly, uncomplicated folk who were only too willing to serve the world-weary urban visitor. The seasonal migration of thousands of American "sports" to the Maritime provinces and the existence of sporting clubs with interests on both sides of the border reinforced this image. Uniform fish and game laws, endorsed by amenable local people eager to serve the genteel cosmopolitan traveller, would secure the transboundary region's reputation as a "sportsman's paradise."

The rural areas of the region were, of course, much more complicated than the static portrait of rustic contentment presented in the tourist literature. Aristocratic notions of proper angling and hunting methods posed a direct challenge to existing patterns of harvesting fish and game, and indeed, to local perceptions of the landscape itself. As the Montreal meeting also made clear, it was difficult to impose from the outside a new moral economy of resource use on the rural population.

ANTI-MODERNISM, TOURISM, AND SPORTING

In the second half of the nineteenth century, tourism emerged as a modern industry in Canada and the United States. It was fuelled in large part by the class and ethnic tensions, the crowding, and the sanitary problems that threatened the late nineteenth-century city and, by contrast, gave credence to the Arcadian vision of the countryside. To the elite city dweller, seaside locales, bucolic villages, and deep forests were imbued with the power to reinvigorate mind and body. As the secretary of the elite Megantic Fish and Game Club noted, rural recreation was therapeutic: "There is a wholesome discipline as well as recuperation in a few weeks of camp life, which rounds out the character of a man, freeing him from many a foolish notion and fitting him for greater usefulness in his calling. The perceptive faculties are quickened, the mind broadened; it ... clears and purifies the spirit and oils the creaking mental machinery."[2] This anti-modern impulse – or "cult of wilderness" as two prominent American historians have labelled the broad movement – attracted thousands of urbanites to remote corners of eastern North America to regain their mental and physical health, and recapture their primitive masculinity.[3]

Momentum had been building in the industry since at least the 1840s, as growing numbers of outdoor enthusiasts ventured forth to trek New Hampshire's White Mountains, fish the famed New Brunswick salmon rivers, or experience the bracing sea breezes on the Maine coast. However, it was not until after 1870 that the infrastructure to support large-scale tourism developed. By this time a comprehensive rail network linking the transborder region was beginning to emerge, providing overnight service to previously inaccessible areas. In the Maritime provinces total railway mileage doubled from 1,600 to 3,200 between 1871 and 1891, and New England's rail network was completed in the early 1890s with the construction of northern Maine's Bangor and Aroostook Railroad. For destinations to which rail service was inconvenient, such as Prince Edward Island, Cape Breton, or the peninsulas of the Maine coast, steamship companies developed routes geared to the tourist trade. Tourist accommodations appeared in tandem with these transportation developments. By the mid-1880s travellers could choose from a wide variety of accommodations – from stately hotels such as the Algonquin in St Andrew's, New Brunswick, and the Poland Spring House in central Maine, to a vast network of rooming houses, rustic cottages, and hunting and fishing camps.

Railroads, steamship lines, and grand hotels aggressively promoted the region's recreational opportunities, creating a mythical landscape of timeless purity. Symbolic links between the region's hardworking farmers, hunters, loggers, and fishers and the flinty soils, vast forests, and open seas from which they drew a living created a complex and multilayered tableau with immense appeal for tourists – and immense economic potential for the tourist industry.

A central focus of this image-making was the idea that the borderlands region was a mecca for angling and hunting. Railroads in particular promoted the region's reputation as a "sportsman's paradise" accessible by efficient luxury transportation and offering the first-rate accommodations and services expected by the well-heeled traveller. The Maine Central Railroad, Bangor and Aroostook Railroad, Grand Trunk Railroad, Intercolonial Railroad, and the Canadian National Railways all published guidebooks lavishly documenting the sporting opportunities, accommodations, outfitting and guiding services, and other amenities available along their lines. And independent authors contributed their share of guides, novels, and magazine articles to this promotional fever.[4]

IMPLEMENTING THE CODE OF THE SPORTSMAN

Any tourist industry, to succeed over time, must at least come close to providing the experiences promised in its advertising; promoters of the "sportsman's paradise" realized that its availability depended upon stable fish and game stocks. In the 1890s a two-week trip to one of the better salmon rivers in New Brunswick cost approximately $450, which exceeded the average yearly income in the rural areas of the province.[5] Tourists were people of considerable means, who were accustomed to – and expected – not only efficient transportation and comfortable accommodations, but also a successful hunting or angling experience. The need to maintain fish and game stocks for the emerging sporting industry was the impetus for intensified fish and game management.

By the late nineteenth century, fish and game legislation already had a lengthy legislative history on both sides of the border. Conservation laws were promulgated in the 1700s as a means of preserving the common forage resources considered essential to extending the settlement frontier into the interior highlands. Massachusetts (which then included Maine) enacted a closed season on deer as early as 1698 and obliged towns to elect deer-reeves. New Hampshire and Vermont enacted similar laws in the mid-1700s. Despite these enactments, however, deer were nearly extinct in New England by the early 1800s; for a time the game laws had remained dormant.[6] In Nova Scotia the first river fishery law, designed specifically to promote upriver settlement by preventing excessive netting at the mouths of rivers and streams, was passed in 1761. The New Brunswick legislature passed similar legislation, as well as a law for the preservation of moose, in 1786, just two years after the colony was created out of the western half of Nova Scotia to welcome Loyalist refugees.[7]

People on both sides of the border began rethinking game protection in the 1850s in response to localized problems of resource depletion. Aghast at the "wanton destruction of Moose and Deer ... made by dogs and men, many of whom are from other States," petitioners in 1853 inspired a law designating a "moose warden" for each county in Maine. Both Nova Scotia and New Brunswick enacted colony-wide fishery acts in the 1850s, to prevent migratory fish runs from being choked off by over-netting at the mouths of the region's more settled rivers. In the next decade each of the borderlands states and provinces continued piecemeal efforts to regulate commercial river fishing, stem sawdust pollution, and compel dam owners to build and maintain fishways. Again the laws were largely ineffective. The lumber industry ignored or resisted the sections pertaining to sawdust and fishways, and as for the fishing regulations, "enforcement was perfunctory, convictions were uncommon, and violators flourished."[8]

These early regulations aimed for the most part to protect commercial salmon, shad, and alewife fisheries, and they ignored sporting interests. Because the commercial fisheries were concentrated on the larger rivers, it was only there that the small complement of commissioners and wardens could hope to enforce the laws. On the American side of the border, these early laws reflected a strong bias against recreational fishing: "Where fishing is followed as an amusement," the Maine commissioners announced in 1870, regulation was simply frivolous. For similar utilitarian reasons, early commissioners favoured forage fishing over tourist interests. Maine's commissioners, for example, opposed an 1875 law closing Moosehead and Brassau lakes to ice-fishing, since, as the commissioners put it, the law would "grant a monopoly of all the trout fishing of Maine to the [summer] guests of the Kineo House at Moosehead Lake." Local inhabitants, they insisted, should be allowed take a few fish on the lakes during winter slack season: "Have they not a sort of prescriptive right?" In New Brunswick and Nova Scotia there had already been pressure to accommodate recreational fishing in the 1850s, on the part of colonial administrators and military officers at the Fredericton and Halifax garrisons, who introduced elite British notions of wildlife management to the colonies.[9]

By the late 1870s fish and game commissioners throughout the region were becoming mindful of the income and prestige that wealthy anglers and hunters brought to rural areas. In 1881 the Maine commissioner repeated stories about a veritable "glut" of bills circulating through Portland banks, due largely to the influx of summer visitors, and recommended: "The point to be considered is how to make the most of this great State's interest." Indeed, Maine was on the forefront of sporting tourism, a fact not lost on the New Brunswick fishery commissioner who jealously remarked that "summer tourist and sportsmen leave weekly $280,000 in Maine and there is no reason why we cannot have as large an amount if we only protect our fish and game."[10] In a similar vein a correspondent to the *Burlington Free Press* remarked in 1892: "Every year that Vermont neglects to maintain or improve the hunting on her hillsides and the fishing in her lakes and streams, thousands of dollars are carried away by her own citizens, and expended in Canada and New York, where they can get the sport they seek, fully protected for their use." Vermont, the writer imagined, had all the makings of an "angler's paradise."[11]

Consistent with the rise of the sporting industry, jurisdictions in the borderlands region began to stiffen their primitive game codes. Conservation laws, which had begun as narrowly defined efforts to protect commercial fisheries, were broadened to include a variety of recreational resources. New Brunswick enacted a closed season for moose in 1865 and extended it in 1872. Three years later the province imposed closed seasons for deer, caribou, partridge, woodcock, and other wildlife. The following year, in the first of many regulations banning traditional harvesting methods, it prohibited the netting of waterfowl and the use of a device known as a "punt gun." New Brunswick experimented with comprehensive fish and game laws in 1878, including provisions for hiring fish and game wardens and prohibitions against a variety of harvesting practices. Vermont (in 1876) and Maine (in 1879) added game protection to the duties of the beleaguered fish commissioners, in response to "widespread complaints about infractions of law." Two years later Maine commissioners called a "congress of sportsmen" from across the state to draft a comprehensive fish and game code, and in 1884 they announced that they had been "called upon to enforce a number of new and stringent laws, that may almost be termed war measures, to ... save the remnant of the game of the Commonwealth." Wardens, they warned, would enforce the laws "to the bitter end." Vermont took action to rein in "a class of murderous fishermen and huntsmen [who] made forest and stream a desert to the sportsman." Between 1884 and 1886 Warden Frank H. Atherton won distinction by facing down a gang of "desperate" Lake Champlain fishermen who had been terrorizing local officials. The state's fish and game commission came into its own under the administration of John W. Titcomb, who served between 1891 and 1902 and again between 1910 and 1914. Titcomb distributed game wardens around the state and kept in close touch through daily reports; he surveyed and posted all ponds and lakes in the state and saw that laws were rigorously enforced.[12]

Gradually the states and provinces increased their funding for conservation agencies and codified irregular and haphazard systems of game laws. In New Brunswick the culmination of this process came in 1893, when the provincial legislature passed its seventy-page *Game Act*, consolidating existing statutes and introducing a number of new regulations. Accompanied by a commitment to enforcement, the 1893 act marked the beginning of modern fish and game administration in the province. The New Brunswick law coincided with similar efforts throughout the region, as commissioners took on the task of perpetuating the "sportsman's paradise."[13]

In 1884 New Brunswick passed an act providing for the leasing of exclusive fishing rights to non-tidal waters owned by the Crown.

Although the act was specific to New Brunswick, it deserves mention here, as it allowed for the development of some of the most powerful sporting clubs in North America, among which were the Megantic Fish and Game Club, with its private preserve spanning the international border, and the "wealthy and aristocratic" Restigouche Salmon Club, which was dominated by New York financiers and by 1890 led the push for tighter regulation of the river fisheries. In 1870 fish culturist George Shepard Page and railroad magnate Jay Cooke inaugurated a similar organization, the Ocquossoc Angling Association, with leased land near Maine's Rangeley Lakes. This elite club, limited to a few dozen members, set up an experimental fish hatchery and lobbied the legislature for a law similar to the 1884 New Brunswick act. The most ambitious private preserve in New England was a 25,000–acre tract located on abandoned farmlands in New Hampshire's Sullivan County. Organized in 1890 by Austin Corbin, it was in its time the largest private game preserve in the United States. Corbin stocked his "sportsman's paradise" with deer, quail, grouse, pheasant, moose, antelope, elk, bison, black forest wild boar, and a few Himalayan goats and surrounded them with thirty miles of wire fence. The preserve incurred a good deal of local antagonism, and, like most game preserves in the northeastern states, was short-lived.[14]

Although New England and the Maritime provinces differed in their experience with private preserves, the organization of scores of fish and game clubs throughout the region was a crucial development in wildlife conservation. The Inglewood Fish and Game Club, founded in 1895 and located on the Musquash River in New Brunswick near the Maine border, was typical of the clubs in the region in that sixty-seven of its eighty-two members were from the greater Boston area, the next largest contingent representing the local Saint John elite.[15] State commissioners helped form the Vermont Association for the Protection and Preservation of Fish and Game in 1874, hoping to increase the value of Vermont's marginal lands: "There are large sections of swampy land in this State which, without the owner's knowledge, are frequented by woodcock and similar game, a pair of which is worth as much when sent to market as a pair of chickens." In this spirit the association restocked the mountains east of Rutland with deer in the early 1870s. In 1890 Commissioner Titcomb headed an effort to reorganize the association as the Vermont Fish and Game League. The new organization took an active role in lobbying the legislature, and its annual outings combined hunting, fishing, dining, and politics – "the latter predominating." Guests at these well publicized events included state and local politicians and luminaries of the stature of William McKinley and Theodore Roosevelt. The Maine State Association for the

Preservation of Fish, chartered in 1875, played a similar role in that state.[16]

Guided by these elite clubs, provincial and state commissioners established a hierarchy of use that favoured recreational over subsistence and commercial forms of resource exploitation. Elite sportsmen adopted British aristocratic notions of hunting and angling, and forged them into what historian John Reiger has called the "code of the sportsman," a gentlemanly code that determined when and how fish and game should be taken. Proponents of the code championed a closed season to allow species to reproduce and advocated giving fish and game a "sporting chance."[17] Traditional practices such as spearing salmon by torchlight, snaring large game animals, running deer with dogs, and netting fish and waterfowl, all of which were common in the region, were roundly condemned. The change was revolutionary. As late as 1860 urban elites and rural market hunters alike had been dogging and jacking deer with virtually no social approbation: "Hunters avail themselves of this peculiarity [the deer's curiosity about light] and hunt them by torchlight in the night time."[18] By the 1880s, however, these and other traditional techniques were considered debasing to the noble arts of hunting and angling, and were systematically outlawed, as the code of the sportsman became the blueprint for modern fish and game management throughout the North Atlantic region.

Underlying the moral exhortations of elite sportsmen lay a powerful economic argument. Philadelphian Jay Cooke, Jr was being less than subtle when, in an effort to have ice-fishing banned in the Rangeley Lakes, he reminded the commissioner: "If there is to be a constant falling off in fish and game, it cannot be expected that ... a class of people will visit the state who ... employ guides and spend large sums for supplies which go the farmers and artisans of the state." Such arguments resonated with tourism promoters, many of whom reduced wildlife management to the simple equation of "how to sell the most game for the most money." In their annual reports, commissioners participated in these economic calculations, commenting, for instance, on the economic value of a moose killed in sport, as opposed to its value realized by a commercial hide hunter. "I think I am within the bounds," the New Brunswick fishery commissioner remarked in 1889, "when I say that one salmon killed by an angler distributes more money in the province than 20 taken in a net."[19]

Joining forces with elite sporting interests had professional advantages for fish and game commissioners. While the code of the sportsman may in retrospect appear scientifically crude and blatantly class-biased, it at least defined a reasonably comprehensive conservation program. More important, it was backed by the political and economic power of an elite sporting fraternity. At a time when provincial, state, and federal governments were reluctant to devote financial resources to wildlife management, wealthy sportsmen, some of whom were also high-level politicians, became valuable allies in extending the scope and power of fish and game commissions. And organizations and individuals frequently spent large sums of money to hire private wardens and operate artificial fish propagation programs. In the 1890s the Restigouche Salmon Club alone annually employed more than two dozen private guardians and spent as much as $5,000 in its efforts to follow through on poaching cases.[20]

The professional profile of fish and game commissioners was also enhanced by their social relationships with the sporting fraternity. Many commissioners were members or regular guests of the most elite sporting clubs in the region and they rubbed elbows with wealthy patrons at annual sporting exhibitions held in cities like Boston and New York. The New Brunswick commissioners, for instance, set up elaborate displays at the Boston show, complete with live animals and authentic Indian guides. The commissioners were dazzled each year, their annual reports suggest, by the respect accorded them by persons of the highest social standing and the numerous invitations they received to attend exclusive banquets and visit elite men's clubs. They were particularly proud in 1895 when they were presented to Governor Walcott in a private reception room at the Boston Sportsmen's Show.[21]

AN UNEVEN RESPONSE

The main difficulty with merging the interests of sporting clubs and public agencies, however, was that it led to a myopic view of the use and preservation of wildlife resources and thus fell far short of full acceptance in rural areas. Popular resistance resulted from aggressive campaigns to criminalize traditional fishing and hunting practices. Forage activities had been an essential element of pioneering life throughout the region, furnishing, as one local history has it, "a very important article of subsistence to the early inhabitants," especially during the years before the forest was cleared for crops. "Trout abounded in the brooks and ponds, and pickerel in the river," according to another local historian, and "one of the pleasures of the early spring, when the ice was breaking up ... was spearing pickerel by the light of the jack, an iron basket filled with burning pine knots, fastened to a rod in the bow of the boat." Hunting and fishing were embedded in local folk culture, and although these practices included a strong element of socializing, there was little inclination to pursue fish and game in a "sportsmanlike" fashion. Traditionally, moose and deer were hunted in March, when the crusted snow impeded their movement, and they were frequently killed by the score in the winter "yards." If the animals left the yards, hunters turned dogs on them. "Incessant and violent barking brought up the gunners," and if the animal tried to escape, the dogs were commanded to seize them by the nose, the legs, or the flanks, and harass them until the hunters approached and dispatched them. One Maine farmer stocked 3,680 pounds of moose meat during a particularly productive winter, which he sold for one cent per pound. "The law regulating the killing of moose," he recalled, was "very loosely enforced."[22]

The conservation strategies of the late nineteenth century required a profound shift in thinking about this forage tradition. To criminalize traditional practices, commissioners encouraged the view that violators were social outcasts, a "class of vagabonds too lazy to work, too cowardly to steal, who ... spear and net the fish upon their spawning beds [and] destroy our fur and game animals ... so long as they can realize the price of a glass of whiskey from their spoil." In New England this strategy echoed resource management concepts of earlier colonial towns, which had set aside a "commons" to be regulated by and for town inhabitants – the "commoners." Maine's 1853 moose law petitioners, for instance, had asked for a general law "by which all foreigners may be prohibited from hunting within the limits of this State."[23] Those who evaded the new laws were derided as outcasts – "rogues," "worthless poachers," or a "class of idle, dissipated men, ready for any wild enterprise." Law-abiding citizens – the commoners – the commissioners hoped, would "aid ... in abating this kind of nuisance" by branding perpetrators as social outcasts. At times game-code violators were identified as "men from other States [who] come into our woods, and in violation of our laws, hunt our deer with packs of hounds, while they feed on our fish." But, with increasing frequency it became the traditional hunter or fisher who was branded as the outsider. Market hunters, the Maine commissioners opined in their 1883 report, were "men without an occupation [among whom] we find the skedaddler, smuggler, thief, firebug, and lazy squatter who lives from what lumber he can steal, berries he can pick, fires he can fight, after setting them, or anything save honest labor." E.J. Phelps, speaking before the Vermont Legislature, suggested that "an average Kanuck with a pound of powder, an ill-bred dog and a jug of whiskey can spoil any game preserve in one season."[24] New Brunswick fish and game commissioners were every bit as eager to "prevent a very dangerous class of pot hunters from crossing our borders and killing indiscriminately the game."[25] This propensity to blame outsiders or foreigners for such depredations contributed to a recognition among fish and game commissioners and sportsmen of the need to standardize harvesting regulations across the region.

One of the targets of this campaign to criminalize traditional forage activity was the Native hunter and fisher. As Henry David Thoreau's *Maine Woods* attests, there was, in both Canadian and New England travel literature, a preoccupation with the supposed primitive qualities of Native men and a reverence for their guiding and woodcraft skills.[26] But on a practical level, white officials and white sportsmen condemned native harvesting techniques such as spearing fish, dogging deer and moose, snaring game, and netting wildfowl as pernicious and unsporting. The opinion of a Nova Scotia commissioner that the "Indian is now the greatest obstacle to contend with in carrying out the Game Law" was frequently expressed on both sides of the border, despite the fact that the Native population of the entire region totalled only around 15,000.[27] In Maine mention of Native hunters first appears in an 1852 petition asking the legislature to prevent Canadian Natives from crossing the border to hunt moose for hides. The fact that several Penobscot Indians from Maine joined the call for exclusionary legislation suggests a territorial dispute with the Canadian St Francis Indians, but it also reveals the growing concern among Native hunters that, as Penobscot John Neptune put it, "the Moose and Deer are fast disappearing from our forests, and a continuance of a few years longer will deprive us of a hunting ground."[28]

The Native signatories to the petition also expressed a great frustration with white hunters who were decimating game in the headwater regions that comprised the Native homelands. Native subsistence patterns were thus circumscribed by twin pressures: white hunters and white game wardens. The Passamaquoddy First Nation, whose homeland spanned the eastern border of Maine and New Brunswick, complained that white officials were making "more strict laws against [their] people until everything [was] taken away from them, their lands, their trees, their hunting grounds." Like traditional white hunters, they harboured a long tradition of hunting with dogs. According to the *Saint Croix Courier*, there was "much sympathy, for various reasons ... for the Indian," but the matter of dogging deer was bound to be criminalized "at no distant day."[29]

Local wardens found Native hunters a politically safe target; it was more acceptable in the local white community to arrest Natives than to catch white poachers. In 1885, for instance, the editor of the *Saint Croix Courier* reported on a band of Pleasant Point Natives hunting deer in the vicinity of Moore's Mills and admonished his readers: "It is the duty of all to see the game protected, and residents of the county are requested to report any cases of violation of the law that may come under their notice."[30] As such prosecutions increased in the 1880s, Natives frequently complained. There were, Indian Agent C.H. Porter admitted, "strong arguments both in law and equity against the punishment of Indians for the violation of such laws," since early treaty rights reserved for them the right to "hunt, fowl, and fish as formerly" on the lands taken by Massachusetts and Maine. Porter recognized that the advance of civilization might compel the state to circumscribe these rights, but he noted: "The loss of the right to hunt and fish is today as great a damage to the Indians as it would have been at any past time, and even more so, and what the State gains without compensating the Indians for their loss, is sheer robbery." One *Courier* article took note of a destitute Native woman and her small children: "The story of their sufferings ... is a pathetic one, and the reflection that, while their children are shivering at home, the Indian men are being pursued by ambitious game wardens who take from them in fines the money that should clothe their children, is not one that the great white race can entertain with pride."[31]

Not surprisingly, Native people were harassed in Canada as well; among other actions, the Canadian federal fishery department systematically eliminated legal salmon fishing for Natives in Quebec, New Brunswick, and Nova Scotia. Officials of the Department of Indian Affairs, in their eagerness to promote farming and dissuade Native people from pursuing the traditional "wandering life," actively assisted local fish and game authorities. Nor were white residents who lived near reserves and competed directly for wildlife resources averse to monitoring illegal native harvesting activities out of self-interest.

Despite the best efforts of conservationists, Native people continued to hunt, fish, and trap. Generations of white domination and misplaced paternalism fine-tuned Natives' ability to resist attempts to change their lives. The strategy of John Cope, a Cape Breton Island Mi'kmaq, is instructive. As the game commissioner for New Glasgow remarked in his 1894 report: Cope "brought out of the woods last winter the carcasses of 15 moose, the majority of which I have every reason to believe he killed himself ... He evaded the law by taking with him several Indians consisting of men and boys. John Martin, Indian, brought out 5 carcasses in the same way." The commissioner for Digby County similarly noted that the trout fishing in his district was "being destroyed by Indians, who catch tons of these fish and sell them to middlemen who ship them on ice to Boston."[32] That Indian agents and wardens "could not get them to believe that the game laws of the province were intended to apply to the Indians" underscores the fact that Native people continued to pursue wildlife with a sense of entitlement that was specifically asserted, as in Maine, on the basis of treaties made with the British colonial administration in the eighteenth century.[33] When the Canadian Minister of Indian Affairs made a national survey of Native fisheries in 1897, for example, he was informed that the Mi'kmaq bands in the northern half of New Brunswick "complain[ed] of being forced to observe the close season [for fishing] and declare[d] that by the treaty which their forefathers entered into with the whites of that time no restrictions were ever to be placed on their right to hunt and fish at all seasons."[34] Native practices were undoubtedly curbed by state regulation, but fishing, hunting, and trapping continued to make up a substantial portion of the Native economy into the twentieth century.

The effect on white hunters and fishers was ambiguous as well. However, it was no mystery why a large segment of the rural population saw the new laws in class terms and responded with varying degrees of acceptance, grudging accommodation, and bitter resentment. The regulations were introduced in an aggressive and unapologetic manner; they sought to end unfettered access to fish and game for tens of thousands of residents in the region; they imposed a generic and artificial moral order on fish and game harvesting; and they interrupted the seasonal rhythm of agriculture, labouring, and foraging, particularly for the poorest class of farmers in the region. A correspondent to the *Maine Farmer* voiced an opinion popular in 1902 when he suggested that those who "toil much for a small return and have no pleasure, are alive to the fact that on their own soil they should have something like equal rights with the wealthy, pleasure loving citizen of Boston or of New York." The same sentiment was expressed more bluntly by the disgruntled New Brunswick resident who characterized the fishing regulations as a "Godless law which takes away the poor man's substance and gives it to wealthy foreigners who treat the settlers like they were brutes."[35]

Class biases were in fact embedded in the region's earliest game laws. Early deer-reeves were chosen by the towns to "inform against those persons who killed deer out of season" – an odious task in communities where neighbours were closely acquainted. Later wardens were often paid through a portion of the fine collected by the justice of the peace, a system that encouraged them to go after those least able to mount a legal defense. Well-known Bangor game dealer Manly Hardy complained: "The rich have, for reasons best known to wardens, been allowed to kill to waste, while poor men who have killed to feed their families have been arrested." Even game commissioners admitted that the "destruction of moose is greater by residents of other States than our own, while arrests and convictions are mostly of our own citizens." In addition, local people objected to the timing of the closed seasons: "When the season is open for gunning, it is the farmer's most busy time ... By the time that the farmer gets his work done up for winter and could shoot a few partridges, it is close time again; and this shows very plainly whom the law is made for."[36] When farmers in Saint John County, New Brunswick, petitioned the government in 1895 to push the legal trout fishing season back to 1 April, to "have a month of fishing before the busy season," they were informed that anglers were "very much against fishing for trout through the ice" and reminded that the localities to which they referred "benefit largely from the visits of great numbers of anglers during the summer."[37] Such responses did little to dispel the notion that the fish and game laws were made to benefit visitors.

In the absence of adequate state funding, the Maritime provinces frequently allowed elite sportsmen and their employees to assume the burden of enforcement. New Brunswick's 1884 act gave leaseholders police and magisterial powers to regulate fishing along the rivers, thereby allowing them to pull up and destroy illegally set nets or arrest poachers. Salmon leaseholders, for example, were required to hire private guardians to protect their waters. In Nova Scotia, the Game and Inland Fishery Protection Society, a private organization founded in the 1850s mainly by officers from the British garrison in Halifax, assumed a leading role in the enactment and enforcement of regulations. Indeed, Nova Scotia's 1887 *Game Act*, published under the direction of that society, allowed private citizens to present affidavits concerning alleged illegal hunting before magistrates, thereby obtaining the power of search and seizure. Under the act, 80 percent of license fees and half of the fines collected from convictions were turned over to the society. Soldiers from the garrison were not required to take out hunting or fishing licenses as long as they were members of the society.[38] Such arrangements heightened the sense of entitlement on the part of elite sportsmen and, for rural residents, further demystified the meaning and intent of the emerging wildlife management regime.

The class biases embedded in the enactment and administration of fish and game law in the region produced a crisis of legitimacy that was expressed in a broad pattern of resistence. Not surprisingly, resistance was strongest in the many marginal farming areas of Northern New England and the Maritimes, where foraging was an integral part of the economy, resources were plentiful, and commercial hunting and fishing persisted. The extent to which fishing and hunting regulations could be thwarted is suggested by a letter from the superintendent of fisheries for the Miramichi District of New Brunswick, who informed his superior in 1897: "Overseer Boyne has 70 nets on hand and Overseer Hogan about as many seized within the last year, while Officer

John Robinson of Newcastle has 39 taken during last winter and this spring, they being seized when no one was present (owners having got out of the way)." The instructions of the Dominion Commission of Fisheries to destroy them "quietly, with as little publicity as possible" reflected the fact that fish and game enforcement was often a difficult and dangerous occupation.[39]

Although the violation of fish and game laws most often took place in a furtive and non-violent manner, violent incidents did occur. Wardens in Nova Scotia and New Brunswick were stoned by men in black face, beaten, or shot at, and on occasion had their equipment destroyed and stolen. On at least two occasions, in 1899 and 1908, federal fishery officers in New Brunswick had their homes and barns burned by poachers in retaliation for a "strict performance of duties." The 1908 incident came days after an officer had seized six nets from a notorious "gang" of poachers; it was, perhaps, a fitting tribute, it being the fortieth anniversary of the federal *Fisheries Act*.[40] In the midst of Maine's so-called Down-East game war, two game wardens were shot and killed in 1884.[41]

While the wardens bore the brunt of the hostility toward the new wildlife management regime, people helping game wardens enforce regulations also put themselves in danger. Along Vermont's Lake Champlain shore, those aiding fish wardens risked having their cattle poisoned or their barns burned. "Very naturally," a Vermont warden remarked, "men of property ... though sympathizing with the purpose of the law, are shy about contributing to its enforcement."[42] Fear of retribution from perpetrators, in addition to the predisposition of many residents against the fish and game laws, made it difficult for commissioners to secure informants in poaching cases. Attempts on the part of sportsmen themselves to impose fish and game laws on the local population could also produce violent confrontations. The most famous incident of this type occurred in New Brunswick in 1888, when the wife of a wealthy angler from Boston was killed by a rifle bullet shot from the bank of the Tobique River by poachers who had been driven off the river the previous evening by gunfire from the same fishing party. The trial of the poachers began with a fifteen-minute defense of the salmon laws by the attorney general of the province, an explicit acknowledgment of the popular dissatisfaction with the regulations.[43]

More difficult to explain was resistance among the region's established farmers, one of whom claimed that Maine was "on the edge of a revolution" in the business of game management. Complaints from farm press editors, agriculture officials, and leaders in the Grange organizations ranged from a variety of petty annoyances involving state funding and trespassing by hunters to fundamental ideological differences about the significance of the rural landscape. In narrow terms, farmers remained unconvinced about the benefits of tourism. Railroad companies, hotels, rum sellers, officials, and guides seemed to reap the rewards of an industry that was to the farmers simply an inconvenience. One Vermonter voiced his frustration that fish and game had been under discussion for years with no noticeable increase in either resource: "If we are not to have fish let us have less talk in the legislature, less law ... less jealousy of spears, nets, pounds and other devices to capture fish. Let us protect the farmer's crops from tramping and not worry about the fish."[44]

It does seem curious that farmers rejected appeals to conserve a forage resource that had been so essential to their pioneering forebears, but in fact they were well aware that these resources had taken on different meaning. By the late nineteenth century, fish and game had been diminished as adjuncts to the farm economy; they were being progressively transformed into forms of property controlled by alien state agents in the interest of nonresident recreations. The change made "every real estate holder a passive tenant and the sportsmen's pleasure the supreme law of the state."[45] Trespass rights to hunt these state-owned fungible resources on private land were particularly galling. City hunters who trampled grain, threatened or frightened livestock, left gates open and campfires burning, and otherwise threatened farm property represented a challenge to the very basis of the agrarian republic: universal petty landownership – the right, as one farmer put it, "to be owners of some portion of God's acres."[46] O.H. Leavitt of Manchester, New Hampshire, summarized the farmers' complaint:

> You are not permitted to kill game on your own land nor catch fish in your own streams, and the dogs of poachers make it unprofitable to keep sheep. Your forests are ruined by fires set by these roving hunters, and you are blamed for not caring for your woodland, and threatened with restrictive laws to define what you shall cut when you want a set of sled stakes ... Under the present operation of the fish and game laws how much better off are the farmers of New England than the peasant tenantry of Europe? What difference does it make who holds a deed of the land when the occupant is only allowed enough to live on from what he digs from the soil, while all the perquisites of nature are reserved for others?[47]

Nothing drove home the challenge to private property as pointedly as the issue of crop damage. Habitat improvement, curbs on market hunting, predator eradication, and experimental introductions brought an explosion in deer population at the end of the century, a phenomenon fish and game officials hailed with enthusiasm but farmers viewed with apprehension. As herds increased and became even more "foolish," complaints about these protected "wards of the state" grew more vigorous. "No law can long be sustained which obliges a man to stand idly by and watch the growing crops, which are his means of subsistence, being destroyed."[48] In this sense, game laws not only threatened private property but they contradicted an agrarian tradition of landscape improvement: the elimination of any natural element that threatened the farmer's livelihood. Laws that denied farmers the right to dispatch deer were a "menace to the agricultural interests."[49]

By the turn of the century farmers were pushing for changes to the game laws and each state and province eventually provided compensation for crops lost to deer. In Vermont, game enthusiast M.E. Wheeler established a private fund to be allocated by the state as compensation for farmers. Maine's fund was administered by Commissioner L.L. Carleton, who, although admitting that "deer destroy perchance now and then a little garden stuff or do some damage occasionally to crops," generally, like his counterparts in other jurisdictions, gave little credence to farmers' complaints about crop damage.[50] To dispatch a marauding deer in New Hampshire, a farmer had to find and notify the commissioners, obtain and pay for a permit, hunt up a licensed guide to witness the killing, and pay the guide for his trouble. In a similar vein, farmers in New Brunswick seeking compensation sometimes had to wait for weeks for an investigation by a game warden, and were warned against taking matters into their own hands. Vermont commissioners were more amenable, since the deer herds introduced by sporting clubs in the 1870s were clearly a "new and unaccustomed nuisance" to farmers. Commissioners responded to the increasing frequency of claims by regulating the season so as to reduce the herds in farm country and make the animals less "foolish."[51] Elsewhere, the results of the program of compensation were mixed, both in alleviating the problem and quelling the farmers' revolt.

The deeper issue among established farmers was whether the borderlands region was to be viewed as a productive, working landscape or as a "sportsman's game preserve" – an extremely sensitive question among farmers bred on the idea of perpetual rural improvement.[52] For generations, farmers had viewed the wildlands – the forests at the headwaters of the region's great rivers – as potential farmlands and hoped for families who would "open these valuable tracts and improve them." Rejecting the cult of wilderness, farmers clung to the vision of pushing back the frontier. The "home, the church, the schoolhouse, the factory and the grange hall represents all that is noblest and sweetest in our civilization, and they must be permitted to advance. Wild animals should not be allowed to bar their progress."[53]

Behind this sentiment lay a recognition that farmers were indeed losing their struggle with the wilderness. Out-migration and farm abandonment touched the core of agrarian pride and brought a "feeling of despondency among all classes of farmers."[54] Given this mood, the call to protect the working landscape was at times hysterical. "Save a farm for your country," urged Maine's H.W. Collingwood: "Don't let the woods claim it again. Don't let the wilderness grab it, but stand by that farm and save it, and fight for it. Save a farm, the noblest work a man can do. Save it for your family and country!"[55] This was the vantage from which the farmer viewed the tourist's veneration of the old, the quaint, the rustic, and the wild as the best the borderlands region had to offer. Out-migration also exacerbated anti-urbanism, since many of those who left the farm were drawn to the city by the very attractions that farmers found so distasteful in the urban sporting community. "A return to the simple habits of our forefathers is not to be expected without a social revolution, and without this we cannot hope for great improvement," one farm improver surmised.[56] The "deserted roads, overgrown pastures, ruins of old farm buildings, [and] plenty of game," celebrated as a paradise by sporting enthusiasts, were seen as signs of failure in the rural communities of the region. Farmers, whose scenic vision was far more utilitarian, preferred "thrifty" farms and neatly cleared fields to the half-abandoned fields and orchards where "partridges and foxes are more numerous than human beings."[57]

Although farm-press editors greeted the tourist industry in the 1870s as a subsidiary source of income for farmers, they soon learned that tourism cut both ways.[58] It validated rural notions of a virtuous folk and a healthy way of life, but its Arcadian vision was static – even nostalgic – at a time when rural easterners were ardently developmental in their approach. The rural landscape, according to the Maine Board of Agriculture, with its "soils, its muck beds, its marine manures, its rocks, its minerals, its fossils, its mines, its quarries of slate and lime and marble, [and] its forest lands," should be peopled by farmers, woodsmen, and factory, quarry, and mill workers, not deer and moose.[59] The vision was fundamentally progressive. According to one New Hampshire local history, the view from the local promontory before the European discovery of North America was, "nothing but dense forests and deep ravines, with no cultivated spot to relieve the monotony of the scene." How different, the writer continued, "the view now enjoyed by the privileged man who gains the summit of Mount Major ... On every side are visible the smiling villages which have sprung up by the waters of the Winnipisogee and Suncook, while he beholds the trackless wilderness as by magic changed into countless, well cultivated farms, and instead of wild beasts that roam the forest, the hills are covered with the joyful flocks and herds."[60]

The challenge to this progressive vision frustrated farmers. The cult of wilderness validated the regression of the frontier and mocked the efforts of pioneering forebears in this most unpromising region. Thus the rhetorical question: "Is the state good for nothing else but to be a hunting ground for the rest of the nation?" became a rallying cry with enduring political force. And it made the analogous query: "Is it any credit to the state that in its vast forests still live the deer, the moose and caribou?" an equally rhetorical question.[61] Maine State Grange Grand Master Obidiah Gardner complained that the Maine exhibit at the 1903 St Louis Fair – a woodland scene with Indians – reinforced "the prevailing opinion that ... Maine [was] composed of icebergs and wild animals."[62]

The first annual meeting of the North American Fish and Game Association clearly demonstrated that, despite three decades of bitterness, violence, and even occasional deaths, elite sportsmen and fish and game commissioners had made little progress in either understanding or acknowledging the fundamental issues behind rural resistance to modern wildlife management. Resolutions were passed to educate and "obtain the sympathy of the public in every way possible" through a "propaganda" campaign in the press. A few delegates made the connection between the closing of common property resources and resistance in the countryside. Collectively, however, the participants remained unrepentant advocates of the code of the sportsman and the elitist ideology that had driven wildlife administration for the past quarter-century. Indeed, their cause had by this time been converted into a progressive crusade, built on an unshakable faith that modern wildlife management was scientifically rational and economically efficient. It would both perpetuate dwindling fish and game stocks and ensure "large disbursements of money among the people, much of it in the wilder and poorer sections, where it is of the greatest value." The solution to what the Maine folklorist Edward Ives has termed the "game war" was not compromise but stricter enforcement, a universal ban on the sale of game meat, further restrictions on traditional harvesting practices and other essentially punitive measures against the "promiscuous killing by pot hunters and market men."[63]

By the second half of the twentieth century, fish and game laws in the northeastern region had achieved a significantly greater level of acceptance. This was partly a result of the policy of compensating farmers for crop damage, the introduction of expensive non-resident license fees and other efforts to make state regulations more equitable. Acceptance was also fostered after 1900 by out-migration from marginal farming areas and the breakdown of traditional patterns of occupational pluralism which incorporated foraging into the seasonal cycle of subsistence. The colonization of prime riverfront properties and wildlands by elite sporting clubs and the progressively strict regulation of commercial and subsistence hunting and fishing had played a part not only in the reorientation of resource use but also in the reconstitution of the rural population.

16

The "Boston States": Region, Gender, and Maritime Out-Migration, 1870–1930

BETSY BEATTIE

In Canada's Maritime provinces the expression "the Boston States" has long been a part of the local lexicon. For some Maritimers the phrase conjures up images of sailing vessels tacking upwind toward Boston with a cargo of hay or oats. Others connect it with ancestral stories of gift packages sent from relatives living and working in the United States. Still others recall their grandparents choosing those words to describe an almost mythic place where, as youths, they had gone to find plentiful jobs, decent wages, and freedom from parental authority, if only for a short time.

Historians of the Maritime provinces have also used the phrase "the Boston States" when writing about the out-migration that took place between Confederation and the Great Depression, years when the Maritimes experienced the net emigration of 300,000 to 500,000 of its residents.[1] Alan Brookes, for example, concluded an article on emigration from Canning, Nova Scotia, with the comment: "For hundreds of thousands of Maritimers, the choice between the burgeoning 'Boston States' and the rapidly declining outports of Nova Scotia was not hard to make."[2] Patricia Thornton, in "The Problem of Out-Migration from Atlantic Canada, 1871–1921," echoed Brookes in writing of "the pull of the neighboring 'Boston States'" on the Maritime populace.[3] Examples like these reveal how much the term has come to symbolize the world that Maritimers envisioned just beyond their borders.

The boundaries of that world were never clearly delineated, however, and even today there is no consensus on the exact meaning of the expression. While the 1998 edition of the *Canadian Oxford Dictionary* defines "Boston States" as "New England," the *Dictionary of Prince Edward Island English* proposes two separate meanings of the phrase: the first, "New England" and the second, "the United States or a portion of it."[4] How could two such divergent definitions have co-existed in the minds of Islanders and by extension, in the minds of other Maritimers as well? One way to begin solving this riddle is to look at where Maritime emigrants went when they left home.

Statistics that measure Maritime-born residents living in the United States are difficult to find because in most U.S. censuses anyone born in Nova Scotia, New Brunswick, or Prince Edward Island was labelled simply as an "English-speaking" or a "French-speaking" Canadian. The exception was the 1880 census, presumably because most of the Maritimers living in the United States at that time had been born before Canadian Confederation in 1867. Table 1, based on population statistics from the 1880 census, presents, in rank order, the six American states that had over 3,000 Maritime-born residents. Although it represents just one year of out-migration, the results are revealing. Whatever the Maritimers' mental image of the "Boston States" may have been, the region to which they migrated was paradoxically either smaller or larger than the boundaries of the six New England States. On the one hand, the preponderant majority of Maritime-born residents in the United States lived in just one state, Massachusetts; a smaller but sizable population were registered in Maine. On the other hand, among the six states with the greatest number of Maritime residents, four – California, Minnesota, New York, and Wisconsin – are not in New England at all.

The heavy concentration of Maritimers in Massachusetts and Maine is not surprising, given the close physical, cultural, and economic connections between the Maritime provinces and the two states. Cross-border travel, trade, and migration between the regions predated European settlement and continued despite wars, embargoes, and political efforts to reorient economic activity to within national boundaries. By the 1880s and 1890s rail and steamship lines also linked the two coastal regions, making population movement from the Maritimes through Maine to Boston even easier and more reliable.[5]

A closer look at settlement patterns within the state of Massachusetts reveals that the area of New England with the highest concentration of Maritime-born residents was even smaller than the total area of Massachusetts and Maine. Table 2 lists the eight cities in Massachusetts with the greatest number of Maritime-born residents as enumerated in the Massachusetts state censuses for 1885, 1905, and 1915. Over the thirty years covered by these censuses only ten different cities appear on these lists, and, with the exception of the fishing port of Gloucester

Table 1 States with Over 3,000 Maritime-born Residents in 1880

State	*No. of residents*
Massachusetts	44,926
Maine	17,849
California	5,388
Minnesota	4,187
New York	3,448
Wisconsin	3,146

Source: United States. Department of the Interior, *Statistics of the Population of the United States at the Tenth Census* (Washington: Government Printing Office, 1883), 492.

Table 2 Eight Massachusetts Cities with the Greatest Number of Maritime-born Residents – 1885, 1905, 1915

1885		*1905*		*1915*	
City	*Population*	*City*	*Population*	*City*	*Population*
Boston	23,724	Boston	29,833	Boston	33,697
Gloucester	3,578	Cambridge	5,135	Lynn	6,821
Cambridge	3,303	Lynn	4,892	Somerville	6,190
Lynn	3,016	Somerville	4,730	Cambridge	5,638
Chelsea	2,295	Gloucester	3,979	Everett	3,197
Somerville	2,033	Everett	2,887	Malden	3,154
Lowell	1,272	Malden	2,818	Gloucester	2,953
Newton	1,123	Chelsea	2,518	Newton	2,357

Source: Massachusetts. Bureau of Statistics of Labor, *The Census of Massachusetts: 1885*. (Boston: Wright and Potter, 1887–88); Massachusetts. Bureau of Statistics of Labor, *The Census of Massachusetts: 1905*. (Boston: Wright and Potter Printing Co., 1908); Massachusetts. Bureau of Statistics of Labor, *The Decennial Census 1915* (Boston: Wright and Potter Printing Co., 1918).

and the cotton mill city of Lowell, which dropped from the list after 1885, all the communities mentioned are within fifteen miles of Boston. Large cities farther inland, like Worcester, Holyoke, and Springfield, had fewer Maritime-born residents in these years than did the smaller Boston-area communities of Everett and Malden. These figures confirm that Maritimers who came to Massachusetts overwhelmingly ended up in Boston or its satellite communities. Measured by density of settlement, the "Boston States" as a destination for Maritime out-migrants was nearly synonymous with the city of Boston itself, only a small fragment of New England.

Nevertheless, as was evident in Table 1, there were also Maritimers who travelled far greater distances when they left home. Some headed to the prairies of the Midwestern states, while others ended up as far away as the Pacific coast. What emerges from these two migration patterns is not a neat picture of a mass movement to one region but a bifurcation of the migrant stream, one to a narrowly defined area along the eastern seaboard and another to regions all across the United States. Put another way, the two destinations were as different as the two definitions of the "Boston States" found in the *Dictionary of Prince Edward Island English.* Who followed which migration path, and why?

The following announcements, which appeared in newspapers from the Maritime provinces in the last three decades of the nineteenth century, are revealing. From the Halifax *Morning Chronicle*, 5 January 1870:

> Emigration – the North-West – Splendid inducements to Emigrants – Wanted 3,000 laborers and 10,000 settlers in the lands of the Lake Superior and Mississippi Railroad in the beautiful State of Minnesota – Good Wages, constant employment, and a farm of 80 acres of magnificent land, for nothing, on the line of an important railway.[6]

From the 4 February 1880 edition of the Charlottetown *Daily Examiner*, this description of job opportunities in Denver: "Carpenters' wages at present are from $2.50 to $3.00 and have every appearance of going higher in spring." Additional opportunities mentioned included openings for brick layers, painters, stone masons, and day labourers.[7]

From the 29 June 1881 issue of the *Trades Journal* of the Provincial Workmen's Association:

> "Sixty Miners lately left the Montague Gold Fields, Halifax Co., to try their fortunes in the mines in New Mexico." Also, "the demand for laborers still continues. About a thousand men ... are wanted to work on railways in the North-West."[8]

And, last, an article in the 3 October 1898 edition of the Amherst, Nova Scotia, *Daily News*:

> In a letter in private hands recently from Boston it is stated that there is so large an influx of young girls from the Blue Nose Land that wages of those who go to live out at service are largely reduced. Daughters of the beautiful Isle where the shamrock grows are the competitors of all others. Notwithstanding all this, others are still on the move in that direction.[9]

These excerpts are just a few of the many notices, advertisements, and cautionary tales published in Maritime newspapers in the late nineteenth century. They informed local residents of the opportunities and pitfalls awaiting prospective migrants and at the same time they reveal to us much about those who left home, where they went, and why. For example, although the tone varied from glowing to gloomy, all these notices mentioned jobs available at the destinations they described; newspaper publishers knew that those who planned to emigrate would be looking for employment. Historians writing about Maritime out-migration, from Marcus Hansen and J. Bartlet Brebner in *The Mingling of the Canadian and American Peoples* to Alan Brookes in his dissertation, "The Exodus," also have made the connection between emigration from the region and the attraction of better employment opportunities than those available in the declining resource-based and shipbuilding economy of the Maritime provinces in the mid- to late nineteenth century.[10] In her article on out-migration from Atlantic Canada, Patricia Thornton has even argued that the attraction of economic opportunities outside the Maritimes induced so many skilled workers to leave the region that their very absence deprived it of the talent needed to develop a strong and modern industrial base.[11]

Many of the occupations described in these articles were of a skilled or semi-skilled nature – jobs such as bricklayers, carpenters, and stonemasons – while others, like railway building, required more brawn than training. However, almost all of the jobs mentioned shared one common feature: they were meant for men. Only in the article describing an overabundance of live-in servants in Boston was there any mention of work for women. But Maritime out-migration in the late nineteenth and early twentieth centuries was not just a male activity. On the contrary, according to Patricia Thornton's research, more women than men left the region in the early years of emigration, and women remained a major component of the migrant stream throughout the period.[12] Thus, women's destinations and the work they did must have had at least as much of a bearing on migration patterns as did the location and type of employment available for men.

As far back as the 1880s the geographer E.G. Ravenstein observed that in England long-distant migration was heavily male-dominated while short-distance, rural-to-urban migration was largely a female phenomenon.[13] Statistics in Tables 3 and 4 point to similar migration patterns for men and women from the Maritimes. Table 3 presents figures for single men and women living in rural and urban areas in New Brunswick and Nova Scotia in 1871. It reveals that even in the early years of industrial development and out-migration single women outnumbered single men in urban areas while in the countryside the

Table 3 Single Men and Women in New Brunswick and Nova Scotia Living in Rural and Urban areas, 1871

	Single Men	*Single Women*	*Sex Ratio Males per 100 Females*
*Rural areas	235,372	228,404	103
*Urban areas	11,783	13,009	91

*Urban areas include the three largest cities in each province: Saint John (pop. 28,805), Portland (pop. 12, 520), and Fredericton (pop. 6,006) in New Brunswick; Halifax (pop. 29, 582), Yarmouth (pop. 5,335), and Dartmouth (pop. 4,358) in Nova Scotia. Roral areas include the rest of the provinces.

Source: Census of Canada, 1870–71 (Ottawa: I.B. Taylor, 1873).

Table 4 Maritime-born Men and Women in Boston 1885, 1895, 1905, and 1915

Year	*Men*	*Women*	*Sex Ratio Males per 100 Females*
1885	9,243	14,481	64
1895	9,713	15,066	64
1905	12,232	17,601	69
1915	13,424	20,273	66

Source: Massachusetts Bureau of Statistics of Labor, *The Census of Massachusetts: 1885* (Boston: Wright and Potter Printing Co., 1887–88); Massachusetts Bureau of Statistics of Labor, *Census of the Commonwealth of Massachusetts: 1895* (Boston: Wright and Potter Printing Co., 1896–1900); Massachusetts, Bureau of Statistics of Labor, *Census of the Commonwealth of Massachusetts: 1905* (Boston: Wright and Potter Printing Co., 1908); Massachusetts Bureau of Statistics of Labor, *The Decennial Census 1915* (Boston: Wright and Potter Printing Co., 1918).

reverse was true. In Boston, as Table 4 demonstrates, the situation was the same: throughout the years of greatest immigration, Maritime-born women heavily outnumbered their male counterparts in this major city. These figures also reveal that Boston, like the Maritime cities, attracted large numbers of single migrants, because married couples and families alone could not have accounted for the great discrepancy in numbers of males and females in the city.

One reason for the disproportionate number of women in cities, especially in Boston, is that most waged work for women in the years between 1870 and 1930 was located in urban areas. In the 1870s and 1880s female paid labour closely mirrored the work a young woman learned as she grew up – jobs involving house cleaning, childcare, needlework, or some form of untrained nursing care. In growing urban areas like Boston, families who could afford it hired others to do this work, and single Maritime women filled this demand. Table 5 groups together similar categories of occupations

Table 5 Types of Occupations of Single Maritime Women in Boston, 1880

Occupation Group	#	%
Religious work	0	.0
Professional	83	2.2
Clerical work	20	.5
Owner/Manager – Business	0	.0
Sales work	56	1.5
Domestic service	2,428	65.4
Service – Institutional	379	10.2
Service – Other	17	.5
Manufacturing	7	.2
Sewing trades	666	17.9
Printing trades	11	.3
Other manufacturing	46	1.2
Total	3,713	99.9*

*Does not add up to 100 percent because percentage figures are rounded off.

Sources: U.S. Census of Population, 1880. Schedule No. 1: Boston, Suffolk County, Massachusetts. In U.S. National Archives and Records Service. *Tenth Census of the United States, 1880.* Washington: NARS, 1960. (Reels 552–62); U.S. Census of Population, 1910. Schedule No. 1: Boston, Suffolk County, Massachusetts. In U.S. National Archives and Records Service. *Thirteenth Census of the United States, 1910.* Washington: NARS, 1982. (Reels 614–26); U.S. Census of Population, 1920. Schedule No. 1: Boston, Suffolk County, Massachusetts. In U.S. National Archives and Records Service. *Fourteenth Census of the United States, 1920.* Washington: NARS, 1992 (Reels 728–43).

that single Maritime women mentioned in the 1880 U.S. nominal census for Boston.

Statistics from the table reveal that of the 3,713 single Maritime women working in the city, 2,428, or 65 percent, were in some form of domestic service, while another 666, or 18 percent, worked in one of the sewing trades as seamstresses, milliners, or tailoresses, and so on. By 1920 job opportunities for women had multiplied as businesses began offering office jobs and sales positions to women, and medical advances had led to the growth of hospitals and development of nurse training programs. These service jobs were also concentrated in cities, and like their counterparts in the 1880s, single Maritime women of the 1920s flocked to these new and varied types of occupations. According to figures on occupational choice compiled from the 1920 U.S. nominal census for Boston and grouped together in Table 6, 4,595 single English Canadian women were employed in a broad array of jobs – 862 in professional positions including teacher and trained nurse, 506 in clerical jobs such as telephone operator and stenographer, and 230 in a variety of sales positions.[14] At the same time 1,243 had still entered domestic service and another 474 still worked in the needle trades.[15]

Table 6 Types of Occupations of Single, English-Canadian Women in Boston, 1920

Occupation Group	#	(%)
Religious work	112	2.4
Professional	862	18.7
Clerical work	506	11.0
Owner/Manager – Business	153	3.3
Sales work	230	5.0
Domestic service	1,243	27.1
Service – Institutional	504	11.0
Service – Other	118	2.6
Other Non-manufacturing employment	13	.3
Manufacturing	93	2.0
Sewing trades	474	10.3
Printing trades	16	.3
Other manufacturing	272	5.9
Total	4,596	99.9*

*Does not add up to 100 percent because percentage figures are rounded off.

Sources: U.S. Census of Population, 1880. Schedule No. 1: Boston, Suffolk County, Massachusetts. In U.S. National Archives and Records Service. *Tenth Census of the United States, 1880.* Washington: NARS, 1960. (Reels 552–62); U.S. Census of Population, 1910. Schedule No. 1: Boston, Suffolk County, Massachusetts. In U.S. National Archives and Records Service. *Thirteenth Census of the United States, 1910.* Washington: NARS, 1982. (Reels 614–26); U.S. Census of Population, 1920. Schedule No. 1: Boston, Suffolk County, Massachusetts. In U.S. National Archives and Records Service. *Fourteenth Census of the United States, 1920.* Washington: NARS, 1992 (Reels 728–43).

But job opportunities alone cannot account for the predominance of women among those who migrated to Boston between 1870 and 1930. For one thing, a growing city like Boston offered an array of jobs for men as well, and many Maritime men took advantage of them. Some who had lost work with the decline in the Maritime wooden ship building industry found work in the shipyards of East Boston.[16] Others took their skills as woodworkers to the city and became carpenters, a trade so dominated by Maritimers in the late nineteenth century that in Boston they were referred to as "Nova Scotia hatchet and saw men."[17] And Boston was just as likely as Denver to have had openings for bricklayers, stone masons, painters, and day labourers. Moreover, it is likely that Denver and other western cities also had a demand for domestic servants, seamstresses, sales clerks, and office workers, yet the notices in Maritimes newspapers rarely mentioned these jobs as inducements to go there.

Ravenstein's description of female-led migration was not only rural-to-urban; it was also short-distant, and distance likely had as much influence on where a young woman went as the job opportunities available there. To be more precise, single Maritime women likely headed to the nearest city that offered them employment. Some went to Halifax, Saint John, and Charlottetown; a greater number went to the nearest major metropolis, Boston. While sons headed anywhere that a suitable job beckoned, daughters stayed closer to home.

There were several reasons for this difference in approach to emigration, all rooted in differing expectations for sons and daughters in late nineteenth- and early twentieth-century North America. Two of the most significant factors were the structure of the pre-industrial family economy and the impact of industrial development on that structure in these years. In the rural, or pre-industrial, family economy all able-bodied members of a household were expected to contribute to the subsistence of the family, whether in the field, the workshop or the home. Though not absolute, there was a clear sexual division of labor: sons helped fathers with farm work, wood cutting, or the pursuit of the family trade; daughters worked with mothers tending gardens, preserving foods, making cloth, sewing garments, and caring for the young and the sick.[18]

Industrialization transformed the family as an economic unit, but it took over a century to complete the process, and in the years between 1870 and 1930 the Maritime provinces were right in the midst of this change. In the 1870s most Maritime residents still lived in the countryside, but urban areas were growing rapidly, and much of what had been created in the home was now produced in factories. Between 1871 and 1891, in Nova Scotia and New Brunswick alone, household production of cloth declined over 55 per cent, from 2,713,059 to 1,211,761 yards.[19] As women's work moved from home to factory, a daughter's ability to contribute to the family economy became more limited. This declining productive capacity, combined with a family's growing need for cash to purchase manufactured goods, impelled Maritimers to re-examine old paternal ideas that required daughters to stay close to home until marriage. Increasingly, young women could only help with family support by earning wages, and the highest paying jobs for them were in urban areas. Many families began to allow daughters to go to work in nearby cities but with the provision that they live under some form of adult supervision. U.S. census statistics on housing of single Maritime women reveal the effectiveness of this provision. Of the 4,157 single Maritime women living in Boston in 1880, 2,697 (over two thirds) were domestic servants while another 543 (13 per cent) boarded with private families.

Proximity to home was also important because until marriage a daughter's primary responsibility was to her parental family. No matter how demanding her job, she could be called home at any time to care for a sick family member or to help with household responsibilities if her mother or sisters could not handle them alone. Even enrollment in a nurse training program did not override family needs, as was evident in application letters to the Boston City Hospital Training School for Nurses in the years between 1886 and 1930. Prospective students were expected to assure the hospital staff that they would have no conflicting family obligations that might cause them to leave the program. The response of Annie Bertha Baker, an applicant from Tremont, Nova Scotia, was typical. She wrote: "Am perfectly free as regards the responsibility of the family, my mother being a widow in good circumstances and one brother and sister living at home."[20]

Furthermore, it was a common practice for young women to leave jobs in the summer to return to the Maritimes to help their families. Summer was the slack season for manufacturing and sales work, so for some daughters going home meant free room and board until work picked up again in fall.[21] But even domestic servants, who could work year-round, sometimes took time off in the summer to help at home, either with the blessing of their employer or with the intention of finding another job in fall. Phebe Ann Sinclair, who worked as a cook in Boston in the 1890s, for example, returned home to Flume Ridge, New Brunswick, for two months every summer to help with household chores.[22] Lillian Wentzel of Upper Foster Settlement, Nova Scotia, received a letter from her former employer in September 1905, asking if she would be coming back to work soon.[23] By contrast, sons who travelled west were far less likely to come home on a regular basis, or, in some cases, at all. In 1892, in response to a request for information on emigration from her community, Sarah Ann Sanford, of Upper Canard, Nova Scotia, testified to her local MP that her son Eben, a farmer in the Dakota Territory, "left this Province twelve years ago and has never been in his native province since."[24] Eben was just fifteen when he left Nova Scotia.

By the early twentieth century the idea of a daughter leaving home to work in Boston and its surrounding communities was no longer novel. On the contrary, it had become so common that going to the "Boston States" took on the aura of a youthful adventure, something not to be missed. As one such migrant later reported to her son, "it was considered that anyone that never got to Boston would die a fool."[25] The work world for young women had changed, with the explosion of new jobs in offices, stores, hospitals, and other institutions. Even more liberating were the new options for living arrangements. Where paternal controls had once been the norm and single Maritime women lived or worked in private families, they could now opt to live in lodging houses. These turn-of-the-century inventions were nothing more than run-down town houses that developers had divided into single rooms to rent with a lodging-house keeper hired as manager. There was no central dining room for family-style meals, few rules other than prompt payment of rent, and no supervision. Most were coeducational. As one contemporary noted, by the 1900s lodging houses had become the preferred form of housing for single working people, in part because they offered "more freedom and a bohemian existence."[26] Another observer commented that "most of the 'British Americans' living in such quarters were from Nova Scotia, with New Brunswick in second place."[27] Among those "British Americans" in 1910 were 2,058 single English Canadian women.[28]

Most of these lodging houses were clustered in a part of the city known as the "South End," where many older homes were available for conversion. The result was a concentration of unmarried youth all living in single rooms with no meals provided or places to meet friends. Businesses soon sprang up to fill these needs. One such institution was the dining room. Carved out of spare basement rooms of lodging houses, these glorified lunch counters sold meal tickets to lodgers for various combinations of breakfasts, lunches, and dinners.[29] Other establishments, of varying degrees of respectability, provided havens for young people to congregate and socialize – places such as beer gardens, dance halls, pool halls, and saloons. Still others – vaudeville theatres and movie houses – offered inexpensive evening entertainment.[30] In addition to these neighbourhood facilities, such major attractions in Boston as the amusement parks at Revere Beach, the Public Gardens, and the Public Library were just a short distance away by trolley or subway.

Not all single Maritime women lived in lodging houses; in 1910 nearly 2,300 still worked in some form of domestic service. Like Jennie Peck of Bear River, Nova Scotia, they still sent money home to help defray family expenses.[31] But even domestics, however confined by their responsibilities, could still use their days off to explore the city, as Jennie herself did on her Sunday-afternoon excursions to the Harvard Arboretum.[32] Small wonder that once Maritime families had loosened the reins on their daughters' behaviour in the city, Boston became a mecca for young, single women from the region.

Boston was not the only city in North America to offer young women better jobs and a more liberated way of life. Lodging, rooming houses, and youth-oriented amusements were just as common in Chicago, for example, as Joanne Meyerowitz has documented in her book *Women Adrift*.[33] Nevertheless, until the 1930s when immigration restrictions and Depression-era unemployment reduced cross-border migration to a trickle, Boston remained the most popular destination for single Maritime women. Some of the same factors that had made Boston attractive to earlier migrants likely contributed to Boston's continued attraction for a second generation of single Maritime women: the persistence of a daughter's responsibility to family needs, the convenient transportation connections, and the historical links that Maritimers had with New England and its major metropolis.

But by the 1910s and 1920s there was an additional tie that bound young women to Boston: the experiences of their own mothers, aunts, and other older female friends and relatives. Some still lived in the city and could ease a newcomer's way to finding housing and employment.[34] Other relatives had returned to the Maritimes with reports of opportunities that the city offered. Ethel Marguerite Chute of Bear River, Nova Scotia, for example, chose to train for nursing in Boston after hearing about the city's opportunities from two of her aunts.[35] And for some daughters, it was the recommendations of their own mothers, who themselves had gone to the city to earn money for family needs and had been transformed by the experience. As Mary Monroe, of Northeast Margaree, Nova Scotia, recalled: "My mother worked in Boston when she was a young girl ... and always said she thought that every young girl should go to the states to find out how other people lived and how they did things."[36]

Mary Monroe's mother used the word "states" but she could just as well have used the expression "Boston States," for she had gone to Boston, and her daughter followed in her footsteps by going to Newton, a Boston suburb. For both mother and daughter, their sex had helped determine their destination, limiting their choices for places to go yet also offering them opportunities for individual growth and freedom not previously available to young women. Like their male counterparts, they had left home primarily for economic reasons – to earn money for their own and their family's sustenance. But there the comparison ended. While a young man's search for employment might have taken him anywhere in North America – from the fisheries of Gloucester to the woods of Minnesota, the mines of Colorado, or the shipyards of East Boston – the nature of women's wage work, and the familial obligations that daughters carried with them when they went away often placed real or psychological boundaries on the distances young women would travel. Thus, while many of the Maritimes' youth headed to the "Boston States" in the period between 1870 and 1930, their choice of destination depended in large part on whether they were sons or daughters. When viewed through the lens of gender, the evolution of disparate definitions of the "Boston States" – "New England" and "the United States or a portion of it" – begins to make sense.

17

Borderlands, Baselines, and Big Game: Conceptualizing the Northeast as a Sporting Region

COLIN D. HOWELL

Borderlands, baseball, and big game! Bluenose sailors, Boston Marathoners, Bobby Gimby, and the Bangor Mall! Other than alliteration, what unites these diffuse examples of northeastern popular culture, from sport to song to shopping expeditions? What might discussion of their interconnectedness offer us beyond a foray into postmodernist eccentricity or unfettered speculation? This study, part of an ongoing project on sporting culture along the Mexican- and Canadian-American borders over the past century, places borderland sporting life, in all its quirkiness, ambiguity, *and* significance, at the centre of historical inquiry rather than at the periphery.

Interest in borderlands studies as a way of inquiring into questions of power, conflict, identity, and cultural formation has grown significantly over the past decade. Along with the process of globalization – the growth of ethnic nationalisms, the seeming fragility and impermanence of existing nation states, and the increasing mobility of peoples, ideas, and capital – the new interest in border relationships reveals a growing fascination with questions of cultural identity (or identities) and issues of national integrity.[1] Nations themselves, we are now told, are invented, imagined communities[2] that have the possibility of being reconceptualized quite differently from the way they are now perceived.

The very meaning of borders in both past and the present is now an issue of considerable controversy. According to W.H. New in *Borderlands: How We Talk About Canada,* borders are metaphorical constructions, and borderlands are "symptomatic of the contemporary condition, a condition of 'interstititality', *in-between-ness*, an experiential territory of intervention and revision."[3] But borders nonetheless distinguish one community from another. One need only think of the recent discourse over the treatment of suspected terrorists to know that borders carry powerful images of identity and differentiation. Borders, then, unite and divide – often at the very same moment.

In a recent article entitled "How Canadians Stopped Worrying and Learned to Love the Americans," Phil Buckner has warned against accepting a notion that borders are "artificial" impediments to closer and more "natural" relations with friendly neighbours.[4] Buckner's argument is a useful counterweight to the attitude of those who would ignore differences in institutional arrangements, social and economic policies, and cultural values that derived from the experience of border making, but his blanket critique of borderlands historiography nonetheless obscures the complex and often ambiguous history of transnational interactions between America and her neighbours to both the north and south. This is especially the case with respect to social and cultural production. In fact, as becomes apparent with respect to sporting life, it is possible to write the history of borderlands interactions and yet maintain one's distance from the contemporary continentalist or global capitalist agenda.

A useful starting point for any discussion of sport in hinterland or borderland regions is the recent literature that has developed around the process of ludic diffusion, or the diffusion of sport. Several sport historians and sociologists have suggested that sporting culture radiates from the more developed nations outward to the rest of the world, and enters host cultures at the elite level, before descending through the social order and eventually reaching the working class and common people.[5] But a top-down approach to the development of popular culture often overlooks the complexity of the process of cultural formation and the lived social, cultural, and economic experience of local communities or hinterland regions, where history is made "on the ground." Of course, these contrasting orientations need not be mutually exclusive. The significance of the history of peoples on the margins and their cultural creativity – their agency, if you like – is that they can be seen as neither dependent upon nor independent of their relationship to the nation or the metropolis. This is particularly evident from a study of the barnstorming baseballists, big-game hunters, Bluenose sailors, and Boston Marathoners, of the interwar years. Baseball, hunting, competitive international schooner races, and Maritime involvement with the Boston Marathon were essential components of the interwar conceptualization of the northeast as a transnational sporting region.

Of course, this imagined sporting community was not the only manifestation of the metropolitan influence over the Maritime provinces that Boston had exerted prior to this period – and would continue to exert more than sixty years after Confederation. Nor did it displace the presence and expression of other allegiances, particularly to Canada, in the sporting culture of the Maritimes. It does appear, however, that the assumption about a transnational northeastern sporting region was the *dominant* construction of the interwar years. The later emergence of nationalist discourses in the 1960s, including Bobby Gimby's musical testimony to Canadian Confederation and the patterns of consumption that encouraged the development of the Bangor Mall, however, undermined such earlier configurations of sporting life in the northeastern borderlands and created new forms of cultural interaction between the Maritimes and New England.

BARNSTORMERS

In 1936, just a year after his retirement from baseball, Babe Ruth climbed aboard the *SS Atlantic* in Portland, Maine, for a vacation trip to Nova Scotia. After arriving in Yarmouth, Ruth spent a few days in the southwestern part of the province in the company of friends and playing golf at the Digby Pines golf course. He then drove through the Annapolis Valley to Halifax before travelling to Westville in Pictou County to give a hitting exhibition. Although many Nova Scotians still recall this visit – and a second one in 1942 when Ruth helped open the new Navy recreation centre in Halifax – Ruth's connection to the Maritimes was more than simply incidental.

Born in Baltimore in 1895, Ruth had grown up along the city's rough-and-tumble waterfront where his parents ran a saloon catering to longshoremen, merchant sailors, roustabouts, and waterfront drifters. Considered an "incorrigible youth," Ruth was consigned for most of his childhood after the age of seven to the Saint Mary's Industrial School for boys, a reform school run by the Xaverian Brothers religious order. The brothers had a lasting influence on Ruth. "It was at St. Mary's," Ruth wrote in his autobiography, "that I met and learned to love the greatest man I've ever known ... Brother Matthias of the Xaverian order." Brother Matthias was born Martin Leo Boutilier in Lingan, Cape Breton, the son of a mining engineer with extensive family connections around the Bras D'Or Lakes. He and his older brother had both grown up playing pick-up baseball before entering the Xaverian brotherhood and following many of their Maritime compatriots before World War I down the road to the "Boston States." Indeed, a number of Ruth's major league colleagues had family in the Maritimes, among them two future Hall-of-Famers: Harry Hooper, whose father was a Prince Edward Island ship's captain, and Harold "Pie" Traynor, whose father, Jimmy, had lived in Halifax before moving to Framingham, Massachusetts. Then, too, there was John Phalen "Stuffy" MacInnes of Gloucester, a member of the Philadelphia Athletics' famed "hundred-thousand-dollar infield," whose family had roots in Cape Breton, and who, after his playing days were over, returned briefly to coach semi-pro baseball in Nova Scotia. And finally, Ruth's first wife, Helen Woodford, whom he met in South Boston, had grown up in Nova Scotia and joined her family in the southward exodus from the Maritimes to Boston.[6]

Of course, given the demands of travel associated with a major league schedule, Ruth had little opportunity for summer visits to the province – in fact for summer vacations of any sort – during his twenty-year career as a major league player. Had he not retired from baseball early in the 1935 season after a disappointing twenty-eight-game stint with the Boston Braves, however, he would no doubt have come to Nova Scotia with the Braves when they visited the province later that summer to play the Maritime champion, Yarmouth Gateways. A mid-season junket to the Maritimes by a major league team would be incomprehensible today, but in the interwar years this was part of a broad tradition of itinerant baseball barnstorming that drew the northeast together as a sporting region, a tradition that endured until the 1950s. Both of Boston's major league clubs, the Braves and the Red Sox, regarded northern New England and the Maritimes as their hinterland and asserted that claim through numerous tours of the region and in their promotional materials. Most of these visits took place at season's end, but in 1935 the Braves came north to St Stephen, New Brunswick, in the middle of their summer schedule with the express purpose of challenging the Maritime champion, and they followed up with a visit to Yarmouth to play the new champions the following summer.

Baseball connections between the Maritimes and New England were nothing new, however. As early as the 1870s, teams and players from the northeast were regular summer visitors to the Maritimes, and by the end of that decade imported professionals were beginning to show up in semi-pro lineups in Halifax, Moncton, Saint John, and Fredericton. Before 1900, travelling teams from Boston and nearby towns such as Haverford, Dorchester, and Lowell, as well as from Portland, Augusta, and Bangor in Maine, had helped create a shared baseball culture within which the border played a rather insignificant role. Various semi-professional leagues such as the Maine–New Brunswick League also spanned the border. In 1912, for example, the Saint John

Marathons (winners of the Maine–New Brunswick league pennant) played a three-game series against the champion Lowell club of the New England League in what amounted to the minor league baseball championship of the Maritimes and New England.

After the war, New England teams flooded the region. In addition to the Braves and Red Sox, Eddie Carr's Auburn Club from Cambridge, Massachusetts, which the Boston *Post* dubbed the "fastest amateur team around Boston," Bob Bigney's South Boston All-Stars, Dick Casey's Neponsett All-Stars, the James A. Roche team of Everett, Massachusetts, Frank Silva's Connecticut Yankees, and touring teams from Arlington, Dorchester, Quincy, Newburyport, Somerville, Malden, Salem, Taunton, and Attleboro would turn Maritime ball diamonds into "burned over districts" of New England baseball barnstorming. They were joined, moreover, by various assemblages of African-American ballplayers from the so-called negro leagues. As Chappie Johnson's Travelling All-Stars, the Philadelphia Colored Giants, the New York Black Yankees, the Ethiopian Clowns, and the Zulu Cannibal Giants barnstormed the province, they gave Maritime fans the opportunity to see leading stars of the negro leagues, such as Bill Jackman and others, playing against their own clubs. Without question the most popular of these teams was Burlin White's Boston Royal Giants, who mixed straight baseball with clownish routines. These routines, or reams as they were called, demonstrated their baseball skills and dramatized their "otherness" as a way of attracting fans to the park. The Giants returned to the Maritimes year after year during the thirties, playing over 300 games against predominantly white local teams. Despite the carnivalesque nature of these tours, which often involved the Giants mocking their white opponents, baseball fans in the Maritimes responded warmly to the Giants, and in the process contributed to an idealized image of the northeast as a region with a shared sporting identity that transcended both the border and the racial divide.[7]

This romanticized transnationalism, of course, stood in contrast to the discourses of betrayal and regional neglect that surrounded the place of the Maritimes within Confederation, and which had been given political expression in the Maritime Rights movement.[8] Indeed, the language of regionalism within Canada and linkages with New England resonated throughout the interwar years in the sporting pages of Maritime newspapers. In addition to the constant coverage of the baseball connection with New England, what is particularly striking is the absence of teams from the rest of Canada from Maritime baseball diamonds in these years. Indeed, the 1935 visit of the Montreal Dow team for two games marks the only instance of a team from elsewhere in Canada playing in the Maritimes and being reported in the region's newspapers during the entire period from the turn of the century to World War II.

BIG GAME HUNTERS

Another component of the interwar imagining of the northeastern borderlands as a sporting region is connected to baseball but not restricted to it. To illustrate, let me return to Babe Ruth. Most Nova Scotians regarded Ruth's visits and those of the touring ball clubs from the United States as an indication of the region's modernity. To get to the Maritimes, these visitors took advantage of improved rail and highway systems. At the same time, the hotly contested matches seemed to demonstrate that Nova Scotians could play on a par with some of the best ballplayers in North America. The need to compete effectively with barnstorming clubs was thus something Nova Scotians took seriously. It is hardly surprising, therefore, that Claude "Dingie" McLeod, the young pitcher who would serve up Ruth's plate offerings in Westville, would take the opportunity to show the crowd that he could strike out baseball's demigod. After a mixture of fastballs on the inside of the plate and curve balls away, Ruth had had enough. He walked out to the mound and told McLeod that he seemed to be missing the point. The crowd was there not to see him strike out, but to watch him hit home-runs. "So just give me some of those big drug store fastballs down the middle like you're supposed to do."[9]

Of course one can find multiple meanings in incidents of this sort. For one thing, Maritimers' perceptions of the significance of these baseball interactions seem to have differed from those of the visitors. The fans in Westville may well have been delighted, even if a little embarrassed, to see one of their own reduce the Babe to the status of a mere mortal. Ruth, on the other hand, had come to the region not because of its modernity or the level of competition that ballplayers in the Maritimes could provide, but rather because it represented to him a natural sporting paradise where he could golf, fish, and hunt to his heart's content and at the same time bask in public adulation. Romantic images of northern New England and the Maritimes as a sportsman's paradise were commonplace in the interwar years, and local newspapers delighted in reporting on hunting trips involving American sporting celebrities. The *Sydney Record* of 13 November 1925, for example, reported on a moose-hunting expedition "40 miles into the wilds of Canada," more specifically into New Brunswick, involving Ruth and three of his baseball buddies. Apparently Ruth did not impress his guide, because he could only walk the first fifteen miles into the bush and needed a horse to complete the other twenty-five.

He did, however, bag his moose, and later regaled the press with his triumph. "As soon as I can get a freight train to carry the head back and get it stuffed, I'll show it to you," Ruth gloated. "The Yankee Stadium is the only place big enough to hold it."[10]

Two years later the press reported on another post-season moose-hunting trip by a group of players from the World Series champion Yankees and some of their former teammates. The players were accompanied by newspaperman William Slocum of the New York *Evening Telegram* and Dr J. Wolford, a big game hunter and baseball devotee from Philadelphia. Wolford had led a group of baseball stars on a hunting trip to New Brunswick in 1924, an expedition that had brought down four bull moose and five deer. On this trip, Jack Doran, a catcher for the Fredericton Tartars, guided the hunters into the woods at Clarendon on the main line of the CPR. This was reported to be the same territory that heavyweight boxer Jack Dempsey had stalked a few years before and where "the fistic star knocked out his first moose."[11] There are a number of similar reports of baseball big game hunters and other celebrities such as Zane Grey stalking the woods of Maine and the Maritimes.[12] Furthermore, the Boston Red Sox star Ted Williams purchased a summer camp on the Miramichi River in order to pursue his avocation as a fly fisherman after his retirement from baseball.

These stories of celebrity hunting trips reinforced musings about the region as a haven for American capitalists who, in seeking out the recuperative benefits of a natural paradise, might in turn come to recognize the potential for future resource development.[13] As Ian McKay has pointed out, the interwar period had witnessed a reconceptualization of the Maritimes as an idyllic paradise, a more authentic and simple place with a population living closer to nature than inhabitants of bustling North American cities. In the wake of deindustrialization and the consequent economic distress of the 1920s and 1930s, the language of industrial progress and modernity that had predominated before the war had given way to antimodernist fantasies about the virtue and innocence of the Maritime folk.[14] Yet the romanticization of rural innocence often carried with it the thirst for commercial advantage. According to Beatrice Hay Shaw's *Nova Scotia: For Beauty and Business*, a 1923 publication promoting the province and its untapped resources, for example, the province offered American businessmen a respite from their hectic lives as well as a resource base ready to be exploited and developed. Shaw's imagery, in fact, bordered on the salacious. She depicted Nova Scotia as the innocent blue-nosed lady-in-waiting sitting patiently for "the man of rod and gun. At this moment [she] holds her arms outspread, and bares her rich bosom to the world, calling to it to come and receive nourishment and life from her ripe breasts."[15]

Indeed, in conceptualizing the northeast as a sporting region, Maritimers created a discourse that married antimodernist assumptions about regional simplicity and a "natural" life-style to a cautious hope of a future transformed by modern technology. Antimodernism might have offered some consolation to a region that was already experiencing the destructive implications of industrial capitalist consolidation and the dismantling of its secondary manufacturing, but this nostalgia did not necessarily imply a rejection of all things modern.

BOSTON MARATHONERS

For most Maritimers, the city of Boston symbolized modernity and opportunity and acted as a safety valve for those unable to make a living in hardscrabble communities throughout the provinces. Centuries of economic interaction beginning in the seventeenth century and a history of widespread out-migration from the Maritimes to the northeastern United States in the decades following Confederation reinforced New England's metropolitan connection to its Maritime hinterland. Moreover, for many Maritimers in the interwar period, Boston seemed to exert a stronger and seemingly more benign influence than either Montreal or Toronto. While Toronto and Montreal were often criticized for their predatory behaviour in an age of deindustrialization, and while the rhetoric of Maritime Rights attributed the shortcomings of Confederation to Central Canada's broken promises, Boston was for many Maritimers literally their second home.

The seemingly benign nature of Boston's metropolitan authority explains in part both the fascination and the considerable involvement that Maritimers had with the Boston Marathon during the interwar years. Interest in marathon running at the turn of the century grew out of the sportive nationalism of the day and the inauguration of the modern Olympic Games in 1896. The brainchild of a French nobleman, Baron Pierre de Coubertin, the modern Olympics were associated with the classical symbols of Greek antiquity, not the least of which was the marathon run. At the 1896 games in Athens, the marathon distance was set at 24.8 miles, the distance a legendary Greek foot-soldier was supposed to have run across the plains of Marathon to carry to Athenians the news of the Greek army's victory over a mighty Persian invasion force. John Graham, manager of the American track and field team at the Athens Games and a member of the Boston Athletic Association (BAA) founded a decade earlier, was so impressed with the majestic spectacle that on his return he set about organizing the first Boston marathon, to be hosted by the BAA in 1897. It has been held annually without interruption ever since.

Boston's significant presence in the turn-of the-century world of track and field was hardly surprising. The first U.S. Olympic team had been an aggregation of students and "gentlemanly amateurs" drawn largely from American northeastern universities, including Princeton, Harvard, Yale, Boston College, and the Massachusetts Institute of Technology. Graham had taken with him a six-man delegation from the Boston Athletic Association, and they were accompanied by James Connolly of Boston's Suffolk Athletic Club. In the twelve track and field events at Athens in 1896, members of the BAA won seven gold medals, and Americans attending the games delivered the club cheer, "B.A.A.–Rah-Rah-Rah," to an approving audience.[16]

Although the first Boston Marathon was won by New Yorker John J. McDermott, Canadians were prominent competitors in the years before World War I. Canadian Ronald MacDonald, a student at Boston College ,won the 1898 race, and two years later a Canadian contingent led by John Caffery of Hamilton took first, second, and third places. Caffery won again in 1901. In 1907 Hamilton-based Onondaga runner Tom Longboat captured the crown. Three years later Fred Cameron of Amherst, Nova Scotia, became the first Boston Marathon champion to hail from the Maritime provinces, leading the race from beginning to end.[17]

Nova Scotia's interest in the Boston race intensified during the 1920s, spurred on by the remarkable success of home-bred marathoners Victor MacAulay of Windsor, Silas McLellan from nearby Noel in Hants County, and Billy Taylor and Johnny Miles from Sydney Mines. Of the four, Miles was the most accomplished, winning the event in 1926 and again in 1929 and becoming, in the words of local sportswriter Gee Ahearne, "the long distance champion runner of the world." Although the victories of Miles overshadowed the careers of MacAulay, McLellan, and Taylor, it is nonetheless worth remembering that Maritimers in the 1920s and 1930s applauded the accomplishments of all these fine runners. MacAulay's top five finish in the 1924 Boston Marathon catapulted him to a spot on the Canadian Olympic team that year. In 1925 he returned to Boston and finished a respectable seventh. Just two weeks after Miles's victory in the 1926 Boston Marathon, McLellan won the annual Italian Athletic Association ten-mile marathon in Lynn, Massachusetts, over Clarence DeMar, a multi-year champion of the Boston race. Billy Taylor finished second to Miles and ahead of DeMar in a race in Halifax in 1927 and joined the others on Nova Scotia's provincial team at Boston the following year. The province's 1928 team wore shirts emblazoned with a red maple leaf surrounded with "Nova Scotia" in large black letters, dramatizing the tension that surrounded the relationship of the Maritimes to the nation itself.[18]

Maritime involvement in the Boston Marathon contributed to the imagining of the northeast as a coherent transnational sporting region. It also gave vent to the ambivalent allegiances and deep frustrations that accompanied postwar economic decline. Both the marathoners themselves and the newspapermen who reported upon them constructed stories that reinforced contemporary discourses about regional identity, national betrayal, and Maritime Rights. In many ways, Maritime sporting heroes and officials of the Maritime Provinces Amateur Athletic Association (MPAAA) became stalking horses of postwar Maritime regionalism. In the summer of 1924, for example, Victor MacAulay charged that Maritime athletes on the Canadian Olympic team had been discriminated against by head coach J.R. Cornelius. MacAulay complained that he had had to wear running shoes that were two sizes too large for him, and that Maritimers had received poor lodgings in comparison with athletes from central Canada and the west.[19] Charges of this sort led J.G. Quigley of the MPAAA to attend a meeting of the Canadian Amateur Athletic Union in 1925 where he called for "Maritime Rights" for the region's athletes.[20] Silas McLellan lodged a similar complaint to that of Victor MacAulay during the 1928 Olympics. The third Canadian to finish in the Olympic marathon that year, McLellan complained that officials of the Canadian Olympic committee had woken him up at 11 o'clock at night to give him a rub-down, and made him sleep in a room with five others. His complaint prompted A.C. Pettipas, Maritime representative on the Canadian Olympic Committee, to protest McLellan's shabby treatment.[21]

Issues of regional alienation and allegiance – not to mention the difficulties involved in making a living in a chronically depressed region where the British Empire Steel Corporation, the main employer in industrial Cape Breton, teetered on financial ruin – were equally evident in the career of Nova Scotia's premiere marathoner of the interwar period. When Johnny Miles, a nineteen-year-old delivery boy from Sydney Mines, won the Boston Marathon in 1926 in his first marathon competition, he became an immediate hero in his native province. For young working-class men such as Miles, running offered an inexpensive means of exercise since it required only a pair of shoes and the time and space to train, and victory in a big event could lead to a steady job. At the same time, the more accomplished a runner became, the heavier the financial costs associated with training. Unlike team sports such as hockey, football, baseball, and lacrosse, track and field offered few opportunities to make money from competition, and amateur athletes like Miles found themselves dependent on financial support from the community in order to defray travel and accommodation cost. In 1926, for example, Miles received financial assistance from his home town and from the Cape Breton Club of Boston, before rewarding his supporters with a victory in the big race.[22]

When Miles and his parents returned from Boston, they were thrown into a dizzying whorl of local functions throughout Sydney Mines, North Sydney, Glace Bay, and Sydney. They also were inundated with invitations to compete in races across the Maritimes and New England. While he could not compete in them all, he did contest nineteen major races in the northeast, until winter brought the 1926 racing season to a merciful close. The price of success was high. In return for financial support and media coverage, Miles and his family were expected to participate in the maintenance of their communities, local, provincial, or regional. The strain of this implied social contract, when combined with Johnny's hunger for success, took its inevitable toll. On 12 June, less than two months after his victory in Boston, Johnny collapsed just 220 yards from the finish line in a ten-mile race in Melrose, Massachusetts. According to the *Halifax Herald*, he suffered from heat exhaustion. Miles's biographer, Floyd Williston, suggested that Johnny had gorged himself on rich pastries at a reception earlier on the day of the race. Neither considered the likelihood that the public appearances associated with Johnny's "social contract" were a factor contributing to his exhaustion.[23]

Just days after Miles's collapse in Melrose, press reports surfaced that he had received offers of financial support from track and field clubs in Boston and Hamilton, Ontario. Johnny's father expressed to the media his concern about the possibility of leaving Sydney Mines, but made it clear that the family would stay in Cape Breton only if he and his son were provided with steady jobs. "There is absolutely no beating about the bush on this score," he told the *Halifax Herald*. "We either get jobs which will not have us tied down hard and fast in order to make a comfortable living or we change our place of residence. Hundreds who found themselves in exactly the same position as we are now have done just this, and why shouldn't we? I have received many promises in order that we might remain in Nova Scotia, but to date they have just been promises."[24] Throughout the summer of 1926, negotiations continued between the Miles family and prospective clubs, and on 13 August the *Halifax Herald* reported that Miles had accepted an offer from the BAA. This report was premature, however. The family eventually declined that offer and returned to Cape Breton.[25]

Over the winter and into the spring of 1927, Johnny trained for the defence of his Boston Marathon title, supported by the Johnny Miles Training Fund set up by the *Halifax Herald.* The candid "Gee" Ahern wrote that the family was in need of "tangible" support and that all well-wishers should "say it with cash." Donations for the fund poured in from all over Nova Scotia and from Johnny's supporters in Boston. The publisher of the *Herald,* William Dennis, believed that support for Miles was warranted because he was both an "asset and advertiser" to a province interested in attracting tourists.[26] An investment in Miles was thus an investment in one's self and one's country. The material circumstances that faced the Miles family were difficult to endure. Even when combined, Miles's father's mining pay and his pay as a clerk could not meet the costs of competing on a regular basis. Nor was it easy to raise money from Cape Breton miners, who faced wage cuts in their struggles with BESCO and themselves relied upon relief from across the country to battle chronic poverty. Still, over $1,500.00 was collected for the Miles family before their departure to Boston to train for the 1927 event.[27]

The 1927 marathon was run in what was unusually hot weather for Boston in April. Miles quickly succumbed, as steaming tar from the hot pavement seeped through the thin base of his shoes. Apparently his father had shaved the bottoms of his sneakers with a straight razor, hoping that thinner soles would translate into a faster time. Before he called it quits at the seventh mile Miles's feet were burned, blistered, and bloodied. He was not alone. More than a hundred runners dropped out because of the heat, including thirty-five before the second mile.[28] Nevertheless, his supporters were quick to criticize. Bill Cunningham, a *Boston Post* sportswriter and friend to Miles, suggested that "Miles should have finished the race if he had to crawl across the line on his hands and knees after the hour of midnight with his bleeding feet wrapped in newspaper."[29] There was initial underlying resentment in the Maritimes as well. It was as if Johnny had reneged on his obligation to those who supported him. Their disappointment quickly healed upon his return to Cape Breton, however. Ten thousand fans turned out to see him defeat Jimmy Henigan, United States ten-mile champion, and Clarence DeMar, eight-time winner of the Boston Marathon (including 1927), in a five-mile race at the Black Diamond track in Glace Bay. On Dominion Day another ten thousand people turned out in Sydney to witness his third-place finish behind Albert Michelson and Jimmy Henigan, and ahead of Clarence DeMar, who finished fourth.[30]

The race in Sydney was one of Miles's last in the Maritimes. In September he left for Hamilton to attend the Olympic trials. After a disappointing ninth-place finish in Hamilton, the Canadian Olympic committee suggested that he was in poor physical condition and requested that he remain there to train. His father also wanted him to stay in Hamilton, where he would work with top-notch trainers in first-class facilities and be given a job at International Harvester inspecting twine.[31] The Hamilton Olympic Club had been trying to recruit him for over a year. Although Miles did not make a formal public announcement that he would be leaving the Maritimes and taking up permanent residence, the invitation from Hamilton and the pressure applied by the Olympic committee made the decision to leave irresistible. His family soon followed him to Ontario, and they purchased a house adjacent to Hamilton Stadium where Miles frequently trained. He finished sixteenth at the Amsterdam Olympics in 1928.

Interestingly, after his departure, Nova Scotians began to cheer instead for runner Billy Taylor. Had Miles gone to Boston he would likely still have been regarded as a Maritimer in the Boston States; but for some, forsaking Nova Scotia for Ontario was tantamount to betrayal. Like Miles, Taylor was also a British immigrant, an ex-miner and ex-grocery clerk from Sydney Mines. After finishing second to Miles and ahead of DeMar in Halifax in 1927, it seemed that Taylor might well be the next Marathon Champion. In 1928 Taylor dominated Maritime races while Miles was winning his share in Central Canada. For Maritimers the 1929 Boston Marathon was Billy Taylor versus Johnny Miles. Miles won the race and set a course record, while Taylor finished sixth.[32] In June the two appeared at the Black Diamond track in Glace Bay. Residents of the colliery districts cheered lustily as Taylor lapped Miles on the seventh mile of a ten-mile race that Taylor went on to win.[33]

While back in Cape Breton for the race Miles finally explained his decision: "I never would have left the Maritime Provinces if there had been anything here for me or any prospects at all for my future ... Every place I went to look for something in my line the answer was we have nothing for you just now."[34] He raced for a few more years and finished fourteenth at the 1932 Olympics before retiring at twenty-six. Miles went on to receive an MBA degree and was employed for forty-three years with International Harvester.[35] Ironically, Taylor also left the region to further his career, moving to Montreal in 1930 to join the distinguished Campbell Park Athletic Club. After several victories, however, he died suddenly from complications after suffering sunstroke at a race in Montreal in June 1931.[36] That both Miles and Taylor finished out their athletic careers in other parts of Canada attests both to their national sensibilities and the limited employment opportunities available to them in Cape Breton. Nevertheless, for most of the interwar period, Maritime sporting connections with New England were more visible than those with the rest of the country.

BLUENOSE SAILORS

In the post-Confederation years,[37] many Maritimers from ports such as Lunenburg, Yarmouth, and Gloucester, Massachusetts, who made their livelihood fishing or sailing the waters of Georges Bank and the Gulf of Maine, or carried on coastal commerce between Nova Scotia and New England, were also tempted down the road to the "Boston States." Not surprisingly, it was their pride in nautical skills or ship building and the sense of competitiveness that accompanied the exploitation of marine resources, that provided the impetus for sporting competition across the international border. In 1905 a 360–nautical-mile sailboat race from Marblehead, Massachusetts, to Halifax was contested for the first time. The Marblehead race was held on a sporadic basis before and after World War I until the Boston Yacht Club and the Royal Nova Scotia Yacht Squadron agreed in 1939 to organize and sponsor the event. The race continues to be run even today on a biennial basis, and in recent years has featured over 100 boats in five divisions.

The connections between the Maritimes and New England were further consolidated after World War I when the schooner *Bluenose*, under the direction of Captain Angus Walters, made her reputation for speed on the open sea. Built in Lunenburg in 1921, the *Bluenose* won every racing competition she entered but one, and over the years established a secure place in regional folklore. The *Bluenose*'s reputation was founded largely upon her successes in the International Fisherman's Trophy Race, a contest first proposed by Colin McKay, one of the region's most influential socialist leaders, as a way of kick-starting the region's struggling postwar economy.[38] Dennis, publisher of the *Halifax Herald* and notable defender of regional causes, whether they involved Maritime Rights or the promotion of Johnny Miles, immediately saw the value of a series of races pitting Canadian fishing schooners against American vessels, in order to settle the claims of fishermen in Lunenburg and Gloucester as to who had the faster fleet. After the American vessel *Esperanto* won the first two races in the fall of 1920, work began on the construction of the *Bluenose* in Lunenburg's Smith and Rhuland shipbuilding yards, and she was launched in time for the 1921 fishing season. Once she met the requirement of a full season in the bank fishery, the *Bluenose* was ready to contest the International Fisherman's Trophy. She won the trophy for the first time in 1921, and never relinquished it until the series was brought to a close by the outbreak of war in 1939.

Dennis's promotion of a race involving fishing schooners at the very time that the fishery was being transformed by the introduction of the gas-powered fishing trawlers was just one manifestation of a broader construction of fishermen and life at sea as the embodiment of Maritime folk identity. According to Ian McKay, as Nova Scotia's postwar culture producers constructed antimodernist images of a sturdy and virile folk, they offered a culture of consolation to a region suffering from de-industrialization and the failed promises of capitalist modernity.[39] It was not only Maritimers who found these romantic images appealing, however. Reporting on the 1922 series involving the *Bluenose* and the American vessel the *Henry Ford*, the Toronto *Globe* described rival captains Angus Walters and Clayton Morrissey as "hard fisted, rollicking sailormen, whose vocation necessitates almost constant defiance of death, [and who] display a brand of sportsmanship that might well be emulated by certain others ... in the sporting eye."[40]

In the first few years of the competition, disputes arose concerning eligibility requirements for the race between those who celebrated the fishermen's skills at sea and members of the yachting fraternity who, in the tradition of the America's Cup competition, were more interested in improvements in racing technology. Dennis agreed that there had to be practical rules for the governing of competition, but insisted: "They should be interpreted and carried out by men who know every phase of the fishing and shipping industry." No yachtsmen, Dennis argued, should "be connected with the competition in any capacity."[41] Earlier, Halifax trustees of the international trophy had barred the Boston schooner *Mayflower* from the race because it had not abided by the rules requiring that vessels be working fishing schooners, and this decision was upheld by the United States Racing Committee, which barred the *Mayflower* from the American elimination finals.

Over the next fifteen years, as the races continued without interruption and disputes over eligibility were held in check, the *Bluenose* came to symbolize the close association of Nova Scotia and New England. Since 1937 the ship's image has been reproduced on the Canadian dime, and the *Bluenose II* was constructed in 1963 in the same shipyards as her predecessor. Although the replica never races, she continues to evoke romantic memories of an earlier age of sail and of past sporting glories.[42] As Cheryl Sullivan has written, "People from all walks of life and from ports all over the world still respond to the romantic past which *Bluenose II* suggests. Millions of people have boarded her, sailed on her, or simply looked at her; and when the time comes for an extensive and expensive refit, it is to these people who feel an emotional connection to the *Bluenose* that the government turns."[43]

CONCLUSION: BOBBY GIMBY AND THE BANGOR MALL

In the interwar period Maritimers and New Englanders developed a sense of a shared sporting culture through connections on sporting diamonds, in hunting grounds, on the ocean, and along long-distance race courses. With the exception of ice hockey, which helped link Canada together through nationwide competition and weekly Hockey Night in Canada radio broadcasts beginning in the 1930s, the emerging national sport culture of the interwar period garnered little support in the Maritimes. Of course, sporting connections between the Maritimes and Canada can be found, especially in regard to Olympic competitions; yet interwar Maritime sporting allegiances were likely to be regional and transnational, rather than pan-Canadian. Only with World War II would the dominant assumption of the northeast as a coherent transnational sporting region begin to give way to alternative constructions. New patterns of consumption – and the growing influence of television – would lead to the perception that the Maritimes truly shared in a Canadian sporting culture. The postwar years also witnessed new patterns of migration that weakened transnational linkages. Instead of making the traditional exodus to New England, Maritimers increasingly left the region in search of jobs in Toronto, and eventually in cities further west.[44] In the 1960s, moreover, amid the heightened nationalism of the day (evident in the flag debate, and the Expo 67 celebrations) the Canadian state took a more active role in the development of a national sporting culture. Canada Games competitions, the coming of two major league baseball franchises, coast to coast television diffusion of hockey and Canadian football, and the marginalization of hunting as a sporting pursuit prompted a re-imagining of the Maritime sporting universe. And so, as Maritimers followed Bobby Gimby in singing about their love of Canada at the "hundredth anniversary of Confederation," or were "goin' down the road" in new directions in search of work and well-being, their once intimate connections with northern New England were displaced by the occasional holiday shopping trip to the Bangor Mall.

18

The Epic of Greater North America: Themes and Periodization in North American History

REGINALD C. STUART AND M. BROOK TAYLOR

Comparative study of New England and the Maritime provinces seems at first glance to raise only regional questions. Are the two areas historically separate or are they a single region? And how do connections and comparisons lead us to resolve such issues? The essays in this volume demonstrate that to pose these questions in a regional setting leads at once to a continental – even a global – context. When Herbert Eugene Bolton wrote in 1932 about the idea of an Epic of Greater America, he argued for a broad historical vision of the Americas in order to offset the focus on the United States that usually passed for American history.[1] Bolton gazed south toward Latin America, not north toward Canada; yet his argument formed part of the intellectual foundations of the "borderlands" approach to Canadian-American affairs. Two problems remained, however. First, once we avoid the significance of national identities, especially the Canadian national identity, what remains may still be U.S. history writ large. And second, in the eyes of the rest of the world, scholarly or otherwise, the twentieth century bestowed a cultural tendency to identify "American" with the United States. So, to borrow from Bolton once again, an effective comparison of the Maritime provinces and the New England states depends in part on our ability to construct an epic of greater North America. And this must include a set of coherent themes and a periodization that allow us to plot historical parallels and shared themes while still respecting national boundaries, the jurisdictions they enclose and the ways in which the neighbouring societies remain distinct.

America. A terminological problem remains. In the eyes of the rest of the world there is only one, and its characteristics are those of the United States. It stands for individualism, capitalism, and power. In the hands of a critic, the modifiers are corrosive, materialistic, unilateral; in the hands of an admirer, free, unrestrained, super. It is the birthplace of the consumer society, mass culture, and globalism. It is a magnet for people seeking refuge and personal advancement. It has the flaws of its virtues. Citizens of the United States are unlikely to be troubled by these perceptions. They can denounce their country's flaws and trumpet their country's virtues with as much verve as anyone abroad. Citizens of Canada, particularly of English-speaking Canada, however, find these perceptions intensely frustrating. If there is but one America, that logic threatens Canada's existence. If America's characteristics are defined by the United States, then Canada has nothing of significance to contribute. Not surprisingly, Canadians have expended a great deal of energy over the years searching for characteristics that are unique and valuable. Indeed, the quest itself may be the Canadian identity.

One consequence of this dichotomy in perceptions between Canada and the United States is the creation of two largely discrete historiographies. Incredibly, except that no one seems to find it incredible, there is no general survey history text of North America. This makes the continent unique in the realm of modern historiography. If there is only one America, the United States, then there is little need for U.S. historians to study or even pay attention to their northern (or southern) neighbour. By the same token, for Canadians a continental approach risks implicit acceptance of continentalism while a distinct historiography offers an implicit assertion of independence. Canadian scholars interested in a broader interpretive framework have had their patriotism questioned, and the questioners have been criticized for letting patriotism get in the way of scholarship.[2]

This is not healthy. It is also confusing for those living outside North America, as one of the authors discovered during two two-year terms teaching in an Area Studies Department in Japan. Such departments, as the name suggests, divide the world into continental or sub-continental areas, such as Latin America, or Southeast Asia. Each has its own survey texts, developed historiography, and scholarly associations. North America is the one area that resists this formula. Why is there no general survey history of North America? Indeed, why are so few thematic surveys set within a continental framework? Non–North American colleagues were puzzled. In their eyes, few countries, integrated at so many levels, were such natural cases for a supra-national analysis. The area had only two, rather than many, countries because

Mexico was part of Latin America. The disparity of scale between Canada and United States would not seem an insurmountable obstacle for an area approach. Indeed the most arresting observation was that the national differences were more rather than less interesting when viewed within a larger continental context.

There are any number of ways one could get at the problem of defining a greater North America. Pollsters, sociologists, and linguists have various angles. Historians should consider what distinguished North Americas historical development, seen first from the external context of the modern world, then from the internal context of cross-border relationships. For the external context, the millennial-ending spate of global histories of the twentieth century offers a useful set of perspectives. Among the most prominent of these works are the multi-authored *Oxford History of the Twentieth Century* and the *Columbia History of the Twentieth Century*, as well as the individual efforts of Eric Hobsbawm, Clive Ponting, and J.M. Roberts.[3]

Hobsbawm was first off the mark in 1994 with *Age of Extremes: The Short Twentieth Century, 1914–1991*. The subtitle's argument generated considerable debate. Do these years better bracket a period than the strictly chronological century? Roberts has his doubts. Is Hobsbawm too Eurocentric? Ponting thinks so. But the arguments are beside the point. How can one possibly impose a global pattern or ethos on so vast a sprawl as a century? The Oxford and Columbia volumes take a different tack. Rather than essay an impossible narrative, they accept the more or less arbitrary nature of the one hundred years between 1900 and 2000, then use them to measure the most significant changes over time. Adopting this approach, it really does not matter where one begins. 1900 makes just as much sense as 1914. The aim is not to establish a turning point but, as Gary Wills writes, to let the most tangible differences over a period of time leap out.[4] One only requires a period extensive enough for the scale of change to be obvious, and for this purpose a century is convenient.

So what changed? The twentieth century's foremost fact is the tripling of the world's population, from 1.63 billion to 6 billion plus, mostly through an extraordinary improvement in what William H. McNeill calls death control. In particular, the application of improvements in medical science, such as sanitation and inoculation, were critical. So, too, was complementary progress in agricultural science coupled with revolutions in communications systems that moved food to markets. Both these required a growth in state structures at municipal, national, and international levels. Starvation, when it occurred, resulted from a failure of markets rather than of food production. The neo-Malthusian fears raised at the United Nations

International Conference on Population held in Cairo in 1994 thus seemed exaggerated.[5]

These breakthroughs not only increased the world population but they also altered the patterns of demographic distribution. Two main trends stand out. First was a movement from rural agricultural to urban industrial or post-industrial societies. Cities actually became healthy places to live. But immigration, not high birth rates, fuelled their growth. Urban living penalized large families and placed a premium on extended education. This had profound implications for family structures, a shift from what Hobsbawm calls the vertical ties of the traditional rural family centred on the patriarchal father, to horizontal ties binding peers, children to children, teens to teens, adults to adults. The freedom among parents to cohabit and split, marry and divorce, is one symbol of the breakdown of the old order. The growth of an international youth culture is another. These are whole new kinds of communities and the phenomenon argues for the globalization of culture in transnational layers.

The second significant trend was a proportional increase in the population of the non-industrialized developing regions coupled with a proportional decline in industrialized developed regions, a particularly pronounced sea change in the post–Second World War period. Between 1950 and 1990 the population of the less developed regions, including China, exploded from about 1.7 billion to over 4 billion. During the same period, the developed regions of Europe, North America, and Japan only grew from .75 billion to 1.25 billion, and fertility rates fell below replacement levels. The geopolitical consequences of this trend are profound. Virtually all of the colonial empires of 1900 disintegrated, to be replaced in astonishing rapidity by a host of new nations. This reconfiguration presented an external challenge to the developed world's political and economic hegemony, and, because of new global migration patterns, brought about internal challenges to its national identities (and residual racism) as industrialized nations became increasingly multicultural.

The developed world's continuing hold over less developed nations is primarily a function of its spreading economic dominance and the military power it supports. For if the growth of the world population is the first pre-eminent fact of the twentieth century, the growth of global wealth is the other. Absolute levels of real per capita income are three or four times higher at the century's end than they were at its beginning. But here, distribution did not favour the developing world. While the economies of the less developed regions grew substantially, and in the case of Asia and Latin America grew faster than those of the developed nations, per capita incomes grew more slowly because of rising populations. Currently, the average income of the three billion inhabitants of Sub-Saharan Africa, India, and China is about one-twentieth of that of the world's twenty-four most developed nations. Convergence between the richest and the poorest has not occurred on a broad scale. It is in the realm of economic power and the imperial power it sustains that the twentieth century truly concluded as "America's century."[6]

This is not a development the general histories of the twentieth century tackle. They chart the size and scope of American dominance and praise or criticize the consequences, but they elide the reasons for it. Olivier Zunz's *Why the American Century?* fills the gap. In what would have been a fine essay in either the Oxford or Columbia volumes, Zunz argues that in the early years of this century the United States produced a fluid and flexible matrix of inquiry for the development and application of technical and managerial expertise. Governments, universities, and corporations collaborated in the pursuit of economically useful knowledge. Equally important, American corporations relied on mass consumption rather than capital investment to fuel the economy. This in turn broke down barriers of religion, class, and, more slowly, race, to create a nation of consumer-citizens. America is the exemplar of techniques of mass marketing now sweeping the globe.[7]

The growth of population and wealth are therefore the two most measurable achievements of the twentieth century, according to the works at hand. Within this context America in many instances had its own particular trajectory; the United States controls nearly one-half of global capitalization and one-quarter of the entire global economy, for instance, despite a population of under 300 million in a world of 6 billion. Beyond that are such themes as immigration, urbanization and suburbanization, and family structures. But perhaps most important in the current context of globalization are greater North America's combined innovations in transportation, communication, and techniques to fashion mass markets and project an imperial consumer culture. The pace varied across the continent and there are asymmetries of scale between Canada and the United States, but general similarities are likely to be more striking than differences in the first instance. What will stand out are divergent approaches to the role of the state and the disparity in wealth generation and distribution and the question of whether there is a relationship between the two. Nevertheless, the external perspective provides one starting point for building an Epic of Greater North America rather than two national histories set side by side.

Internally, the received historiography of North America at first blush presents a barrier to the development of a continental perspective. Despite the national lines usually employed by historians, however, the past reveals endless cross-border migrations and meanderings, and trade in goods, systems, and services. Equally important, a continental melange of values, institutions, ideas, and amusements through nearly two centuries have rendered the political boundary anywhere from porous to irrelevant, depending upon where you look and when. Such connections have drawn the attention of certain groups of historians, and the Epic of Greater North America can draw upon a substantial literature in cross-border studies accumulated over the past eighty years. This literature falls into three distinct phases.

First, foreign affairs specialists, particularly in Canadian-American relations, thought in a continental framework because they studied bilateral history. Further, "Canadian-American relations," which the Carnegie scholars defined, has over time incorporated a diverse range of diplomatic, economic, political, social, intellectual, and cultural themes and topics.[8] The premise remains, however, that of two nation-states in dialogue on the road to resolving issues, and making executive policies. Second, comparative scholars such as Seymour Martin Lipset, have put themes and topics into a cross-border context.[9] Third, borderlanders straddle the political boundary in carefully defined zones of cross-border interaction, be they to examine history, commerce, literature, or populations.[10]

The Carnegie scholars under James T. Shotwell's leadership from the 1920s to the 1940s challenged the national streams of North American history. Broad narratives emerged as a by-product, most of them written by Canadians, which saw North American history broken into periods based on political/diplomatic events. Edgar McInnis in 1945 and Bruce Hutchinson in 1955, as their tables of contents show, drew political and diplomatic threads through successive crises over borders, resources, trade agreements, conflict, and alliances. This political/diplomatic periodization moved through Hugh Keenleyside and Gerald Brown in 1952 to the first modern text by Edelgard Mahant and Graeme Mount in 1989.[11]

In company with other branches of historical study, examinations of Canadian-American relations proliferated and fragmented after 1970. Narratives appeared less often but became more important because a growing mountain of material had to be mastered and blended to achieve any overall understanding. Commercial and economic studies, both general and specific, proliferated, and did not always fit neatly into the historical rhythms of politics and diplomacy. Journalist Lawrence Martin of the *Globe and Mail* in 1982 cast the story in pairs of presidents and prime ministers from Ulysses S. Grant and John A.

Macdonald to James E. Carter and Pierre Trudeau. The personal proved mostly political, and made no advance toward a North American history. Richard Gwyn of the *Toronto Star* analysed issues and themes in a North American context, on the other hand, and juxtaposed Canada against the United States in the context of greater North America.[12] This was new. But almost all these and other authors viewed the cross-border story from a Canadian perspective, so a sense emerged that Canada had in both overt and unspecific ways been dominated by the United States, made dependent, to the cost of the country, its people, and future. The binational asymmetry of power and wealth combined with occasional moralizing over the flaws of the United States also tended to mask the social and ideological commonalities that bound Canadian and U.S. history. However real our differences, we have become far less foreign to each other than to peoples outside North America, cultural heritage notwithstanding, and that includes the British.

Recent Canadian-American narratives suggest that the traditional political and diplomatic threads might become even less significant over time as ever more diverse commercial, social, and cultural events, issues, and themes get drawn into the story. Political boundaries and the jurisdictions remain, but perceptions of their significance seem to be in flux. The periodization derives from the internal history of Canada rather than a history of the relationship, as Jack Granatstein and Norman Hillmer suggested. Robert Bothwell, however, used a political theme to create an alternate periodization. John H. Thompson and Stephen J. Randall offered the most comprehensive narrative yet published, but still employed a political/diplomatic periodization.[13]

Certain specialized studies offered alternative ways to approach North America's past. Gordon Stewart examined American trade and economic policy makers' goals and his periodization put the Treaty of Paris (1783), Reciprocity (1854), American refusal of reciprocity with Canada (1892), Canadian refusal of reciprocity with the United States (1911), and mutual agreement in Free Trade (1988) as signposts for eras in the historical flow. Seymour Martin Lipset's sociological approach compared and contrasted a series of cultural and social topics based on data from the 1970s and 1980s. He began with founding moments for Canada and the United States in the political-ideological schism of the 1760s and 1770s: Whig and Tory. This dichotomy, whatever its utility for the late eighteenth and early nineteenth centuries, lost any explanatory power by 1900 at the latest. By Lipset's date of publication (1989) such an historical view was blatantly anachronistic.[14]

Historical geographers offered a perspective that suggested a greater North America, although a journalist, Joel Garreau, of the *Washington Post,* offered the first popular rendition of a regional reconfiguration that ignored national boundaries. He identified nine nations in North America, although he never implied they would become nation-states. He argued on socio-cultural and economic grounds that Ecotopia in the Pacific Northwest, [Greater] New England in the Atlantic Northeast, and a mid-continental breadbasket, for examples, made greater sense than bisecting those regions by a political border. And that is precisely how historical geographer D. W. Meinig's *magnum opus* approaches North America's past. He explores how human use of space changed over time and produced cross-border regions and communities by 1920. The technologies of communication are central to his explanation and thesis. Modes of transport, in particular, on oceans, lakes, rivers, and canals, railroads on regional and transcontinental scales, and (in his final volume to come) road and air travel are the engines of his interpretation of historical/spatial evolution. All regions in North America, including the British provinces and then Canada, Mexico, and even Caribbean islands and territories farther offshore, became part of an integrated North America with the expansive, dynamic, and powerful United States as the core and primary engine. By implication, intellectual, social, and cultural themes evolved in the same spaces, albeit in different ways. Political boundaries still marked national jurisdictions, but these mattered less to Meinig than the ways in which communities formed.[15] At the same time, his first volume had an exo-continental perspective, whereas his second volume adopted a continental vantage point. The third volume, which covers 1867–1920, is U.S.-centered. Perhaps, once completed, Meinig's work may constitute the nearest case we have of the Epic of Greater North America, but so far he has progressively identified a U.S. centre and Canadian and Central American adjuncts.

This quickens the need for coordinating time frames into a flexible yet descriptive periodization to accommodate the warp and woof of greater North American history because many disciplines now work on this front, fragment the story, and complicate the problem of synthesis, as a glance through the *American Review of Canadian Studies, The Canadian Review of American Studies,* and other periodicals and conference agendas shows. This diverse work must be digested and blended with the received literature. Alongside the national historiographies, we also need an Epic of Greater North America to synchronize our understanding with twentieth century developments. The massive cross-border bibliography and historiographical proliferation since the 1960s mostly kept implications of the continental context at arm's length. The political boundary demarks a complex cultural, social, intellectual, commercial and security, at times metaphorical, zone as well as a jurisdictional divide. Imagine the political border removed, however, and borderland communities can be redefined and reshaped endlessly in cultural, social, and economic terms.

To render such complexity manageable within a broad interpretive scheme that incorporates regions such as the Atlantic northeast is no easy task. Can we simply take everything we have and recast it into an Epic of Greater North America?[16] Not, in our view, without two fundamental tools. First, we need a comparative analytical template; and second, we need a meaningful periodization scheme to interrelate time and space, history's two dimensions. Historians of either country could protest that once inside a North American framework, their national experience will fade and transform. Canadianists in particular fear such an eclipse because the political, economic, social, and cultural asymmetry of the United States and Canada threaten to leave at the end of the day only the United States as America. But why should that be so? Historians juxtapose Germany and Belgium in Europe, Brazil and Ecuador in Latin America, and Korea and China in Asia, so why not the United States and Canada in North America?

A survey of existing studies of Canada and the United States in North America suggests, for example, that we can portray the two countries in terms of a series of layers and sub-strata. These identify fundamental cross-border themes for comparative analysis. The four principal themes evident in the historiographical categories that weave into the narrative syntheses we have are political/diplomatic, economic, social, and cultural.

Political and diplomatic means the presence of elected leaders, policy makers, and bureaucrats in national, and provincial and state jurisdictions as well as transnational organizations. Because both countries are continental federations, this layer has expanded, ramified, and evolved through time and space from the Atlantic Northeast to the Pacific Northwest. Sub-strata include an array of cross-border institutions, such as the International Joint Commission, the North American Free Trade Association, or the North American Aerospace Defense command. Informal associations, such as regional governors' and premiers' conferences; intelligence and police work, such as the Royal Canadian Mounted Police and Federal Bureau of Investigation liaisons; or the cooperative work of the Immigration and Naturalization Service with Canada Customs and Revenue are some sub-strata in operation, and cases could be enumerated endlessly. The sheer volume of informal agencies, departments, and organizations that operate continuously in a cross-border fashion would defy tabulation.

Economics entails all forms of cross-border business, trade, and finance, in services as well as commodities, often, but not always, managed by formal agreements, from the Reciprocity of 1854 to the North American Free Trade Agreement in 1993 and the work-in-progress of the Free Trade Association of the Americas. Here sit banking partnerships and mergers, currency management, investments and stock market regulation and interaction, and countless corporate liaisons and partnerships. Cross-border trade within North American companies constitutes a substantial portion of all Canadian-American exchange. Continental transportation systems, on water, road, rail, or in the air have paired, partnered, linked, and merged over time. These examples sit within all the historical phases of industrialization and its ramifications. In the twentieth century, the growth of mass commodity producers and consumers, and the continental merchandising system intertwined with North America's popular culture. The way the two national economies have become virtually one illustrates the range and complexity of this layer.[17] Sub-strata include the rise of bureaucratic management, services such as advertising and insurance, communications such as telegraph, the mails, telephone, broadcasting, and the Internet.

"Social" subsumes peoples, ethnic groups, immigration and settlement patterns in a three-way context: national, continental, and cross-border. Over time both countries clearly became multi-ethnic and inclusive in similar ways at similar times, despite shared racism against non-whites. The "mosaic versus melting pot" clichés must be abandoned because they cannot describe, if they ever did, distinctive social realities. Other sub-strata include urbanization and suburbanization, and shifting rural and urban/suburban balances of demographic distribution. Religious diversity and structures, revivalism and fundamentalism, legal assumptions and practices, definitions of crime and approaches to correction and punishment, and social reform movements all fit here as well. The roles of private institutions and public policy for education at all levels offer a final example, and link with the cross-border migrations of students and professionals moving among home, colleges, universities, and employment.

"Cultural" means values, ideas, and identities from local through regional to national and bi-national. Here, too, sit intellectual creativity and practice, from the habits and mores of daily living and diversion, to elite sensibilities and preoccupations. This is less the spectrum from lowbrow to highbrow than the emergence of a shared culture of mass consumption of commodities and entertainment genres that now typify North American life both here and in the rest of the world. In truth, both elite and mass culture are cosmopolitan, and express and shape national identities whatever the particular product, whether print, sound, shape, image, or performance. Sport as recreation and entertainment rests here along with tourism and vacationing. Canada and the United States now seem on this layer joined at the hip, the protests of Canadian cultural nationalists notwithstanding. The process of how virtually any product or activity has become a commodity originated in greater North America in the twentieth century and spread from there into a global context.

The layers and sub-strata are like crystals in a kaleidoscope. Rotate the tube and different patterns emerge. Daniel J. Boorstin, for example, ignored customary periodization to show how Americans after 1867 sorted themselves into malleable national communities bound by invisible strands of production, marketing, consuming, and servicing. At the same time, they drifted in and out of statistical lumps depending upon taste, location, occupation, income levels, and education.

No Canadian scholar has attempted such a study, but one could, perhaps by building on the insights of Harold Innis. Work within a comparable time frame would likely produce a similar result because of accelerating communications in North America since the mid-nineteenth century. For example, it seems likely that by 1925 continental habits in entertainment and reading, as studies of vaudeville, radio, film, and newspapers suggest, constituted a cross-border development where political jurisdiction had a marginal influence. With the advent of television, and now the Internet, mass North American communities of viewers and users have emerged almost simultaneously. The Canadian Radio and Telecommunications Commission notwithstanding, after 1970 the political border became largely irrelevant in this example as a unified North American history of communications, as well as specific Canadian and U.S. histories, unfolded.

Our categories of cross-border studies exhibit a default flow among these layers, as their periodization suggests. The political and diplomatic layer seems dominant because scholars of Canadian-American relations accept national policy making as the primary governing force over economic, social, and cultural interaction. Politics and interests, whether economic, social, or cultural, interact, and the government of the day produces trade agreements or other legislation that determines how the cross-border relationship unfolds. Borderlands scholars have applied this theme within a regional, cross-border context, but, like a handful of comparative scholars, also work up from local, social, and cultural, as well as economic, layers. The emphasis on politics and diplomacy seems out of phase with current realities, such as emerging regionalisms in the post–North American Free Trade era. So, how can we adjust the unpredictable and ever-shifting kaleidoscope without doing violence to the fabric of cross-border history?

To begin with, we suggest a revision of the default order of the layers. Both the internal and external perspectives indicate the particular importance of transportation and communication, and the application of technology. These developments permitted the convergence of mass markets and consumerism, the culture of commodification. These themes, we would argue, constitute the foundation, which interacts with and informs social as well as economic activity. Only then would we move on to politics and diplomacy. The constitutional and legal power of politicians and bureaucrats notwithstanding, they respond to as much as they shape the cross-border forces of our time, and the same might be said of much of the past century. In Canadian-American affairs, we have witnessed leaders scramble to manage dispersed, diverse, and disparate cultural, social, and economic forces within federal jurisdictions over which in the end they have at best shared control. Ask who is in charge of cross-border relations in the year 2005, and the answer is everyone and no one because of the volume, extent, and complexity of cross-border linkages in all layers of the relationship.

Notice that the political jurisdictions will abide. For example, Canada and the United States have always been liberal societies, but they administer their liberalism differently. The former has a communitarian bias and presumes the need to temper by policy individual freedoms. The latter has an individualist bias and presumes the need to temper by policy when individual freedoms are threatened or abused. We must not reiterate and embellish the received template of cross-border history, but rather cross-link the layers and sub-strata, with an eye for distinctions into an integrated periodized template on which to write the Epic of Greater North America.

Periodization is the second major requirement. Most studies use political and diplomatic events to subdivide North American history, which means that economic, social, and cultural themes get inserted piecemeal and their innate historical rhythms disappear. It seems to us that transportation and communications, in the practical sense of moving people, goods, and ideas, rather than in any theoretical sense, offer an encompassing periodization. From European outreach and plantings in the seventeenth century to the electronic era twenty-first century, five successive, but overlapping, eras seem clear.

During the first period, humans, animals, currents, or the wind moved people, ideas, commodities, and information in what amounted to a six-kilometre-an-hour world. By the late eighteenth century, human ingenuity had wrought a second era, served by canals, more efficient vessels, and roadways. A third, mechanical, era appeared as the railroad augmented previous patterns. Accumulating innovations increasingly mechanized long-distance exchanges of people, goods and ideas, while traditional methods remained in urban regions. By the 1870s in eastern North America mechanical power propelled people, goods, and ideas in a complex web among all major cities, and towns. The first British provincial railroad was built to link Montreal with Portland, Maine. Railroad maps of the 1850s show a northeastern grid that embraced the British provinces. The transcontinental grid of 1900 criss-crossed the border in regional patterns. By 1930 a continental road system developed to carry ever-growing numbers of motorized cars and trucks engaged in long and short distance communications of people and goods.

The fourth period, North America's electrical era, began when telegraph lines marched beside railroads in the 1850s and 1860s, expanded with telephones, first in urban, then rural regions, and culminated with wireless broadcasting and reception. So, by the 1950s all communications operated in three dimensions. A North American sphere, not separate Canadian and U.S. realms, provided a spatial context within which this era in the epic of Greater North America unfolded.

The fifth and current era, the electronic age, progressively diversified an established North American communications system by the 1930s, when a North American radio system came into place. Canada mixed public and private broadcasters in radio and television, while the U.S. system was all private, or privately supported. Broadcasters and their sponsors reached North American audiences by 1960, although distance and asymmetry meant that Canadian broadcasters could not penetrate much beyond the northern tier of U.S. states. Microwave, cable, and satellite networks further eroded national political controls. Policy makers chased and worked around public tastes. Current high technology communications ignores political boundaries in the worlds of commerce, services, marketing, investment, education, and entertainment.

The modern history of periodicals suggests a case study that interweaves our layers. Samuel Moffett noted the variety of U.S. newspapers and magazines in Montreal and Toronto in 1907. By then, Canadian periodicals, like their U.S. counterparts, had mostly become commercial publications in the age of big business. Rising urban literacy, the growth of leisure time, and an expanding middle class created what proved infinitely variable continental communities of readers. A proliferating variety of special interest magazines linked producers and consumers through advertising. Location, income levels, or national jurisdiction mattered less than interests, so magazines on homemaking, mechanics, sailing, sports, among many others, found cross-border readerships. Despite Canadian government attempts to treat periodicals as a culture subject to protectionism, the 1998 contretemps over magazines suggests that for most magazines nationality is irrelevant. Such publications can therefore offer a nexus to coordinate cultural, social, and economic themes and periods in North American history.[18]

Many other specific topics can be reinterpreted in a continental context as aspects of the Epic of Greater North America. For example, studies of francophones in Canada and the United States have assumed the border as a barrier. This has relegated Franco-America to lesser significance than it deserves. France operated in a North American context in the seventeenth and eighteenth centuries. The 1755–62 Acadian dispersal rippled from Nova Scotia to other British colonies and as far as Louisiana, where Acadians survived as Cajuns and formed modern links with Maritime kinfolk. The would-be Republic of Madawaska was a North American event. French migrated to Maine in the lumber trade, and from there ranged as far afield as Michigan and Wisconsin where their descendants remain, and Franco-Americans fought in the U.S. Civil War. French from Lower Canada/Quebec in the middle and later years of the nineteenth century migrated to work in cotton and other industries and formed expatriate groups in New England that mostly assimilated over time. Beginning in the 1950s, young people in Quebec embraced the ideas, themes, and products of American popular and mass culture in a way that further suggests the French experience as, among other things part of greater North America.[19]

The history of Blacks in Canada and the United States can be similarly rewritten into a North American context. Black settlement in Nova Scotia, on a substantial scale, began with the British evacuation from New York in 1783 after U.S. Independence. Although many left for Sierra Leone, others arrived from Chesapeake Bay plantations, liberated by British raiding forces during the War of 1812. The U.S. slavery controversy spilled over political boundaries, with Black refugees being harboured in Lower Canada and even British Columbia. Most of these refugees returned to the United States during and after the war, but Blacks in Canada retained links with those in the United States, and drew inspiration from the modern U.S. Civil Rights movement.[20]

Tracing connections between the Maritime provinces and New England states, borderlands historians have begun to rewrite the histories of regions into case studies of greater North America. The Atlantic Northeast offers rich potential in this respect because of the deep cultural, social, and economic linkages that have in some respects bound provinces and states into a shared history. Graeme Wynn, for example, traced the cultural bonds between the Maritime provinces and New England states so as to suggest that, while political boundaries mattered after Confederation in 1867, cultural, social, and economic regional identities survived and endured. Greg Marquis detailed these themes during the U.S. Civil War era. Karl McNeil Earle has recently brought Newfoundland and Labrador into this context. Regional interest in "Atlantica" on the part of business people, politicians, and academics reflects a desire to restore what proponents see as historical north-south linkages artificially sundered by Confederation.[21] Each borderland region that emerged in the east-to-west development of both countries offers a similar opportunity for consideration of an Epic of Greater North America.

P.A. Buckner has raised concerns about a continental approach to North American history in general, and the Borderlands Project in particular. Scholars pursuing either agenda exclusively may slide into geographical determinism, or even a deterministic continentalism. In post 9/11 North America, a continental approach also risks portraying alternatives, national or otherwise, as unnatural, artificial, even anachronistic. Dangers also await those writing from the perspective of the nation state, where excesses of nationalism and impatience with limited identities have worked themselves out. Limited identities, too, pose a danger. Each approach has its own set of slippery slopes. Selecting to study within one context rather than another is not an entirely neutral decision for any historian to make. Such selections also hold out rewards for scholarship generally, however, and we maintain that it is no longer sustainable to ignore the rich possibilities of the continental context. So, many years after Herbert Bolton broached the concept, an Epic of Greater North America still holds its original promise.

19

Peeping Through the Cracks: Seeking Connections, Comparisons, and Understanding in Unstable Space[1]

GRAEME WYNN

We are all borderlanders now. Or so we are told by two much-quoted theorists of our time, Arjun Appadurai and Homi Bhabha. Highly educated, highly intelligent, re-located, transculturated individuals, both Appadurai and Bhabha read outward, it seems to me, from their own experience, to interpret the world at the turn of the millennium. For Appadurai, much impressed by the space-shrinking, border-jumping powers of today's means of electronic communication, nation-states – and the boundaries that are so essential to defining them – are increasingly irrelevant in a postmodern, postcolonial and (soon to be) postnational world. Networks, not nations, are fast becoming our prime grids of affiliation. Bhabha sees much the same present and future. But he characterizes our circumstances rather differently. For Bhabha, borderlands are symptomatic of the contemporary condition. In his view, we all live in between. We are interstitial creatures occupying fluid spaces of transgression and revision. Now, I readily confess to finding much of this theorizing suspect, and Homi Bhabha, in particular, difficult to read and harder to understand. Elsewhere, Bhabha claims, if I recall, that a boundary is not a line at which something stops, but a line at which something begins to become present. Being rather literal-minded and a geographer at that, I think after some puzzlement that it all depends which way you are heading. But let me avoid this niggling disciplinary doubt by staying a while precisely where Bhabha and Appadurai claim we all are: betwixt and between.[2]

To attend the conference at which the first version of these ideas was presented, I travelled from the Canadian province of British Columbia to the U.S. state of Maine. I crossed a continent, and an international boundary. The journey was swift and easy. Still, I felt its effects – in jet-lag and in the countless, sometimes disquieting, ways in which, it seems to me, the United States differs from Canada. When I make this journey, I know, I feel in my very bones, that I have crossed something of importance – not a Rubicon to be sure, but not nothing either. I am also conscious that I could – and that others do – look at all of this rather differently. I could say that I live in Cascadia – though I prefer to think of it with Joel Garreau and Ernest Callenbach as a somewhat larger, less commercially orientated realm called Ecotopia. Either way, Cascadia and Ecotopia are extensive territories spanning the 49th parallel on the west coast of the continent, whose inhabitants (those who coined these regional names would insist) have distinct economic interests and hold particular environmental attitudes. Then I could go on to observe that northern Maine is a place that seems rather familiar to me, because it is notably similar to one I know well and that I have long sought to understand: Maritime Canada. In this view, the flanks of the continent do indeed begin to look like interstitial space in Bhabha's sense. Not only that. Brook Taylor and Reg Stuart argue, in chapter 18 of this collection, that most of the world's citizens regard the differences that some Canadians hold dear, the differences by which Canadians separate themselves from Americans, as far less important than the attributes common to all people between the Rio Grande and the Tundra. There are, clearly, significant challenges and baffling questions in all of this.[3]

In exploring connections in what we should perhaps be thinking of as eastern interstitial space (where once we saw a boundary and where, before that, as Béatrice Craig reminds us, there was no boundary, real or remarked), and in pursuing comparisons – which hold open the possibility of difference as well as of similarity – between and among parts of that space, the chapters of this book offer an immensely rich variety of perspectives. Eighteen papers cover eleven thousand years of history, in parcels ranging from a couple of years to several millennia in duration. They deal with a substantial fraction of the globe, in portions ranging from the North Atlantic triangle (to recycle an old phrase), to the St John Valley. They reflect deep research and careful conceptualization. They draw upon anthropology, archeology, folklore, history, and political science. By one – far too simple and syntactically awkward – reckoning, the papers in this volume offer a range of approaches to historical topics: chronological, retrospective, conceptual, imaginative, statistical, contextual, environmental, familial, cultural, intellectual, comparative, ethnic, cultural production, gender, and continental. But they warrant more than such curt characterization, so let me add a little flesh to this reckoning by connecting these essays to those spawned by an earlier gathering on a similar theme, before drawing some comparisons between the two events.

In their introductory essay, Stephen Hornsby and John Reid allude to a relatively long history of engagement with the broad theme of this volume, dating back to 1938, when Harold Innis was in Orono to offer some observations about Canadian-American relations, and it is to that history that I first turn. More specifically, the meeting from which these papers emerged bears comparison to the 1987 conference that produced *The Northeastern Borderlands: Four Centuries of Interaction* (published in 1989).[4] To compare these two events (and the books that resulted from them) is to reveal that much has changed in fifteen years. Two commentators from the 1987 meeting – Robert Babcock and David Sanger – gave papers at the meeting in 2000. None of the 1987 presenters were invited back in that capacity, although John Reid reappeared as co-organizer, a definite elevation in the order of things. Moving in the other direction, another of the presenters from 1987 returned in 2000 to sweep up the bits at the end. All of this means that a chorus of fresh, new voices has joined the debate initiated in 1987. By my count, Betsy Beattie, Elizabeth Mancke, and Bill Wicken had not completed their doctoral theses when the Northeastern Borderlands conference was held. Deborah Trefts and Joshua Smith, who likewise contributed greatly to the discussions of 2000, were still engaged in doctoral studies at that date. That such scholars as these are engaging questions that some of us thought worth spending time on several years ago is cause for a certain satisfaction. Indeed, my delight at this changing of the guard, and at the contributions made to this volume by younger scholars reminds me of the title of a Mavis Gallant short story, "In Youth is Pleasure."[5]

From connections to comparisons.[6] Several trails blazed in 1987 were revisited in 2000; other papers in this volume open important new directions for consideration in the twenty-first century. Between old and new, it is also clear that one trail has gone rather cold. At the 1987 event, George Rawlyk gave a long paper to the work of John Bartlet Brebner, but Brebner is given scant mention here. This may not be significant, but it certainly strikes me as of passing interest that one of the great students of the northeast, of the links between New England and Atlantic Canada, and of the North Atlantic world (which is back in vogue as a focus of scholarly attention) has apparently entered the ranks of the nearly forgotten.

The 1987 conference and the volume that emerged from it were somewhat shorter than the conference of 2000 and this book. Those who presented papers in 1987 were assigned a portion of the puzzle. Four centuries of interaction in the Northeastern Borderlands were divided up among five speakers: John Reid and Harold McGee were asked to deal, for the most part, with the pre-1762 period; George Rawlyk dealt with the late eighteenth century; I was asked to speak to the nineteenth century; and Margaret Conrad spoke on the late nineteenth and early twentieth centuries. Together we hoped that these papers blazed some trails. Those who revisited them in 2000 pushed those trails a good deal further into the woods of our unknown, and made them a lot clearer than we were able to do in 1987.

Harold McGee worried in 1987 at the tight time-frame within which we worked. Four centuries of borderland interaction, he said quite categorically, was too narrow a template; we needed to think seriously about prehistory, and the a long period of interaction among people of the northeast before 1600. David Sanger, who was the commentator on McGee's paper in 1987, certainly endorsed those sentiments, and he extends this important line of inquiry into prehistoric territory in the opening paper of this collection. John Reid's 1987 reflections on the complex interplay of peoples in the Northeast during the colonial period were seen by the three editors of the *Northeastern Borderlands* volume as descriptions of a "benign articulation." From the vantage point of 2000, and on the basis of some of the arguments presented in this volume, "benign" may not have been the best way of describing what Reid was discussing. Perhaps he was not entirely happy with the phrase, borrowed from Donald Meinig, even in 1987.[7] In any event, several of the points that Reid made then have been elaborated – and carried forward – by papers in this volume. Although they are very different in scale and intent, the papers by Elizabeth Mancke and Geoffrey Plank engage the notion of interplay and move in important new directions.

Thinking about nineteenth century New England in 1987, I went lickety-split through a great bundle of material to offer a sketch of what I called, in echo of John Bartlet Brebner, "Greater New England of the 19th Century." I suggested that this Greater New England was realized in a number of dimensions – of experience, of economy, of the primitive and the romantic, and of attitudes and artifacts – and marked in a number of ways. Some of the papers in this volume might be sorted according to these same categories. With respect to the Greater New England of experience, for example, Béatrice Craig, Jacques Ferland, and Sandy Ives add something important to my earlier sketch. In respect of economy, Jacques Ferland, again, and Julian Gwyn do the same. In terms of the primitive and romantic, I count

Dick Judd and Bill Parenteau as offering new insights. Perhaps it is not too much of a stretch to see Craig's and David Sutherland's and Joshua Smith's papers as dealing with some of the attitudes that I alluded to very briefly. But all of this is only to acknowledge that my ideas were preliminary, and that colleagues have pushed again down indistinct old trails, extending them and carrying forward our understanding of nineteenth and twentieth century interactions between New England and the Maritime region. Finally, to end these comparisons, let me note that Betsy Beattie follows Margaret Conrad's 1987 essay in exploring the exodus of Maritimers to New England between 1870 and 1920, but she adds new dimensions to the story, specifically by emphasizing gender and separating out the different experiences of young men and young women in this migration.

These, then, are a few of the ways in which the work included in this volume is connected to what went before. In each case, earlier understandings have been refined and nuanced, and territories that were skipped by in 1987 have been more fully explored. But this volume also offers several completely new trails blazed into formerly little-considered territories. There was very little in the 1987 volume on the urban, whereas Bob Babcock's contribution here is a comparative study of two important urban centres. Scott See's exploration of ethnicity, nativism, and violence also brings an important new perspective to events in this region. In emphasizing environmental issues, Deborah Trefts investigates a topic that is crucially important – both to our potential readers and to the wider public to whom we should speak – a subject that was substantially ignored in 1987. Colin Howell makes sport and light of a fascinating subject, and his essay demonstrates how important these dimensions of cultural experience are to defining the region. Again, these were missed almost completely in *The Northeastern Borderlands.* Nor does that volume hold anything quite as bold and ingenious and as encompassing as Elizabeth Mancke's wide-horizon sketch of the multiple centres and multiple overlappings that she uses to so deftly characterize the evolving patterns of the early Northeast. In sum, then, the essays gathered here enhance understanding of New England, of the neighbouring Maritime provinces, and of the Maritime–New England borderland. They also challenge readers to think anew and productively about the region and about scholarship relating to it.

Yet some of the central challenges implicit in the focus of this volume have been given less attention than they deserve. This is especially true if we think about the conference that produced this volume as a "follow-up" to the 1987 meeting. Let me come to this point somewhat obliquely. There is a rather large arch that marks the border crossing between Canada and the United States along the Highway 99–Interstate 5 route from British Columbia to Washington state. It is, I hasten to add, a single arch, and its colour is not golden. On this structure, the Peace Arch, are carved the words "Children of a Common Mother." Anyone passing this way by road must see this inscription. It is, in its way, a theorization of the boundary. It is a theorization that I have often wondered about. When I first saw it – some three decades ago, and a little more English than I am now – I thought that this was a most impolite characterization of the maternal figure to whom homage was being paid. Since then I have been informed that my reading of the inscription was not the one that those who carved the monument intended. They, it seems, wished to recognize that although the line had to be marked, it was a line that lay between siblings, between new nations that were branches of the same tree – a sturdy English oak, perhaps.[8]

At the turn of the millennium, I still wonder about this theorization. I do so in part because I wonder what happened to Quebec in all of this, and in part because it seems so hopelessly out of date. One leaves Vancouver, where 35 per cent of the population is foreign-born, where half the school-age population has English as a second language, and where 80 percent of the foreign born are from Pacific Rim countries – China, Taiwan, Hong Kong, and so on – to confront this claim of shared descent with a certain amount of puzzlement.[9] If it cannot hold internally, how can this theorization have meaning on a continental scale? Perhaps, in this respect, Homi Bhabha was right about our living in interstitial space, about borders not being what they used to be, about things all being rather mixed up, and about lines such as that between the United States and Canada being less significant than they once were. Certainly the line no longer divides the kinds of spaces that shaped the thinking of those who created the monument. Perhaps, too, Bhaba is telling us that since we take boundaries such as this for granted we no longer need worry very much about marking them, in the way that those who commissioned the Peace Arch did.

All of this leads me to note – a point I wish to make forcefully – that the very idea of boundaries and borderlands that framed the 1987 conference, and that was surely on the conceptual horizon as the 2000 meeting was planned, is neither explicitly engaged with, nor theorized, in most of the papers gathered here. This worries me. It does so, not because it radically detracts from the quality of the papers as explorations of their particular topics but because it seems to me to reflect a certain, perhaps unconsidered, acquiescence in the Appadurai-Bhabha position that everything is in-between these days. From this perspective the border is easily taken for granted. Then it is a short step to the conclusion that there is little need to theorize it or about it. And from there we can simply proceed to explore dimensions of this unstable space that seem interesting or significant to us – or alternatively choose to make links and connections across it the foci of our work – without stepping back and thinking about the implications either of the boundary line or of the claim that it is fast fading into insignificance.

My concern about these things is reflected in some ways in Craig's essay and heightened not a little by my memory of Phil Buckner's observations at the 1987 conference. Serving as the final commentator on that meeting, Buckner elected to correct or chastise some of those who gave papers there.[10] In essence he urged caution about what was then described as the Borderlands Project. He saw in this initiative a kind of late manifest destiny and lamented a tendency to "argue that the things people have in common regardless of which side of the border they live on are more important than the things that divide them." The border was not at all meaningless, in Buckner's estimation, and was far from "an undesirable barrier to the free flow of people, goods, and ideas" as some implied.

I, too, would insist that if we fail to think – and quite hard – about what we are engaged with when we study and talk about boundary regions, if we fail (in some sense) to theorize borderlines and borderlands, to contextualize them as Craig does and to worry about the ways in which others theorize them, we are probably encouraging – by omission rather than commission, by the unreflective, easy acceptance of the views of others whose experience is not necessarily universal – a conviction that the boundary really does not matter very much. This is what got under Buckner's skin in 1987 and it is a stance that should yet (I hope) raise the anxiety of many Canadians in the twenty-first century.

We need to be cautious about the notion that borderlands are places where people come harmoniously and unthinkingly together in this age of globalization, of transnationalism, and of the death of the nation-state – or at least in the age that is so often described by those kinds of terms. I know I argued in 1987 that the New England–Maritime provinces border was porous in many ways. The papers collected here, make it clear that porosity was manifest in ways other than those I identified. But Buckner's reminder was a salutary one because he wanted us to see that borders do matter.

Earlier, I referred to Gallant's story "In Youth is Pleasure." In that story the protagonist, Linette Muir, crosses the border from the United States into Canada. She says, "I expected to sense at once an air of calm and grit and dedication, but the only changes were from prosperous to shabby, from painted to unpainted, from smiling to dour. I was entering a poorer and curiously empty country, where the faces of the people gave nothing away." Now I am pretty sure that none of those attending the New England–Maritime Canada conference from north of the proverbial 49th parallel would have wanted that paragraph emblazoned on their jackets for their return to Canada. Nor, given the sizable number of Canadian comedians who have made Americans laugh in the last few years, are Canadians likely to take kindly to the notion that they are more dour than their American cousins. Still, Gallant's short story reminds us that the boundary is "real" and discernible in a number of ways, although not all of these are ways that we might immediately call to mind.

On the face of it, Ms. Muir's commentary on the visibility of the boundary may seem trivial. But it points to wider and deeper ramifications. It reflects a sense in which people and place are mutually constituted, a view that affords history a role in the formation of human societies and individual lives, and a conviction that (for good or ill) it makes a difference where one lives. All of this is, of course, in direct challenge to some visions of the twenty-first century, including that of Appadurai, which insist that rampant processes of globalization will essentially obliterate national identities. In this view, virtual communities linking people with shared interests across friction-free electronic space will supersede those based on territory and/or proximity. Thus the "global village" (of which Marshall McLuhan spoke so famously) – or "Cascadia" – will be realized.[11]

Some decades ago, at about the same time as McLuhan was announcing the emergence of the global village, Canadians were much more concerned about the porosity or otherwise of the border, and about the survival of their country, than seems to be the case today. At the time, several commentators offered up wickedly witty aphorisms about the border to their compatriots. One, which has popped up in various forms, suggested that Canada was unthinkable without its border with the United States of America.[12] If we accept this, it would seem that any undermining of the border *qua* border, any move to make it less consequential, is bound to erode the "thinkability" of Canada.

In 1968 the well-known historian Maurice Careless put a rather different spin on much the same idea. He said: "There could not be a Canada without the United States, and may not be a Canada with one." This was at a time of great concern about the influence of American corporations, about branch plants taking over the Canadian economy, and about the threat to Canadian autonomy implied by these developments. Even the prime minister equated his country's vulnerability to that of a mouse abed with an elephant. Similar concerns echoed in a suite of books with titles such as Ian Lumsden's *Close the 49th Parallel*, but they have now all but disappeared from the public imagination, from public discourse – and even from university reading lists. Perhaps I am just a voice from the past, an intellectual dinosaur who somehow, and with a few others such as Mel Hurtig and Maude Barlow, escaped extinction. However, I cannot help but think that the concerns spawned by foreign investment and talk of the global village thirty years ago warrant discussion if not full resurrection in this age of neo-classical/neo-liberal economic policy, of NAFTA, the WTO, and so on.[13]

I have no answers on these matters, only concerns. I think it important that Canada offer alternatives to the United States in a number of ways, and that those alternatives be seen and cherished. I am not, in short, prepared to go quietly into the good night forsaking the conviction that – despite our laments about the erosion of their historical knowledge and of their sometimes woeful lack of preparation for university level scholarship in history and geography – people who live in Canada and in the United States should still attend to different histories and have different sensibilities. In sum, it is fine to think about connections, but not at the expense of inquiry into the differences and the ways in which these connections are constructed. I think we see some of this in the work presented here. Deborah Trefts's exploration of the fisheries crisis provides a convenient means of illustrating the claim, though I hope that I do not distort her measured point by placing my own particular emphasis upon it. In suggesting that Canadians opted for regulation and government and control and that Americans placed their faith in science in seeking to solve the fisheries crisis, I think Trefts may be pointing to some dimensions of the differences between the two countries upon which I have digressed too long. I think, too, that Colin Howell's reflections upon the construction and then, if you will, the deconstruction of the sporting region of the Northeast by a different set of technologies and a different set of national agendas is a reflection that we live and work in this borderland territory in an ever-shifting, certainly far from constant, matrix of influences. It is as well, I would insist, to pay attention to these, as well as to the distinctiveness of the elements brought together in this construct, the transborder region.

Let me move on. One of the things that surprises me about the work collected here is that despite the title of the gathering that spawned this volume – "Connections and Comparisons" – relatively little attention is given here to explicit comparisons. Connections we had in abundance. The authors of these essays seemed to take it for granted that the Northeast was marked by connections or movements of one sort or another – of young ladies and women, of tannery workers, of baseball players, or by whatever links the particular topic might entail. They pay much less attention to comparative analysis of the sort undertaken by Bob Babcock, although Trefts's paper is more explicitly comparative than most in trying to follow the responses of governments on both sides of a borderline to a single crisis.

Babcock referred to Mark Bloch as one of his points of inspiration and guidance in pursuing comparative methodology.[14] It is worth pausing for a moment to think about Bloch's approach and the ways in which it has moved in and out of focus among historical and other scholars in the last little while. Certainly comparative history – comparative anything for that matter – is not particularly easy. It has often been seen as a good thing to do, but because it so frequently requires familiarity (for historians) with at least two sets of archives, (for sociologists) with two different societies, and so on, there are clearly disincentives to undertaking it. Indeed it was in respect of these very issues that the American historian Raymond Grew observed, some twenty-five years ago, that comparison was "more widely admired than consciously practiced." In this, comparative history might be compared with the connoisseurship of fine wines: much talked about, but rarely practised with accomplishment. But this discrepancy reflects the difficulties of comparative history; it does not mean that it should not be pursued. After all, the majority of us with uneducated palates can still find considerable pleasure (or solace) in a bottle of wine.[15]

How then to proceed? A couple of the papers collected here offer some pointers. To expand on these beginnings, however, it is worth turning, briefly, to what others have had to say about comparative work – and by extension to thinking about borderlands issues – on the basis of their own inquiries in different parts of the world. I have no desire to turn these reflections into an annotated bibliography, but it seems to me that in addition to Bloch we might consider George Frederickson, who has studied race relations in South Africa, the American south, and elsewhere and taken the view with respect to comparative studies that these are best orchestrated around the nation-state. This is a position that he seems to hold with some passion, but it may no longer be as justifiable as he believes it to be. Frederickson has certainly been critical of other approaches in advancing his attachment to comparison at the national level. Thus he has taken issue with Theda Skocpol, a sociologist who favoured what she called "macrosocial analysis" as a path to comparative insight. By this Skocpol meant that comparative work should identify the major economic, social, and political features of the two realms on which it concentrates and then isolate the discrete variables that make a difference on each of these axes. Frederickson liked this no more than what he termed the cultural approach – a strategy for dealing with differences in culture, identity, and so on between nations or regions. For Frederickson the cultural approach implied the embrace of radical exceptionalism, the easy position that in the end every culture is unique. Here, he says, people mistakenly rest content with demonstrating uniqueness by contrast, rather than seeking to understand the differences between places, cultures, or nations in any fuller way.[16]

Even this brief summary is enough to suggest that work across borderlands, whether on connections or through comparisons, is a challenge. Many of the papers gathered here avoid explicit engagement with the comparative problematic. I think some of them are the poorer for this. Compared with what might have been, they contribute little to the investigation of differences, to thinking about what difference the border made (or makes), and to considering different ways of meeting the challenges of working across borders and in a comparative frame. Several questions thus remain, perhaps they will lure a rising generation of scholars to blaze new and revealing trails toward their answers over the next fifteen years. Certainly I am convinced that there are models in work undertaken elsewhere to provide direction for such investigations. There is also a receptive audience for the insights likely to flow from inquiries sensitive both to the challenges of comparison and to the importance of scale in their examination of this northeastern corner of the continent. Consider that the Australian historian Ian Tyrell insisted (in the *American Historical Review* in 1991) on the relevance of comparison at the subnational level when seeking to understand certain kinds of developments, certain types of political and social movements, and so on. In some ways Tyrell's article might stand as a modest manifesto for work on the region at the heart of our concerns here. As a group, students of the northeast should be in a position to speak to some of the issues that he raised. We should also be engaging – as Elizabeth Mancke is – with debates raised again just a few years ago in a special issue of the *Journal of American History*. Contributors to this "symposium" called "The Nation and Beyond" gave comparative study a new and trendy spin by labelling it transnational history, or transnationalism, and putting it in the context of globalization.[17]

The time is ripe for serious engagement with borderlands studies or transborder issues across the width of the continent, and there are ways in which concerns hinted at in the pages of this volume can be brought to bear on wider issues that are getting some play at a fairly abstract level. One demonstration of this lies in the fact that this book deals with parts of two nations, but with parts of two nations that are themselves components of a wider Atlantic world – a central theme of Mancke's paper. Clearly, then, inquiries and arguments centred in this corner of the continent can be connected with and brought to bear on issues that are fast becoming (if not always for the most impeccable of reasons) quite important in wider scholarly discourse. In any event, I would urge more careful and explicit comparative work, as well as inquiry in wider, innovative, and more speculative veins to encourage a rethinking of both the region and the linkages between the different parts. Here lie, I suspect, some productive ways forward.

Let me begin to conclude these reflections by unpacking my earlier allusion to Maurice Careless. That 1968 quote came from an essay that he titled "Hooray for the Scars and Gripes." It was in a book called *The New Romans*, edited by A.W. Purdy.[18] A.W. Purdy, better known as Al Purdy, died on Good Friday, 2000, a few days before the New England–Maritime Canada conference began. A Canadian poet much revered by many in literary circles and by those who know him from some of his earlier work such as "The Country North of Belleville," Purdy had had cancer for some time, and his last poem was a reflection on his home and native land. The title, "Her Gates Both East and West: Wanderings in Canada in the Century before the Millennium," suggests the ambition of this work.[19] I refer to all of this – Purdy through Careless and "Her Gates Both East and West" – to extract a line from this poem. Purdy is describing Canada here, but I want to turn this quotation to our borderland. He calls Canada "a country that no man may comprehend / asking the same questions as in ages past." This is the Canada of the new millennium.

In thinking a little bit about new questions for borderlands studies, or studies of the Northeastern region, I am encouraged, as it were, to peep through the cracks, to offer some glimpses of the (or at least *a*) future. I draw inspiration from Purdy in seeking to do this because it seems to me that although the fact that we have entered a new millennium may have very little significance for scholarship, by coincidence of timing we are also entering a scholarly environment in which many of the basic, even taken-for-granted terms of scholarly practice are open for debate. To the extent that we engage with these new approaches, we are asked to forsake old ways for the new. Whatever the territories of our inquiry, it seems certain that they can no longer be fully comprehended by "asking the same questions as in ages past."

Perhaps I should acknowledge that I am a geographer, and that my views on these matters may be somewhat different from those of most of the scholars whose papers are gathered here. Like several other disciplines, human geography has been thrown into considerable ferment in the last ten years or so by the widespread and enthusiastic embrace of a group of ideas referred to variously as critical theory, or postmodernism, or poststructuralism. In truth, the list of theoretical stances goes on and I shall neither run it to completion nor offer an exegesis of all of these ideas here. There is an ever-growing literature to which those who wish deeper immersion may turn.[20] Let me say, too briefly and too simply, that these ideas lay serious challenge to what their advocates are inclined to call the "Enlightenment Project"; they draw into question the transparency of language; they raise questions about how we know what we know; and they evince skepticism both about knowledge and the possibility of gaining anything more than partial, limited, and "situated" understanding. These are ideas that we ignore, in the twenty-first century, at some peril of being dismissed for asking questions whose answers no longer hold much interest.

This said, I do not intend my remarks to stand as a Trojan horse from which Foucault, Derrida, and other critical theorists will descend with their armies of followers to capture and dominate Northeastern studies. Indeed I would urge vigilance against such an outcome, because I fear there has been altogether too much bandwagon jumping among geographers impressed by the glitter and pizzazz of the passing parade. An attitude of healthy skepticism is as warranted here as elsewhere. It is quite possible that some of these emperors' new clothes are less fine than the chorus of approbation for them would imply. But, that caveat registered, I am also persuaded that a number of interesting questions and insights are brought to the fore by these new approaches. Further, it seems to me that, with one or two exceptions, these ideas have not been enough in evidence in the papers delivered here. Where they are discernible, they have, in a sense, to be imputed because they are not declared explicitly. I happen to think that this is preferable to introducing every observation with a bow to the pantheon before proceeding with what one wants to say. Yet because I see relatively little engagement with these approaches, and because I think they are worth some consideration, I offer a few thoughts about ways in which facets of this critical, theoretical arsenal might be incorporated productively into transborder and historical studies in the northeast. I do so by turning attention, briefly, to work engaged with another border and its associated borderlands.

Colin Howell, alone among contributors to this volume, draws attention to the fact that the United States has another border than the one that separates it from Canada. That border is, of course, along the Rio Grande – the border with Mexico and beyond with Central and South America. I am fully conscious that this is a very different realm than the one with which these papers are concerned. However, I want to think for a while with two books that I take as representative of a larger body of writing produced by a group of Latin American scholars whose studies are more informed by critical theoretical ideas than most work on the northeastern region, and whose approaches reveal some exciting new interpretive possibilities. Each of these books explicitly seeks to combine traditional historical inquiry with insights derived from social theory. The first, *The Fence and the River* by Claire Fox, is a smart treatment, in the cultural studies vein, of the U.S.-Mexico border. The second, a voluminous tome of essays brought together under the editorship of Gilbert Joseph, Catherine LeGrand, and Ricardo Salvatore and bearing the title *Close Encounters of Empire: Writing the Cultural History of U.S.-Latin American Relations*, ranges much more widely and reflects a broader spectrum of engagement with recent theoretical ideas.[21]

Lest all of this seem hopelessly remote from Machias and Cape Breton, the winter ferry ride to Port aux Basques, and the northeastern section of the world's longest undefended border, let me remind you that, like Canadians, residents of central and southern America feel the power and imperial character of the United States. Latin Americans joke, as Canadians do, that when the United States sneezes they get pneumonia. More to the point, there are a number of parallels between historical scholarship on Latin America and that on the Atlantic region of Canada. In desperately abbreviated form: Latin American history has moved from an emphasis on diplomatic-commercial relations between the United States and Latin American countries to embrace modernization and diffusion theory, dependency theory, political economy, and the so-called cultural turn. Broadly analogous changes in Maritime Canadian studies can be traced from the Carnegie series on Canadian-American relations (referred to as the Shotwell Series by Reg Stuart and Brook Taylor). In the Carnegie work, the emphasis was very much on diplomatic and commercial history. Industrialization and modernization have been important themes in the history of the Maritime provinces after Confederation, and questions of dependency have loomed large in discussions of the "de-industrialization" that began before the Great Depression. Obviously modernization and dependency in the Maritime regional context had as much to do with Central Canada as they did with the United States. The fit is not perfect. But it is less loose than first impressions might suggest. After all, Eric Sager has traced several ways in which interpretations of the Atlantic region's past have been influenced by writing on and from Latin America. Let me then try to suggest some of the ways in which my chosen exemplars of Latin American historical inquiry succeed in posing interesting new questions, breaking important interpretive ground, and demonstrating ways in which new approaches might add to the range and subtlety of what is being done in this corner of the continent.[22]

Claire Fox offers a fascinating and intelligent reading of a diverse set of representations of the U.S.-Mexican border. Her inquiring gaze ranges across popular culture to weave postcards, films, documentary videos, novels, performance art, and speculative fiction into a lucid reflection on the intricate and contested history of the border in the twentieth century, and particularly its last three decades. For those concerned with the northern border of the United States, the book opens on a familiar note, with a discussion of the "cultural exemption" debate during the NAFTA and GATT negotiations of the early 1990s. It then considers the deployment, by protectionists and free-traders, of two common icons – the fence and the river – in portrayals of the border as a prototype of what free trade would bring. After a third chapter connecting these representations with earlier ones, chapters four and five consider movement and migration as prominent motifs in narratives about the border region. This summary alone is sufficient to suggest some broad parallels between – some underlying themes threaded through – the stories of borders north and south; perhaps it is enough to encourage the adoption (or adaptation) of Fox's perspective in studies of the northeastern border, or perchance to inspire a NAFTA-compatible comparative foray or two.

Of course, the details and substance of these stories, the lived realities of life along these borders of the United States with Mexico and Canada, differ enormously. Comparison can only go so far. But Fox's work, rooted in cultural theory, resonates in other registers as well as this. She began her work with an explicit intention to "investigate the relationship between regionally based texts and political and economic transformations taking place at the global level." She came to realize that her original conceptual framework – based on the notion of discrete social groups interacting across the borderline – "underestimated the complex reality of the border as a 'contact zone' with a long history of transculturation." And she grew to understand not only the importance of scale – "from the international to the regional and the urban" – in studying the border, but also how these realms might be "traversed interchangeably by individual and collective subjects." Border zones are complex places, and Fox full well understands this.

Finally, it should be noted that Fox's close engagement with the culture and politics enveloping this particular line persuaded her of the dangers and distortions inherent in "the current tendency on the part of postmodernist intellectuals to universalize the phenomenon of 'border crossing.'" This point is of particular, and – if I might be so brazen – double, import. Clearly the lesser of its glories is that it echoes my earlier claims about the need for caution in underestimating the relevance of nation-states and borders in the twenty-first century. More significantly, it is an important reminder that postcolonial scholarship "may too readily license a panoptic tendency to view the globe through generic abstractions devoid of nuance."[23] This is the last thing that historians, historical geographers, and other scholars of the past and of the northeastern region should be moving toward. And it is precisely because she is knowledgeable about her research site, thoughtful about her methodology, and judicious in her conclusions that Fox has written a path-breaking study that should provoke thought and suggest new research directions to students of the northeastern corner of the continent.

Close Encounters of Empire is a completely different order of business. Ranging across a vast territory, from Central America through the "southern cone," it offers a rich smorgasbord of case studies united by little other than their authors' interests in bringing the insights of recent theoretical writing to bear on particular histories. Impossible to summarize, remote from most of what little I know, and beyond my competence to judge, these essays strike me by turns as audacious, engaging, intriguing, pleasing, and even puzzling. Fortunately, the editors of the volume have taken their responsibilities seriously and provided an extended introduction that situates the work of their contributors in a broad historical framework. I borrow shamelessly from this introduction to suggest three ways in which new – and more traditional – approaches can be brought into productive engagement. Each of these brief commentaries begins, in a sense, with a stark contrast. Each juxtaposes approaches to understanding the past (and present). These pairings might be seen as binaries; indeed, their elements are sometimes portrayed as polar opposites. But I wish, in each case, to suggest with Joseph, LeGrand, and Salvatore, that such a template is too rigid, that the elements of each pairing are complementary rather than incompatible, and that a blurring of the borders between them can open fertile ground for future inquiry.

The first couplet is culture/political economy. This is now a commonly remarked contrast, especially among those who advance a cultural approach to historical and contemporary scholarship. Typically, they represent culture and political economy as opposites. The cultural approach is seen to rest upon textual analysis, as being concerned with the cultures of encounter, and as paying long-overdue attention to contingency, and fragmentation. Its emphasis is on understanding every culture on its own terms, on respecting otherness and on celebrating difference. Because naming is arbitrary and the world humans know cannot be said to be anchored in reality, the ambitions of social science are false, and scholarship is properly about "understanding social meanings of a social world." Political economy, by explicit contrast, is said to be focused on economic development and much given to unilinear interpretations. At worst, it is described as being wedded to a structural, deterministic view of economic processes that gives scant agency to humans. Yet, emphasizing extremes and portraying these approaches as antithetical strikes me as radically unfortunate. To be sure, some political economists have neglected to pay much attention to culture and have emphasized supply and demand, trade, and the material relations of production in their concern to explain "who gets what and why." Economic growth, production and consumption, the distribution of wealth in society, and political struggles over production and distribution have been the stock-in-trade of much political economy. These are not unimportant matters. Reversing the critique, it could be said that these things figure little – if at all – in most work in the cultural studies vein. But this is a sterile debate. These are different, not exclusive approaches; they reveal distinct facets of the whole. Moreover, as Joseph et al. point out, political economy and culture are ambiguous theoretical categories that refer to concrete social domains and to abstract dimensions thereof. It seems to me that little is to be gained by touting the value of one over the other. Rather, it would appear that scholars steeped in knowledge about particular places, whether gained from archives, field investigation, or other approaches, who hold questions of social justice (long fundamental to political economy) as important, are well situated to absorb insights from the "cultural turn" into their scholarship. By the same token – although the challenge associated with the development of deep and grounded understanding of particular parts of the earth's surface is perhaps greater here – there is surely room for consideration of economic and political (and geographical and social) processes alongside the cultural. No matter from which direction it is undertaken, a creative, thoughtful combination of perspectives from both sides of this somewhat artificial and overemphasized divide – a new synthesis – holds the promise of moving understanding forward.

The second pairing, of meta-narratives and mini-stories, again turns on the sense, inherent in the new critical theoretical literature, that the world is an immensely complex place, and that it is improper to impose overarching interpretations upon it. Just as Political Economy is identified with modernist master narratives (of "Development" for example) and Cultural Studies is portrayed as sensitive to postmodern concerns with difference and multiple, fragmented stories, so this polarity is dismissive of traditional scholarship in history and the humanities more generally. It is so for its avowed tendency to impose integrative plot lines, coherent, united actors (society's power brokers, at worst the proverbial "dead white male" cohort), and tidy, unified interpretations, upon the world. Rather, it is argued, the world should be represented as it is, through multi-stranded, poly-vocal accounts, full of divided subjects, and replete with fragmented social fields. But this way lies frustration – or Babel. If the world is as complex as it is said to be – and it probably is – then the challenge of doing justice to all viewpoints and all voices is overwhelming. Moreover, most of us, I would guess, crave perspective on the buzzing, perplexing world of everyday existence and on the past that helps us hold on to the present – even if only to dispute that perspective. Again the sharp contrast developed for the purposes of retrospective critique is unfit to mark the road ahead. It is not necessary to polarize determinism and contingency, or systemic analysis and fragmentary description in thinking about the conduct of social inquiry. Indeed, to do so is to misrepresent the way in which we experience the world. Surely the way forward is again through the middle ground. The most cogent critiques of modernist assumptions should point the way to more probing and critical engagements with the past. But we must be careful to avoid ditching good historical babies with the proverbial bath water here. It seems to me that many elements of this critique are overplayed. If they have any valence at all it is with certain types of social scientific analysis rather than with the best of scholarship in history and the humanities. Rather than feeling cowed by criticism, I would suggest that we consider turning the most insightful elements of this faultfinding to advantage – as several contributors to *Close Encounters* do – to render our best practices even better by offering more nuanced, more varied, and more inclusive accounts than most of those we have conjured to date.

My third dyad offers more of the same. It turns on a tendency in the critical theoretical literature to emphasize complexity and fluidity of subjects and locations and to downplay the fact that these complex pieces are inescapably parts of larger wholes. To put this another way, current theoretical preoccupations tend to move the emphasis of scholarly inquiry away from "structures" to focus on "agency." Having just sought to save babies in the bathwater, here I think we should be careful not to miss the forest for the trees. Now as ever we need to understand the complex architecture of both the parts and the wholes in our work. And, again, I find excellent examples of scholarship that does this in the pages of *Close Encounters.* Deeply informed about the histories of their own small parts of Latin America, these authors have asked new questions – as well as questions the same as in ages past – of their sources. They have adjusted their conceptual frameworks and spoken to the preoccupations of the new millennium in ways that in many respects exemplify the proudest traditions of historical inquiry. Insofar as we seek models to inspire and (re)direct our own work on the northeastern corner of the continent, we might well spend a little time in close encounter with the pages of *Close Encounters*, to think about connections and comparisons of a different sort than those with which most of the papers presented here have been concerned, and to reflect upon the particular and still abundant challenges of comprehending the northeast corner of the continent.

Notes

CHAPTER ONE

1 C.P. Stacey, *The Undefended Border: The Myth and the Reality* (Ottawa: Canadian Historical Association, 1953).

2 Rising Lake Morrow, ed., *Conference on Educational Problems in Canadian-American Relations* (Orono: University of Maine Press, 1939). For background on the Carnegie series of conferences, see Carl Berger, *The Writing of Canadian History: Aspects of English-Canadian Historical Writing Since 1900* (Toronto: University of Toronto Press, 1976), 137–59.

3 Harold A. Innis, "Economic Trends in Canadian-American Relations," in Morrow, ed., *Conference on Educational Problems*, 96–107, esp. 106–7.

4 See Charles R. Acland and William J. Buxton, "Continentalism and Philanthropy: A Rockefeller Officer's Impressions of the Humanities in the Maritimes, 1942," *Acadiensis*, 23:2 (Spring 1994), 72–93, esp. 83–5; Alfred Goldsworthy Bailey, *Culture and Nationality: Essays by A.G. Bailey* (Toronto: McClelland and Stewart, 1972), 5–6; Judith Fingard, "Focusing on their Roots: University of New Brunswick Historians and Regional History," *Acadiensis*, 30:1 (Autumn 2000), 38–40.

5 David C. Smith, *The First Century: A History of the University of Maine, 1865–1965* (Orono: University of Maine at Orono Press, 1979), 235–6.

6 P.A. Buckner, "Acadiensis II," *Acadiensis*, 1:1 (Autumn 1971), 8.

7 Alice R. Stewart, "Recent Historical Literature and the New England-Atlantic Provinces Region," *Acadiensis*, 1:1 (Autumn 1971), 90–3.

8 See the forum articles collected in *Acadiensis*, 30:1 (Autumn 2000).

9 Stephen J. Hornsby, Victor A. Konrad, and James J. Herlan, eds., *The Northeastern Borderlands: Four Centuries of Interaction* (Fredericton: Acadiensis Press, 1989).

10 Herbert Eugene Bolton, *The Spanish Borderlands: A Chronicle of Old Florida and the Southwest* (New Haven: Yale University Press, 1921); Bolton, "The Epic of Greater America," *American Historical Review*, 38 (1932–33), 448–74.

11 Lauren McKinsey and Victor Konrad, *Borderlands Reflections: The United States and Canada* (Orono: Canadian-American Center, University of Maine, 1989); Roger Gibbins, *Canada as a Borderlands Society* (Orono: Canadian-American Center, University of Maine, 1989); Seymour Martin Lipset, *North American Values and Institutions in Canada and the United States* (Orono: Canadian-American Center, University of Maine, 1990); also Clark Blaise, *The Border as Fiction* and Russell Brown, *Borderlines and Borderlands in English Canada: The Written Line* (Orono: Canadian-American Center, University of Maine, 1990). In addition, a collection of essays was published: Robert Lecker, ed., *Borderlands: Essays in Canadian-American Relations* (Toronto: ECW Press, 1991).

12 Jeremy Adelman and Stephen Aron, "From Borderlands to Borders: Empires, Nation-States, and the Peoples in Between in North American History," *American Historical Review*, 104 (1999), 814–41, esp. 815–17.

13 See Richard White, *The Middle Ground: Indians, Empires, and Republics in the Great Lakes Region, 1650–1815* (New York: Cambridge University Press, 1991).

14 Evan Haefali, "A Note on the Use of North American Borderlands," *American Historical Review*, 104 (1999), 1222–5; Christopher Ebert Schmidt-Nowara, "Borders and Borderlands of Interpretation," Ibid., 1226–8; John R. Wunder and Pekka Hämäläinen, "Of Lethal Places and Lethal Essays," Ibid., 1229–34; Jeremy Adelman and Stephen Aron, "Of Lively Exchanges and Larger Perspectives," Ibid., 1235–9.

15 Bolton, "The Epic of Greater America," 448–74; Marc Bloch, "Pour une histoire comparée des sociétés européennes," *Revue de synthèse historique*, 46 (1928), 15–50. The text of Bloch's essay (without the original notes) is available in English translation in Frederic C. Lane and Jelle C. Riemersma, eds., *Enterprise and Secular Change: Readings in Economic History* (Homewood, Illinois; Richard D. Irwin, Inc., 1953), 494–521; see also William H. Sewell, Jr, "Marc Bloch and the Logic of Comparative History," *History and Theory*, 6 (1967), 208–18.

16 Ian Tyrrell, "American Exceptionalism in an Age of International History," *American History Review*, 96 (1991), 1031–55.

17 David Thelen, "The Nation and Beyond: Transnational Perspectives on United States History," *Journal of American History*, 86 (1999–2000), 965–75, esp. 967.

18 Ibid., 974–5.

19 D.W. Meinig, *The Shaping of America: A Geographical Perspective on 500 Years of History* (4 vols., New Haven: Yale University Press, 1986–2004). The influence of Meinig's work is discussed, for example, in Tyrrell, "American Exceptionalism," 1040–1, and in Bernard Bailyn, "The Idea of Atlantic History," *Itinerario*, 21:1 (1996), 19–44. For a further recent example of the interaction of historical geography and history, see the "Oceans Connect" issue of *Geographical Review*, 89:2 (1999), which proposes the use of oceanic space as an alternative framework to national perspectives. Of especial relevance are Jerry H. Bentley, "Sea and Ocean Basins as Frameworks of Historical Analysis," Ibid., 215–24; Martin W. Lewis, "A Maritime Response to the Crisis in Area Studies," Ibid., 161–8; and Elizabeth Mancke, "Early Modern Expansion and the Politicization of Oceanic Space, Ibid., 225–36.

20 Ian Tyrrell, "Making Nations/Making States: American Historians in the Context of Empire," *Journal of American History*, 86 (1999–2000), 1027.

21 See Berger, *The Writing of Canadian History*, 213–18, 241–2.

22 Berger, *The Writing of Canadian History*, passim; M. Brook Taylor, *Promoters, Patriots, and Partisans: Historiography in Nineteenth-Century English Canada* (Toronto: University of Toronto Press, 1989); Ronald Rudin, *Making History in Twentieth-Century Quebec* (Toronto: University of Toronto Press, 1997); Jean-Marie Fecteau, "Between Scientific Enquiry and the Search for a Nation: Quebec Historiography as Seen by Ronald Rudin," *Canadian Historical Review*, 80 (1999), 641–66; Jean-Paul Hautecoeur, *L'Acadie du discours: pour une sociologie de la culture acadienne* (Québec: Les Presses de l'Université Laval, 1975); Jacques Paul Couturier, "'L'Acadie, c'est un détail': Les représentations de l"Acadie dans le récit national canadien," *Acadiensis*, 29:2 (Spring 2000), 102–19.

23 While this is not the place for a detailed exposition of recent debates in Canadian historiography, a sense of their texture can be obtained from such diverse criticisms of pluralist approaches as those expressed in J.L. Granatstein, *Who Killed Canadian History?* (Toronto: HarperCollins, 1998), Jocelyn Létourneau, "L'avenir du Canada: par rapport à quelle histoire?" *Canadian Historical Review*, 81 (2000), 230–59, and Bryan D. Palmer, "Of Silences and Trenches: A Dissident View of Granatstein's Meaning," *Canadian Historical Review*, 80 (1999), 676–86; in such vigorous rejoinders as those delivered in A.B. McKillop, "Who Killed Canadian History? A View from the Trenches," *Canadian Historical Review*, 80 (1999), 269–99, and by a number of the authors represented in Mariana Valverde et al., "On the Case: *Explorations in Social History*: A Roundtable Discussion," *Canadian Historical Review*, 81 (2000), 266–92.

24 Ramsay Cook, "Canadian Centennial Cerebrations," *International Journal*, 22 (1967), 663.

25 For fuller discussion, see P.A. Buckner, "'Limited Identities' Revisited: Regionalism and Nationalism in Canadian History," *Acadiensis*, 30:1 (Autumn 2000), 11–15; John G. Reid, "Writing About Regions," in John Schultz, ed., *Writing About Canada: A Handbook for Modern Canadian History* (Scarborough, Ontario: Prentice-Hall, 1990), 71–96; see also the observations in Ramsay Cook, "'Identities Are Not Like Hats,'" *Canadian Historical Review*, 81 (2000), 260–5.

26 P.A. Buckner, "The Borderlands Concept: A Critical Appraisal," in Hornsby, Konrad, and Herlan, eds., *The Northeastern Borderlands*, 152–8; Buckner, "How Canadian Historians Stopped Worrying and Learned to Love the Americans!" *Acadiensis*, 25:2 (Spring 1996), 117–40.

27 Graeme Wynn, "Peeping Through the Cracks: Seeking Connections, Comparisons, and Understanding in Unstable Space," chapter 19 in this volume.

28 See the recent study by Francis M. Carroll, *A Good and Wise Measure: The Search for the Canadian-American Boundary 1783–1842* (Toronto: University of Toronto Press, 2001).

29 The issue of comparative development is broached in Kris E. Inwood, "Maritime Industrialization from 1870 to 1910: A Review of the Evidence and its Interpretation," in Inwood, ed., *Farm, Factory, and Fortune: New Studies in the Economic History of the Maritime Provinces* (Fredericton: Acadiensis Press, 1993), 169–70.

30 Wynn, "Peeping Through the Cracks," 306.

CHAPTER TWO

1 Space does not permit a systematic review of the entire 11,000 years of the pre-European period; neither can this synthesis reflect all regions at any one time, because of the uneven nature of the record. Indeed, for the Maritimes over half of the record remains undocumented. Chronology in this paper is expressed in radiocarbon years ago or BP, standing for "before the present" Convention sets this at AD 1950. Although calibration curves that permit corrections from radiocarbon years to calendar years (AD/BCE) are available, few published papers in the Maritime Peninsula have employed this technique. To avoid confusion, the more conventional presentation is used in this essay.

2 The date of entry continues to be a contentious topic despite assertions by some scholars to the contrary. In this essay I take the position that the actual date is largely irrelevant for the Maritime Peninsula because of the glacial ice covering the region.

3 George F. MacDonald, *Debert: A Palaeo-Indian Site in Central Nova Scotia, Anthropology Papers.* (Ottawa: National Museums of Canada, 1968).

4 Arthur, E. Spiess, James W. Bradley, and Deborah Wilson, "Paleoindian

Occupation in the New England-Maritimes Region: Beyond Cultural Ecology," *Archaeology of Eastern North America* 26 (1998), 201–64.

5 Christopher Ellis, Albert C. Goodyear, Dan F. Morse, and Kenneth B. Tankersley, "Archaeology of the Pleistocene-Holocene Transition in Eastern North America," *Quaternary International* 49/50 (1998), 151–66.

6 Spiess, Bradley, and Wilson, "Paleoindian Occupation in the New England-Maritimes Region," 201–64.

7 Ronald B. Davis and George L. Jacobsen, Jr, "Late Glacial and Early Holocene Landscapes in Northern New England and Adjacent Areas of Canada," *Quaternary Research* 23 (1985), 341–68.

8 Richard M. Gramly, *The Vail Site: A Paleo-Indian Encampment in Maine* (New York: Buffalo Society of Natural Sciences, 1982); MacDonald. *Debert: A Palaeo-Indian Site in Central Nova Scotia.*

9 Stephen Loring, "On the Trail of the Caribou House: Some Reflections on Innu Caribou Hunters in Northern Ntessinan (Labrador)." In Lawrence Jackson and Paul Thacker, *Caribou and Reindeer Hunters of the Northern Hemisphere.* (Aldershot: Ashgate Publishing Ltd., 1997), 185–220.

10 Spiess, Bradley, and Wilson, "Paleoindian Occupation in the New England-Maritimes Region," 201–64.

11 Ibid.

12 MacDonald, *Debert: A Palaeo-Indian Site in Central Nova Scotia.*

13 Stephen G. Pollock, Nathan D. Hamilton, and Robson Bonnichsen, "Chert from the Munsungun Lake Formation (Maine) in Palaeoamerican Archaeological Sites in Northeastern North America: Recognition of Its Occurrence and Distribution," *Journal of Archaeological Science* 26 (1999), 269–93.

14 Ellis, Goodyear, Morse, and Tankersley, "Archaeology of the Pleistocene-Holocene Transition in Eastern North America," 151–66; Spiess, Bradley, and Wilson, "Paleoindian Occupation in the New England-Maritimes Region," 201–64.

15 Red ochre-covered artifacts, probably from burials, have been found in Ontario and further west. Ellis, Goodyear, Morse, and Tankersley, "Archaeology of the Pleistocene-Holocene Transition in Eastern North America," 151–66.

16 Ibid.

17 Claude Chapdelaine, ed., *Il y a 8000 ans à Rimouski: Paléoécologie et archéologie d'un site de la culture plano*, vol. 22, *Paléo-Québec* (Montréal: Recherches Amérindiennes au Québec, 1994).

18 Stephen A. Davis and David Christianson, "Three Paleo-Indian Specimens from Nova Scotia," *Canadian Journal of Archaeology* 12 (1988), 190–6.

19 Belinda J. Cox and James B. Petersen, "The Varney Farm (36–57 Me): A Late Paleoindian Encampment in Western Maine," *The Maine Archaeological Society Bulletin* 37, no. 2 (1997), 25–48.

20 David Sanger, William R. Belcher, and Douglas C. Kellogg, "Early Holocene Occupation at the Blackman Stream Site, Central Maine." In Brian S. Robinson, James B. Petersen and Anne K. Robinson, eds., *Early Holocene Occupations in Northern New England* (Augusta, Maine: Maine Historic Preservation Commission, 1992), 149–61.

21 William A. Ritchie, *The Archaeology of New York State* (New York: Natural History Press, 1965).

22 David G. Anderson, "Models of Paleoindian and Early Archaic Settlement in the Lower Southeast," in D.G Anderson and K.E. Sassaman, eds., *The Paleoindian and Early Archaic Southeast* (Tuscaloosa, Alabama: The University of Alabama Press, 1996), 29–57; Ellis, Goodyear, Morse, and Tankersley, "Archaeology of the Pleistocene-Holocene Transition in Eastern North America," 151–66.

23 Dena F. Dincauze, *The Neville Site, Peabody Museum Monographs* (Cambridge, Massachusetts: Harvard University Press, 1976).

24 James A. Tuck, "The Archaic Period in the Maritime Provinces." In Michael Deal and Susan Blair, eds., *Prehistoric Archaeology in the Maritime Provinces: Past and Present Research* (Fredericton: The Council of Maritime Premiers, 1991), 29–65; Tuck, "The Northeastern Maritime Continuum: 8000 Years of Cultural Development in the Far Northeast," *Arctic Anthropology* 12, no. 2 (1975), 139–47; James V. Wright, *A History of the Native People of Canada, Volume I (10,000–1,000 B.C.)*. Paper 152, Mercury Series, Archaeological Survey of Canada (Ottawa: Canadian Museum of Civilization, 1995).

25 Brian S. Robinson, "Early and Middle Archaic Period Occupation in the Gulf of Maine Region: Mortuary and Technological Patterning," in Brian S. Robinson, James B. Petersen, and Ann K. Robinson, eds., *Early Holocene Occupation in Northern New England*, 63–116.

26 For an extended review of the discussion, see Bruce J. Bourque, *Diversity and Complexity in Prehistoric Maritime Societies* (New York: Plenum Press, 1995).

27 Brent M. Murphy, "Researching the Early Holocene on the Maritime Provinces," MA thesis, Memorial University of Newfoundland, 1998; David Sanger, "Gilman Falls Site: Implications for the Early and Middle Archaic of the Maritime Peninsula," *Canadian Journal of Archaeology* 20 (1996), 7–28.

28 Michel Plourde, "Cap-De-Bon-Désir: Is the Early Archaic in the Eastern St. Lawrence Valley Related to the Gulf of Maine Archaic Tradition?" Paper presented at the Canadian Archaeological Association, Ottawa,

2000; Plourde, "Une composante de l'archaïc ancien au Cap-De-Bon-Désir, Grandes-Bergeronnes," *Archéologiques* 13 (1999), 1–11.

29 James B. Petersen, *Archaeological Testing at the Sharrow Site: A Deeply Stratified Early to Late Holocene Cultural Sequence in Central Maine*, Occasional Papers in Maine Archaeology, No. 8 (Augusta, Maine: Maine Historic Preservation Commission, 1991); James B. Petersen, Nathan D. Hamilton, David Putnam et al., "The Piscataquis Archaeological Project: A Late Pleistocene Occupational Sequence in Northern New England," *Archaeology of Eastern North America* 14 (1986), 1–18.

30 Nathan Hamilton and John Mosher, "Rumford Falls: A Holocene Cultural Sequence in Northwestern Maine," Report on file, Maine Historic Preservation Commission, Augusta, Maine.

31 From our modern perception, the transition from the elegant chipped chert artifacts to the rather unprepossessing metamorphic tools can lead to ideas of devolution. However, the technology is no less sophisticated, as techniques used to work chert cannot be used to flake the metamorphic rocks. Expressed in terms of adaptation to the changed environments, the new technology represents a reasonable alternative.

32 For a review of Archaic food bone remains see, Arthur E. Spiess, "Archaic Period Subsistence in New England and the Atlantic Provinces," in Robinson, Petersen, and Robinson, eds., *Early Holocene Occupation in Northern New England*, 163–85.

33 Marshes are defined as wetlands with open water supporting aquatic plants, fish, birds, amphibians, reptiles, and mammals such as muskrat, beaver, and moose.

34 David Sanger, Alice R. Kelley, and Heather Almquist, "Geoarchaeological and Cultural Interpretations in the Lower Penobscot Valley, Maine," in John Hart and David Cremeens, eds., *Current Topics in Northeast Geoarchaeology*, 135–50.

35 Heather Almquist-Jacobson and David Sanger, "Paleogeographic Changes in Wetland and Upland Environments in the Milford Drainage Basin of Central Maine, in Relation to Holocene Human Settlement History," in John Hart, ed., *Current Northeast Paleoethnobotany* (Albany, New York: New York State Museum, 1999), 177–90.

36 Heather Almquist, Ann.C. Dieffenbacher-Krall, Riley Flanagan-Brown, and David Sanger "The Holocene Record of Lake Levels of Mansell Pond, Central Maine, USA," *The Holocene* 11 (2)(2001), 189–201.

37 Brian Robinson, "A Regional Analysis of the Moorehead Burial Tradition: 8500–3700 B.P.," *Archaeology of Eastern North America* 24 (1996), 95–148.

38 Robert E. Funk, "Holocene or Hollow Scene? The Search for the Earliest

Archaic Cultures in New York State," *The Review of Archaeology* 17, no. 1 (1996), 11–25.

39 For a review of the history of this idea see, James B. Petersen and David E. Putnam, "Early Holocene Occupation in the Central Gulf of Maine Region," in Robinson, Petersen and Robinson, eds., *Early Holocene Occupation in Northern New England*, 13–61.

40 Ritchie, *The Archaeology of New York State.*

41 David Sanger, "Culture Change as an Adaptive Process in the Maine Maritimes Region," *Arctic Anthropology* 12, no. 2 (1975), 60–75; Tuck, "The Archaic Period in the Maritime Provinces," 29–65.

42 Steven L. Cox, "Site 95.20 and the Vergennes Phase in Maine," *Archaeology of Eastern North America* 19 (1991), 135–61; James B. Petersen, "Preceramic Archaeological Manifestations in the Far Northeast: A Review of Current Research," *Archaeology of Eastern North America* 23 (1995), 207–30; Brian S. Robinson, "Projectile Points, Other Diagnostic Things, and Cultural Boundaries in the Gulf of Maine Region," *Maine Archaeological Society Bulletin* 36 (1996), 1–24; Sanger, "Gilman Falls Site: Implications for the Early and Middle Archaic of the Maritime Peninsula," 7–28; David Sanger and Bonnie Newsom, "Middle Archaic in the Lower Piscataquis River, and Its Relationship to the Laurentian Tradition in Central Maine," *The Maine Archaeological Society Bulletin* 40, no. 1 (2000), 1–22.

43 The Laurentian tradition, so named because its originator, William Ritchie, thought its origins lay to the north and the Laurentian Mountains, was conceived as a basic adaptation to the northern hardwood forests of Lake Champlain and the St Lawrence Valley. Ritchie, *The Archaeology of New York State*; William A. Ritchie, "The KI Site, the Vergennes Phase and the Laurentian Tradition," *The Bulletin of the New York State Archaeological Association* no. 42 (1968), 1–5. Recently, J.V. Wright has suggested the term "Middle Great Lakes–St Lawrence Culture" to refer to basically the same phenomenon. James V. Wright, *A History of the Native People of Canada*, vol. I, Mercury Series, Archaeological Survey of Canada Paper 152 (Ottawa: Canadian Museum of Civilization, 1995).

44 Cox. "Site 95.20 and the Vergennes Phase in Maine," 135–61.

45 James B. Petersen, Brian S. Robinson, Daniel F. Belknap, James Stark, and Lawrence K. Kaplan, "An Archaic and Woodland Period Fish Weir Complex in Central Maine," *Archaeology of Eastern North America* 22 (1994), 197–222.

46 Historic Mi'kmaq fish traps were described by early French visitors N. Denys and Diereville. Harald E. Prins, *The Mi'kmaq: Resistance, Accommodation, and Cultural Survival. Case Studies in Cultural Anthropology* (Fort Worth: Harcourt Brace & Company, 1996), 29.

47 James B. Petersen and Nancy Asch Sidell, "Mid-Holocene Evidence of *Curcurbita* Sp. from Central Maine," *American Antiquity* 61 (1996), 685–98.

48 Robinson, "Projectile Points, Other Diagnostic Things, and Cultural Boundaries in the Gulf of Maine Region," 1–24; David Sanger, "An Analysis of Seasonal Transhumance Models for Pre-European State of Maine," *Review of Archaeology* 17, no. 1 (1996), 54–8; Sanger and Newsom, "Middle Archaic in the Lower Piscataquis River, and Its Relationship to the Laurentian Tradition in Central Maine," 1–22.

49 Bourque, *Diversity and Complexity in Prehistoric Maritime Societies.*

50 A number of the papers presented in the proceedings of the 1974 Smithsonian Institution conference on the Late Archaic reflect the debate. William W. Fitzhugh, "Introduction," in William W. Fitzhugh, ed., *Papers from a Symposium on Moorehead and Maritime Archaic Problems in Northeastern North America* (Washington, DC: Arctic Anthropology, 1975), 1–6.

51 In a comparison of Hirundo and Turner Farm assemblages it was pointed out that roughly contemporary assemblages displayed fundamental differences that could not be explained by environment alone. David Sanger, Ronald B. Davis, Robert G. MacKay, and Harold W. Borns, Jr, "The Hirundo Archaeological Project: An Interdisciplinary Approach to Central Maine Prehistory," in Walter B. Newman and Bert Salwen, eds., *Amerinds and Their Paleoenvironments in Northeastern North America* (New York: New York Academy of Sciences, 1977), 457–71.

52 Relative sea-level curves for the Maritime Peninsula vary. For mid-coast Maine, where the evidence for coastal Late Archaic sites is best preserved, a detailed curve is available. Walter A. Barnhardt, Walter R. Gehrels, Daniel F. Belknap, and Joseph T. Kelley, "Late Quaternary Relative Sea-Level Change in the Western Gulf of Maine: Evidence for a Migrating Glacial Forebulge," *Geology* 23, no. 9 (1995), 317–20. A relative sea-level curve for the Gulf of St Lawrence exhibits basically the same phenomenon. Heiner Josenhans and Scott Lehman, "Late Glacial Stratigraphy and History of the Gulf of St. Lawrence, Canada," *Canadian Journal of Earth Sciences* 36 (1999), 1327–45.

53 Bourque, ed., *Diversity and Complexity in Prehistoric Maritime Societies.*

54 Daniel F. Belknap, "Geoarchaeology in Central Coastal Maine," in Bourque, ed., *Diversity and Complexity in Prehistoric Maritime Societies*, 275–391; John G. Crock, James B. Petersen, and Ross M. Anderson, "Scalloping for Artifacts: A Biface and Plummet from Eastern Blue Hill Bay, Maine," *Archaeology of Eastern North America* 21 (1993), 179–92; David Sanger, "Maritime Adaptations in the Gulf of Maine," *Archaeology of Eastern North America* 16 (1988), 81–99; David Sanger and Douglas C. Kellogg, "Prehistoric Archaeology and Evidence of Coastal Subsidence on the Coast of Maine," in Walter A. Anderson and Harold Borns, eds.,

Neotectonics of Maine (Augusta, Maine: Maine Geological Survey, 1989), 107–26; Christopher J. Turnbull and Patricia M. Allen, "A Review of *Maritime Provinces Prehistory* by James Tuck," *Canadian Journal of Archaeology* 12 (1988), 250–60.

55 Bourque, ed., *Diversity and Complexity in Prehistoric Maritime Societies.*

56 Ibid.; Douglas A. Byers, *The Nevin Shellheap: Burials and Some Observations, Papers of the R.S. Peabody Foundation* (Cambridge, Massachusetts: Peaboby Museum, 1979); Wendell S. Hadlock, "The Taft's Point Shell Mound at West Gouldsboro, Maine," *The Robert Abbe Museum Bulletin* 5 (1939); Sanger, "Culture Change as an Adaptive Process in the Maine Maritimes Region," 60–75.

57 Michael Brigham, Robert N. Bartone, Jessica A. Reed, and Ellen Cowie, "Introduction to the Archaeological Phase III Excavations at NTOLONAPEMK, the Eastern Surplus Company Superfund Site, 96–02," *The Maine Archaeological Society Bulletin,* Vol. 41 (2), 27–39.

58 David Sanger and Stephen A. Davis, "Preliminary Report on the Bain Site and the Chegoggin Archaeological Project," in Deal and Blair, eds., *Prehistoric Archaeology in the Maritime Provinces: Past and Present Research,* 59–71.

59 A recent report of numerous plummets and other Late Archaic artifacts eroding from the head of the Bay of Fundy may cause a revision when more is known. Patricia Allen, personal communication, 2000.

60 This position has been most clearly articulated by Bruce Bourque. Bourque, ed., *Diversity and Complexity in Prehistoric Maritime Societies,* 231–3.

61 Brian S. Robinson, "Archaic Period Burial Patterning in Northeastern North America," *The Review of Archaeology* 17, no. 1 (1996).

62 Norman Clermont and Claude Chapdelaine, *Île Morrison: Lieu sacré et atelier de l'archaïque dans l'outaouais,* vol. 28, *Paléo-Québec* (Montréal: Recherches Amérindiennes au Québec, 1998).

63 David Sanger, *Cow Point: An Archaic Cemetery in New Brunswick,* vol. 12, Mercury Series (Ottawa: Archaeological Survey of Canada, National Museums of Canada, 1973); James A. Tuck, ed., *Ancient Peoples of Port Au Choix, Social and Economic Studies* (St John's: Institute of Social and Economic Research, 1976).

64 James E. Anderson, "The Human Skeletons," in Tuck, ed., *Ancient People of Port Au Choix,* 124–31; also, Johan Jelsma, *A Bed of Ochre* (Amsterdam: Rijksuniversiteit Groningen, 2001).

65 Sanger, *Cow Point: An Archaic Cemetery in New Brunswick.*

66 For a review see Bourque, ed., *Diversity and Complexity in Prehistoric Maritime Societies.*

67 Anonymous, *Maine Prehistoric Survey Site Forms* [CD-ROM]. Maine Historic Preservation Commission, 7 February 2000 [cited February 7, 2000].

68 David W. Black, "Rum Beach and the Susquehanna Tradition in the Quoddy Region, Charlotte County, New Brunswick," *Canadian Journal of Archaeology,* 24 (2000), 89–105; Michael Deal, "Late Archaic and Ceramic Period Utilization of the Mud Lake Stream Site, Southwestern New Brunswick," *Man in the Northeast* 32 (1986), 67–94; Tuck, "The Archaic Period in the Maritime Provinces," 29–65.

69 Bourque, ed., *Diversity and Complexity in Prehistoric Maritime Societies*; Sanger, "Culture Change as an Adaptive Process in the Maine Maritimes Region," 60–75; David Sanger and Bruce J. Bourque, "The Rise and Fall of the Susquehanna Tradition in the Maine-Maritimes Provinces Region," paper presented at the Eastern States Archaeological Federation, Wilmington, Delaware, 1986; Tuck, "The Archaic Period in the Maritime Provinces," 29–65.

70 Brian S. Robinson, "A Regional Analysis of the Moorehead Burial Tradition: Groups and Boundaries on the Gulf of Maine," PhD thesis, Brown University, 2000.

71 Sanger, "Culture Change as an Adaptive Process in the Maine Maritimes Region," 60–75; Bourque, ed., *Diversity and Complexity in Prehistoric Maritime Societies.*

72 Patricia M. Allen, "The Oxbow Site: An Archaeological Framework for Northeastern New Brunswick," in M.G. Hanna and B. Kooyman, eds., *Approaches to Algonquian Archaeology, Proceedings of the Thirteenth Annual Conference* (Calgary: University of Calgary Archaeological Association, 1982), 119–34; James B. Petersen and David Sanger, "An Aboriginal Ceramic Sequence for Maine and the Maritime Provinces," in Deal and Blair, eds., *Prehistoric Archaeology in the Maritime Provinces: Past and Present Research,* 113–70.

73 James V. Wright, *A History of the Native People of Canada: Volume II (1,000 B.C.-A.D. 500),* paper 152, Mercury Series (Ottawa: Canadian Museum of Civilization, 1999).

74 Christopher, J. Turnbull, "The Augustine Site: A Mound from the Maritimes," *Archaeology of Eastern North America* 4 (1976), 50–62.

75 Stephen A. Davis, "The Ceramic Period of Nova Scotia," in Deal and Blair, eds., *Prehistoric Archaeology in the Maritime Provinces: Past and Present Research,* 93–108.

76 Douglas Rutherford, "The Ceramic Period in New Brunswick," in Deal and Blair, eds., *Prehistoric Archaeology in the Maritime Provinces: Past and Present Research,* 109–19; Rutherford, "Reconsidering the Middlesex Burial

Phase in the Maine-Maritimes Region," *Canadian Journal of Archaeology* 14 (1990), 169–81.

77 Wright, *A History of the Native People of Canada: Volume II.*

78 Susan Blair, "Feeling the Elephant: Early Maritime Woodland Components from South Central New Brunswick," paper presented at the Canadian Archaeological Association, Ottawa 2000.

79 Ives Goddard, "Eastern Algonquian Languages," in B.G. Trigger, ed., *Handbook of North American Indians–Northeast* (Washington, DC: Smithsonian Institution, 1978), 70–7; Franklin T. Siebert, "The Original Home of the Proto-Algonquian People," in *Contributions to Anthropology: Linguistics I (Algonquian)* (Ottawa: National Museum of Canada, 1967), 13–47.

80 Stuart J. Fiedel, "Correlating Archaeology and Linguistics: The Algonquian Case," *Man in the Northeast* 41 (1991), 9–32.

81 This attack on the "*In situ*" hypothesis of Iroquoian culture, which has been favoured for nearly fifty years, (see Wright, *A History of the Native People of Canada: Volume II*), has engendered much discussion. For a summary of differing views, see Norman Clermont, "The Origin of the Iroquois," *The Review of Archaeology* 17, no. 1 (1996), 59–62; Dean R. Snow, "Migration in Prehistory: The Northern Iroquoian Case," *American Antiquity* 60, no. 1 (1995), 59–79.

82 Rutherford, "The Ceramic Period in New Brunswick," 109–19. Rutherford does not suggest a migration to explain the differences.

83 Petersen and Sanger, "An Aboriginal Ceramic Sequence for Maine and the Maritime Provinces," 113–70.

84 Christopher Borstel, *Archaeological Investigations at the Young Site, Alton, Maine*, Occasional Publications in Maine Archaeology, No. 2 (Augusta, Maine: Maine Historic Preservation Commission, 1982); Karen E. Mack, David Sanger, and Alice R. Kelley, *The Bob Site: A Multicomponent Archaic and Ceramic Period Site on Pushaw Stream, Maine*, Occasional Papers in Maine Archaeology. No. 12 (Augusta: Maine Archaeological Association and Maine Historic Preservation Commission, 2002); Bonnie Newsom, "Ceramic Period Archaeology Along the Lower Piscataquis River, Maine," MSc thesis, Institute for Quaternary Studies, University of Maine, 1999. For a more comprehensive review, see also Petersen and Sanger, "An Aboriginal Ceramic Sequence for Maine and the Maritime Provinces," 113–70.

85 For alternative views see Bruce J. Bourque, "Radiocarbon Dating and the Little Gap," paper presented at the Canadian Archaeological Association, Ottawa 2000; Spiess and Petersen, "End of the Susquehanna Tradition circa 3000 BP, in Maine"; paper also presented at CAA, Ottawa.

86 Douglas C. Kellogg, "Statistical Relevance and Site Locational Data," *American Antiquity* 52, no. 1 (1987), 143–50; Kellogg, "Why Did They Choose to Live Here? Ceramic Period Settlement in the Boothbay, Maine, Region," *Northeast Anthropology* 48 (1994), 25–60; David Sanger,

"Testing the Models: Hunter-Gatherer Use of Space in the Gulf of Maine, USA," *World Archaeology* 27 (1996), 512–26.

87 The majority of well-defined coastal semi-subterranean houses occur between Penobscot Bay and Passamaquoddy Bay. William R. Belcher, "The Archaeology of the Knox Site, East Penobscot Bay, Maine," *Maine Archaeological Society Bulletin* 29, no. 1 (1989), 33–46; Stephen A. Davis, *Teacher's Cove: A Prehistoric Site on Passamaquoddy Bay*. vol. 1, *New Brunswick Archaeology Series* (Fredericton: Historic Resources Administration, 1978); David Sanger, *The Carson Site and the Late Ceramic Period in Passamaquoddy Bay, New Brunswick*, vol. 135, Mercury Series (Ottawa: Canadian Museum of Civilization, 1987); Sanger, "An Introduction to the Prehistory of the Passamaquoddy Bay Region," *American Review of Canadian Studies* 16, no. 2 (1986), 139–59; Sanger, "Prehistory of Passamaquoddy Bay: A Summary," *Maine Archaeological Society Bulletin* 11, no. 2 (1971), 14–19.

88 Examples of faunal lists from coastal sites abound. They reflect the heterogeneity in subsistence and settlement strategies. For examples, see William R. Belcher, "Prehistoric Fish Exploitation in East Penobscot Bay, Maine: The Knox Site and Sea-Level Rise," *Archaeology of Eastern North America* 17 (1989), 175–90; David W. Black, *Living Close to the Ledge: Prehistoric Human Ecology of the Bliss Islands, Quoddy Region, New Brunswick, Canada.* Occasional Papers in Northeastern Archaeology, vol. 6 (Dundas: Copetown Press, 1992); Sanger, *The Carson Site and the Late Ceramic Period in Passamaquoddy Bay, New Brunswick*; Sanger, "Testing the Models: Hunter-Gatherer Use of Space in the Gulf of Maine, USA," 512–26; Arthur E. Spiess and Robert Lewis, *The Turner Farm Fauna: 5000 Years of Hunting and Fishing in Penobscot Bay, Maine*, Occasional Publications in Maine Archaeology, no. 11 (2001); Frances L. Stewart, "Seasonal Movements of Indians in Acadia as Evidenced by Historical Documents and Vertebrate Faunal Remains from Archaeological Sites," *Man in the Northeast* 38 (1989), 55–77; Turnbull and Allen, "A Review of *Maritime Provinces Prehistory* by James Tuck," 250–60.

89 Pierre Biard, "Relation of New France, and the Jesuit Father's Voyage to That Country," in Reuben Thwaites, ed., *Jesuit Relations and Allied Documents* (Cleveland: Burrows Brothers, 1896).

90 Davis, "The Ceramic Period of Nova Scotia," 93–108.

91 Dean R. Snow, *The Archaeology of New England* (New York, NY: Academic Press, 1980), 43.

92 Speck credits F. Eckstorm for a repetition of Biard's account. Frank G. Speck, *Penobscot Man* (Philadelphia: University of Pennsylvania Press, 1940), 36.

93 Sanger, "An Analysis of Seasonal Transhumance Models for Pre-European State of Maine," 54–8; Sanger, "Testing the Models: Hunter-Gatherer Use of Space in the Gulf of Maine, USA," 512–26.

94 Rutherford, "The Ceramic Period in New Brunswick," 109–19; Stewart, "Seasonal Movements of Indians in Acadia as Evidences by Historical Documents and Vertebrate Faunal Remains from Archaeological Sites," 55–77; Turnbull and Allen, "A Review of *Maritime Provinces Prehistory* by James Tuck," 250–60.

95 James B. Petersen, "Fiber Industries from Northern New England: Ethnicity and Technological Traditions During the Woodland Period," in James B. Petersen, ed., *A Most Indispensable Art* (Knoxville: University of Tennessee Press, 1996), 100–19.

96 For a detailed evaluation of the evidence, see Sanger, "An Analysis of Seasonal Transhumance Models for Pre-European State of Maine," 54–8. A recent piece of evidence in further support of summer inland occupation comes from the recognition of pottery scraps, typically residues from pottery manufacture, a warm weather activity when the clay can be air-dried prior to firing. Newsom, "Ceramic Period Archaeology Along the Lower Piscataquis River, Maine."

97 Fredrik Barth, "Introduction," in F. Barth, ed., *Ethnic Groups and Boundaries* (Boston: Little, Brown and Company, 1969), 9–38, 12.

98 Tanner offers an excellent analysis. Adrian Tanner, *Bringing Home Animals* (London: C. Hurst & Company, 1979).

99 For example, early in the seventeenth century Father LeJeune recorded that the Montagnais did not feed bones to the dogs, and often burned them for fear of offending the Spirit Masters. Thwaites, ed., *The Jesuit Relations and Allied Documents:* 73 vols. (Cleveland: Burrows Brothers, 1896–1901) vol 6, 163, 211, 213, 217, 219. Speck notes that bear bones were incinerated among the Innu. Franklin G. Speck, *Naskapi* (Norman: University of Oklahoma Press, 1935), 104.

The prohibition was often recorded in Mi'kmaq country by early observers. As late as 1911 a Mi'kmaq informant reflected the concern that if one allows dogs to chew game animal bones, "It will bring starvation to you even if you pitch the bone to a dog." Wilson D. Wallis and Ruth S. Wallis, *The Micmac Indians of Eastern Canada* (Minneapolis: University of Minnesota Press, 1955), 107.

100 Anonymous, "Zoological Sketches," *The Halifax Monthly Magazine* 1831, 145–51, 149.

101 Frank Speck, "Penobscot Tales and Religious Beliefs," *The Journal of American Folklore* 48 (1935), 1–107.

102 Bone calcines at temperatures above 400°C. The hydroxyapatite fraction of Hirundo bone was fused, indicating temperatures of >800°C. James A. Knight, "Differential Preservation of Calcined Bone at the Hirundo Site, Alton," MSc thesis, Institute for Quaternary Studies, University of Maine, 1985. Discussion with forest ecologists indicates that the hypothesis of natural fires attaining temperatures in the 800°C

range is unlikely unless the ground is covered with huge piles of slash. Therefore, it seems unlikely that the calcined bone in archaeological sites is the product of natural or wild fires.

103 F. Stewart, personal communication, 2000. After an examination of food bone from a Passamaquoddy Bay shell midden site, Stewart concluded: "Food bone wastes were not purposely disposed of by burning." Frances L. Stewart, *Faunal Remains From the 1979 Excavations at the Minister's Island Site (Bgdr:10) of New Brunswick.* Manuscript on file (Fredericton: Department of Tourism, Recreation and Heritage, 1980), 7. Jeffery D. Sommer, *Investigation of the Faunal Remains from the Todd Site (17–11), Muscongus Bay, Maine,* MSc thesis, Institute for Quaternary Studies, University of Maine, Orono, 1997. K. Sobolik, personal communication, 2000; Spiess, "Archaic Period Subsistence in New England and the Atlantic Provinces," 163–85.

104 S. de Champlain, "The Voyages of the Sieure de Champlain," in H. Biggar, ed., *The Works of Samuel De Champlain* (Toronto: The Champlain Society, 1922), 204–469 [1613], 327.

105 A review of southern New England illustrates a very complex social situation. Kathleen J. Bragdon, *Native People of Southern New England, 1500–1650* (Norman: University of Oklahoma Press, 1996).

106 David Demeritt, "Agriculture, Climate and Cultural Adaptation in the Prehistoric Northeast," *Archaeology of Eastern North America* 19 (1991), 183–202.

107 Vincent O. Erickson, "Maliseet-Passamaquoddy," in B.G. Trigger, ed., *Handbook of North American Indians-the Northeast,* vol. 15 (Washington DC: Smithsonian Institution, 1978), 123–36; Prins, *The Mi'kmaq,* 27, 28.

108 Franklin G. Speck, "The Eastern Algonkian Wabanaki Confederacy," *American Anthropologist* 17 (1915), 492–508. Brought together in times of political emergencies, this institution continues today as a means of maintaining social, political, and family ties. Kinship terminology (fictive in most instances), such as "brother" applied to tribal emissaries, extended even to positioning the junior Mi'kmaq delegate in a cradle board.

109 I wish to acknowledge the assistance of a number of people assisted with the preparation of this paper. Stephen Bicknell produced the artifact photographs. John Mosher kindly made available his notes on treatment of animal bones taken from *The Jesuit Relations* and other sources. Discussions with Arthur Spiess and Kristin Sobolik helped with bone distributions. Micah Pawling brought to my attention the reference on burning of deer bones in Nova Scotia. Ann Dieffenbacher-Krall solicited a number of opinions on ground temperatures achieved during forest fires. Susan Blair permitted me to examine unpublished collections from New Brunswick.

CHAPTER THREE

1 The major exception is Harold A. Innis's staple thesis; see *The Fur Trade in Canada: An Introduction to Canadian Economic History*, rev. ed. (Toronto: University of Toronto Press, 1952). For the importance, but limitations, of the staples thesis see R. Cole Harris, ed., "Preface," *Historical Atlas of Canada*, vol. 1, *From the Beginning to 1800* (Toronto: University of Toronto Press, 1987). The author is grateful to Stephen Hornsby, John Reid, Tina Loo, Bob McDonald, and anonymous readers, all of whom offered thoughtful criticisms and constructive suggestions for improving this essay.

2 See Michael Mann, *The Sources of Social Power*, vol. 1, *A History of Power from the Beginning to A.D. 1760* (Cambridge: Cambridge University Press, 1986), 1–33. The following paragraph is an application of Mann's idea to an imperial context.

3 R. Cole Harris, "The Pattern of Early Canada," *The Canadian Geographer/Le géographe canadien* 31, 4 (1987), 290–8; and Nicholas Canny, "The Origins of Empire: An Introduction," in Canny, ed., *The Oxford History of the British Empire*, vol. 1, *The Origins of Empire: British Overseas Enterprise to the Close of the Seventeenth Century* (Oxford: Oxford University Press, 1998), 1–33, emphasize colonization as the central component of empire building.

4 John G. Reid, *Acadia, Maine, and New Scotland: Marginal Colonies in the Seventeenth Century* (Toronto: University of Toronto Press, 1981); Gillian Cell, *English Enterprise in Newfoundland, 1577–1660* (Toronto: University of Toronto Press, 1969); and Andrew Hill Clark, "New England's Role in the Underdevelopment of Cape Breton Island during the French Regime, 1714–1758," *The Canadian Geographer* 9 (1965), 1–12.

5 Peter E. Pope, *Fish into Wine: The Newfoundland Plantation in the Seventeenth Century* (Chapel Hill: University of North Carolina Press, 2004).

6 For example, see C. Grant Head, *Eighteenth Century Newfoundland: A Geographer's Perspective* (Toronto: McClelland & Stewart, 1976); W. Gordon Handcock, *'Soe Longe as there comes noe women': Origins of English Settlement in Newfoundland* (St John's: Breakwater, 1989); and John Mannion, "The Waterford Merchants and the Irish-Newfoundland Provisions Trade, 1770–1820," in Donald H. Akenson, ed., *Canadian Papers in Rural History*, vol. 3 (Gananoque, Ontario: Langdale Press, 1982), 178–203.

7 For the embedding of this idea in colonial American history see D.W. Meinig, *The Shaping of America: A Geographical Perspective on 500 Years of History*, vol. 1, *Atlantic America, 1492–1800* (New Haven: Yale University Press, 1986), 85–109; John J. McCusker and Russell R. Menard, *The Econ-*

omy of British America, 1607–1789 (Chapel Hill, North Carolina: University of North Carolina Press, 1985), 91–116. The entrenchment of the New England paradigm in Maritime history dates from John Bartlet Brebner's work in the early twentieth century. See in particular *New England's Outpost: Acadia before the Conquest of Canada* (New York: Columbia University Press, 1927) and *The Neutral Yankees of Nova Scotia: A Marginal Colony during the Revolutionary Years* (New York: Columbia University Press, 1937). Brebner was influenced by the continentalist, rather than imperial, approach to Canadian history; see Carl Berger, *The Writing of Canadian History: Aspects of English-Canadian Historical Writing since 1900*, 2d ed. (Toronto: University of Toronto Press, 1986), 140–59. For its recent application in Canadian history, see Graeme Wynn, "A Province Too Much Dependent on New England," *Canadian Geographer* 31: 2 (1987), 98–113.

8 Edward Shils, "Center and Periphery," in *Center and Periphery: Essays in Macrosociology* (Chicago: University of Chicago Press, 1975), 3–16. For its application in British America, see Jack P. Greene, *Peripheries and Center: Constitutional Development in the Extended Polities of the British Empire and the United States 1607–1788* (Athens, Georgia: University of Georgia Press, 1986).

9 For reconceptualizations of imperial space in the nineteenth century, see Daniel W. Clayton, *Islands of Truth: The Imperial Fashioning of Vancouver Island* (Vancouver: University of British Columbia Press, 2000); and R. Cole Harris, ed., *The Resettlement of British Columbia: Essays on Colonialism and Geographical Change* (Vancouver: University of British Columbia Press, 1997).

10 Reid, *Acadia, Maine, and New Scotland*; and Cell, *English Enterprise in Newfoundland, 1577–1660*.

11 Harris, ed., "Preface," *HAC* 47–50 and Plates 19–28.

12 David B. Quinn, "Newfoundland in the Consciousness of Europe in the Sixteenth and Early Seventeenth Centuries," in *Explorers and Colonies: America, 1500–1625* (London: Hambledon Press, 1990), 301–20; Selma Barkham, "The Basque Whaling Establishments in Labrador 1536–1632, A Summary," *Arctic* 37, no. 4 (1984), 515–19; and John Mannion and Selma Barkham, "The 16th Century Fishery," *HAC*, 1:Plate 22. The involvement of the Portuguese in the sixteenth-century fishery has recently been challenged; see Darlene Abreu-Ferreira, "Terra Nova through the Iberian Looking Glass: The Portuguese-Newfoundland Cod Fishery in the Sixteenth Century," *Canadian Historical Review* 79 (1998), 100–15.

13 Quinn, "Newfoundland in the Consciousness of Europe," 303–9, 319–20.

14 Kenneth R. Andrews, *Trade, Plunder and Settlement: Maritime Enterprise and*

the Genesis of the British Empire, 1480–1630 (Cambridge: Cambridge University Press, 1984), 304–7; and Mannion and Barkham, "The 16th Century Fishery," *HAC*, 1:Plate 22.

15 Quinn, "Newfoundland in the Consciousness of Europe," 301–20.

16 A Report from the Committee of Secrecy Appointed by Order of the House of Commons to Examine Several Books and Papers laid before the House relating to the late Negotiations of Peace and Commerce, etc. Reported on the Ninth of June, 1715 (London, 1715); John G. Reid, "1686–1720: Imperial Intrusions," in Phillip A. Buckner and John G. Reid, eds., *The Atlantic Region to Confederation: A History* (Toronto: University of Toronto Press, 1994), 80–1, 93–4; J.K. Hiller, "The Newfoundland Fisheries Issue in Anglo-French Treaties, 1713–1904," *Journal of Imperial and Commonwealth History* 24 (1996), 1–23; and Frederic F. Thompson, *The French Shore Problem in Newfoundland: An Imperial Study* (Toronto: University of Toronto Press, 1961), 7–8.

17 Bruce J. Bourque and Ruth H. Whitehead, "Trade and Alliance in the Contact Period," in Emerson W. Baker et al., eds., *American Beginnings: Exploration, Culture, and Cartography in the Land of Norumbega* (Lincoln, Nebraska: University of Nebraska Press, 1994), 131–47; and Ralph Pastore, "The Sixteenth Century: Aboriginal Peoples and European Contact," in Buckner and Reid, eds., *The Atlantic Region to Confederation*, 22–39.

18 Bruce Trigger, *Natives and Newcomers: Canada's 'Heroic Age' Reconsidered* (Kingston and Montreal: McGill-Queen's University Press, 1985), 111–63; Pastore, "The Sixteenth Century: Aboriginal Peoples and European Contact," 22–39; and Bourque and Whitehead, "Trade and Alliances in the Contact Period," 131– 47.

19 Trigger, *Natives and Newcomers*, 172–83; John G. Reid, "Political Definitions: Creating Maine and Acadia," in Baker et al., eds., *American Beginnings*, 173–9; and Alaric Faulkner and Gretchen F. Faulkner, "Fort Pentagoet and Castin's Habitation: French Ventures in Acadian Maine," (ibid.), 217–40.

20 Trigger, *Natives and Newcomers*, passim.

21 Reid, *Acadia, Maine, and New Scotland*, 14; Charles McLean Andrews, *The Colonial Period of American History*, 4 vols. (New Haven: Yale University Press, 1934–38), 1:82–4; Cecil T. Carr, ed., *Select Charters of Trading Companies A.D. 1530–1707* (London: B. Quariteh, 1913), 53. The charter of Virginia divided the territory into two overlapping segments; the London branch of the company had rights in the area from 34–41° and the Plymouth branch had rights in the area from 38–45° north latitude. In 1620 a separate charter was granted to the Council of New England for the area from 40–48° north latitude, thus extending its interest into the territory of the largely defunct Newfoundland Company; see Andrews,

The Colonial Period, 82–4. The charter of New Scotland (1624) was defined by the physical landscape, a point of pride of Sir William Alexander, who made the claim "mine be the first National Patent that ever was cleerly bounded within America by particular limits upon the Earth." See Reid, *Acadia, Maine, and New Scotland*, 23–4.

22 Ralph Pastore, "The Collapse of the Beothuk World," *Acadiensis* 19:1 (1989), 51–71; and "Fishermen, Furriers, and Beothuks: The Economy of Extinction," *Man in the Northeast*, 33 (1987), 47–62.

23 Archibald M. MacMechan, ed., *A Calendar of Two Letter-Books and One Commission-Book in the Possession of the Government of Nova Scotia, 1713–1741* (Halifax: Herald Printing House, 1900), 85, 88, 101, 110, 134, 140, and 246.

24 Hiller, "The Newfoundland Fisheries Issue," 1–23; and Thompson, *The French Shore Problem in Newfoundland*.

25 The other significant factor is the power of native peoples and the decisions that colonizing powers made to interact with them.

26 Reid, *Acadia, Maine, and New Scotland*, 14–18.

27 Cell, *English Enterprise in Newfoundland*, 53–7, 108–25, quote on 54.

28 W.J. Eccles, *France in America*, rev. ed. (Markham, Ontario: Fitzhenry and Whiteside, 1990), 19.

29 Leslie Choquette, *Frenchmen into Peasants: Modernity and Tradition in the Peopling of French Canada* (Cambridge: Harvard University Press, 1997), 249–60.

30 Elizabeth Mancke and John G. Reid, "Elites, States, and the Imperial Contest for Acadia," in John G. Reid et al., *The 'Conquest' of Acadia, 1710: Imperial, Colonial, and Aboriginal Constructions* (Toronto: University of Toronto Press, 2004), 25–47.

31.Mancke and Reid, "Elites, States, and the Imperial Contest for Acadia"; Eccles, *France in America*, 63–94; John Mannion and Gordon Handcock, "The 17th Century Fishery," *HAC*, 1:Plate 23; J.S. McLennan, *Louisbourg: From its Foundation to its Fall* (London: Macmillan, 1918); B.A. Balcom, *The Cod Fishery of Isle Royale, 1713–1758* (Ottawa, 1984); and Christopher Moore, "Cape Breton and the North Atlantic World in the Eighteenth Century," in Kenneth Donovan, ed., *The Island: New Perspectives on Cape Breton History* (Fredericton: Acadiensis Press, 1990), 31–48.

32 Jack P. Greene, "'A Posture of Hostility': A Reconsideration of Some Aspects of the Origins of the American Revolution," *Proceedings of the American Antiquarian Society* 87 (1977), 27–68.

33 Andrew Hill Clark, *Acadia: The Geography of Early Nova Scotia to 1760* (Madison: University of Wisconsin Press, 1968), 99–108; Reid, *Acadia, Maine, and New Scotland*, 103–4; and Jean Daigle, "Acadian Marshland Settlment," *HAC*, 1:Plate 29.

34 Emerson W. Baker and John G. Reid, "Amerindian Power in the Early

Modern Northeast: A Reappraisal," *William and Mary Quarterly*, 3rd ser., 61 (2004), 77–106.

35 Reid, *Acadia, Maine, and New Scotland*, 103–4, 118.

36 Elizabeth Mancke, "Imperial Transitions," in Reid et al., *The 'Conquest' of Acadia*, 178–202.

37 Ibid; Joseph J. Malone, *Pine Trees and Politics: The Naval Stores and Forest Policy in Colonial New England* (Seattle: University of Washington, 1964), 10–27; and Robert Greenhaigh Albion, *Forests and Sea Power: The Timber Problem of the Royal Navy, 1652–1862* (1926; rpt., Hamden, Connecticut: Archon, 1965), 238–55.

38 Brebner, *New England's Outpost*, 166–75; Winthrop P. Bell, *The 'Foreign Protestants' and the Settlement of Nova Scotia* (Toronto: University of Toronto Press, 1961).

39 Elizabeth Mancke, "Another British America: A Canadian Model for the Early Modern British Empire," *Journal of Imperial and Commonwealth History* 25 (1997), 1–25.

40 Cell, *English Enterprise in Newfoundland*, 53–80.

41 John Mannion, Gordon Handcock, and Alan Macpherson, "The Newfoundland Fishery, 18th Century," *HAC*, 1:Plate 25; and Jerry Bannister, *The Rule of the Admirals: Law, Custom, and Naval Government in Newfoundland, 1699–1832* (Toronto: University of Toronto Press, 2003).

42 A Report from the Committee of Secrecy (1715).

43 Robert V. Wells, *The Population of the British Colonies in America before 1776* (Princeton: Princeton University Press, 1975), 259–96; and J.M. Bumsted, "1763–1783: Resettlement and Rebellion," in Buckner and Reid, eds., *The Atlantic Region to Confederation*, 165.

CHAPTER FOUR

1 *R. vs. Marshall, Canadian Native Law Reporter* 4 (1999), 181.

2 This controversy is covered in Ken Coates, *The Marshall Decision and Native Rights* (Montreal and Kingston: McGill-Queen's University Press, 2000).

3 CBC Radio News, "Native Band says it will fish in Bay of Fundy," 13 April 2000.

4 See, for instance, Tom Porter, "Traditions of the Constitution of the Six Nations," in Leroy Little Bear et al., eds., *Pathways to Self-Determination: Canadian Indians and the Canadian State* (Toronto: University of Toronto Press, 1984), 14.

5 Chicago, Newberry Library, Ayers Collection, "Recensement general fait au mois de novembre mille sept cent huit." (France, Archives nationales, Archives des colonies, C11B, 6:77r); "Recensement des sauvages dans l'isle Royale et de la peninsule de l'acadie qui sont ... en 1722," 27

décembre 1722; Ibid., G1 466, no. 71, "Recensement fait cette presente anné du nombre des sauvages ... 1735."

6 Great Britain, Public Record Office (hereafter PRO) CO 42/1:364r, "Etat des sauvages de la Riviere St. Jean appelles Amalecites, quelquefois Canibas ou Abenaquis," enclosed in Gov. James Murray to Board of Trade, 26 June 1764.

7 "Return of Indians and their Familys that are and have Been in the Service of the United States by order of Col. Allen ... at Machias July 28, 1780," in Frederic Kidder, ed., *Military Operations in Eastern Maine and Nova Scotia During the Revolution* (Albany: Joel Munsell, 1867), 284.

8 James Wherry, "Documents Relating to the History of the Passamaquoddy Indian Presence in Charlotte County, New Brunswick," (Fredericton, 1981), 6–10. My thanks to George Matthews of St Stephen, New Brunswick, for bringing this collection of documents to my attention.

9 PRO, CO 42/1:364r.

10 Nova Scotia Archives and Records Management, RG 1/7: doc. 22, Passamaquoddy to Philipps, 23 November 1720.

11 PRO, CO 217/18:18r-21r, "Treaty of Peace and Friendship concluded with the Delegates of the St. Johns and Passamaquoddy Tribes of Indians," 23 February 1760.

12 "Diary of Sergeant John Burrell, 1759–60," in *Acadiensis* 5 (1905), 294.

13 These issues are explored in Sidney L. Harring, *Crow Dog's Case: American Indian Sovereignty, Tribal Law, and United States Law in the Nineteenth Century* (Cambridge: Cambridge University Press, 1994), 25–34.

14 The text of the treaty is in PRO, CO 217/18:18r-31r.

15 PRO, CO 217/20:103r, Benjamin Gerrish's Accounts, 17 November 1760.

16 For the 1726 treaty, see PRO, CO 217/5:3r-5r; for the 1749 treaty, *Indian Treaties and Surrenders*, vol. 2 (Ottawa: Queen's Printer, 1891), 200–1. These treaties are explained in William C. Wicken, *Mi'kmaq Treaties on Trial: History, Land, and Donald Marshall Junior* (Toronto: University of Toronto Press, 2002), and Stephen E. Patterson, "Indian-White Relations in Nova Scotia, 1749–61: A Case Study in Political Interaction," *Acadiensis* 23:1 (Autumn 1993), 23–59.

17 Eric Hobsbawm, *Nations and Nationalism Since 1780: Programme, Myth, Reality* (Cambridge: Cambridge University Press 1990).

CHAPTER FIVE

1 The Wabanaki Confederacy was a political grouping dating back at least to the seventeenth century, that linked native groups in what is now Maine with others in the Maritime region. In addition to the Wulstukwiuk, its members included the Mi'kmaq, the Penobscot, and the Eastern Abenaki peoples.

2 While not always asking the question overtly in bold terms, several scholars have asked whether the colonies that remained loyal to the British during the American Revolution differed fundamentally from those that rebelled, even in the years before 1763. This question is raised implicitly by George Rawlyk's *Nova Scotia's Massachusetts: A Study of Massachusetts–Nova Scotia Relations, 1630 to 1784* (Montreal: McGill-Queen's University Press, 1973), by Barry Moody's "A Just and Disinterested Man: The Nova Scotia Career of Paul Mascarene, 1710–1752" (PhD. diss., Queen's University, 1976), and by Elizabeth Mancke's recent articles, including "Early Modern Imperial Governance and the Origins of Canadian Political Culture," *Canadian Journal of Political Science* 32 (1999) 3–20; and "Another British America: A Canadian Model for the Early Modern British Empire," *Journal of Imperial and Commonwealth History* 25 (1997) 1–36. This question is also implicated in the extensive literature on the position of the loyal colonies during the war of the American Revolution. For an overview of that literature, see Mancke's "The American Revolution in Canada," in Jack P. Greene and J.R. Pole, eds., *A Companion to the American Revolution* (Oxford: Blackwells, 2000), 503–10.

3 For a provocative discussion of this issue see Léon Thériault, "Acadia from 1763 to 1990: An Historical Synthesis," in Jean Daigle, ed., *Acadia of the Maritimes: Thematic Studies from the Beginning to the Present* (Moncton: Chaire d'études acadiennes, 1995).

4 Council minutes, 15 July 1755, in Thomas B. Akins, ed., *Selections from the Public Documents of the Province of Nova Scotia* (Halifax: Charles Annand, 1869), 258–9.

5 Pierre de Rigaud, marquis de Vaudreuil de Cavagnial to ministry, 1 June 1756, in Placide Gaudet, ed., "Acadian Genealogy and Notes," *Report Concerning Canadian Archives for the Year 1905* (Ottawa: National Archives of Canada, 1906), 179–81.

6 William Martin, "Description of the St. Johns River in Nova Scotia, March 11, 1758," LO 6939, Huntington Library.

7 See also John Knox, *Journal of Captain John Knox*, ed., Arthur G. Doughty (Toronto: Champlain Society, 1914), vol. 1, 281–2; William Shirley to Charles Lawrence, 13 March 1756, in Akins, ed., *Selections*, 428–37.

8 Knox, *Journal*, vol. 1, 176. The British and the New Englanders did make a few other, more concerted efforts during this three-year period to establish a military presence in the area, including one intriguing, aborted effort in 1756, in which they tried to attack the Acadians by surprise by disguising themselves as French. See Lawrence to Shirley, 18 February 1756, RG 135, doc. 25, Public Archives of Nova Scotia; Vaudreuil to ministry, 1 June 1756, in Gaudet, ed., "Acadian Genealogy and Notes," 179–81, esp. 180.

9 See Robert Monckton, "Report of the Proceedings of the Troops," *Collec-*

tions of the New Brunswick Historical Society 5 (1904) 165–75; Knox, *Journal*, vol. 1, 262; M.A. MacDonald, *Rebels and Royalists: The Lives and Material Culture of New Brunswick's Early English-Speaking Settlers, 1758–1783* (Fredricton: New Ireland Press, 1990), 13–23.

10 Robert Monckton to commanding officer at Halifax, 6 October 1758, AB 727, Huntington Library; Monckton to James Abercromby, 15 October 1758, AB 764, Huntington Library.

11 Monckton, "Report," 170–2; Knox, *Journal*, vol. 1, 268–9; Robert Hale's *Chronicle*, 1757–1761, French and Indian War Papers, Folio vol. 2, 24, American Antiquarian Society.

12 For an account of the November expedition, see Knox, *Journal*, vol. 1, 279–81.

13 Knox, *Journal*, vol. 1, 296–8; Jeffery Amherst to William Pitt, 19 April 1759, *Collections of the New Brunswick Historical Society* 5 (1904) 174–5; Hale's *Chronicle*, Folio vol. 2, 28.

14 Knox, *Journal*, vol. 1, 297.

15 Journal of Enoch Poor, 6 April 1759 to 12 May 1760, HM 610, Huntington Library; Hale's *Chronicle*, Folio vol. 2, 40.

16 "Diary of Sergeant John Burrell," *New England Historical and Genealogical Register* 59 (1905) 352–4; Journal of Enoch Poor.

17 "Diary of Sergeant John Burrell," 353. See also Hale's *Chronicle*, Folio vol. 2, 43.

18 Journal of Enoch Poor.

19 "Diary of Sergeant John Burrell," 353. The makeup of the family appears in the Journal of Enoch Poor.

20 Burrell sets the number at 30, Poor at "50 or 60." "Diary of Sergeant John Burrell," 353; Journal of Enoch Poor.

21 Amherst to Lawrence, 5 February 1760, in Akins, *Selections*, 467–9.

22 "Diary of Sergeant John Burrell," 354.

23 Ibid.

24 Muriel K. Roy, "Settlement and Population Growth," in Jean Daigle, ed., *The Acadians of the Maritimes: Thematic Studies* (Moncton: Centre d'études acadiennes, 1982), 125–61, at 154.

25 See Fred Anderson, *A People's Army: Massachusetts Soldiers and Society in the Seven Years' War* (New York: Norton, 1984), 65–6.

26 "Diary of Sergeant John Burrell," 354.

27 Journal of Enoch Poor.

28 An expedition to the Passamaquoddy region left the fort in March 1760. "Diary of Sergeant John Burrell," 354. Poor also reports on this expedition.

29 Knox, *Journal*, vol. 1, 268.

30 When Burrell finally left Fort Frederick to return to his home in Massachusetts, he was brought first to Annapolis Royal and then proceeded on

the same ship to Boston. "Diary of Sergeant John Burrell," 354. Similarly, when Poor wrote letters home, he sent them to Annapolis Royal, with instructions that they be transmitted from there to Boston. See Journal of Enoch Poor.

31 "Diary of Sergeant John Burrell," 352.

32 Ibid., 353.

33 Ibid., 354.

34 John Frye to Thomas Hutchinson, 23 April 1760, CO 5/58, "Records of the British Colonial Office, class 5 [microform]," edited by Randolph Boehm (Frederick, Maryland: University Publications of America, 1983–84), pt. 3, reel 5, frame 473.

35 Monckton, "Report," 168–9; Knox, *Journal*, vol. 1, 271–2.

36 See Journal of Enoch Poor.

37 "Diary of Sergeant John Burrell," 353.

38 Ibid.

39 Journal of Enoch Poor. As a result of inflation, the value of pound notes in Massachusetts varied depending on when they were issued. "Old tenor" notes were those produced before 1738. They were the most valuable, and even after the colonial government stopped making them, they were used as a standard of value.

40 "Diary of Sergeant John Burrell," 352.

41 Monckton, "Report," 167.

42 Journal of Enoch Poor.

43 Ibid; see also Hale's *Chronicle*, Folio vol. 2, p. 35.

44 Journal of Enoch Poor.

45 Ibid. In this passage Poor initially wrote the word "fall," crossed it out, and replaced it with "bay."

46 Ibid.

47 "Diary of Sergeant John Burrell," 352.

48 Journal of Enoch Poor.

49 "Diary of Sergeant John Burrell," 352.

50 Journal of Enoch Poor; "Diary of Sergeant John Burrell," 353. Poor's account provides the most detail.

51 Other New Englanders would arrive to settle in the valley in the 1760s, including some veterans who had fought elsewhere in North America during the Seven Years' War. See D. Murray Young, "Planter Settlements in the St. John Valley," in Margaret Conrad, ed., *They Planted Well: New England Planters in Maritime Canada* (Fredericton: Acadiensis Press, 1988), 29–35; MacDonald, *Rebels and Royalists*, 24–42.

52 For a sense of strategic thought concerning the river, see Shirley to Lawrence, 13 March 1756, Akins, ed., *Selections*, 428–37.

53 See Lawrence to Shirley, 18 February 1756, RG 135, doc. 25, Public Archives of Nova Scotia; Vaudreuil to ministry, 1 June 1756, in Gaudet, ed., "Acadian Genealogy and Notes," 179–81.

54 Knox, *Journal*, vol. 1, 268; see also Shirley to Lawrence, 19 March 1756, Akins, ed., *Selections*, 437–9; Lawrence to George Montagu Dunk, Earl of Halifax, 2 February 1757, Peter Force Collection, 8A/54, Library of Congress.

55 Monckton, "Report," 172.

56 Journal of Enoch Poor.

57 For an account of British efforts to remove the Acadian refugees from the Miramichi region (a campaign very similar to the one on the Saint John) see James Murray to James Wolfe, 24 September 1758, CO 5/53, "Records," pt. 3, reel 3, frame 670. After 1763 Acadians were permitted to stay in various parts of the province of Nova Scotia, but only rarely in the St John valley. See Council minutes, 5 July 1763, Akins, *Selections*, 338; Richard Bulkeley to John Anderson and Francis Peabody, Akins, *Selections*, 357.

58 Knox, *Journal*, vol. 1, 297.

59 In his instructions to Silvanus Cobb in winter of 1749–50, Cornwallis offered a bounty of £10 for the scalp of "every Indian you shall destroy." In the same document he offered a reward of £50 for the apprehension of Le Loutre. Ronald Rompkey's account of this episode, in his introduction to *Expeditions of Honour: The Journal of John Salusbury in Halifax, Nova Scotia, 1749–1853* (Newark: University of Delaware Press, 1982), 40, is inaccurate in this respect. See Instructions for Silvanus Cobb, 13 January 1749/50, CO 217/9, doc. 209, The National Archives, Kew.

60 See, for example, Robert Dinwiddie to Shirley, 29 July 1755, in R.A. Brock, ed., *The Official Records of Robert Dinwiddie*, 2 vols. (Richmond: Virginia Historical Society, 1884), 2:130–1.

61 William Thynne to John Campbell, 4th Earl of Loudon, February 12, 1756, LO (NA) 823, Huntington Library. See also Thynne to Loudon, 27 February 1756, LO 861, Huntington Library.

62 See William Sparke to Loudon, 25 August 1756, LO (NA) 1584, Huntington Library; Phineas Lyman to Loudon, 9 September 1756, LO (NA) 1753, Huntington Library; John Campbell, 4th Earl of Loudon to William Johnson, 10 September 1756, LO (NA) 1760, Huntington Library; Peter Wraxall, "Information of a party of Indians who brought in two French scalps," September 1756, LO (NA) 1938, Huntington Library.

63 William Henry, 1st Baron Lyttleton of Frankley to Loudon, 19 February 1757, LO (NA) 2865, Huntington Library. See also Henry Bouquet to Loudon, 25 August 1757, LO (NA) 4308, Huntington Library.

64 Order given at Montmorenci, 9 July 1759, "Instructions for Young Officers by Colonel Wolfe," Manuscript copy, Newberry Library. Reprinted in *General Wolfe's Instructions to Young Officers* (London, 1780), 89; "An Accurate and Authentic Journal of the Siege of Quebec," in A.G. Doughty and G.W. Parmelee, eds., *Siege of Quebec*, (Quebec: Dussault & Proulx, 1901), 4:279–94, esp. 288–9. See also "A Journal of the Expedition up the River

St. Lawrence," (ibid.), 5:1–11, 6–7; "Journal of Major Moncrief," (ibid.), 5:23–58, at 45–6; John Montrésor, "Journal of the Siege of Quebec," (ibid.), 4:301–34, at 329; "Journal abrégé de la campagne de 1759," (ibid.), 5:282–301, at 293.

65 Circular letter of Lawrence, 11 August 1755, *Collections of the Nova Scotia Historical Society*, 3 (1883), 82.

66 Charles Lawrence to James Abercromby, 31 March 1758, AB 95, Huntington Library.

67 Abstract of Dispatches from Canada, in E.B. O'Callaghan, ed., *Documents Relative to the Colonial History of the State of New York*, 15 vols. (Albany: Weed, Parsons, 1850–53), 10:427; Claude Godfrey Coquard to his brother, 1757, in E.B. O'Callaghan, ed., *Documents Relative to the Colonial History of the State of New York*, 10:528; Charles Lawrence to William Shirley, 18 February 1756, in Akins, ed., *Selections*, 297; *Boston Evening Post*, 15 March 1756; *Pennsylvania Gazette*, 18 March 1756; Knox, *Journal*, 1:115.

68 See Loudon to William Pitt, 25 April 1757, LO (NA) 3467, Huntington Library.

69 See especially Peregrine Thomas Hopson, Minutes in regard to a descent proposed to be made upon the island, 11 July 1757, LO (NA) 3688, Huntington Library. Reprinted in Stanley Pargellis, ed., *Military Affairs in North America, 1748–1765* (New York: American Historical Association, 1936), 302–10, esp. 305–6.

70 See Amherst to Edward Whitmore, 28 August 1758, CO 5/53, "Records," pt. 3, reel 3, frame 647.

71 For an enthusiastic statement, see Benjamin Hallowell to Loudon, 17 February 1759, LO (NA) 6042, Huntington Library.

72 See Philip Lawson, *The Imperial Challenge: Quebec and Britain in the Age of the American Revolution* (Montreal: McGill-Queen's University Press, 1990).

73 William Arbuthnot to Thomas Pownall, 1 April 1760, CO 5/58, "Records," pt. 3, reel 5, frame 299.

74 Statement of Ebenezer Redfield, 17 May 1760, CO 5/58, "Records," pt. 3, reel 5, frame 577; Statement of Arbuthnot and others, 5 May 1760, CO 5/58, "Records," pt. 3, reel 5, frame 569; Pownall to Amherst, 12 May 1760, CO 5/58, "Records," pt. 3, reel 5, frame 470; Joseph Gerrish Jr. to Pownall, 12 May 1760, CO 5/58, "Records," pt. 3, reel 5, frame 482; Arbuthnot to Pownall, 6 May 1760, CO 5/58, "Records," pt. 3, reel 5, frame 563.

75 Arbuthnot to Pownall, 6 May 1760, CO 5/58, "Records," pt. 3, reel 5, frame 563; Pownall to Amherst, 12 May 1760, CO 5/58, "Records," pt. 3, reel 5, frame 470; Gerrish to Pownall, 12 May 1760, CO 5/58, "Records," pt. 3, reel 5, frame 482.

76 Petition of John Buxton and others, May, 1760, CO 5/58, "Records," pt. 3, reel 5, frame 567; Arbuthnot to Pownall, n.d., CO 5/58, "Records," pt. 3, reel 5, frame 573; Petition of Arbuthnot and others, CO 5/58, "Records," pt. 3, reel 5, frame 575; Hutchinson to Amherst, CO 5.58, "Records," pt. 3, reel 5, frame 594. Burrell was finally relieved in July, after fifty new recruits arrived at Fort Frederick from New England. See Amherst to Hutchinson, 7 June 1760, CO 5/58, "Records," pt. 3, reel 5, frame 596; Hutchinson to Amherst, 21 June 1760, CO 5/59, "Records," pt. 3, reel 5, frame 768; Hutchinson to Amherst, 7 July 1760, CO 5.59, "Records," pt. 3, reel 5, frame 773.

77 Arbuthnot to Pownall, 3 March 1760, CO 5/58, "Records," pt. 3, reel 5, frame 298.

78 Amherst to Edward Whitmore, 18 May 1760, CO 5/58, "Records," pt. 3, reel 5, frame 445.

79 *The Oxford English Dictionary* (2d. ed., Oxford: Clarendon Press, 1989), vol. 7, 330.

80 See Anderson, *A People's Army,* 187–95.

CHAPTER SIX

1 For the socioeconomic history of the St John Valley before 1870, see my following articles: "Migrant Integration in a Frontier Society: The Madawaska Settlement, 1800–1850," *Histoire sociale–Social History,* 38 (November 1986), 277–98; "Agriculture and the Lumberman's Frontier: The Madawaska Settlement, 1800–1870," *Journal of Forest History,* 12 (July 1988), 125–37, reprinted under the title "Occupational Pluralism in British North America," in J.M. Bumsted, ed., *Interpreting Canada's Past, vol. 1, Pre-Confederation* (Toronto: University of Toronto Press, 1993), 366–94; "Agriculture et marché au Madawaska, 1799–1850," *The River Review/La revue rivière,* 1 (1995), 13–38; "Agriculture in a Pioneer Region: The Upper St. John Valley in the First Half of the Nineteenth Century," in Kris Inwood, ed., *Farm, Factory and Fortune: New Studies in the Economic History of the Maritime Provinces* (Fredericton: Acadiensis Press, 1993), 17–36; "Le développement agricole dans la haute vallée du St Jean en 1860," *Revue de la Société historique du Canada,* 3 (1993), 13–26; "The Homespun Paradox: Market-oriented Production of Cloth in Eastern Canada in the Nineteenth Century" (with J. Rygiel and Elizabeth Turcotte), *Agricultural History,* 76 (winter 2002), 28–57; "Survival or Adaptation? Domestic Rural Textile Production in Eastern Canada in the Nineteenth Century" (with J. Rygiel and Elizabeth Turcotte), *Agricultural History Review,* 49, Part II (Autumn 2001), 140–71; "La transmission des patrimoines fonciers dans le Haut St-Jean au XIXe siècle," *Revue d'histoire de l'Amérique française* (décembre, 1991); "Land Transmission Practices

among Northern Maine French Canadians in the Nineteenth Century," in Peter Benes, ed., *New England–New France, 1600–1850* (Boston: Boston University, 1992), 68–80.

For material culture, see Jane L. Cook, *Coalescence of Style: The Ethnic Heritage of St. John River Valley Regional Furniture, 1763–1851* (Montreal: McGill-Queen's University Press, 2001); and for elites, see Sheila M. Andrew, *The Development of Elites in Acadian New Brunswick 1861–1881* (Montreal: McGill-Queen's University Press, 1996). For borderlands studies, see Stephen J. Hornsby and John G. Reid, "Introduction" to this volume.

2 Maine State Archives, Report of the commissioners to investigate alleged illegal voting, created by resolution, R 1878 C93.

3 "British" in the context of early nineteenth-century North America was a rather vague term. It could refer to the British from Britain, but also to his or her Majesty's subjects in British North America. The latter included all of Britain's possessions in North America. Until 1867, the term "Canada" applied only to present day Quebec (Lower Canada) and Ontario (Upper Canada). New Brunswickers were *not* "Canadians." The latter were often referred to as "Provincials" by European British and by Americans. In this paper, the term "British" is used in its nineteenth-century meaning, and refers to British subjects of European or North American extraction.

4 Patrick Campbell, *Travels in the Interior Inhabited Parts of North America in the Year 1791 and 1792* (Edinburgh, 1793), 80–110; John Mann, *Travels in North America, Particularly in the Provinces of Upper and Lower Canada and New Brunswick and in the States of Maine, Massachusetts and New York* (Glasgow, 1824; Reprinted Fredericton, 1978), 36–41; Lieutenant E.T. Coke, *A Subaltern's Furlough: Descriptive of Scenes in Various Parts of the United States, Upper and Lower Canada, New Brunswick and Nova Scotia during the summer and autumn of 1832* (London, 1833), 349–64, in Gerald M. Craig, ed., *Early Travellers in the Canadas, 1791– 1867* (Toronto: Macmillan, 1955), 97–110.

5 [James Lumsden], *American Memoranda, by a Mercantile Man during a short Tour in the Summer of 1843* (Glasgow 1843):

"Along the Madawaska river the country is principally settled by a class of the poorest Irish squatters I ever saw: if an acre or two of potato ground is cleared, it is all the poor creatures seem to care for; and their chief means of subsistence is derived from occasional employment in assisting the lumberers on the river ... From Temiscouata Lake to Little Falls, you scarcely see a respectable habitation. With the exception of two or three small farm houses, there are nothing but log huts and miserable dwellings."

6 Park Holland, Surveyor of the Bingham Purchase. Park Holland, *Life and Diary* (Bangor Historical Society, 1790). Another traveller who did not

think the St John Valley's ethnic makeup deserved more than a passing mention was George Head, *Forest Scenes and Incidents in the Wilds of North America, being a Diary of a Winter's Route from Halifax to the Canadas* (London, 1829), 63–136. Head made his trip in 1815.

7 Donald E. Graves, ed., *The War Journal of Lieut. John Le Couteur, 104th Foot: "Merry Hearts Make Light days"* (Ottawa: Carleton University Press, 1993), 99.

8 Arcadia was a region of ancient Greece considered to be a rural paradise. The term has since been used to refer to an idealized rural community characterized by innocence, peacefulness, and simplicity.

9 Le Couteur, 99.

10 Peter Fisher, *History of New Brunswick* (Saint John: New Brunswick Historical Society, 1921; first published 1825), 52–7.

11 [Peter Fisher] *Notitia of New Brunswick for 1836, and extending into 1837, comprising Historical, Geographical, Statistical and Commercial Notices of the province, by an inhabitant* (Saint John, 1838).

12 Fisher, *History of New Brunswick*, 53.

13 *Notitia*, 98.

14 Maine State Archives, Land Office records, Journal of George W. Coffin, Massachusetts land agent, Journey up to the St John River, September and October 1825.

15 Report of Charles S. Davies, Esq, agent appointed by the executive of the State of Maine to Enquire into and Report upon certain facts relating to aggressions upon the rights of the State, and of individual citizens thereof by inhabitants of the province of New Brunswick, 31-1-1828.

16 Report of Charles S. Davies, 15.

17 The petitions and land grants are in the Provincial Archives of New Brunswick (PANB), RS108, Land petitions and application books, Microfilm reel F1024, Petition of Augustin Leblanc and others to Governor Parr of Nova Scotia, 24-11-1784; Reel F1025, petition of Amand and Francis Cormier, 5-4-1785; Reel F1029, petition of Augustin White and other French inhabitants, 10-3-1785; Reel F1032, memorial of French settlers, 28-6-1786; petition of Francis Violet, 28-08-1786; F1033, petition of Arthur Nicholson 6-4-1786 and 16-7-1787; petition of J.B. Cormier, 1787; petition of Benjamin Davis et al., 25-5-1787; petition of J.B. Cir et al., 1-6-1787; petition of Charles Lambert, 20-4-1787; petition of Joseph and Marie Cormier, 20-6-1787; F1034, petition of Richard Vandenburgh, 1787; Reel F1035, petition of John Martin et al., 1-7-1788 , 31-7-1788 and 10-10-1788; Reel F1036, petition of William Lockyer, 5-2-1789; petition of Joseph Thibodo et al., 21-12-1789; petition of Joseph Sear 26-8-1789 and 14-11-1789. See also Raoul Dionne, *La colonisation Acadienne au Nouveau Brunswick 1760–1860* (Moncton: Université de Moncton, Chaire d'études acadiennes, 1989). The land

sales between Lower St John Acadians and other individuals are in PANB, York County registry office, Book 1–4, 1785–1815, microfilm reel 5618; For the secondary literature on the topic, see Mason Wade, "The Loyalists and the Acadians," in Edward Shriver, ed., *The French in New England, Acadia and Quebec: Proceedings of a Conference held at the University of Maine at Orono, May 1972* (Orono, Maine: New England–Atlantic Provinces–Quebec Center, 1973), 7–22; W.O. Raymond, "The First Governor of New Brunswick and the Acadians of the River St. John," in *Proceedings and Transactions of the Royal Society of Canada*, 3d ser. vol. 8 (1914), 415–52 (this a particularly well-documented piece by the individual who edited the Deane and Kavanagh report for the *Collections* of the New Brunswick Historical Society); Béatrice Craig, "Early French Migrations to Northern Maine, 1785–1850," *Maine Historical Society Quarterly*, 25 (Spring 1986), 230–47.

18 Edward Kavanagh, "Wilderness Journal," *Maine History News*, vol. 16, no. 2, 3, 4 (April, July, October 1980), 3–7, 8–11, 15–16.

19 W.O. Raymond, ed., "State of the Madawaska and Aroostook settlements in 1831, Reports of John G. Deane and Edward Kavanagh to Samuel Smith, Governor of the State of Maine," New Brunswick Historical Society, *Collections*, 9 (1914), Descriptive part, 452–84; original, at the Maine State Archives. Reprinted in Thomas Albert's *Histoire du Madawaska* (Québec: Imprimerie franciscaine missionnaire, 1921).

20 Deane and Kavanagh, Report, 454.

21 Ibid., 453.

22 See Raymond's introduction to Deane and Kavanagh, Report, cited above. See also the testimonies in Trial of John Baker, transcript, in John Francis Sprague, *The Northeastern Boundary Controversy and the Aroostook War* (Dover, Maine: Observer Press, nd), 76–92. For appointments as civil parish officials, see PANB, Minutes of the County Council, York County 1818–1833 and Carleton County 1833–1850.

23. *Republican Journal*, (Belfast, Maine) 1 December 1831; also, *Republican Journal*, 3 September 1840; the latter is reprinted from the *Bangor Democrat* (nd).

24 Bancroft's narrative must have been publicly known even earlier, as the *Maine Republican* concluded an article on the Madawaska French with a reference to it in 1843. *Republican Journal*, 29 December 1843.

25 *Republican Journal*, 29 December 1843. This did not fit the evidence either. See my articles on Madawaska economy at the beginning of the nineteenth century listed in note 1.

26 *Republican Journal*, 29 December 1843.

27 Deane and Kavanagh, Report, 460; see also *Republican Journal*, 27 January 1843, for an echo of this opinion.

28 "Report of the Commissioners appointed under resolve of February 21,

1843, to locate grants and determine the extent of possessory claims under the late treaty with Great Britain."

29 "Report of the Committee upon Education in the New Settlements, 1847," in *Legislative Documents of the State of Maine*, 1847, 52–7.

30 "Final report of the Superintendent and Instructor of School in the Madawaska Settlement for the year 1844," in *Legislative documents of the State of Maine*, 1844, 2. The "Report of the land commissioners" for 1844 expressed the same belief.

31 "It will be a long time before they accustom themselves to the machinery of our institutions and a longer time before their distinct nationality is effaced or lost." *Republican Journal*, 29 December 1843.

32 For instance, Deane and Kavanagh, Report, 459; Charles Davies, Report, 15; Fisher, *History of New Brunswick*, 53.

33 "Report of the Commissioners on the Settlement of the Public Land of Maine," (Augusta, Maine: Sprague-Owen and Nash, 1870), 7 and 72; "Final Report of the Superintendent ... for the year 1844," 8.

34 James Doyle, *North of America: Images of Canada in the Literature of the United States, 1775–1900*, (Toronto: ECW Press, 1983), 17–18, 21–6, 31, 67.

35 Ibid., 28–9.

36 Ibid., 25–6.

37 "Report of the Committee upon education in the new settlement," 52–7: "On its newest parts, the State borders very largely upon foreign provinces in which free schools do not exist and as emigration is always to a greater or lesser degree taking place, there is a constant influx of ignorance and educational indifference within the bounds of the state. Especially does this current flows in upon us from the valley of the St. John."

38 *Kennebec Journal* (Augusta, Maine), 12 November 1858; Edward H. Ellwell, *Aroostook, with some Account of the Excursion Thither of the Editors of Maine in the Year 1858 and 1878* (Portland: Transcript Printing Co., 1878). Ellwell relied upon the editor of the *Maine Evangelist* for his comments on Madawaska; I could not trace any surviving contemporary issues of this paper.

39 This is evident when one compares the cadastral and survey maps of this area at different points in time.

40 Béatrice Craig, "Le développement agricole dans la haute vallée du St. Jean en 1860," *Revue de la Société historique du Canada*, 3 (1993), 13–26.

41 Ellwell, *Aroostook*.

42 Charles Lanman, *Adventures of an Angler in Canada, Nova Scotia and the US* (London, 1848).

43 Lanman, 234.

44 Ibid., 236.

45 Charles Hallock, "Aroostook on the Madawaska," *Harper's Monthly Magazine,* vol. 27 (1863), 688–98.
46 Ibid., 696.
47 Ibid., 695.
48 "Report of the Commissioners on Claims of Settlers on Proprietors' Land," 62.
49 "Report of the Commissioners on Claims of Settlers and Proprietors," 7.
50 Edmund Ward, *An Account of the St. John and its Tributary Rivers and Lakes* (Fredericton, 1841), 84–9.
51 Abraham Gesner, *New Brunswick with Notes for Emigrants,* 178–81; see also 212–15, 224–9, 332–5, 378–88 for soil, climate, currency, pioneering, etc.
52 James Finlay Weir Johnston, Report on the Agricultural Capabilities of the Province of New Brunswick (Fredericton, 2nd ed., 1850); Johnston, *Notes on North America,* 1851, ch. 3, 67–82.
53 Ward, *An Account of the St. John,* 87.
54 Ibid., 88.
55 Gesner, *New Brunswick with Notes,* 180.
56 Ibid., 332.
57 Ibid., 333.
58 Ibid., 180, 333.
59 Ibid., 180.
60 Ibid., 333.
61 Ibid., 334.
62 Johnston, *Notes on North America,* 70.
63 Ibid., 67.
64 Ibid., 80.
65 Ibid., 81.
66 Ibid., 72.
67 Ibid., 68.
68 For a good critique of European literature about Quebec farming, which was plagued by the same misconceptions, see R.M. McInnis, "A Reconsideration of the State of Agriculture in Lower Canada in the First Half of the Nineteenth Century," *Canadian Papers in Rural History,* vol. 3 (1983), 4–49.
69 Mark Overton, *Agricultural Revolution in England: The Transformation of the Agrarian Economy, 1500–1850* (Cambridge: Cambridge, 1996), 77; Gregory Clark, "Productivity Growth without Technical Changes in European Agriculture, Reply to Komlos," *Journal of Economic History,* XLIX (December 1989), 979–91.
70 Johnston, *Notes on North America,* 70.
71 Charles S. Lugrin, *Victoria County,* Appendix to the Journal of the House of Assembly of New Brunswick, 1972.

72 Ibid., xi.

73 Ibid., xiii.

74 Ibid., vii.

75 Early historian C.L. Hatheway's book contains absolutely no comment about the ethnic makeup of the Madawaska settlement: C.L. Hatheway, *The History of New Brunswick from its First Settlement, Containing a Geographical Description of the Province* (Fredericton, 1846), 43–7. Tourist Campbell Hardy, lieutenant in the Royal Artillery, tried to turn his attempt at getting food from people who spoke no more English than he did French into an amusing anecdote: Lieut. Campbell Hardy, *Sporting Adventures in the New World, or Days and Nights of Moose Hunting in the Pine Forest of Acadia,* 2 vols. (London: Hurst and Blackett, 1855), I, 138; William Thomas Baird, who had visited the Madawaska settlement in 1838, gives a purely descriptive account, and mentions that young men from the New Brunswick elite used to board with Madawaska families to learn French: William Thomas Baird, *Seventy Years of New Brunswick Life: Autobiographical Sketches* (Saint John, New Brunswick, 1890), 54, 89–94; Isaac Stephenson, who had lived in the vicinity of Woodstock before moving to Wisconsin, also makes no comment about the Frenchness of the upper Saint John Valley settlers in his memoirs: Isaac Stephenson, *Recollections of a Long Life* (Chicago, 1915), 1–56.

76 Reginald Horsman, *Race and Manifest Destiny: The Origins of American Racial Anglo-Saxonism* (Cambridge: Harvard University Press, 1981), esp. chaps. 3, 5, and 6.

77 Ibid., 62–77.

CHAPTER SEVEN

1 Continuous trade between Acadia/Nova Scotia and New England dates from the 1650s, when skins were the principal commodity. These are not dealt with here, as these furs, largely Maliseet-harvested, came from territory later called New Brunswick. Nova Scotia's exports of skins to New England stopped in 1776 and resumed only in the 1830s when the trade was restricted to seal skins, all of which were first imported from Newfoundland before being re-exported. See especially National Archives (NA), CUST12/1–22 and CUST16/1.

2 Manuscripts for studying Nova Scotia's economy are found principally in three archives: the NA in Kew, the Nova Scotia Archives and Records Management (NSARM) in Halifax, and the Library and Archives Canada (LAC) in Ottawa.

The NA holds detailed customs house trade statistics, shipping lists, and some merchant correspondence and petitions. See NA, CUST16/1. James F. Shepherd and Gary M. Walton, *Shipping, Maritime Trade, and the*

Economic Development of Colonial North America (Cambridge: Cambridge University Press, 1972). NA, CUST17/10–17, for trade and shipping for Nova Scotia–Cape Breton with the United States, 1787–95; NA, CUST6/1–21, for imports, 1832–52; NA, CUST12/1–22, for exports, 1832–53; NA, CUST34/291–5, 644–77, Board of Customs papers relating to Nova Scotia–Cape Breton, c1786–c1855; CO217/44, 217/78–9; CO221/28–35; HO76/1–2; T1/360, 369, 379, 387, 393, 411, 416, 424, 447; T64/84. See Julian Gwyn, ed., *Nova Scotia Naval Office Shipping Lists, 1730–1820*, 3 reels (Yorkshire: British Association for American Studies, 1982). Derived from reports prepared in London and Halifax to provide details of Nova Scotia's recorded external trade and shipping, some of these data were published as appendices to Nova Scotia's annual *House of Assembly Journals and Proceedings* [hereafter HAJP], and later in the dominion Parliament's sessional papers.

NSARM holds the lighthouse shipping lists, and several miscellaneous trade data occasionally required by the colonial government. The Halifax data cover 1778–1839; those for Shelburne, 1789–1832; for Yarmouth, 1797–1837; for Liverpool, 1804–72; and for Sydney, 1825–39. My data base includes more than 17,100 vessel movements for 1778–1839. RG1/248, 307, 379; RG31–105/1 (6–39), RG31–105/2 (1–13), RG31–105/3 (1), RG31–102/2 (15); Liverpool Port Books. Examples include: Halifax trade and shipping, 1801–28 in NSARM, RG13/40; Pictou trade and shipping, 1833–52. NSARM, RG13/12b, 14c, 16e, 17f. NSARM also retains civil court case files, including that of the vice-admiralty court to 1792. These provide details of wartime-captured vessels and peacetime disputes, many involving New Englanders. Papers of Nova Scotia merchants, especially of those trading principally to the United States, are absent from the several hundred volumes of pre-1870 mercantile ledgers in Nova Scotia's archives. This lacuna can occasionally be filled by documents relating to times when traders and merchants became involved in legal proceedings, either launched by the Crown in smuggling matters or as between merchants in commercial disputes. If the proceedings took place before the Court of Chancery, where evidence was submitted only in writing, the record for an individual cause will occasionally include the original evidence in the form of mercantile correspondence and ledgers. Julian Gwyn, "Capitalist, Merchants and Manufacturers in Early Nova Scotia, 1769–1791: The Tangled Affairs of John Avery, James Creighton, John Albro and Joseph Fairbanks," in Margaret Conrad, ed., *Intimate Relations: Family and Community in Planter Nova Scotia* (Fredericton: Acadiensis Press, 1995), 190–212.

The LAC holds Halifax vice-admiralty court records from 1793 onward. Referring to some 1,100 ships captured at sea to 1815, they include a broad range of papers of special interest to New England commercial undertakings, as two-thirds of the ships involved were either built or owned in New England. The LAC is also the most important repository in Canada for microfilm copies of pre-Confederation materials found in British archives. Bruce G. Wilson, ed., *Manuscripts and Government Records in the United Kingdom and Ireland Relating to Canada*, (Ottawa: National Archives of Canada, 1992).

Such manuscripts allow us only to know what goods were freighted, their value and volume, details of ships, the names of their masters, and sometimes their owners. This is little, indeed, as we know nothing of their thoughts or their business acumen, and can only guess at their expectations. Still, we know nothing of their profits and losses, the only thing that mattered to them.

3 Andrew Hill Clark, "New England's Role in the Underdevelopment of Cape Breton Island during the French Regime, 1713–1758," *Canadian Geographer*, 9 (1965), 1–12.

4 Julian Gwyn, "The Impact of Louisbourg upon the Economy of Massachusetts, 1745–49" in D.A. Muise, ed., *Papers and Abstracts for a Symposium on Ile Royale During the French Regime* (Ottawa: National Museum of Man, 1972), and "War and Economic Change: Louisbourg and the New England Economy in the 1740s," in Pierre Savard, ed., *Mélanges d'histoire du Canada français offerts au professeur Marcel Trudel* (Ottawa: University of Ottawa Press, 1978), 114–31. Donald F. Chard, "The Impact of Ile Royale on New England, 1713–1763" (PhD diss., University of Ottawa, 1976); and Christopher Moore, "Merchant Trade at Louisbourg, Ile Royale," (MA thesis, University of Ottawa, 1977).

5 Christopher Moore, "Cape Breton and the North Atlantic World in the Eighteenth Century," in Kenneth Donovan, ed., *The Island: New Perspectives on Cape Breton History, 1713– 1990* (Sydney: University College of Cape Breton Press, 1990), 30–48; Moore, "The Other Louisbourg: Trade and Merchant Enterprise in Ile Royale, 1713–58," *Histoire sociale-Social History*, 12 (1979), 79–96, especially Table 3. See also Donald Chard, "The Price and Profits of Accommodation: Massachusetts-Louisbourg Trade, 1713–1745," in Philip C.F. Smith, ed., *Seafaring in Colonial Massachusetts* (Boston: Colonial Society of Massachusetts, 1980), 131–51.

6 Moore, "Merchant Trade at Louisbourg, Ile Royale," Table 2.10.

7 David B. Flemming, *The Canso Islands: An 18th Century Fishing Station* (Ottawa: National Historical Sites Service, 1977. Manuscript Report 308).

8 Julian Gwyn, "The Royal Navy in North America, 1712–1776," in Jeremy Black and Philip Woodfine, eds., *British Navy and the Use of Naval Power in the Eighteenth Century* (Leicester: Leicester University Press, 1988), 129–47.

9 For 1721, 1723–26, 1730: NA, CO217/4, f. 44, 278, 294, 299v–301v,

CO217/5, f. 6, 231v–232v; CO221/28, f. 13–14. There were only fifty ships listed at Canso in 1739 all from New England. CO217/6, f. 340–5, when Captain Peter Warren described the "English fishery at Canso [as] much decayed ... within these ten years past." Julian Gwyn, ed., *The Royal Navy and North America: The Warren Papers, 1736–1752*, vol. 118 (London: Navy Records Society, 1973), 12.

10 Julian Gwyn "Financial Revolution in Massachusetts: Public Credit and Taxation, 1692–1774," *Histoire sociale-Social History*, 17 (1984), 59–77.

11 Gwyn, "War and Economic Change: Louisbourg and the New England Economy in the 1740s," 128–9; and Gwyn, "Shipbuilding for the Royal Navy in Colonial New England," *American Neptune*, 48 (1988), 22–30.

12 Boston Custom House records, The Athanaeum, Boston.

13 Such vessels almost invariably left in ballast, as Nova Scotia's exports for many years were inconsequential. Lewis R. Fischer, "The Fruits of Stability: Merchant Shipping and Societal Growth in Pre-Revolutionary Halifax," in W.A.B. Douglas, ed., *Canada's Atlantic Connection* (Ottawa: mimeographed, 1984), 1–29; and Lewis R. Fischer, "Revolution without Independence: The Canadian Colonies, 1749–1775," in Ronald Hoffman et al., *The Economy of Early America: The Revolutionary Period 1763–1790* (Charlottesville: University Press of Virginia, 1988), 88–125. Ships from New York and Pennsylvania combined amounted only to 12.5% of Halifax entries. NA, CO221/28.

14 Between 1752 and 1765, 29.3% of ships and 24.7% of tonnage sailing to North American ports from Boston cleared for Nova Scotia. Murray G. Lawson, "The Routes of Boston's Trade, 1752–1765," *Transactions of the Colonial Society of Massachusetts*, 38 (1948), 81–120.

15 Julian Gwyn, "The Impact of Military Spending on the Colonial American Money Markets, 1760–1783," *Historical Papers-Communications historiques* (1980), 77–99; and Gwyn, "British Government Spending and the North American Colonies, 1740–1775," *Journal of Imperial and Commonwealth History*, 8 (1980), 74–84.

16 Julian Gwyn, "Economic Fluctuations in Wartime Nova Scotia, 1755–1815," in Margaret Conrad, ed., *Making Adjustments: Change and Continuity in Planter Nova Scotia 1759–1800* (Fredericton: Acadiensis Press, 1991), 60–88.

17 Loudoun Papers. Henry E. Huntington Library, San Marino, California.

18 Gerrish accounts, 1757–73. NA, ADM17/150.

19 Jean Daigle, "Nos amis les ennemis: les relations commerciales entre l'Acadie et le Massachusetts, 1670–1711" (PhD diss., University of Maine-Orono, 1975).

20 John Dewar Faibisy, "The Effects of American Privateering upon Nova Scotia during the American Revolution" (PhD diss., University of Massachusetts, 1972) lists 223 vessels, making for or departing Nova Scotia's

ports, libelled in New England courts. Reproduced in Michael J. Crawford, ed., *Naval Documents of the American Revolution*, vol. 10 (Washington: Naval Historical Center, 1996), 1201–10.

21 Gwyn, "Economic Fluctuations," 64–9.

22 Marion Robertson, *King's Bounty. A History of Early Shelburne Nova Scotia* (Halifax: Nova Scotia Museum, 1983), 120.

23 Details of shipments from New England of building supplies from 1749 onward are found in the Naval Officers' Shipping Lists for Halifax. NA, CO221/28.

24 Neil MacKinnon, *This Unfriendly Soil: The Loyalist Experience in Nova Scotia 1783–1791* (Montreal: McGill-Queen's University Press, 1986), 151–5.

25 *Folger & Starbuck v Holmes*, NSARM, RG36a/111, a source unknown to Margaret Ells, "The Dartmouth Whalers," *Dalhousie Review* (April 1935), 85–95; or C. Bruce Fergusson, "The Southern Whale Fishery, 1775–1804," *Collections of the Nova Scotia Historical Society*, 32 (1959), 79–124; or Gerald S. Graham, "The Migration of the Nantucket Whale Fishery: An Episode in British Colonial Policy," *New England Quarterly* (1935), 179–202.

26 NA, CUST17/11, 18–9; CUST17/12, 30–1; CUST17/13, 30–1.

27 Graeme Wynn, "A Region of Scattered Settlements and Bounded Possibilities: Northeastern America 1775–1800," *Canadian Geographer*, 31 (1987), 319–38; "A Province Too Much Dependent on New England," *Canadian Geographer*, 31 (1987), 98–113; and his "New England's Outpost in the Nineteenth Century" in Stephen Hornsby et al., eds., *The Northeastern Borderlands: Four Centuries of Interaction* (Fredericton: Acadiensis Press & Canadian-American Center, University of Maine, 1989), 64–90.

28 *The Statistical History of the United States from Colonial Times to the Present* (New York: Basic Books, 1976), 29.

29 Julian Gwyn, "Rum, Sugar and Molasses in the Nova Scotia Economy, 1770–1854," in James Morrison and James Moreira, eds., *Tempered by Rum: Rum in the History of the Maritime Provinces* (Halifax: Pottersfield Press, 1988), 112–31.

30 29 Geo III, c.14; Richard John Uniacke, ed., *The Statutes at Large Passed in the Several General Assemblies held in His Majesty's Province of Nova Scotia ... 1758 to 1804* (Halifax: 1805), 275–6.

31 NA, CUST17/13.

32 Little was recorded before a customs sub-collector became resident at Windsor in 1833. Petition of Louis W. Wilkinson and fifty others to Board of Customs, 1843. NA, CUST34/651.

33 $1.20–$1.60 a ton. NA, CUST34/651.

34 Details from Nova Scotia Lighthouse Shipping List. NSARM, RG31–105/1 (13).

35 Inward to Nova Scotia 33.1% (31,865 tons) of vessels, outward from Nova Scotia 26.1% (32,389 tons). NA, CUST17/12, 30–1.

36 As with the trade data for 1790, details for Cape Breton and Nova Scotia have been combined. The crews numbered 1,833 men and boys. Seventy-seven of the ships were captured prize vessels, whose average was 70.8 tons. NA, CUST17/12, 225.

37 By 1808 the merchant fleet had grown by half to 33,220 measured tons, while the number of ships expanded by 58% to 684. Between 1786 and 1808, some 894 ships were newly built, totalling 57,885 measured tons. Details in NA, CUST17/12–30.

38 The year before $4,575 in prize cocoa had been shipped from Nova Scotia to the United States. NA, CUST17/16–17.

39 Massachusetts, forty-four; Connecticut, twenty-six; Maine, twenty-one; Rhode Island, thirteen; New Hampshire, four; and one unspecified. Julian Gwyn, "Treatment of American Prize Vessels by the Halifax Vice-Admiralty Court, 1793–1812" (Annapolis: Thirteenth Naval History Symposium, 1997).

40 Faye Margaret Kert, *Prize and Prejudice: Privateering and Naval Prize in Atlantic Canada in the War of 1812* (St John's: International Maritime Economic History Association, 1997).

41 D.A. Sutherland, "1810–20: War and Peace," in Phillip A. Buckner and John G. Reid, eds., *The Atlantic Region to Confederation: A History* (Toronto: University of Toronto Press, 1994), 241; Walter R. Copp, "Nova Scotian Trade During the War of 1812," *Canadian Historical Review*, 18 (1937), 141–55.

42 Data on ship entries is found for Halifax (1815, 1817, 1821, 1825–27, 1832–34, 1839), Yarmouth (1815, 1821, 1824–27, 1830, 1832, 1834, 1837, 1839), Liverpool (1815–17, 1824–28, 1830, 1832–34, 1837, 1839–72), Shelburne (1815, 1817, 1825, 1827–28, 1830, 1834, 1837, 1839), and Sydney (1825, 1827–28, 1830, 1832–34, 1837–38).

43 Details from Naval Officers' Shipping Lists data base.

44 The year 1835 saw 618 British ships and 215 foreign (35%) involved in this trade, while in 1865, 2,832 vessels were British and 502 foreign (15%).

45 Eric W. Sager and Gerald E. Panting, *Maritime Capital: The Shipping Industry in Atlantic Canada 1820–1914* (Montreal: McGill-Queen's University Press, 1990), 98.

46 Marilyn Gerriets and Julian Gwyn, "Tariffs, Trade and Reciprocity: Nova Scotia, 1830–1866," *Acadiensis* 25:2 (Spring 1996), 62–81.

47 To Board of Customs, 20 October 1846. NA, CUST34/664, f. 426v–7.

48 Julian Gwyn, "Imports and the Changing Standard of Living in Nova Scotia, 1832–1872," *Nova Scotia Historical Review*, 11 (1991), 43–64.

49 When the U.S. tariff rose to $1.75 a ton in 1842, American ships from

European ports refused to load coal in North Sydney, believing that the freight would not pay the cost. NA, CUST34/644, f. 143. Tariff rose to 30% in 1846, and declined to 24% in 1857 and 20% in 1864. Julian Gwyn, "'A Little Province Like This': The Economy of Nova Scotia Under Stress, 1812–1853," *Canadian Papers in Rural History*, 6 (1988), 219; and "Golden Age or Bronze Moment? Wealth and Poverty in Nova Scotia: the 1850s and 1860s," *Canadian Papers in Rural History*, 8 (1992), 206; Marilyn Gerriets, "The Rise and Fall of a Free-Standing Company in Nova Scotia: The General Mining Association," *Business History* (1992), 46–7.

50 Weymouth district petitioners to John Hood, secretary to the Board of Customs, New Edinburgh, 8 August 1843. NA, CUST34/664, f. 269v.

51 Gwyn, *Excessive Expectations*, 189–91.

52 NSARM, RG1/40.

53 Gwyn, *Excessive Expectations*, 119.

54 Ibid., 77.

55 Ibid., 75–6.

56 Ibid., 74.

57 Study of American naturalization papers helps to identify among American citizens those Nova Scotians who fished for New Englanders. Wayne M. O'Leary, *Maine Sea Fisheries: The Rise and Fall of a Native Industry, 1830–1890* (Boston: Northeastern University Press, 1996), 359. Perhaps not too much should be made of this, as 9.6% of officers and 7.2% of crew in the Canadian merchant fleet were American-born. Data for masters covered 1863–91 for the merchant fleets of Pictou, Yarmouth, and Halifax, while that of the crews included as well the merchant fleet of Saint John. Eric W. Sager, *Seafaring Labour: The Merchant Marine of Atlantic Canada 1820–1914* (Montreal: McGill-Queen's University Press, 1989), 146, 152.

58 Francklin to Board of Trade, 30 September 1766. NSARM, RG1/78. George Rawlyk, *Nova Scotia's Massachusetts: A Study of Massachusetts-Nova Scotia Relations 1630 to 1784* (Montreal: McGill-Queen's University Press, 1973), 224; Graeme Wynn, "A Province Too Much Dependent on New England," *Canadian Geographer*, 31 (1987), 98–113.

59 Andre Gunder Frank, *On Capitalist Underdevelopment* (London: Oxford University Press, 1975).

60 Gwyn, *Excessive Expectations*, passim.

61 Rawlyk, *Nova Scotia's Massachusetts*, xiii.

62 Despite four MA theses: George Frederick Butler, "Commercial Relations of Nova Scotia with the United States, 1783–1830" (Dalhousie, 1934); Ernest Clarke, "Relations between Nova Scotia and the United States, 1754–1870" (Toronto, 1934); Malcolm James Mercer, "Relations between Nova Scotia and New England, 1815–1867, with Special Reference to Trade and the Fisheries" (Dalhousie, 1938); and Ian Leonard

MacDougall, "Commercial Relations between Nova Scotia and the United States of America, 1830–1854" (Dalhousie, 1961).

63 One early such example relates to the 1745 Louisbourg prize money which was rerouted within a year into New England mortgages. Julian Gwyn, "Money Lending in New England: The Case of Admiral Sir Peter Warren and His Heirs, 1730–1805," *New England Quarterly*, 44 (1971), 117–34.

CHAPTER EIGHT

1 John O. Coote, *The Norton Book of the Sea* (New York: W.W. Norton & Co., 1989), 332.

2 Joshua Marsden, *The Narrative of a Mission to Nova Scotia, New Brunswick, and the Somers Islands* (Plymouth Dock, England: J. Johns, 1816), 56–7 Canadian Institute for Historical Microproductions (CIHM) microfiche 21227].

3 Marcus Rediker and Peter Linebaugh, *The Many-Headed Hydra: Sailors, Slaves, Commoners, and the Hidden History of the Revolutionary Atlantic* (Boston: Beacon Press, 2000).

4 Joshua Marsden, *Grace Displayed: An Interesting Narrative of the Life, Conversion, Christian Experience, Ministry and Missionary Labors of Joshua Marsden* (New York, the author, 1813) [CIHM microfiche 48054].

5 Stephen Humbert, *The Rise and Progress of Methodism in the Province of New Brunswick, from its Commencement until About the Year 1805* (Saint John: L.W. Durant, 1836), 35–6 [CIHM microfiche 57341].

6 Christopher Hill, *Liberty Against the Law: Some Seventeenth-Century Controversies* (New York: Penguin Press, 1996), 113; David Phillipson, *Smuggling: A History 1700–1970* (Newton Abbot: David & Charles, 1973), 92–3.

7 Emilia Viotti da Costa, *Crowns of Glory, Tears of Blood: The Demerara Slave Rebellion of 1823* (New York: Oxford University Press, 1994), 7–15.

8 E.P. Thompson, *The Making of the English Working Class* (New York: Pantheon Press, 1976), 389.

9 For St Mary's, see Christopher Ward, "The Commerce of East Florida During the Embargo, 1806–1812: The Role of Amelia Island," *Florida Historical Quarterly* 68:2 (1989), 160–79. For Heligoland see Judith Blow Williams, *British Commercial Policy and Trade Expansion, 1750–1850* (Oxford: Clarendon Press, 1972), 357–8.

10 *Annals* I, 299 (May 9, 1789) quoted in Leonard D. White, *The Federalists: An Administrative History* (New York: The Macmillan Company, 1956), 460.

11 For the burning of the *Gaspee*, see Neil R. Stout, *The Royal Navy in America, 1760–1775* (Annapolis, Maryland: Naval Institute Press, 1973), 141–3.

12 Hill, *Liberty Against the Law*, 113.
13 Brian Cuthbertson, *The Old Attorney-General: A Biography of Richard John Uniacke* (Halifax: Nimbus Publishing Limited, 1980), 76–7.
14 Alan Taylor, "The Smuggling Career of William King," *Maine Historical Society Quarterly*, 17 (Summer 1977), 19–38.
15 Francis Jennings, *The Creation of America: Through Revolution to Empire* (Cambridge: Cambridge University Press, 200), 134.
16 Hill, *Liberty Against the Law*, 112.
17 Adam Smith, *An Inquiry Into the Nature and Causes of the Wealth of Nations* (Chicago: Encyclopaedia Britannica, 1952), 397.
18 Jean Lunn, "The Illegal Fur Trade Out of New France, 1713–1760," *Canadian Historical Association Annual Report 1939*, 61–75.
19 Naomi Griffiths, "The Golden Age: Acadian Life, 1713–1748," *Social History* [Canada] 17:33 (1984): 21–34.
20 Victor L. Johnson, "Fair Traders and Smugglers in Philadelphia, 1754–1763," *Pennsylvania Magazine of History and Biography* 83:2 (1959), 125–49.
21 Lance R. Grahn, *The Political Economy of Smuggling: Regional Informal Economies In Early Bourbon New Granada.* (Boulder: Westview-Press, 1997).
22 Jerry W. Cooney, "'Doing Business in the Smuggling Way': Yankee Contraband in the Rio de la Plata," *American Neptune* 47:3 (1987): 162–8.
23 James Fenimore Cooper, *Ned Myers; or A Life Before the Mast* (New York: Stringer and Townsend, 1854), 123.
24 Gerald S. Graham, "The Gypsum Trade of the Maritime Provinces: Its Relation to American Diplomacy and Agriculture in the Early Nineteenth Century," *Agricultural History*, 12 (April 1938): 209–23.
25 Frances Stafford, "Illegal Importations: Enforcement of the Slave Trade Laws Along the Florida Coast, 1810–1828," *Florida Historical Quarterly* 46:2 (1967), 124–33.
26 Jennings, *Creation of America*, 80, quoting John J. McCusker and Russell R. Menard, *The Economy of British North America, 1607–1789*, (Chapel Hill: University of North Carolina Press, 1991), 77.
27 See E.P. Thompson, "The Moral Economy of the English Crowd in the Eighteenth Century," *Past and Present*, 50 (1971), and Linebaugh and Rediker, *Many-Headed Hydra.*
28 Geoffrey Morley, *The Smuggling War: The Government's Fight Against Smuggling in the 18th and 19th Centuries* (Stroud, Gloucestershire: Alan Sutton Publishing, Ltd., 1994).
29 Parliament, First Report from the Committee Appointed to Enquire into the Illicit Practices Used in Defrauding the Revenue (London: 1783), 6–7.
30 Neville Williams, *Contraband Cargoes: Seven Centuries of Smuggling* (Hamden, Connecticut: Shoe String Press, 1961), 147.

31 Total of £235,988: £15,788 for the cavalry regiments; see Williams, *Contraband Cargoes,* 151; £220,220 for the customs establishment; see Parliament, First Report, 7.

32 Williams, *Contraband Cargoes,* 204–19; Morley, *Smuggling War,* 124–62.

33 Ibid., 180–7.

34 Ibid., 204; Morley, *Smuggling War,* 158–62.

35 Cal Winslow, "Sussex Smugglers," in Douglas Hay, Peter Linebaugh, John G. Rule, E.P. Thompson, and Cal Winslow, eds., *Albion's Fatal Tree: Crime and Society in Eighteenth-Century England* (London: Allen Lane, 1975), 149.

36 Williams, *Contraband Cargoes,* 206.

37 Thompson, *Making of the English Working Class,* 355; Hill, *Liberty Against the Law,* 113.

38 Phillipson, *Smuggling,* 105.

39 F.F. Nicholls, *Honest Thieves: The Violent Heyday of English Smuggling* (London: Heinemann, 1973), 217.

40 Bruce J. Bourque and Ruth H. Whitehead, "Trade and Alliances in the Contact Period," in Emerson Baker, ed., *American Beginnings: Exploration, Culture, and Cartography in the Land of Norumbega* (Lincoln, Nebraska: University of Nebraska Press, 1994), 131–47.

41 Robert H. Lord, John E. Sexton, and Edward T. Harrington, *History of the Archdiocese of Boston, in the Various Stages of its Development, 1604 to 1943* (New York: Sheed and Ward), 589.

42 Alaric Faulkner and Gretchen Fearon Faulkner, *The French at Pentagoet, 1635–1674: An Archaeological Portrait of the Acadian Frontier* (Augusta and Fredericton: The Maine Historic Preservation Commission and the New Brunswick Museum, 1987), 28, 168.

43 John G. Reid, "An International Region of the Northeast: Rise and Decline, 1635–1762," in Stephen J. Hornsby, Victor A. Konrad, and James J. Herlan, eds., *The Northeastern Borderlands: Four Centuries of Interaction* (Fredericton: Acadiensis Press, 1989), 15.

44 Ibid., 17.

45 Hugh F. Bell, "'A Melancholy Affair' – James Otis and the Pirates," *American Neptune* 31:1 (1971), 23.

46 Ibid., 35–7.

47 J.M. Bumsted, "1763–1783: Resettlement and Rebellion," in Phillip A. Buckner and John G. Reid, eds., *The Atlantic Region to Confederation: A History* (Toronto: University of Toronto Press, 1998), 162–3.

48 Henry St John to Capt. Gidoin, 20 July 1766 (United States Naval Academy Manuscript Collection, Annapolis, Maryland).

49 James S. Leamon, *Revolution Downeast: The War for American Independence in Maine* (Amherst: University of Massachusetts Press, 1993), 178.

50 Leamon, *Revolution Downeast,* 138–9.

51 Roger Paul Nason, "Meritorious but Distressed Individuals: The Penobscot Loyalist Association and the Settlement of the Township of St. Andrews, New Brunswick, 1783–1821." MA thesis, University of New Brunswick, 1982, 143–4.

52 Lodge and Armstrong to the Board of Trade, 9 September 1787, BT6/59, quoted in Gerald S. Graham, *Sea Power and British North America, 1783–1820: A Study in British Colonial Policy* (Cambridge: Harvard University Press, 1941), 154–5.

53 Williams, *British Commercial Policy*, 218–51.

54 Benedict Anderson, *Imagined Communities: Reflections on the Origins and Spread of Nationalism* (Revised edition, London: Verso, 1991).

55 In two incidents the cannon of Fort Sullivan fired on smugglers. The first was on 7 November 1813 (see National Archives RG 21, "Federal District Court Records, Maine District," *United States v. the Sloop Venture*, National Archives and Records Administration, Waltham, Massachusetts [hereafter as RG 21/MeDC]). The second occurred in April 1814; see David Zimmerman, *Coastal Fort: A History of Fort Sullivan, Eastport, Maine* (Eastport, Maine: Border Historical Society, 1984), 38. Sentries, however, frequently fired their muskets at smugglers in this period.

56 Alan Taylor, "Centers and Peripheries: Locating Maine's History," *Maine History* 39:1 (Spring 2000), 5–8; for an analysis of how juries aided smugglers, see Douglas Lamar Jones, "'The Caprice of Juries': The Enforcement of the Jeffersonian Embargo in Massachusetts," *American Legal History*, 24 (1980), 307–30.

57 J.C. Arnell, "The Superintendent of Trade and Fisheries for Nova Scotia and the Armed Vessels *Union* and *Hunter*," *Mariner's Mirror* 55:4 (November 1970), 395–410.

58 Dave McIntosh, *The Collectors: A History of Canadian Customs and Excise* (Toronto: NC Press Limited, 1984), 235.

59 Stephen Humbert to Lt. Gov. George S. Smyth, August 18, 1820, Provincial Archives of New Brunswick RS 24, Provincial Archives, Fredericton, New Brunswick (hereafter as PANB RS 24).

60 Graham, "The Gypsum Trade," 209–23.

61 Ibid., 221.

62 W.S. MacNutt, *New Brunswick: A History, 1784–1867* (Toronto: Macmillan, 1963; paperback reprint, 1984), 173–6.

63 Humbert to Smyth, August 18, 1820, PANB RS 24. See chapter 10 for a detailed account of the Plaster War.

64 See David McCrone, *The Sociology of Nationalism: Tomorrow's Ancestors* (London and New York: Routledge, 1998), 86, for a consideration of the idea that the state creates the nation.

65 *United States v. John Clap of New York*, "Final Record Book U.S. District Court, Maine," National Archives RG 21, District Court Records, Maine

District, National Archives and Records Administration, Waltham, Massachusetts (hereafter as RG 21).

66 Frances W. Gregory, *Nathan Appleton: Merchant and Entrepreneur, 1779–1861* (Charlottesville, Virginia: University Press of Virginia, 1975), 87–106, passim.

67 Graham, *Sea Power*, 155.

68 *New England Palladium* (Boston), 28 February 1809.

69 See deposition of John W. Bradley, *U.S. v. A Quantity English Goods*, December term, 1812, RG 21/MEDC.

70 John Young to William Young, 6 February 1815 in D.C. Harvey, "Pre-Agricola John Young, or a Compact Family in Search of Fortune," *Collections of the Nova Scotia Historical Society* 32 (1959), 135.

71 David S. Macmillan, "Christopher Scott: Smuggler, Privateer and Financier," *Canadian Banker* 78:3 (1971), 23–6.

72 "Sir Samuel Cunard," *Dictionary of Canadian Biography*, vol. 9 (Toronto: University of Toronto Press, 1972), 173.

73 Sellers, *Market Revolution*, 14–15, 73.

74 Patrick Clinch to John Saunders, September 4, 1835, Ms. in "Edward Winslow Papers," Special Collections, Harriet Irving Library, University of New Brunswick, Fredericton, New Brunswick.

75 Winslow, "Sussex Smugglers," 149; Hill, *Liberty Against the Law*, 111; Graham, *Sea Power*, 153; Morley, *Smuggling War*, 58–9.

76 Graham, *Sea Power*.

77 See Graham, *Sea Power*, 168–173.

78 Humbert, *Rise and Progress of Methodism*, 35.

79 Case file, *S. Humbert, claimant of Sloop Industry, apt. v. the United States*, May Term 1812, National Archives RG 21, Circuit Court Records, Massachusetts District.

80 "Stephen Humbert," *Dictionary of Canadian Biography* VII, 424–5.

81 MacNutt, *New Brunswick*, 175, wrote: "The breaking up of the [plaster] trade 'on the lines' implied a small-scale war."

82 *Royal Gazette* (Fredericton), 30 May 1820.

83 Humbert to Thomas Wetmore, August 18, 1820, PANB, RS 24.

84 MacNutt, *New Brunswick*, 175.

85 Humbert to Smyth, 16 October 1820, PANB, RS 24.

86 Smith, *Wealth of Nations*, 180.

87 Winslow, "Sussex Smugglers," 159.

CHAPTER NINE

1 *Rule and Misrule of the English in America* (London: Colburn & Co., 1851) 2:319–21.

2 For a selection of anti-Catholic diatribes, see Rev. Robert Sedgwick, *The*

Papacy: The Idolatry of Rome (Halifax: Wesleyan Conference Steam Press, 1859); Rev. Andrew King, *The Papacy: A Conspiracy Against Civil and Religious Liberty* (Halifax: Wesleyan Conference Steam Press, 1859); Rev. J.L. Murdoch, *The Causes Which Since the Reformation Have Led to the Revival and Increase of Popery* (Halifax: Wesleyan Conference Steam Press, 1859).

3 H.M. Richey, *The Spirit of Popery, and the Duty of Protestants in Regard to Public Education* (Halifax: Wesleyan Conference Steam Press, 1859), 36.

4 Scott W. See, "Nineteenth-Century Collective Violence: Toward a North American Context," *Labour/Le Travail* 39 (1997), 13–38.

5 Stephen J. Hornsby, Victor A. Konrad, and James J. Herlan, eds., *The Northeastern Borderlands: Four Centuries of Interaction* (Fredericton: Acadiensis Press, 1989), 7.

6 For a recent example of this argument, see Jeremy Adelman and Stephen Aron, "From Borderlands to Borders: Empires, Nation-States, and the Peoples in Between in North American History," *American Historical Review* 104 (1999), 814–41.

7 Ethnic and religious confrontations in Saint John, Fredericton, and Woodstock were explored in the author's monograph, *Riots in New Brunswick: Orange Nativism and Social Violence in the 1840s* (Toronto: University of Toronto Press, 1993).

8 Conflict in the borderlands region has been explored in Theodore M. Hammett, "Two Mobs of Jacksonian Boston: Ideology and Interest," *Journal of American History* 62 (1976), 845–68; Wilfred J. Bisson, *Countdown to Violence: The Charlestown Convent Riot of 1834* (New York: Garland Publications, 1989); and See, *Riots in New Brunswick.* For a broader discussion of nativism and riots, see David Grimsted, *American Mobbing, 1828–1861* (New York: Oxford University Press, 1998), 218–45.

9 John Higham, *Strangers in the Land: Patterns of American Nativism, 1860–1925*, 2d ed. rev. (New Brunswick, New Jersey: Rutgers University Press, 1988). Higham revisited his work in "Another Look at Nativism," *Catholic Historical Review* 44 (1958), 148–50; and "The Strange Career of *Strangers in the Land*," *American Jewish History* 76 (1986), 214–26. For another history of nativism in the United States, see Ray Allen Billingham, *The Protestant Crusade, 1800–1860: A Study of the Origins of American Nativism* (New York: Macmillan, 1938).

10 For a useful analysis of historical literature on nativism, see James M. Bergquist, "The Concept of Nativism in Historical Study Since *Strangers in the Land*," *American Jewish History* 76 (1986): 125–41. Works include John R. Mulkern, *The Know-Nothing Party in Massachusetts: The Rise and Fall of a People's Movement* (Boston: Northeastern University Press, 1990); and Jean H. Baker, *Ambivalent Americans: The Know-Nothing Party in Maryland* (Baltimore: Johns Hopkins University Press, 1977). Note also Elliott J. Gurn, "'Good-bye Boys, I Die a True American': Homicide, Nativism,

and Working-Class Culture in Antebellum New York City," *Journal of American History* 74 (1987): 388–410. For a study that concentrates on the nativists' reactions to the Irish, see Dale T. Knobel, *Paddy and the Republic: Ethnicity and Nationality in Antebellum America* (Middletown, Connecticut: Wesleyan University Press, 1986).

11 Howard Palmer, "Strangers in the Land: A Canadian Perspective," *American Jewish History* 76 (1986), 122. See also Howard Palmer, *Patterns of Prejudice: A History of Nativism in Alberta* (Toronto: McClelland & Stewart, 1982); James T. Watt, "Anti-Catholic Nativism in Canada: The Protestant Protective Association," *Canadian Historical Review* 48 (1967), 45–58; Marilyn Barber, "Nationalism, Nativism and the Social Gospel: The Protestant Church Response to Foreign Immigrants in Western Canada, 1897–1914," in Richard Allen, ed. *The Social Gospel in Canada* (Ottawa: National Museums of Canada, 1975), 186–226.

12 W.L. Morton, "Victorian Canada," in W.L. Morton, ed., *The Shield of Achilles: Aspects of Canada in the Victorian Age* (Toronto: McClelland & Stewart, 1968), 314–16; William Westfall, *Two Worlds* (Montreal: McGill-Queen's University Press, 1988).

13 For European examples, see George Rudé, "The Gordon Riots: A Study of the Rioters and Their Victims," *Transactions of the Royal Historical Society* (1956): 93–114; Natalie Zemon Davis, "The Rites of Violence: Religious Riot in Sixteenth-Century France," *Past and Present* 59 (1973): 51–91; John Stevenson, *Popular Disturbances in England, 1700–1870* (London: Longman, 1979), 137–42, 276–7; and Frank Neal, *Sectarian Violence: The Liverpool Experience, 1819–1914* (Manchester: Manchester University Press, 1988).

14 Cecil J. Houston and William J. Smyth, *Irish Emigration and Canadian Settlement: Patterns, Links, and Letters* (Toronto: University of Toronto Press, 1990), 3; Donald MacKay, *Flight from Famine: The Coming of the Irish to Canada* (Toronto: McClelland & Stewart, 1990), 290–1.

15 Discussions of these dynamics are found in two works by J.R. Miller: "Anti-Catholicism in Canada: From the British Conquest to the Great War," in Terrence Murphy and Gerald Stortz, eds., *Creed and Culture: The Place of English-Speaking Catholics in Canadian Society, 1750–1930* (Montreal: McGill-Queen's University Press, 1993); and "Bigotry in the North Atlantic Triangle: Irish, British and American Influences on Canadian Anti-Catholicism, 1850–1900," *Studies in Religion* 16 (1987), 289–301.

16 See, *Riots in New Brunswick,* 53–5; A.J.B. Johnston, "Popery and Progress: Anti-Catholicism in Mid-Nineteenth-Century Nova Scotia," *Dalhousie Review* 64 (1984), 146; Kenneth Duncan, "Irish Famine Immigration and the Social Structure of Canada West," *Canadian Review of Sociology and Anthropology* 2 (1965), 26–7; Terrence Murphy, "The Emergence of Maritime Catholicism, 1781–1830," *Acadiensis* 13 (1984), 44.

17 *Weekly Chronicle*, 18 July 1851.
18 Rev. J.L. Murdoch, *The Causes Which Since the Reformation Have Led to the Revival and Increase of Popery* (Halifax: Wesleyan Conference Steam Press, 1859), 22 [italics in the original]; *Loyalist*, 24 September 1847; *Church Witness*, 6 July 1853.
19 John Earle's address, House of Assembly, 13 April 1850, in *Reporter*, 10 May 1850; editorials, *Loyalist*, 16 July, 17 September, 15 October 1847.
20 *Protestant and Evangelical Witness*, 4 April, 6 June 1863; *Prince Edward Islander*, 22 July 1864.
21 G.R.C. Keep, "The Irish Adjustment in Montreal," *Canadian Historical Review* 31 (1950): 39–40.
22 A description of the quarantine station is found in Marianna O'Gallagher, *Grosse Ile: Gateway to Canada, 1832–1937* (Ste-Foy: Carraig, 1984).
23 Ronald Rudin, *The Forgotten Quebecers: A History of English-Speaking Quebec, 1759–1980* (Quebec: Institut québécois de recherche sur la culture, 1985), 95–6; Robert J. Grace, *The Irish in Quebec: An Introduction to the Historiography* (Quebec: Institut québécois de recherche sur la culture, 1993), 56. St John's, Newfoundland, also had a substantial Irish-born population in the mid-nineteenth century, but Irish immigration diminished after the 1830s. See Michael Staveley, "Population Dynamics in Newfoundland: The Regional Patterns," in John J. Mannion, ed., *The Peopling of Newfoundland* (St John's: Institute of Social and Economic Research, Memorial University of Newfoundland, 1977), 53–5.
24 Rudin, *Forgotten Quebecers*, 83–7; James M. O'Leary, *History of the Irish Catholics of Quebec: Saint Patrick's Church to the Death of Rev. P. McMahon* (Quebec: Daily Telegraph, 1895), 9. For a study of nineteenth-century canal workers, see Peter Way, *Common Labour: Workers and the Digging of North American Canals, 1780–1860* (Cambridge: Cambridge University Press, 1993).
25 MacKay, *Flight from Famine*, 321.
26 Grace, *The Irish in Quebec*, 60–70; Herbert B. Ames, *The City Below the Hill* (1897; reprint ed., Toronto: University of Toronto Press, 1972).
27 *Six Lectures Delivered in the Round Room of the Rotunda, Dublin* (Toronto: Donogh and Brother, 1853).
28 Report of the Commissioners Appointed to Inquire into the Conduct of the Police Authorities on the Occasion of the Riot at Chalmers' Church on the 6th of June, 1853 (Quebec: R. Campbell, 1854), 103.
29 Ibid.
30 Letter from Mayor Tessier to local commander, 8 June 1853, in British Military "C Series," vol. 318, National Archives of Canada [NAC].
31 For a thorough assessment of the military's role in the riot, see Elinor Kyte Senior, *British Regulars in Montreal: An Imperial Garrison, 1832–1854* (Montreal: McGill-Queen's University Press, 1981), 109–33.

32 Sir Edward James Alexander, *Passages in the Life of a Soldier, or, Military Service in the East and West* (London: Hurst and Blackett, 1857), I:173.
33 *The Riot and Outrage of 9th June in Montreal* (Montreal: F.W. Campbell, 1853), 16.
34 Ibid., 4.
35 Ibid., 22.
36 Ibid., 14.
37 Although not signed, the fairly balanced *The Riot and Outrage of 9th June* was clearly written by a Protestant. The other, *Remarks on the Deplorable Events Which Took Place in the Haymarket Square, on the 9th June, 1853* (Montreal: J.C. Becket, 1853), was signed "A Protestant."
38 *Remarks on the Deplorable Events*, 16.
39 Petition from Methodist and Episcopal Church Ministers, 13 September 1853, in RG4, C1, v. 339 [NAC].
40 Grace, *The Irish in Quebec*, 126. See also Canada East, Provincial Secretary's Office Correspondence, File #49 [NAC]; Philippe Sylvain, "L'affaire Corrigan à Saint-Sylvestre," *Les Cahiers des Dix* 42 (1979): 125–44.
41 Canada East, Provincial Secretary's Office Correspondence, File #49 [NAC].
42 James H. Mundy, *Hard Times, Hard Men: Maine and the Irish 1830–1860* (Scarborough, Maine: Harp Publications, 1990), 78–80.
43 *Bangor Daily Whig and Courier*, 9 June 1851.
44 See the 2 June 1855 *Portland Advertiser* for an example of abolition resolutions that were passed by a local Know-Nothing convention.
45 Allan R. Whitmore, "'A Guard of Faithful Sentinels': The Know-Nothing Appeal in Maine, 1854–1855," *Maine Historical Society Quarterly* 20 (1981), 161.
46 Nancy Skoglund, "Assault on John Bapst," in Richard S. Sprague, ed., *A Handful of Spice: Essays in Maine History and Literature* (Orono: University of Maine Press, 1968), 119.
47 *Eastern Argus*, 10 July 1854; *Portland Advertiser*, 24 May 1854, 12 July 1854; Mundy, *Hard Times, Hard Men*, 138–41, 148–51.
48 Frank L. Byrne, *Prophet of Prohibition: Neal Dow and His Crusade* (Madison: State Historical Society of Wisconsin, 1961), 51.
49 *Bangor Daily Whig and Courier*, 21 April 1855.
50 Henry S. Clubb, *The Maine Liquor Law: Its Origin, History, and Results* (New York: Fowler and Wells, 1856), 43–7.
51 "The Law of the Riot. The Portland Riot," in George S. Hale and John Codman, eds., *Monthly Law Reporter* (Boston: Crosby and Nichols, 1856), 376.
52 Ibid., 377.
53 Accounts of the riot vary significantly. The *Eastern Argus* of 4 June 1855 criticized Dow's actions and claimed that the fracas never reached a level

that warranted deadly fire from the police and troops. Conversely, the *Portland Advertiser* of 4 June 1855 applauded the actions of the mayor, police, and militia in containing a potentially disastrous riot.

54 *Portland Advertiser,* 4 June 1855.

55 "The Law of the Riot. The Portland Riot," 381–4.

56 Ibid., 380.

57 *Eastern Argus,* 4 June 1855; *Portland Advertiser,* 4 June 1855.

58 "The Law of the Riot. The Portland Riot," 385.

59 *Eastern Argus,* 5 June 1855.

60 *Portland Advertiser,* 12 June 1855.

61 "The Law of the Riot. The Portland Riot," 386; *Eastern Argus,* 13–28 June 1855; *Portland Advertiser,* 13 June-4 July 1855.

62 Report of the Committee of Investigation of the Riot, in the City of Portland (Portland: Benjamin D. Peck, 1855), 5. According to one account, Poor narrowly escaped injury during the riot when he inadvertently passed near City Hall and a bullet pierced his hat. See *Eastern Argus,* 4 June 1855.

63 *Report of the Committee of Investigation of the Riot,* 34.

64 Ibid., 43–4. [italics in original]

65 Ibid., 47.

66 Ibid., 41. See also *Eastern Argus,* 4 June 1855.

67 *Report of the Committee of Investigation of the Riot,* 15–33.

68 Joseph Ware, *Review of the Testimony Taken Before the Second Inquest on the Body of John Robbins* (Portland: 1855), 9–32.

69 Ibid., 1.

70 Ibid., 3.

71 Ibid., 5.

72 Ibid., 6.

73 Dow maintained that Robbins had been the ringleader of another Portland riot in 1849. See *Portland Advertiser,* 12 June 1855. Another example of a defence of Robbins's character is found in *Eastern Argus,* 11 June 1855.

74 Ware, *Review of the Testimony,* 9–32.

75 *Eastern Argus,* 8 October 1849.

76 *Portland Daily Advertiser,* 7 May 1849.

77 "The Law of the Riot. The Portland Riot," 363.

78 Ibid., 364.

79 Ibid., 366.

80 *Portland Advertiser,* 4 June 1855.

81 *Eastern Argus,* 7 June 1855.

82 *Novascotian,* 19 July 1852; A.J.B. Johnston, "The 'Protestant Spirit' of Colonial Nova Scotia: An Inquiry into Mid-Nineteenth-Century Anti-Catholicism," MA thesis, Dalhousie University, 1977; Johnston, "Popery

and Progress," 147; Terrence M. Punch, "Irish Halifax: The Immigrant Generation, 1815–1859," *Ethnic Heritage Series* 5 (1981), 6–7.

83 A.J.B. Johnston, "Nativism in Nova Scotia: Anti-Irish Ideology in a Mid-Nineteenth-Century British Colony," in Thomas P. Power, ed., *The Irish in Atlantic Canada 1780–1900* (Fredericton: New Ireland Press, 1991), 24–5.

84 *Christian Messenger*, 10 September 1847.

85 *Novascotian*, 2 November 1857.

86 D. Campbell and R.A. MacLean, *Beyond the Atlantic Roar: A Study of the Nova Scotia Scots* (Toronto: McClelland & Stewart, 1975) 20–3, 51–2, 55–60, 69–70, 74, 221–2.

87 Punch, "Irish Halifax," 38–9, 46.

88 *Morning Chronicle*, 9 December 1856.

89 *Chronicle*, 19 June 1856, cited in J. Murray Beck, *Joseph Howe: The Briton Becomes Canadian* (Montreal: McGill-Queen's University Press, 1983), 110.

90 *Novascotian*, 15, 29 December 1856.

91 *Parliamentary Debates*, Nova Scotia House of Assembly, 9, 10, 11, 12 February 1857.

92 Johnston, "Nativism in Nova Scotia," 28–9.

93 *Morning Chronicle*, 14 May 1859.

94 Peter T. McGuigan, *Peoples of the Maritimes: The Irish* (Tantallon, Nova Scotia: Four East Publications, 1991), 32–3.

95 *Presbyterian Witness and Evangelical Advocate*, 7 June 1856.

96 "Circular: To the Public," in Millner Papers, New Brunswick Museum.

97 *Parliamentary Debates*, Nova Scotia House of Assembly, 14 February 1857; quote from *Presbyterian Witness*, 3 January 1857.

98 *The Christian Instructor and Missionary Register of the Presbyterian Church of Nova Scotia* (Halifax: James Barnes, 1858), in MG100, vol. 211, Public Archives of Nova Scotia. Formed in March 1857, the organization attempted to garner the support of Protestant religious leaders as well as politicians and concerned citizens. It drew heated debate in the assembly, wherein Howe argued that there had been no need for such an organization in the 1840s because of the relative peace and the absence of Catholic social and political influence in the colony. However, Howe found the Protestant Alliance's rationale rooted to the famine migration and the Gourlay Shanty disturbance. See *Parliamentary Debates*, Nova Scotia House of Assembly, 14 February 1859. Defunct by 1860, the Alliance failed because many Protestant ministers found it too political in orientation and the intense nativist response appeared to have run its course.

99 *Novascotian*, 29 December 1856.

100 *Novascotian*, 9 March 1857.

101 Joseph Howe, *To the People of Nova Scotia* (Halifax: 1857), 3.
102 *Casket*, 19 March 1857.
103 *Morning Chronicle*, 17 June 1856; *Novascotian*, 24 June 1856.
104 *The Church Times*, 10 January 1857, cited in Punch, "The 'Protestant Spirit' of Colonial Nova Scotia," 257.
105 *Morning Chronicle*, 12 November 1857.
106 For a provocative study of Irish stereotypes, see L.P. Curtis, Jr, *Apes and Angels: The Irishman in Victorian Caricature* (Devon, England: David & Charles, 1971).
107 See Allan Greer, "The Birth of the Police in Canada," in Allan Greer and Ian Radforth, eds., *Colonial Leviathan: State Formation in Mid-Nineteenth-Century Canada* (Toronto: University of Toronto Press, 1992), 17–49.
108 Whitmore, "The Know-Nothing Appeal in Maine," 157.

CHAPTER TEN

1 Abraham Gesner, *The Industrial Resources of Nova Scotia* (Halifax, 1869), 19–20.
2 Julian Gwyn, *Excessive Expectations: Maritime Economy & the Economic Development of Nova Scotia, 1740–1870* (Montreal: McGill-Queens University Press, 1998).
3 J.M. Beck, *The Government of Nova Scotia* (Toronto: University of Toronto Press, 1957), 83–5.
4 D.A. Sutherland, "Halifax Merchants and the Pursuit of Development, 1783–1850," *Canadian Historical Review*, v. 59/1 (March 1978), 1–17; Julian Gwyn, "'A Little Province Like This': The Economy of Nova Scotia under Stress, 1812–1853," *Canadian Papers in Rural History*, 6 (1988), 192–225; Robert Morgan, "'Poverty, Wretchedness, and Misery': the Great Famine in Cape Breton, 1845–1851," *Nova Scotia Historical Review*, 6: 1 (June 1986), 88–104.
5 R.H. McDonald, "Nova Scotia Views the United States, 1784–1854" (PhD diss., Queen's University, 1974), 228–38.
6 S.F. Wise and R.C. Brown, *Canada Views the United States* (Toronto: Macmillan, 1967) argue that visceral anti-Americanism had largely died by mid-century all across British North America. For an exception, see the assembly speech of Martin I. Wilkins, as reported in *Morning Chronicle* (Halifax), 3 June 1854.
7 This theme is explored broadly by A.A. Den Otter, *The Philosophy of Railways: The Transcontinental Railway Idea in British North America* (Toronto: University of Toronto Press, 1997).
8 J.M. Beck, *Joseph Howe*, vol. 2 (Kingston: McGill-Queen's University Press, 1983), 32–4. Gesner's praise of railroads appears in his *Industrial*

Resources, 17. The flowery rhetoric on what railroads had done for New England comes from John Howe, president of the Boston & Maine Railroad, in a letter to Joseph Howe, 24 September 1851, found in National Archives of Canada, MG24, B29, vol. 1, f. 835.

9 D.A. Sutherland, "James W. Johnston," *Dictionary of Canadian Biography* (DCB), vol. 10 (Toronto: University of Toronto Press, 1972), 383–8.

10 The lure California exerted on mid-nineteenth century Nova Scotians is demonstrated by the curious career of William A. Smith who, in the west, transformed himself into Amor de Cosmos. For his life see R.A.J. McDonald and H.K. Ralston, "Amor de Cosmos," DCB, vol. 12 (Toronto: University of Toronto Press, 1990), 237–43. A somewhat parallel experience involving a Nova Scotian migration to Australia's goldfields, led by Reverend Norman McLeod, is told in Flora McPherson, *Watchman Against the World* (Wreck Cove, Cape Breton: Breton Books, 1993).

11 *British Colonist* (Halifax), 27 August 1850; *Acadian Recorder* (Halifax), 31 August 1850; *Novascotian* (Halifax), 2 September 1850.

12 *Acadian Recorder*, 13–20 July, 31 August 1850; *Novascotian* 15–22 July, 5–26 August 1850.

13 M. Gerriets and J. Gwyn, "Tariffs, Trade and Reciprocity, Nova Scotia, 1830–1866," *Acadiensis*, 25:1 (Spring 1996), 62–81.

14 In addition to the shipping columns of Nova Scotian newspapers, see Public Archives of Nova Scotia [PANS], United States Consular Despatches (Halifax), 1833–1854, which include details on both vessels and cargoes moving between Halifax and American ports, most notably Boston, New York, and Philadelphia.

15 For American material appearing in Nova Scotian newspapers, see as examples, *Sun* (Halifax), 9 January 1850; *Novascotian*, 11 February 1850; *British Colonist*, 6 April 1850; *Sun*, 27 May 1850; *British Colonist*, 22 June 1850; *Novascotian* 15 July 1850; *British Colonist*, 7 September 1850; *Sun*, 21 October 1850; *Acadian Recorder*, 2 November 1850. A sketch of Fuller is found in F.S. Cozzens, *Acadia, or, a Month with the Bluenoses* (New York, 1859), 24. Nova Scotian use of New England as a model for reform of its schools was called for by the colony's first Superintendent of Education; see Nova Scotia, *Journals and Proceedings of the House of Assembly* (JPHA) 1851, appendix 53.

16 *Sun*, 2, 12, 17, 21 June 1850. A profile of Nugent is provided by J.M. Beck, "Richard Nugent," DCB, vol. 8, 656–8.

17 *Novascotian*, 23 December 1850; 6, 20 January 1851. Biographic detail on Sprott (1780–1869) is contained in G.W. Sprott, *Memorials of the Rev. John Sprott* (Edinburgh, 1906).

18 *Morning Journal* (Halifax), 7 August 1854; *Sun*, 15 December 1854.

19 As quoted in the *Novascotian*, 29 July 1850.

20 *Novascotian*, 5 August 1850.

21 Beck, *Howe*, vol. 2, 16–25

22 Ibid., 26–50.

23 Ibid., 51–3.

24 Ibid., 53–4.

25 The situation facing Nova Scotia at the end of the 1840s was summarized by Lieutenant-Governor John Harvey in his "General Description of Nova Scotia in 1848," PANS Annual Report, 1947 (Halifax: PANS, 1948), 14–42. Ben Forster, *A Conjunction of Interests: Business, Politics and Tariffs, 1825–1879* (Toronto: University of Toronto Press, 1986) maintains that Nova Scotia was the least protectionist part of British North America. See also R.H. McDonald, "Nova Scotia and the Reciprocity Negotiations, 1846–1854," *Nova Scotia Historical Quarterly*, 7: 3 (September 1977), 205–35.

26 William Young papers, PANS, MG1, v. 3362, f. 14, W.H. Merritt to Young, 4 July 1849; Young to Merritt, 9 August 1849; PANS, RG3, Nova Scotia Executive Council minutes, 8 August 1849 ; Colonial Office [CO] 217, v. 202, f. 211, John Harvey to Lord Grey, 7 September 1849

27 H.A. Innis, *The Cod Fisheries* (Toronto: University of Toronto Press, 1978), 323–56. For contemporary accounts of American encroachment on Nova Scotia's inshore fisheries, see Gesner, *Industrial Resources*, 105–9 and PANS, United States consular despatches (Halifax), T.B. Livingston to the Secretary of State, 1 March 1850. Demands that American be excluded from coastal waters are contained in PANS, RG1, v. 260, #32, David Allison to J.B. Uniacke, 9 April 1851.

28 Young's trip proved controversial among his peers, some of whom thought he had revealed too much to the Americans. On this quarrel, see Nova Scotia, JPHA, 1851, appendix 20; PANS, RG1, v. 259, #39, Young to Henry Bulwer, 17 June 1850; #53, Nova Scotia Executive Council minutes, 2, 9 July 1850. A portrait of William Young which stresses the opportunistic side of his character is found in J.M. Beck, "William Young," DCB, vol. 11, 943–9.

29 Nova Scotia, JPHA 1851, appendix 20, Harvey to Lord Elgin, 25 July 1850.

30 Background on the early stages of reciprocity negotiations is provided in D.C. Masters, *The Reciprocity Treaty of 1854* (Toronto: McClelland & Stewart, 1963), 4–7; Irene W.D. Hecht, "Israel D. Andrews and the Reciprocity Treaty of 1854: A Reassessment," *Canadian Historical Review*, 44:1 (December 1953), 313–29.

31 See Nova Scotia, JPHA, 1852, appendix 17 for the petition of 20 January 1852, wherein Halifax merchants argued for naval assistance against American fishermen. Initial local enthusiasm over British interventions is expressed in *Novascotian*, 14, 26 July, *Morning Chronicle* (Halifax), 14 August 1852; *British Colonist*, 31 July 1852.

32 Arrival of the USS *Mississippi* under Commodore Matthew Perry is reported in *Novascotian*, 18 August 1852. London policy is spelled out in CO 217, v. 209, f. 200, Elgin to Admiral Seymour, 29 July 1852.

33 Nova Scotia, JPHA, 1852, appendix 25.

34 The rage in Halifax over what was seen as a sellout of Nova Scotia's claims to the inshore fisheries is articulated in *Morning Chronicle*, 2 September 1852; *Novascotian*, 6 September 1852; *Sun*, 6 September 1852; *British Colonist*, 7 September, 5 October 1852.

35 Beck, *Howe*, vol. 2, 67–71. See also Den Otter, *Philosophy of Railways*, 84–7 and Rosemarie Langhout, "Developing Nova Scotia: Railways and Public Accounts, 1848–1867," *Acadiensis*, 14:2 (Spring 1985), 3–28.

36 Masters, *Reciprocity Treaty*, 27–45.

37 The pressure put on Young and his evasive responses are revealed by his correspondence; see particularly PANS, MG22, v. 733, #458, Moses Perley to Young, 3 June 1854; #462, Francis Hincks to Young, 5 June 1854; #473, Young to Perley, 10 June 1854; #474, Young to E.B. Chandler, 10 June 1854.

38 Charles Tansill, *The Reciprocity Treaty of 1854* (Baltimore, 1922), 58–70 argues that the concessions demanded by Nova Scotia were sought by Elgin but, except for coal, refused by the Americans. That source also argues that I.D. Andrews used state department funds, funnelled through agents such as E.G. Fuller of Halifax, to buy support for the treaty in the colonial press. On the last point, see also Hecht, "I.D. Andrews," 321–2. For diverse opinions in Halifax papers about what had been negotiated, see *Sun*, 10–13 June 1854; *Novascotian*, 26 June 1854; *Acadian Recorder*, 1 July 1854.

39 Masters, *Reciprocity Treaty*, 52–4. For resigned comments in the Halifax press about the pressure being applied by both metropolitan powers to secure Nova Scotia's ratification of the treaty, see *Acadian Recorder*, 7 October 1854; *British North American* (Halifax), 13 October 1854; *Morning Chronicle*, 14 November 1854; *Acadian Recorder*, 18 November 1854.

40 Nova Scotia Assembly debates, as reported in *Novascotian*, 13 December 1854.

41 CO217, v. 214, f. 33, Nova Scotia Legislative Council to the Crown, 13 December 1854.

42 Nova Scotia Assembly debates, *Novascotian*, 13, 25 December 1854. The treaty passed by a margin of 32 to 10 in the Assembly and 16 to 2 in the Council, ibid., 13–18 December 1854.

43 Nova Scotia's mid-1850s economic recovery and the optimism it generated are discussed in D.A. Sutherland, "Nova Scotia's Response to the Crystal Palace: the Provincial Industrial Exhibition of 1854," *Journal*, Nova Scotia Historical Society, vol. 3 (2000), 72–84.

44 Assembly debate on the future of British North America occurred in Feb-

ruary 1854 but was not reported until much later. See the coverage provided by the *Morning Chronicle* between 23 May and 20 June 1854. The quotes from Howe and Johnston appear in *Morning Chronicle,* 23 May and 15 June 1854. The letter signed "A Nova Scotian" is contained in *British North American,* 10 November 1854.

45 Post-Confederation secessionist sentiment is discussed in C.D. Howell, "W.S. Fielding and the Repeal Elections of 1886 and 1887 in Nova Scotia," *Acadiensis,* 17:2 (Spring 1989), 55–72; for the dynamics of mid- to late-nineteenth-century emigration to the United States, see A.A. Brookes, "The Golden Age and the Exodus: the Case of Canning, Kings County," ibid., 11:1 (Autumn 1981), 57–82; on the Loyalist myth see Murray Barkley, "The Loyalist Tradition in New Brunswick: The Growth and Evolution of an Historical Myth, 1825–1914," ibid., 4:2 (Spring 1975), 3–45. The meaning of the term "whitewashed Yankee" is discussed in Joseph E. Garland, *Bear of the Sea* (Halifax: Nimbus, 2001), 174–5.

CHAPTER ELEVEN

1 David Harvey, *The Condition of Postmodernity. An Enquiry into the Origins of Cultural Change* (Cambridge, Massachusetts: Blackwell, 1990).

2 The following papers have relevance to the history of this family enterprise: Jacques Ferland, "Solidarity and Estrangement among Canadian Leather Workers: Sole Leather Tanning at Grand Lake Stream Maine, 1871–1880," December 1988, a paper presented at the Australian-Canadian Labour History Conference, Sydney, Australia; Jacques Ferland, "Canadian Working-Class Estrangement in Maine's Sole Leather Tanning Industry: The Poetry and Local Correspondence of Martin Butler, 1878–1889," May 1990, a paper presented at the Atlantic Canada Studies Conference, Orono, Maine; Jacques Ferland, "A Borderlands Industrial Empire of the Northeast: The Shaw Brothers and the Sole Leather Tanning Industry, 1863–1884," October 1991, a paper presented at the Biennial Conference of the Association for Canadian Studies in the United States, San Francisco; Jacques Ferland, "Along the Paths of Commodity Production: The Labour Process as a Perceptual Field," December 1993, a paper presented at the Australian-Canadian Labour History Conference, Sydney, Australia.

3 William Cronon offers a thought-provoking perspective on the complementarity between the industrial heartland and its resource-extracting hinterland in *Nature's Metropolis: Chicago and the Great West* (New York: W.W. Norton, 1991).

4 For pertinent conceptual observations on rural industrialization and labour process development in the hinterland, see Jacques Ferland and

Chris Wright, "Rural and Urban Labour Processes: A Comparative Analysis of Australian and Canadian Development," *Labour/ Le Travail* 38 (Fall 1996).

5 The expression "tradition-bound" is drawn from Jonathan C. Brown, *A Socioeconomic History of Argentina, 1776–1860*, Cambridge Latin American Studies (Cambridge: Cambridge University Press, 1979), 51. On the notion that tanning was a backward industry, see Peter C. Welsh, "A Craft That Resisted Change: American Tanning Practices to 1850," *Technology and Culture* IV (Summer 1963), 299–317; Peter C. Welsh, *Tanning in the United States to 1850: A Brief History* (Washington, DC: Smithsonian Institution, 1964). Focusing mostly on both institutional development and technological evolution, Lucius F. Ellsworth argues for his part that important changes began early in the century but that industry-wide response to these conditions only came in the 1890s. L.F. Ellsworth, *Craft to National Industry in the Nineteenth Century: A Case Study of the Transformation of the New York State Tanning Industry* (New York: Arno Press, 1975), 15.

6 Graeme Wynn, *Timber Colony: A Historical Geography of Early Nineteenth Century New Brunswick* (Toronto: University of Toronto Press, 1981), 9.

7 Contemporary treatises of tanning techniques and implements include, among many others: Julia De Fontenelle and F. Malepeyre, *The Arts of Tanning, Currying, and Leather-Dressing* (Philadelphia: 1852; edited by Campbell Morfitt); J. Leander Bishop, *A History of American Manufactures from 1608 to 1860* (Philadelphia: 1868); Charles Thomas Davis, *The Manufacture of Leather* (Philadelphia: 1885); Alexander Watt, *Leather Manufacture: A Practical Handbook of Tanning, Currying and Chrome-Leather Dressing* (London: 1906); International Library of Technology, *Packing-House Industries, Manufacture of Leather, Manufacture of Soap* (Scanton: 1913) Folio 22: 40; (United Shoe Machinery Corporation) "Hides and Leather Working Machinery," unpublished manuscript (Beverley, Massachusetts: c 1919) Folio A: History.

8 Andrew Ure, *A Dictionary of Arts, Manufactures and Mines* (New York: 1842) 769; "On the Processes of Tanning, Leather-Dressing, and Dying, Etc. from Aikin's Dictionary of Chymistry," in Dr Thomas P. Jones, *The Franklin Journal, and American Mechanics' Magazine; Devoted to the Useful Arts, Internal Improvements, and General Science*, vol.1 (Philadelphia: 1826) 119.

9 Estimates of bark consumption vary widely because of the relative thickness of green hides, the weight differential between dry and green hides, and the diverse physicochemical properties of bark. See the following contemporary estimates: Julia de Fontenelle and F. Malepeyre, *The Arts of Tanning*, 208 and 210; Jonathan C. Brown, *A Socioeconomic History of Argentina*, 55; "Extract from an account of the Prattsville Tannery in 'Hunt's Merchant's Magazine,'" *Journal of the Franklin Institute* vol. XIV (1847), 270.

10 "Extract from an account of the Prattsville Tannery." The Prattsville main tannery building covered an area 530 feet long, 48 feet wide, and two and a half storeys high, for a productive capacity of 300 vats. Post–Civil War tan yards in the state of Maine and the province of Quebec seldom exceeded this length but often doubled its breadth to hold between four and seven hundred vats. See, for example, *Saint Croix Courier* (St Stephen, New Brunswick) 1 June 1871; *The Calais Times* (Calais, Maine) 15 June 1883; *Bangor Daily Whig and Courier*, 16 September 1871. See also marginal annotation of census enumerator for the Roxton Falls tan yard, Shefford County, Quebec, 1861 census manuscript.

11 Canadian Patent Office Record, Patent No. 1661 – Miller (James,) of the Parish of St Pie, in the County of Bagot, for "The discovery of the art of manufacturing from tan-bark a substance for tanning and dying purposes, to be called 'Miller's Extract of Tan-Bark.'" Quebec, dated 12 March, 1864.

12 "The Tannery Industry," Tenth Annual Report of the Bureau of Industrial and Labor Statistics for the State of Maine 1896 (Augusta, Maine: 1897), 72.

13 Helen H. Foster and William Streeter, *Only One Cummington* (Cummington, Massachusetts: 1974), 262; H. Elmer Miller, *Sketches and Directory of the Town of Cummington* (West Cummington, Massachusetts: 1881), 38.

14 Ellsworth, *Craft to National Industry*, 135–48.

15 (Baker Library) R.G. Dun, Massachusetts Ledgers, vol. 46, Hampshire Co., 41–3; Ellsworth, *Craft to National Industry*, 141.

16 Penobscot County Court House, Deed of Registry, see especially vol. 241, 349–51, and vol. 282, 563; (Baker Library) R.G. Dun, Hampshire Co., vol.46, 44; R.G. Dun, Boston, vol. 77, 250. Also, Ferland, "A Borderlands Industrial Empire," 5–6.

17 US Census, Products of Industry, Maine, 1860. Located in Detroit, Plymouth, Burnham, Dexter and Acton, Maine, the Shaws' leather output (1,140 tons) and gross income ($159,653) in 1859–60 were both greater than the aggregate output (1,103 tons) and gross income ($84,888) of their combined competitors William Plaisted, A. Webb and Company, H. and H.R. Hunt, A.H. Buzzell, C.P. Church, Chancy Case, and S. Lothrop.

18 (Baker Library) R.G. Dun, Canada East, Montreal, vol. 5, 9. Even though the terms of their co-partnership were only registered in Canada on 27 January 1863, the Shaws began their Canadian operations in 1859, when they purchased a tannery at Roxton Falls from John Pratt and Company of Montreal.

19 Jean-Pierre Kesteman, Peter Southam, and Diane Saint-Pierre, *Histoire des Cantons de l'Est* (Sainte-Foy, Québec: Institut québécois de recherche sur la culture, 1998), 230–31.

20 The author has consulted the deed records in counties Shefford,

Drummond, Arthabasca, Brome, and Missisquoi to reconstitute the Shaws' sole leather tanning operations in the Eastern Townships of Quebec. These public records were further corroborated by the early handwritten ledgers of R.G. Dun in Boston and punctual research was further conducted in local newspapers, manuscript census records, and the municipal records of Roxton Falls. The Shaw creditors also conducted research in Quebec deed records in 1883. Their findings were published in "Report of the Committee of Creditors of F. Shaw & Bros. On the Affairs of the Firm," (Boston: 18 October 1883), Schedule I: "Tanneries and Land, in Province of Quebec," 85–8. See also Jacques Ferland, "Evolution des rapports sociaux dans l'industrie canadienne du cuir au tournant du 20e siècle" (PhD dissertation, McGill University, 1986).

21 The author has consulted the deed records in counties Penobscot and Washington to reconstitute the Shaws' sole leather tanning operations and real estate in eastern Maine. Additional sources include the R.G. Dun records, local newspaper articles and news items from Bangor, Calais, and Eastport, Maine, and St Stephen, New Brunswick, and the "Report of the Committee of Creditors of F. Shaw & Bros. On the Affairs of the Firm," particularly Schedule A: "Tannery Properties," and Schedule D: "Lands." The extent to which the Shaw family exerted control over residential life in these tanning communities is examined in Jacques Ferland, "Solidarity and Estrangement," and Jacques Ferland, "Canadian Working-Class Estrangement in Maine's Sole Leather Tanning."

22 For practical reasons, the commodification of hemlock bark was done mostly from the month of May to as late as August. It is then that bark peeling and yarding crews could best carve out from the felled hemlock trees sheets of bark, being further required to pile them on skids and to "cut, skid and swamp all roads necessary for the hauling of said bark" in December and January. Primary sources on bark peeling include legal documents such as: State of Maine, Washington County, Superior Judicial Court, Jan. Term AD 1884, "John K. Ames v. Fayette Shaw et als., Declaration," 1–2; "Report of Evidence," 3. 10, 23. See also Maine Bureau of Labor Statistics, "The Tannery Industry," 74.

23 The 22 October 1881 edition of the Carleton *Sentinel* gives a detailed physical description of the Woodstock extract mills, as well as a history of this new technology. See also "Report of the Committee of Creditors," Schedule A, 16–27; Schedule D, 63–5.

24 "Report of the Committee of Creditors," Schedule A: "New York Tanneries," 29–30; Exhibit F: "Assets at New York State Tanneries," 111; Schedule D: "Lands in New York," 65–6.

25 "Extract from an account of the Prattsville Tannery," 269: Zadock Pratt estimated the ecological impact of turning half a million hides into sole leather at 475,200 hemlock trees and 6,666 acres of good bark land.

26 Carleton *Sentinel*, 22 October 1881.
27 (Baker Library) R.G. Dun, "Early Handwritten Credit Reporting Ledgers of the Mercantile Agency," vol. 88, Massachusetts, 197.
28 R.G. Dun, Canada East, Montreal, 22 April 1874; also, "Report of the Committee of Creditors."
29 "Report" of C.O. Billings, in "Report of the Committee of Creditors," 5–10.
30 *Evening Transcript* (Boston), 18 October 1883: "The titles to the tanneries and lands situated in New York State, and known as the St. Regis and St. Lawrence tanneries, stand in the name of Shaw Bros. & Cassils."
31 R.G. Dun, Boston, Massachusetts, vol. 77, 375, 1 November 1877, and 401, 6 June 1879; vol. 88, 197, 12 January 1882 and 15 February 1883.
32 "Report" of C.O. Billings, Chairman of the Creditors' Committee in "Report of the Committee of Creditors," 8.
33 The "Shaw Failure" was followed with much interest in borderland communities such as St Stephen, New Brunswick, and Calais, Maine. The *Saint Croix Courier*, published in St Stephen, dutifully reported on this case on a regular basis between 1883 and 1887.
34 "The Shaw Failure," *Saint Croix Courier*, 8 November 1883.
35 "Report" of C.O. Billings, 10–11. The Chairman initiated "legal proceedings" but did not act on the legal advice he received because "no results could be reached prior to this meeting."
36 "Report of the Committee of Creditors," schedules B, E, and H.
37 "Report of the Committee of Creditors," Exhibit H: "F. Shaw & Bros. of Vanceboro', Maine," and Schedule E: "Lands – Vanceboro' firm."
38 F. Shaw and Brothers, letter "To the Creditors of F. Shaw and Brothers," dated Boston, 1 November 1883, in "Report of the Committee of Creditors," 9.
39 F. Shaw and Brothers, letter, 9.
40 Saint John *Daily Telegraph*, 2 August 1880.
41 As reported and quoted in the Carleton *Sentinel*, 18 September and 27 November 1880.
42 Carleton *Sentinel*, 27 November 1880.
43 *Saint Croix Courier* (St Stephen, New Brunswick), 13 December 1883.
44 Ibid., 29 November 1883.
45 Ibid., 29 November 1883.
46 Ibid., 20 March 1884.
47 Ibid., 2 September and 2 December 1886.
48 M.H. Watkins, "A Staple Theory of Economic Growth," in W.T. Easterbrook and M.H. Watkins, eds., *Approaches to Canadian Economic History* (Toronto: McClelland & Stewart, 1967), 62–4.

CHAPTER TWELVE

* I am grateful to R. Marvin McInnis, Richard Judd, Scott See, and the publisher's anonymous commentators for their many helpful comments on previous drafts. Dr. Thomas Gaffney of the Portland Public Library provided invaluable aid during my explorations into the Maine city's nineteenth-century economic and social history.

1 S.A. Saunders, *The Economic History of the Maritime Provinces* (Fredericton: Acadiensis Press, 1984). Originally published in 1939.

2 "Economic Growth in the Atlantic Region, 1880 to 1940," in David Alexander, ed., *Atlantic Canada and Confederation: Essays in Canadian Political Economy* (Toronto: University of Toronto Press, 1983), 51–78.

3 Philip Wood, "Barriers to Capitalist Development in Maritime Canada, 1870–1930: A Comparative Perspective," in Peter Baskerville, ed., *Canadian Papers in Business History, Vol. 1* (Victoria: University of Victoria Public History Group, 1989), 33–58.

4 For reviews of the literature from varying perspectives, see James B. Cannon, "Explaining Regional Development in Atlantic Canada: A Review Essay," *Journal of Canadian Studies* 19:3 (Fall 1984), 65–86; Kris E. Inwood, "Maritime Industrialization from 1870 to 1910: A Review of the Evidence and its Interpretation," in K. Inwood, ed., *Farm, Factory, and Fortune: New Studies in the Economic History of the Maritime Provinces* (Fredericton: Acadiensis Press, 1993), 149–170; Eric Sager, "Dependency, Underdevelopment and the Economic History of the Atlantic Provinces," *Acadiensis* 17:1 (Autumn 1987), 117–37; T.W. Acheson, "The Maritimes and 'Empire Canada'," in David Bercuson, ed., *Canada and the Burden of Unity* (Toronto: 1977), 87–114; E.R. Forbes and D.A. Muise, eds., *The Atlantic Provinces in Confederation* (Toronto: University of Toronto Press, 1993), chapters 3–7.

5 Saunders, *Economic History of the Maritime Provinces.*

6 James Kierstead, *The Theory of Economic Change* (Toronto: Macmillan, 1948), 269–81. On financial markets, see James D. Frost, "The 'Nationalization' of the Bank of Nova Scotia, 1880–1910," *Acadiensis* 12 (Autumn 1982), 3–38.

7 L. McCann and A. Gunn, *Heartland and Hinterland: A Regional Geography of Canada* (Scarborough: Prentice Hall Canada, 3rd ed., 1998), 19, 32.

8 T.W. Acheson, "The National Policy and the Industrialization of the Maritimes," *Acadiensis* 1, (Spring 1972), 1–28. See also Acheson, "The Maritimes and 'Empire Canada,'" in Bercuson, ed., *Canada and the Burden of Unity*, 87–114.

9 E.R. Forbes, "Misguided Symmetry: The Destruction of Regional Transportation Policy for the Maritimes," in Bercuson, ed., *Canada and the Burden of Unity*, 60–86.

10 R.E. George, *A Leader and a Laggard* (Toronto: University of Toronto Press, 1970).

11 David Frank, "The Cape Breton Coal Industry and the Rise and Fall of the British Empire Steel Corporation," *Acadiensis* 7:1 (1977), 3–34.

12 William H. Sewell, Jr, "Marc Bloch and the Logic of Comparative History," *History and Theory* 6:2 (1967), 215.

13 Jane Jacobs, *The Life and Death of North American Cities* (New York: Random House, 1961), *passim.*

14 For the history of Saint John from its founding to the Confederation period, see T.W. Acheson, *Saint John: The Making of a Colonial Urban Community* (Toronto: University of Toronto Press, 1985). For Portland there is the outdated volume by A. Moulton, *Portland by the Sea* (1926), but see also Robert H. Babcock, "Economic Development of Portland (Me.) and Saint John (NB) During the Age of Iron and Steam, 1850–1914," *American Review of Canadian Studies* IX (Spring 1979), 3–37; and Babcock, "Private vs. Public Enterprise: A Comparison of Two Atlantic Seaboard Cities, 1850–1925," chap. 3 in G.A. Stelter and A.F.J. Artibise, eds., *Power and Place: Canadian Urban Development in the North American Context* (Vancouver: UBC Press, 1986), 51–81.

15 John A. Watt, "Uneven Regional Development in Canada: A Study of Saint John, N.B., 1880–1910," unpublished PhD diss., University of Waterloo, 1981, 170.

16 "Locomotives by Fleming's Foundry," typescript #462, New Brunswick Museum, Saint John (hereafter NBM); "The Phoenix Foundry (St. John, NB) and George Fleming," typescript in the author's possession.

17. Scrapbook #1, Myy 286, NBM; (Saint John) *Progress* 15 December 1888; R.G. Dun Credit Reports, vol. 9, Saint John, 357, 603 Baker Library, Harvard University (hereafter BLHU).

18 See Richard F. Dole, "The Portland Company," *Railroad History* 139 (Autumn 1978), 5–38; Michael J. Sheehy, "John Alfred Poor and International Railroads: The Early Years to 1860," unpublished MA thesis, University of Maine, 1974, 57–8; E.H. Elwell, *The Successful Business Houses of Portland* (Portland: W.S. Jones, 1875), 119–20.

19 BLHU, R.G. Dun Credit Reports, vol. 14, Maine, 294; vol. 15, Portland, 399; W. B. Willis, *History of Portland* , 730.

20 BLHU, R.G. Dun Credit Reports, vol. 20, Portland, 41, 303.

21 For additional details, see Babcock, "Economic Development of Portland (Me.) and Saint John (NB)," passim.

22 BLHU, R.G. Dun Credit Reports, Portland, vol. 20, 290; vol. 16, 484; *Mining & Industrial Journal,* 23 March, 6 April 1883, 17 July, 25 September 1885, 30 April 1886, 18 November 1887; 21 December 1888; 19 July 1889; 29 August, 12 September 1890; 7 August 1891; 23 September 1892; 15 September 1893; 19 January 1894; 3 September 1897; 2 September 1898; 23 November 1900; August 1904; August

1905. See also Maine, Bureau of Industrial and Labor Statistics, *Report,* 1898, 119.

23 *Industrial Journal,* 25 September, 11 December 1885; 9 April 1886; 15 July 1887; 6 April, 6 July, 21 December 1888; 15 March, 3 May 1889; 28 February, 6 June, 29 August, 26 December 1890; 3 April, 31 July 1891; 15 January, 29 April, 29 July, 22 November 1892; R.G. Dun Credit Reports, Portland, vol. 15, 589.

24 *Industrial Journal,* 25 September, 11 December 1885; 9 April 1886; 15 July 1887; 6 April, 6 July, 21 December 1888; 15 March, 3 May 1889; 28 February, 6 June 29 August, 26 December 1890; 3 April, 31 July 1891; 15 January, 29 April, 29 July, 22 November 1892; BLHU, R.G. Dun Credit Reports, Portland, vol. 15, 589.

25 BLHU, R.G. Dun Credit Reports, vol. 16, Portland, 505 (quotation); Victor S. Clark, *History of Manufactures in the United States* Vol. 2, (New York: Peter Smith, 1949), 262–3.

26 BLHU, R.G. Dun Credit Reports, vol. 16, Portland, 395, 505, 606; *Maine Mining Journal,* 25 August 1882; *Mining & Industrial Journal,* 9 March, 21 December 1883; 8 February 1884; *Industrial Journal,* 11 July, 26 December 1884; 9 January, 24 July 1885; 26 November, 24 December 1886; 22 April 1887; 6 April, 12 October 1888; 30 August, 29 November 1889; 9 March 1894; 6, 20 October, 1 December 1899; 9 March, 29 June, 17 August, 2 November 1900, August 1902; November, December 1903; October 1904.

27 R.F. Dole, "Portland Company," 13; *Maine Mining Journal* , 20, 27 January, 3, 17, 24, 31 March, 12 May, 2, 9 June, 14 July, 11, 25 August, 22 September, 27 October 1882; 5 January, 2 February, 30 March, 29 June, 13 July 1883; 8 February, 7 March, 4 July, 22 August, 12 September 1884; *Industrial Journal,* 13 February, 14, 21 August 1885; 22 January, 19 February, 26 March, 30 April, 11 June, 16 July, 3, 10 September, 22 October, 3 December 1886; 15 July, 16 December 1887; 30 March, 27 April, 8 June, 20 July, 31 August 1888; 18 October 1889; BLHU, R.G. Dun Credit Reports, vol. 15, Portland, 633 (23 April 1883).

28 "The Phoenix Foundry," n.p.; "Locomotives by Phoenix Foundry," NBM, *Daily Morning News,* 17 March 1870.

29 BLHU, R.G. Dun Credit Reports, vol. 9, Saint John, 10, 102, 150, 308, 343, 562, 591 (quotations).

30 *Daily Telegraph* 20 July 1875; *Daily News,* 29 September 1875; *Daily Sun,* 9 September 1881; *Monetary Times,* 27 May 1883; *Montreal Herald,* 21 May 1884 (quotation); in Merchants & Industries Scrapbook #535, NBM; *Mining & Industrial Journal,* 22 September, 10 October 1882; 26 January, 16 February, 21 September 1883; 17 October 1884; *Daily Sun,* 15, 27 June 1885; *Industrial Journal,* 18 September 1885; 25 June 1886; 28 January, 21 October 1887.

31 Ian Sclander, clippings, #87, NBM.
32 E.H. Willis, "Report on the Manufacturing Industries of Certain Sections of the Maritime Provinces," Canada, House of Commons, *Sessional Papers* #37 (1886), 91.
33 V.S. Clark, *History of Manufactures,* vol. 2, 674.
35 *Industrial Journal,* 8 June, 20 July 1888. The major railways marginalized the Portland Company's rolling stock by replacing wooden freight cars with pressed-steel ones.
36 *Saint John Globe,* 24 October 1891; Watt, "Uneven Regional Development," 182.
37 *Daily Telegraph,* 16 November 1887; *Saint John Globe,* 20 June 1895, in Merchants & Industrial Scrapbook #535, NBM; *Industrial Journal,* 24 March 1893.
38 See Clark, *History of Manufactures,* vol. 2, 132, 183, 485; *Industrial Journal,* 3 February 1888, 3 January 1890, 2 January, 25 December 1891, 1 January, 24 June 1892.
39 *Industrial Journal,* 14 December 1894.
40 Ibid., 18 September 1896; Maine, Bureau of Industrial and Labor Statistics, *Report,* 1899; Clark, *History of Manufactures,* vol. 2, 782–3.
41 *Industrial Journal,* 27 February 1885; 29 January, 14 May 1886.
42 Flyer in Portland Company collection, vol. 24, no. 178, Maine Historical Society (hereafter MHS).
43 *Industrial Journal,* 23 March 1888.
44 Ibid., May 1902.
45 Ibid., 19 August, 9 September 1887.
46 Portland Company Directors' Records, 10 August 1889, Box. 57, MHS; *Industrial Journal,* 30 August 1889; Portland Board of Trade, *Journal,* vol. III (June 1890), 47.
47 *Industrial Journal,* 2 October 1891.
48 Ibid., 11 December 1891, August 1901.
49 Ibid., 28 October 1892, 30 June 1893, 23 November 1894, 11 September 1896, 3 September 1897.
50 Ibid., 19 May, 30 October 1899 (quotation).
51 Ibid., 5 October 1900, June 1901.
52 Ibid., May 1902.
53 See data in Table 5.
54 *Industrial Journal,* 23 November 1900, February 1902.
55 Ibid., August 1904, August 1905.
56 Ibid., 16 February 1900, May 1910, March 1911.
57 Ibid., 9 March 1900, August 1902, November 1903, October 1904, January 1910; Maine Department of Industry & Labor, Report, 1919–20.
58 Maine, Department of Industry & Labor, Report, 1919–20, p. 37.
59 Maine, Bureau of Industry & Labor, Report, 1901, 91.

60 Maine, Department of Industry & Labor, *Report*, 1901, 85–92.

61 Burton Glendenning, "Crown Land Timber Regulations and the Introduction of the Pulp and Paper Industry to New Brunswick," (unpublished paper, 1983); *Industrial Journal*, 9 September 1898; Watt, "Uneven Regional Development," 199; *Labour Gazette* 5 (November 1904), 448; 5 (June 1905), 1306; 6 (November 1905), 615; *Daily Sun*, 12 May 1905.

62 Bill Parenteau, "The Woods Transformed: The Emergence of the Pulp and Paper Industry in New Brunswick, 1918–1931," *Acadiensis* 22:1 (Autumn 1992), 5–43; Parenteau, "The Pulp and Paper Industry," Part IV of "The New Brunswick Forest Heritage: A History of the Forest Industries, 1780–1930," unpublished manuscript prepared for Parks Canada, 1994, 221–32.

63 *Industrial Journal*, 10 September 1886, 17 June 1887.

64 This paragraph is condensed from Babcock, "Private vs. Public Enterprise: A Comparison of Two Atlantic Seaboard Cities, 1850–1925," in Stelter and Artibise, eds., *Power and Place: Canadian Urban Development in the North American Context*, 51–81.

65 See Wylie, "When Markets Fail: Electrification and the Maritime Industrial Decline in the 1920s," *Acadiensis* 17(1987).

66 G. Wynn, "Places at the Margin: The Atlantic Provinces," in *Heartland and Hinterland: A Regional Geography of Canada* (Scarborough: Prentice Hall Canada, 3rd ed., 1998), 193.

67 See L.D. McCann, "Metropolitanism and Branch Businesses in the Maritimes, 1881–1931," *Acadiensis* 13 (Autumn 1983), 112–25.

CHAPTER THIRTEEN

1 Edward D. Ives, *Joe Scott: The Woodsman-Songmaker* (Champaign: University of Illinois Press, 1978), especially 412–24. See also Ives, *Larry Gorman: The Man Who Made the Songs* (Bloomington: Indiana University Press, 1964; reprinted Fredericton: Goose Lane, 1993); *Lawrence Doyle: The Farmer-Poet of Prince Edward Island* (Orono: University of Maine Press, 1971); *"Drive Dull Care Away": Folksongs from Prince Edward Island* (Charlottetown: Institute for Island Studies and Champaign: University of Illinois Press, 1999).

2 There is an immense scholarly literature on these ballads, but G. Malcolm Laws's two studies are probably the best starting place: *Native American Balladry*, Revised edition (Philadelphia: American Folklore Society, 1864), *American Balladry from British Broadsides* (Philadelphia: American Folklore Society, 1957).

3 The first scholarly notice given to this Maine-Maritimes connection was by Horace P. Beck; see his "Folksong Affiliations of Maine," *Midwest Folklore* VI (Fall, 1956), 159–66.

4 For an old but still valuable general history of the American lumber industry, see James E. Defebaugh, *The History of the Lumber Industry in America*, 2 vols. (Chicago: The American Lumberman, 1906). For Maine, Richard G. Wood, *A History of Lumbering in Maine 1820–1861* (Orono: University of Maine, 1935); David C. Smith, *A History of Lumbering in Maine 1861– 1960* (Orono: University of Maine, 1972). For the Canadian side of the story, see Donald McKay, *The Lumberjacks* (Toronto: Ryerson Press, 1978).

5 Ives, *Joe Scott*, 380.

6 For more on Billy Allen and his songs, see Franz Rickaby, *Ballads and Songs of the Shantyboy* (Cambridge: Harvard University Press, 1926), xxix–xxxvii.

7 *PI* referred specifically to Prince Edward Islanders, but was easily extended to include anyone from the Maritimes.

8 Ives, *Joe Scott*, 387.

CHAPTER FOURTEEN

1 This paper is based on research undertaken in Canada and the United States for my doctoral dissertation. I am indebted to faculty and staff of the Canadian-American Center at the University of Maine and of Dalhousie University's Law School and Marine Affairs Program for their generosity in hosting me for extended periods. The recognition and support of the following institutions are also greatly appreciated: Yale University's School of Forestry and Environmental Studies and Center for International and Area Studies; the Sea Grant College Programs of Connecticut, Maine, and Woods Hole Oceanographic Institution; the Canada–U.S. Fulbright Program; the Organization of American States; the Canadian Embassy in Washington, DC; the Teresa & H. John Heinz III Foundation; the Maritime Studies Program of Williams College and Mystic Seaport; and the Andrew W. Mellon Foundation.

2 I have coined the name "Greater Gulf of Maine Region" (GGOMR) and delineated its boundaries. The GGOMR extends east from the Connecticut River to Bedford Basin. The former empties into eastern Long Island Sound in the state of Connecticut, and the latter is bordered on two sides by the Halifax-Dartmouth metropolitan area in the province of Nova Scotia. The region encompasses the watersheds, inshore waters, and marine waters therein, including the offshore fishing banks between and including Georges and Sable Island Banks, the Scotia-Fundy shelf, the Bay of Fundy, the Gulf of Maine proper, and the waters between and including Nantucket Sound and the easternmost portion of Long Island Sound.

3 Massachusetts Fish Commission, Fourth Annual Report 1869, 61–2.

4 The *inshore* or *coastal* fisheries were generally conducted in small, unprotected boats within three nautical miles of land. *Nearshore* or "shore fishing," the first of the two phases of deep-sea fishing, occurred between three and thirty nautical miles from the coast. These trips rarely exceeded two weeks and were often shorter; see Joseph W. Smith, *Gleanings from the Sea: Showing the Pleasures, Pains and Penalties of Life Afloat with Contingencies Ashore* (Andover, Massachusetts: Published by the author, 1887), vii.

5 Depending upon the species and location, during and after the 1870s and 1880s, the answer to the North Atlantic conundrum was "no" for menhaden and adult Atlantic (sea) herring (including Georges Bank herring), and for sturgeons, oysters, and lobsters. Due to length restrictions, however, this essay does not assess fisheries policy making after 1869 for Canada or after 1872 for the United States.

6 Customary international law since the early seventeenth century and the findings of Queen Victoria's Royal Commission on the Sea Fisheries (1865) gave credence to this myth. Hugo Grotius, the influential Dutch jurist, politician, and counsel to the Dutch East India Company (1583–1645), claimed that marine fishes were inexhaustible and espoused the doctrine of *mare liberum*, freedom of the seas. Prominent jurists took issue with him, yet his perspective prevailed in customary international law well into the twentieth century. British biologist and fishery investigator Thomas Henry Huxley (1825–1895), chair of the Royal Commission on the Sea Fisheries, is widely credited with having asserted a similar view; see Hugo Grotius, *De Jure Praedae Commentarius*, translation of 1604 manuscript by G. Williams edited by J. Scott (Oxford: Clarendon Press, 1950); "Extracts from the Report of the Commissioners Appointed to Inquire into the Sea-Fisheries of the United Kingdom; Presented to Both Houses of Parliament by Command of Her Majesty. London, 186[5]," in Commissioner Spencer F. Baird, Report on the Condition of the Sea Fisheries of the South Coast of New England in 1871 and 1872: Part I, United States Commission of Fish and Fisheries (Washington, DC: Government Printing Office, 1873), 145–8.

7 For example, in an article published in June 1854 in *Revue des Deux Mondes* and translated by Gamaliel Bradford three years later for a temporary commission appointed by the Massachusetts Legislature to investigate fish-culture (aquaculture), Jules Haime refuted these assumptions:

> Fisheries have often been called the agriculture of the waters, as if seas, lakes, and rivers were inexhaustible store-houses of food, where, without fear of ever impoverishing them, man might continue to take and destroy forever, bounded only by his wants and desires. This definition is false, because founded on a false view of the case. Fishery [*sic.*]

> is not the agriculture of the waters; it is only the harvesting. The waters are a source of production extremely powerful, but by no means infinite; and that the harvest may be always certain and abundant, it should be prepared by regular sowing, if it is true, according to the expression of M. de Quatrefages, that fish may be multiplied by sowing in the same manner as grain.

Jules Haime, "The History of Fish-Culture in Europe from its Earlier Records to 1854," in U.S. Commission of Fish and Fisheries, Annual Report II 1872–1873, 465, 465–9. Also see, H.W. Johnston, "Appendix: Special Report on the Distress Among Nova Scotia Fishermen," in *Reports on the Fisheries, Etc., of the Dominion of Canada* (Ottawa: Department of Marine and Fisheries, 1868), 11–15; "On the Limits of Artificial Culture, and the Possible Exhaustion of Sea Fisheries," in Massachusetts Fish Commission, *Fourth Annual Report 1869*, 61–2; "Fisheries on the Coast of Massachusetts," in Massachusetts Fish Commission, Fifth Annual Report 1870, 73–74; "European Authorities on the Subject of Regulating the Fisheries By Law," in Baird, Sea Fisheries of the South Coast of New England, 139–45; Theodore Soudakevicz, "Report on the Progress of Pisciculture in Russia, 1. – The Decrease of Food-Fishes," in U.S. Commission of Fish and Fisheries, Annual Report II 1872–1873, 493–5.

8 William Cronon, *Changes in the Land: Indians, Colonists, and the Ecology of New England* (New York: Hill and Wang, 1983), 22.

9 Robert C. Beardsley, Bradford Butman, W. Rockwell Geyer, and Peter Smith, "Physical Oceanography in the Gulf of Maine: An Update," in G.T. Wallace and E.F. Braasch, eds., *Proceedings of the Gulf of Maine Ecosystem Dynamics Scientific Symposium and Workshop* (Hanover, New Hampshire: Regional Association for Research on the Gulf of Maine (RARGOM) Report, 97–1, 1997), 41–2.

10 Cronon, *Changes in the Land*, 20–1, 76–7, 165–9.

11 William Wood, *New-England's Prospect* (London, 1634), 1967 reprint, 35.

12 Cronon, *Changes in the Land*, 76, 168; Robert G. Albion, William A. Baker, and Benjamin W. Labaree, *New England and the Sea* (Middletown: Wesleyan University Press, 1972), 15.

13 Bartholomew Gosnold and his crew (1602), for instance, were so impressed by the multitude of cod in the waters off southeastern Massachusetts that Gosnold called the extensive peninsula he found Cape Cod. Crewmember John Brereton marvelled that the water in which he and his companions took cod was "but seven fathoms [11 m] … and within less than a league of the shore, when in Newfoundland they fish in forty or fifty fathoms waters, and far off." The chronicler of George Weymouth's expedition (1605), James Rosier, claimed that the cod encountered off the Maine coast were "much greater, better fed, and abundance

with train" (oily livers). George Popham and Raleigh Gilbert (1607) agreed; no one aboard their ships had ever seen codfish "so large and great"; see Lorenzo Sabine, Report on the Principal Fisheries of the American Seas, Prepared for the Treasury of the United States (Washington, DC: Robert Armstrong, 1853), 94–5; Douglas R. McManis, *Colonial New England: A Historical Geography* (New York: Oxford University Press, 1975), 14–22; Faith Harrington, "*Wee Tooke Great Store of Cod-fish*: Fishing Ships and First Settlements on the Coast of New England, 1600–1630," in Emerson W. Baker, Edwin A. Churchill, Richard D'Abate, Kristine L. Jones, Victor A. Konrad, and Harold E. L. Prins, eds., *American Beginnings: Exploration, Culture, and Cartography in the Land of Norumbega* (Lincoln: University of Nebraska Press, 1994), 197, 191–216.

14 Harrington, "*Wee Tooke Great Store of Cod-fish*," 192–3.

15 Ibid., 193.

16 John C. Pearson, ed., *The Fish and Fisheries of Colonial North America: A Documentary History of the Fishery Resources of the United States and Canada, Part II: The New England States* (Washington, DC: U.S. Fish and Wildlife Service, Department of the Interior, and National Oceanic and Atmospheric Admi-nistration, 1972), 181–6, 225; Harrington, "*Wee Tooke Great Store of Cod-fish*," 208.

17 Pearson, ed., *Fish and Fisheries of Colonial North America, New England*, 180–1, 194, 194–A, 195, 227, 325; Joseph W. Collins and Richard Rathbun, "The Sea Fishing Grounds of the Eastern Coast of North America from Greenland to Mexico," in George Brown Goode, ed., *The Fisheries and Fishing Industries of the United States: Section III, The Fishing Grounds of North America with Forty-nine Charts* (Washington, DC: Government Printing Office, 1887), Charts nos. 8 and 10.

18 See Pearson, ed., *The Fish and Fisheries of Colonial North America, Part I: The Canadian Atlantic Provinces*; Pearson, ed., *Fish and Fisheries of Colonial North America: New England*.

19 Leslie W. Scattergood and S.N. Tibbo, *The Herring Fishery of Atlantic Canada* (Ottawa: Fisheries Research Board of Canada, 1959), 4–6; Pearson, ed., *Fish and Fisheries of Colonial North America: New England*, 186; Lorenzo Sabine, Report on the Principal Fisheries of the American Seas: Prepared for the Treasury Department of the United States (Washington, DC: Robert Armstrong, 1853), 192.

20 When the Pilgrims reached Cape Cod in 1621 they were unaware that in 1616 a lethal, highly contagious, three-year epidemic of European origin – probably chickenpox – had decimated native American populations within a twenty- to thirty-mile-wide swath along the coast from Narragansett Bay in western Rhode Island to Penobscot Bay in eastern Maine. Native Americans in the vicinity of Boston Harbor suffered the most. Indigenous salmon production has been estimated at 14 to 15 million tons per year. Where fishing had occurred – mainly with spears, weirs, and nets – an

average of 580 pounds was taken every square mile. Theodore Steinberg has surmised that the anadromous fish runs in the Charles River "may well have been in the middle of a fantastic renewal caused by the depopulation of the native people." It is probable that anadromous fish runs elsewhere in the Boston area and in rivers and streams throughout the affected region likewise increased; see R.W. Dunfield, *The Atlantic Salmon in the History of North America* (Ottawa: Department of Fisheries and Oceans, 1985), 1; Theodore Steinberg, *Nature Incorporated: Industrialization and the Waters of New England* (New York: Cambridge University Press, 1991), 26; Cronon, *Changes in the Land*, 85–90.

21 Dunfield, *Atlantic Salmon*, 10, 12, 25, 28, 40, 46–fn28; Joint Commission, Report of the Joint Commission Relative to the Preservation of the Fisheries in Waters Contiguous to Canada and the United States (Ottawa: S.E. Dawson, Printer to the Queen, 1897), 3–4, 10–11; Thomas F. Knight, *Pamphlets on the Fishes and Fisheries of Nova Scotia. No. III. River Fisheries* (Halifax: A. Grant, 1867), 1–2.

22 Wood, *New-England's Prospect*, 38.

23 Pearson, ed., *Fish and Fisheries of Colonial North America: New England*, 625, 227–8.

24 Connecticut Fish Commission, Fourth Annual Report 1869–1870, 7; Dunfield, *Atlantic Salmon*, 9–10; Anthony Netboy, *Salmon: The World's Most Harassed Fish* (Tulsa, Oklahoma: Winchester Press, 1980), 172.

25 Cronon, *Changes in the Land*, 21, 168–9.

26 See, for example, McManis, *Colonial New England*, 113–16; Cronon, *Changes in the Land*, 120–1, 160; Thomas R. Cox, *This Well-Wooded Land: Americans and their Forests from Colonial Times to the Present* (Lincoln: University of Nebraska Press, 1985), 44; Anthony N. Penna, *Nature's Bounty: Historical and Modern Environmental Perspectives* (Armonk, New York: M.E. Sharpe, 1999), 4, 7–8, 16–18, 21–30, 41.

27 See McManis, *Colonial New England*, 89, 114; Cronon, *Changes in the Land*, 149–51; Penna, *Nature's Bounty*, 9, 17, 28, 41.

28 See John Smith, *A Description of New England* (London, 1616) in Pearson, ed., *Fish and Fisheries of Colonial North America: New England*, 280; Lewis H. Morgan, *The American Beaver and His Works* (1868), reprinted in Penna, *Nature's Bounty*, 135–8; Penna, *Nature's Bounty*, 158–9; Richard N.L. Andrews, *Managing the Environment, Managing Ourselves: A History of American Environmental Policy* (New Haven: Yale University Press, 1999), 46–7; McManis, *Colonial New England*, 132; Ann Vileisis, *Discovering the Unknown Landscape: A History of America's Wetlands* (Washington, DC: Island Press, 1997), 16–17.

29 John R. Stilgoe, *Common Landscape of America: 1580 to 1845* (New Haven: Yale University Press, 1982), 317; Cox, *This Well-Wooded Land*, 176; Dunfield, *Atlantic Salmon*, 43, 57.

30 See Steinberg, *Nature Incorporated,* 26–7, 33–4, 36–7; Vileisis, *History of America's Wetlands,* 32–3, 48–9; Harry Thurston, *Tidal Life: A Natural History of the Bay of Fundy* (Camden East, Ontario: Camden House Publishing Co., 1990), 83–5; David D. Platt, ed., *Rim of the Gulf: Restoring Estuaries in the Gulf of Maine* (Rockland, Maine: Island Institute, 1998), 100–1; Michael Burzynski and Anne Marceau, *Fundy: Bay of the Giant Tides* (Alma, New Brunswick: Fundy Guild, 1994), 16–17; Philip W. Conkling, ed., *From Cape Cod to the Bay of Fundy: An Environmental Atlas of the Gulf of Maine* (Cambridge: The MIT Press, 1995), 123–7.

31 See Penna, *Nature's Bounty,* 159–67; Andrews, *Managing the Environment,* 109–13; Steinberg, *Nature Incorporated,* 205–39; Martin V. Melosi, *The Sanitary City: Urban Infrastructure in America from Colonial Times to the Present* (Baltimore: The Johns Hopkins University Press, 2000), 113, 141, 162.

32 Report of the Joint Commission, 3.

33 Raymond A. McFarland, *A History of the New England Fisheries with Maps* (New York: University of Pennsylvania, 1911), 121; Harold A. Innis, *The Cod Fisheries: The History of an International Economy* (Toronto: Ryerson Press, 1940), 206–7, 211, 222; Lesley Choyce, *Nova Scotia: Shaped by the Sea* (Toronto: Penguin Books, 1996), 138–9.

34 Choyce, *Nova Scotia,* 138–9.

35 Dunfield, *Atlantic Salmon,* 62.

36 W.S. MacNutt, *New Brunswick, A History: 1784–1867* (Toronto: Macmillan, 1963), 88, 162; Dunfield, *Atlantic Salmon,* 20, 98; Rosemary E. Ommer, "The 1830s: Adapting their Institutions to their Desires," in Phillip A. Buckner and John G. Reid, eds., *The Atlantic Region to Confederation: A History* (Toronto: University of Toronto Press, 1994), 285.

37 MacNutt, *New Brunswick,* 1, 20, 32, 39, 41, 47, 58, 88.

38 Choyce, *Nova Scotia,* 138; Dunfield, *Atlantic Salmon,* 62, 69, 71–2, 99, 105; Anthony Netboy, *The Atlantic Salmon: A Vanishing Species?* (Boston: Houghton Mifflin, 1968), 350.

39 Moses H. Perley, "Report Upon the Fisheries of the Bay of Fundy," in Reports on the Sea and River Fisheries of New Brunswick (Fredericton: J. Simpson, 1852), 128; Dunfield, *Atlantic Salmon,* 67–8.

40 W.A. Spray, "Perley, Moses Henry," in *Dictionary of Canadian Biography, vol. 9: 1861– 1870* (Toronto: University of Toronto Press, 1976), 628–30; Perley, "Fisheries of the Bay of Fundy," 91–178.

41 Knight, *River Fisheries,* 2; Knight, *Report on the Fisheries of Nova Scotia* (Halifax: A. Grant, 1867), 17.

42 *Statutes of New Brunswick* 1851, 14 Vict., c. 31; *Statutes of New Brunswick* 1863, 26 Vict., c. 6.

43 Dunfield, *Atlantic Salmon,* 123–4.

44 *Statutes of Nova Scotia* 1853, 16 Vict., c. 17; *Statutes of Nova Scotia* 1866, 29

Vict., c. 36; Dunfield, *Atlantic Salmon*, 134, 155; Knight, *Fishes and Fisheries of Nova Scotia*, 31–2, 40, 66–71, 80.

45 Cronon, *Changes in the Land*, 136, 149–52; Douglas R. McManis, *Colonial New England: A Historical Geography* (New York: Oxford University Press, 1975), 89; Mark D. Bertness, *The Ecology of Atlantic Shorelines* (Sunderland, Massachusetts: Sinauer Assoc. Inc., 1999), 180.

46 Marshall McDonald, "The Connecticut and Housatonic Rivers and Minor Tributaries of Long Island Sound," in Goode, ed., *Fisheries and Fishery Industries of the United States*, Sec V., vol. I, 660–1; Cronon, *Changes in the Land*, 136, 155; Dunfield, *Atlantic Salmon*, 42–3; Netboy, *Atlantic Salmon*, 321–2.

47 Dunfield, *Atlantic Salmon*, 34, 43; for native American use of nets, see Steinberg, *Nature Incorporated*, 170.

48 Dunfield, *Atlantic Salmon*, 43–4, 57, 78–9.

49 In March 1775, the British Parliament enacted the *New England Restraining Act*, which effectively banned the colonies' vessels from fishing the offshore grounds until peace was signed in 1783. During the war schooners were turned into privateers, used for naval purposes, tied up at wharves, or hauled from the sea. Only a dozen were afloat by the early 1780s; see Samuel Eliot Morison, *The Maritime History of Massachusetts: 1783–1860* (Boston: Houghton Mifflin Co., 1921), 147; Daniel Vickers, *Farmers and Fishermen: Two Centuries of Work in Essex County, Massachusetts, 1630–1850* (Chapel Hill: University of North Carolina Press, 1994), 265–6.

50 Dunfield, *Atlantic Salmon*, 57–8.

51 Sabine, *Principal Fisheries of the American Seas*, 192–3.

52 Netboy, *Atlantic Salmon: Vanishing*, 322; Dunfield, *Atlantic Salmon*, 57–8.

53 Dunfield, *Atlantic Salmon*, 79.

54 Stilgoe, *Common Landscape of America*, 317, 325–6, 331–2; Louis C. Hunter, *A History of Industrial Power in the United States, 1780–1930, Volume One: Waterpower in the Century of the Steam Engine* (Charlottesville: The University of Virginia Press, 1979), 186.

55 Morison, *Maritime History of Massachusetts*, 214.

56 Wood (1634) described the Merrimack as: "the best place … lying 8 miles beyond [Agowam], where is a river twenty leagues navigable, all along the riverside is fresh marshes, in some places three miles broad. In this river is sturgeon, salmon, and [striped] bass, and diverse other kinds of fish." Wood, *New-England's Prospect*, 340.

57 Steinberg, *Nature Incorporated*, 166–204, 205–39.

58 Cronon, *Changes in the Land*, 152; Dunfield, *Atlantic Salmon*, 148.

59 McFarland, *History of the New England Fisheries*, 177–82, 201–2, 207–10.

60 George Brown Goode, "The Fresh Halibut Fishery," in Goode, ed., *Fisheries and Fishery Industries of the United States*, Sec. V., vol. 1, 3–89; George H. Proctor, *The Fishermen's Memorial and Record Book* (Gloucester: Proctor

Brothers, Publishers, 1873), 67–8, 77, 82, 96; Proctor Brothers, *The Fishermen's Own Book* (Gloucester: Proctor Brothers, 1882), 50; McFarland, *History of the New England Fisheries,* 278–9, 282–4; James B. Connolly, *The Port of Gloucester* (New York: Doubleday, Doran & Company, 1940), 185.

61 Proctor Brothers, *Fishermen's Own Book,* 6–7, emphasis added.

62 Smith, *Gleanings from the Sea,* 122.

63 According to the American Fish Bureau headquartered in Gloucester: "In the early history of the fishing industry of New England, the business was carried on in small vessels or boats, that from the abundance of fish had no occasion to go far from shore. In those days the near shore fishing grounds along the New England coast were well supplied with all the desirable varieties of salt water fish, and were of great value to the producer. The same, probably, might be said of the near shore fishing grounds of the British Provinces at that date." American Fish Bureau (1887), in Smith, *Gleanings from the Sea,* 288.

64 Vickers, *Farmers and Fishermen,* 276; McFarland, *History of the New England Fisheries,* 181; see generally, Wayne M. O'Leary, *Maine Sea Fisheries* (Boston: Northeastern University Press, 1996).

65 Joseph Gough, *A Historical Sketch of Fisheries Management in Canada* (Halifax: Department of Fisheries and Oceans, Scotia-Fundy Region, 1993), 13.

66 Morison described the evolution of the Massachusetts fleets as follows:

> A regional readjustment in the fishing industry went on between 1835 and 1855. Boston, the second greatest fishing port in 1837, gradually went out of the business, and no other town on Boston Bay but Hingham owned a fishing schooner in 1855. The South Shore and the Merrimac declined; the North Shore remained stationary. The only regions which increased their fleet during these eighteen years were Cape Cod, and her rocky rival Cape Ann. The latter's fishing fleet in 1837 was less than half that of Cape Cod. But in the next twenty years Cape Ann caught up. The population of Gloucester and Rockport (separated in 1840) more than doubled between 1820 and 1855 … But concentration was the tendency of the age, and "the harbor" (Gloucester) gradually absorbed all Cape Ann fisheries.

Morison, *Maritime History of Massachusetts,* 302–3.

67 Ibid., 304–5.

68 McFarland, *History of the New England Fisheries,* 59, 66; Albert C. Jensen, *The Cod* (New York: Thomas Y. Crowell Co., 1972), 162.

69 Charles G. Atkins, "The River Fisheries of Maine" in Goode, ed., *Fisheries and Fishery Industries of the United States,* Sec. V, vol. I, 695, 727.

70 Massachusetts Fish Commission, Sixth Annual Report 1871, 79–270.

71 For Massachusetts see Appendix: "A Collection of the Laws of Massachu-

setts Relating to Inland Fisheries, From the year 1623 through the year 1871," in Massachusetts Fish Commission, Sixth Annual Report 1871, 79–270.

72 Atkins, "River Fisheries of Maine," 727.

73 Massachusetts Fish Commission, Sixth Annual Report 1871, 228.

74 Massachusetts Commissioners for the Artificial Propagation of Fish, Report of Commissioners Appointed Under Resolve of 1856, Concerning the Artificial Propagation of Fish, with Other Documents (Boston: William White, 1857), 13.

75 New Hampshire Legislature, Report of the Select Committee on the Fisheries (Concord: George E. Jenks, 1865), 3; New Hampshire Fish Commission, First Annual Report 1865–1866, 3–4.

76 Charles G. Atkins, "On the Salmon of Eastern North America, and its Artificial Culture," in U.S. Commission of Fish and Fisheries, Annual Report II 1872–1873, 226.

77 Atkins, *Salmon of Eastern North America,* 226.

78 Connecticut Fish Commission, First Annual Report 1866–1867, 17.

79 U.S. Commission of Fish and Fisheries, Annual Report IV 1875–1876, 14.

80 Connecticut Fish Commission, First Annual Report 1866–1867, 17, emphasis added.

81 Department of Marine and Fisheries, First Annual Report 1868, 10–11; W.A. Spray, "Mitchell, Peter," in *Dictionary of Canadian Biography, vol. 12: 1891–1900* (Toronto: University of Toronto Press, 1990), 741; Gough, *A Historical Sketch of Fisheries Management in Canada,* 13–14.

82 Thomas F. Knight, *Pamphlets on the Fishes and Fisheries of Nova Scotia. No. II. Shore and Deep Sea Fisheries* (Halifax: A. Grant, 1867), 61; Knight, *River Fisheries,* 53–62; Knight, *Fishes and Fisheries of Nova Scotia,* 10, 24–8.

83 H.W. Johnston, "Appendix: Mr. Johnston's Report," in Reports on the Fisheries, Etc., of the Dominion of Canada (Ottawa: Department of Marine and Fisheries, 1868), 1–4.

84 William H. Venning, "Appendix: Mr. W.H. Venning's Report" (10 October 1867), in Reports on the Fisheries, Etc., of the Dominion of Canada (Ottawa: Department of Marine and Fisheries, 1868), 14–15.

85 Ibid., 9, 11–12, 17, 20, 23.

86 Ibid., 10–11, 21–28.

87 Although weirs were usually constructed of brush or of boards, rather than netting, they were commonly referred to as "nets." All four types of fixed nets are described in detail in Baird, Sea Fisheries of the South Coast of New England, 260–72.

88 Two categories of nets were used: movable and fixed. Movable nets included the seine and the gill-net. The *seine,* which enclosed the fish,

was hauled to shore or gathered in the open water. The *gill-net* could be fixed or drifting. It was designed so that the heads of the fish could pass through the mesh, but their bodies could not. When they tried to withdraw, the net held their gills securely. Fixed nets included traps, pounds, and weirs. Some, such as the *trap*, a very simple but sturdy pound that was unique to the exposed waters of Narragansett Bay, particularly the Seaconnet River area, had to be looked after constantly. It was suitable for capturing the fish that entered, but not for retaining them until their removal was convenient, as were *pounds* and *weirs*. *Seines* could ensnare huge numbers of fish when the conditions were favourable, but *pounds* and *weirs* captured even more since they did not have to be tended. Thousands of barrels of fish could be caught at one time, especially the species at the heart of the controversy; see Baird, Sea Fisheries of the South Coast of New England, XXIV–XXV, XXVII.

89 Frederick W. True, "The Pound-Net Fisheries of the Atlantic States," in Goode, ed., *Fisheries and Fishery Industries of the United States* Sec. V, vol. I, 597.

90 Fixed nets were also used in the capture of river herrings, shad, salmon, and striped bass. The anadromous fisheries problem overlapped with the inshore problem near the mouths of rivers frequented simultaneously by both types of fish, and during the annual coastal migrations of certain river species – as when *shad* swept along the shoreline each spring.

91 Dean Conrad Allard Jr, *Spencer Fullerton Baird and the U.S. Fish Commission* (New York: Arno Press Inc., 1978), 69–73; E.F. Rivinus and E.M. Youssef, *Spencer Baird of the Smithsonian* (Washington, DC: Smithsonian Institution Press, 1992), 142–3.

92 William Healey Dall, *Spencer Fullerton Baird, A Biography, Including Selections from his Correspondence with Audubon, Agassiz, Dana, and Others* (Philadelphia: J.B. Lippincott Co., 1915), 416–18.

93 Allard, *Spencer Fullerton Baird*, 76–7.

94 Elmer Charles Herber, *Correspondence Between Spencer Fullerton Baird and Louis Agassiz – Two Pioneer American Naturalists* (Washington, DC: The Smithsonian Institution, 1963) 8; Allard, *Spencer Fullerton Baird*, 55–7, 75, 77; Tim D. Smith, *Scaling Fisheries: The Science of Measuring the Effects of Fishing, 1855–1955* (Cambridge: Cambridge University Press, 1994), 44, 46.

95 Robert V. Bruce, *The Launching of Modern American Science, 1846–1876* (New York: Alfred A. Knopf, 1987), 49.

96 Dall, *Spencer Fullerton Baird*, 417, 419–20; Allard, *Spencer Fullerton Baird*, 77; *Congressional Globe*, 41st Cong., 2nd sess., 1869–1870, ix.

97 *Congressional Globe*, 41st Cong., 3rd sess., 1870–1871 (9 February 1871), Appendix, 398.

98 Baird, Sea Fisheries of the South Coast of New England, XIII, XVII–XVIII, 1–6.

99 Baird, *Sea Fisheries of the South Coast of New England,* XII–XVII, 7–72; Allard, *Spencer Fullerton Baird,* 69, 88–9; Dall, *Spencer Fullerton Baird,* 424–5.

100 Allard, *Spencer Fullerton Baird,* 119–25; U.S. Commission of Fish and Fisheries, Annual Report II 1872–1873, 757.

101 U.S. Commission of Fish and Fisheries, Annual Report II 1872–1873, ii–iv, vi–vii; Allard, *Spencer Fullerton Baird,* 364.

102 U.S. Commission of Fish and Fisheries, Annual Report II 1872–1873, vi, x–xi; George Brown Goode, "Herring," in *The Fisheries and Fishery Industries of the United States,* Sec. I, Natural History of Useful Aquatic Animals, with an Atlas of Two Hundred and Seventy-seven Plates – Text (Washington, DC: U.S. Government Printing Office, 1884), 553–5.

103 Mitchell, who served as Minister of Marine and Fisheries from 1867–1873, furnished documentation and authorization for Baird's investigation, as well as permission to take fish by any method he chose, whether or not it was legal in Canada. Whitcher and Venning provided personal letters on his behalf; see Baird, Sea Fisheries of the South Coast of New England, iii-vi.

104 Knight, *Fishes and Fisheries of Nova Scotia,* 16.

105 Cod fishing vessels from Lunenburg, Nova Scotia, that had been operating along the Labrador Coast switched in 1869 from hand-lines to the trawl-lines that were already being used experimentally off southwestern Nova Scotia. Lunenburg's mackerel vessels quickly adopted purse seines to increase the efficiency and size of their catches; see B.A. Balcom, *History of the Lunenburg Fishing Industry* (Lunenburg: Lunenburg Marine Museum Society, 1977), 17–18.

106 U.S. Commission of Fish and Fisheries, Annual Report II 1872–1873, lx, xii.

107 Baird, Sea Fisheries of the South Coast of New England, VII.

108 Ibid., XXXII.

109 Ibid., VII.

110 Prior to 1870, fixed net fishers from Cape Cod to Montauk Point, Long Island, sold thousands of barrels of scup and sea bass to farmers for use as manure; see U.S. Commission of Fish and Fisheries, Annual Report XXVIII 1902, 269.

111 Baird, *Sea Fisheries of the South Coast of New England,* VII.

112 U.S. Commission of Fish and Fisheries, Annual Report II 1872–1873, xi–xiii.

113 Baird had previously surmised that insufficient prey was the primary reason for the disappearance of the fish that had furnished southern New England's coastal communities with their summer food supply. While lobbying Congress for a federal inquiry in January 1871, he had postulated that although cod and mackerel were not typically caught in

pounds, their abundance depended upon the inshore fishes that had diminished – particularly "scup, tautog, herring, sea bass, striped bass, &c." (*Congressional Globe*, 41st Cong., 3rd sess., 1870–1871, 585.)

114 Maine Fish Commission, Sixth Annual Report 1872, 8.

115 *Statutes of Canada* 1868, 31 Vict. c. 60.

116 The Dominion *Fisheries Act* specifically repealed New Brunswick's *Act relating to the Coast and River Fisheries* and its *Act to encourage the formation of Oyster Beds*, which had not been enforced. Regulations promulgated under either law, which were consistent with the federal *Fisheries Act*, remained in effect until amended or superseded by federal regulations. Federal fishery officers were empowered to enforce these provincial regulations and those of Nova Scotia. The provisions in Nova Scotia's *Revised Statutes* concerning the river, coast, and deep-sea fisheries continued into force for several years; see *Statutes of Canada* 1868, 31 Vict. c. 60, 20, 21.

117 Baird, Sea Fisheries of the South Coast of New England, XXXIII, 133–4.

118 Allard, *Spencer Fullerton Baird*, 96–8; Baird, Sea Fisheries of the South Coast of New England, XXXIV.

119 Allard, *Spencer Fullerton Baird*, 121, 125–7; U.S. Commission of Fish and Fisheries, Annual Report II 1872–1873, xvi; U.S. Commission of Fish and Fisheries, Annual Report IV 1875–1876, 11–12; *Congressional Globe*, 42nd Cong., 2nd sess., 1871–1872, 627–30.

120 U.S. Commission of Fish and Fisheries, Annual Report IV 1875–1876, 3; XVII *Stat.* 350, ch. 415 (1872); *Congressional Globe*, 42nd Cong., 2nd sess., 1871–1872, 807.

121 U.S. Commission of Fish and Fisheries, Annual Report II 1872–1873, xvi–xix, 757.

122 Maine Fish Commission, Sixth Annual Report 1872, 5–6; U.S. Commission of Fish and Fisheries, Annual Report II 1872–1873, iv–v; Atkins, *Salmon of Eastern North America*, 242.

123 U.S. Commission of Fish and Fisheries, Annual Report II 1872–1873, 763–71.

124 U.S. Commission of Fish and Fisheries, Annual Report II 1872–1873, xviii-xxiii, 765; Atkins, *Salmon of Eastern North America*, 242–57, 262–7; Maine Fish Commission, Sixth Annual Report 1872, 16; Massachusetts Fish Commission, Seventeenth Annual Report 1882, 14.

125 Richard Rathbun, "Report Upon the Inquiry Respecting Food-Fishes and the Fishing-Grounds," in U.S. Commission of Fish and Fisheries, Annual Report XVI 1888–1889, XLIV.

126 U.S. Commission of Fish and Fisheries, Annual Report II 1872–1873, xvi–cii.

127 XVII *Stat.* 513, ch. 227 (1873).

128 See, for example: Department of Marine and Fisheries, Third Annual Report 1869–1870, 78.

CHAPTER FIFTEEN

1 Report of the Convention of the North American Fish and Game Protective Society (Montreal, 1900).

2 Bishop Heber, *Guide Book to the Megantic, Spider and Upper Dead River Regions of the Province of Quebec and the State of Maine* (*The Official Guide Book of the Megantic Fish and Game Club*) (Boston, 1897), 17–18.

3 T. Jackson Lears, *No Place of Grace: Antimodernism and the Transformation of American Culture, 1880–1920* (New York, 1981); Roderick Nash, "The Cult of Wilderness," in Nash, ed., *Wilderness and the American Mind*, 3rd edition, (New Haven: Yale University Press, 1982).

4 See, for example, William G. MacFarlane, *Where Breezes Blow: An Illustrated Guide to St. John and Fredericton* (St John: Mason & MacFarlane, 1895).

5 Canada, Sessional Papers, 1891, no. 24, 8a, "Report of the Salmon Fisheries on the Baie des Chaleurs," Annual Report of the Department of Marine and Fisheries, appendix, 30–1.

6 David Goodsell Gale, "The History of the Vermont Fish and Game Commission, 1866–1960, and the Importance of its Operations to the State," MA thesis (University of Vermont, 1963), 97; Florence J. Perry, "From Colonization and Depredation to Conservation and Education: Progress Report of the Vermont Fish & Game Department," 1894, reference files, Vermont State Archives, Montpelier, Vermont.

7 *Statutes of Nova Scotia* (1761), 2 George III, ch. 2; *Statutes of New Brunswick* (1786), 27 George III, chs. 20, 33; Moses Perley, *The Sea and River Fisheries of New Brunswick* (Fredericton, 1851); Thomas F. Knight, *The River Fisheries of Nova Scotia* (Halifax, 1867); R.W. Dunfield, *The Atlantic Salmon in the History of North America* (Ottawa: Department of Fisheries and Oceans, 1985); Provincial Archives of New Brunswick (PANB), Northumberland County Council Records, RS153, Special Session of the Peace, 18 June 1809.

8 "Petitions (printed) of Ruben Gregg...," January 1843, ch. 173, box 281 (1853), Maine State Archives, Augusta; "Petition of John Armstrong and others for the amendment of an act, entitled an act for the preservation of moose and deer," 27 February 1854, envelope 23, box 234 (1854), Maine State Archives; *New England Farmer*, 6 March 1869; Helenette Silver, *A History of New Hampshire Game and Furbearers*, New Hampshire Fish and Game Department survey report no. 6 (Concord, New Hampshire: Evans Printing Company, 1957), 83; Dunfield, *The Atlantic Salmon*; D. Wilson, "Report on the Salmon Fisheries in Certain Rivers of New Brunswick, 1862," in *Journals of the New Brunswick House of Assembly*, 1863, appendix, 1–30; Gilbert Allardyce, "The Vexed Question of Sawdust: River Pollution in Nineteenth-Century New Brunswick," *Dalhousie Review*, 52 (1972), 171–90.

9 Fourth Annual Report of the Commissioner of Fisheries, 1870 (Augusta:

Sprague, Owen & Nash,1870), 5; Report of the Commissioners of Fisheries and Game of the State of Maine, 1880 (Augusta: Sprague & Son, 1880), 5; Ninth Annual Report of the Commissioners of Fisheries of the State of Maine, 1875 (Augusta: Sprague, Owen & Nash, 1875); W. Ross King, *The Sportsman and Naturalist in Canada* (London, 1866); Moses Perley, "Sea and River Fisheries of New Brunswick"; Robert Day, "The British Garrison at Halifax: Its Contribution to the Development of Sport in the Community," in Morris Mott, ed., *Sport in Canada: Historical Readings* (Toronto: Copp Clark, 1989).

10 "Report of the Commissioner of Fisheries," in Annual Report of the New Brunswick Crown Land Department (1887), 9.

11 Report of the Commissioner of Fisheries and Game of the State of Maine, 1881 (Augusta: Sprague & Son, 1882), 7; Joseph Auld to *Burlington Daily Free Press,* 2 November 1892.

12 *New Brunswick Acts,* 1878, *An Act for the Protection of Certain Birds and Animals,* 127–33; Perry, "From Colonization and Depredation," 12; Arthur F. Stone, *The Vermont of Today, with Its Historic Background, Attractions and People,* vol. 2 (New York: Lewis Historical Publishing Company, 1929), 714; Report of the Commissioners of Fisheries and Game of the State of Maine, 1880 (Augusta: Sprague & Son, 1880), 3; Report of the Commissioners of Fisheries and Game, of the State of Maine, 1881 (Augusta: Sprague & Son, 1882), 9; *Maine Farmer,* 3 January 1884; *Vermont Watchman and State Journal,* 16 May 1877, 22 November 1882, 29 October 1884; *Rural Vermonter,* 3 December 1886.

13 *New Brunswick Acts,* 1893, *An Act to Consolidate and Amend Several Acts for the Protection of Certain Birds and Animals,* 92–162; Report of the Commissioners of Fisheries and Game of the State of Maine, 1883 (Augusta: Sprague & Son, 1883), 11–12

14 *New Brunswick Acts,* 1884, *An Act to Regulate the Leasing of the Fishery Rights in the Non-Tidal Waters Pertaining to the Crown as Riparian Proprietor of Ungranted Crown Lands, and for the Protection of the Fisheries,* 9–13.

15 "Activities and By-laws of the Inglewood Fish and Game Corporation," 1898.

16 *Burlington Daily Free Press,* 16 November 76; *Vermont Watchman and State Journal,* 16 May 1877; *Vermont Watchman and State Journal,* 13 November 1878; Gale, "History of the Vermont Fish and Game Commission," 38–40, 197; Luther B. Johnson, *Eighty Years of It, 1869–1949* (Randolph, Vermont: Luther B. Johnson, 1949), 187; Stone, *Vermont of Today,* vol. 2, 715; *Forest and Stream* 2 (19 February 1874): 24; Silver, *History of New Hampshire Game and Furbearers,* 120–2; *Maine Farmer,* 1 January 1870, 6 March 1875.

17 John Reiger, *American Sportsmen and the Origins of Conservation* (Norman, Oklahoma, 1977); see also, James Tober, *Who Owns the Wildlife?: The Polit-*

ical Economy of Conservation in Nineteenth-Century America (Westport Connecticut: Greenwood Press, 1981); Richard Judd, *Common Lands, Common People: The Origins of Conservation in Northern New England* (Cambridge: Harvard University Press, 1997)

18 *Burlington Free Press,* 10 May 1869.

19 Annual Report of the Maine Inland Fish and Game Commission, 1904, 74; "Report of the Inspector of Fisheries," in Annual Report of the New Brunswick Crown Land Department, 1889, 98.

20 Bishop Heber, *Guide Book to the Megantic, Spider and Upper Dead River Regions*; Activities and By-laws of the Inglewood Fish and Game Corporation; "Report of the Inspector of Fisheries," in Annual Report of the New Brunswick Crown Land Department, 1892, appendix B, 19.

21 "Report of the Chief Game Commissioner," 1898, in Annual Report of the New Brunswick Crown Land Department, 1898, 115.

22 Charles H. Bell, *History of the Town of Exeter, New Hampshire* (Boston: J.E. Farwell & Co., 1888), 47; Fred E. Crawford, *The Life and Times of Oramel Crawford: A Vermont Farmer, 1809–1888* (n.p., by the author, 1952), 26; John Langdon Sibley, *History of the Town of Union* (Boston: Banjamin B. Mussey, 1851), 391–2; A.N. Somers, *History of Lancaster, New Hampshire* (Concord, New Hampshire: Rumford Press for the town, 1899), 100; *Maine Farmer,* 23 March 1872.

23 Ruben Gregg petition; John Armstrong petition.

24 Sixth Annual Report of the Commissioner of Fisheries of the State of Maine, 1872 (Augusta: Sprague, Owen & Nash, 1872), 5; Fourth Annual Report of the Commissioners of Fisheries of the State of Maine, 1870 (Augusta: Sprague, Owen & Nash,1870), 7–8; Seventh Annual Report of the Commissioners of Fisheries of the State of Maine, 1873 (Augusta: Sprague, Owen & Nash, 1873), 6–7; Eleventh Annual Report of the Commissioners of Fisheries of the State of Maine, 1877 (Augusta: Sprague, Owen & Nash, 1877), 17; Thirteenth Report of the Commissioner of Fisheries of the State of Maine, 1879 (Augusta: Sprague, Owen & Nash, 1879), 28–9; Report of the Commissioners of Fisheries and Game of the State of Maine, 1883 (Augusta: Sprague & Son, 1883), 19; *Burlington Free Press,* 16 November 1876.

25 "Report of the Chief Game Commissioner," 1897, in Annual Report of the New Brunswick Crown Land Department, 1897.

26 Henry D. Thoreau, *The Maine Woods* (Boston: Houghton, Mifflin and Co., 1892); on the glorification of native culture by tourists, see Patricia Jasen, *Wild Things: Nature, Culture and Tourism in Ontario, 1790–1914* (Toronto: University of Toronto Press, 1995); Bill Parenteau, "'Care Control and Supervision': Native People in the Canadian Atlantic Salmon Fishery," *Canadian Historical Review,* vol. 79 (1998), 1–35.

27 *Report of the Secretary of the Inland Fishery Protection Service,* 1894, 11.

28 "Petition of N.G.G. Barrows and 70 others praying for a law against the destruction of Moose," 21 February 1852, ch. 274, box 271 (1852); "Petition of John Neptune & 14 others for law to prevent destruction of Moose," 5 March 1852, ibid.; *Calais Advertiser,* 23 September 1874.

29 *Saint Croix Courier,* 29 January 1874, 8 October 1885, 29 April 1886. We are deeply indebted to Jacques Ferland for providing the materials cited.

30 *Saint Croix Courier,* 12 March 1885. We are deeply indebted to Jacques Ferland for providing the materials cited.

31 C.H. Porter, Agent, Passamaquoddy Indians, Calais, 30 November 1886; *Saint Croix Courier,* 17 December 1885. We are deeply indebted to Jacques Ferland for providing the materials cited.

32 Report of the Secretary of the Inland Fishery Protection Service, 1894, 6, 11.

33 National Archives of Canada (NA), Records of the Department of Indian Affairs, RG 10, vol. 8862, file 1/18–5, pt. 1, W.D. Carter, Indian Agent, to J.D. McLean, Secretary of Indian Affairs, 7 March 1898.

34 NA, Records of the Department of Indian Affairs, RG 10, vol. 3908, file 107,297, pt. 1, W.D. Carter to J.D. McLean, 21 January 1898.

35 *Carleton Sentinel,* 1 September 1888.

36 *Act for the better observance of the Lord's Day,* 16 May 1865, chapter 253 (1865), Massachusetts State Archives, Boston; Silver, *History of New Hampshire Game and Furbearers,* 90; Report of the Commissioners of Fisheries and Game of the State of Maine, 1883 (Augusta: Sprague & Son, 1883), 12; "Reply to 'Special,'" and "Those Ninety Deer," Notebook: Father's Articles and About Game," 618 f3, Fannie Hardy Eckstorm Collection, Northeast Folklore Center, University of Maine, Orono; *Maine Farmer,* 16 April, 1 October, 1903.

37 NA, Record of the Department of Fisheries, RG 23, vol. 281, file 2124, John A. Chesley, Overseer, St John, to J. Costigan, Minister of Fisheries, 19 October 1895; Costigan to Chesley, 26 October 1895.

38 "Constitution and By-Laws of the Game and Inland Fishery Protection Society of Nova Scotia, to which is added the Acts relating to the Preservation of Game" (Halifax, 1889).

39 NA, Record of the Department of Fisheries, RG 23, vol. 247, file 1588, R.A. Chapman Inspector, to Dominion Commissioner of Fisheries, 26 July 1897; Dominion Commissioner of Fisheries to Chapman, 9 November 1897.

40 NA, Record of the Department of Fisheries, RG 23, vol. 326, file 2773, Guy Carr, Fishery Overseer, Compton Station, New Brunswick, to Deputy Minister of Fisheries, 29 May 1899; R.E. Venning, Deputy Minister of Fisheries to Guy Carr, 3 August 1899; vol. 247, file 1588, P. Robichaud, Overseer, Inkerman Parish, Gloucester County, to R.A. Chapman, Inspector, 17 November 1908; Chapman to R.E. Venning, 19 November 1908.

41 Edward D. Ives, *George Magoon and the Down East Game War: History, Folklore and the Law* (Urbana, Illinois: University of Illinois Press, 1988).

42 *Rural Vermonter*, 3 December 1886.

43 *St John Globe*, 20 August, 21 August 1888; *Carleton Sentinel*, 2 October 1888.

44 *Boston Herald, in Maine Farmer*, 20 February 1902; *Maine Farmer*, 23 February 1899, 17 May 1900; Silver, *History of New Hampshire Game and Furbearers*, 102; *Vermont Watchman and State Journal*, 10 January 1883.

45 *Maine Farmer*, 8 August 1901.

46 "Farmers vs. Sportsmen," *Forest and Stream* 2 (14 May 1874), 210. See *Maine Farmer*, 29 January 1903.

47 O.H. Leavitt in *Maine Farmer*, 9 February 1899.

48 *Maine Farmer*, 31 December 1885, 25 October 1900.

49 C.H. Abbott in *Maine Farmer*, 24 January 1900.

50 Gale, "History of the Vermont Fish and Game Commission," 126–7; *Maine Farmer*, 8 August 1901.

51 Leavitt in *Maine Farmer*, 9 February 1899; *Maine Farmer*, 11 April 1907; Silver, *History of New Hampshire Game and Furbearers* (quoting fish and game report), p. 102; PANB, Records of the Minister of New Brunswick Crown Lands, RS 105, box #5, T.G. Loggie, Deputy Minister of Crown Lands to Denis Doyle, Newcastle, 4 and 9 October 1909; Loggie to Richard Melanson, Bathurst, 31 August 1909; Loggie to Alfred Melanson, Bathurst, 31 August 1909.

52 Z.A. Gilbert in *Maine Farmer*, 26 February 1903.

53 *Maine Farmer*, 15 October 1903.

54 Gilbert, "Changes in Our Farming," Eighteenth Annual Report of the Secretary of the Maine Board of Agriculture, 1873 (Augusta: Sprague, Owen & Nash, 1873), 6–8.

55 Collingwood, "Saving a Farm," Agriculture of Maine: Forty-fourth Annual Report of the H.W. Secretary of the Board of Agriculture for the Year 1900 (Augusta: Kennebec Journal Print, 1901), 73.

56 *Maine Farmer*, 24 October 1874.

57 James Walter Goldthwait, "A Town that Has Gone Downhill," *Geographical Review* 17 (October 1927), 542.

58 *Maine Farmer*, 24 June 1876.

59 "Secretary's Report," Fourth Annual Report of the Secretary of the Maine Board of Agriculture, 1859 (Augusta: Stevens & Sayward, 1859), 40.

60 Daniel Lancaster, *The History of Gilmanton* (Gilmanton, New Hampshire: Alfred Prescott, 1845), 13–14.

61 *Maine Farmer*, 26 July 1900.

62. "Obidiah Gardner's Address," *Maine Farmer*, December 17, 1903. See *Maine Farmer*, 26 July 1900.

63 Report of the Convention of the North American Fish and Game Protective Society (Montreal, 1900).

CHAPTER SIXTEEN

1 Kari Levitt, in *Population Movements in the Atlantic Provinces,* estimated that New Brunswick, Nova Scotia, and Prince Edward Island suffered a net out-migration of 341,000 persons between 1881 and 1921, while Patricia Thornton, in her article "The Problem of Out-migration from Atlantic Canada, 1871–1921," suggests that between the 1860as and the 1920s the region's net loss of population was nearer to 500,000. See Kari Levitt, *Population Movements in the Atlantic Provinces* (Fredericton: Atlantic Provinces Economic Growth Council, 1960); Patricia Thornton, "The Problem of Out-migration from Atlantic Canada, 1871– 1921," *Acadiensis* 15, 1 (Autumn 1985):18.

2 Alan A. Brookes, "The Golden Age and the Exodus: the Case of Canning, Kings County," *Acadiensis* 11, 1 (Autumn 1981): 82.

3 Thornton, "Problem of Out-Migration," 30.

4 *The Canadian Oxford Dictionary* (Toronto: Oxford University Press, 1998), 161; T.K. Pratt, (ed.), *Dictionary of Prince Edward Island English* (Toronto: University of Toronto Press, 1988), 21–2.

5 *Historical Atlas of Canada, Volume II: The Land Transformed, 1800–1891* (Toronto: University of Toronto Press, 1993), plate 26; Arthur L. Johnson, "Boston and the Maritimes: A Century of Steam Navigation" (PhD dissertation, University of Maine, 1971), passim.

6 *Halifax Morning Chronicle,* 5 January 1870.

7 *Charlottetown Daily Examiner,* 4 February 1880.

8 Provincial Workmen's Association, *Trades Journal,* 29 June 1881.

9 *Amherst (Nova Scotia) Daily News,* 3 October 1898.

10 Marcus Lee Hansen and John Bartlet Brebner, *The Mingling of the Canadian and American Peoples* (New Haven: Yale University Press, 1940); Alan Alexander Brookes, "The Exodus: Migration from the Maritimes to Boston During the Second Half of the Nineteenth Century" (PhD diss., University of New Brunswick, 1978).

11 Thornton, "Problem of Out-Migration."

12 Ibid., 18–19.

13 E.G. Ravenstein, quoted in Everett Lee, "A Theory of Migration," *Demography* 3 (1966): 47–8.

14 As noted earlier, by the twentieth century the U.S. census only divided Canadians into two groups according to the language they spoke. However, the Massachusetts State Census continued to list the Maritime provinces as places of birth until 1915, and figures from that census confirm that most of the English Canadians in Boston were from the Mari-

time provinces. In 1905, for example, there were a total of 47,554 English Canadians in the city of which 33,769, or 71 per cent, were from the Maritime provinces. Thus, one can consider census data on single English Canadian women as indicative of the behaviour of single Maritime women.

15 Betsy Beattie, *Obligation and Opportunity: Single Maritime Women in Boston, 1870–1930* (Montreal: McGill-Queen's University Press, 2000), 139–43.

16 Alan A. Brookes, "Out-Migration from the Maritime Provinces, 1860–1900: Some Preliminary Considerations," *Acadiensis* 5:2 (Spring 1976): 46.

17 Sam Bass Warner, *Streetcar Suburbs: The Process of Growth in Boston (1870–1900)*, 2nd ed., (Cambridge: Harvard University Press, 1978), 129.

18 Scholars first observed the workings of the family economy in the peasant families of Europe from the sixteenth through the nineteenth centuries, as capitalism transformed social and economic relations in the European countryside and survival on farms was increasingly difficult for all but those with land holdings large enough to produce a surplus for commercial sale. In recent years North American social historians have demonstrated that both rural and urban poor families, faced with the commercialization of agriculture and industrial capitalist development in nineteenth-century North America, used similar strategies to survive subliving wages and inadequate farm production. For a synthesis of the findings of historians on how families in Europe and North America adapted the family economy to an urban, industrial setting, see Michael Anderson, *Approaches to the History of the Western Family, 1500–1914* (London: Macmillan, 1984), 78–80. For examples of how Canadian rural families used the family economy as a survival strategy, see the essays in Daniel Samson, *Contested Countryside: Rural Workers and Modern Society in Atlantic Canada, 1800–1950* (Fredericton: Published for the Gorsebrook Research Institute for Atlantic Studies by Acadiensis Press, 1994); and Marjorie Griffin Cohen, *Women's Work, Markets, and Economic Development in Nineteenth-Century Ontario* (Toronto: University of Toronto Press, 1988).

19 Beattie, *Obligation and Opportunity*, 129.

20 Letter of application to the Boston City Hospital Training School for Nurses from Annie Bertha Baker of Tremont, Nova Scotia, 1894, Box 2, Folder 3, Boston City Hospital Training School Records, Nursing Archives, Mugar Library, Boston University, Boston.

21 Carroll Wright, *The Working Girls of Boston* (Boston: Wright and Potter, 1889; reprint New York: Arno and the *New York Times*, 1969), 99–101.

22 Letter from Margaret Vail Neal to Neil Sinclair, 30 October 1931.

23 Letter from Mary A. Sheldon, West Newton, Massachusetts, to Lillian Wentzel, Upper Foster Settlement, Nova Scotia, 25 September 1905.

24 Sarah Ann Sanford, Upper Canard, Nova Scotia, as quoted in Brookes, "Golden Age and the Exodus," 80.

25 Quotation of Harriet Barry included in a letter written to the author by her son Carroll H. Snell, Riverview, New Brunswick, 26 November 1988.

26 Albert Benedict Wolfe, *The Lodging House Problem in Boston* (Cambridge: Harvard University Press, 1913), 52.

27 Robert A. Woods, *The City Wilderness: A Settlement Study by Residents and Associates of the South End House* (Boston: Houghton Mifflin, 1898), 49.

28 Beattie, *Obligation and Opportunity,* 113.

29 Wolfe, *Lodging House Problem,* 32.

30 Ibid.

31 Beattie, *Obligation and Opportunity,* 135; Jennie Peck, interview with the author, 21 May 1989, Bear River, Nova Scotia.

32 Jennie Peck, interview with the author.

33 Joanne J. Meyerowitz, *Women Adrift: Independent Wage Earners in Chicago, 1880–1930* (Chicago: University of Chicago Press, 1988).

34 For example, Anita Saunders of Middleton, Nova Scotia, came to train as a nurse at McLean Hospital near Boston, and at first she was very homesick. She found comfort and encouragement from an old Sunday school teacher who lived in the city. "I would call her when I'd get down ... and she'd come over and talk with me," Anita reported. Anita Saunders, interview with the author, 14 January 1989, Weston, Massachusetts.

35 Information on Ethel Marguerite Chute taken from a letter to the author and a questionnaire filled out by her nephew Carroll Snell, February 1989.

36 Mary Monroe Hart, interview with the author, 30 May 1989, North East Margaree, Nova Scotia.

CHAPTER SEVENTEEN

1 See, for example, Jeremy Adelman and Stephen Aron, "From Borderlands to Borders: Empires, Nation States, and Peoples in Between in North America," *American Historical Review,* 104, 3 (June 1999), 814–41; and the articles by David Thelen, Bruno Ramirez, Ian Tyrrell, Robin Kelley, and Mauricio Tenorio Trillo in "The Nation and Beyond. International Perspectives on United States History. A Special Issue," in *The Journal of American History,* 86:3 (December 1999), 965–1187. Masao Miyoshi, "A Borderless World? From Colonialism to Transnationalism and the Decline of the Nation State," *Critical Inquiry* (Summer 1993), 726–51, discusses the erosion of the nation-state in the context of the globalizing process.

2 Benedict Anderson, *Imagined Communities: Reflections on the Origin and Spread of Nationalism* (London: Verson, rev. ed. 1991: orig. pub. 1983).

For a similar discussion in a Canadian context, see Daniel Francis, *National Dreams: Myth, Memory, and Canadian History* (Vancouver: Arsenal Pulp Press, 1997).

3 William New, *Borderlands: How We Talk About Canada* (Vancouver: UBC Press, 1998), 27.

4 Phillip Buckner, "How Canadian Historians Stopped Worrying and Learned to Love the Americans," *Acadiensis*, 25:2 (Spring 1996), 117–40.

5 Allen Guttmann, *Games and Empires: Modern Sports and Cultural Imperialism* (New York: Columbia University Press, 1994).

6 Ruth's upbringing and his connection to the Maritimes are chronicled in Robert Creamer, *Babe: The Legend Comes to Life* (New York: Simon and Schuster, 1974); Robert Ashe, *Even the Babe Came to Play: Small-Town Baseball in the Dirty 30s* (Halifax: Nimbus, 1991; William Humber, "Babe Ruth Comes to Canada in Search of ??", *Saskatchewan Historical Baseball Review* (1996) 24–35; and Colin Howell, "The Man who Taught the Bambino: The Mystery of Brother Matthias," in William Humber and John St James, eds., *All I Thought About Was Baseball: Writings on a Canadian Pastime* (Toronto: University of Toronto Press, 1996), 149–52.

7 The baseball connection between New England and the Maritimes is addressed in fuller detail in Colin Howell, *Northern Sandlots: A Social History of Maritime Baseball* (Toronto: University of Toronto Press, 1995).

8 Ernest R. Forbes, *The Maritime Rights Movement, 1919–1927: A Study in Canadian Regionalism* (Montreal and Kingston: McGill-Queen's University Press, 1979).

9 Ashe, *Even the Babe Came to Play*, 102–3; Howell, *Northern Sandlots.*

10 *Sydney Record*, 13 November 1925.

11 Ibid., 21 October 1927; *Halifax Herald*, 1 November 1924.

12 See, for example, the lengthy article entitled "Where Gun, Canoe and Fishing Rod are the Tourist's Joy," in a special tourist edition of the *Halifax Herald*, 24 March 1925.

13 James Morrison, "American Tourism in Nova Scotia, 1871–1940," *Nova Scotia Historical Review*, 2:2 (December 1982), 40–51.

14 Ian McKay, *The Quest of the Folk: Antimodernism and Cultural Selection in Twentieth-Century Nova Scotia* (Montreal and Kingston: McGill-Queen's University Press, 1994).

15 Beatrice M. Hay Shaw, *Nova Scotia: For Beauty and Business* (Halifax: Royal Print and Litho Ltd., 1923), vii.

16 Mark Dyreson, *Making the American Team: Sport Culture, and the Olympic Experience* (Urbana and Chicago: University of Illinois Press, 1998), 40–6.

17 A brief history of the Boston Marathon and the results of each race can be found at the official Boston Marathon website, *www.bostonmarathon.org/history.htm.* I am also indebted to my student research assistant

Daniel Macdonald for collecting material relating to the career of Johnny Miles used in this essay.

18 *Halifax Herald*, 5 April 1928.
19 Ibid., 29 July 1924.
20 Ibid., 19 September 1925.
21 Ibid., 3 September 1928.
22 Ibid., 13, 17 April 1926; Williston, *Johnny Miles: Nova Scotia's Marathon King* (Halifax: Nimbus, 1990), 2.
23 *Halifax Herald*, 14 June 1926; Williston, *Johnny Miles*, 35.
24 *Halifax Herald*, 29 June 1926.
25 Ibid., 13 August 1926.
26 Ibid., 7, 9, 19, 25 March 1927.
27 Ibid, 7 April 1927.
28 Williston, *Johnny Miles*, 44–5; Tom Derderian, *Boston Marathon: The History of the World's Premier Running Event* (Urbana, Illinois: Human Kinetics Publishers, 1990), 112–14; *Halifax Herald*, 20, 21 April 1927.
29 Derderian, *Boston Marathon*, 114.
30 *Halifax Herald*, 2 July 1927.
31 Ibid., 10, 19, 24 September 1927.
32 Ibid., 15, 18, 19, 20 April 1929.
33 Ibid., 13 June 1929.
34 Ibid., 10 June 1929.
35 Derderian, *Boston Marathon*, 133.
36 Williston, *Johnny Miles*, 75–6.
37 Alan Alexander Brooks, "The Exodus: Migration from the Maritimes to Boston During the Second Half of the Nineteenth Century," PhD diss., University of New Brunswick, 1977; Patricia Thornton, "The Problem of Out-migration from Atlantic Canada, 1871–1921: A New Look," *Acadiensis*, 15:1 (Autumn 1985), 3–34: Betsy Beattie, "'Going up to Lynn': Single, Maritime-Born Women in Lynn, Massachusetts, 1879–1930," *Acadiensis*, 22:1 (Autumn 1992), 65–86.
38 Ian McKay, "Of Karl Marx and the Bluenose: Colin Campbell McKay and the Legacy of Maritime Socialism," *Acadiensis*, 27:2 (Spring, 1998), 3–25.
39 McKay, *Quest of the Folk*.
40 Toronto *Globe*, 24 October 1922.
41 Ibid., 27 October 1922.
42 James Marsh, "The Bluenose."
43 Cheryl Sullivan, "The Paradox of *Bluenose II*: Antimodernism, Capitalism and the Legacy of the Schooner *Bluenose* in Nova Scotia," *Nova Scotia Historical Review* (1997), 2–22.
44 Gary Burrill, *Away: Maritimers in Massachusetts, Ontario and Alberta: An Oral History of Leaving Home* (Montreal and Kingston: McGill-Queen's University Press, 1992).

CHAPTER EIGHTEEN

1 Herbert E. Bolton, "The Epic of Greater America," *American Historical Review*, 38 (1933), 448–74.

2 Rohitt Aggarwala, "Non-Resident Me: John Bartlet Brebner and the Canadian Historical Profession," *Journal of the Canadian Historical Association*, New Series, 10 (1999), 237–77. See also Stephen G. Tomblin, "Shifting Boundaries and Borderlands Discourses," *Acadiensis*, 23 (Autumn 1993), 200, and P.A. Buckner, "Canadian Historiography and American Canadian Relations," *Tsukuba Seminar on Canadian Studies*, 6 (1994), 21–35.

3 Eric Hobsbawm, *Age of Extremes: The Short Twentieth Century, 1914–1991* (London: Abacus Books, 1995); Michael Howard and William Roger Lewis, eds., *The Twentieth Century* (New York: Oxford University Press, 1998); Clive Ponting, *The Twentieth Century: A World History* (New York: Henry Holt, 1998); David Reynolds, *One World Indivisible: A Global History Since 1945* (New York: W.W. Norton, 2000); J.M. Roberts, *Twentieth Century: The History of the World 1901 to the Present* (London: Allen Lane, 1999).

4 Garry Wills, "A Reader's Guide to the Twentieth Century," *New York Review of Books*, 15 July 1999, 24–8.

5 See W.H. McNeill, *The Global Condition: Conquerors, Catastrophes, and Community* (Princeton: Princeton University Press, 1992), and *A World History* (New York: Oxford University Press, 1999).

6 This summary draws on Hobsbawm's and the other broad studies cited above.

7 Olivier Zunz, *Why the American Century?* (Chicago: University of Chicago Press, 1998). See also Thomas L. Friedman, *The Lexus and the Olive Tree: Understanding Globalization* (New York: Anchor Books, 2000).

8 John Herd Thompson and Stephen J. Randall, in *Canada and the United States: Ambivalent Allies* (3rd ed.; Montreal and Kingston: McGill-Queen's University Press, 2002), offer the most comprehensive survey of Canadian-American relations in this respect. For a more political-diplomatic orientation see J.L. Granatstein and Norman Hillmer, *For Better or For Worse: Canada and the United States to the 1990s* (Toronto: Copp Clark Pitman, 1991). See also Carl Berger, "Internationalism, Continentalism, and the Writing of History: Comments on the Carnegie Series on the Relations of Canada and the United States," in R.A. Preston, ed., *The Influence of the United States on Canadian Development: Eleven Case Studies* (Durham, North Carolina: Duke University Press, 1972), 32–54; revised for *The Writing of Canadian History: Aspects of English-Canadian Historical Writing Since 1900* (2nd ed.; Toronto: University of Toronto Press, 1986).

9 Seymour Martin Lipset, *Continental Divide: The Values and Institutions of the United States and Canada* (New York: Routledge, 1990).

10 Lauren McKinsey and Victor Konrad, *Borderlands Reflections: The United States and Canada* (Orono, Maine: The Borderlands Project, 1989); Roger Gibbins, *Canada as a Borderlands Society* (Ibid., 1989); Clark Blaise, *The Border as Fiction* (Ibid., 1990); Russell Brown, *Borderlines and Borderlands in English Canada: The Written Line* (Ibid., 1990); Robert Lecker, ed., *Borderlands: Essays in Canadian-American Relations* (Toronto: ECW Press, 1991). See also W.H. New, *Borderlines: How We Talk about Canada* (Vancouver: University of British Columbia Press, 1998); for a recent appraisal, see Maureen Apel Molot, "Does the 49th Parallel Matter Any More?" and Steven Lee, "Real Borders in a Not So Borderless World," Chapters 1, 11, in Molot and Fen Hampson, eds., *Vanishing Borders: Canada Among Nations 1999* (Don Mills, Ontario: Oxford University Press, 2000).

11 Edgar McInnis, *The Unguarded Frontier* (New York: Russell and Russell, 1941); Bruce Hutchinson, *The Struggle for the Border* (Toronto: Longmans, 1955); Hugh L. Keenleyside and Gerald S. Brown, *Canada and the United States: Some Aspects of their Historical Relations* (New York: Alfred A. Knopf, 1952); Edelgard E. Mahant and Graeme S. Mount, *An Introduction to Canadian-American Relations* (Scarborough, Ontario: Nelson Canada, 1989).

12 Lawrence Martin, *The Presidents and the Prime Ministers: Washington and Ottawa Face to Face: The Myth of Bilateral Bliss, 1867–1982* (Toronto: Doubleday, 1982); Richard Gwyn, *The 49th Paradox: Canada in North America* (Toronto: McClelland & Stewart, 1985).

13 Granatstein and Hillmer, *For Better or for Worse* ; Robert Bothwell, *Canada and the United States: The Politics of Partnership* (Toronto: University of Toronto Press, 1992); Thompson and Randall, *Canada and the United States: Ambivalent Allies.*

14 Gordon T. Stewart, *The American Response to Canada since 1776* (East Lansing: Michigan State University Press, 1992); Lipset, *Continental Divide,* chapter 1.

15 Joel Garreau, *The Nine Nations of North America* (Boston: Houghton Mifflin, 1981); D.W. Meinig, *The Shaping of America: A Geographical Perspective on 500 Years of History: Atlantic America, 1492–1800* (New Haven: Yale University Press, 1986); Meinig, *The Shaping of America: A Geographical Perspective on 500 Years of History: Continental America 1800–1867* (Ibid., 1993); Meinig, *The Shaping of America: A Geographical Perspective on 500 Years of History: Transcontinental America, 1850– 1915* (Ibid., 1998).

16 See Lewis Hanke, ed., *Do the Americas Have a Common History? A Critique of the Bolton Theory* (New York: Alfred A. Knopf, 1963). In this collection, George Brown prepared the only essay on Canada in the context of the

volume's overwhelmingly Latin American and United States dominated definition of pan-Americanism.

17 Thomas J. Courchene and Colin Telmer, *From Heartland to North American Region State: The Social, Fiscal and Federal Evolution of Ontario* (Toronto: Faculty of Management, University of Toronto, 1998); Alan F.J. Artibise, "Cascadian Adventures: Shared Visions, Strategic Alliances, and Ingrained Barriers in a Transborder Region," paper, "On Brotherly Terms: Canadian American Relations West of the Rockies," University of Washington, 1996.

18 Samuel E. Moffett, *The Americanization of Canada*, Introduction by Allan Smith (Toronto: University of Toronto Press, 1972); Paul Rutherford, "Made in America: The Problem of Mass Culture in Canada," in David H. Flaherty and Frank E. Manning, eds., *The Beaver Bites Back? American Popular Culture in Canada* (Montreal and Kingston: McGill-Queen's University Press, 1993) 260–80; Theodore Peterson, *Magazines in the Twentieth Century* (Urbana: University of Illinois Press, 1964); Dallas W. Smythe, *Dependency Road: Communications, Capitalism, Consciousness* (Norwood: Ablex Publishing Company, 1981); Mary Vipond, "Canadian Nationalism and the Plight of Canadian Magazines in the 1920s," *Canadian Historical Review*, 58 (March 1977), 43–64.

19 Alfred Olivier Hero, Jr, *Louisiana and Quebec: Bilateral Relations and Comparative Sociopolitical Evolution, 1673–1993* (Lanham: University Press of America, 1995); Diane Pacom, "Bring French in North America: Quebec Culture and Globalization," *American Review of Canadian Studies*, 31 (Autumn 2001), 441–8; Damien-Claude Bélanger, *Canada, French Canadians, and Franco-Americans in the Civil War Era (1861–1865)* (Marianopolis College: www2.marianopo...ry/frncdns/studies/dcb/default.htm); G. Bouchard and Y. Lamonde, *Québécois et américains: la culture Québécoise aux XIX et XX siècles* (Saint Laurent: Fides, 1995).

20 Richard Itor, "The Backlash and the Quiet Revolution: The Contemporary Implications of Race and Language in the United States and Canada," in David M. Thomas, ed., *Canada and the United States: Differences that Count* (Peterborough, Ontario: Broadview Press, 1993), 141–64; Robin Winks. *Blacks in Canada: A History* (Montreal: McGill-Queen's University Press, 1971); James W. St G. Walker, *Racial Discrimination in Canada: The Black Experience* (Ottawa: University of Ottawa Press, 1985).

21 Graeme Wynn, "New England's Outpost in the Nineteenth Century," in Stephen J. Hornsby et al., eds., *The Northeastern Borderlands: Four Centuries of Interaction* (Orono and Fredericton: Canadian-American Center and Acadiensis Press, 1989), 64–90; Greg Marquis, *In Armageddon's Shadow: The Civil War and Canada's Maritime Provinces* (Montreal and Kingston: McGill-Queen's University Press, 1998); Karl McNeil Earle, "Cousins of a

Kind: The Newfoundland and Labrador Relationship with the United States," *American Review of Canadian Studies*, 28 (Winter 1998), 387–411.

CHAPTER NINETEEN

1 My title needs a brief gloss. "Connections and Comparisons" is obvious; it is taken from the subtitle of the conference from which these remarks derive. I use "unstable space" to characterize the in-betweenness of borderlands with which I begin my discussion. "Peeping through the cracks" reflects my growing sense in Orono in 2000 (a sense derived from an observation of V.V. Nabokov's) that as commentator on two days of papers delivered at the New England–Maritime Canada conference I seemed to think like a genius in the middle of the night; that in the predawn hours I imagined myself writing like a man of letters; and that, in the cold light of day I would but speak like a child. So I saw no recourse (borrowing from Nabokov once more) than to speak memory after peeping through the cracks in my recollections of all that had been said. I came by Nabokov's observations on the elusiveness of the creative spirit in an account of an interview with English novelist Zadie Smith: S Lyall, "A Good Start," *The New York Times Book Review*, 30 April 2000, 8. See also V.V. Nabokov, *Speak, Memory* (New York: Putnam, 1966).

2 Arjun Appadurai, *Modernity at Large: Cultural Dimensions of Globalization* (Minneapolis and London: University of Minnesota Press, 1997); Homi Bhabha, *The Location of Culture* (London: Routledge, 1994).

3 International Centre for Sustainable Cities, with the Cascadia Institute and the Discovery Institute, *Opportunities for Achieving Sustainability in Cascadia*, (Vancouver: ICSC, 1994); Joel Garreau, *Nine Nations of North America* (New York: Avon Books, 1981); E. Callenbach, *Ecotopia: The Notebooks and Reports of William Weston* (Berkeley: Banyan Tree Books, 1975).

4 Stephen J. Hornsby, Victor A. Konrad, and James J. Herlan, eds., *The Northeastern Borderlands: Four Centuries of Interaction* (Fredericton: Acadiensis Press, 1989).

5 M. Gallant, "In Youth is Pleasure," in *The Moslem Wife and Other Stories* (Toronto: McClelland & Stewart, 1994), 136–55.

6 What follows draws structure, at least, from C.M. Judd and A.J. Ray, eds., *Old Trails and New Directions: Papers of the Third North American Fur Trade Conference* (Toronto: University of Toronto Press, 1980).

7 D.W. Meinig, *The Shaping of America: A Geographical Perspective on 500 Years of History* (New Haven: Yale University Press, 1986).

8 W.H. New, *Borderlands: How We Talk About Canada* (Vancouver: University of British Columbia Press, 1998), 35–6, briefly mentions the Peace Arch; see also his "On the Border," *Canadian Literature*, 144 (1995), 4–7. I am indebted to my colleague Bill New and his "Borderlands" lectures, which

pointed me to several themes explored here, and particularly to the Gallant short story.

9 D. Hiebert, "Immigration and the Changing Social Geography of Greater Vancouver," *BC Studies*, 121 (Spring 1999), 35–82 and his "Immigration and the Changing Canadian City," *The Canadian Geographer*, 44:1 (2000), 25–43.

10 P.A. Buckner, "The Borderlands Concept: A Critical Appraisal," in Hornsby, Konrad and Herlan, eds., *The Northeastern Borderlands*, 152–8. Buckner restated some of these concerns in "How Canadian Historians Stopped Worrying and Learned to Love the Americans!" *Acadiensis*, 15:2 (1996), 117–40.

11 M. McLuhan (with Q. Fiore), *The Medium is the Massage* (New York: Bantam, 1967). See also M. McLuhan and B.R. Powers, *The Global Village: Transformations in World Life and Media in the 21st Century* (New York: Oxford University Press, 1989). Cole Harris has offered a spirited defence of Canadian distinctiveness vis-à-vis the United States, characterized by Appadurai in "Postmodern Patriotism: Canadian Reflections," *The Canadian Geographer* 45:1 (2001), 193–207. The opportunity to read this essay in draft form, after the Connections and Comparisons conference, pointed me to Appadurai's book and allowed me to refine some of the observations offered in Orono.

12 New, *Borderlands*, 6 attributes one version of this to M. Kuester, *Canadian Studies: A Literary Approach* (Bochum: Universitätsverlag Brockmeyer, 1995).

13 I. Lumsden (ed.), *Close the 49th Parallel, etc.: the Americanization of Canada* (Toronto: University of Toronto Press, 1970).

14 M. Bloch, "Toward a Comparative History of European Societies," trans. J.C. Riemersma, in F.C. Lane and J.C. Riemersma, eds., *Enterprise and Secular Change: Readings in Economic History* (Homewood, Illinois: 1953), 494–521. See also A.O. Hill and B.H. Hill Jr, "Marc Bloch and Comparative History," *American Historical Review*, 85:4 (1980), 828–46, with "Comment," by W.H. Sewell Jr, and S.L. Thrupp, 847–53, and "Reply," 854–7; and W.H. Sewell, "Marc Bloch and the Logic of Comparative History," *History and Theory*, 6 (1967), 208–18.

15 R. Grew, "The Case for Comparing Histories," *American Historical Review*, 85, 4 (1980), 763–78; see also his "The Comparative Weakness of American History," in *Journal of Interdisciplinary History*, 16 (1985), 87–101.

16 G.M. Frederickson, "From Exceptionalism to Variability: Recent Developments in Cross-National Comparative History," *Journal of American History*, 82 (1995), 587–604; T. Skocpol and M. Somers, "The Uses of Comparative History in Macrosocial Inquiry," *Comparative Studies in Society and History*, 22 (1980), 174–97. For an example of Frederickson's work, see *The Arrogance of Race: Historical Perspectives on Slavery, Racism and Social*

Inequality (Middletown, Connecticut: Wesleyan University Press, 1988). See also the special issue comprised of articles on "The Nation and Beyond: Transnational Perspectives on United States History," *Journal of American History*, 86 (1999).

17 I. Tyrell, "American Exceptionalism in an Age of International History," *American Historical Review*, 96:4 (1991), 1031–56; see also comment by M. McGerr, "The Price of the 'New International History,'" 1056–67 and the reply by Tyrell, 1068–72. For some exemplification, see I.R. Tyrell, *True Gardens of the Gods: Californian-Australian Environmental Reform, 1860–1930* (Berkeley: University of California Press, 1999).

18 J.M.S. Careless, "Hooray for the Scars and Gripes," in A.W. Purdy, *The New Romans: Candid Canadian Opinions of the United States* (New York: St. Martin's Press, 1968), 35.

19 P. Lane, "We've lost one of our greatest voices," *Globe and Mail* 25 April 2000, R1. "Her Gates Both East and West," was published for the first time as a sidebar to this memoir. Regular publication was in *Beyond Remembering: The Collected Poems of Al Purdy* (Madeira Park, British Columbia: Harbour Publishing, 2000). See also "It's the writing itself that is the most rewarding," *Globe and Mail*, 25 April 2000, R2.

20 I have reflected at greater length on these matters in "A Fine Balance? Geography at the Millennium," *The Canadian Geographer*, 43:3 (1999), 220–43.

21 C.F. Fox, *The Fence and the River: Culture and Politics at the U.S. – Mexico Border*, Cultural Studies of the Americas, vol. I (Minneapolis: University of Minnesota Press, 1999; G.M. Joseph, C.C. LeGrand, and R.D. Salvatore, eds., *Close Encounters of Empire: Writing the Cultural History of U.S.-Latin American Relations* (Durham, North Carolina: Duke University Press, 1998).

22 E. Sager, "Dependency, Underdevelopment and the Economic History of the Atlantic Provinces," *Acadiensis*, 7:1 (1987), 117–37.

23 A. McClintock, *Imperial Leather: Race, Gender, and Sexuality in the Colonial Conquest* (New York: Routledge, 1995).

Index